Pirchei Publishing
164 Village Path / P.O. Box 708
Lakewood, New Jersey 08701
(732) 370-3344
www.shulchanaruch.com

Product Produced & Compiled by YPS:
Rabbi Shaul Danyiel & Rabbi Ari Montanari
www.lionsden.info/YPS

THE YESHIVA PIRCHEI SHOSHANIM SHULCHAN ARUCH LEARNING PROJECT

# The Noahide Laws – Lesson One
# Introduction

**© Yeshiva Pirchei Shoshanim 2017**
This shiur may not be reproduced in any
form without permission of the copyright holder.

## Outline of This Lesson:

1. Misconceptions & Tragic Histories
2. Jews & Non-Jews
3. Law & Love
4. Summary

# Introduction to the Noahide Laws

## Misconceptions & Tragic Histories

Judaism is greatly misunderstood. Admittedly, Judaism appears strange when compared to other faiths. Whereas Christianity, Islam, and other religions seek adherents, and openly preach and proclaim the trueness of their faiths, Judaism appears to do the opposite. It seems turned in on itself and quietly unconcerned with the spiritual wellbeing of non-Jews. Judaism also seems, to the outsider, to be preoccupied with the minutiae of obscure law. This has given rise to the myth that Judaism is a religion of "justice," devoted to the worship of a "vengeful God."

These misconceptions are, for the most part, the result of an 1800 year campaign of marketing and persecution by the Church who sought to replace the original Torah with their own ideology.

The Christian world invested tremendous effort in quashing Torah teachings and thought. They subjected Jews to persecution, exile, torture, and even death. Jews were forced into ghettos and frequently prohibited from teaching or printing Torah thought and teachings. As the oppressors outlawed Jewish and non-Jewish interactions, they simultaneously accused the Jews of being separatist and aloof. As the persecutors locked the Ghetto gates, they accused the Jews of being secretive and insular.

Persecution formed the basis for a propaganda that only fueled further harassment and discrimination. This condition was the norm for most of the Jewish world until only 70 years ago.

Since after the Holocaust, Jews have enjoyed religious freedom unlike anything experienced for the past 2000 years. With the decline of official oppression and discrimination, it is only now that Torah can be discussed, studied, and taught freely.

## Jews & Non-Jews

Judaism is not unconcerned with non-Jews, nor is it aloof to the spiritual needs of the world at large. For the past 2000 years, however, these matters could not be discussed openly in any meaningful way. It is only recently that the Jewish community has been able to freely discuss the Torah's vision of the world. It is not a vision for Jews alone, but a vision for all mankind.

At Sinai the Torah was revealed and given to the Jewish people. It sealed the covenant between the Jewish people and the Creator of the universe. However, the Sinaitic covenant was neither the first nor the only agreement stuck between God and man. As testified to within the Torah itself, God established covenants with Adam and Noah.

Today, the Torah provides for two ideal relationships with God. One is that of the Jew, known as Judaism, governed by the covenant of Sinai. The other is that of the gentile, originally[1] governed by the covenants of Noah and Adam, known as the Noahide covenant.

## Law & Love

The Torah, Judaism, and by extension, the Noahide laws, are concerned with action. Mere belief in God or principles is not enough. The Torah requires us to actualize; to perform God's will in this world. How, though, do we know God's will? The answer is: *mitzvos*.

Both of the covenants include *mitzvos* – divine commandments – expressing God's expectations of man. The Sinatic, Jewish covenant includes 613 *mitzvos*, divine laws. The Noahide covenant contains 7 categories of *mitzvos* (commandments) which include over 30 *mitzvos* in total.

---

[1] As we shall see in future lessons, the original Adamic/Noahic covenant was eventually subsumed under the authority of the Sinaitic covenant.

But, why laws? Are not ethics enough? The Torah, as we shall see, contains both ethics and laws. Yet, there is a big difference between laws and ethics. Ethics are guiding moral principles having broad application. They are values commonly held, but whose interpretation easily becomes subjective. Laws, however, are specifically defined guidelines that mold and create societies; laws have the effect of putting everyone on the same page. They create commonality and community. Ethics need laws to impose structure, commonality, and to preserve their meaning. However, law without ethics is meaningless.

But isn't Judaism, or for that matter Noahism, a religion of love? If the covenants are motivated by love, then why does God want us to follow laws? The question itself is fundamentally flawed. Creation was, by default, the ultimate act of love and kindness. As we will learn in later lessons, God created the universe in order to bestow his goodness. Therefore, all of His actions are ultimately for the sake of our good, and all are acts of love. This includes His covenants, both the Sinaitic and the Noahide.

The idea that love and law are opposites is a fiction. It is part of the historical campaign of marketing and persecution discussed above. The church long portrayed the Torah as a covenant of law while claiming that their religion as one of love. The Torah views love and law as two sides of the same coin. Without any restraint, boundaries, or guidance, love is a destructive force, smothering force. Similarly, strict untempered justice is terrifying and unbearable. Law tempered by love, and love tempered by law, is God's ideal formulation.

The *mitzvos* – the divine commandments – give structure and expression to the underlying beliefs, ethics, and values of God's Torah. By fulfilling the *mitzvos*, we connect and become part of our Creator's will. In this sense, the *mitzvos* are far more than just laws – they are a direct means of connecting to God.

Therefore, the *mitzvos* must be studied, pursued, loved, and performed with tremendous joy and thankfulness for the opportunities that they present.

From a metaphysical standpoint, the fulfillment of *mitzvos* contributes to the rectification of God's creation. By fulfilling the *mitzvos*, we draw the light of God into the world and bring it closer to perfection.

## Legal Systems in Theory and Reality

The Torah is not only a religious system, but is also a system of national, civil, and interpersonal law. As with all systems of law, it carries penalties for violations. Throughout this course we will frequently discuss the penalties for violation of the Noahide laws. **These discussions are, today, mainly theoretical**. The reason for knowing the penalties of the transgressions today is so we can compare the relative severity of the transgressions. A transgression with a light penalty is, generally, a lesser transgression than one with a severe penalty. From such comparisons, we can determine which course of action to take in pressing circumstances.

This same method of analysis is used by Jews in the study of Jewish law.

Unfortunately, this discussion of penalties, necessary to the study of the Noahide laws, has sometimes given rise to anti-Semitic myths and misunderstandings. These are the most frequent questions asked about the Noahide laws:

**Noahides Law is discriminatory because it imposes the death penalty for non-Jews for any transgression of the Torah.**

> There are very few transgressions of Noahide law that incur capital punishment. As we shall see, the Noahide laws include 7 categories of transgressions, for which only about a dozen specific actions incur capital punishment. By comparison, Jewish law has about 35 categories which incur capital punishment, with over 100 specific transgressions for which a Jew could be put to death. Furthermore, Noahides are only executed via beheading, the quickest and most painless method of Torah-mandated executions. Jews, though, may also be burned to death, strangled, or stoned – penalties that <u>may not</u> be given to Noahides. Additionally there are dozens of Jewish transgressions for which Jews are punished with 40 lashes. Jews may also receive *kares* – spiritual excision – one of the most severe penalties found in the Torah. Non-Jews <u>do not</u> receive lashes or *kares*. <u>The Torah's legal system is, generally, more stringent in its judgment and treatment of Jews than of non-Jews</u>.[2]

---

[2] See also Sanhedrin 59a.

## Will I be put to death for transgressing the Noahide laws?

The death penalty was only ever given 1) in Israel, 2) when the Jews had full sovereignty over their land, and 3) when the Sanhedrin was fully functioning. Today, even though Israel is in Jewish hands, this is only a political restoration. It is not the level of religiously valid possession required to allow theocratic rulership of the land. Furthermore, there is no Sanhedrin today to administer the death penalty (the Sanhedrin cannot be restored until messianic times). Another important point is that the Noahide legal system primarily charges Noahides with the administration of justice, not Jews.

You can also view things this way: if Jews are not liable to capital punishment today, then Noahides are certainly not either. As we have seen, Jewish law is, generally, more severe than Noahide law.

In short – though there were times in the past when an Noahide in Israel could, in theory, receive the death penalty, it can never be happen today.

## Weren't Noahides put to death more often than Jews in ancient Israel?

There are no statistics as to the demographics of those executed. However, given that Noahide law cannot be more severe than Jewish law, it is a strange assumption to make. As well, the circumstances necessary to actually obligate someone to execution are very specific; in fact they are so specific that execution was rarely ever decreed. The Talmud records:

*A court that executes at a rate of one person every seventy years is considered murderous.*[3]

The commentaries explain that even one person every 70 years was a frequency beyond the pale of possibility, indicating that the court was far too severe in its approach. Consider as well that just because someone commits a crime deserving the death penalty, they may not actually receive it. This is the case in American law as well.

## Isn't a Non-Jew put to death for studying Torah? Also, isn't a Jew allowed to steal from a non-Jew? Isn't a Jew allowed to lie to a non-Jew, but not to another Jew? Isn't a Jew allowed to kill a non-Jew? Isn't a Jew allowed to charge a non-Jew interest, yet not to another Jew?

---

[3] See Mishnah Makkos 1:10.

We grouped these allegations together because they all suffer from the same problem: they are all assumptions based on either mistranslations or decontextualized Talmudic quotes. Realize this: <u>the Talmud does not state the final law for Jews.</u> This allegation is a long-held anti-Semitic myth. The Talmud is an encyclopedia of conversations and explorations pertaining to Torah Law. It <u>DOES NOT</u> represent conclusive Jewish belief or practice. A Talmudic conversation may quote 50 different opinions without explicitly indicating clearly which one is conclusive. The Church has, for centuries, cherry-picked those statements which could be used as propaganda against the Jews. The conclusive opinions of the Talmud are recorded in commentaries and codes, especially in the *Shulchan Aruch*, The Code of Jewish Law, complied by Rabbi Yosef Karo in the 16$^{th}$ century. The importance of the Talmud is that it presents the methodology of correct Torah interpretation and study. The *Shulchan Aruch* decides according to the Talmudic opinions that prohibit a Jew from stealing, lying to, or harming a non-Jew. Additionally, a non-Jew is not actually put to death for studying Torah.

One of the above allegations, however, is true. A Jew may not charge interest to another Jew, but may do so to a non-Jew. By the same token, though, non-Jews may charge interest to Jews, so it is something of a false criticism.

## Summary of This Lesson

1. At Sinai, God gave the Torah to the Jewish people, entrusting them with 613 divine commandments. At the same time God reaffirmed through Moses that the 7 Laws of the Children of Noah still applied to all of mankind.

2. The Torah is therefore a divine revelation not only for the Jewish world, but also for the non-Jewish world with regard to the 7 Laws of the Children of Noah.

3. Although the creation of the world and the giving of the Torah were acts of love, this does not preclude the role of law.

4. The *mitzvos* – divine commandments – give shape and direction to our expressions of love and worship of God, while they also inform us as to God's will.

5. Although the 7 Laws of the Children of Noah are a fundamental part of Torah thought, they have not been discussed or taught much in the past 1800 years. This is largely the effect of persecution and ghettoization, which limited interactions with non-Jews and the restrictions placed on the study and teaching of Torah.

THE YESHIVA PIRCHEI SHOSHANIM SHULCHAN ARUCH LEARNING PROJECT

# The Noahide Laws – Lesson Two

© **Yeshiva Pirchei Shoshanim 2017**
This shiur may not be reproduced in any
form without permission of the copyright holder.

164 Village Path, Lakewood NJ 08701 732.370.3344
164 Rabbi Akiva, Bnei Brak, 03.616.6340

## Outline of This Lesson:

1. Ancient Noahide History
2. Aimé Pallière & R' Eliyahu Benamozegh
3. Vendyl Jones
4. R' Menachem Mendel Schneersohn, The Lubavitcher Rebbe
5. The Aftermath of The Rebbe's Call
6. The *Sefer Sheva Mitzvos HaShem*
7. State of Noahide Outreach Today
8. Role of This Course
9. Summary

# *An Overview of Noahide History*

## Ancient Noahide History

It is obvious that there was a divine law in place prior to the giving of the Torah. After all, murder must have been prohibited, for Cain was punished for killing Abel.[1] The generation of the flood was punished for widespread robbery, among other lapses.[2] The cities of Sodom and Gomorrah were destroyed for extensive wickedness[3] and, in particular, sexual misconduct.[4]

We see, therefore, that God had expectations for man prior to the giving of the Torah. The Torah itself enumerates these expectations in many places:

> *God blessed them and God said to them: "Be fruitful and multiply…"*
> Genesis 1:28 see also Genesis 9:1

> *…but of the Tree of Knowledge of Good and Bad you must not eat…*
> Genesis 2:17

---

[1] Genesis 4:1-12

[2] Genesis 6:5-13

[3] Genesis 13:13, 18:20 – 22; See Yalkut Shimoni: Bereishit 83, Sanhedrin 109a and Genesis Rabbah 50 for further examples of the cruelty and sin of Sodom and Gemorah.

[4] Genesis 19:5.

> *But flesh, with its soul, its blood, you shall not eat.*
> Genesis 9:4

Though ancient sources are scarce, there are references from the time of the second temple onwards to non-Jewish worshipers of the Jewish god. These non-Jewish worshipers, known as the *Phebomenoi* (φοβουμενοι τον θεον), or Heaven-Fearers,[5] apparently adhered to the Noahide laws. Besides Talmudic and Mishnaic references, their existence is also cited in the first century C.E. writings of [Joesphus Flavius](#).[6] At about the same time, the Roman satirists Gaius Petronius Arbiter and Decimus Iunius Iuvenalis mocked those Romans who adopted Jewish beliefs and philosophy yet refused circumcision and full conversion.

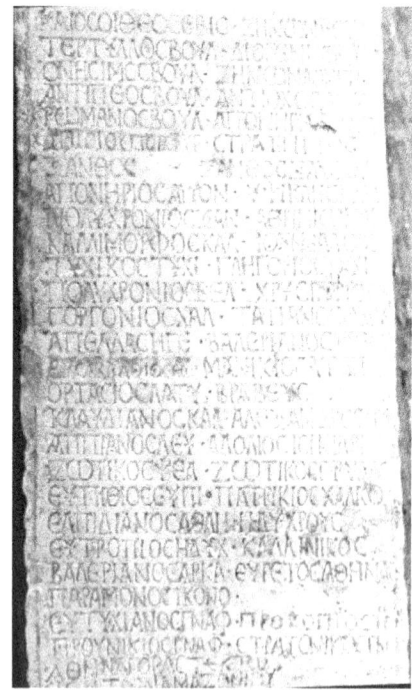

The most important archaeological evidence pertaining to Noahides was discovered in 1976 in Aphrodisias, Turkey. Two inscriptions (see image, left), dating from approximately 210 C.E., were discovered in an ancient synagogue. The first inscription is a list of synagogue founders, all with Jewish names common to the period. The second inscription, however, is a list of non-Jewish names such as Zeno, Athenogoras, and Diogenes. This inscription is prefaced with the words: "And these are those who are God Fearers..." A similar inscription was discovered in the ancient ruined synagogue of Sardis, Turkey. This inscription lists three groups: Jews, converts, and observers of the Noahide laws. We know almost nothing about these ancient groups or their specific modes of observance.

With the ascent of church power and increasing persecution and dispersion of the Jewish community, Noahism fell by the wayside. With the exception of a few individual exceptions, the Noahide faith did not reappear again until the late 19th and early 20th century.

---

[5] Alternatively, known as *sebomenoi* (σεβομενοι), *theosebes* (θεοσεβης) or *theophobes* (θεοφοβεἰς) in some sources.

[6] *The Jewish Wars* II: 454, 463, and VII: 45; *Antiquities* XIV: 110 and XX: 41; *Against Apion* I: 166,167, and II: 282.

## Aimé Pallière & Rabbi Eliyahu Benamozegh

Noahism reemerged a religious identity in the late 19th century through the meeting of Aimé Pallière (1868-1949, photo below) and Rabbi Eliyahu Benamozegh (1822-1900, photo left). Pallière had lost faith in Catholic doctrine and began a personal search for religious truth. After being exposed to authentic Torah study in his home town of Lyon, he became interested in converting to Judaism. For family reasons, conversion was a remote option and Pallière found himself in deep spiritual crisis. His friends in the Jewish community suggested that he contact Rabbi Eliyahu Benamozegh, Rabbi of the Sephardic community of Leghorn, Italy.

R' Benamozegh offered Pallière a solution in the form of the Noahide laws:

*We Jews have in our keeping the religion destined for the entire human race, the religion to which the Gentiles are subject and by which they are to be saved, as were our Patriarchs before the giving of the Law. Could you suppose that the true religion which God destines for all humanity is only the property of a special people? Not at all. His plan is much greater than that. The religion of humanity is no other than "Noahism," not because it was founded by Noah, but because it was through the person of that righteous man that God's covenant with humanity was made. This is the path that lies before your efforts, and indeed before mine, as it is my duty to spread the knowledge of it also.*[7]

Though they only met once, Pallière and R' Benamozegh corresponded extensively over the next three years until R' Benamozegh's passing. Their exchanges formed the core of Pallière's book *Le sanctuaire inconnu, The Unknown Sanctuary*, which developed many ideas proposed by R' Benamozegh in his *Israël et l'Humanité, Israel and Humanity*.

Pallière and Benamozegh's thought influenced many to consider the Noahide laws as a religious faith. Subsequently, a few Noahide societies appeared in Europe devoted to the study of Pallière and Benamozegh's works. However, this movement came to an abrupt end with the advent of World War II.

It is important to note that, while Pallière and Benamozegh's conception of the Noahide laws is of historical importance, it is not entirely consonant with Jewish

---

[7] Aimé Pallière in *Le sanctuaire inconnu*.

theology and outlook. R' Benamozegh's theology could be, generously, called unconventional. Throughout his career R' Benamozegh, and Pallière to a large extent, was trying to create a "universalist" theology of Judaism.

This idea sought to resolve conflicts between Jewish, Christian, Moslem, and even pagan beliefs into a single unified Jewish theology.[8] Benamozegh used the Noahide laws as an important element in this goal. Their writings are of some historical importance. However, their vision of Noahism, both in practice and identity, presents many issues.[9]

## Early 20th Century

In the early 20th century a few major Torah scholars authored studies on the Noahide laws. These are important touchstones for anyone looking to attain a thorough understanding of the Noahide precepts. The two most significant are the *Kuntres Ner Mitzvah*, by Rabbi Meir Dan Plotzki (published in his larger work, the *Kli Chemda*) and the discussion of the Noahide Laws in the *Mitzvos HaShem* by Rabbi Yonasan Shteif.

Throughout the 20th century, Noahide issues were discussed sporadically by a number of Torah authorities. Most notably, Rabbi Moshe Feinstein, one of Judaism's greatest decisors of Torah law, wrote several important responsa on the Noahide laws. This material is found in many places in his *Igros Moshe* and is foundational to a practical understanding of the Noahide laws.

---

[8] The liberality of Benamozegh's theology, as evidenced in *Israël et l'Humanité* and in his other writings, is often problematic. Despite their popularity in Noahide circles, his writings are almost entirely unknown to mainstream Judaism. They have only recently become known to contemporary authorities and experts as a result of increased interest in the Noahide laws.

[9] An example is Pallière's own conception of Noahide practice, which was somewhat different than what might be expected. Though a Noahide, he admits in *Le sanctuaire inconnu* that he remained a practicing Catholic, even accepting regular communion. Several explanations have been offered of Pallière's apparently dual religious allegiances. However, these explanations all fail for one of two reasons: either 1) they are based on erroneous assumptions about Christianity, or 2) they are based on a flawed understanding of the laws of idolatry as they apply to non-Jews. Indeed, there is no satisfactory way of explaining Pallière's practice within the context of standard Torah thought. However, his situation is acceptable, perhaps even laudable, within the context of R' Benamozegh's universalist view of religion. This is one example of the many difficulties underlying R' Benamozegh's approach.

## Vendyl Jones (1930 – 2010)

Vendyl Jones was arguably the most important figure in the resurrection of Noahism as a religious identity. Jones began his career as pastor of a Baptist church. He resigned his pulpit in 1956 after wrestling with deep doubts as to his Christian faith. Though he held advanced degrees in theology and biblical studies, Vendyl decided to restart his entire religious education from scratch. Moving his family to South Carolina, he enrolled in classes at a local Talmud Torah (Jewish elementary school). As he gained facility in Torah study and Hebrew, he sought guidance from local rabbis in observance of the Noahide laws. Jones steadily developed a very sophisticated Noahide religious identity grounded firmly in Torah study and worldview.

In the 1960's Jones became deeply involved in archaeological pursuits, eventually moving his family to Israel to continue his studies at Hebrew University. Over the next three decades he embarked on a number of important excavations.

Through his lectures on biblical archaeology, publications, lectures, and weekly classes, he not only inspired innumerable non-Jews to explore Noahism, but also brought the Noahide laws back onto the rabbinic radar. Since the destruction of the temple, awareness of the Noahide laws had waned. As well, rabbinic familiarity with these laws had become correspondingly scarce. Vendyl's personal quest to understand the Noahide obligations inspired many rabbis to reopen these long abandoned areas of study.

As a result of his sincere beliefs and honest quest for truth, Vendyl is regarded by many Noahides and Rabbis as the father of the modern Noahide movement.

## Rabbi Menachem Mendel Schneersohn (1902 - 1994)

In 1984 Rabbi Schneersohn (the last leader of the Chassidic court of Lubavitch), called upon the larger Rabbinic community to engage in the study and dissemination of the Noahide laws. His article, published in the rabbinic journal *HaPardes*,[10] made a deep impression within his own movement, Chabad-Lubavitch. Many Chabad Rabbis began studying and teaching the Noahide laws in earnest (indeed Chabad Lubavitch has long held an edge in the study and teaching of this material). The Rebbe also spoke and wrote on the Noahide laws, outlining many of the fundamental principles. His teachings were collected and published as *Kol Bo'ai HaOlam* by Rabbi C. Miller.

The Rebbe further encouraged the creation of authoritative compendia of Noahide law. However, such a work did not materialize until only recently.

## The Aftermath of the Rebbe's Call

Though many in Chabad Lubavitch embraced the Rebbe's call-to-action, Rabbi Schneersohn's article was largely ignored by the rest of the Jewish world. This lack of response must be viewed in the context of the time. 1984 was only 39 years after the catastrophic destruction of European Jewry. At that time, the Jewish world was engaged in an intense struggle to re-establish Torah education and observance in the US. As well, the Jewish community was deeply involved in outreach to the vast population of unaffiliated American Jews. It was "all hands on deck" time for the Jewish community. Given limited resources and pressing needs, Noahide outreach was not a priority.[11] Additionally, the rabbinic community did

---

[10] *Sheva Mitzvot Shel Benai Noach*, *HaPardes* 59:9 (5745)

[11] Lubavitch, it should be noted, was far ahead of other Jewish groups in post-holocaust rebuilding. If any group was, at that time, in a position to reach out to Noahides it certainly would have been Lubavitch,.

not find Rabbi Schneersohn's key argument (that there exists today a Torah obligation to seek non-Jewish observance of the Noahide laws) convincing.[12]

While the Jewish mainstream did not embrace Noahide outreach, the fringe of the Jewish world took a deep interest in it. These groups, however, often taught interpretations of the Noahide laws that were heavily colored by their own ideologies and beliefs. Additionally, many of these organizations realized that, by teaching the Noahide laws in a way that catered to what non-Jews wanted to hear, they could build a support base among non-Jews. These groups, for the most part, had not succeeded in finding an audience within the Jewish world. With the Noahide laws, they had a tool to build support and followers for their own agendas.

## The Late 20th Century

By the late 1990's and early 2000's, a number of things were occurring in the Jewish and Noahide worlds:

- **Among Non-Jews** – Beginning in the late 20th century the non-Jewish world has experienced a wave of disillusionment with Christianity. Many ex-Christians, feeling betrayed by their religious upbringing, sought connection with the Torah, coming to view it no longer as the "Old Testament," but as the "Original Testament." In the American south and southwest, in particular, non-Jews began approaching Rabbis seeking to understand the Torah.

- **In the Jewish Mainstream** – Although the Jewish world is still engaged heavily in establishing itself and reaching out to unaffiliated Jews, increasing interest from non-Jews has pushed Noahism "onto the radar." A number of important Torah scholars and experts on Torah law have recently turned their attention to Noahism.

- **Awareness of the Fringe** – As the Jewish mainstream has become increasingly aware of the Noahide movement, it has also become aware of problems and inaccuracies in the way the Noahide laws have been taught. Unfortunately, due to the mainstream's two-decade absence from Noahism,

---

[12] For a critical survey of the sources involved, see Rabbi Michael J. Broyde's "The Obligation of Jews to Seek Observance of Noahide Laws by Gentiles: A Theoretical Review" in *Tikkun olam: social responsibility in Jewish thought and law*. Edited by David Shatz, Chaim I. Waxman and Nathan J. Diament. Northvale, N.J. : Jason Aronson, 1997.

the Noahide movement had become a feeding ground for many fringe groups. These groups have succeeded in selling themselves to Noahides as valid authorities on Torah and Noahism. In the early 2000's, these fringe groups started to come under fire from the Jewish mainstream. Their response has been to wage increasingly desperate and eccentric campaigns to hold onto their Noahide supporters.

Between the increasing numbers of Noahides, and the problems with how Noahism had been presented by many groups, it became clear that something was missing. To date, no one had undertaken a significant, practical analysis of the totality of Torah literature on the Noahide laws. Without such an analysis, anyone discussing the Noahide laws was doing so "in a vacuum." It also meant that there was no standard by which ideas could be compared to determine their legitimacy. This situation confirmed the Rebbe's tremendous foresight in calling for a full, authoritative compendium of Noahide law.

## The *Sefer Sheva Mitzvos HaShem* – The Seven Divine Commandments

In the late 20th century, Ask Noah International (ANI) took the initiative to fulfill the Lubavitcher Rebbe's desire for a complete exposition of Noahide law. They tasked the well-known Jerusalem scholar, Rabbi Moshe Weiner, with the *halakhic* (Torah law) research and writing of the work. This monumental project cumulated with the publication in Hebrew of the first major *halakhic* (practical) exploration of Noahide laws and beliefs: the *Sefer Sheva Mitzvos HaShem*. This three-volume work was the first major presentation of the foundational principles of the Noahide Laws.

His work is a survey of nearly everything written in classical Torah sources on the Noahide laws, how they are to be understood, and how they are to be fulfilled. The most important achievement of the *Sefer Sheva Mitzvos* is that it successfully distills a framework for determining legitimate Noahide practice and identity.

We must keep in mind that for over 1500 years observance of the Noahide laws did not exist as a religious identity. Whatever this observance may have once been, it effectively went extinct in the 4th century. Like Judaism, Noahism has foundational principles upon which it is built. These principles are found in the core texts of the Torah and Talmud. In order to rebuild Noahism, these foundational principles must be brought out into the light. Any attempt to resurrect adherence to the Noahide laws without a solid textual foundation is doomed to fail. Yet, with these foundations in place, the beliefs and identities of Noahism can be rebuilt and made to flourish.

Before the publication of the *Sefer Sheva Mitzvos HaShem*, the Noahide movement had only a limited scholarly resources upon which to grow and rebuild. The publication of the *Sefer Sheva Mitzvos HaShem* is also important in that it provided a point of contact between mainstream Judaism's scholarly community and the Noahide movement, reintroducing this subject to the arena of *halakhic* (Torah law) discourse.

In 2011, selections of the *Sefer Sheva Mitzvos HaShem* were translated and published in English as *The Divine Code*.

Since its publication a number of further studies have been produced. Of particular importance is the *Toldos Noach* by Rabbi Eliezer Baruch.

## The Current Situation

The Noahide movement today is deeply polarized. There are essentially two approaches:

- **Approach #1: Noahism as Judaizing** – The approach advocated by many groups outside of the Jewish mainstream has been one of Judaizing: encouraging non-Jews to imitate Jewish practices and symbols (such as Shabbat observance, building *sukkot*, etc.) This approach is problematic for two reasons:

    o 1) **Torah Law** – There are a number of principles of Torah law, established from time immemorial, that restrict Judaizing, the imitation or adoption of Jewish practices by non-Jews. The transgression of these rules is severe; some even carry the penalty of death at the hands of heaven! Rather than help and assist Noahides in developing and establishing a positive, uniquely non-Jewish relationship with God, many of the aforementioned groups have simply offered non-Jews Jewish rituals and claimed that they are legitimate "Noahide observances." When challenged as to the legitimacy of this approach, these groups have resorted to increasingly strange defenses of their actions.

    o 2) **An Existential Contradiction** – Advocating the imitation of Jewish practices as an expression of Noahide identity creates an existential problem. If the Noahide laws represent God's will and the Torah's relevance for all of mankind, then they must have universal meaning. Why then should we define the Noahide laws using the narrow, specific experiences of the Jewish people? For example, let's look at the Torah's festivals. The Jewish observances of the festivals are uniquely bound up with the history and experience of the Jewish people. Yet, the Mishnah[13] tells us that the festivals also have universal relevance. The universal meaning and the Jewish meaning of the festivals, though, is not always the same. Sukkot is an excellent example of this duality. The Mishnah[14] tells us that the world is judged for water on Sukkot. Additionally, Sukkot is also the holiday on which Israel gave offerings to gain atonement for the non-Jewish nations. These aspects of the holiday are universal and directly relevant to Noahides. However, the building of and dwelling within a *sukkah* (the festive booths built on the holiday) is unique to Israel alone. After all, dwelling within a *sukkah* commemorates the return of the clouds of glory after the building of the tabernacle in the wilderness. By encouraging Noahides to adopt Jewish observances (i.e. building a *sukkah*), the universal meaning of the holiday is constricted and supplanted with the specific Jewish meaning. If the Noahide laws are universally relevant, then their meaning must be kept universal and not constrained to the Jewish experience. Encouraging non-Jews to imitate Jewish rituals creates an existential conflict. Is Noahism about the universal experience of mankind, or is Noahism defined only by the Jewish experience?

- **Approach #2: Defining Boundaries** – In what appears to be a reaction to the first approach, many in the mainstream Jewish world have taken a very conservative stance. These groups have sought to define observance of the Noahide laws primarily by what it is not and what it cannot be. Their mission is to explain where the boundaries lay between Judaism and the Noahide laws, and to draws the lines that Noahides may not cross. From a scholarly perspective, the details of this approach are absolutely correct. However, this approach overlooks an important need: **the need to positively express one's faith**. There is great value and necessity in defining the boundaries of a Noahide's identity. However, such a negative definition does not provide much of a route for positive religious expression. This craving for positive religious expression has been specifically exploited by the first approach. The first approach offers non-Jews positive affirmations of their faith via imitations of Jewish ritual. Though illegitimate from a perspecive of Torah law, this imitation of Jewish ritual fulfills a vitally important spiritual need. Additionally, by not providing a positive model for the growth of observance of the Noahide

---

[13] Rosh HaShanah 1:2.

[14] Ibid.

laws, this second approach may drive away those non-Jews looking for an authentic approach to Torah.

In summary, the central issue concerning the Noahide laws today is that of finding positive, acceptable modes of non-Jewish religious expresson. Approach #1 offers Noahides a positive expression of their faith by encouraging them to imitate Jewish ritual. Though deeply problematic, this approach fills an important need. Approach #2 is aboslutely correct from a perspective of Torah belief and law, yet does not meet the religious needs of many non-Jews.

## The Approach of this Course

This course does not seek to enter into the debate between the two aforementioned approaches (although we may occasionally point out issues and questions raised by both approaches). This course takes a practical, source-based approach with the following goals:

- To clarify the exact definition and identity of a "Noahide" in our times,

- To explain the fundamental principles of Noahism and the derivation of the Noahide laws,

- To explain the universal themes of the Torah and holidays and the ways in which Noahides may give legitimate, positive expression to these themes within the expectations of Torah law,

- To define which areas of the Noahide laws need more growth on behalf of the Noahide community to create positive expressions of their faith.

The goal of this course is not to be the definitive, final word on the Noahide laws. Instead, this course seeks to provide Noahides and the rabbinic community with a foundation, a sense of direction, and with clearly defined goals.

## Summary of the Lesson

1. There is evidence, both written and archaeological, of communities of Noahide adherents from biblical times through the 3rd century CE. The Church's ascent to power eliminated these communities. Until the 19th century, Noahide observance and identity would remain rare.

2. In the late 19th and early 20th century Aimé Pallière & Rabbi Eliyahu Benamozegh reintroduced Noahide observance to Europe. Their writings on the role of the Noahide laws in modern society are important. However, their vision of Noahide identity and practice is heavily colored by Universalist religious thought prevalent in Europe at the time.

3. In the second half of the 20th century, Vendyl Jones became the impetus and rallying point for the resurgent interest in Noahide observance, leaving a deep impact on the course of the Noahide movement.

4. Rabbi Menachem M. Schneersohn in 1984 called upon the rabbinic community to study and teach the Noahide laws to gentiles. While Rabbis within his own movement embraced this call, most of the rabbinic community did not follow suit.

5. There are two polarized approached to Noahism today. One, from outside the Jewish mainstream, encourages imitation of Jewish ritual. The other, seeks to define the boundaries of Noahism. Both approaches contain flaws and merits. The biggest issue with them both, however, is that they do not provide guidance for legitimate, positive expressions of Noahide faith.

6. Rabbi Moshe Weiner, in 2001, began compiling the *Sefer Sheva Mitzvos HaShem*, [the Seven Divine Commandments] the first major compilation and analysis of authentic sources pertaining to the Noahide laws.

THE YESHIVA PIRCHEI SHOSHANIM SHULCHAN ARUCH LEARNING PROJECT

# The Noahide Laws – Lesson Three

**© Yeshiva Pirchei Shoshanim 2017**
This shiur may not be reproduced in any
form without permission of the copyright holder.

164 Village Path, Lakewood NJ 08701 732.370.3344
164 Rabbi Akiva, Bnei Brak, 03.616.6340

## Outline of This Lesson:

1. Non-Jews in the Torah: Many Identities
2. Idolaters & Idolatry
3. *Ger Tzedek*
4. *Ben Noach, Bat Noach, Bnei Noach*
5. *MiChakhmei Umos HaOlam* – Of the Wise of the Nations
6. *MiChasidei Umos HaOlam* – Of the Pious of the Nations
7. How Does One Become a Noahide?
8. *Ger Toshav*

# Gentile Identities in the Torah

## Introduction

Non-Jewish religious identity is a complicated matter that will be examined in detail in future lessons. However, it is important at this point to provide working definitions of the various non-Jewish identities found throughout the Torah and Talmud.

## Non-Jews in the Torah: Many Identities

Words have very different meanings when used in technical versus colloquial contexts. For example, "accurate" and "precise" are used in everyday speech to mean the same thing. However, they have very different meanings in a scientific context. Similarly, most people hear "challah" and think of the braided loaves of bread used on the Sabbath. However, in the Talmud and other works that determine religious practice "challah" refers specifically to the dough tithe given to *Kohanim*, priests, in the times of the temple (see Numbers 15:17-21).

The Torah uses many terms for non-Jews and, within the context of Jewish law, these terms have very specific meanings. However, the use of these terms in Kabbalistic (mystical), Midrashic, and other non-legal writings is much less controlled. It takes a trained, experienced Rabbinic scholar to determine when these terms have their legal and practical meanings versus colloquial and metaphoric connotations.

## Idolaters & Idolatry

The Torah and Jewish law are, by necessity, very concerned with defining idolatry and the identity of the idolater. Anyone who worships idols is, of course, an idolater. Idolatry, however, manifests itself in a number of forms. It can be either as modes of worship or systems of belief. Engaging in idolatrous practices, such as bowing before a statue, are prohibited even if one doesn't believe in what he is doing.

Similarly, idolatrous beliefs, such as believing that God manifests or has ever manifested Himself corporeally, are prohibited.

An idolater is referred to using a variety of terms in the Torah and Talmud, the most common being *Akum*. *Akum* is an acronym for **A**veid **K**okhavim **U**-**M**azalos – one who serves stars and constellations. However, it is used to refer to any idolater and is sometimes a general term for non-Jews. A lesser known term is *nochri*, which carries a similar connotation.

## *Ger Tzedek* – A Righteous Convert

The word *Ger* has many meanings. The verb root from which it derives implies sojourning. However, in its noun form it means a "stranger" or "outsider." When used alone, *Ger* almost always means a convert. When *Ger* is in any way used together with the word *Toshav*, it means a *Ger Toshav*, something entirely different than a convert (we will discuss *Ger Toshav* at length in future lessons). The Talmud devotes extensive analysis to determining correct interpretations of the Torah's use of the term *Ger*. For clarity, the Talmud qualifies its own use of *Ger* with the term *Tzedek*, meaning a righteous convert. The term *Ger Tzedek*, as used in the Talmud and codes of Jewish law, means exclusively a full convert to Judaism.[1]

If a *ger tzedek* is a full convert to Judaism, then why does the Talmud call them a *ger tzedek* and not simply a "Jew?" The reason is that a convert is not 100% identical to a born Jew. For example, a female convert may not marry a *Kohen* (descendant of Aharon).[2] A convert may also not serve in a position of communal authority (such as being a synagogue Rabbi)[3] nor sit on a *beis din* (Rabbinic tribunal). For the purposes of discussing the laws involved, the Talmud must have some way to distinguish a convert from a born Jew. We should note also, that is no other term in Hebrew for convert – only *Ger Tzedek*.

---

[1] The term *Ger Tzedek* is used in five places in the Babylonian Talmud (Bava Metzia 71a, Bava Metzia 111b, Gittin 57b, Yevamos 48b, and Sanhedrin 96b) and twice in the Jerusalem Talmud (*Bava Metzia* 5:4 and 9:10).

[2] Maimonides, *Issurei Biah* 18:1.

[3] Maimonides, *Hilchos Melakhim* 1:4.

## Ben Noach, Bat Noach, Bnei Noach

*Ben Noach* and *Bat Noach* mean, respectively, a Son of Noah and a Daughter of Noah. *Bnei Noach* is the plural form of both of these terms. In English, the term used for a *Ben* or *Bat Noach* is Noahide. These are generic terms for any non-Jew who keeps the Seven Mitzvos for any reason or motivation. There are different types of *Bnei Noach*:

- *MiChakhamei Umos HaOlam*
- *MiChasidei Umos HaOlam*

## MiChakhmei Umos HaOlam – The Wise Ones of the Nations

One who keeps the Seven Mitzvos because they are logical and make societal sense is called *MiChakhamei Umos HaOlam* – From the Wise Ones of the Nations. Such a *Ben Noach* receives only a very limited portion in the World to Come[4] for his observance. He receives most of his merit in this world.[5]

## MiChasidei Umos HaOlam – The Pious Who Receive a Share in the World to Come

The Talmud in Sanhedrin 105a proves that the *Umos Ha-Olam*, the gentile nations, have a share in the World to Come if they are *Chasidim*, pious. Therefore, a non-Jew who keeps the Seven Mitzvos (Commandments) is called *MiChasidei Umos HaOlam*, of the Pious Non-Jews, and he receives reward in the World to Come. However, he only merits this reward if he accepts and observes his *mitzvos* from the viewpoint that they were transmitted and reaffirmed to the world via Moses at Sinai.

One who keeps the Seven Mitzvos only on account of the original covenant with Adam and Noah will still receive reward. However his reward will be of a lesser form and he will not be considered *MiChasidei Umos HaOlam*, of the Pious Non-Jews.

---

[4] The future messianic era.

[5] The nature of the reward for "The Wise Ones" is subject to many interpretations. The many discussions of the subject would certainly agree, though, to the description we have provided here. See Maharal in *Tiferes Yisrael* and *Derech HaShem* II:4.

## How Does One Become a *Ben Noach*?

To become a Noahide, one must accept the Seven Mitzvos upon himself from a conviction that they are divinely ordained, having been commanded to the world by God, through Moses, who reaffirmed the covenant sealed with Adam and then Noah. By accepting the Seven Mitzvos as such, one becomes *MiChasidei Umos HaOlam*, a Pious Gentile, and the highest status attainable by a *Ben Noach*.

While any personal acceptance of the Seven Mitzvos is sufficient, it makes logical sense to capture the intention of the acceptance in the form of a verbal oath enumerating the 7 mitzvos and stating one's motivation in accepting them. Any text accomplishing these goals is sufficient.

For example:

> *I accept upon myself the Seven Commandments of the Children of Noah, including the general and specific prohibitions of idolatry, murder, theft, sexual immorality, blasphemy, eating of flesh torn from a living animal, and the general and specific commandments to establish a system of justice, as commanded to Noah, Adam, and their descendants, by the mouth of The Holy One, creator of the universe, as reaffirmed and transmitted by His servant Moses at the giving of the Torah at Sinai.*

One is not required to accept the *mitzvos* before any Jewish Court (*Beis Din*),[6] court, or assembly of other persons. Any personal or private acceptance of the Seven Mitzvos is sufficient. Nevertheless, it is a good idea to make a verbal acceptance before witnesses.

## *Ger Toshav* - A Non-Jew who resides in the land of Israel

The term *ger toshav* has created special confusion for modern Noahides and will be discussed at length in a future lesson.

The *ger toshav* is referred to in many places in the Torah:

- Exodus 12:43-45 – *This is the decree of the Passover offering… a resident* [Toshav] *and a hired laborer may not eat of it.*

- Lev. 25:6 – *The land's yield of the sabbatical year shall be yours to eat, yours… and the residents'* [Toshav] *who sojourns* [Ger] *among you.*

---

[6] A Jewish rabbinic court of three judges. A *Beis Din* judges matters of religious and monetary law in the Jewish community.

- Lev. 25:35 – *...you shall strengthen him, the convert or the resident* [Toshav].

- Lev. 25:40 – *Like a laborer or a resident* [Toshav] *he shall be with you, until the jubilee year he shall work with you.*

- Lev. 25:45 - *...also, from among the children of the residents* [Toshav] *who dwell* [Ger] *with you...*

- Lev. 25:47 – *If the means of a sojourner* [Ger] *who resides* [Toshav] *among you...*

- Num. 35:15 – *For the children of Israel, the convert, and the resident* [Toshav] *among them...*

The term *ger*, from the Hebrew root *gar*, meaning "to sojourn," refers to an alien, a stranger, or an immigrant. *Toshav* means "reside." A *ger toshav* is, therefore, a resident alien: a non-Jew who resides in the land of Israel among the Jewish people. However, the Torah tells us:

*They [idolaters] shall not dwell in your land lest they cause you to sin against Me and worship their gods.*[7]

We see that a *ger toshav* must give up his idolatrous beliefs and practices in order to live in Israel.

How is this accomplished practically? How far must a non-Jew go in disavowing idolatry so that he may reside in Israel? The Talmud[8] explains that the prospective *ger toshav* must come before a *Beis Din* (Jewish religious court) and accept upon himself to faithfully observe the seven Noahide laws.

However, the Talmud[9] and later authorities tell us that there is no status of *ger toshav* in our days.

Nevertheless, some rabbis have instructed Noahides to accept the status of *ger toshav* even today. Others have not sought to confer *ger toshav* status, but have required potential Noahides to nevertheless accept their commandments before a *Beis Din* (Jewish Rabbinical court). Both of these are unnecessary as we will see in future lessons.

---

[7] Exodus 23:33.

[8] *Avodah Zarah 64b*.

[9] *Arakhin 29a*.

The *halakhah* (decisive religious law) is that there is no need or benefit for one to accept the Seven Mitzvos before a *Beis Din*. Such an acceptance before a *Beis Din* will have no effect whatsoever on the *Ben Noach's* religious status, ability to fulfill his *mitzvos*, or the merit he receives for fulfilling the mitzvos.

## Summary of the Lesson

1. Idolatrous thoughts, practices, and beliefs are all prohibited. An idolater is called an *akum*. Sometimes the term *nokhri* is used, but it is uncommon.

2. A *ger tzedek* is a non-Jew who has undergone conversion to Judaism. It has no other definition.

3. A *Ben Noach* is a male Noahide. A *Bat Noach* is a female Noahide. *Bnei Noach* are Noahides.

4. *MiChasidei Umos HaOlam* – a Pious One of the Nations – is a *Ben Noach* who has accepted the Seven *Mitzvos*. His acceptance is tied to the revelation at Sinai – he accepts the Noahide laws as an extension of this revelation. In return, he receives the full merit of "one who is commanded and fulfills" and merits a share in the World to Come.

5. One, who accepts the Seven *Mitzvos* based upon logic or moral (yet non-religious) basis is praised, yet receives no reward in the World to Come.

6. One becomes a *Ben Noach* by accepting the Noahide laws upon himself. There is no special form of this acceptance. However, a verbal oath makes sense. For practical reasons, it is a good idea that the oath be made before a witness.

THE YESHIVA PIRCHEI SHOSHANIM SHULCHAN ARUCH LEARNING PROJECT

# The Noahide Laws – Lesson Four

**© Yeshiva Pirchei Shoshanim 2017**
This shiur may not be reproduced in any
form without permission of the copyright holder.

164 Village Path, Lakewood NJ 08701 732.370.3344
164 Rabbi Akiva, Bnei Brak, 03.616.6340

# Outline of This Lesson:

1. The Uniqueness of the Torah Tradition
2. The Jewish View of *Tanakh* (Scripture)
3. The Prophets & Writings
4. The Many Facets of Torah
5. Torah *She-Baal Peh* – The Oral/Experiential Torah
6. Mesorah - Transmission
7. Writing Down the Oral Law
   a. The Mishnah (Teaching)
   b. The Gemorah (Learning)
   c. The Talmud
8. Other Torah Texts
   a. Midrash
   b. Mystical Texts
9. Rabbinic Authority
10. Deciding *Halakhah* (Practice)
11. Eras of Torah Scholarship & Authority
    a. The *Gaonim*
    b. The *Rishonim*
    c. The *Koviim*
    d. The *Acharonim*
12. In Summary

# Interpreting the Torah

## The Uniqueness of the Torah Tradition

In the next several lessons, we are going to study the seven Noahide laws, how they are derived, and how they structure and shape the Divine vision for mankind. Since this exploration will be rooted in the ancient texts that make up Torah thought and theology, we must first introduce these texts and explain their purpose and how they work.

Although the seven Noahide laws have their origins in Adam and Noah, God chose to transmit and preserve them via Moses and the giving of the Torah at Sinai. This placed the Seven *Mitzvos* within the structure and system of Torah study and learning. Therefore, the seven Noahide laws must be interpreted and understood within the context of the Torah.

**This point cannot be stressed enough: Jewish, and therefore Noahide, study and interpretation of the Torah is unique and unlike the study of any other religious texts.**

The uniqueness of the traditional approach to Torah interpretation cannot be emphasized enough. Jewish biblical interpretation exists in a completely different universe than non-Jewish modes of biblical interpretation. In fact, they overlap so little that no amount of background in biblical studies can prepare one for the unique approach that has been used by the Jewish people for centuries since the Torah's giving at Sinai.

As we shall see in this lesson, the term "Torah" encompasses far more than what could ever be put into writing. At Sinai, Moses received not only the Torah, in all of its various forms, but he also received a divinely ordained method of study and interpretation.

This larger conception of the Torah, along with its method of study, forms the basis of the two true religious paths ordained for mankind: Judaism, and the Noahide laws.

## The Jewish View of *Tanakh* (Scripture)

In many non-Jewish (by implication, non-Noahide) religions, the *Tanakh*,[1] the Torah, Prophets and Writings, are all treated with equal authority. Some even treat the later prophets with greater authority than the Torah itself.

This is not how Torah is viewed by those of Jewish, and by extension, Noahide faith. We view the Torah, Prophets, and Writings as hierarchical – there is an order of greater and lesser authority.

At the pinnacle of this hierarchy are the five books of the written Torah – the *Chumash*[2]. They are the final, permanent, crystallization of God's will for mankind. The Torah will never be replaced or superseded by any other future covenant or revelation.

In the textual realm, the Torah is the primary text for deriving law and practice for both Jews and Noahides.

## The Prophets & Writings

If the Torah is the ultimate revelation of God's will, then what is the need for later prophecy?

The main purpose of prophecy was to correct the people when they strayed from proper conduct or allegiance to the Torah. Therefore, the prophets and writings contain a treasure trove of moral inspiration and contemplation.

As for their practical interpretation, the prophets and writings do not come to, God forbid, alter or emend the Torah; The Torah is eternal and perfect. Rather, the Prophets and Writings play a supporting role. They are often used to clarify

---

[1] The complete Hebrew Bible is referred to as the *Tanakh*. The word is an acronym for *Torah* (Five Books of Moses), *Neviim* (Prophets), and *Kesuvim* (Writings).

[2] The word *Chumash* is the common term for the Five Books of Moses. It is a Hebrew word that means "fifths" – a reference to the five books.

the meanings of certain proper nouns that occur in the Torah. They are also used as support, yet not proof, of Rabbinic laws, customs, and interpretations.

## The Many Facets of Torah

The Five Books of Moses (the *Chumash*) is the most succinct possible written expression of Torah. However, the written Torah is only a gateway, an entry point into the larger world of Torah. The Torah is so vast, so all encompassing, that it is impossible to be entirely captured in writing.

Committing ideas to writing has many advantages – it creates permanence and a basis for interpretation. However, certain things cannot be expressed effectively in writing. For example, learning to sew, or paint from text alone is virtually impossible. One must be taught by someone with greater knowledge then himself. He must also be shown examples and have certain techniques demonstrated.

The situation is no different when trying to capture the infinite will of God in the finite language of man. A close reading of the Torah reveals many ambiguous, unclarified statements and terms. For example:

- *And it shall be for a sign upon your hand, and as* totafot *between your eyes; for with a mighty hand did the LORD bring us forth out of Egypt.* – Exodus 13:6

    o   The word *totafot* occurs in two similar passages (Deuteronomy 6:8 and 11:18), yet is not defined nor does it have any helpful Hebrew cognates.

- Similarly, The Torah writes: *…When you shall say 'I want to eat meat'… you shall slaughter of your herd and flock, according to how I have commanded you."* – Deuteronomy 12:20-21

    o   The Torah is referring to some method of slaughter commanded by God; however the Torah nowhere records this method.

- *This month shall be for you the first of the Months* – Exodus 12:2.

    o   What month is being referred to? Egyptian months (where the Jews lived), or Chaldean months (where Avraham came from). Is the Torah talking about Lunar or Solar months?

- *Let no man leave his place on the seventh day* – Exodus 16:29.

- What "place" may man not leave on the Sabbath? His home? His City? His recliner?

- Jethro instructed Moses to appoint judges and to: *enjoin upon them the laws and the teachings, and make known to them the way they are to go and the practices they are to follow.* – Exodus 18:20.

  - If the written Torah is complete and the only guiding force for man, then what is left for Moses to instruct? As well, the phrase: *…make known to them the way they are to go…*, informs us that there is some system or method by which judges are to rule.

Despite all of these ambiguities, the Psalms refer to the Torah as perfect:

*The Torah of God is perfect, restoring the soul…*[3]

How can a perfect text contain so many ambiguities? The answer is that *Torah* is not merely the text of the Torah. There is an orally transmitted, experiential component to the Torah, one which clarifies the ambiguities and, in combination with the written text, is called *perfect*.[4]

The Torah itself explicitly alludes to this larger conception of the Torah in Leviticus 26:46: *These are the statutes and the ordinances, and the* Toros [plural of Torah] *that God has given…*

If the written Torah was the only expression of Torah, then the verse would simply read: *This is the Torah that God has given*!

## Torah She-Baal Peh – The Oral/Experiential Torah

The Oral law exists for a number of reasons:

- It explains concepts that cannot be fully captured in writing,
- It defines unusual or rare terminology,

---

[3] Psalms 19:8.

[4] Albo, *Sefer HaIkkarim* III: 23. For other proofs to the necessity of an orally transmitted component of the Torah, see *Kuzari* 3:35; *Moreh Nevuchim* I:71; Rashbatz in *Mogen Avos Chelek HaFilosofi* II:3; Rashbash Duran in *Milchemes Mitzvah, Hakdama* I. See also Rashi to *Eruvin* 21b s.v. *VeYoser*; *Gur Aryeh* to *Shemos* 34:27.

- Most importantly, it provides a system of interpretation. This system of interpretation is crucial because it gives us three things:

    1) It guides us in the application of the Torah to new situations and new scenarios,

    2) It gives us standards and guidelines by which we can evaluate the legitimacy of interpretations and applications of the Torah, and

    3) It provides a means by which we can reconstruct any details of correct observance should it become blurred or forgotten due to exile and oppression.

## *Mesorah* - Transmission

The most important element in validating interpretations of the written and oral Torah is the concept of *Mesorah*. *Mesorah* is the greatest proof to the authenticity of any concept, practice, or interpretation.

*Mesorah* is a hard concept to translate. The closest translation is probably "transmission," the giving over of information. It refers to an unbroken chain of transmission from the revelation at Sinai until the present time. Authenticity of concepts and practices is strongly based upon *Mesorah*.

For example, the word *totafot* occurs in three similar passages: Exodus 13:6, Deuteronomy 6:8 and 11:18. The oral component of Torah tells us that *totafot* are *Tefillin*, phylacteries, the black boxes containing scriptural parchments which are worn by Jewish men during morning prayers. The oral component also tells us the complicated details of their writing and manufacture. For example: the boxes must be perfectly square and both the boxes and straps must be black. Yet, how do we know this is correct?

First and foremost – we know it is correct because we believe in the correctness of the oral component of the Torah. On top of that though, *Mesorah* tells us it is correct because there has never been a time since the giving of the Torah when *Tefillin* were made or conceived of in any other way.

Another example is kosher slaughter. The Torah tells us that there is a method of correct slaughter (see above and Deuteronomy 12:20-21). Yet, the Torah does not define this method. The oral Torah, though, provides us with great detail on the process, anatomical, and technical requirements for kosher slaughter. We know this to be correct based on the authority of the oral Torah and based on the fact that there has never been a time since Sinai when kosher slaughter was done any other way.

It should be noted here that *Mesorah* carries more weight than even archaeological evidence. Archaeology is concerned with reconstructing forgotten things based upon a minute amount of evidence. *Mesorah* is known information transmitted from generation to generation without having been forgotten. When there is a known break in *Mesorah*, the chain of transmission, and it has a practical effect on observance, we do not attempt to resurrect the *Mesorah* based on archaeological evidence. For example, knowing which cities in Israel were walled in ancient times is important for a number of laws. We rely on *Mesorah*, transmitted knowledge, to determine which cities were walled. Archaeological evidence is insufficient proof.

## Writing Down the Oral Law

For much of Jewish History, the oral Torah was not written down. It was part and parcel of the culture of a unified people living in a single location. Its integrity was also maintained by a central authority, the Sanhedrin. However, as the threat of exile loomed large and the Sanhedrin's authority waned under Roman persecution, the Rabbis realized that the transmission of Torah study and *Mesorah* was in danger[5].

They began to write down as much of the material as possible. Their vision for this redaction was two-fold:

1) To create a representative literature of the oral component of Torah in a form that was compact and efficient for study and memorization, and

2) Create a statement of the oral law that, by way of study, would teach and preserve the correct method of Torah study and interpretation.

The final product of this effort was the *Mishnah*.

---

[5] See *Temura* 14b.

| | |
|---|---|
| **The Mishnah (Teaching)** | The *Mishnah*, "Teaching," was sealed by Rabbi Judah the Prince[6] in about 220 CE. It's almost 600 chapters were divided into 6 orders, and each order into smaller divisions called *Masechtos,* Tractates. Each tractate was divided into chapters, and each chapter into smaller divisions, called *Mishanyos* – teachings. The Mishnah was quickly accepted as the authoritative representative statement of the oral Torah[7]. |
| **The Gemorah (Learning)** | If the *Mishnah* is the Teaching, then the *Gemora* is the "Learning." Once the *Mishnah* was complete, the rabbis immediately began teaching it in the academies of study. Their lessons on the *Mishnah* explained the relationship between the oral and the written Torah, the methods of interpreting both, and the practical conclusions. These studies in the *Mishnah* are called *Gemora,* "Learning." Eventually, all of the *Gemorah* was collected and written down alongside the Mishnah. The two side-by-side, are called the Talmud. The Talmud was completed between the 5th and 6th centuries. |
| **The Talmud** | As mentioned above, the Talmud is a two-part work comprised of the *Mishnah*, a representative statement of the oral Torah, and the *Gemorah*, a vast collection of studies on the *Mishnah*. After the diaspora, the two centers of Torah study were Bavel (modern day Iraq) and, to a much lesser degree, Israel. Each of these centers produced their own editions of the Talmud. |

- *Talmud Bavli* – The Babylonian Talmud. The collection of studies produced just over the border of Israel in Bavel. The greatest of the Jewish scholars had been exiled to Bavel. Their Talmud is considered far more authoritative and reliable than the Yerushalmi Talmud. When people refer to the Talmud, they are usually referring to the Talmud Bavli.

- *Talmud Yerushalmi* – The Jerusalem Talmud. The collection produced by the small scholarly remaining in Israel after the exile. They suffered terrible privation and hardship and worked under very difficult conditions. Their Talmud is generally considered inferior to its Babylonian-produced counterpart. One problem is that we lack a definitive text for the Jerussalem Talmud. There are numerous versions, many of which

---

[6] "The Prince" is an honorific on account of Rabbi Yehudah's tremendous scholarship and piety.

[7] There are two other collections of material from the oral Torah that are similar to the *Mishnah*. These collections are called the *Tosefta* and *Braisa*. The *Braisa* are teachings not included in the *Mishnah* because they either did not meet the standards of compactness and pedagogical value, or they did not fit constructively into the overall goals of the *Mishnah*. The *Tosefta* is a collection of supplementary material to the Mishnah. Both the *Braisa* and *Tosefta* carry significant authority.

contradict each other. Additionally, vast sections of the Jerusalem Talmud have been lost or were never completed.

The Babylonian Talmud is the authoritative source-text for Torah law and study. Occasionally, when an issue in the Babylonian Talmud is uncertain, the Jerusalem Talmud is used for clarification or to find consensus.

## Other Torah Texts

**Midrash**  The *Midrash*, "Exposition," is the oral Torah's interpretations of many non-Legal aspects of the Torah. It includes ethical, theological, and moral meditations upon the text of the Torah. It also fills in many missing details of the Torah narrative. **While the *Midrash* may be used to clarify details of Talmudic interpretations, it is important to remember that we very rarely base law or practice solely upon Midrash.**

**Mystical Texts**  Mystical, philosophical, and metaphysical ideas are part and parcel of the Torah. There are a vast number of mystical texts, yet the one that reigns supreme is the *Zohar*, "The Book of Splendor." The *Zohar* is a medieval compilation of *Midrashim* from the school of Rabbi Shimon bar Yochai – an early mystic who appears throughout the Talmud.

The *Zohar* is the cornerstone of the *Kabbalistic* (mystical) study of the Torah. The *Zohar* does, to a limited degree, influence the practical observance of *Halakhah* (religious practice and law). However, only the greatest experts in Torah are able to discern when and how mystical concerns affect real practice.

**The *Zohar* is an exceedingly difficult text that cannot be understood at face value. It should only be studied under the guidance of one who is an expert in its intricacies or by someone who has sufficient grounding in the rest of Torah literature.**

## Rabbinic Authority

Experts in the above texts have been given authority to decide issues of practice. This is found in numerous places in the Torah text itself (i.e. Ex. 18:20, Deuteronomy 16:18 and 17:8–13). Not only this, but they have also been given the authority to make decrees to safeguard the laws of the Torah. Their authority is also hierarchical.

## Deciding *Halakhah* (Actual Practice)

The system of deciding religious practice, *Halakhah*, is part and parcel of Torah. The system of *Halakhah* exists to preserve the *Mesorah* and to fill in gaps when they occur. Not all rabbis are capable of deciding matters of *Halakhah*. Those who are capable are known as *poskim* ("decisors," or singular *posek*) or *Dayanim* (judges – singular *Dayan*). A *posek* or *Dayan* must:

- Be fluent in the hierarchies of Torah authority and rules of derivation and interpretation,
- Have a mastery of the source material,
- Possess sufficient scholarship to understand how a decision in one area will affect the "homeostasis" of the entire *halakhic* system,
- Thoroughly understand the boundaries of *Mesorah* and evaluate decisions in its context.

The structure of rabbinic authority in exile is a meritocracy. The greater and more accomplished a scholar, the greater the authority he holds. Generally, no scholar today may overrule an accepted decision from an authority in an earlier era of Torah scholarship.

## Eras of Torah Scholarship and Authority

Since the destruction of the Temple and worldwide dispersion of the Torah community, there has been a constant global effort to unify and preserve Torah observance in exile. The Torah world has gone through many stages in accomplishing that goal.

**The *Gaonim* (The Respected or Eminent Ones) 700 to 1000 CE**

From about the $7^{th}$ until the $11^{th}$ century (when the Jewish community began to spread beyond the Middle East, settling in Spain, Africa, France, and Germany) the exile communities corresponded frequently with the *Gaonim*, the leaders of the remaining academies of Torah study in the Middle East. The *Gaonim* answered questions and compiled guidelines for them on prayer and holiday observances.

| | |
|---|---|
| **The *Rishonim*** **(The Early Scholars)** **1000 to 1500 CE** | The Jewish community eventually abandoned the Middle East as its centers of scholarship shifted to Spain, Germany, and France. The scholars in these countries established their own schools and produced producing extensive, foundational commentaries on the Talmud and the Torah. They were known as the *Rishonim*. |
| **ature *Koviim* (The Establishers)** **1500 to 1680 CE** | The *Koviim* sought to collect and systematize all of the scholarship produced in the diaspora to produce a unified statement of Torah law in the exile. Their work is the basis of all Jewish practice today. The most important of the *Koviim* is Rabbi Yosef Karo (1488 – 1575). He collected, studied, compiled, and systematized every known piece of Torah thought produced since the exile. His magnum opus was the *Shulchan Aruch*, the Set Table - a complete statement of Jewish practice in exile. It is a massive work based upon the thought of thousands of Torah scholars working for over 1000 years. It is the basis of Jewish practice today. |
| **The *Acharonim*** **(The Later Scholars)** **1680 to 2013?** | With the *Shulchan Aruch's* acceptance, the rabbinic world now had a launch pad – a universal foundation – from which to work. There was a sudden explosion in all areas of Torah scholarship. The generations of scholars following the *Koviim* are known as the *Acharonim*. |

## Summary of the Lesson

1. The tradition of Torah study and interpretation that has been passed down to us from Sinai is unique and unlike the methods of scriptural study used by other non-Jewish and non-Noahide faiths.

2. *Tanakh*, the Hebrew Scriptures, is viewed as hierarchical. The *Chumash*, the 5 Books of Moses, sits at the top of this hierarchy. It is eternal and cannot be changed. Later prophets and writings cannot modify the revelation of Sinai.

3. The Torah cannot be understood without the oral/experiential component to "make it whole." We know that this component is correct because of *Mesorah* – a chain of transmission – it has been handed down to us in an unbroken chain since the giving of the Torah.

4. Due to regional instability and the impending exile, the Rabbis decided to commit as much of the oral component of the Torah to writing as possible. This compilation, completed about 220 CE, is the *Mishnah* (Teaching). The study and analysis of the *Mishnah* was eventually recorded as well. This is called the *Gemora* (Learning).

5. The *Gemora* and *Mishnah* together, side-by-side, is the Talmud. The two communities of Jerusalem and Bavel each produced their own editions of the Talmud. The Babylonian (Bavel) Talmud is far superior and more reliable than the Jerusalem Talmud. It forms the basis of Talmudic study today.

6. Torah observance and practice is only decided based on the Talmud, the written Torah, and the long tradition of interpretation and study by qualified scholars. The Midrash is the oral law's exposition on the ethical, philosophical, and homiletic parts of Torah. Practice cannot be decided from Midrash.

7. There are many works on the *Kabbalistic*, mystical aspects, of the Torah. It takes tremendous wisdom and background to understand these works.

8. The Torah grants authority to qualified rabbinic scholars.

9. Torah scholarship has passed through a number of eras in exile as scholars sought to create a unified diaspora observance of Torah.

THE YESHIVA PIRCHEI SHOSHANIM SHULCHAN ARUCH LEARNING PROJECT

# The Noahide Laws – Lesson Five

**© Yeshiva Pirchei Shoshanim 2017**
This shiur may not be reproduced in any
form without permission of the copyright holder.

164 Village Path, Lakewood NJ 08701 732.370.3344
164 Rabbi Akiva, Bnei Brak, 03.616.6340

## Outline of This Lesson:

1. Introduction to this Lesson
2. Sources of the Noahide Laws & Principles of Deriving Them
3. Explicit Commandments
    a. To Adam & Noah
    b. Commandments Recorded Before Sinai
4. Implicit Commandments
5. Repetitions at Sinai
6. Noahide vs. Jewish Law
7. Post-Sinai Commandments
8. Applying the Principles
9. How Many Noahide Laws Are There?
10. The Earliest Source
11. Statements of the 30 Noahide Laws
    a. Rabbi Shmuel bar Chofni Gaon
    b. Rabbi Menachem Azaria da Fano
12. In Summary

# Deriving the Noahide Laws I

## Introduction

In the previous lesson we got a "birds-eye" view of the landscape of Torah learning. We reviewed many of the core texts and how they have shaped the observance and study of the Torah in the diaspora. We also discussed the chain of Torah transmission and the authority of authentic Torah interpretation.

In this lesson, we are going to look at how the Noahide laws fit into the landscape of Torah learning, how they are derived from the Torah, and how they are interpreted. This lesson is an important precursor to discussing the Noahide laws in practice.

## The Sources of the Noahide Laws

Until this point in this course, we have translated the Hebrew word *mitzvah* as "commandment." However, this translation doesn't fully capture the essence of *mitzvah*. **A *mitzvah* is best defined as an expression of God's will. Any expression of God's will or desire, whether stated explicit or merely intimated, is a *mitzvah*.** This is true for both the 613 *mitzvos* given to the Jews and the seven Noahide *mitzvos* given to all mankind.

The seven Noahide laws are not explicitly stated in any one place in the Torah. For that matter, neither are many of the other commandments of the Torah. The Noahide laws are communicated in a number of ways and in a number of places before the revelation at Sinai.

## Explicit Commandments

**To Adam & Noah**  Before the giving of the Torah, there were a number of commandments given to all of mankind via Adam and Noah:

> *God blessed them and God said to them, "Be fruitful and multiply, fill the earth and subdue it; and rule over the fish of the sea, the bird of the sky, and every living thing that moves on the earth."* Genesis 1:28

> *Therefore a man shall leave his father and his mother and cling to his wife and they shall become one flesh.* Genesis 2:24

> *But flesh, with its soul, its blood, you shall not eat.* Genesis 9:4

> *However, your blood that belongs to your souls I will demand, of every beast I will demand it; but of man, of every man for that of his brother, I will demand the Soul of man. Whoever sheds the blood of man, by man shall his blood be shed... And you, be fruitful and multiply; teem the earth and increase upon it.* Genesis 9:4-7

It appears that these commandments were intended for all mankind because they were given to the progenitors of the Human race.

God further instructed Abraham and his descendants in His will, right up until the Exodus from Sinai. For example, He commanded Abraham in the *mitzvah* of circumcision (Genesis 17:10). Many further commandments were given in Egypt prior and during the liberation. See Exodus 12 and 13 which enumerate the many laws of the Passover sacrifice and other *mitzvos*.

However, not all of these expressions of divine will are directed at all people. The commandments given to Noah and Adam are clearly relevant to all people.

However, those given to Abraham and his descendants are limited to them alone. For example, see Genesis 17:10 – 13:

> ...*Every male* **among you** *shall be circumcised... At the age of eight days every male* **among you** *shall be circumcised. He that is* **born in your household**... *shall be circumcised.*

We see that the Torah limits this commandment to the members of Abraham's family.[1]

---

[1] See Sanhedrin 59b for an extensive discussion of whether these commandments applied to all or only some of Abraham's descendants.

This is the first factor in deriving the Noahide Laws:

**Not all commandments from before the giving of the Torah were intended for all people. Some are universal; others are only for the families and descendants of the patriarchs of the Jewish people.**

## Commands Recorded Before Sinai Were Not Always Given Before Sinai

*Therefore, until this day, the children of Israel do not to eat the displaced sinew on the hipsocket, for he struck Jacob's hip-socket on the displaced sinew.* Genesis 32:33

It seems that a commandment was given at this point prohibiting the sciatic sinews. The Talmud, however, notes an oddity.[2] In this verse the Torah uses the term "children of Israel." This is surprising because Jacob would not have his name changed to "Israel" until Genesis 35:10, well after the events discussed here.

The Talmud discusses this oddity, concluding that the commandment against eating the sinew was in fact given at Sinai. Yet, since eating the sinew is prohibited as a commemoration of Jacob's struggle, Moses recorded the *mitzvah* in its relevant place in Genesis.

The language …*until this day*… is explained by the same reasoning.

Our second factor in deriving the Noahide laws is:

**Not all *mitzvos* written before Sinai (Exodus Ch. 20) were necessarily commanded before the revelation at Sinai took place**

## Implicit *Mitzvos*

God often expresses His will clearly. Sometimes, however, God's will is derived by implication or example. For example, God tells Noah that he is going to destroy the world on account of its being "filled with robbery" and having "corrupted its way upon the earth.[3]" See Genesis 6:11 – 13.

---

[2] See the Mishnah on Chullin 100b and Gemora to Chullin 101b.

[3] Sanhedrin 56b -57a. Even though this is not the definitive derivation, it is one of a number of similar derivations by way of implication.

By implication, robbery and "corrupting its way…" must be abhorrent and punishable. By seeking to understand the exact parameters and boundaries of these two issues, we can discern God's will for his creation.

There are many other places in the Torah, prior to Sinai, where God's will is similarly implied.

This leads us to our third principle in understanding the Noahide laws:

**A few of the Noahide laws are not directly commanded, but are rather implied by the history of God's relationship with man.**

## Repetitions at Sinai

Some of the Noahide laws, whether communicated explicitly or by implication, are repeated by God when giving the Torah at Sinai (i.e. against murder and theft). Others (i.e. *Be fruitful and multiply*...) are not. If these are universal laws already incumbent upon mankind, then what is the point of repeating them at Sinai? And, if there is some need for their repetition, then why are only some of them repeated?

The Rabbis of the Talmud[4] discuss this question in depth, comparing examples, looking at specific cases, and eventually derive the only conclusions that make sense and are consistent with the rest of the Torah:

1. **A *mitzvah* applying to Noahides and repeated at Sinai applies to both Noahides and Jews,**

2. **A *mitzvah* applying to Noahides and not repeated at Sinai only applies to Jews.**

God repeated the Noahide laws at Sinai for several reasons. The giving of the Torah modified many aspects of the original Noahic covenant (this will be discussed in greater detail later in this course). Among the changes it caused, was that it revised the universal quality of many *mitzvos* given before Sinai. Once the Torah was entrusted to Israel, all commandments given before Sinai ceased to be universal and, instead, applied only to the Jews (Rule 2). However, God wanted the universal quality of certain *mitzvos* to "carryover" into the post-Sinai world (Rule 1). Another reason is that God wanted to place specific universal laws clearly under the umbrella of Torah learning and interpretation.

---

[4] Sanhedrin 59a.

## Jewish vs. Noahide Law

The Talmud, in its analysis of the Noahide laws, derives another principle: **There is nothing permitted to a Jew which is forbidden to a Noahide.** This rule, directly related to the two that we just learned, applied only to matters of prohibition. For example, a there is no food that is kosher for a Jew, yet not kosher for a Noahide. This rule does not apply to positive commandments.

## Many Commandments Given to Israel Modify the Parameters of the Noahide Laws

The last general principle to know is this: Commandments given to the Jews at Sinai modify the application of the Noahide laws. For example, take the following verse:

*Anyone who blasphemes the name of God shall be put to death… as well as the convert and the native born.* Leviticus 24:16

This verse is discussing the punishment for those who curse God. God has many names. This verse is teaching that execution is only applied to one who curses God's true name. While blaspheming lesser names is nonetheless prohibited, a native born Jew and convert are not put to death for doing so.

However, the Talmud is bothered by the phrase *…convert and the native alike.* Obviously, this verse must be speaking to the Jewish people – after all, it is being given at Sinai! So, why does the Torah need to specify to us that it only applies to converts and native born Jews? The reason is that the verse wishes to exclude Noahides from its teaching. The verse is saying that only Jews are executed for cursing one of God's true names, and are not executed for cursing lesser names. However, Noahides are executed for cursing even lesser names of God.

## Applying the Principles

By overlying all of these principles, and filtering the Torah through them, the Noahide laws and their structure begins to emerge. However, it takes tremendous scholarship and intense knowledge of the texts and methods involved to derive all of the laws. The good news is that the rabbis of the Talmud have recorded much of this analysis for us. Much of it is concentrated in tractate Sanhedrin 56 to 60.

This specific lesson, being an overview, is not the place to map out in detail the derivation of each of the Noahide laws. We will, however, discuss their derivation throughout this course as we explore the laws in depth.

## How Many Noahide Laws Are There?

Applying the Talmud's principles of derivation, we discover that there are about 30 Noahide laws. The Talmud itself in tractate Chullin 92a confirms this number. However, the Talmud in tractate Sanhedrin 56a tells us that there are only 7 Noahide laws. So, how many are there - 7 or 30?

Rabbi Aharon HaLevi of Barcelona explains the contradiction in his *Sefer HaChinuch* 424:

> *Make no mistake in the enumeration of the Seven Noahide Laws which are well known and recorded in the Talmud. They are but categories which contain many particulars. For example, you will find sexual prohibitions grouped into one category. This category, however, has many specifics such as the prohibitions of ... homosexuality or bestiality. Similarly, with regards to idolatry they have one command with numerous parts...*

## The Earliest Reference to the Noahide Laws

The Talmud notes that the earliest reference to the laws is in an apparently unrelated verse.

In Genesis 1:29 God gives every tree to Adam for food:

> *God said, "... every tree that has seed bearing fruit. It shall be to you for food."*

The same idea is repeated shortly thereafter in Genesis 2:16:

> *And the L-rd, God, commanded the man, saying: "Of every tree of the garden you may surely eat."*

However, this repetition is strange. For one, the Torah never repeats itself without purpose. A repetition must add something not previously known. Another issue is the language of the verse. If God is giving Adam the trees as food, then why does God have to ...command the man...? The Talmud notes these oddities, also noting that the original Hebrew verse divides into seven clauses. The sages, in Sanhedrin 56b, conclude that each clause is a subtle reference to one of the Seven Noahide Laws:

| Number | Transliteration | English Translation | Talmudic Explanation |
|---|---|---|---|
| 1 | *Va-yatzav*... | And He commanded... | The word *va-yatzav* is typically used for commandments that maintain civil justice, as in Genesis 18:19. It is out of place here. In this verse it is understood by the Talmud to imply the need for a judicial system. |
| 2 | ...*Adonoy*... | ...the L-rd... | This apparently superfluous use of God's holy name implies a teaching about the holiness of God's name. From here the Talmud derives the prohibition of blasphemy. |
| 3 | ...*Elohim*... | ...God... | Why repeat the reference to God here? Furthermore, this term for God is a generic one. When this term is used for the One True God, it is in reference to God's role as judge. However, it is often used generically as a reference to false Gods, as in Exodus 20:3: "You shall have no other gods." Used in this context, and juxtaposed with God's true name, the Talmud understands it as a reference to the prohibition of idolatry. |
| 4 | ...*al ha-Adam*... | ...unto Adam... | The word Adam means both the name of the first man and is the generic term for humankind. Used here in conjunction with two divine names, it implies the sanctity of human life, as in Genesis 9:6: "Whoever sheds the blood of man..." Therefore, it alludes here to the sanctity of life and prohibition of murder. |
| 5 | ...*laymor*... | ...saying... | Introducing a commandment with the term "saying" is associated with precepts pertaining to sexual morality or immorality as in Jeremiah 3:1 |
| 6 | ...*mi-kol eytz ha-gan*... | ...of every tree of the garden... | God qualified His permission to eat of "every tree," limiting it to those "of the garden," implying that the fruit of other |

| | | | |
|---|---|---|---|
| | | | trees is prohibited. This restriction of benefit by virtue of God's rights as owner implies, conceptually, the prohibition of theft. |
| 7 | *Akhol tokhayl.* | …you shall surely eat. | This expression is what is called *lashon kafula*, a double expression, where a verb is doubled in two forms. These unusual expressions always imply the exclusion of something. In this case, the verse implies that one may eat of the trees of the garden, but specifically may not eat of something else; namely, a limb taken from a living animal. |

## THE SEVEN NOAHIDE LAWS

The seven laws are mostly prohibitions. However, many commentators interpret each prohibition as implying a positive *mitzvah* as well. These are the basic seven laws:

1) Man must establish a judicial system.

2) The prohibition of blasphemy (cursing the name of God). Correspondingly, one must honor the name of God.

3) The prohibition of idolatry (polytheism). Correspondingly, it is a positive mitzvah to believe in and reinforce the unity and singularity of God.

4) The prohibition of murder. By implication, there is a positive mitzvah to sustain and preserve life.

5) The prohibition of incest and sexual immorality. The positive corresponding mitzvah is modesty and sexual purity.

6) The prohibition of theft. One must, therefore, respect and safeguard the property of others.

7) The prohibition of eating a limb torn from a living animal. Therefore, one must only eat of a properly deceased animal.

## Statements of the 30 Noahide Laws

The earliest surviving statement of the Noahide laws with their expanded derivations is from the Torah commentary of Rabbi Shmuel ben Chofni Gaon (d. 1034, Sura, Iraq):

### I. Idolatry[5]

1) Belief in the unity of God

2) Prohibition of idolatry

3) To offer ritual sacrifices

4) To honor one's father and mother[6]

5) Prohibition of worshiping the Molekh

6) Prohibition of witchcraft

7) Prohibition of soothsaying and soothsayers

8) Prohibition of conjuring and conjurers

9) Prohibition of sorcery and sorcerers

10) Prohibition of sciomancy

11) Prohibition of demonomancy

12) Prohibition of theurgy

13) Prohibition of necromancy

### II. Blasphemy

14) Prohibition of blasphemy

15) To Pray

---

[5] Note that the order of items in this list has been changed slightly from the original manuscript in order to more closely group similar items.

[6] The placement of this mitzvah at this point in the list seems odd. It will be discussed in a future lesson.

16) Prohibition of false oaths

### III. Murder

17) Prohibition of suicide

18) Prohibition of murder

### IV. Sexual Immorality

19) Prohibition of adultery

20) To engage in formal marriages

21) Prohibition of incest with a sister

22) Prohibition of homosexuality

23) Prohibition of bestiality

24) Prohibition of castration

### V. Not to Eat a Limb Torn From a Living Creature

25) Prohibition of eating the limb of an animal that died naturally

26) Prohibition of eating the limb of a living animal

27) Prohibition of eating or drinking blood

28) Prohibition of crossbreeding animals[7]

### VI. Justice

29) To establish courts of justice[8]

### VII. Theft

30) Prohibition of theft and robbery

---

[7] Its position in this list will be discussed in a future lesson.

[8] The original manuscript is damaged here. By reconstructing R' Shmuel ben Chofni's derivations, and via elimination, we can conclude that justice must be the missing *mitzvah*.

Rabbi Menachem Azaria da Fano (1548 to 1620) presented his derivations in his *Asara Maamarot*:

### I. Idolatry

1) Prohibition of idolatry

2) Prohibition of offering a child to the Molekh

3) Kosem divination[9]

4) Meonen divination[10]

5) Not to interpret omens.

6) Prohibition of sorcery, sorcerers, and witchcraft.

7) Not to use charms or incantations

8) Not to consult mediums

9) Not to consult oracles

10) Prohibition of necromancy

### II. Sexual Immorality

11) Prohibition of incest, homosexuality and bestiality

12) To Be fruitful

13) To Multiply

14) Not to grant legal recognition to homosexual marriages

15) Not to crossbreed animals

16) Prohibition of castration

17) Not to graft trees

### III. Murder

---

[9] A form of ancient divination.

[10] A form of soothsaying.

18) Murder

19) Striking a Jew

### IV. Blasphemy

20) Not to curse the name of God

21) To honor the Torah and Torah scholars

22) To study the parts of the Torah relevant to Noahide observance

### V. Theft

23) Robbery and theft

24) The probation of studying parts of the Torah only relevant to Jewish observance[11]

### VI. Establishing courts of justice

25) To establish courts of justice

26) The prohibition of observing the Sabbath[12]

### VII. Limb from a living animal

27) Prohibition of consuming a limb torn from a living animal

28) Not to eat the blood of a living creature

29) Not to eat from an animal that died on its own

30) Not to eat human flesh

---

[11] Since these parts of the Torah were given on to Israel as an inheritance, studying them is akin to stealing.

[12] The Sabbath was only commanded to the Jewish people, not to the non-Jewish world. Its position in this place in the list will be discussed in a future lesson.

Later authorities[13] have added further derivations to these lists.[14]

These lists are neither the definitive nor final derivations of the Noahide laws. They are only statements of the core principles. As later authorities have pointed out, living the laws in practice requires further exploration and subdivision of the *mitzvos*.[15]

In the next lesson we will address guiding principles unique to each category of the Noahide laws.

## Preparing the Foundation:

**At this point, we are laying the groundwork needed to begin the full study of the Noahide laws. Although we are devoting much discussion to the legal aspects of the Noahide laws, we must remember that the *mitzvos* are not just legal decrees. They are expressions of Divine will. We will explore the deeper aspects of the Noahide laws shortly. However, a solid grasp of these basic principles is important to fully appreciate the deeper aspects of the 7 *mitzvos*.**

## Summary of the Lesson

1. God expresses his will in many ways in the Torah. Any expression of God's will, whether explicit or implicit, is a *mitzvah*.

2. Not all commandments given before the giving of the Torah were intended for all people. Some are universal; some are only for the families and descendants of the patriarchs of the Jewish people.

3. Not all *mitzvos* written before Sinai were actually commanded before Sinai.

4. Many of the Noahide laws are not directly commanded, but are rather implied by the interactions and conversations between God and man.

---

[13] Rama, Ran, Rav Saadia Gaon, for example.

[14] I.e. charity, levirate marriage, tithes, and others.

[15] See, for example, Rabbi Aharon Lichtenstein's excellent book *The Seven Laws of Noah*, who expands the basic laws further into about 66 precepts.

5.  1) A mitzvah told to Noahides and repeated at Sinai applies to Noahides and Jews, and 2) a mitzvah told to Noahides and not repeated at Sinai only applies to Jews.

6.  There is nothing permitted to a Jew which is forbidden to a Noahide.

7.  Many commandments given to Israel modify the parameters of the Noahide laws.

8.  The seven laws are actually categories that include a number of subordinate details. The total number of basic laws is about 30. However, this number is much higher when considering the details of their application.

THE YESHIVA PIRCHEI SHOSHANIM SHULCHAN ARUCH LEARNING PROJECT

# The Noahide Laws – Lesson Six

**© Yeshiva Pirchei Shoshanim 2017**
This shiur may not be reproduced in any
form without permission of the copyright holder.

164 Village Path, Lakewood NJ 08701 732.370.3344
164 Rabbi Akiva, Bnei Brak, 03.616.6340

## Outline of This Lesson:

1. Introduction

2. The Importance of Maimonides

3. Later Authorities and the Noahide Laws

4. The Importance of Torah Study

5. Introductions to the Seven Noahide Laws

    a. *Dinim*

    b. Positive or Negative Commandment?

    c. Torah Law vs. Civil Law

    d. Talmud Sanhedrin 56b

# Deriving the Noahide Laws II

## Introduction

In the last lesson we reviewed the rules and trends governing the derivation of the Noahide laws. We saw that the "7 laws" are actually 7 categories of principles expressing God's will for all humanity. We also saw that the *Gaonim* (scholars in the Middle East from about 589 to 1038 CE) and *Rishonim* compiled statements of the expanded Noahide laws. In this lesson, we will continue with the derivation of the Noahide laws and talk about unique aspects of each of the 7 categories.

## Rabbi Moshe bar Maimon (Maimonides or The Rambam, 1140 – 1205 C.E.)

Until the modern era, the most sophisticated elaboration of the Noahide laws was found in the *Mishnah Torah* (also known as the *Yad HaChazaka*) of Rabbi Moshe bar Maimon (also known as Maimonides or the Rambam). The *Mishnah Torah* is a far-reaching and detailed systemization of *Halacha* (Torah practice and law). Although it is not the definitive work on Torah law (that would be Rabbi Yosef Karo's *Shulchan Aruch* completed in 1555) it has exerted more influence on the codification of Torah law than any other work since the sealing of the Talmud.

What sets the *Mishnah Torah* apart from other codes is its scope. Torah scholars before and after Maimonides tend to limit their studies only to the practical *mitzvos* (commandments). However, the *Mishnah Torah* seeks to explain every law of the Torah, whether it applies nowadays or not. The Noahide observances, since they were not a practical subject of study for much of Jewish history, were not given much attention by other authorities. However, Maimonides examines them in detail. His writings are of the utmost importance for studying the Noahide laws.

However, three points must be kept in mind when studying Maimonides's writings:

1) Maimonides's word is not the final word. What he writes, though, is of the utmost importance for study and understanding.

2) Maimonides writes "in a vacuum." This means that he does not always indicate where or when a given idea applies or if it is relevant nowadays. Also, Maimonides never indicates his sources. When studying his works, one must always determine his sources, if the given law applies today or only in the future, and if it applies in Israel, the Diaspora, or both. Many of his writings regarding non-Jews and Noahides do not apply in our times. However, this is not always apparent from the text.

3) Maimonides's writings on the Noahide laws are not found in any one place. Though mostly concentrated in chapters 9 and 10 of *Hilkhos Melakhim*, many are scattered among numerous other topics. Also, laws in one location often modify those in another. A student must know the complete picture to fully understand Maimonides's thought.

**Although Maimonides is the most important writer on the Noahide laws, his writings cannot be taken at face value. They require detailed analysis and explanation before they can be applied practically.**

## Later Authorities

Understandably, authorities after Maimonides remained focused on practical matters affecting the Jewish community in exile. Much of Maimonides's Noahide writings do not find their way into later works. The *Shulchan Aruch* (the authoritative summation of Jewish law), for example, contains only scant reference to Noahide issues.

However, the Noahide laws are frequently discussed in the responsa literature. Responsa (in Hebrew *She'elos u-Teshuvos*, "questions and answers") are collections of questions to famous *poskim* (decisors of Jewish law) and their responses. Since the exile, Jews around the world have sent their most difficult queries on thought and practice to the *poskim*. Thankfully, the *poskim* wrote back and their responses were preserved for posterity. While the codes of law are general guides to practice, the responsa literature illustrates actual cases of "Torah in-action."

Throughout Jewish history, many questions were asked to *poskim* about the Torah's expectations for non-Jews. After Maimonides's writings, the responsa literature is the most important collection of sources for studying the Noahide laws.

In summary: The Talmud explains the references and derivation of the Noahide laws from the text of the Torah. It does not list all of the laws, only some as examples. The *Gaonim* (i.e. R' Shmuel bar Chofni Gaon) compiled lists of the laws and their subdivisions. Maimonides elaborated upon the Noahide laws and how they fit into the larger scope of Torah law. His writings are foundational for any study of the Noahide laws. The *poskim* (later authorities) provide guidance and insights into the "real-world" application of the Noahide laws.

## The Importance of Torah Study

All of this may seem like a lot of work to come to an understanding of religious belief and practice. However, the effort involved is not unique to the Noahide laws. The derivation of Jewish law is also incredibly detailed, requiring scholarship and tremendous mental acuity. Why do we need to put so much thought and effort into it, though? Why, some ask, couldn't God just tell us all the rules?

A fundamental belief of Judaism and Noahism is that God wants us to study the Torah deeply and exhaustively. By doing so we engage directly with God's eternal will. The deeper we delve into the Torah, the more we connect with and understand God. Remember – God wants us to engage with him and he wants to engage with us.

**If prayer is our speaking to God, then Torah study is God speaking to us.**

Also, practically speaking, a mere list of rules can easily come to be ignored. However, something into which one has delved and invested his whole being becomes deeply ingrained. Ingrained, studied material is neither easily ignored nor forgotten.

## Introductions to the Seven Categories

This lesson and the following ones will provide a brief overview of general concepts unique to each of the Seven Categories of Noahism.

## *Dinim* – The Requirement to Exercise Justice

**Positive or Negative Commandment?**

*And Dinah the daughter of Leah, whom she had borne unto Jacob, went out to see the daughters of the land. Shechem the son of Hamor the Hivite, the prince of the land, saw her; and he took her, and lay with her... two of the sons of Jacob, Simeon and Levi, Dinah's brethren, took each man his sword, and came upon the city unawares, and slew all the males. The sons of Jacob came upon the slain, and spoiled*

*the city, because they had defiled their sister... And Jacob said to Simeon and Levi: 'You have aggrieved me, and made me hateful to the inhabitants of the land...'*
Genesis 34

Maimonides[1] explains that the entire city of Shechem was put to death for failing to bring Dinah's assailants to justice; the entire city transgressed the *mitzvah* of *dinim* – the requirement to exercise justice.

Nachmanides, however, perceives a big problem with this interpretation. The Talmud[2] teaches that Noahides are only liable for the death penalty for transgressing a negative commandment (meaning a prohibition – a *thou shalt not*). The failure of Shechem to try the alleged perpetrators is the transgression of a positive (*thou shalt*) *mitzvah* – the commandment to establish and carry out justice. Since it is the transgression of a positive *mitzvah*, then why did Shechem deserve death?

The Meiri provides an insightful answer from the Talmud itself. The Talmud[3] tells us that the Seven Noahide laws are listed as prohibitions, negative commandments. The Talmud itself questions this idea, though, asking: If all of the Noahide laws are prohibitions, then why is *dinim* included? Is not *dinim*, the requirement to carry out justice, a positive commandment? The Talmud answers that the Noahide laws are merely listed according to their negative, prohibitive qualities. In truth, though, the Noahide laws are not 100% prohibitive in nature. Similarly, *dinim*, the requirement to establish courts, is not a purely positive commandment. It includes both positive and negative aspects.

In one sense it requires the establishment of courts and enforcement of the laws (the positive aspects). It also prohibits perversions of justice and the allowance of crime to run rampant (the negative, prohibitive aspects). Therefore, by not trying the crimes against Dinah, Shechem violated the negative/prohibitive aspect of *dinim*, and for this deserved death.

Based upon this understanding of *dinim*, we see that *dinim* includes laws pertaining to the establishment and operation of a legal system (*thou shalts*) and prohibitions to prevent perversions and laxity (*thou shalt nots*). As a general rule, the Seven Noahide laws, despite being termed as prohibitions, contain positive as well as negative *mitzvos*.

---

[1] *Hilchos Melakhim 9:14.*

[2] Sanhedrin 57a teaches that they are liable for transgressing any *mitzvah* for which they were forewarned. Later, on 59a, it is clarified that this only applies to the negative *mitzvos*.

[3] Sanhedrin 58b-59a.

**THE YESHIVA PIRCHEI SHOSHANIM SHULCHAN ARUCH PROJECT**
**THE NOAHIDE LAWS | DERIVING THE NOAHIDE LAWS II | LESSON 6**

**Torah Law vs. Civil Law**

By what standard do Noahide courts establish themselves, create, try and enforce their laws? Shall they base their *dinim*, legal systems, on their own logic and needs of the time? Or, perhaps, should their laws be based on Torah law?

Nachmanides holds that the Noahide legal system is based upon the same system outlined by the Torah for Jews.[4] According to his opinion the same laws governing loans or partnerships between Jews would apply to loans and partnerships between Noahides.[5]

If Nachmanides's opinion is the rule, then today's secular courts are not fulfilling the *mitzvah* of *dinim*. Therefore, Noahides cannot sue in secular court and must use either a *beis din* (Jewish religious court) or a specially convened court of Noahides who are experts in their laws.

However, Maimonides[6] disagrees with Nachmanides:

> *It devolves upon the judges to create equitable rules, appropriate for each country, according to the ways in which the nations currently handle such matters… "The law of the land is the law."*

The civil courts and the laws they establish fulfill the mitzvah of *dinim* for Noahides. According to the Ri Anatoli and Maimonides, it is not necessary for the particular laws of the Noahide courts to match the details of Torah law as given to the Jews. Therefore modern courts are 100% satisfying the requirement of *dinim* and it is a *mitzvah* for Noahides to use them.

The Rama explains these differences of opinion as having their source in the Talmud.

**Talmud**
**Sanhedrin 56b**

> *L-rd God commanded man, saying "Of every tree of the garden you may surely eat.*
> Genesis 2:16

The Talmud explains that Rabbi Yochanan learns *dinim* from the word *Vayatzav – And he commanded…*, relating the use of the word here to its use in Genesis 18:19:

---

4 See Nachmanides's commentary to Genesis 34:35. Of course, there are obvious exceptions to this rule to which even Nachmanides would agree.

5 There would be some slight differences with regard to interest charged or paid, but the laws would fundamentally be the same.

6 Maimonides's take on the matter is not immediately apparent in his writings. Nevertheless, his position can be derived by implication. As a result, most major *poskim* see this issue as part of a larger disagreement between Maimonides and Nachmanides as to the nature and scope of *dinim*. See Shu"t *Maharam Shick* OC 142, *Shu"t Maharsham* IV: 86; *Avnei Nezer* CM 55.

> *For I have known him, that he will **command** his children and his household after him that they will keep the way of God, to do righteousness and justice.*

This verse is pertaining to Abraham's household and their observance of God's law. Since no complete code of civil law had yet been given at the time of Abraham, then this verse must be referring to any logically derived system of civil law. Therefore, *dinim* is satisfied by the establishment of any logically derived, well regulated system of law.

However, Rabbi Yitzchok derives *dinim* from the word *Elokim*, God:

> *L-rd **God** commanded man, saying "Of every tree of the garden you may surely eat.*
> Genesis 2:16

Rabbi Yitzchok relates the word's use here to the use of the word *Elokim* in Exodus 22:7:

> *The master of the house shall approach the **judge**…*

In this verse the word *Elokim* means "judge," and implies a system of civil law (*Elokim* may have either meaning depending on context). Since this verse is pertaining to laws after the giving of the Torah, then it must be referring to an established legal system: the Torah legal system. By connecting the reference to *dinim* in Genesis 2:16 to this verse in Exodus 22:7, Rabbi Yitzchok is telling us that Noahide courts must follow the civil laws set forth in the Torah.

So: Nachmanides appears to hold like Rabbi Yochanan. Maimonides, though, appears to hold like Rabbi Yitzchok.

The discussion continues among later authorities. The Rama concludes like Rabbi Yochanan and the Nachmanides: certain aspects of civil law are fundamentally the same between Jews and non-Jews; it follows the Torah's mandates. Many other later authorities take the same view[7].

However, many formidable *poskim*[8] conclude like Maimonides: The laws established by the secular courts are sufficient for Non-Jews.

Whose opinion is definitive? The answer to this question requires more space than we have here. It will be discussed in later lessons on civil and monetary laws.

---

[7] There are others who share this opinion. See for example, *Tumim* 110:3 and *Minchas Chinuch* 414 & 415, *Chasam Sofer* CM 91.

[8] See *HaEmek Shaylah* #2:3; *Chazon Ish*, Bava Kamma 10:1

## Summary of the Lesson

1. Maimonides delved extensively into the Noahide laws in his *Mishnah Torah*. This medieval exposition on Torah law is the most influential work since the sealing of the Talmud and, by far, the most important work for the study of the Noahide laws. However, it is by no means the final, definitive word on either Jewish or Noahide practice

2. Much of the material needed for a complete practical understanding of the Noahide laws comes from the writings of the *poskim*, the later decisors of Jewish law.

3. Why do the Noahide laws require so much study and intense analysis? The answer is that all Torah requires intense study and analysis. Not only is it needed from an intellectual standpoint, in order to refine and clarify matters, but it is also a spiritual exercise that ingrains the Torah within us.

4. The seven Noahide laws, although termed and listed as prohibitions, contain both positive and negative *mitzvos*. For example, *dinim* both requires the establishment of courts (a positive commandment) and the prevention of perversion of justice (a negative commandment).

5. Whether the requirement of *dinim*, Noahide civil law, is fulfilled by today's secular courts or only by courts exercising Torah law is a matter of extensive discussion among the authorities.

THE YESHIVA PIRCHEI SHOSHANIM SHULCHAN ARUCH LEARNING PROJECT

# The Noahide Laws – Lesson Seven

© **Yeshiva Pirchei Shoshanim 2017**
This shiur may not be reproduced in any
form without permission of the copyright holder.

**164 Village Path, Lakewood NJ 08701 732.370.3344**
**164 Rabbi Akiva, Bnei Brak, 03.616.6340**

## Outline of This Lesson:

1. Introduction

2. Blasphemy

    a. Definition

    b. Belief in God

    c. Prayer

3. Idolatry

    a. Definition

    b. *Shituf*

    c. *Shituf*, Christianity & Islam

    d. Creating New Religions

# Deriving the Noahide Laws III

## Introduction

In the last lesson we reviewed some general principles of the Noahide laws. Most importantly, we saw that the seven categories include both positive and negative commandments. In this lesson we will continue with the commandments of Blasphemy and Idolatry and look at the unique aspects of each.

## Blasphemy

**Definition** This specific prohibition of blasphemy is called such only for lack of an appropriate English term with which to translate the original Hebrew. In English, the word "blasphemy" is often used interchangeably with "heresy." Alternatively, many use "blasphemy" to mean "taking the L-rd's name in vain." However, neither of these uses conveys the intent of the actual Hebrew prohibition. The definition of this prohibition is found in *Leviticus 24:15-16*:

>...*Ish ish ki* **yekaleil** *elokav ve-nasah cheto.*
> **Venokeiv** *sheim HaShem mos yumas.*

> "...Any man who **curses [yekaleil]** God shall bear his sin.
> And one who is ***nokeiv*** the name of God shall be put to death."

The first time the Torah mentions this sin it uses the word *yekaleil*, which clearly means *he curses*. In fact, this is the term used most often in connection with this transgression. However, in verse 16 the Torah uses the odd word *nokeiv*.

The *Mishnah*[1] explains that *nokeiv* refers to cursing God using His own divine name in the formula of: may XXXXX curse (or smite) XXXXX. This is the specific definition of blasphemy warranting the death penalty.

The Talmud[2] expands the scope of this prohibition to include all divine names or appellations for God's divine attributes.

Numerous other prohibitions are included under the umbrella of blasphemy. These include not desecrating, destroying, or erasing God's name, using God's name inappropriately, and many others.

**Belief in God**

As we noted in the previous lesson, the Seven Noahide laws are enumerated according to their negative ("thou shalt not") aspects. Nevertheless, they contain many positive ("thou shalt") qualities.

Rabbi Reuven Margolies, an eminent 20th century scholar, observes an important such nuance in *Margolios HaYam*,[3] his masterful commentary on tractate Sanhedrin (where most of the Noahide laws are discussed):

> *It is astonishing that there is no mention here [in the Seven Noahide] laws of the foremost principle, the fundamental of all fundamentals: belief in God! ... It is belief in God that must serve as the foundation for all* mitzvos *and prohibitions... It seems as though belief in God is subsumed in the category of blasphemy.*

That belief in God is required of Noahides is iterated by many authorities;[4] however the proposition that it falls under the category of blasphemy is surprising. Wouldn't it make more sense for belief in God to be subsumed within the laws of idolatry?

Rabbi Aharon Lichtenstein, in his book *The Seven Laws of Noah*, asks the same question and offers a very good answer.[5] The laws against idolatry regulate man's relationship to the physical world, keeping this world's meaning and value in perspective. However, the laws against blasphemy define the nature and

---

[1] Sanhedrin 56a.B

[2] Sanhedrin 56a.

[3] *Margolios HaYam* on Sanhedrin 56a #25.

[4] See Rabbeinu Nissim Gaon's *Hakdama* to Tractate Berachos, where he says that belief in God is required via logic, being implicit in the very fabric of the Noahide code. The *Sefer HaChinuch Aseh* 430 likewise lists it as part of the Noahide code, but does not state his reasoning.

[5] P. 78.

boundaries of man's relationship with his Creator. Therefore, belief in God and all other elements of the man/God interaction are included under blasphemy.

**Prayer**  Prayer, following this rule, should therefore be included under blasphemy. However, is there an obligation for Noahides to pray? Rabbi Nissim Gaon[6] implies such, writing:

> *Not all of the Seven Laws and their derivations require revelation. For example – the obligation to recognize God, to obey Him, and the obligation to* **serve** *him – all of which are rational and can be logically derived.*

The Hebrew term used by Rabbi Nissim for serving God, *le-avdo,* usually refers specifically to prayer. The *mitzvah* of Prayer for Noahides is further implied by *Isaiah 56:7*:

> *My house shall be called a house of prayer for all peoples.*

On this verse Rashi notes: *Not for Israel alone.* Also, Rabbi Shmuel ben Chofni Gaon, in his exposition of the Noahide laws,[7] includes prayer as an obligation as do many later authorities. Yet, even those few later authorities who do not reckon prayer an actual obligation nevertheless agree that it is proper and that Noahides are rewarded for it.[8]

The study of Torah, being intrinsic to the man/God relationship, is also included under the rubric of blasphemy.[9] By extension is the *mitzvah* to honor the Torah and its Torah scholars.

## Idolatry

**Definition**  The prohibition of idolatry, for both Jews and non-Jews, contains many nuanced details explaining the distinction between idolatrous thoughts and idolatrous deeds. Both of these are prohibited in different ways.

The exact details involved in pinning down idolatrous thoughts vs. deeds will be covered in this course in the appropriate place.

Maimonides writes that any act of idol worship that is a capital offense for Jews is likewise a capital offense for Noahides.[10] In general, this establishes similarities

---

[6] Ibid.

[7] Discussed in an earlier lesson.

[8] *Igros Moshe* OC II:25.

[9] See the Rama MiFanu's list of the 30 Noahide laws brought at the end of Lesson 6.

between Jews and Noahides with regard to the laws of idolatry. We say "in general" because there are a few important exceptions. One of these differences is the issue of *Shituf*. *Shituf* is the belief in some other (false) deity in addition to believing in the one true God.[11]

**Shituf**

While *Shituf* is a prohibited belief for Jews, its relevance to Noahides and non-Jews is nuanced and often a source of much confusion.

Maimonides[12] and many later authorities[13] condemn *shituf* as outright idolatry even for non-Jews. According to these authorities, there is no such thing as *shituf*; *shituf* is simply indistinguishable from idolatry. However, Tosafos[14] and many other Rishonim and Acharonim[15] disagree. According to those who permit *shituf*, it is permitted only according to very specific conditions:

1) The Torah views non-Jewish belief in another god in addition to the true God to be mistaken. It is not a prohibition, but it is unrighteous and one who does so, though not viewed as a sinner, is not considered *MiChasidei Umos HaOlam*[16] – of the Pious Nations of the World - and will not receive his full reward for observing the Noahide laws.

2) *Shituf* pertains only to **belief** in a secondary divine being, <u>not</u> to the **worship** of a secondary god. Any expression of worship for this secondary deity is prohibited as idolatrous practice.[17]

3) It is only the belief in another god in addition to the true God that is not punishable. Conflation of the true God with another entity or the assigning of corporeality to the true God creates issues of actual idolatry. The Torah definition of idolatry is not only limited to the worship of idols, but pertains to how we conceive and represent the nature of the one true God.

---

[10] *Hilchos Melakhim* 9:2.

[11] It should be noted that there is a vast amount of literature on this topic – enough for many, many books.

[12] See *Hilchos Avodas Kokhavim* 1:2, *Hilchos Teshuvah* 3:7, and many other places.

[13] *Noda b'Yehudah* II YD 148; *Shaar Efraim* 24; *Pri Megadim* YD 65:45; *Shut Chasam Sofer* OC 84.

[14] Sanhedrin 63b and Bechoros 2b.

[15] *Piskei HaRosh* Sanhedrin Ch. 7 and others. See also *Darkhei Moshe* OC 156; *Shulchan Aruch* OC 156; *Pischei Teshuvah*, Y.D. 147:2; *Mor u'Ketziah* 224; *Shoel uMeishiv* Tanina I:51; *Seder Mishnah Yesodei HaTorah* 1:7.

[16] See *Sefer Sheva Mitzvos HaShem* I:1 *haara* 9.

[17] This is the universal conclusion of the authorities. See *Noda BiYehudah* II:148; *Minchas Chinuch* 26 & 86; *Shaar Efraim* 24. See also *Chasam Sofer* gloss to *Shulchan Aruch* OC 156.

### Shituf, Christianity & Islam

Many have tried to qualify Christianity as an acceptable belief for non-Jews using the concept of *shituf*. Though true that many authorities have stated Christianity is acceptable for non-Jews, this opinion must be put in context.

The status of Christianity in the eyes of the Torah is often complicated. There have been thousands of pages written on this topic, and even a basic survey of the literature is far beyond the scope of this course. In short: Christianity has many elements that are clearly idolatrous from a Torah perspective (i.e. its various rituals and modes of worship), but some that are difficult to pin down (i.e. is it truly monotheistic or polytheistic?).

Historically, Sephardic Rabbis, living in Muslim-ruled lands, were free to rule stringently. They criticized Christian belief as outright idolatry. However, rabbis living in Christian lands had to be very clever and cautious in what they said and wrote. Given the shadow of the church and the ever-present threat of exile and death, they were not able to freely voice their views on Christianity. They had to take a tempered approach. In these Rabbis' theological writings they often declare Christian belief *shituf* and therefore acceptable for non-Jews. However, in their writings on *halakha*, Torah law, they often implied that Christian ritual and worship was to be treated as idolatry.[18] They were often able to get these views past censors because *halachic* (legal) writings were not so thoroughly vetted as the church censors usually lacked sufficient understanding of the material.

Were it not for the threat of the church, these Ashkenazi rabbis very well may have taken the stringent view of their Sephardi co-religionists and condemned Christianity as idolatry.

Nevertheless, even if Christian belief is *shituf*, the practice of Christianity would remain idolatrous. The practical conclusion, for a number of reasons, is that Christianity is to be treated as absolute idolatry.[19]

Namely, it is not merely the worship of another secondary deity, but it is an idolatrous conception of God Himself.[20] Therefore, Christianity is to be treated as absolute idolatry for non-Jews in both belief and practice.[21]

---

[18] See Rama YD 141:1 and 150 who rules that crosses to which a non-Jew has bowed are prohibited as idolatrous images. This is a subtle yet definitive statement since such a conclusion is only possible if, fundamentally, the Rama held that the concept of the trinity is idolatrous.

[19] See *Hilchos Avodas Kokhavim* 9:4, *Maachalos Assuros* 11:7, *Hilchos Melachim* 11:4. See also Rambam's *Perush HaMishnayos* to the beginning of tractate *Avoda Zarah* (note, however, that the modern editions are heavily censored). See also *Minchas Elazar* I:53-3; *Yechaveh Da'as* IV:45. An extensive list of opinions is brought in *Yayin Malchus*, pp. 234-237.

[20] See the *Vikuach* of Nachmanides. See also his commentary on the Torah to Deut. 16:22. The idea that God ever took on corporeal manifestation, had a mother, was born, or exists as a tripartite deity are all heretical concepts according to the Torah.

What about Islam? Islam is not idolatrous[22] and, sometimes, has strong theological resonance with Torah thought and belief.[23] From the perspective of the prohibition of idolatry, it is 100% monotheistic[24].[25] However, Islam presents a different problem altogether.

**Creating New Religions**

Both Jews and non-Jews are enjoined against the creation of new religions.[26] One who creates a new religion is, by default, rejecting belief in the truth of the Torah, Moses (the greatest prophet in history), and in God's authority. The Torah, containing both the Noahide and Jewish laws, were given to stand for all eternity. The Torah states this in no fewer than 24 places![27]

---

[21] It should be pointed out that believing Christians do not themselves have the status of full idolaters. See *Shulchan Aruch*, Y.D. 148:12; *Shut Yehudah Yaaleh* YD 170.

[22] *Maachalos Assuros* 11:7; Tur YD 124; *Beis Yosef* YD 146; Rama YD 146:5; YD 124:6; Taz YD 124:4; *Shach* YD 124:12; See *Ben Ish Chai* on *Parshas Balak* for a discussion of the issues. There are a few who hold that Islam is prohibited as idolatry. It seems that this is due to certain customs of the Haj. See note 24.

[23] For example, a Jew or Noahide may not enter a Church for any reason because it is a place of idolatry (see *Igros Moshe* YD 3:129-6 and many, many others), yet it is permissible to enter and even pray within a mosque (*Avnei Yashfei* 1:153 quoting Rav Elyashiv, *ztz"l*; *Yabia Omer* VII YD 12:4; and others). In fact, a Muslim contemporary of Maimonides, the historian Ibn al-Qifti, records that while in Egypt Maimonides would occasionally pray in a Mosque (see al-Qifti's *Tarikh al-Hukama*). Of course, this is not an ideal situation and may have been done only in special circumstances. One recent authority, Rabbi Boruch Efrati, has advised traveling Jews to pray in airport mosques (a common amenity overseas) rather than pray among the hustle and bustle of the terminal. This ruling, though, pertains only to praying in the physical space of the mosque. One may not take part in actual Islamic prayer services. It must be noted, however, that another recent authority, the *Shu"t Tzitz Eliezer* XIV:91, cites the Ran (see note 24 below) and prohibits Jews, or for that matter Noahides, from entering mosques. Although his opinion is not agreed to by other authorities, all agree that one should not enter a mosque without a compelling need or reason.

[24] While the belief system of Islam is acceptably monotheistic, many customs of the Haj (Mecca pilgrimage) are problematic. This may be the reasons for the Ran to Sanhedrin 61b and other dismissals of Islam. See also Meiri to *Avodah Zarah* 57a.

[25] However, an interesting difference emerges with regard to teaching Torah. Maimonides writes in a responsum (ed. Blau #149) that because Christians accept the Torah as part of God's revelation (albeit as the "old testament"), there are unique permits and leniencies with regard to Jews teaching them Torah. Yet, because Islam rejects the Torah's authenticity (substituting the Quran), Jews may not teach Torah to Moslems.

[26] *Hilchos Melachim Perakim* 8 & 10.

[27] Exodus 12:14, 12:17, 12:43, 27:21, 28:43, Leviticus 3:17, 7:36, 10:9, 16:29, 16:31, 16:34, 17:7, 23:14, 23:21, 23:31, 23:41, 24:3, Numbers 10:8, 15:15, 19:10, 19:21, 18:23, 35:29, Deuteronomy 29:28.

New religions denying the eternal authority of the Torah are not to be given legitimacy. This principle would apply equally to Christianity, Islam, Buddhism or any religion coming after the Torah, regardless of whether or not these religions observe all or part of the Noahide laws.[28]

In the same vein, neither a Noahide nor a Jew may alter the religion set forth for him by the Torah. To do so is also a rejection of the Torah, God's will, and the de facto creation of a new religion. For example, a Noahide may not observe holy days not commanded to him. This would include such holidays as the Sabbath or Passover; these days were commanded only to the Jewish people.[29] Similarly, the *mezuzah* and *Tefillin* are symbols commanded only to Jews and not to Noahides.[30] To observe may constitute the creation of a new religion and one would receive no reward for their observance.

However, Noahides may observe any commandment given to the Jews that:[31]

1) Has a logical reason behind it, and

2) Is of positive benefit to the person or society.

However, his intent cannot be to undertake the commandment solely because he believes it is a religious commandment.[32] If that were his underlying reason, he would be in error, for the commandment is only for the Jews and not for Noahides.

Arguably the foremost authority on Jewish Law in the 20th century, **Rabbi Moses Feinstein** ztz"l emphatically wrote that a Noahide who decides to keep Torah commandments intended only for the Jews receives no reward or blessing for his actions.[33]

---

[28] See *Igros Moshe* YD II:7.

[29] See *Hilchos Melachim* 10:9; Meiri to Sanhedrin 58b.

[30] See Radvaz to *Hilchos Melachim* 10. The Yerushalmi, Peah 1:1 brings a story about Rebbe giving a mezuzah to Artavan, the Persian King. This story is often understood, erroneously, as proof that a non-Jew may hang a *mezuzah*. For a discussion of this *gemarah's* halachic relevance, see *Shu"t Ginas Veridim*, OC II:28. See also *Shu"t Beer Sheva* 36; *Beer Heitiv* YD 286:5; *Shaarei Teshuva* 157; *Sefer HaEshkol* cited in *Pischei Shearim*, p. 252.

[31] *Hilchos Melachim* 10:10

[32] See Radvaz to *Hilchos Melachim* 10.

[33] *Igros Moshe* YD II:7.

As we shall see, though, this does not preclude Noahide observance of any other *mitzvos* of the Torah. We will examine this issue in great depth in a future lesson.

To summarize: One cannot be a Christian Noahide because Christianity is idolatrous in both belief and practice. One cannot be a Moslem Noahide because Islam is a new, post-Torah religion and therefore denies the eternality of Torah. What is more, one cannot even be a "Jewish" Noahide. The Noahide path is not a way for non-Jews to participate in Jewish ritual or religion. It is a way for them to be non-Jews according to God's will: as Noahides.

In the next lesson, we will continue our overview of the seven categories.

## Summary of the Lesson

1. The specific sin of blasphemy is cursing God, or any of his attributes, with one of His own divine names. For Noahides this is expanded to include the desecration of God's name and other prohibitions.

2. Among the positive aspects of the category of blasphemy are the requirements of prayer, belief in God, and other fundamentals of faith.

3. The prohibition of idolatry exists in both thought and deed.

4. Most of the laws of idolatry are the same for Jews and Noahides. A significant difference is *Shituf* – the belief in the true God plus other subordinate deities. *Shituf* is permitted for non-Jews, yet not for Jews.

5. *Shituf* is only permitted to non-Jews as a system of belief. Non-Jews may not, however, worship in practice any God other than the One True God.

6. There are no religions today that are *Shituf*. Even Christianity is not *Shituf*, but actual idolatry.

7. Islam is theologically acceptable to Torah belief, however it is an erroneous faith for non-Jews in that it was created after the Torah was given.

8. The creation of new religions is prohibited in that it is de facto rejection of the Torah. Furthermore, neither Jews nor non-Jews may add to what has been bequeathed to them.

9. Noahides may accept any additional *mitzvos* provided that those *mitzvos* are logical and beneficial to society and the individual. Furthermore, they

cannot accept these *mitzvos* solely from religious motivations. Otherwise, their acceptance would constitute adding to their Noahide faith.

THE YESHIVA PIRCHEI SHOSHANIM SHULCHAN ARUCH LEARNING PROJECT

# The Noahide Laws – Lesson Eight

© **Yeshiva Pirchei Shoshanim 2017**
This shiur may not be reproduced in any
form without permission of the copyright holder.

164 Village Path, Lakewood NJ 08701 732.370.3344
164 Rabbi Akiva, Bnei Brak, 03.616.6340

## Outline of This Lesson:

1. Introduction
2. Incest
3. Homicide
4. Theft
5. A Limb Torn From a Living Creature
6. Summary

# Deriving the Noahide Laws IV

## Introduction

In the last lesson, we reviewed general principles of the Noahide laws of idolatry and blasphemy, their unique details, and their positive aspects. In this lesson we will conclude our overview with the remaining prohibitions of incest, murder, theft, and a limb torn from a living creature.

Please keep in mind that this lesson, as well as the previous few, are only overviews introducing the general principles of the seven categories. Later lessons will be devoted to the specific observance of these categories.

## Incest

The category of incest is fundamentally concerned with preserving the sanctity of the male/female relationship and the integrity of the family unit. As with all of the Noahide laws, it includes a fundamental prohibition, ancillary related prohibitions, and positive precepts.

As all of the seven Noahide categories, it also includes positive precepts pertaining to marriage, divorce, reproduction, modesty, and interactions between the genders.

## Homicide

The prohibition of murder, along with that of a limb torn from a living animal, has the fullest and most explicit expression of all the Noahide laws:

> *I shall avenge your life's blood. From the hand of any beast I shall avenge it and from the hand of man. From the hand of man for his brother I shall avenge life. For anyone who sheds the blood of man by man shall his blood be shed for man was created in the image of G-d.*
> Genesis 9:5-6

While murder is the fundamental prohibition here, this category also includes issues such as injury, euthanasia of the terminally ill, suicide, and abortion. Also included are the implied positive *mitzvos* of preserving life and the rules pertaining to self-defense.

A surprising inclusion under the category of homicide is the laws of speech. For Jews, there are detailed expectations as to what one person may say about another. Damaging or negative language is strictly prohibited without a compelling reason. Though Noahides are not obligated in these laws, these are precepts having a logical reason and benefit for society. Such *mitzvos* may be voluntarily accepted by Noahides. Furthermore, many authorities[1] learn from the story of Tamar and Judah[2] that Noahides are specifically prohibited from causing embarrassment to each other. It seems, therefore, that Noahides should observe the laws of speech either because it is logical and beneficial or because of an actual prohibition against causing embarrassment.

## Theft

Theft is possibly the largest and most comprehensive area of the Noahide laws. It covers virtually every conceivable facet of monetary and property law as well as the whole gamut of business, commercial, employment, and real estate law.

This category further includes the prohibitions of kidnapping, rape, and other socially destructive acts.

The laws of theft are not solely relevant to the above areas, but also apply to ideology. They dictate the boundaries of Torah tradition for Jews and Noahides and preserve the integrity of the two traditions.

The positive qualities of theft include respecting and protecting the property of others, conducting one's business honestly, and preserving social integrity.

---

[1] I.e. Shut *Divrei Yatziv* YD 51.

[2] Genesis 38:25.

## *Eiver Min HaChai* - A Limb Torn From a Living Creature

The Talmud lists this as one of the 7 laws implied by Genesis 2:16 (the earliest source for the Noahide laws). However, this presents us with a problem. In the Talmud[3], Rabbi Yehudah in the name of Rav points out that Adam was not allowed to eat meat in the Garden of Eden, as it is written:

> *And God said: 'Behold, I have given you every herb yielding seed that is upon the face of the earth and every tree in which is the fruit of a tree yielding seed- to you they shall be for food. And to every beast of the earth, every fowl of the air, and to everything that creeps upon the earth that has a living soul: every green herb for food.' And it was so.*
> Genesis 1:29-30

What then is the point of commanding Adam regarding a limb torn from a living creature if Adam was not allowed to eat meat? Furthermore, why does the Talmud derive the prohibition of a limb torn from a living animal from Genesis 2:16? After all, this commandment (as well as the permission to eat meat) is explicitly dictated to Noah to after the flood:

> *And God blessed Noah and his sons, and said to them: 'Be fruitful, multiply, and replenish the earth. And the fear and dread of you and shall be upon every beast of the earth, and upon every bird of the air, and upon all that teem upon the ground, and upon the fish of the sea. Into your hand they are delivered. Every moving thing that lives shall be for food for you; as the green herb have I given you everything.*

> **Only flesh with the life thereof, which is the blood thereof, shall ye not eat.**
> Genesis 9:1-4

**Maimonides**   Maimonides offers a simple explanation: while all seven *mitzvos* are referenced in Genesis 2:16, only the first six were actually commanded to Adam. The seventh commandment, a limb from a living animal, was only given at the time of Noah. This explanation also tells us why the seven *mitzvos* are called the seven "Noahide Laws;" they were completed with the giving of the seventh mitzvah to Noah.

However, Tosafos[4] offers an alternate explanation.

---

[3] Sanhedrin 59b.

[4] Tos. Sanhedrin 56b DH *Achol Tochal*.

**Tosafos**  According to *Tosafos*, *Genesis 1:29-30* only prohibited Adam from killing animals in order to eat their flesh. Adam was nevertheless allowed to eat the flesh of animals that died naturally.

Despite this permission, God specifically prohibited Adam from eating flesh torn from an animal while it was still living. The later verse, *Genesis 9:1-4* (addressed to Noah), expanded the permission of man to eat meat by allowing animals to be killed for their meat.

The law of flesh torn from a living animal only applies to birds and mammals, whether domesticated or wild. It does not apply to fish, crustaceans, insects, or other such creatures.[5]

Included within this category also are precepts regarding cruelty to animals, animal husbandry, and cross-breeding plant species.

## Summary

The seven Noahide laws are actually categories. Each one, called in the name of its basic prohibition, includes a body of related laws. Even though the Talmud enumerates the Noahide laws according to their prohibitions, they include many positive requirements as well.

Many of the categories of Noahide law overlap with Jewish law. Some areas of Noahide law are parallel to Jewish law, being essentially the same in concept and purpose, but having different sources and applications. Still, many other elements of Noahide law are based upon simple logic and practicality.

Since the time of Maimonides, *poskim* (decisors of Torah law) have examined and answered numerous questions of Torah law for both Jews and non-Jews around the world. Their writings are the primary sources available for building a comprehensive and practical understanding of Noahide observance.

---

[5] *Maachalos Asuros Perek 5*.

## Summary of the Lesson

1. Incest includes the prohibitions of incest, homosexuality, bestiality, and adultery.

2. The positive implications of the prohibition of incest are the requirements of marriage, divorce, modesty, and rules pertaining to reproduction.

3. Homicide includes laws of murder, self-defense, injury, euthanasia of the terminally ill, suicide, and abortion.

4. The positive elements of the prohibition of homicide include preserving live and care of those who are ill.

5. The prohibition of theft covers a vast area including business, real estate, employment, kidnapping, and rape.

6. The positive aspects of theft include preserving social integrity and order as well as respecting and protecting the property of others.

7. The law of a limb torn from a living animal was either given in the times of Noah (according to Maimonides) or to Adam (according to Tosafos).

8. This law applies only to mammals and birds. It does not apply to sea creatures (even mammalian) or to insects or crustaceans.

9. This law also includes precepts pertaining to animal husbandry, agriculture, and animal welfare.

THE YESHIVA PIRCHEI SHOSHANIM SHULCHAN ARUCH LEARNING PROJECT

# The Noahide Laws – Lesson Nine

**© Yeshiva Pirchei Shoshanim 2017**
This shiur may not be reproduced in any
form without permission of the copyright holder.

164 Village Path, Lakewood NJ 08701 732.370.3344
164 Rabbi Akiva, Bnei Brak, 03.616.6340

## Outline of This Lesson:

1. Introduction
2. Defining *Ger Toshav*
3. The Prohibition of Non-Jewish Residency in Israel
4. Non-Idolatrous Gentiles in Israel
5. The *Ger Toshav*
6. The Benefits of *Ger Toshav*
7. How Does a Non-Jew Become a *Ger Toshav*?

# Noahide Identity I – Ger Toshav

## Introduction

The most important question to answer before getting into the practical observance of the Noahide laws is: What is a Noahide? It is a deceptively simple question because it involves a very complicated answer – an answer vital to the practical fulfillment of the Noahide laws. In the next few lessons we will examine this question in great depth. It involves the study of many apparently unrelated topics and an array of sources in order to get to our conclusion. **Note: Much of the material in this and the next two lessons will be advanced material.**

## The Ger Toshav Question

**The Prohibition of Non-Jewish Residence in Israel**

In Deuteronomy 7:1-2, God commands to the Jewish people:

*When the Lord, your God, shall bring you into the land when you go to possess it, and shall cast out many nations before you – the Hittite, and the Girgashite, and the Amorite, and the Canaanite, and the Perizzite, and the Hivite, and the Jebusite, seven nations greater and mightier than you – and when the Lord, your God, shall deliver them up before you, you shall smite them. You shall completely destroy them. You shall make no covenant with them **nor show them favor.***

From this last verse, *…nor show them favor*, the Talmud *Avodah Zarah* 20a derives a number of prohibitions, one of which is the prohibition of settling idolaters in the land of Israel. Maimonides[1] proposes Exodus 23:33 as the reason for these

---

[1] *Hilchos Avodas Kokhavim 10:6.*

injunctions:

> They [idolaters] shall not dwell within your land lest they cause you to sin against Me and worship their gods.

Maimonides summarizes the *halakha*, practice, derived by the Talmud from these verses:[2]

> It is forbidden to sell them homes and fields in Israel. In Syria, one may sell them homes, but not fields.
>
> One may rent them homes in Israel, provided that a neighborhood [of idolaters] is not established. Fewer than three [homes] does not constitute a neighborhood. It is, however, forbidden to rent them fields. In Syria, one may rent them fields…
>
> …It is permitted to sell them houses and fields in the Diaspora, because it is not our land.
>
> Even when it is permitted to rent [houses to idolaters], it is not permitted to rent to them for use as a dwelling, because they will bring idols into them, as [the Torah in Deuteronomy 7:26] states: "Do not bring an abomination into your home." It is, however, permitted to rent them homes to use as storehouses.
>
> It is forbidden to sell them fruit, grain, or other produce while it is attached to the earth. One may sell [them] after they have been harvested or on the condition that they will be harvested, and then he must harvest them.
>
> Why is it forbidden to sell them land or anything attached to the land? Because [the Torah in Deuteronomy 7:2] states: "Do show them favor." [Which the Talmud points out may also be read as:] "Do not give them a resting place in the land." As long as they do not have a resting place in the land, their stay will be a temporary one…
>
> It is also forbidden to give them a present.

The *Shulchan Aruch* and all other codifiers rule in agreement with Maimonides that it is prohibited for idolaters to settle permanently in Israel.[3] This rule however, only applies when Israel has sovereignty and authority over the non-Jews in its land.[4]

---

[2] *Hilchos Avodas Kokhavim 10:3-4.*

[3] *Yoreh Deah 151:8.* While all agree that this is true for selling property to non-Jews in Israel, there is much disagreement about renting property to non-Jews even outside Israel. The custom appears to be to rely upon the lenient authorities who permit rentals to non-Jews.

[4] *Hilchos Avodas Kokhavim 10:6.*

## Are Non-Idolatrous Gentiles Permitted to Reside in Israel?

Maimonides's last statement, regarding gifts, is curious on account of the following verse:

*You shall eat not eat improperly slaughtered meat – you shall give it to the* ger *within your gates so that he may eat it…* (Deuteronomy 14:21)

This verse instructs the Jew to gift improperly slaughtered meat to a *ger*. Now, we might assume that this *"ger* within your gates" is a convert to Judaism. However, this cannot be so, because a convert is like a born Jew in his obligation to observe the dietary laws. If, however, this verse speaks of a non-Jew, then it must refer to a non-Jew who is not an idolater. Otherwise, how is a Jew allowed to gift the meat to the non-Jew? As we just learned, a Jew may not favor an idolater with gifts!

## The *Ger Toshav*

From this verse and many others, we see that the Torah anticipates the presence of non-idolatrous gentiles in Israel, referring such individuals as *ger toshav*:

- Exodus 12:43-45 – *This is the decree of the Passover offering… a resident [toshav] and a hired laborer may not eat of it.*

- Lev. 25:6 – *The land's yield of the sabbatical year shall be yours to eat, yours… and the residents' [toshav] who sojourns [ger] among you.*

- Lev. 25:35 – *…you shall strengthen him, the convert or the resident [toshav].*

- Lev. 25:40 – *Like a laborer or a resident [toshav] he shall be with you, until the jubilee year he shall work with you.*

- Lev. 25:45 - *…also, from among the children of the residents [toshav] who dwell [ger] with you…*

- Lev. 25:47 – *If the means of a sojourner [ger] who resides [toshav] among you…*

- Num. 35:15 – *For the children of Israel, the convert, and the resident [toshav] among them…*

The term *ger*, from the Hebrew root *gar*, meaning "to sojourn," refers to an alien, a stranger, or an immigrant. *Toshav* means "reside." A *ger toshav* is, therefore, a resident alien: a non-Jew who resides in the land of Israel among the Jewish people.

## The Benefits of a *Ger Toshav*

A survey of the Midrashic, Mishnaic, Talmudic, and *halakhic* literature reveals that the *ger toshav*, though not Jewish, enjoys many of the benefits reserved for Jews who live in Israel. However, the *ger toshav* is also bound by many of the same restrictions that apply to idolaters.

Let's first examine the residency of a *ger toshav*. Unlike an idolater, a *ger toshav* is allowed to settle, even permanently, in Israel. However, his dwelling there is subject to a number of conditions:

- The *ger toshav* must be settled in a place where he can make a living or practice his trade.[5]

- A *ger toshav* was not permitted to live near the borders of Israel, but only well into the interior.[6]

- A Jew may sell land in Israel to a *ger toshav*.[7]

- Once settled, the Jews may not force a *ger toshav* to move from one place to another.[8] It is, however, permitted to relocate him if the move is of substantial benefit to him.[9]

- A *ger toshav* may not reside in Jerusalem.[10]

The Jewish community is commanded with a general obligation (derived from Leviticus 25:35) to sustain a *ger toshav*. Such is not the case with idolaters. The Jewish community is prohibited from providing medical treatment or even saving the life of an idolater.[11]

---

[5] *Sifrei* to Deuteronomy 23:17. See also *Maseches Geirim* 3:4, by way of implication.

[6] *Sifrei* to Deuteronomy 23:17; *Maseches Geirim* 3:4.

[7] *Sefer HaChinuch 94*.

[8] *Sifrei* ibid.

[9] *Malbim* to Deuteronomy 23:17; *Sifrei* ibid.

[10] *Tosefta Negaim 6*; Maimonides, *Hilchos Beis HaBechira 7:14*. However, *Sifrei* to Deuteronomy 23:17 and *Hagahos Raavad* to *Hilchos Issurei Biah 14:8* hold that a *ger toshav* may not live within the boundaries of any established city. Maimonides and *Tosefta*, though, only prohibit the dwelling of a *ger toshav* within Jerusalem, making no mention of any restriction upon living anywhere else. If Maimonides agreed with the *Raavad*, then why would Maimonides need to single out a prohibition against living in Jerusalem? It appears, therefore, that Maimonides does not acknowledge a general prohibition against residing in cities. See *Maggid Mishneh* to Maimonides, *Issurei Biah 14:8*. See also *Zayis Raanan* and *Zera Avraham* ibid.

[11] Maimonides, *Hilchos Avodas Kochavim 10:1-2*. Maimonides qualifies this ruling, writing that Jews may offer an idolater medical treatment if denial of it would disrupt the peace. However, a Jew may only do so for fee and not for free.

"Sustaining" a *ger toshav* includes the following:

- The Jews are commanded to sustain the *ger toshav* and to ensure his welfare in the same way they would for a fellow Jew.[12] For example: if he is in danger we must do whatever possible to save him.[13] So too, he must be supported with charity, if needed.[14]

- Since Jews are commanded to ensure his welfare, they may even provide the *ger toshav* with free medical care if necessary.[15]

- A Jew may, even on Shabbos, assist a *ger toshav* in giving birth.[16]

- Jews may give gifts to a *ger toshav*.[17]

- Jews may go beyond the minimal social graces required for peace when interacting with a *ger toshav*. This is not the case with idolaters, for whom we may only show the minimal degree of courtesy needed to maintain peace and civility. A *ger toshav*, though, may be treated with the same etiquette, kindness, and grace afforded to other Jews.[18]

The Torah also commands the Jews in a number of *mitzvos* ensuring the *ger toshav* a degree of equanimity in civil and monetary law.[19] These *mitzvos* also guarantee specific protections for the earned wages of a *ger toshav*.[20]

There is also an obligation for the Jews to establish courts to adjudicate disputes between *ger toshav* according to their Noahide laws.[21]

---

[12] *Pesachim 21b*; *Avodah Zara 65a*; Maimonides, *Hilchos Zekhiyah UMatana 3:11* and *Hilchos Melakhim 10:12*.

[13] *Ramban* in his gloss to the *Sefer HaMitzvos*, Mitvah Aseh 16.

[14] Maimonides, *Hilchos Matnas Aniyim 7:1*.

[15] Maimonides, *Hilchos Avodas Kokhavim 10:2*.

[16] Maimonides, *Hilchos Shabbos 2:12*. However, we may not violate the Shabbos to do so.

[17] *Pesachim 21b*; *Avodah Zara 65a*; Maimonides, *Hilchos Avodas Kokhavim 10:4*; *Tur*, *Choshen Mishpat* 249.

[18] *Gittin 62a*.

[19] *Maseches Gerim 3:2*; *Yerushalmi* Yevamos 8:1; *Sifrei* Deuteronomy 23:17.

[20] *Sifrei* Deuteronomy 24:14; *Maseches Geirim 3:3*; *Yerushalmi* Yevamos 8:1; *Bava Metzia 111b*; Maimonides, *Hilchos S'khirus 11:1*.

From the Jewish perspective, the *ger toshav*, since he does not worship idols, is not subject to laws based upon concerns for idolatry. For example, we do not accept an oath from a regular non-Jew because he will likely swear in the name of his false deity. However, we may accept an oath from a *ger toshav*.[22] The wine of idolaters, because it is of religious significance to them, is prohibited for both benefit and consumption. However, the wine of *a ger toshav* is only prohibited for consumption.[23] It should be noted that there are a few other instances in Torah law, unrelated to idolatry, in which a *ger toshav* is regarded differently than an idolater.[24]

In every other respect, though, a *ger toshav* is treated like an idolater.[25] In a number of instances in which we might have thought otherwise, the sources make certain to reinforce this point:

- A Jew may lend to a *ger toshav* on interest.[26]

- A Jew who must sell himself into servitude may only sell himself to another Jew or to a convert. He may not serve a *ger toshav*.[27]

- The *shemitta* year[28] does not cancel the debts[29] of a *ger toshav*.[30]

---

[21] See *Maimonides, Hilchos Melakhim 10:11*. The *Radbaz* ad loc. notes that the Jewish obligation is only when the *ger toshav* have not established their own courts.

[22] Exodus 23:13; *Tosafos Kesubos 94a*.

[23] This prohibition of consumption is part of many dietary restrictions aimed at limiting social interaction between Jews and non-Jews. Maimonides, *Hilchos Maachalos Asuros 11:7*; *Shulchan Aruch, Yoreh Deah 124:2*.

[24] See, for example Maimonides, *Hilchos Rotzeach 5:3-4* on the exile of a *ger toshav* who unintentionally kills another *ger toshav* or an indentured servant.

[25] *Avodah Zarah 64b*.

[26] Mishnah, *Bava Metzia 70b* and Talmud, *Bava Metzia 71a*; Maimonides, *Hilchos Melaveh Ve-Loveh 5:1*.

[27] Maimonides, *Hilchos Avadim 1:3*.

[28] The seventh, sabbatical year of the seven-year agricultural and tithing cycle. See Exodus 23:10-11.

[29] Cancellation of debts is an effect of the *shemitta* year. See Deuteronomy 15:1 – 3.

[30] *Sifrei* Deuteronomy 15:3.

- If a Jew sells his indentured servant to a *ger toshav*, the Jew is forced to buy him back, even if at an exorbitant price, and to grant him his freedom.[31]

- Biblically, a *ger toshav* is like a non-Jew with regard to the laws of tzaraas – he does not become impure.[32] However, there are a number of rabbinic decrees creating exceptions for a *ger toshav*.[33]

- A *ger toshav* may not partake of the Passover sacrifice.[34]

- Jews many not accept funds from a *ger toshav* for the rebuilding or upkeep of the Temple complex.[35]

- Jews have no commandment to correct or rebuke a *ger toshav*.[36]

## How Does a Non-Jew Become a Ger Toshav?

The Talmud in Avodah Zarah 64b records a three-way dispute as to how a gentile becomes a *ger toshav*.

- Rabbi Meir – A *ger toshav* is a non-Jew who has, before three Torah Scholars, accepted upon himself to not worship idols.

- *Chachomim* (the majority of sages) – a *ger toshav* is a non-Jew who, before three Torah Scholars, accepts upon himself to observe the seven Noahide laws.

---

[31] Gittin 44a; Maimonides, Hilchos Avadim 8:5; Shulchan Aruch YD 267:80.

[32] Mishnah, *Negaim* 3:1; Maimonides, Hilchos Tumas Tzaraas 9:1.

[33] For example, they are decreed Rabbinically impure for the *tzaraas* of houses and garments. See the Rash to *Negaim 3:1*; Rosh, Raav, to *Gittin* ibid.; Tos. Yom Tov *Gittin 3:1* and 11:1; *Mishnah LeMelech Tumas Tzaraas 14:11*. A *ger toshav* is also equal to a non-Jew with regard to the *Ziva* impurity. See *Tosefta Zavim 2*.

[34] Mechilta, Exodus 12:45; *Maimonides*, Hilchos Korban Pesach 9:7 (see *Raavad* and *Kesef Mishnah* as well); *Sefer HaChinuch 14*; Minchas Chinuch *13:2*; Sefer Mitzvos HaGadol, *Lav 354*.

[35] *Maimonides*, Hilchos Shekalim 4:8 from Ezra 4:3 and Nechemiah 2:20.

[36] Rashi to *Sanhedrin 75a*. This is difficult considering that Maimonides holds of an obligation to compel observance of the Noahide laws (Hilchos Melakhim 8:10-11). It may be that this obligation is only in force until the non-Jew has accepted the seven laws. After that point, he is liable for his own observance of them.

- *Acherim* (the others) – A *ger toshav* is a non-Jew who has accepted all of the commandments of the Torah save one: the prohibition of eating *neveilos*, meat that has not been properly slaughtered according to Torah law.

Multiple opinions may be acceptable in matters of history or homiletics,[37] yet we can only accept a single idea as binding in matters of practice.[38] One of the many rules for deciding *halakhah*, practice, is that the opinion of the majority is decisive.[39] The *Chachomim*, being the majority, are therefore the *halakhah*, practice.[40]

As expected, later scholars[41] decide the *halakhah*, practice, in accordance with the *Chachomim*: a *ger toshav* is a non-Jew who has accepted, before three scholars, the observance of the seven Noahide laws. Yet, one scholar, Rashi, is inconsistent in his definition of a *ger toshav*. In a number of places[42] Rashi appears to define *ger toshav* using Rabbi Meir's criteria.[43] Strangely, though, Rashi rules like the *Chachomim* in *Avodah Zarah 24b*. What then does Rashi actually hold? Scholars have taken the position that Rashi must hold like the *Chachomim*. After all, the idea that Rashi would deviate from the basic tenets of Talmudic interpretation is troubling. The difficulty lies in explaining the occasions on which Rashi appears to follow Rabbi Meir.

Many great scholars have tried to unravel Rashi, yet no single approach has succeeded.[44] The most famous explanation of Rashi is that of the *Beer Sheva*.[45] He

---

[37] See Maimonides's *Perush HaMishnayos* to *Sotah 3:5*, *Sanhedrin 10:3*, and *Shevuos 1:4*. See also *Tosafos* to *Yoma 5b*, *Chagigah 6b*, and *Sanhedrin 15b*. See also *Maharitz Chayes* to *Yevamos 86b*.

[38] See *Avodah Zara 7a*; Yerushalmi, *Sanhedrin 4:2*; *Soferim 16:5*; Rif, *Sanhedrin 12b*; Rosh, *Sanhedrin 4:6*; *Mevo HaTalmud*. See also Tur, *Choshen Mishpat 25*; Shach, *Choshen Mishpat 25:9*; Teshuvos *Rashba* 1230.

[39] See *Chullin 11a*.

[40] See Shmuel HaNagid *Mevo HaTalmud*.

[41] See notes below.

[42] I.e. *Avodah Zarah 64b*, *Sanhedrin 96b*, *Yevamos 48b*.

[43] It should be pointed out that Rabbeinu Gershom to *Kerisus 9b* appears to define a *ger toshav* similarly to Rashi and Rabbi Meir. Nevertheless, his opinion, like Rashi's, is not accepted as *halakhah*.

[44] See *VeShav HaKohen 37*. In a well-known responsum, the *Veshav HaKohen* cites these many attempts in an admirable effort to find consistency in Rashi. He is unable to do so, however, and concludes that Rashi requires further study.

[45] *Beer Sheva* to *Sanhedrin 96b*. *Beer Sheva* is a commentary on the Talmud in the style of *Tosafos*. Authored by Rabbi Yissaschar Ber Eulenberg (1550-1623), chief justice of the rabbinic court of Gorizia, Italy.

explains that *Avodah Zarah 64b* (the aforementioned source of the three opinions as to the criteria for a *ger toshav*) is part of a larger Talmudic conversation about when Jews are obligated to support a non-Jew who lives among them within Israel.[46]

According to the *Beer Sheva*, Rashi agrees with the *Chachomim* only with regard to providing support to a *ger toshav*. However, the *Beer Sheva* explains that Rashi follows Rabbi Meir's opinion for all other matters affecting the *ger toshav*.

The *Beer Sheva's* explanation works well for many instances where Rashi appears to espouse Rabbi Meir. However, it is contradicted by Rashi's comments to Arakhin 29a. There, Rashi seems to apply Rabbi Meir's criteria even for the sake of defining a *ger toshav* for communal support.[47]

Maimonides,[48] the *Arbah Turim*,[49] and the *Shulchan Aruch*[50] all record the position of the *Chachomim* as conclusive: to become a *ger toshav* a non-Jew must accept the seven Noahide laws upon himself before a *beis din*, a tribunal of three qualified scholars.

---

[46] *Avodah Zarah 64b – 65a*. Although this passage quotes Rabbi Meir's opinion, the view of Rav Yehudah brought therein is nevertheless pertinent.

[47] For other attempts at resolving Rashi's understanding of the criteria for a *ger toshav*, see the responsa *VeShav HaKohen* 37 and *Margolios HaYam* ad. loc. See also Rabbi Yaakov Kaminetzky's *BeInyan Ger Toshav* in *Sefer HaZikaron LeZekher Moreinu veRabbeinu ha-Gaon R. Rafael Boruch Sorotzkin*, pp. 198-200. See also Rabbi Moshe Shternbuch in *Edut*, No. 6 (Adat II 5749), p. 30.

[48] *Hilchos Melachim 8:10-11*, *Hilchos Avodas Kokhavim* 10:6, *Hilchos Issurei Biah* 14:8, and *Hilchos Shabbos* 20:14.

[49] *Yoreh Deah 124* – see *Bais Yosef* ad loc.

[50] *Yoreh Deah 124:2*.

THE YESHIVA PIRCHEI SHOSHANIM SHULCHAN ARUCH LEARNING PROJECT

# The Noahide Laws – Lesson Ten

© **Yeshiva Pirchei Shoshanim 2017**
This shiur may not be reproduced in any
form without permission of the copyright holder

## Outline of This Lesson:

1. Does Ger Toshav Apply Today

2. A 20th Century Problem

# Noahide Identity II
# Ger Toshav Today

## When Does the *Ger Toshav* Status Apply?

The Talmud[1] notes a similarity of language between the verses describing an indentured servant and a *Ger Toshav*:

- Indentured Servant: Deuteronomy 15:16 – *In the event that he says to you: "I will not leave you," because he loves your household and **because it is a benefit to him**...*[2]

- *Ger toshav*: Deuteronomy 23:17 – *He shall dwell with you in your midst, in whichever place he will choose from your cities **because it is a benefit to him**...*

This similarity of language, called a *gezeira shava*[3] in the system of Talmudic interpretation, indicates that the two concepts share similarities. In this case, the law of the *ger toshav* is similar to the law of freeing an indentured servant: it only

---

[1] *Arakhin* 29a.

[2] In the Jubilee year all indentures servants were freed. This verse speaks of a servant who rejects freedom, whishing instead to remain with his master. See note 55, below.

[3] *Gezeira shava*, an "equivalent decree" is one of the methods of scriptural exegesis revealed along with the Torah at Sinai.

applies when the Jubilee cycle[4] is in full observance. Maimonides codifies this qualification as law[5] and it is accepted as such by all later authorities.

Since full observance of the Jubilee year ceased around 600 BCE,[6] no *ger toshav* have been accepted by Israel since that time. Of course, this means that acceptance of *ger toshav* is not possible in our times, as Maimonides writes:

> *Even if a non-Jew comes and accepts upon himself the entire Torah with the exception of but a minor detail, we still do not accept him [as a ger toshav],*[7]

and,

> *A* ger toshav *may only be accepted in a time when the Jubilee year is in full observance. When the Jubilee year is not in full observance, we can only accept full converts.*[8]

## A 20th Century Problem: Non-Jewish Residence in Israel

What is meant by "we do not accept them?" This is an extremely important question and one that has immediate relevance. As we saw above, idolaters are prohibited from residing in Israel. However, this prohibition only applies when the Jews have rulership over Israel and the non-Jews therein. It appears that this criterion is based on political sovereignty, and not on any redemptive qualification such as the end of the exile or rebuilding of the temple. Given the establishment of the state of Israel, the prohibition of non-Jewish residency must again be in force.

However, we have no Jubilee observance and, therefore, cannot grant *ger toshav* status. If this is the case, then how can any non-Jews reside in Israel? Must not they be forcibly removed?

---

[4] The Jubilee cycle is the 50 year agricultural and legal cycle observed during ancient times. It is no longer observed in our times (see note 53). In the 50th year, the Jubilee year, all indentured servants were freed. See Leviticus 25:39 – 40.

[5] Hilchos Issurei Biah 14:8.

[6] See Maimonides, Hilchos Shemitta 10:8. The Jubilee year is only observed when the tribes are dwelling in their territories. With the exile of Gad and half of Manasseh in about 600 BCE, observance of the cycle ceased.

[7] *Hilchos Issurei Biah ibid.*

[8] Hilchos Avodas Kochavim 10:6.

To answer this question, we must take a very close look at the identity of a *ger toshav*. Becoming a *ger toshav* has three broad effects on a non-Jew:[9]

1) He is granted permission to reside in Israel,

2) He becomes entitled to support from the Jewish community, and

3) He is treated differently from an idolater with regards to many laws.[10]

A basic reading of Maimonides's statement of the laws pertaining to a *ger toshav* implies that acceptance of the seven Noahide laws before a *beis din* is needed to convey all three effects. However, according to Maimonides's chief disputant, the Raavad,[11] things are not so simple:

> *This [the Maimonides's] interpretation is closed and sealed, failing to explain what is meant by "we do not accept* ger toshav *unless the Jubilee year is observed," nor what is to be done with the* mitzvos *of a* ger toshav... *Rather, these are the* mitzvos *that are not in affect when the Jubilee is not observed (some of them create leniency for him [the non-Jew], and some create stringency): When the Jubilee is not observed, he [the non-Jew] may even reside within cities [in Israel]... this is the leniency. We have no obligation to support him – this is the stringency.*

According to the *Raavad*, the inability of the courts to accept a *ger toshav* in our times is only for the purpose of obligating the Jewish community to sustain the *ger toshav*.[12] It appears that, even without acceptance of the Noahide laws before a *beis din*, a gentile may nevertheless live in Israel provided that he keeps the Noahide laws. This is also the understanding of *Tosafos*[13], the Rashba,[14] and the *Kesef Mishnah*.[15] The *Kesef Mishnah* explains, however, that a careful reading of Maimonides reveals that Maimonides would even agree with the *Raavad*: that

---

[9] It may be argued that there are more effects than these three. Listing them all, however, is more an exercise in taxonomy than one relevant to this discussion. For the sake of brevity, I have chosen to represent the identity of the *ger toshav* using these three broad effects. The point is that the identity of a *ger toshav* includes many facets which are, to a degree, independent of each other.

[10] As we shall see, it is possible that 3 and 1 are really one in the same.

[11] Hilchos Issurei Biah 14:8.

[12] This is similar to the *Beer Sheva*'s attempt to explain Rashi's inconsistencies in defining a *ger toshav*.

[13] To *Avoda Zarah 65a*.

[14] Responsa I: 182.

[15] Hilchos Avodas Kochavim 10:6.

acceptance before a *beis din* is only needed for the sake of entitling the non-Jews to support. It is not needed to allow a non-Jew to live in Israel.[16]

Therefore, when the authorities conclude that we do not accept *ger toshav* in our times, it means that a *ger toshav* cannot today bind the Jewish community to support and protect him in Israel.

Yet, if acceptance before a *beis din* is only needed to qualify one for communal support, then why does a *ger toshav* receive the other two benefits – of residency and as a non-idolater?

The answer is that these two factors (which are actually one-in-the-same) are automatic consequences of the non-Jew's rejection of idolatry. They are not a result of his acceptance of the Noahide laws before a *beis din*. Recall that the purpose of prohibiting non-Jewish residency in Israel was:

*They [idolaters] shall not dwell within your land* **lest they cause you to sin against Me and worship their gods.**[17]

If a non-idolatrous gentile wishes to live in Israel, there is no danger of him corrupting the faith of the Jewish populace. Therefore, the prohibition against his residency should not apply.

Put succinctly: every *ger toshav* may be a non-idolatrous resident, but every non-idolatrous resident is not necessarily a *ger toshav*.

The majority of authorities[18] who have tackled the question of non-Jewish residency in the modern state of Israel have relied upon this interpretation of *ger*

---

[16] See *Tzafnas Paneach* to *Hilchos Issurei Biah 14*; See also *Rashba's Toras HaBayis*; *Bais Yosef* to YD 124.

[17] Exodus 23:33. See *Hilchos Avodas Kochavim ibid*.

[18] *Sheelas Shlomo II:433* who cites this as the opinion of Rav Tzvi Yehudah Kook as well; *Mishpat Kohen 61*; *Mishnas HaMedinah* p. 65; *Siach Nachum* 93. This opinion is relied upon by most authorities who have weighed the issue. A number of other permissive factors have been offered as well. For example, Rav A. I. Kook in *Iggros Ra'ayah 89* (as well as *Mishpat Kohen 58*) and Rav I. Herzog in *Shut Heichal Yitzchak EH 1:12* (and in *Techumim II*, p. 172) cite the *Meiri* (to *Bava Kama 113a* and *Yoma 84b*) that the prohibition against non-Jewish residence does not apply to civilized people; indeed they have an automatic, collective status of *ger toshav*. This opinion is problematic for at least four reasons. First, is that the *halakhah* prohibiting non-Jewish residency is intended to protect the integrity of Jewish faith and practice (as per Exodus 23:33 – see Maimonides, *Hilchos Avodas Kokhavim 10:6*). If so, then why should we be concerned as to whether or not the non-Jew is uncivilized? The second issue is that the Meiri's views on the *halakhic* status of non-Jews are unique and controversial. They have very little precedent or acceptance in Torah literature. The third problem is with the general use of the Meiri as a *halakhic* source. Shortly after the completion of his commentary in the late 13th century, almost all of his manuscripts were lost. They remained undiscovered until the 1920's. Having been outside the stream of *halakhic* debate and development

*toshav* (that a non-Jew only need to not worship idols)[19] to permit the residency of non-Jews in Israel.[20]

We must keep in mind that the necessity for deciding, in practice, the exact definition of *ger toshav* has only become pertinent since the establishment of the state of Israel. Prior to this time, Torah scholars offered many possible understandings of the *ger toshav* (as we shall soon see).

---

for so long, never having been seen by the *Tur*, *Shulchan Aruch*, *Shach*, *Taz*, etc., the acceptability of his opinions as *halakhically* dispositive is difficult. Fourth, the Meiri's position is in the severe minority and is contradicted by both earlier and later authorities. See *HaPardes 26*, pp. 7-13. Rabbi Menachem Kasher, *HaTekufah HaGedolah* Ch. 13, proposes an alternative reason to permit non-Jewish settlement in Israel: that the prohibition of non-Jewish residency does not apply today because Jewish rulership of the land is not complete. According to R. Kasher, it seems that non-Jewish residency is only a problem once the messianic redemption has occurred. However, R. Kasher alone espouses this view and it is not quoted or entertained by later scholars.

[19] Of course, this position requires an examination of the monotheistic statuses of both Christianity and Islam. Islam is relatively easy to deal with. However, defining Christianity's monotheistic status is no easy task. It appears that the burden of this determination is what drove some of the minority of the *halakhic* opinions on non-Jewish residency to rely upon the Meiri. By doing so, one avoids the question of Christianity's status altogether. For the purposes of residency, however, most of the authorities mentioned in note 69 find enough doubt as to the overall communal status of Christianity to allow Christians to reside as non-idolaters.

[20] However, what about the restrictions that dictate where a *ger toshav* may reside? Since the residence of a non-Jew is dependent on his rejection of idolatry, then all of those restrictions should apply equally to contemporary non-idolatrous gentiles. The current circumstances of Israel, though, are not comparable to those of ancient times. For example, the holiness of the cities and of Jerusalem is not as it once was. Therefore, non-Jewish residence in these places may be allowed.

THE YESHIVA PIRCHEI SHOSHANIM SHULCHAN ARUCH LEARNING PROJECT

# The Noahide Laws – Lesson Eleven

© **Yeshiva Pirchei Shoshanim 2017**
This shiur may not be reproduced in any
form without permission of the copyright holder.

## Outline of This Lesson:

1. Introduction
2. Two Very Difficult Paragraphs From Maimonides
3. Identifying the Problems
4. Making Sense of the Paragraphs 10 & 11

# Noahide Identity III
# Ger Toshav Today

## Introduction

Having clarified the identity of a *ger toshav*, we now turn our attention to Noahide identity. We will soon see how the two relate to each other. The term *ben Noach* (Noahide), or *Bnei Noach* (the plural of Noahide) occurs in about fifty places in the Talmud and Rashi. However, it is used primarily in its simple meaning, "a child of Noah," as a generic term for all non-Jews. Is it possible that the term *ben Noach*, Noahide, implies more? Is there an actual, positive identity called "Noahide?"

## Two Very Difficult Paragraphs

**HILKHOS MELAKHIM 8:10-11**

The answer to this question depends upon two frightfully difficult paragraphs in Maimonides's *Mishneh Torah*,[1] his code of Torah law. Here are the two paragraphs in full:

[Note: The bracketed letters have been inserted for ease of reference]

§10. *[A]Moses our Teacher gave over the Torah and Mitzvos only to the Jewish people, as it is written: "It is an inheritance to the congregation of Jacob" (Deut. 33:4). And all who wish to convert from among the nations, "as you are, so shall the convert be before the Lord" (Num. 15:15). However, for those who do not wish to accept Torah and Mitzvos, we do not force them to do so.*

*[B] And so too it was commanded to Moses by the Almighty to force the peoples of the world to accept the commandments charged to the children of Noah. [C]All who do not accept them shall be executed. One who accepts them is called a* Ger Toshav.

---

[1] Hilchos Melakhim 8:10-11.

§11. *[D] All who accept the Seven Mitzvos and are careful to observe them are called MiChasidei Umos HaOlam (of the Pious Peoples of the World) [E] and they have a share in the World to Come. [F] This is provided that one accepts and observes them because they were commanded to him by the Holy One, in his Torah, and [G] reaffirmed by Moses. [H] However, one who observes them based on intellectual reason alone is neither called a Ger Toshav nor MiChasidei Umos HaOlam (of the Pious Peoples of the World). He is, rather, "of the wise ones" of the gentiles.*²

## Identifying the Problems

Using the reference letters inserted into the text, let's go through the difficulties point-by-point.

[A] *Moses our Teacher gave over the Torah and Mitzvos only to the Jewish people, as it is written: "It is an inheritance to the congregation of Jacob" (Deut. 33:4). And all who wish to convert from among the nations, "as you are, so shall the convert be before the Lord" (Num. 15:15). However, for those who do not wish to accept Torah and Mitzvos, we do not force them to do so.*

> This section is fairly innocuous, stating simply that the Torah is the unique possession of the Jews, yet all who want to convert and become Jewish may voluntarily do so. Additionally, no gentile may be coerced into converting.

[B] *And so too it was commanded to Moses by the Almighty to force the peoples of the world to accept the commandments charged to the children of Noah.*

> Our paragraphs are capstones to a chapter dealing with the conquest of the land of Israel. For example, §1 of this chapter opens:
>
>> When the army's troops enter the territory of gentiles, conquering them and taking them captive…
>
> §9, immediately preceding our selection, reads:

---

² The text of this last phrase differs in the *editio princeps* (Rome, 1480) and almost all subsequent printed editions. These versions read : … *one who observes them based on intellectual reason alone is neither called a* Ger Toshav *nor* MiChasidei Umos HaOlam *(of the Pious Peoples of the World),* **and is not** *"of the wise ones" of the gentiles.* This is almost certainly the error of a careless copyist (the mistake being in the transcription of a single letter). Many of the earliest manuscript versions read … *He is, rather, "of the wise ones" of the gentiles.* Later scholars also cite this version of the text as correct. See Teshuvos Maharam Alashkar 117, Rav Yosef ben Shem Tov's *Kevod Elokim* 29a, and, more recently, Iggros Reiyah I:89. Recent critical editions of Maimonides have corrected this text to read … *He is rather "of the wise ones" of the gentiles.* See Rabbi Shabtai Fraenkel's edition of the *Mishneh Torah*. See also the editions prepared by Rabbi Yosef Qafih and Yeshivat Or Vishua.

> *Similarly, a treaty cannot be made with a city which desires to accept a peaceful settlement until they deny idol worship, destroy their places of worship, and accept the seven universal laws commanded Noah's descendants. Any gentile who does not accept these commandments must be executed if he is under our authority.*

§10 and §11, therefore, are clarifying the requirement of these conquered peoples to accept the Noahide laws. Yet, if we are speaking about the conquest of Israel, then why does Maimonides use the phrase ... *to force the peoples of the world...?* Maimonides is not speaking only about the gentile inhabitants of Israel, but about the gentiles of the world!

[C] *All who do not accept them shall be executed. One who accepts them is called a* Ger Toshav.

> This requirement for execution is difficult to understand. The most obvious problem is it has no apparent source. Furthermore, if we understand [B] as requiring forced acceptance of the Noahide laws upon all the peoples of the world, then [C] would require the execution of anyone who refuses. [C] Would even mandate the execution of those who fulfill the Noahide laws, yet who never accepted them formally before a *beis din*. This yields a startling conclusion. See [H]:
>
>> [H] However, *one who observes them based on intellectual reason alone is neither called a* Ger Toshav *nor* MiChasidei Umos HaOlam *(of the Pious Peoples of the World). He is rather "of the wise ones" of the gentiles.*
>
> We see that a person who observes the Noahide laws based on reason alone is not someone who has accepted these laws before a *beis din*. Therefore, according to [B] and [C] such a "wise one of the gentiles" would also be executed for failing to accept the Noahide laws.
>
> The net result of this simple reading of Maimonides is to erase the identity of the *ben Noach*, the Noahide, entirely. According to such a reading, the only available options to a gentile are conversion to Judaism, becoming a *ger toshav*, or being executed!

§11 only creates more problems for us:

[D] *All that accept the Seven Mitzvos and are careful to observe them are called* MiChasidei Umos HaOlam *(of the Pious Peoples of the World)*

The classification of *MiChasidei Umos HaOlam*, of the Pious Peoples of the World, has no clear Talmudic precedent.[3] This is only true, however, of our modern editions of the Talmud. Sanhedrin 110b discusses the reward earned by "the children of the wicked of the idolaters." Rashi, commenting on this passage, similarly refers to the merit of the children "of the righteous of the idolaters." In both instances, the *Mesoras HaShas*[4] indicates that earlier versions of the texts, both the Talmud and Rashi, read "the children of the nations of the world," and "the pious peoples of the world," respectively. It is likely that our modern text is the product of an offended church censor.

What is odd, though, is the tying of this status of *MiChasidei Umos HaOlam*, of the Pious Peoples of the World, to the acceptance of the Noahide laws.

[E] *and they have a share in the World to Come.*

This passage presents little that is surprising. The Talmud has already demonstrated that gentiles receive reward for fulfilling their *mitzvos*.[5] However, we again have the question: why is the receiving of the eternal reward of the world to come dependent on the status of *MiChasidei Umos HaOlam*, of the Pious Peoples of the World, and becoming a *ger toshav*?

[F] & [G] *This is provided that one accepts and observes them because they were commanded to him by the Holy One, in his Torah, and reaffirmed by Moses.*

Maimonides requires acceptance of the Noahide laws based upon Sinaitic revelation, rejecting the validity of acceptance based upon the original Noahic[6] covenant. Without acceptance based on Sinaitic revelation, a gentile does not receive reward in the World to Come for fulfilling his Noahide obligations.

---

[3] In Chullin 92a, Rav Yehuda uses the term *tzadikei umos ha-olam*, the righteous of the gentile nations, in his interpretation of Zecharia 11:13. Rav Yochanan in the name of Rav Shimon Ben Yehotzadak, however, says that it refers to the righteous of Israel. See Maharsha and Rashi with the Hagahos HaBach.

[4] Marginal gloss authored by Rabbi Yehoshua Boaz (d. Italy 1557). It provides cross references and critical notes to the Talmudic text.

[5] Bava Kama 38a; Sanhedrin 105a.

[6] Maimonides and Tosafos disagree as to whether or not all seven Noahide laws were given to Adam (the view of Tosafos Sanhedrin 56b, d.h Achol Tochal, and possibly Rashi to Sanhedrin 57a, d.h. l'Mishri Basar), or if only the first six were given to Adam and only the seventh given to Noah (the view of Maimonides, Hilkhos Melakhim 9:1). My favoring of the term "Noahic" rather than "Adamic" for the original covenant is not meant to imply one view over another. I use "Noahic" for its consonance with the term "Noahide," which is the common descriptor for these laws.

[H] However, *one who observes them based on intellectual reason alone is neither called a* Ger Toshav *nor* MiChasidei Umos HaOlam *(of the Pious Peoples of the World). He is, rather, "of the wise ones" of the gentiles.*[7]

> Maimonides informs us that not only is acceptance based upon the Noahic covenant insufficient, but even fulfillment of the Noahide laws based upon reason or logic is unacceptable. One who observes the Noahide laws based upon reason[8] does not merit being called pious, but only wise.[9] Furthermore, one who observes his laws based upon reason appears precluded from receiving any reward – Maimonides only grants reward to one who accepts the laws based on belief in Sinaitic revelation (see [D] and [E] above).

## Making Sense of Maimonides's §10 and §11

The issues in §10, of forcing acceptance and executions, we will deal with later. The immediate issue, the question of Noahide identity, requires an unraveling of §11:

> 11. [D] *All who accept the Seven Mitzvos and are careful to observe them are called* MiChasidei Umos HaOlam *(of the Pious Peoples of the World)* [E] *and they have a share in the World to Come.* [F] *This is provided that one accepts and observes them because they were commanded to him by the Holy One, in his Torah, and* [G] *reaffirmed by Moses.* [H] *However, one who observes them based on intellectual reason alone is neither called a* Ger Toshav *nor* MiChasidei Umos HaOlam *(of the Pious Peoples of the World).* [I] *He is, rather, "of the wise ones" of the gentiles.*

Rabbi Yosef Karo, author of the *Shulchan Aruch*, notes that there is no apparent textual source for this paragraph, writing: "it appears to me that our master made this statement as a result of his own deduction…[10]" Despite this lack, Rabbi Karo agrees with Maimonides's conclusions.[11]

---

[7] See note 2, above, on the text of this final phrase.

[8] Apparently, meaning as a concept of natural law or social necessity.

[9] The term *MiChachmei Umos HaOlam*, of the wise of the nations, has Talmudic precedent. It appears in *Pesachim 94b* and *Rosh HaShanah 12a* in a discussion of the secular wisdom of the gentiles.

[10] *Kesef Mishnah* ad loc.

[11] The inability to locate sources for Maimonides's rulings does not automatically disqualify them. See the responsa of the *Rivash*, *Maharalbach*, and *Rosh* who discuss many examples.

Without a textual source,[12] scholars have been left to speculate as to Maimonides's reasoning.[13] However, the *Sefer Toldos Adam*[14] records a curious story about Rabbi Shlomo Zalman of Volozhin (brother of the famed Rabbi Chaim of Volozhin). A visiting Sephardic Rabbi asked Rabbi Zalman to explain several difficult sections from Maimonides's writings. When asked about the source of our §11, the author tells us that Rabbi Zalman offered up the following Midrash:

> *Rabbi Chisda Said: I have heard that the pious of the nations of the world have a share in the world to come. However, we have not been taught so with regard to the wise men of the nations of the world. Who is a pious man from among the nations of the world? He who accepts the seven commandments because they are written in the Torah. A wise man from among the nations of the world, however, is one who observes them based upon his own reason.*

*Sefer Toldos Adam*, however, does not identify this *midrash*. In fact, since his quotation of it, no one has ever succeeded again in locating it.

In the 20th century, however, the manuscript of a lost *Midrash*, the *Mishnas Rebbi Eliezer*, was discovered and published.[15] The *Mishnas Rebbi Eliezer*[16] includes the following passage:

---

[12] Maimonides, in his *Teshuvos HaRambam* I:148 (ed. Blau 1957) references our §10 and §11, alluding to a *Braisa shel Rebbi Eliezer ben Yaakov* as his source. However, Maimonides seems to tie this source only to the idea of forcing acceptance of the Noahide laws (§10). Additionally, no one has every located this *Braisa shel Rebbi Eliezer ben Yaakov*. See note 15, below.

[13] See, for example, the letter from Rabbi Yaakov Emden in Moses Mendelssohn's *Gesammelte Schriften*, No. 16 (Berlin, 1929). Rabbi Emden exchanged correspondence on the interpretation of §10 with Moses Mendelssohn, the intellectual father of Reform Judaism. Mendelssohn was deeply unsettled by this paragraph and wrote to Emden seeking assistance. Rabbi Emden proposed three possible derivations; however, these are difficult to understand and poorly supported.

[14] By Rabbi Yechezkel Feivel. VI 35a. The *Sefer Toldos Adam* is a biography of Rabbi Shlomo Zalman of Volozhin.

[15] *Mishnas Rebbi Eliezer oh Midrash Sheloshim VeShtayim Middos*. Ed. H. G. Enelow. Bloch Publishing New York, 1933. As mentioned in note 12, Maimonides mentions a *Braisa shel Rabbi Eliezer ben Yaakov* in connection with §10. However, this *Braisa shel Rabbi Eliezer ben Yaakov* cannot be the same text as the *Mishnas Rebbi Eliezer*. For one, the *Mishnas Rebbi Eliezer* contains no material similar to that of §10. Additionally, the *Mishnas Rebbi Eliezer* is attributed to Rabbi Eliezer ben Yossi HaGlili, not ben Yaakov. Furthermore, Maimonides was aware of the *Mishnas Rebbi Eliezer* as a text independent of the *Braisa shel Rabbi Eliezer ben Yaakov*. We know this because Maimonides quotes it explicitly as the *Mishnas Rebbi Eliezer ben Yossi HaGlili* in his *Sefer HaMitzvos, Mitzvos Aseh* 5. There is an extant manuscript of a *Braisa shel Rabbi Eliezer* (MS Vatican). However, this text appears to be part of the *Mishnas Rebbi Eliezer* (of ben Yossi HaGlili) and not the *Braisa shel Rabbi Eliezer ben Yaakov*. Michael Higger, writing in *The Jewish Quarterly Review*, Vol. 27, No. 1 (Jul., 1936), pp. 63-67, identifies the rediscovered *Mishnas Rebbi Eliezer* as a comingling of two earlier texts: the *Midrash Agur* and this *Braisa Shel Rabbi Eliezer*. Admittedly, there is some confusion as to the title of the *Mishnas Rebbi Eliezer*, it being referred to by a number of names in the literature. See,

> *The Chasidei Umos HaOlam [the Pious of the gentile nations] are only called pious when they when they fulfill the seven mitzvos commanded unto the children of Noah in all of their details.* **This is provided that they do so saying "we fulfill them because our father Noah commanded us by the mouth of the Mighty One."** *If they do so, then they merit the World to Come just as does a Jew. This is so even though they do no keep the Shabbos and Festivals for, after all, they were not commanded in them. But, if they observe them [the seven mitzvos] saying "we heard them from so-and-so" or* **if they observe them in accordance with their own reason... then they receive their reward only in this world.** [Emphasis added.]

This text is the closest parallel in any ancient rabbinic text to our Maimonidean §10. Viewed against the *Midrash* quoted in *Sefer Toldos Adam*, it appears that the *Sefer Toldos Adam*'s *Midrash* is either a corrupted or poorly recalled version of this *Mishnas Rebbi Eliezer*.

Is the *Mishnas Rebbi Eliezer* Maimonides's source for his §10? It is certainly possible. After all we know that Maimonides was familiar with it.[17] However, there are two obvious differences between the *Mishnas Rebbi Eliezer* and that of Maimonides's §10. The first is that the *Mishnas Rebbi Eliezer* requires acceptance of the Noahide laws because of Noahic revelation, not Sinaitic. The second is that the *Mishnas Rebbi Eliezer* mentions reward in this world for those who keep the Noahide laws according to their own reason. Maimonides makes no such statement.

Whether or not the *Mishnas Rebbi Eliezer* was relied upon by Maimonides, it nevertheless attests to a tradition validating Maimonides's concepts.

However, it is also possible that Maimonides's reasoning is entirely based upon a famous Talmudic passage in *Bava Kamma 38a*.

---

*Encyclopedia Talmudit*, VI, 290, 11 on the identification of the *Braisa shel Rebbi Eliezer, Mishnas Rebbi Eliezer*, and other texts.

[16] Enelow, p. 121.

[17] Maimonides quotes from it in his *Sefer HaMitzvos, Mitzvos Aseh* 5.

THE YESHIVA PIRCHEI SHOSHANIM SHULCHAN ARUCH LEARNING PROJECT

# The Noahide Laws – Lesson Twelve

© **Yeshiva Pirchei Shoshanim 2017**

This shiur may not be reproduced in any
form without permission of the copyright holder.

**164 Village Path, Lakewood NJ 08701 732.370.3344**
**164 Rabbi Akiva, Bnei Brak, 03.616.6340**

## Outline of This Lesson:

1. Introduction

2. *Bava Kamma* 38a

3. *Bava Kamma* 38a & The *Mishnas Rebbi Eliezer*

4. *Chiddushei HaGriz,* The *Ohr Somayach,* & Rabbi Malkiel Tannenbaum

5. Understanding Maimonides

# Noahide Identity IV
# What is a Noahide?

## Introduction

The term *ben Noach* (Noahide) or *Bnei Noach* (the plural of Noahide) occurs in about fifty places in the Talmud and Rashi. However, it is used primarily in its simple meaning, "a child of Noah," as a generic term for all non-Jews. Is it possible that the term *ben Noach*, Noahide, implies more? Is there an actual, positive identity called "Noahide?"

## Bava Kamma 38a

According to the Talmud, God altered the reward that Noahides may earn for their *mitzvos*. Quoting Habakkuk 3:6, Talmud *Bava Kama 38a* offers the following interpretation:

> "He [God] arose and judged the land; He saw and released the nations."[1]

> [Talmud:] He [God] saw the seven commandments that the descendants of Noah had accepted upon themselves. Since they did not observe them, he released them.

According to Rav Yosef this passage teaches that God released the non-Jews from the obligation of the Noahide laws. However, the other sages reject this interpretation because it is illogical. The gentiles should be punished for neglecting their laws, not rewarded by being released from them!

---

[1] The Talmud understands the word *va-yatir*, "tremble," also meaning "he released."

Mar, Son of Ravina, proposes another possibility: that even if the gentiles fulfill all their commandments they will never receive reward for doing so. The implication, of course, is that they will still suffer punishment for not keeping their *mitzvos*.
The Talmud also rejects this interpretation, citing Leviticus 18:5 as proof that non-Jews do receive reward for keeping their commandments:

> *"That man shall perform and gain life…"*

> *[Talmud:] The verse does not state Kohen, Levi, or Israel, but "Man," meaning Jews as well as gentiles.*

A third interpretation settles the question. In tractate *Kiddushin*[2] the Talmud explains that the reward of a person who fulfills an obligatory *mitzvah* is greater than the reward of one who fulfills a voluntary *mitzvah*.[3] The Talmud here, in *Bava Kamma* 38a, concludes that God altered the nature of the reward that gentiles would receive for keeping their commandments. Although gentiles are still obligated to observe the Noahide laws, the Talmud is telling us that the reward they receive is only the lesser reward of one who fulfills a commandment voluntarily.

## Bava Kamma 38a & the Mishnas Rebbi Eliezer

It appears from the Talmud that gentiles can only receive the lesser reward (of one who fulfills a voluntary commandment), and have no way to merit the greater reward of one who fulfills an obligatory commandment. However, the *Mishnas Rebbi Eliezer* tells us that this is not so. If we compare the Talmud's conclusions to the *Mishnas Rebbi Eliezer*, we see that the latter grants the Talmud's lesser reward to those who keep the Noahide laws based upon their own reason. It grants the greater reward to those who keep the Noahide laws because of Noahic revelation. The *Mishnas Rabbi Eliezer* also tells us that the Talmud's lesser reward is the temporary reward of this world and the greater reward is the eternal reward of the world to come.

---

[2] 31a.

[3] The rationale is that someone who voluntarily performs a *mitzvah* receives less reward because he did not satisfy any specific will of God. However, one who performs an obligatory commandment has satisfied God's specific will and is rewarded commensurately (see *Tosafos HaRosh* and *Chiddushei HaRitva* to *Kiddushin* 31a; see also *Tosafos Tokh*). Another explanation is that the *yetzer hora* – the evil inclination – opposes the performance of an obligatory commandment more than it opposes a non-obligatory commandment. Accordingly, one must pay more attention and expend more effort in the proper fulfillment of an obligatory *mitzvah* (see *Tosafos to Avodah Zarah 3a*, D.H. *Gadol* and *Tosafos HaRosh* to *Kiddushin* 31a).

## Chiddushei HaGriz, the Ohr Somayach, and Rabbi Malkiel Tannenbaum

In the late 19th and early 20th centuries, a number of authorities on Maimonides – Rabbis Yitzchok Zeev Soloveitchik,[4] Meir Simcha HaKohen,[5] and Malkiel Tannenbaum[6] – independently advanced nearly identical interpretations of §11 that relate it directly back to *Bava Kamma* 38a.[7] Their understanding not only illuminates Maimonides, but also clarifies our understanding of the Talmud.

They explain that the gentile nations were originally bound in their observance of the Noahide laws by force of a Noahic covenant.[8] Iteration of the Noahide laws at Sinai, however, transferred the authority of this original Noahic covenant, to Sinai. Noahides would now be bound in their covenant not because of Adam and Noah, but because of Moses transmitting of the Torah at Sinai. Therefore, when the Talmud states that God "released" the gentiles, it means that He released them from the binding force of the original covenant. In order to become obligated in this new Sinaitic covenant, a gentile must accept the Noahide laws anew. After all, the Jews had to accept their covenant. Once a gentile does so, he becomes obligated in the Noahide laws and receives his reward as one who is obligated.

Until a gentile accepts this new, Sinaitic affirmation, are we to say that he has no obligation at all to keep the Noahide laws? The Talmud tells us that this is not so. Though the authority of the original Noahic covenant ceased, gentiles are still punished for transgressing the Noahide laws. Were this not the case, gentiles would be profiting from having long neglected the Noahide laws.

The punishment meted for not observing the laws is, therefore, a legal technicality so that non-Jews should not profit by their transgression. The force of the original covenant, however, is no longer binding. Therefore, there is no covenantal imperative for any gentile to observe the Noahide laws until he accepts the Sinaitic reaffirmation of these laws. Until a gentile makes such an acceptance, any observance of the Noahide laws is voluntary, and his reward (the temporary reward of this world) is commensurate with this fact.

---

[4] *Chiddushei Riz HaLevi, Mikhtavim,* last letter.

[5] *Chiddushei Ohr Somayach* to *Hilkhos Issuei Biah* 14:7.

[6] Published posthumously in *Torah SheBaal Peh XV* (1973). Rabbi Tannenbaum (1847 – 1910) was the Rabbi of Lomze, Poland, and a famed *posek*, decisor of Torah law.

[7] A near identical understanding of *Bava Kama* 38a, predating these scholars by about 600 years, is also proposed by Rabbi Yom Tov Asevilli in his *Chiddushei HaRitva* to *Makkos* 9a.

[8] See note 6 above.

Once a gentile accepts the Noahide laws as per the Sinaitic reaffirmation, he becomes bound by them and receives the higher reward of one who fulfills obligatory commandments.

## Understanding Maimonides

Maimonides could have derived §11 from this understanding of the Talmud *Bava Kamma* 38a. All that remains then is to explain the equating of the Talmud's greater reward with that of the World to Come. The *Mishnas Rabbi Eliezer* may serve as a source for just that.

But what about Maimonides's requirement that gentiles accept their laws based on Sinaitic reaffirmation rather than the original Noahic covenant? Maimonides's disagreement with the *Mishnas Rebbi Eliezer* on this point is not surprising. The Talmud and its commentaries discuss the nullification of the original Noahic covenant and reaffirmation of the Noahide laws in Sanhedrin 59a. This is necessary to explain the repetition of the Noahide laws at Sinai. Maimonides states his view clearly in his *Commentary on the Mishnah*:[9]

> *All that we do or do not do is solely because of the command of the Holy One, blessed is He, through our teacher Moses, may peace be upon him, and not because the Hole One, blessed is He, stated it to any prophet who came before him. For example, we do not eat limbs torn from living animals because God forbade it to Noah, but rather because Moses forbade it to us at Sinai by affirming that [it] remains in effect. Similarly, we do not circumcise because our forefather Abraham, may peace be upon him, circumcised himself and his household, but rather because the Holy One, blessed is He, commanded us through Moses, may peace be upon him. So too with the sciatic nerve; we do not obey this prohibition because of our forefather Jacob, but because of the command of our teacher Moses, may he rest in peace.*

We see here that Maimonides acknowledges that the Noahide laws were binding before Sinai. However, Maimonides is telling us that their covenantal status changed from Noahic to Sinaitic at the giving of the Torah. While this paragraph speaks of the Jewish obligation to keep the original Noahide laws based on Sinaitic revelation, §11 clarifies that this is also true of the Noahide obligation.

On this interpretation of Maimonides, and the requirement that Noahides accept their obligations based upon the Sinaitic reaffirmation, there is very little disagreement among later authorities.[10]

---

[9] To *Chullin* 7:6.

[10] See Chazon Ish *Sheviis* 24:2 and to *Hilkhos Avodas Kokhavim* 65:2. Ritva and Ramban to *Makkos* 9b; *Teshuvos* HaRashbash 543; Zvi Hirsch Chajes in *Toras HaNeviim* 11; *Zekhusa D'Avraham* 21; *VeShav HaKohen* 38.

Lastly, how do we explain Maimonides's omission of reward for one who observes these commandments based on reason? The sources we have cited thus far agree that the "wise people of the nations" receive reward for their observance of the Noahide laws (it is, though, only the lesser temporary reward of this world). They explain that Maimonides's omission does not imply his rejection of the concept. It is likely, given that §11 is discussing an obligation upon the gentiles to accept the Noahide laws based on Sinaitic revelation, that it was not the place to discuss any reward for non-acceptance of these laws. Additionally, since the Talmud has already drawn clear conclusions regarding the lower reward, Maimonides is coming only to explain the mechanism by which non-Jews may merit the eternal reward of the World to Come.

THE YESHIVA PIRCHEI SHOSHANIM SHULCHAN ARUCH LEARNING PROJECT

# The Noahide Laws – Lesson 13

**© Yeshiva Pirchei Shoshanim 2017**
This shiur may not be reproduced in any
form without permission of the copyright holder.

**164 Village Path, Lakewood NJ 08701 732.370.3344**
**164 Rabbi Akiva, Bnei Brak, 03.616.6340**

## Outline of This Lesson:

1. How Does a Noahide Accept the Sinaitic Aspects of the Noahide Laws?

2. Possible Answers

3. Maimonides's Own Words

4. How Does One Become a Ben Noach?

# Noahide Identity V
# Becoming a Noahide

## How Does a Non-Jew Accept the Sinaitic Aspect of the Noahide Laws?

There is one further question that, for our purposes, is very important: is §11 a continuation of §10, or is §11 independent of §10?
§10 states:

> *And so too it was commanded to Moses by the Almighty to force the peoples of the world to accept the commandments charged to the children of Noah. All who do not accept them shall be executed. One who accepts them is called a* Ger Toshav.

Immediately thereafter §11 opens with:

> *All who accept the Seven Mitzvos and are careful to observe them are called* MiChasidei Umos HaOlam *(of the Pious Peoples of the World) and they have a share in the World to Come.*

If we assume that §11 is a continuation of §10, then it would mean that a gentile must accept the Noahide laws before a *beis din* and become a *ger toshav* in order to be *MiChasidei Umos HaOlam*. If this is the case, then no gentile today can become *MiChasidei Umos HaOlam* because we do not currently accept *ger toshav*.

Yet, if §11 is independent of §10, then a gentile can become *MiChasidei Umos HaOlam* even by private acceptance of the Noahide laws (provided that this acceptance is based on Sinaitic revelation). In such a case, acceptance of the Noahide laws is independent of the laws of a *ger toshav*. This reading would therefore allow for a Noahide identity independent of *ger toshav*.

## Possible Answers

For modern Noahides, resolution of this question is vitally important. There are a number of approaches:

**Rabbis Betzalel Zolti and Rabbi Yosef Kahaneman**

- Rabbis Betzalel Zolti[1] and Rabbi Yosef Kahaneman[2] – Their view is the most radical and is based upon a super-literal reading of §10 and §11. The crux of their approach is that *ger toshav* is a religious status somewhere between that of Jew and non-Jew. Accordingly, they interpret acceptance of the Noahide laws before a *beis din* as a conversion to a new religion: *ger toshav*. This new religious identity includes the right to live in Israel, to be supported by the Jewish community, and to become *MiChasidei Umos HaOlam*. According to this view, the various parts of the *ger toshav* identity do not exist independent of each other nor do they exist absent this "conversion." This approach sees §11 as a continuation of §10.

  However, they admit that their opinion is only theoretical because we cannot accept *ger toshav* in our times. Modern Noahides are then left with only one option: to be in the lesser category of one who fulfills a commandment voluntarily: of the "wise" of the nations.

  We must reject this interpretation for two reasons: 1) the majority of scholars interpret *ger toshav* as a legal construct, not as a religious identity,[3] and 2) this approach is contrary to the practical halakhic reliance upon the *Raavad* and *Kesef Mishna's* understanding of Maimonides discussed in Section I, above.

**The Brisker Rav & Rav Raphael HaKohen**

- Rabbis Yitzchok Zeev Soloveitchik[4], the Brisker Rav, and Raphael HaKohen Susskind[5] – They adopt a very literal reading of Maimonides. Yet, unlike Rabbis Zolti and Kahaneman, they treat *ger toshav* as a purely legal status and not as a conversion. This legal status, however, is one indivisible whole: acceptance of the Noahide laws before a *beis din* is needed for residency, support, and every other facet of *ger toshav*.

---

[1] *Mishnas Yaavetz* 3. Rabbi Zolti (1920 – 1982) was elected as chief Rabbi of Jerusalem in 1977 and was a highly regarded authority on Torah law.

[2] *Kuntres Divrei Torah*. Cited in *Minchas Asher* I:7.

[3] See *Chiddushei Ri"z Soloveitchik, Mikhtavim*, final letter; *Ohr Somayach* to *Hilkhos Issurei Biah* 14:7; *Chazon Ish* ad loc. Rabbi Asher Weiss in his *Minchas Asher* I: 7 cites the proofs of Rabbi's Kahaneman and Zolti, yet demonstrates convincingly that they are not conclusive.

[4] *Chiddushei Ri"z Soloveitchik, Mikhtavim*.

[5] *VeShav HaKohen* 38.

Therefore, Rabbis Soloveitchik and Susskind also view §11 as a continuance of §10. They also require acceptance of the Noahide laws before a *beis din* in order to become *MiChasidei Umos HaOlam*. However, Rabbis Soloveitchik and Susskind agree that this is not possible in our times because we do not today accept *ger toshav*.

As with the opinion of Rabbis Zolti and Kahaneman, we must also reject that of Rabbis Soloveitchik and Susskind. Their literalist reading of Maimonides also precludes relying upon the opinions of the *Raavad* and *Kesef Mishnah* to explain the residency of non-Jews in modern day Israel.

**The Ohr Somayach**

- Rabbi Meir Simcha HaKohen of Dvinsk[6] – Rabbi Meir Simcha agrees with Rabbi Soloveitchik that *ger toshav* is not a conversion to a new religious identity, but a purely legal construct. Like the *Raavad* and *Kesef Mishnah*, the Rabbi Meir Simcha maintains that the various facets of *ger toshav* may exist independent of each other. However, Rabbi Meir Simcha does not address our specific question: is acceptance of the Noahide laws before a *beis din* needed to become *MiChasidei Umos HaOlam*? His view allows for two possibilities: 1) That a Noahide may accept the commandments on his own and become *MiChasidei Umos HaOlam*, or 2) that even though acceptance before a *beis din* for support is not possible today, it is nevertheless required, even today, to become *MiChasidei Umos HaOlam*.

This second possibility is intriguing. Even though *ger toshav* is a purely legal construct, the fact that the various aspects of it exist independently allow for even the identity of *MiChasidei Umos HaOlam* to exist independently. Yet, the identity of *MiChasidei Umos HaOlam* is fundamentally different than the other elements of *ger toshav*. It is inherently a matter of religious identity. Perhaps then, accepting the Noahide laws to become *MiChasidei Umos HaOlam* is a type of religious conversion independent of the other aspects of *ger toshav*. This certainly makes sense considering that acceptance of the Noahide laws is essentially the acceptance of a new, Sinaitic covenant.

When a gentile wishes to convert to Judaism, the most important requirement is his acceptance before a *beis din* of the Sinaitic covenant of the 613 commandments. May we may then infer that acceptance of the Sinaitic aspect of the Noahide Laws by gentiles should also require acceptance before a *beis din*?

Although the logic behind this possibility is appealing, it does not hold up to scrutiny. A non-Jew's acceptance of the seven *mitzvos* is fundamentally

---

[6] *Ohr Somayach* to *Hilkhos Issurei Biah* 14:7.

different from conversion to Judaism. Conversion to Judaism requires the acceptance of new commandments to which the prospective convert has no obligation. However, acceptance of the Noahide laws involves the acceptance of laws which were the material of a prior covenant. In fact, non-Jews receive reward (the lesser type of this world) for fulfillment of the Noahide laws even without having accepted them as per the Sinaitic reaffirmation. Therefore, if a Noahide wishes to accept the Sinaitic Noahide covenant, he is not accepting a completely new body of law, only modifying his covenantal obligation. Also, a non-Jew who accepts the Noahide laws due to the Sinaitic covenant remains a non-Jew. The only practical change is in the nature of his reward. When a non-Jew becomes a Jew, however, the conversion confers an entirely new legal, metaphysical, and spiritual identity. Lastly, the requirement of a *beis din* for the sake of Jewish conversion is derived from Numbers 15:16: *One* Mishpat *[judgment] shall be for you and the convert*. The word *Mishpat* indicates a comparison between conversion and legal proceedings: just as *Mishpat*, judgment, requires a *beis din* then so too does conversion to Judaism. This derivation is only made with regard to full conversion and nothing else.

**Rabbi Malkiel Tannenbaum**

- Rabbi Malkiel Tannenbaum[7] – Rabbi Tannenbaum is one of the scholars who contributed the above-discussed interpretation of Maimonides's §11 and *Bava Kamma* 38a. His statement is one of the most eloquent and prompts an interesting question. Why would acceptance of the Sinaitic reaffirmation of the Noahide laws be predicated on becoming a *ger toshav*? If Noahides must accept this Sinaitic reaffirmation, then tying acceptance to *ger toshav* makes it impossible for them to accept it unless we may accept *ger toshav*. There is no apparent reason for the two to be related. It must be, therefore, that §11 discusses Noahides in general, independent of *ger toshav*. Since Noahide identity is independent of *ger toshav*, there is no reason to assume that one must accept the Noahide laws before a *beis din*.

***Sefer Sheva Mitzvos HaShem***

- Rabbi Moshe Weiner in the *Sefer Sheva Mitzvos HaShem* - Rabbi Weiner, after surveying the various readings of Maimonides, concludes that personal acceptance of the Noahide laws is sufficient to become *MiChasidei Umos HaOlam*. In his conclusion, he offers a proof from Maimonides, *Hilchos Melakhim*.[8]

    > *If a* ben Noach *who was converted, circumcised, and immersed in a mikveh desires to revert back to his previous status as a ger toshav, we do not listen to him. He remains a Jew in every way or must be executed.*

---

[7] See note 23, above.

[8] 10:3.

> *And if he was a minor [under the age of 12 or 13] and immersed by the beis din [for the sake of conversion], he may renounce his conversion when he attains majority [the age of 12 or 13] and assumes the status of a ger toshav.*

The law is that a minor may not convert to Judaism on his own because, as a minor, he cannot make such a commitment. Rather, the *beis din* oversees his conversion as a minor, but allows him to choose his identity upon adulthood. If he chooses to renounce Judaism at this time, he may do so. Rabbi Weiner draws our attention to the fact that the child automatically *...assumes the status of a ger toshav,* upon renouncing his conversion. Rabbi Weiner notes that this does not make sense for we do not currently accept *ger toshav*! Obviously, the answer is that Maimonides is only speaking of a time when we accept *ger toshav*. However, writes Rabbi Weiner this cannot be so. In every other instance in which Maimonides invokes *ger toshav*, he is careful to note that it does not apply in our times. Maimonides, though, makes no such qualification here. Therefore, Maimonides must hold that the *ger toshav* status of a minor who rejects his conversion does in fact exist in our times. However, the child attains this status without having to accept the seven laws anew before a *beis din*. Rabbi Weiner concludes that one who accepts the Noahide laws without acceptance before a *beis din* attains some partial identity as a *ger toshav*, even in our times, and is thus *MiChasidei Umos HaOlam*.[9]

## Maimonides's Own Words

To the above, I will add Maimonides's own words[10] penned in response to a question as to the merit non-Jews receive:

> *As for your question about the gentile nations, you should know that God desires the heart and that matters follow the heart's intentions. Therefore, our Rabbis, Sages of truth, peace be upon them, have said "the pious of the gentile nations have a share in the World to Come." This is if they have achieved that which is proper to achieve of knowledge of the Creator... then without a doubt, anyone who has improved his soul*

---

[9] With great respect for Rabbi Weiner's tremendous work, I must humbly admit that this proof is far from convincing for two reasons. For one, there are other places where Maimonides discusses *ger toshav* in a context that clearly does not apply today (See, for example, *Hilchos Rotzeach ve-Shemiras HaNefesh* 5:3-4; *Hilkhos Issurei Biah* 14:5; *Hilkhos Shekalim* 4:8). In these instances, Maimonides makes no explicit qualification as to whether or not he is speaking about a time when *ger toshav* are accepted. Instead, we may determine this fact simply from context. In our passage above, we can tell from the references to execution that this law does not apply to our times. Second, Maimonides iterates numerous time for us that *ger toshav* only applies when the Jubilee year is observed. Maimonides may very well intend this rule as intrinsic to the definition of *ger toshav*, and, therefore, did not always feel the need to reiterate this qualification.

[10] *Teshuvos HaRambam VeIgrosav* (Leipzig, 1859) II 23b.

> *with correct virtues, wisdom, and faith in the Creator, blessed is He, is certainly among those destined for the world to come…*

Nowhere here does Maimonides require acceptance of the Noahide laws before a *beis din* in order to merit eternal reward. In fact, Maimonides mentions no such requirement in any of his writings. To the contrary, Maimonides states explicitly in this letter that the merit of the World to Come, the identity of *MiChasidei Umos HaOlam,* is dependent on the heart – upon personal acceptance of the Noahide laws as per the Sinaitic reaffirmation.

There is not a single source, anywhere, in all of Torah Literature, which mandates acceptance of the Noahide laws before a *beis din* in order to become *MiChasidei Umos HaOlam* in our days. This idea is a possibility merely implied by how one reads the juxtaposition of Maimonides's two paragraphs.

The *halakhic,* practical, conclusion is that acceptance of the Noahide laws before a *beis din* is not required for one to become *MiChasidei Umos HaOlam.* If a Noahide insists upon accepting his obligations before a *beis din*, it is certainly not prohibited for him to do so. This acceptance, however, conveys no status of *ger toshav* because this status cannot be conferred in our times. .

## How Does One Become a *Ben Noach*?

To become a Noahide, one must accept the Seven Mitzvos upon himself from a conviction that they are divinely ordained, having been commanded to the world by God, through Moses, who reaffirmed the covenant sealed with Adam and then Noah. By accepting the Seven Mitzvos as such, one becomes *MiChasidei Umos HaOlam*, a Pious Gentile, and the highest status attainable by a *Ben Noach*.

While any personal acceptance of the Seven Mitzvos is sufficient, it makes logical sense to capture the intention of the acceptance in the form of a verbal oath enumerating the 7 mitzvos and stating one's motivation in accepting them. Any text accomplishing these goals is sufficient.

For example:

> *I accept upon myself the Seven Commandments of the Children of Noah, including the general and specific prohibitions of idolatry, murder, theft, sexual immorality, blasphemy, eating of flesh torn from a living animal, and the general and specific commandments to establish a system of justice, as commanded to Noah, Adam, and their descendants, by the mouth of The Holy One, creator of the universe, as reaffirmed and transmitted by His servant Moses at the giving of the Torah at Sinai.*

One is not required to accept the *mitzvos* before any Jewish Court (*Beis Din*),[11] or assembly of other persons. Any personal or private acceptance of the Seven Mitzvos is sufficient. Nevertheless, it is a good idea to make a verbal acceptance before witnesses.

## Summary of Lessons

1. When the Jubilee year was fully observed (until about 600 BCE) a non-Jew could come before a *beis din*, rabbinic tribunal, and pledge his acceptance of the Noahide laws. By doing so, he obligated the Jewish community to support and sustain him. He also enjoyed certain rights of residency and other entitlements.

2. The status of ger toshav ceased to exist about 2600 years ago.

3. With the establishment of the modern state, *poskim* (authorities on Torah law) had to clarify which aspects of *ger toshav* identity were practical and which were only theoretical. Since the status no longer exists, what was to be done with all the non-Jews who owned land in Israel?

4. The conclusion of the majority of *poskim* is that appearing before a *beis din* and becoming a *ger toshav* was only necessary to entitle the non-Jew to support from the Jewish community. In order to live or own land in Israel, one only needs to be a monotheistic, non-idolater.

5. The practical, *halakhic*, conclusion is that ger toshav and Noahide are two independent identities. We cannot always learn from one to the other. While every *ger toshav* is a de facto Noahide, every Noahide is not a *ger toshav*. After all, ger toshav does not exist anymore in our times.

6. Maimonides learns from *Bava Kamma 38a* and, possibly, the *Mishnas Rebbi Eliezer*, that a non-Jew must accept the Noahide laws because at Sinai their authority was transferred to the Torah. A non-Jew who accepts this new Sinaitic obligation becomes fully obligated in the Noahide laws and received the eternal merit of the World to Come. This acceptance is personal, and does not require acceptance before a *beis din*.

---

[11] A Jewish rabbinic court of three judges. A *Beis Din* judges matters of religious and monetary law in the Jewish community.

7. A non-Jew, who observes the Noahide laws, yet without them as a Sinaitic obligation, is essentially observing the laws voluntarily. He receives only the reward of this world and does not merit the eternality of the world to come. Nevertheless, he is held liable for transgression of the laws.

THE YESHIVA PIRCHEI SHOSHANIM SHULCHAN ARUCH LEARNING PROJECT

# The Noahide Laws – Lesson Fourteen

© **Yeshiva Pirchei Shoshanim 2017**
This shiur may not be reproduced in any
form without permission of the copyright holder.

## Outline of This Lesson:

1. Maimonides Hilkhos Melakhim 10:9 & 10

2. The Sources

3. Maimonides According to the Radbaz

# Chiddushei Dat I – A Fundamental Principle

## Introduction

*Chiddushei Dat* is a principle fundamental to the identity of Noahides and the observance of the Noahide laws. However, it is a concept difficult for many Noahides to grasp. To those unfamiliar with the mechanics of the Torah, it appears to impose restrictions upon Noahide practice. *Chiddushei Dat*, though, does no such thing. It defines and protects the boundaries of what makes a Noahide a Noahide, preserving it as its own identity. Jews have a parallel, similar concept called *Baal Tosif*. *Baal Tosif* defines what *mitzvos* Jews may and may not do and the degree to which they may modify or adopt new practices. In this lesson we will introduce the concept of *Chiddushei Dat* and explain just how important it is to keeping the Noahide laws.

## Maimonides *Hilkhos Melakhim* 10: 9 & 10

Once again, we need to confront two difficult paragraphs in the writings of Maimonides:

§9 *A non-Jew[1] who delves into the Torah is obligated to die. They should only be involved in the study of their seven commandments.*

*Similarly, a non-Jew who rests, even on a weekday, observing that day similarly to a Shabbat, is obligated to die. Needless to say, this is also the case if he creates a festival for himself.*

*The general rule governing these matters is this: they may not originate a new religion or create/perform* mitzvot *for themselves based on their own reasoning. Either convert and accept all the* mitzvot *or uphold their commandments without adding or detracting from them.*

*If a gentile delves into the Torah or Shabbat, or innovates a religious practice, he is beaten, punished, and informed him that he is obligated to die for his actions. However, he is not actually executed.*

> §9 is telling us, in no uncertain terms, that a non-Jew may not observe the Shabbat, the Jewish festivals, or voluntarily keep any *mitzvah* of the Torah in which he is not commanded. It is clear that this is a serious matter. Why is so dire, though, to deserve such a severe penalty?

§10 *Should a non-Jew wish to perform one of the Torah's other* mitzvos *in order to receive merit/benefit, we should not prevent him from doing so even according to all of its details. If he brings an animal to be sacrificed as a burnt offering, we should accept it.*

> §10 teaches us that a non-Jew may voluntarily perform a mitzvah in which he is not commanded as long as he does so "for reward." What is the need for this curious qualification?

*If a non-Jew who keeps the seven* mitzvot *gives charity, we should accept it from him. It appears to me that it should be given to the Jewish poor, for the non-Jew receives his sustenance from the Jewish community who is obligated to support him. In contrast, if a regular non-Jew gives charity, we should accept it from him and give it to the non-Jewish poor.*

## The Sources

Let's go through the Maimonides again, this time looking at his sources and some problems posed by his words:

§9 *A non-Jew who delves into the Torah is obligated to die. They should only be involved in the study of their seven commandments.*

---

[1] Many printed editions of the *Mishnah Torah*, being heavily censored, read *akum*, meaning *idolater*. However, almost all early manuscripts and critical editions read *goy*, a generic term for anyone who is not Jewish.

The Talmud in Sanhedrin 59a learns from Deuteronomy 33:4 that the Torah is the unique heritage of Israel. As such, parts of it may not be studied by non-Jews and even Noahides. The exact details of this prohibition will be examined extensively in a future lesson.

*Similarly, a non-Jew who rests, even on a weekday, observing that day similarly to a Shabbat, is obligated to die. Needless to say, this is also the case if he creates a festival for himself.*

Sanhedrin 58b teaches that all mankind was originally prohibited from keeping Shabbat. The divine rest of Shabbat was God's alone. At Sinai, however, Israel was commanded to partake in the divine rest of Shabbat as a sign of their unique covenant with God. This is the meaning of Exodus 31:13:

> *You shall speak unto the Children of Israel, saying: you must keep my Shabbat, for it is a sign between me and the Children of Israel*

In the Torah, the Hebrew word "Shabbat" may refer to the Shabbat, the seventh day, or any day upon which labor is prohibited by the Torah. This would include festivals. Noahides and the Shabbat/Festivals will be discussed extensively in a future lesson.

*The general rule governing these matters is this: they may not **originate a new religion** or create/perform mitzvot for themselves based on their own reasoning. Either convert and accept all the mitzvot or uphold their commandments without adding or detracting from them.*

The words in bold are, in Hebrew, the term *chiddushei dat*. From where does Maimonides derive this concept?

*If a gentile delves into the Torah or Shabbat, or innovates a religious practice, he is beaten, punished, and informed him that he is obligated to die for his actions. However, he is not actually executed.*

§10 *Should a non-Jew wish to perform one of the Torah's other mitzvos in order to receive merit/benefit, we should not prevent him from doing so even according to all of its details. If he brings an animal to be sacrificed as a burnt offering, we should accept it.*

Why does the non-Jew's motivation in doing a particular *mitzvah* mitigate the prohibition of *chiddushei dat*? Obviously, there are boundaries to this concept. What are they?

*If a non-Jew who keeps the seven mitzvot gives charity, we should accept it from him. It appears to me that it should be given to the Jewish poor, for the non-Jew receives his sustenance from the*

Jewish community who is obligated to support him. In contrast, if a regular non-Jew gives charity, we should accept it from him and give it to the non-Jewish poor.

> It is curious that this paragraph is here instead of in Maimonides's section on the laws of charity.

## Maimonides *Hilkhos Melakhim* 10: 9 & 10 According to the Radbaz

The most significant early explanation of this passage is from the Radbaz, Rabbi Dovid ibn Abi Zimra:

**§9** *A non-Jew who delves into the Torah is obligated to die. They should only be involved in the study of their seven commandments.*

*Similarly, a non-Jew who rests, even on a weekday, observing that day similarly to a Shabbat, is obligated to die. Needless to say, this is also the case if he creates a festival for himself.*

> The Radbaz quotes Rashi, who writes in his commentary on the Talmudic source[2] that "rest" means any kind of rest for any reason. However, the Radbaz adds "This is if he establishes a day for rest; however, occasional cessation from labor is not prohibited."

*The general rule governing these matters is this: they may not* **originate a new religion** *or* **create/perform** *mitzvot for themselves based on their own reasoning. Either convert and accept all the mitzvot or uphold their commandments without adding or detracting from them.*

*If a gentile delves into the Torah or Shabbat, or innovates a religious practice, he is beaten, punished, and informed him that he is obligated to die for his actions. However, he is not actually executed.*

**§10** *Should a non-Jew wish to perform one of the Torah's other* mitzvos *in order to receive merit/benefit, we should not prevent him from doing so even according to all of its details. If he brings an animal to be sacrificed as a burnt offering, we should accept it.*

> The Radbaz writes:

---

[2] Sanhedrin 58b.

> *If he wants to perform a mitzvah, saying that he has an obligation in the matter, we do not allow him to do so. However, he may perform it in order to receive reward as one who performs a mitzvah voluntarily. This is why he [Maimonides] is careful to write: "... in order to receive merit/benefit..."*

If a non-Jew performs a *mitzvah* under the belief that God has any expectation or desire for his *mitzvah*, it is tantamount to creating a new *mitzvah* for himself. After all, all *mitzvahs* are God's desires and will for our actions. If the performance of a *mitzvah*, though, is not tied to this belief, and only to the desire for reward, then the non-Jew may perform the *mitzvah*. The Radbaz adds:

> *However, mitzvos requiring unique levels of holiness and ritual purity, such as* Tefillin, Torah *scrolls, and* Mezuzos, *I have deliberated and concluded that we should be strict and not permit them [to non-Jews].*[3]

To summarize, the Radbaz holds:

- A non-Jew may not establish a particular day as a fixed time to rest from labor. The type of labor or the reason for the rest does not matter. The Radbaz is quoting and agreeing with Rashi on this point.

- A non-Jew may voluntarily perform any other *mitzvah*, provided that he does so knowing that God has no desire or expectation for his action. Any other motivation, i.e. reward, is permissible.

- A non-Jew who performs a *mitzvah* (in which he is not obligated) under the misguided belief that God desires him to do so transgresses *chiddushei dat* – he is adding a *mitzvah* to the Noahide Laws and, effectively, creating a new religion for himself.

There are a number of authorities, coming both before and after, who appear to confirm the Radbaz's interpretation:

- The Meiri to Sanhedrin 59a – A non-Jew who performs other mitzvos of the Torah is to be honored like a *Kohen Gadol*, a high priest.[4]

---

[3] The *halakhah* is like the Radbaz for these items. See Maimonides *Hilkhos Tzitzis 3:9* who rules against selling or providing a Noahide with *Tzitzis*. The Rama YD 291 also prohibits a Jew from providing a non-Jew with a *mezuzah* scroll. Although the Talmud Yerushalmi Peah 1:1 mentions that Rebbi Yehudah gifted a *mezuzah* scroll to a gentile king, the *Pri Megadim* in *Ginas Veridin OC II: 28* demonstrates that this incident is not relevant to whether or not Noahides may observe the mitzvah of *mezuzah*.

[4] As we shall see, this opinion is rejected by later authorities. The writings of the Meiri were almost completely unknown to the Torah world until the 20th century. Not having been seen for almost

- Maimonides himself, in a number of places, appears to confirm the Radbaz. For example, he writes[5] that a non-Jew who does the *mitzvah* of circumcision receives reward.[6] Most important, however, is what he writes in his commentary to the Mishnah:[7] *For what reason is their [the non-Jews] Terumah tithe and sanctified offerings valid? Because even though they have no mitzvah, if they do such a small thing they receive some reward…*[8]

- *Biur Halakha* 304:3 – The *Biur Halakha*, in explaining a difficult passage in the *Mogen Avraham*, writes that a *ger toshav* may accept any additional *mitzvos* he chooses at the time of his "conversion" to *ger toshav*. The *Biur* explains that the prohibitions on keeping Shabbat only apply to a *ger toshav* who did not accept Shabbat when he stood before a *beis din*. Note, that he views *ger toshav* as a religious rather than a legal status.[9]

However, the Radbaz's opinion and those of the others sages quoted above, is not the final word. As we shall see, there are a number of difficult questions posed by Maimonides.

## A Big Contradiction

Maimonides's condition, that Noahides may only accept additional *mitzvos* for the sake of reward, presents us with a big problem.

---

500 years, they never became part of the *halakhic* process. Their practical relevance is, therefore, questionable. See *Igros Moshe EH* I: 63 and *Chazon Ish, Igros* I: 32 as to our reliance upon long-lost or newly discovered manuscripts.

[5] Responsa 124 (Friemann ed.)

[6] A proof cannot be derived from this, however. Circumcision was not one of the *mitzvos* commanded at Sinai; its origins are more complicated. Rabbi Moshe Weiner discusses circumcision as an exception to the rule of Noahides and mitzvos in *The Divine Code*, 2nd ed., pp. 67 – 72.

[7] *Terumos* 3:9.

[8] However, even this may be explained as an exception. Tithing and offerings are matters of practical benefit and are, as we shall see, exceptions rather than rules.

[9] This opinion is also difficult. As we have seen in prior lessons, ger toshav does not fully apply today. Furthermore, most *poskim* reject *ger toshav* as a religious identity. Also, many later *poskim*, such as *Igros Moshe* OH V: 18 and *Shevet HaLevi* I: 64, point out that there are other, simpler explanations of the *Mogen Avraham*.

The Talmud[10] is unambiguously clear on this point: Noahides who, for the sake of reward, perform *mitzvos* in which they are not obligated do not receive reward for doing so.

How do we resolve this contradiction? We will examine the issue more closely in the next lesson.

---

[10] Rosh HaShanah 4a; Bava Basra 10b

THE YESHIVA PIRCHEI SHOSHANIM SHULCHAN ARUCH LEARNING PROJECT

# The Noahide Laws – Lesson Fifteen

© **Yeshiva Pirchei Shoshanim 2017**
This shiur may not be reproduced in any
form without permission of the copyright holder.

## Outline of This Lesson:

1. *HaRav HaGaon* Moshe Feinstein, *ztz"l*
2. The Source of *Chiddushei Dat*
3. Voluntarily Keeping Other *Mitzvos*
4. Rav Moshe's Reading of Maimonides & the Radbaz
   a. The Most Important Point
5. To Summarize Rav Moshe
6. Rav Moshe Weiner in the *Sefer Sheva Mitzvos HaShem* (The Divine Code).

# Chiddushei Dat II – Rav Moshe Feinstein, ztz"l

## HaRav HaGaon Moshe Feinstein, ztz"l

Rabbi Moshe Feinstein was one of the two most important *poskim* [authorities on Torah law] of the 20th century. Reb Moshe was a towering scholar whose influence, authority, and writings impacted the life of all Torah-observant Jews world-wide. He was particularly important to North American Jewish communities. A prominent American *posek* recently described Rav Moshe as the "Maimonides of American Jewry."

In the middle decades of the 20th century, Rabbi Feinstein penned a number of letters[1] addressing Noahide practice. He devotes several paragraphs to specifically untangling the concept of *Chiddushei Dat*.

A full overview of Rav Moshe's analysis would require far more space than we have allotted here. Translations of Rav Moshe's letters are being prepared as an appendix to this course. We will present here a summary of Rav Moshe's writings on the subject.

---

[1] *Igros Moshe* OC II:25, V:18, YD I:3, I:6, II:7, II:8, III:90, IV:51:1, CM II:69.

## THE SOURCE OF CHIDDUSHEI DAT

Just as Noahides have *Chiddushei Dat*, Jews have a similar prohibition to *Chiddushei Dat* called *Baal Tosif*, which specifically prohibits Jews from creating new *mitzvos* or adding to and modifying existing *mitzvos*.[2] Non-Jews, however, do not have the prohibition of *Baal Tosif*. In fact, we only know of the Noahide prohibitions against Torah study and Shabbat observance because of specific Torah verses from which these prohibitions are derived.[3] From where, then, does Maimonides derive the general prohibition of *Chiddushei Dat*?

Rav Moshe explains that there are commonalities in the underlying reasons behind these prohibitions. For example, the Talmud and Midrash both describe the study of Torah (in an impermissible manner) and keeping Shabbat as misappropriations of *mitzvos* commanded only to Israel. By analyzing these commonalities, the other writings of Maimonides, and many other sources, Rav Moshe concludes that *Chiddushei Dat* is not only the underlying reason for the Noahide prohibitions of Torah study and Shabbat observance, is a general principle governing Noahide practice. This is why Maimonides writes: *The general rule governing these matters is this…*

Rav Moshe explains that Shabbat observance and certain types of Torah study are singled out because they are the most severe transgressions for Noahides and the only ones involving the death penalty. Note, however, that this penalty is at the hands of heaven and not administered by an earthly court. This is what Maimonides means when he writes: *…he is obligated to die for his actions. However, he is not actually executed.*

## VOLUNTARILY KEEPING OTHER MITZVOS

Rav Moshe notes a peculiar issue in §10 and the Radbaz's interpretation:

**§10** *Should a non-Jew wish to perform one of the Torah's other* mitzvos *in order to receive merit/benefit, we should not prevent him from doing so even according to all of its details.*

> **Radbaz:** *If he wants to perform a mitzvah, saying that he has an obligation in the matter, we do not allow him to do so. However, he may perform it in order to receive reward as one who performs a mitzvah voluntarily. This is why he [Maimonides] is careful to write: "… in order to receive merit/benefit…"*

---

[2] See Deuteronomy 13:1. Maimonides discusses this prohibition in his *Sefer HaMitzvos, Lavin 313*. See also *Sefer HaChinuch 454*. *Baal Tosif* applies when one attributes these additions or modifications to Torah authority. The rabbis, however, are specifically empowered by the Torah to establish safeguards and decrees, as discussed in an earlier lesson.

[3] The Torah source prohibiting Noahides from studying certain parts of the Torah will be discussed in the near future.

As we mentioned in the previous lesson, the Talmud explicitly states that a non-Jew who performs a Jewish *mitzvah* for the sake of reward does not actually receive reward for his *mitzvah*. How are we to explain this contradiction?

There is a classical debate in the Talmud as to whether or not a Jew who performs a *mitzvah* in which he is not obligated is considered pious or foolish.[4]

The Talmud Yerushalmi, Shabbos 1:2, states that a Jew who performs a *mitzvah* in which he is not obligated is a *hedyot* – a foolish person. However, there are numerous examples in Rabbinic literature[5] of people receiving praise for performing such *mitzvos*! Why is the performance of a voluntary *mitzvah* sometimes called praiseworthy and sometimes called foolish? The answer lies in the nature of "non-obligation:"

- Sometimes, a *mitzvah* exists but an individual is not obligated to actually fulfill it. For example, all Jews are commanded in the *mitzvah* of Tefillin. Nevertheless, women are exempted from wearing *Tefillin*.[6] Theoretically, if a woman dons *Tefillin* in the right way and with the right intention, she may receive reward and she is not called a *hedyot*. This example, it should be noted, is only theoretical. For many reasons in *halakha*, women do not wear *Tefillin*.

- Rav Moshe discusses the relationship of a Jewish child under the age of 12 or 13 to the *mitzvos*. Below these ages, children are not obligated in the *mitzvos*. Nevertheless, a Jewish child is still bound in the covenant of the *mitzvos* even though their specific obligations are not yet in force. Rav Moshe writes that children receive reward for these voluntary mitzvos.

- In a case when no *mitzvah* exists for a person, but he performs the *mitzvah* anyway, such a person is called a *hedyot* – a foolish person. In this situation, the person is called foolish because their action is not holy and holds no spiritual value. For example: on sukkot there is a *mitzvah* for Jews to eat and sleep in the sukkah. If it is raining, though, one is exempted from eating and sleeping in the *sukkah*.

---

[4] See Bava Kamma 87a; Talmud Yerushalmi Shabbat 1:2.; see also Kiddushin 30a.

[5] *Shulchan Aruch* OC 639:2 praises one who drinks even water in his sukkah. However, drinking water in a sukkah is not a *mitzvah*! For resolutions to this specific case, see *Biur Halacha* to end of OC 639; Vilna Gaon to *Mishnayos Brachos* I: 3.

[6] It is a general principle of Torah law that all Jewish women are exempt from any positive, time-bound commandment.

The Rama[7] writes that a Jew who decides to sit in a *sukkah* despite the rain is called a *hedyot*. In the case of rain, the *mitzvah* of eating and sleeping in the *sukkah* is not suspended; rather, it ceases to exist entirely. In such a case, the sitter is merely sitting outside in the rain! Rather than being a holy act, their "*mitzvah*" has become a foolish one! Nachmanides writes similarly:[8]

> In the Talmud Yerushalmi it is stated: "Anyone who performs a mitzvah in which he was not commanded from the Torah is a hedyot." This is discussing someone who performs a mitzvah to which he has absolutely no connection whatsoever. Then, he is, in effect, **adding to the Torah.** However, one who does a mitzvah of the Torah according to its proper performance even though he was not commanded in it, such as women, receives reward.

Nachmanides adds to the definition of *hedyot*. A Jew who performs a *mitzvah* that in which he has no obligation is called foolish because he thinks that he is acting piously. However, he may actually be committing a transgression: adding to the Torah!

To fully appreciate the concepts of *Baal Tosif* and *hedyot*, we need to understand the idea of *Bitul Hayeshus* – the nullification of ego and will.

### BITUL - MY WILL VS. GOD'S WILL

Who defines for us what actions are holy or not? Can we decide that an act is holy or a *mitzvah* on our own? No, we cannot. The entire concept of *mitzvos* is that God has defined for us what is meaningful and holy and what is not meaningful and holy. Therefore, our will is, to a large degree, irrelevant. Our duty as servants of *HaShem*, God, is *Bitul Hayeshus* - to nullify our will in the search for and servitude of His will. We must strive to understand God's will, learn to recognize it, and learn how to fulfill it according to its specific details. The objective guidepost for determining God's will and its fulfillment is the study of the Torah according to the principles of Torah elucidation handed down from time immemorial.

In certain areas, God has given the man leeway to beautify the *mitzvos*, or to declare certain things as holy or "set aside" for service to God. However, if a Jew decides to do a *mitzvah* where it clearly does not apply, that Jew is "forcing" his will upon God.

---

[7] Shulchan Aruch OC 639:7.

[8] *Chiddushim* to *Kidushin* 31a. This is the reading found in most standard editions of Nachmanides. However, there are some editions that read: …*one who does a mitzvah of the Torah according to its proper performance even though he was not commanded in it, such as women or* **gentiles**, *receives reward*. The Birkei Yosef YD 333:1 quotes Nachmanides as: …*such as women or* **idolaters**. Some modern critical editions include have placed the word "gentiles" in brackets. The inclusion of this reference to non-Jews is suspicious. Not only does not make any sense in context, but its pattern of inclusion in older does not indicate a clear chain of transmission.

If a Jewish farmer in the Midwest decides to not work his field on the *shemitta* (sabbatical) year[9], insisting that he is doing it for God, he is called a *hedyot*. For one, the *mitzvah* only exists in Israel. God's desire is only that the Holy land rest in the sabbatical year; not any other land. To rest another, non-holy land in the sabbatical year is to diminish the importance of Israel and the *mitzvah* of *shemitta*. Second, our farmer is endangering his livelihood, which is foolish. Lastly, if he loses his farm or creates tension among his family or business associates because of his "religious" obstinacy, then it causes a *Chillul HaShem* – a desecration of the Torah.

All of the foregoing applies to Jews. The Jewish people are very stringently enjoined against forcing their will upon *HaShem*.

If this is case for Jews, Rav Moshe's writings beg us to wonder why things should be any different for Noahides? After all, there are not two Torahs!

It is vitally important for anyone wishing to adopt a Noahide identity to embrace this point: **there are not two Torahs**. The same mechanics that govern Jewish observance of the 613 mitzvos also govern the Noahide observance of the 7 *mitzvos*. Just as the Jews have *Baal Tosif*, the Noahides have *Chiddushei Dat*. The concept of *hedyot* applies equally to both.

## Rav Moshe's Reading of Maimonides and the Radbaz

§9 *A non-Jew*[10] *who delves into the Torah is obligated to die. They should only be involved in the study of their seven commandments.*

*Similarly, a non-Jew who rests, even on a weekday, observing that day similarly to a Shabbat, is obligated to die. Needless to say, this is also the case if he creates a festival for himself.*

> These two prohibitions are unique because they are the most severe. This is why they are singled out by the Talmud and Maimonides.

*The general rule governing these matters is this: they may not originate a new religion or create/perform* mitzvot *for themselves based on their own reasoning.*

> The prohibition of *Chiddushei Dat* is not limited to Shabbat, Festivals, and Torah study, but applies to all mitzvos of the Torah. *Chiddushei Dat* is

---

[9] See Leviticus 25 for the verses defining this *mitzvah*.

[10] Many printed editions of the *Mishnah Torah*, being heavily censored, read *akum*, meaning *idolater*. However, almost all early manuscripts and critical editions read *goy*, a generic term for anyone who is not Jewish.

transgressed whether a non-Jew creates a new religious practice for himself, or behaves as if he is obligated in the other mitzvos of the Torah.

*Either convert and accept all the* mitzvot *or uphold their commandments without adding or detracting from them.*

**THE MOST IMPORTANT POINT**

This point is perhaps the most important yet: the prohibitions of *Chiddushei Dat* do not exist to reduce or restrict the identity of a Noahide. Similarly the prohibition of *Baal Tosif* does not exist to reduce or restrict the identity of a Jew. Instead, *Chiddushei Dat* exists to define the boundaries of a Noahide's relationship with his creator. It delineates where Judaism ends and the Noahide laws begin.

A Noahide may drink from the same well as Judaism and share its core beliefs and values, yet he has an identity wholly separate and distinct from Judaism. Noahides have their own special *mitzvos* and missions in the world, as the Jews have theirs. The Noahide Laws are not a "Judaism for non-Jews." Neither is being a Noahide a way for non-Jews to participate in Judaism. For the non-Jew who wishes to observe Jewish rituals or festivals in a Jewish manner, Maimonides teaches that conversion to Judaism is his only option.

*If a gentile delves into the Torah or Shabbat, or innovates a religious practice, he is beaten, punished, and informed him that he is obligated to die for his actions. However, he is not actually executed.*

This is talking about a case when the non-Jew lives under Jewish sovereignty. He is liable to punishment for observing these *mitzvos*. Specifically, he is liable to death at the hands of heaven.

§10 *Should a non-Jew wish to perform one of the Torah's other* mitzvos…

The prohibition of performing other Torah *mitzvos* is nowhere as severe as for the Shabbat, festivals, or Torah study. In fact, a non-Jew may choose to perform other Torah commandments subject to specific conditions. These conditions are the boundaries of *Chiddushei Dat*.

*Should a non-Jew wish to perform one of the Torah's other* mitzvos… This indicates that a non-Jew may only occasionally perform other Torah *mitzvos*. If a non-Jew decides to regularly observe one of the *mitzvos*, he has effectively added a religious observance and transgresses *Chiddushei Dat*.

*…in order to receive merit/benefit…*

The Radbaz writes: *If he wants to perform a mitzvah, saying that he has an obligation in the matter, we do not allow him to do so. However, he may perform it in order to receive reward as one who performs a mitzvah voluntarily. This is why he [Maimonides] is careful to write: "… in order to receive merit/benefit…"*

Rav Moshe explains that any spiritual motivation makes the *mitzvah* a religious act. This is even if the *mitzvah* is performed only occasionally. Therefore, the only permissible motivation can only be ulterior. However, what ulterior, non-spiritual, motives could there possibly be for keeping kosher or many other *mitzvos*? Maimonides is telling us that, although the non-Jew may not perform the *mitzvah* from a sense of spiritual connection or need, he may for the obligation of receiving reward. This sets the threshold for permitted motivation in performing one of the Torah's *mitzvos*. However, Rav Moshe explains this is only pertaining to the motivation. The non-Jew does not actually receive reward for doing the *mitzvah*. This is because the Talmud explicitly learns that non-Jew does not receive reward if he performs a mitzvah as such.

Nevertheless, mitzvos that provide a logical or tangible, real-world benefit may certainly be adopted. We will elaborate on this idea in a moment.

*… we should not prevent him from doing so even according to all of its details.*

Unlike Shabbat, festivals, and certain types of Torah study, we must do not stop a non-Jew from trying to do the *mitzvah*. However, this implies that we should neither encourage nor assist a non-Jew in doing so.

*If he brings an animal to be sacrificed as a burnt offering, we should accept it.*

Rabbeinu Nissim Gaon writes:[11]

> *Not all of the Seven Laws and their derivations require revelation. For example – the obligation to recognize God, to obey Him, and the obligation to serve him – all of which are rational and can be logically derived.*

Certain aspects of Noahide worship and practice are permitted or proper not because they are commanded in the Torah, but because they are compelled by logic and basic, common, religious needs. Therefore, Rav Moshe points out that certain *mitzvos* and religious acts are certainly permitted and they may even be done according to all their Torah details. Such *mitzvos* would include prayer and certain types of offerings and tithes.

---

[11] Introduction to Tractate Brachot.

## To Summarize Rav Moshe

- Noahides may not keep Shabbat or study those parts of Torah prohibited to them. The details of these prohibitions will be discussed shortly.

- Noahides should not be encouraged to perform any other *mitzvos* of the Torah.

- If a Noahide insists on performing a *mitzvah* to which he is not commanded, it is permitted provided that his motivation is not at all spiritual. In such a case, he may even perform the *mitzvah* according to all of its details.

- Even so, a Noahide should not perform such a *mitzvah* regularly because then, regardless of his motivation, it constitutes the establishment of a new religious practice.

- The *mitzvah*, however, has no spiritual merit or meaning. Any feeling of connection or spiritual elevation one may sense is illusory.

- Nevertheless, there are certain spiritual practices, such as prayer, that are permitted to Noahides and for which they are rewarded.

## Rav Moshe Weiner in the *Sefer Sheva Mitzvos HaShem* (The Divine Code)

After reviewing the many interpretations of Maimonides, Rabbi Weiner decides the *halakha*, law, in accordance with Rav Moshe. However, Rabbi Weiner elucidates[12] Rav Moshe's position further. He explains that there are many *mitzvos* whose performance need not be motivated by spirituality or reward, but have an immediate real-world benefit. It is possible, and perhaps laudable (and in some instances, even obligatory), for Noahides to perform these *mitzvos*.

Maimonides writes:

> Should a non-Jew wish to perform one of the Torah's other mitzvos **in order to receive merit/benefit,** we should not prevent him from doing so even according to all of its details.

---

[12] See *The Divine Code*, 2nd ed. Pp. 64 – 74. Rabbi Weiner's conclusions in this area are endorsed by Rabbis Chaim Kanievsky and Zalman Nehemiah Goldberg.

Rabbi Weiner explains that the word *sekhar* may be understood as "merit" or "benefit." Rabbi Weiner explains that Maimonides's use implies "benefit." Therefore, if a Noahide wishes to adopt a *mitzvah* that provides direct, real-world material or social benefit, it is permitted and, perhaps, even praiseworthy to do so. A Noahide may practice such a *mitzvah* regularly and according to all of its Torah details.

*Mitzvos* having real-world material or social benefit would include all of those that are *Bein adam le-chaveiro*, between man and man, such as:

- Honoring one's parents,

- *Tzedaka* (charity),

- Observing the prohibitions against *Tzaar Baalei Chayim*, animal cruelty,

- Observing the laws of prohibited speech.

- There are many other examples that we will discuss in this course.

There are a number of religious observances that are between man and God, *Bein Adam le-Makom*, that may also be observed, as will be discussed later on.

Rabbis Weiner and Feinstein's conclusions on *Chiddushei Dat* outline the guiding principles determining whether or not a Jewish *mitzvah* may be practiced by a Noahide.

## Summary of Lessons

1. Besides their *mitzvos*, Noahides may only regularly practice Torah *mitzvos* that are:

    a. Compelled by logic,

    b. Provide material or social benefit to the world, society, or the individual,

    c. Such *mitzvos* may be practiced according to all of the Torah's details.

2. Noahides may not practice any other *mitzvah* of the Torah:

    a. Regularly, regardless of motivation,

b. Even occasionally if he is spiritually motivated to do so,

3. Any *mitzvah* unique to Jewish identity or requiring the unique holiness of Israel may not be performed by a Noahide under any circumstances. These include:

   a. Mezuzah,

   b. Tefillin,

   c. Torah Scroll

   d. Tzitzis

   e. These specific *mitzvos* will be discussed in greater detail in a future lesson.

4. Noahides may not in any way observe Shabbat or the Festivals. However, there are some exceptions that will be discussed in a future lesson.

5. There are restrictions on what Torah may be studied by Noahides.

6. **The prohibitions of *Chiddushei Dat* do not exist to reduce or restrict the identity of a Noahide. Similarly the prohibition of *Baal Tosif* does not exist to reduce or restrict the identity of a Jew. Instead, *Chiddushei Dat* exists to define the boundaries of Noahide practice. It clearly delineates where Judaism ends and Noahism begins.**

7. **A Noahide may drink from the same well as Judaism and share its core beliefs and values, yet his identity is wholly separate and distinct from Judaism. Noahides have their own special *mitzvos* and missions in the world, as the Jews have theirs. The Noahide laws are not a means of "Judaism for non-Jews." Neither is being a Noahide a way for non-Jews to participate in Judaism. For the non-Jew who wishes to observe Jewish rituals or festivals, Maimonides teaches that conversion to Judaism is his only option.**

THE YESHIVA PIRCHEI SHOSHANIM SHULCHAN ARUCH LEARNING PROJECT

# The Noahide Laws – Lesson Sixteen

© **Yeshiva Pirchei Shoshanim 2017**
This shiur may not be reproduced in any
form without permission of the copyright holder.

## Outline of This Lesson:

1. Introduction

2. Obligations in Prayer

3. Texts of the Prayers

    a. The *Siddur*, the Jewish Prayer book

    b. The Psalms – The Universal Prayer book

    c. Modern Collections of Noahide Prayers

4. Practical Advice: How to Pray

5. Index of Suggested Psalms

# Noahide Prayer: Daily Prayer I

## Introduction

Our first sixteen lessons have been devoted to foundational concepts for understanding the sources, derivations, and guiding principles of the Noahide laws. With this sixteenth lesson we will now delve into the practical aspects of being a Noahide.

The first lesson in this new section will cover Noahide prayer.

## Obligations in Prayer

**Jewish Obligations in Prayer**

In Judaism, prayer exists on two levels: fixed communal prayer and personal spontaneous prayer. The fixed communal prayers require Jews to gather and pray three times each day facing east toward Jerusalem. These prayers are not personal prayers, but are fixed prayers with specific texts that are said on behalf of the Jewish community. These prayers were established in place of the thrice daily sacrifices offered in the temple. Personal prayer, however, is spontaneous and may be said in any language, using any words, and at any time one wishes.

Both forms of prayer are required and expected by God for the Jewish people.

| **What about Noahides?** | Neither the Talmud nor Maimonides mentions prayer of any type as being an obligation for Noahides.

At least one early authority, however, did recognize such an obligation. Rav Shmuel ben Chofni Gaon, in his commentary on the Torah,[1] lists prayer as one of the expanded obligations of the Noahide laws.

A contemporary of Rav Shmuel ben Chofni Gaon, Rabbeinu Nissim Gaon, does not list prayer as an obligation, but he implies such, writing:[2]

*Not all of the Seven Laws and their derivations require revelation. For example – the obligation to recognize God, to obey Him, and the obligation to* **serve** *him – all of which are rational and can be logically derived.*

The Hebrew term used by Rabbeinu Nissim for serving God, *le-avdo*, is usually understood as a specific reference to prayer. It is possible, though, that Rabbeinu Nissim is using the term *le-avdo* in its more general sense, meaning simply *to serve*. Nevertheless, the general idea conveyed by the passage is a concept true to both Jewish and Noahide thought: **that we are obligated to observe many principles by force of logic and reason alone, without any specific revelation**.

For example, Jews are required to make blessings before and after eating and drinking. The Talmud[3] explains that the source of this obligation is logic rather than revelation.

Similarly, the obligation for Noahides to pray is not sourced in any particular textual derivation, but is rooted in reason.

Curiously, though, it is not mentioned in the writings of Maimonides or in the Rema Mi-Fanu's statement of the Noahide laws.[4] This omission is odd considering that non-Jewish prayer is referred to many times in *Tanakh*, Scripture. For example:

---

[1] Commentary to Genesis 34:12. Chofni's Torah commentary was entirely forgotten until its rediscovery in the Cairo Geniza. It even appears to have been unknown to Rav Shmuel's contemporaries. Originally in Arabic, it was not translated and published until 1978.

[2] Introduction to Tractate *Brachos*.

[3] *Brachos* 35a.

[4] The Rama Mi-Fanu's list was brought and discussed in an earlier lesson. It seems that R' Shmuel ben Chofni's expansion of the Noahide laws was unknown to Maimonides and Rama Mi-Fanu.

> *My house shall be called a house of prayer **for all peoples**.*[5]

On this verse Rashi remarks that the temple is a house of prayer not only for Jews but for all peoples. Also:

> *Praise the L-rd, **all nations**, extol Him **all the peoples**.*[6]

We see from these versus that prayer is expected for non-Jews as well.

Rav Moshe Feinstein *ztz'l*,[7] in a responsum on Noahide practice,[8] puts prayer into perspective. According to Rabbi Feinstein, Noahides have no regular obligation to pray (this is in contrast to Jews who are required to pray daily facing east). Rather, all Noahide prayer is of the unfixed and personal type mentioned above.

For Noahides, prayer is only a *mitzvah* when performed in response to personal needs or circumstances. If one experiences challenges for which he does not pray, his lack of response is tantamount to a denial of God as the sovereign ruler of all things and all events. When one does pray in such circumstances, it demonstrates reliance and belief in the Creator.

When a Noahide prays to give thanks or praise absent a personal need, he still receives reward for such prayer even though it is not of the same nature as prayer prompted by personal needs.

It appears that many early authorities do not list prayer as an obligation due to its free, unfixed nature and due to its being derived from reason rather than revelation or textual exegesis.[9]

In summary:

- Jews have regular obligations to pray regardless of their personal needs or circumstances.

---

[5] Isaiah 56:7.

[6] Psalms 117:1.

[7] Rabbi Moshe Feinstein (b. Russia, 1895 – d. New York, 1986) was the foremost Torah authority of his generation and one of the most important scholars of the past 200 years. His magnum opus, the responsa *Igros Moshe*, continues to exert tremendous influence on Jewish thought and practice worldwide.

[8] *Igros Moshe* II: 25.

[9] See Nachmanides's commentary on Maimonides's *Sefer HaMitzvos* regarding whether or not prayer should even be included among the 613 mitzvos for Jews.

- Noahides have no regular obligation to pray. Rather, prayer as a response to personal needs or circumstances is obligated by force of reason. For this prayer they receive reward for having performed a *mitzvah*;

- Nevertheless, prayer in praise of God for His might and for having created all things is still a *mitzvah* and rewarded even though it is entirely voluntary.

## Texts of the Prayers

As with all personal prayers, there are no fixed texts for Noahide prayer. Since all Noahide prayer is essentially personal prayer, it is ideally expressed using sincere words from the heart.

However, we all sometimes need help jump-starting our prayers. In such cases, using a text can be of tremendous help.

**The *Siddur* - Using the Jewish Prayer book**

Many Noahides have asked about using the standard Jewish prayer book, the *Siddur*, for their personal prayers.

The core liturgy of the siddur was established in the 4th century BCE by the Anshei Kenesses HaGedola, the Men of the Great Assembly. This was a group of scholars and prophets under the leadership of Ezra who rebuilt and reestablished Jewish practice in the Holy Land following the destruction of the first temple. After the destruction of the second temple, the prayer book underwent a number of subsequent revisions to reflect the circumstances of diaspora Judaism.

The result is a prayer book specifically tailored to the unique obligations and needs of the Jewish community in exile. As such, most of the *siddur* is not relevant to Noahides.

For example, the *siddur* is replete with prayers for "the return to Israel," and prayers invoking the merit of Abraham, Isaac, and Jacob. A Noahide cannot recite these passages since Noahides do not have a share in the land of Israel or in the heritage of Abraham, Isaac, and Jacob. Additionally, many passages refer to *mitzvos* that only apply only to those with Jewish lineage.

For these reasons, it is advisable that Noahides do not use the Jewish prayer book. Nevertheless, there are a few sections of universal application. We will look at these in our next lesson on prayer.

**The Psalms – The Universal Prayer book**

Instead, many rabbis have advised Noahides to use the book of Psalms, *Tehillim*, as an aid to prayer. The book of Psalms is a collection of the personal prayers of King David and many other great people.[10] This "universal prayer book" gives voice to even the most subtle and nuanced needs of the soul. At the end of this lesson we have attached an index of Psalms suitable for many occasions.

**Modern Collections of Noahide Prayers**

Despite the *Siddur's* general inapplicability to Noahides, it contains some material of universal relevance. In the past decade many attempts have been made to adapt this material into a regular order of Noahide prayers. In the next lesson on prayer we will examine these collections and suggested orders of Noahide prayers as well as excerpts from the siddur.

## Practical Advice: How to Pray

Prayer is more than just speaking to God – it is the establishing of a relationship. Like all relationships, it takes time, work, and communication. Our sages and *tzaddikim* (righteous ones) have established certain benchmarks for prayer to help us maximize our potential.

1) **Identify your prayer.** A prayer will always fall into one of the three categories below. Identifying your prayer will help you to better understand the prayer's purpose and guide your speech. The sages have identified three modes of prayer:

    a. **Praise** – Praising God for the abilities that are unique to Him alone. For example: praising God for his creation of the sun and the heavens, or for His ability to give life and heal sickness.

    b. **Requests** – Asking God for one's needs or for the needs of others. This includes both spiritual and physical needs.

    c. **Thanks** – Expressing gratitude to God for all that He has done on behalf of the petitioner. For example, health, family, friends and livelihood.

---

[10] See *Bava Basra* 14b. It is a popular misconception that King David was the author of the Psalms. Though true that he authored many of them, he also edited the final collection, choosing to include many writings from earlier authors.

2) **Prayer should be verbalized.** By verbalizing our prayers we are forced to give voice and articulation to our most important concerns. Articulating them via speech gives honor to both the prayer and to God the recipient.[11]

3) **Set aside regular times for reflection and prayer.** Though Noahides are not obligated in set times for prayer, establishing regular times for prayer spiritual reflection is intrinsic to the spiritual life of Jew and Noahide alike. This personal time should be fixed, regular, and sacred. The place should be somewhere private, quiet, and respectful. Some people will set aside time daily, others weekly. The beauty of being a Noahide is that you know what you have to do, but have a good amount of freedom to personalize it.

4) **Make a point of praying for all of your needs throughout the day.** God provides EVERYTHING. Even things appearing to come solely by the hand of man are still provided by God. Therefore, it is appropriate to pray for **all** of one's needs, whether great or small, physical or spiritual, silly or serious. Anything a person has is only a result of God.

5) **Prayer is directly and only to the one true God and creator of all things.** The Noahide Laws and Judaism both reject the idea of praying to or through any intermediary. Additionally, we only pray envisioning God as a single unity, not an entity with multiple forms or expressions. These concepts of a disparate God or of an intermediary are idolatrous and prohibited for Jews and Noahides alike. **All you need to connect with God is you, your prayers, and God.**

## Index of Suggested Psalms

The following index of Psalms is compiled from a number of sources. You will find slight variations in practice and custom as to which Psalms are recited on which occasions.

When multiple psalms are given for one particular need, it is preferable that they all be said. This may be done either all at once or over a period of time. This is only a

---

[11] See *Igros Moshe* OC II: 25 that Noahides should verbalize their prayers. Purely mental prayer, even by Jews, is used only in extenuating circumstances.

recommendation, however. A little said with concentration and intent is better than a lot said without.

**NOTE: Non-Jewish editions of the Psalms often use numberings that differ from the traditional Hebrew division of the psalms. The numbers below reflect the original numberings. We suggest the Artscroll Hebrew/English edition of the Psalms (Artscroll item# TEHH) available from www.Artscroll.com.**

- Daily Psalms

    - Psalms for daily recitation: 67, 100, 145, 146, 150, and 20 – These appear in the Siddur and are recited daily by Jews as well.

    - Psalms for Specific Days:

        - In addition to the regular daily psalms, each day has its own specific psalm alluding to the work of creation accomplished on that day. The Psalm for the seventh day depicts the future messianic era. Each of these psalms was recited by the Levites on its corresponding day in the ancient temple. Today we continue the tradition of reciting these daily songs:

            - Sunday 24
            - Monday 48
            - Tuesday 82
            - Wednesday 94
            - Thursday 81
            - Friday 33
            - Saturday 92

- For after a full meal – a full meal is defined as one at which bread was eaten.

    - Psalm 67 or 104.

- For God's Guidance: 16, 19, 139

- For a Livelihood: 23, 34, 36, 62, 65, 67, 85, 104, 121, 136, 144, 145

- For Success: 57, 112, 122

- For a Favorable Judgment: 7, 35, 93

- For Help in Times of Need: 16, 20, 25, 26, 38, 54, 81, 85, 86, 87, 102, 130, 142

- For Being Rescued: 124

- For Thanksgiving for a Miracle: 18

- For Repentance: 51, 90

- To Find One's Spouse: 32, 38, 70, 71, 121, 124

- On the Day of One's Marriage: 19

- To Have Children: 102, 103

- Upon Giving Birth: 20

- For Recovery From Illness: 6, 30, 41, 88, 103

- To Express Gratitude: 21, 25, 26, 38, 54, 81, 85, 86, 87, 102, 130, 142

- For Peace: 46

- When the land of Israel is in Danger: 83, 130, 142

- For a Safe Journey: 91

- At a cemetery 33, 16, 17, 72, 91, 104, 130 (letters of the name of the deceased from 119)

## Summary of This Lesson:

1. Noahides have an obligatory *mitzvah* to pray in response to their needs and circumstances. This prayer has no fixed texts or set times.

2. It is proper to offer other prayers of praise or gratitude. These voluntary prayers are likewise personal and have no fixed times or texts.

3. The Siddur, the Jewish prayer book is mostly inapplicable to non-Jews. It contains some universal sections which we will examine in a later lesson.

4. The book of Psalms is the universal prayer book and the most widely suggest text for Noahide prayer.

5. There are three types of prayer:

    a. Requests

b. Praises

   c. Thanks

6. Prayer should be verbalized rather than performed in thought alone.

7. One should set aside regular times for spiritual reflection and prayer.

8. One should pray for ALL things, whether physical, spiritual, great or small.

9. One should pray only and directly to God, no to or through any other entity.

THE YESHIVA PIRCHEI SHOSHANIM SHULCHAN ARUCH LEARNING PROJECT

# The Noahide Laws – Lesson Seventeen

**© Yeshiva Pirchei Shoshanim 2017**
This shiur may not be reproduced in any
form without permission of the copyright holder.

## Outline of This Lesson:

1. Introduction
2. The Siddur
3. Noahide Prayerbooks
4. Other Details of Prayer

# Noahide Prayer: Daily Prayer II

## Introduction

In the previous lesson on prayer (Lesson 17) we looked at the ideas behind Noahide prayer, practical suggestions, and the book of Psalms. In this lesson we are going to delve into the sections of the Siddur – the Jewish prayer book – which are universal to both Jews and Noahides. We will also and look at recent compilations of prayers. We are also going to begin our discussion of blessings on food and other benefits.

## The *Siddur*

As we mentioned in the last lesson, the *siddur* is not intended nor does it try to be a prayer book for both Jews and Noahides. It is uniquely tailored to the concerns of a Jewish community in exile. Therefore, much of its content does not apply to Noahides. The issue, however, goes beyond non-application; were non-Jews to use many of the prayers in the *siddur,* they would be praying falsely. For example, to say a prayer which includes the petitioner as part of Israel is a mistake because Noahides are not part of Israel. Though this seems like a minor detail, consider the verse from Psalms[1]:

*One who utters falsehood shall not stand before me.*

Therefore, before saying any prayers found in the *siddur*, a Noahide must assess whether or not the particular prayer is relevant to non-Jews.

---

[1] 101:7

The following list of prayers is relevant to both Jews and non-Jews and found in all standard editions of the Siddur. I have been very conservative in selecting these passages. Certainly there are many others that can arguably be included. Nevertheless, I have chosen the ones upon which everyone can agree.

To iterate what has been stated before: these are only suggestions. For Noahides, ideal prayer is personal, heartfelt, and unique to the needs of the individual. These prayers are suggestions that may be helpful in developing an approach, language, and familiarity with prayer.

Page numbers refer to the locations of these prayers in the Artscroll Classic Siddur, Nusach Ashkenaz (Ashkenaz Liturgy):

- **Page 3: Upon Arising in the Morning**. The siddur discusses a ritual hand-washing performed by Jews upon arising. This is not applicable to Noahides. However, the two short prayers said here are relevant.

    o Upon arising, one should say: *Modeh Ani – I gratefully thank you...*

    o Once one has relieved himself, washed his face, and completed the regular waking routine, he should say: *Reishis Chochmah – The beginning of wisdom....*

- Once one is dressed and has his thoughts gathered, he should then continue with: **Page 13: *Adon Olam – Master of the Universe.***

    o This famous hymn was penned in the 11th century by Rabbi Shlomo ibn Gabirol. The first part speaks of God the creator and transcendent king, while the second addresses God as the personal, immanent God of salvation and comfort. This classic text is recited before daily prayers and often after Shabbos and holiday prayers as well.

- **Morning Blessings**. As we shall see in upcoming lessons it is proper (yet not compulsory) for Noahides to recite many types of blessings. For the most part, Noahides can use the text for these blessings found in the Siddur.

    o **Page 15: Last paragraph – Blessing of *Who fashioned man with wisdom...***

        ▪ This blessing praises God for creating the wondrous machine of the body and for maintaining its balance and function each day.

- Jews say this at some point after relieving themselves in the morning and after every such occasion throughout the day. Noahides may certainly do the same.

  o **Page 19: Top of page –** *My God, the Soul...* This praises God for safeguarding our souls and restoring our spiritual and physical vitality every morning.

  o **Page 19: The order of the Morning Blessings.** These will require some adaptation for Noahide use. The exact reasons behind these blessings and why they need emendation will be explained in the live lesson.

    - The second blessing, ...*for not having made me a gentile*, should be omitted.

    - The third, ...*for not having made me a slave*, should be omitted.

    - Whether male or female, the fourth blessing should be ... *for having made me according to His will.*

    - The remaining blessings through ...*who gives strength to the weary* on page 21 may be said without alteration. There are, however, two exceptions. One should omit the blessings that concludes with ...*who girds Israel...* and ...*who crowns Israel...*

- **Morning Psalms.** The next section of the Siddur is a collection of Psalms praising God.

  o **Page 59:** *Boruch SheAmar – Blessed is He who Spoke.* This blessing opens the daily recitation of Psalms. Noahides may precede their psalms with this blessing. Tradition tells us that this prayer fell from heaven and was transcribed about 2400 years ago. It is one of the deepest and most multi-layered parts of the liturgy.

  o **Page 67: Psalm 145** proceeded by the opening versus: *Praiseworthy...*

  o Page 71: Psalm 146

  o Page 75: Psalm 150

- Page 83: *Yishtabach – May your name be praised forever...* This prayer concludes the recitation of psalms. Noahides may recite it, but it is proper to omit the phrase ...*the God of our forefathers*.

- **Page 91 – The *Shema*.** There is a lot of debate as to whether or not Noahides may say the *Shema*. On one hand, the *Shema* is composed of passages from the Torah, which are perfectly acceptable for Noahides to read and recite. On the other hand, the *Shema* is a prayer – a pledge of allegiance – and thus much more than a recitation of scripture. Having consulted with a number of experts and *poksim* (decisors of Torah law), the following is recommended:

    - **Bottom of Page 91:** *Hear O' Israel: The Lord our God, The Lord is One!* If Noahides wish to recite the *Shema*, then they should say the entire verse interpreting it as a statement of allegiance to the God of Israel and recognition that He is the one true God. This is preferable to omitting the "Hear O' Israel" and only reciting he second part of the verse. It is forbidden to replace "Israel" with "Noah" because it is rewriting a verse of the Torah. An even better course of action is to compose a text that accomplishes the same purpose as the Shema. The reason Jews recite the Shema is as an acceptance of G-d's sovereign kingship; it is a religious "pledge of allegiance." The verse itself is only a means to doing this. Therefore, it is best advised that Noahides compose a text that expresses a Noahide acceptance of God's kingship. Therefore, one will fulfill the intent and spirit of the Shema while avoiding the difficulties posed by using the Jewish texts.

    - **Top of page 93, first paragraph.** From *You shall love...* to ... *arise* may be recited. However, the last verses containing the commandments of *Tefillin* and *mezuzah* should be omitted as a matter of propriety, not prohibition.

    - **The remaining parts of the Shema should be omitted.**

- **Pages 163 to 169: The Psalms of the Day.** The appropriate Psalm of the day may be said.

Note that the *Amidah / Shemonah Esrei*, the central liturgy of the siddur, is not included in the above list. Authorities on Torah law are unanimous in their conclusion that this prayer, instituted to replace Jewish temple sacrifices, should not be said by Noahides.

## Noahide Prayer Books

It is not known if ancient Noahides had any unique liturgies or particular prayers. As we mentioned at the start of this course, the ancient Noahides disappeared in the 3rd century leaving no written evidence of liturgy.

However the absence of evidence of such liturgies is not proof that such liturgies did not exist. After all, most set prayers at that time were said from memory. In fact, the Jewish community didn't even compile written prayer books until the 9th century.

The lack of uniquely Noahide prayers is acutely felt by both Noahides and Jews involved in Noahide study. In response, many collections of Noahide prayers have been authored over the past two decades.

Many of these compilations are excellent, while some make fundamental mistakes.

Having reviewed all of the publications available today, I would most recommend a small, pocket-sized booklet entitled ***Prayers, Blessings, Principles of Faith and Divine Service for Noahides*** by Rabbis Moshe Weiner and Immanuel Shochet (available online from Amazon.com).

This small booklet contains original and adapted liturgy, blessings, grace after meals, and other prayers for *Bnei Noach*. All of the material is meticulously researched and highly consistent with the underpinning legal and theological concerns of Noahism. Nevertheless, one must keep in mind that Noahide prayer is ideally meaningful, personal prayer. Therefore, even this prayer book should not be treated as a rigid, concrete text. Rather, it is an aide that you should feel free to adapt and personalize as needed.

## Other Details of Prayer

- Though one does not need to pray loudly, it is important to at least articulate his prayers through speech.[2]

- One should ideally use his own prayers. However, if helpful, one may use other relevant texts composed by those who believe in HaShem and in his Torah. One

---

[2] *Igros Moshe* OC II: 25.

should not use prayers composed by idolaters or commonly offered to idolatry. This is even if one's intent is to pray to the true God. This type of prayer is comparable to offering a defiled sacrifice before God.[3]

- Similarly, one should not pray to God in a *Makom Avodah Zarah* – a place of idol worship. This would include a church, a chapel in which there is a cross or crucifix, a Buddhist temple, or any place containing idolatrous imagery. Even though Islam is an unacceptable religion, a Noahide may pray in a mosque.[4]

- One should not pray within sight or odor of excrement or other bodily waste.

- One should pray in a clean, respectable environment. One may not pray in a bathroom, slaughterhouse, or other such place.

- One should not pray before adults or children who are nude or immodestly clothed.

- Though Noahides have no fixed obligations in prayer, it is nevertheless appropriate to establish regular times for prayer and reflection.

## Summary of This Lesson

1. In prayer, one must be very careful not to utter any words of falsehood.

2. Much of the Siddur is specific to the exile Jewish community and specifically addresses their concerns. Therefore, Noahides cannot use most of the material contained therein.

3. Nevertheless, the Siddur contains some universal material that Noahides may use for their daily prayers.

4. While ancient communities may have had specific Noahide liturgies, any actual evidence has been lost to history.

5. Recent authors have compiled and composed collections of Noahide prayers.

---

[3] Igros Moshe Ibid.

[4] Although Islam is monotheistic, it rejects the Torah as the final revelation and authority.

6. When one prays, he should do so in a place and manner that is respectable.

7. Prayer should be verbal and aloud.

# The Noahide Laws – Lesson Eighteen

THE YESHIVA PIRCHEI SHOSHANIM SHULCHAN ARUCH LEARNING PROJECT

© **Yeshiva Pirchei Shoshanim 2017**
This shiur may not be reproduced in any
form without permission of the copyright holder.

## Outline of This Lesson:

1. Introduction & Types of Mitzvos
   a. The Three Classes of Mitzvos
2. The Source For Making Blessings
   a. The Blessing After Meals
   b. The Blessing For Torah & Certain Species
   c. Other Blessings
3. The Jewish vs. The Noahide Obligation to Make Blessings
4. Types of Brachos, Blessings
5. What does it mean to Bless God?
6. Texts of the Blessings
7. The Blessings After Meals
   a. A Noahide Grace After Meals

# Noahide Prayer: Blessings I

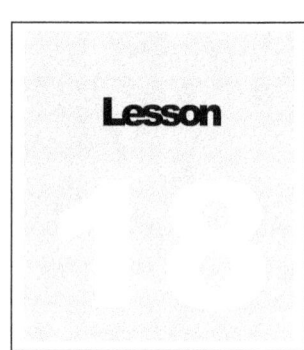

## Introduction & Types of *Mitzvos*

**NOTE: Throughout this lesson, references such as *(Siddur, p. 31)* refer to page numbers in the *Artscroll Classic Edition of the Siddur, Nusah Ashkenaz*.**

As mentioned in previous lessons, Noahides may adopt any Jewish *mitzvah* in all its details provided that the *mitzvah* is logical or provides a tangible benefit to society, oneself, or the world as a whole.

Among the *mitzvos* compelled by logic, for example, is prayer.

However, these *mitzvos* compelled by logic or benefit are of a different nature than other Noahide *mitzvos*.

**THREE CLASSES OF MITZVOS**

*Mitzvos*, in general, are divided into three classes:

1) *Mechuyeves* – *Mitzvos* that one must do. For example, the *mitzvos* involved with establishing justice and courts are *Mechuyeves*. They are obligatory and one is liable for their neglect.

2) *Reshus* – *mitzvos* that are optional. This means that the *mitzvah* exists and applies to a person; however one is not punished or liable for neglecting the *mitzvah*. If one performs such *mitzvos*, then he is accorded reward and merit for doing so.

3) *Mitzvos* which have no application to a person. Some *mitzvos* are entirely inapplicable to some people. For example, Kohanim, the temple priests, have commandments unique to them alone. Their *mitzvos* are inapplicable

to other Jews. Other Jews may not even adopt these *mitzvos* voluntarily. It is very risky and spiritually dangerous to adopt *mitzvos* to which one has no connection. At best, one receives no merit for doing so. At worse, one may receive divine punishment. This is true for both Jews and Noahides. One should be very cautious when adopting practices to which one has no obligation or connection.

The 7 *Mitzvos* of Noah and their subdivisions generally fall into the first category – those of obligatory *mitzvos*. Jewish *mitzvos* which have no connection to Noahides (i.e. most dietary laws or the observance of many Jewish holidays) fall into the third group.

Noahide *mitzvos* compelled by logic or practical benefit generally fall into the second category. One does not need to perform such *mitzvos*, but it is preferable and logical to do so.

## The Source of Blessings

It is an obligatory *mitzvah* (a *mechuyeves*) for Jews, to give blessings (*brachos* in Hebrew) to God before partaking of any benefit this world has to offer. What is the origin of this practice? Is it from the Torah or from the Rabbis?

**Blessing after Meals**

With regard to one blessing in particular, the *Birkas HaMazon* (*Blessing After Meals* – Siddur, p. 184 at the bottom) we know its obligation comes from the Torah. The Torah states:

> *You shall eat, be satisfied, and bless God your Lord*
> *for the good land that He has given you.*[1]

From here we learn a biblical obligation to bless God after meals.[2]

---

[1] Deuteronomy 8:10.

[2] The Talmud clarifies that a proper meal is one at which bread is eaten.

**Blessing For Torah & Certain Species**

Two further blessings, the one said before learning Torah (Siddur, p. 17) and the *MaEyn Shalosh* (Siddur, p. 201), a blessing said after eating certain species of fruit, grains, or wine, *may* be biblical in origin. However, pinning it down precisely is difficult.[3] Very generally, most authorities view the blessings for learning Torah as biblical in origin. However, there is no clear consensus as to the origin of the *MaEyn Shalosh*.

**Other Blessings**

What about the many other blessings (see Siddur, pp. 223, 225, 229 – 231)? The Talmud concedes that all other blessings, though obligatory, are only rabbinic in origin. Their authority is compelled by logic alone, not by any particular biblical decree, as the Talmud states:

> *Though not a command of God, it is a logical obligation upon a person.*[4]

God gave us this world to partake of and to serve Him through it. Every time that we benefit from this world, we are partaking of God's kindness as Creator. It only makes sense, therefore, to acknowledge God the Giver. As support for this line of reasoning, the Talmud invokes a subtle contradiction in the verses of the Psalms:

> *Rabbi Levi noted a contradiction between two verses. One states, "The earth and its fullness belong to God.[5]" Another verse says, "The heavens belong to God, but the earth He gave to man.[6]" He resolved the contradiction by stating that one verse refers to the status of the world before reciting a Bracha and the other to after its recitation. Said Rabbi Chanina Bar Pappa: When one derives enjoyment from this world without a Bracha, it is as if he has stolen from God!*

Before one eats a fruit, the fruit belongs to God – He created it, nurtured it, and brought it to this place in its existence. One cannot partake of that fruit unless he "redeems" it by making a blessing upon it, thanking God for the benefit one is about to receive. Otherwise, his partaking of the fruit is akin to stealing!

---

[3] The nature of the *Maeyn Shalosh*, the blessing said after certain grains, fruits, and wine, is difficult to determine because of a biblical ambiguity. Deuteronomy 8:10, which states the command to bless after a meal, also includes a list of the items for which one is recited to recite this blessing. For this reason, the Rashba and Rosh hold it is biblical in origin (see Bais Yosef 209). However, the Rambam, Taz (209:3) and others hold of a different reading of the verse, and conclude that it is rabbinic in origin. There is no clear consensus on the matter. With regard to the blessings over learning Torah, although the source is very unclear, most authorities treat them as biblical in origin. The question of rabbinic vs. biblical origin is more than merely academic; it has occasional practical applications for Jews.

[4] Berachos 35a.

[5] Psalms 24:1

[6] Psalms 115:16.

Incidentally, this Talmudic passage illustrates a concept mentioned back in Lesson 5. We saw there that *mitzvos* are only learned and proved from the Torah and not from the Prophets and Writings. The Prophets and Writings exist to elaborate and elucidate our understanding of the Torah. They also provide support and insight into Rabbinic decrees. Note that the Talmud does not use these Psalm verses as "biblical" proof for making blessings. Instead they are used as support to a Rabbinic proposition based on religious logic.

## The Jewish Obligation vs. the Noahide Obligation

For Jews, making blessings over benefit is an obligatory *mitzvah*. Even though almost all blessings are rabbinic in origin (with the exception of the blessing after a meal and, possibly, a few others), a Jew is nevertheless required to make them. Neglecting *Brachos* is considered a transgression for a Jew.

Since the whole idea of *Brachos* is rooted in religious logic, for Noahides it falls into the second category mentioned above: *Reshus*, voluntary *mitzvos*.

What about the blessing after meals, though? Isn't this blessing biblical in origin? Yes – it is. However, this blessing was only commanded to Jews, not to Noahides. Nevertheless, the idea of making a blessing after meals is compelled by the same religious logic that compels all other blessings.

## Types of *Brachos*

The Maimonides,[7] based upon the Talmud, identifies three categories of blessings/*Brachos*:

1) **Blessings over benefit** (Siddur p. 225). These include blessings over food, drink, spices, etc.

2) **Blessings over *mitzvos*** (Siddur p. 227). Since God's commandments exist to benefit mankind, Jews make blessings when coming to fulfill the commandments. The formula of these types of blessings is the well-known: *Blessed are you are God, ruler of the universe, who has hallowed us with His commandment of…*

3) **Blessings of thanks, praise, and gratitude** (Siddur p. 229).

---

[7] *Hilchos Brachos* 1:4

Categories 1 and 3 are the most relevant to Noahides. The second category, however, is complicated even for Jews. There are many details as to the exact wordings of these types of blessings. Furthermore, not all *mitzvos* require blessings at all times. Some never do. Since the second category is generally inapplicable for Noahides, we will focus our attention on the first and the third.

## What Does It Mean to Bless God?

Before going further, let's stop for a minute and consider a basic question: What does it mean to "Bless God?"

If the idea of *Brachos/blessings* is to express gratitude and thanks, then why blessings are worded "Blessed are you…" instead of "Thanks and gratitude unto you…?"

Furthermore, if God is the source of all blessings, then who are we to "bless" God? God, after all, has no lack or deficiency. He is perfect!

This question has been asked by many scholars and many answers have been provided, all of which point in the same direction:

- **Yad Ketanah**:[8] Saying *Blessed are you…* is an acknowledgement that God is the source of the concept of blessing.

- **Rashba**[9]: Included in the concept of a *bracha* is the admission that He is ruler over all, and everything is from Him. As it says in the Talmud: *A person must bless God for the bad just as he must bless Him for the good."* This is because the word *bracha* comes from the word *breicha*, meaning *reservoirs of water* – an allusion to the primordial waters of creation and the source of all things.

- **Chizkuni**:[10] The word *Baruch,* when applied to God, is used like a greeting implying supreme praise. It is not to be understood in the regular sense of the word *blessed*.

---

[8] Commentary on Maimonides by Rabbi Dov Berish Gottlied, d. 1796.

[9] Responsa I: 423. Rashba is an acronym for Rabbi Shlomo ben Aderet, d. 1310. Rashba was a prolific commentator on the Talmud and a renowned posek.

[10] To Genesis 24:27. The Chizkuni is a famed commentary on the Torah written in c. 1240 by Rabbi Chizkiyhu ben Manoach.

- **Chaim of Volozhin:**[11] The word *bracha* implies burgeoning abundance. Even the letters of the world, **Beis**, **Reish**, and **Kaf**, imply such. The numerical value of the letters is a progression of multiples of 10:[12]

    **Beis** = 2
    **Kaf** = 20
    **Reish** = 200

This sampling of interpretations all indicate that *blessed*, when referring to God, is a statement of praise for God as the source of all blessing and abundance. It implies not only acknowledgement and gratitude, but the recognition that God is the unique, sole provider of all things.

## Texts of the Blessings

The text of the blessings was first recorded by Ezra and his assembly in about 350 B.C.E. Their texts were the result of tremendous study, contemplation, debate, and prayer. This effort imbued the texts of the blessings with a holiness and authority that endures until today.

Writes the Rambam and many others:

> *It is not appropriate to alter them [the texts of the blessings] or to add or subtract from any of them. Anyone who deviates from the text that the Sages instituted for blessings is mistaken.*[13]

However, the sages instituted their texts for the Jewish community, not for the Noahide community. So, what texts should Noahides use for their blessings?

On one hand, Noahides may use any text for blessings provided that it satisfies the core idea of a blessing: to acknowledge God as the creator of all things who bestows benefit to His creation.

However, let us recall for a moment that the compelling reason for blessings is the same for both Noahides and Jews: a compelling religious logic. Considering this, the texts formulated by Ezra should be sufficient for Jews as well as Noahides. For this reason it is not only permissible, but perhaps even preferable, for

---

[11] *Nefesh HaChaim* II: 2. Rabbi Chaim of Volozhin (d. 1821) was the foremost disciple of Rabbi Elijah Kramer, the famed Vilna Gaon.

[12] See Maharal *Tiferest Yisrael* 34 and *Netzach Yisrael* 45.

[13] Ibid. 1:5.

Noahides to use the established texts of the blessings as found in the Jewish siddur. Furthermore, it is also preferable to make the blessings according to the same rules that govern Jewish practice.

## The Blessing after Meals

An exception to using the Jewish texts exists with regard to the blessing said after meals (Siddur p. 185, bottom).[14] This blessing was originally a single paragraph composed by Moses. Over time, three more paragraphs were added. Each of the four paragraphs speaks of matters pertaining solely to the Jewish obligation to bless after meals and the unique connection between the Jewish people and the land of Israel. It is therefore incorrect for Noahides to use this text.

**A Noahide Grace after Meals**

A little known fact is that the Midrash actually records a Noahide blessing for after meals! We are taught that Abraham, who excelled in offering hospitality to guests, would never ask his guests to thank him or pay him. Rather, Abraham only asked that his guests recite a blessing of thanks to God. The blessing he taught them was:

> *Blessed is the God of the universe from whose bounty we have eaten.*[15]

It appears that this was recited after any filling meal, whether or not bread was eaten. For Noahides, it is advisable that this blessing be said after any filling, sit-down meal, following the precedent of Abraham.

This blessing may be enhanced by adding Psalms 67 or 104 before it.

Recently, many texts have been composed for Noahides for after meals.[16] Many of these texts are very good, yet should be used in addition to the blessing mentioned above and preferably recited before it.

In the next lesson, we will explore the actual blessings to use and the rules governing their use.

---

[14] Another exception exists with regard to the blessing *MaEyn Shalosh*, said after certain fruits, grains, and wine. We will look at this exception in a future lesson.

[15] Bereshis Rabbah 54.

[16] Rabbis Moshe Weiner and J. Immanuel Schochet have written an excellent text that may be found in their pamphlet: *Prayers, Blessings, Principles of Faith, and Divine Service for Noahides*.

## Summary of This Lesson

1. There are three types of mitzvos: 1) Obligations one must do, 2) *Mitzvos* that one should do, yet for which one is not liable for neglecting, 3) *Mitzvos* to which one has no connection.

2. Noahide practices compelled by logic or adopted voluntarily for practical benefit fall in the second category of *mitzvos* mentioned above. This includes prayer and making blessings on benefit.

3. Very few blessings have their sources in the Torah. Most blessings were decreed upon the Jewish community by the Rabbinic authority. However, no blessings were ever required of the Noahide community.

4. Nevertheless, the logic that compelled the Rabbinic decree requiring Jew to make blessings applies equally to the Noahide community. However, making blessings is not obligatory – it is, rather, a preferable and meritorious practice.

5. Blessings are either made over benefit, over mitzvos, or as praise. Only the first and last types are applicable to the Noahide community.

6. God does not need us to bless him because he is perfect and needs nothing. When we "bless God" it is an acknowledgment of His role as the source of all blessing and benefit.

7. The texts of the blessings as established by Ezra and his assembly are, for the most part, applicable to both Jewish and Noahide blessings.

8. There are a few notable exceptions to use of Jewish *bracha*/blessing texts by Noahides. A major one is the Jewish text for the blessing after meals, *Birkas HaMazon*. This blessing speaks of concerns unique to the Jewish spiritual position. Instead, Noahides should use the Noahide text recorded in the Midrash. This text may be enhanced by adding psalms or especially composed texts.

THE YESHIVA PIRCHEI SHOSHANIM SHULCHAN ARUCH LEARNING PROJECT

# The Noahide Laws – Lesson Nineteen

© **Yeshiva Pirchei Shoshanim 2017**
This shiur may not be reproduced in any
form without permission of the copyright holder.

## Outline of This Lesson:

1. Introduction

2. Blessings on Benefit

    a. Blessings Over Food & Drink

        i. Before-Blessings

            1. Bread
            2. Grain Foods
            3. Wine
            4. Fruits
            5. Veggies
            6. All Other Foods

        ii. Guiding Principles

    b. The Blessing After Eating

            7. The Blessing Taught by Abraham

    c. Blessings on Aromas

            8. Spices
            9. Fragrant Trees & Their Flowers
            10. Fragrant Grasses, Herbs, and Flowers
            11. Fragrant Fruits

3. Blessings of Praise & Gratitude

            12. Lightening
            13. Thunder
            14. Rainbows
            15. Oceans

16. Things Beautiful
17. Things Grotesque or Exotic
18. Fruit Trees in Bloom
19. Outstanding Torah Scholar
20. Outstanding Secular Scholar
21. Gentile King
22. Seeing One Who Has Recovered From Mortal Sickness
23. Good News
24. Bad News
25. Miracles

# Noahide Prayer: Blessings II

## Introduction

In the last lesson we saw the rationale for Noahides to make blessings. We also learned that it is acceptable and, perhaps, even preferable for Noahides to use the texts of the blessings established by Ezra and the *Anshei Kenesses HaGadolah* (Men of the Great Assembly) for this purpose. In this lesson we are going to examine each of the blessings and how it is applied. The governing laws of the blessings presented here are the same as those practiced by Jews. However, some necessary adjustments have been made. These changes are indicated in the footnotes.

For ease of reference, we have numbered the texts of the blessings.

## Blessings over Food and Drink

Blessings over food and drink are said both before and after eating or drinking.

**A BREAD MEAL**

**The Main Meal**

A bread-based meal usually has two parts: the main meal, and the "after meal," at which drinks and deserts are served.

Many verses in Tanach speak of the primacy of bread as the basic foodstuff of man. Because of its unique status, bread has the ability to "exempt" other foods eaten at the meal from requiring a blessing.

This means that, if you eat a meal at which bread is served, you only need to make a blessing over the bread at the outset of the meal.[1] No further blessings are

---

[1] You may notice that Jews wash their hands in a ritual manner before making the blessing over bread. This practice is related to commemorating specifically Jewish temple purity rituals.

required on anything else served. The only exception is wine because it too is uniquely distinguished in Tanach.

**What is Called Bread?**

For the purpose of this blessing, bread is defined as having been made from a flour of either wheat, barley, rye, oats or spelt, kneaded with water, and baked. Whether or not the bread is leavened makes no difference.[2] Bread includes pita, bagels, Kaiser rolls, Matzah, etc.[3]

1) The blessing over bread is: ***Blessed are you, our God, sovereign of the universe, who brings forth bread from the earth.***

This blessing, like most blessings, is in the present tense because God is constantly creating and bestowing His kindnesses up His creation.

**The After-Meal**

Desserts, including after-meal drinks such as coffee, tea, or a digestive, are not included as part of the main meal. Therefore, they are not covered by the blessing over bread and would require their own blessings.

## Other Blessings on Food & Drink

### Blessings over Any Grains or Food Made From Grains

Any food made from wheat, barley, rye, oats, spelt, or rice <u>that is not bread</u> receives the following blessing:

2) ***Blessed are you, our God, sovereign of the universe, who creates many species of sustenance.***

This blessing would be made on crackers, rice cakes, pasta, pop tarts, cereals, oatmeal, etc.

Should you have a food that is a mixture of grain and something else, always make the blessing on the grain-based food and do not make a blessing on the other food. For example: when eating shredded wheat cereal with milk, make the above blessing on the shredded wheat only and do not make a blessing on the milk. This is, again, due to the prominence of grains.

### For Wine (Including Grape Juice)

---

Noahides should not practice this ritual washing. Normative washing of the hands with soap and water for cleanliness is perfectly acceptable.

[2] Small crackers, like Ritz or saltines, receive the blessing #2 below, despite their similarity to Matza.

[3] Pita chips and bagel chips, though, would only require blessing #2 below.

Tanach praises grape products in many places, elevating wine as the most prominent of all beverages. For this reason, we have a special blessing for it:

> 3) *Blessed are you, our God, sovereign of the universe, who creates the fruit of the vine.*

### Blessings on Fruits and Vegetables

The Torah divides produce into two botanical categories: trees and ground vegetation. A tree is defined by the Talmud as any plant whose stalk and branches remain from season to season. Ground vegetation is any plant whose stalk or branches wither back and must regrow each season.[4]

According to these definitions, bananas and strawberries are the fruits of ground vegetation. Apples, pears, oranges, and lemons, on the other hand, are the produce of trees. The Torah has established separate blessings for the fruits of each type of plant.

### The Fruit of the Tree

For the fruit of trees the blessing is:

> 4) *Blessed are you, our God, sovereign of the universe, who creates the fruit of the tree.*

This is the correct blessing for apples, oranges, pears, blueberries, plums, peaches, nectarines, lemons, grapefruit, etc.

### The Fruit of the Ground [Vegetation]

For the fruit of ground vegetation, which includes most vegetables, the blessing is:

> 5) *Blessed are you, our God, sovereign of the universe, who creates the fruit of the earth.*

This blessing would be made over tomatoes, potatoes, peppers, broccoli, cauliflower, strawberries, melons and gourds, eggplant, etc.

### For All Other Foods & Drinks

For all foods and drinks which do not require one of the above blessings, the following blessing is used:

> 6) *Blessed are you, Lord, our God, sovereign of the universe, through whose word all things came into being.*

---

[4] The Talmud lists many other criteria for identifying ground vegetation and trees. We have listed here only the most common feature. With some exotic fruits, such as papaya and passion fruit, their classification can get tricky. In these cases we have to rely on more obscure Talmudic criteria.

## Guiding Principles of Before-Blessings

1) There is no minimum amount for recitation of a before-blessing; a blessing is proper even for the minutest amount that is consumed.

2) Once one has made the blessing, he should not speak between the conclusion of the blessing and tasting the food or drink.

3) There is a principle of economy of blessings. We always try to make blessings in the most efficient way possible. If you have a fruit salad that contains apples, oranges, pears, and blueberries, all of which can be covered by blessing #4 above, the one should make one blessing on the whole mixture.

4) When you have many foods before you, you should always make the blessing on the one you prefer or desire most at that moment. The only exception is bread – if you plan on eating bread then you should make that blessing first and thereby "exempt" all other foods (remember- economy of blessings).

5) If one has no particular preference for any of the foods before him, and bread is not part of the meal, then he should make the blessings in the order listed above starting with blessing #2. Meaning, one should first make the blessing over grain foods (#2), then wine (#3), then fruit of trees (#4), fruit of ground vegetation (#5), and lastly, all other foods (#6). For example, if one has a fruit salad before him that contains oranges, and strawberries, he should pick out an orange, make the blessing upon it (#4) and then pick out a strawberry and make the blessing upon it (#5). This hierarchy of blessings is based on the degree to which various foods are given prominence and praise in Tanach.

6) When a grain food occurs in mixture with other foods, one only needs to make a blessing on the grain food (#2). For example, apple pie would only require #2, not a #2 and a #4.

7) One should preferably make his blessing over a whole food item rather than a partial one. If one has half-an-apple and a whole apple before him, he should make the blessing on the whole apple.

8) One should hold the food or drink in his hand (or on his fork) while he makes the blessing.

9) A food which is added merely as a spice or flavor does not require its own blessing. When eating French fries and ketchup one only needs to make a #5 on the French fries.

10) Similarly, if a food contains a number of ingredients wherein one is clearly primary and the others are secondary, one only makes the blessing on the primary. For example, one only makes a #2 on the noodles in a lasagna. If one is eating a beef stew with very tiny pieces of vegetables, but big chunks of meat, then the blessing should only be made over the meat (#6). If the ingredients are all of equal prominence, one should make the unique blessing called for by each ingredient.

11) Any food normally requiring a special blessing (#2 through #5) that has been completely liquefied or otherwise rendered unrecognizable only required a #6. Pringles is a good example – they get a #6

12) If you are every unsure as to what blessing to say, or have forgotten what to do, then make a #6. In a pinch it will cover anything.

**After Blessings**

We also bless God after having partaken of his benefit. This blessing is in many ways a greater expression of thanks than the fore-blessing.

As mentioned in Lesson 15, the *Midrash* records a blessing after meals that was taught by Abraham to non-Jews:

**7) Blessed is the God of the universe, of whose bounty we have eaten.**

This blessing should be said any time one has eaten any amount and feels satisfied.[5] It may be enhanced with the addition of Psalms or other specifically composed texts. These additional texts should be added before the blessing.

## Blessings on Aromas

The following are blessing on various types of aromatic benefit. There is no after-blessing for these blessings.

If you are ever in a pinch and don't know which one to say, or are uncertain as to what you are smelling, use #8.

---

[5] After-blessings differ greatly between Jews and Noahides. This is because the text of most after-blessings is unique to Jews alone. Furthermore, the existence of this Midrashic blessing trumps the use of any of the Jewish after-blessings by Noahides.

**Upon Smelling Spices (Cloves, Cinnamon, Nutmeg, etc) or Natural Incenses:**

> *8) Blessed are you, our God, sovereign of the universe, who creates species of spices.*

**Upon Smelling Fragrant Trees and their Flowers**

Here we apply the same definition of trees mentioned above for the blessings on fruit. This blessing would be said over any tree or flower with a woody stalk (i.e. roses):

> *9) Blessed are you, Lord, our God, sovereign of the universe, who creates fragrant trees.*

**Upon Smelling Fragrant Grasses, Herbs, and Their Flowers**

Here we apply the same definition used above for ground vegetation. This blessing would be used when smelling lemongrass, tulips, or orchids:

> *10) Blessed are you, Lord, our God, sovereign of the universe, who creates fragrant grasses.*

**When Smelling Fragrant Fruits (i.e. an Esrog)**
> *11) Blessed are you, Lord, our God, sovereign of the universe, who gives good fragrance to fruits.*

## Blessings of Praise and Gratitude

**Upon Seeing Lighting**

This blessing, as the one on thunder and rainbows, may only be said once per rainstorm. In order to say it twice, the sky would have to clear completely and then another storm roll in. Or, a person would travel to a place where there is another storm

> *12) Blessed are you, Lord, our God, sovereign of the universe, who fashions the work of creation.*

This blessing is also said whenever one sees exceptionally impressive natural phenomena such as giant mountains, shooting stars, or great rivers. It is also said when one experiences an earthquake. However, in these cases, it can only be said after 30 days have passed since the last time the phenomenon was experienced. This 30-day rule will be discussed more below.

### Upon Hearing Thunder

13) *Blessed are you, Lord, our God, sovereign of the universe, whose power and might fills the world.*

### Upon Seeing a Rainbow

The rainbow was given as a sign of God's promise never to destroy the world again after the flood of Noah. Therefore, we recite the following blessing upon seeing the rainbow. We only recite it when we can see both ends of the bow in the sky:

14) *Blessed are you, Lord, our God, sovereign of the universe, who remembers the covenant, is faithful to His covenant, and who fulfills His word.*

### Upon Seeing the Ocean

**30-DAY RULE**

According to many, this blessing should also be said upon seeing the Mediterranean Sea. This blessing, and many of the following, is only said after thirty days have elapsed since the last time the sighting or event occurred. This is to preserve the freshness and impact of the blessing. For example: a person sees the ocean and makes the blessing. 15 days later, he sees the ocean again. This time, he should not recite a blessing. He only says another blessing if 30 days passes since this last sighting (which amounts to 45 days from the last time he made the blessing).

15) *Blessed are you, Lord, our God, sovereign of the universe, who makes the great sea.*

### Upon Seeing Things of Unsurpassed Beauty

This blessing is reserved for seeing exceptionally beautiful people, landscapes, or other such creations. The 30 day rule applies to this blessing.

16) *Blessed are you, Lord, our God, sovereign of the universe, who has such in His world.*

### Upon Seeing Things Strange and Grotesque

This blessing is reserved for seeing animals or people that are strange or deformed. The 30 day rule applies to this blessing.

17) *Blessed are you, Lord, our God, sovereign of the universe, who varies the forms of his creations.*

### Upon Seeing Fruit Trees in Bloom

This blessing may only be recited once a year, in the spring, and upon flowering fruit trees:

18) *Blessed are you, Lord, our God, sovereign of the universe, into whose world, lacking nothing, He created good creatures and trees, for the benefit of man.*

## Upon Seeing an Outstanding Torah Scholar

This blessing is reserved for the very few, very special leaders of the Torah world. There are, at most, less than 10 people in the world for whom this blessing would be said. The 30 day rule applies to this blessing.

19) *Blessed are you, Lord, our God, sovereign of the universe, who has apportioned his wisdom to those who hear Him.*

## Upon Seeing an Extraordinary Secular Scholar

Like the blessing above, it is reserved for very few people. This is made upon seeing the Albert Einstein's and Isaac Newtons of the world (I know one leading Rabbi who said it when he met Steven Hawking). At least one authority, though, holds that it may be said for any Nobel Prize winner. The 30 day rule applies to this blessing.

20) *Blessed are you, Lord, our God, sovereign of the universe, who has given of his wisdom to flesh and blood.*

## Upon Seeing a Gentile King

To merit this blessing, the ruler must 1) rule lawfully, 2) cannot be overruled, and 3) has absolute power over the life and death of his subjects. There are virtually no heads of state in our times who meet these qualifications. The custom today is to recite an altered form of the blessing, omitting the references to God's kingship. This makes it merely a statement of praise and not an actual blessing. The 30 day rule applies to this blessing.

21) *Blessed is he who has given of his glory to flesh and blood.*

## Upon Seeing, for the First Time, a Friend Who Has Recovered From a Mortal Illness

22) *Blessed is the merciful one, sovereign of the universe, who has given you to us and not to the dust.*

## Upon Hearing News That Benefits Oneself and Others

23) *Blessed are you, our God, sovereign of the universe, who is good and does good!*

**Upon Hearing Extremely Bad News, Such as the Death of a Person, or News of a Calamity or Plague:**

24) *Blessed is the true judge.*

**If One Has Experienced a Miracle in a Certain Place**
If a person believes that he has benefitted from a miracle, then the following blessing is recited each time he is in the place where the miracle occurred. However, it is only recited if one visits the place once every 30 days or more. If one visits the place more regularly than every 30 days, the freshness of the experience will quickly wear off.

25) *Blessed are you, Lord, our God, sovereign of the universe, who performed a miracle for me in this place.*

THE YESHIVA PIRCHEI SHOSHANIM SHULCHAN ARUCH LEARNING PROJECT

# The Noahide Laws – Lesson Twenty

© **Yeshiva Pirchei Shoshanim 2017**
This shiur may not be reproduced in any
form without permission of the copyright holder.

164 Village Path, Lakewood NJ 08701 732.370.3344
164 Rabbi Akiva, Bnei Brak, 03.616.6340

## Outline of This Lesson:

1. Introduction

2. Non-Jewish Torah Study: Praiseworthy or Prohibited?

    a. Sanhedrin 59a – Full Text

    b. Analysis

    c. Conclusion

3. Liable to Death

    a. Rambam

4. Types of Torah & Types of Torah

    a. Meiri

5. Delving Vs. Learning

    a. Machaneh Chaim

6. What May Be Studied

    a. Written Torah

    b. Oral Torah & Works on Law

7. Do Noahides Make a Blessing on Torah Study?

# Torah Study I

## Introduction

Do Noahides have a *mitzvah* of Torah study? The answer is "no," but with a very big asterisk. As with many topics, our understanding is enhanced by first examining the Jewish *mitzvah*. As mentioned in an earlier lesson, not all *mitzvos* apply to all Jews at all times. Nevertheless, every Jew is explicitly commanded to study the entire Torah and all of the *mitzvos*.

However, there is no place where Noahides are commanded to study Torah. To the contrary, we find that the Noahide laws actually restrict non-Jewish study of Torah. Furthermore, there are prohibitions in Jewish law on what Torah Jews may teach to Noahides.

When examining the topic of Torah study for non-Jews, we have to look at three factors:

1) What the Noahide laws restrict non-Jews from studying,

2) What Jewish law restricts Jews from teaching, and

3) The positive aspects of non-Jewish Torah study mentioned in the sources.

## Non-Jewish Torah Study: Praiseworthy, or Prohibited?

The main source for the status of non-Jewish Torah study is a Talmudic passage from Sanhedrin 59a. We will first examine the complete passage, and then break it down line-by-line as understood by the primary Talmudic commentaries:

**SANHEDRIN 59A - FULL TEXT**

[Material in brackets has been inserted by the editor and translator]

[Proposition:] *Rabbi Yochanan said: A non-Jew who delves into Torah is liable to death, as it says: "The Torah was commanded through Moses as* **the inheritance** *of the Children of Jacob."* It is an inheritance for the Jews, not for the Non-Jews.

- [Question:] *Why is this [prohibition] not included explicitly in their seven laws?*
    - [Answer #1:] *One explanation is that* **"the inheritance"** *prohibits Non-Jews from delving into Torah because it would constitute stealing.*
    - [Answer #2:] *Another explanation is that the word for* **"the inheritance"** *should be read as "betrothed." Therefore, a non-Jew who studies Torah is considered as having committed adultery with a betrothed woman.*

[Challenge to the Proposition:] *They* [the other Rabbis] *challenged this teaching from a Braisa:*[2]

*Rabbi Meir would say: From where do we know that even a non-Jew who delves into Torah study is like a Kohen Gadol* [high priest]? *For it is written: "...that* **Adam**, *a man, shall keep them and live through them."*[3] *The verse does not say that a Kohen, Levi, or Yisrael, shall do and live through them, but rather "a man."*

- [Answer and resolution:] *There, in the Braisa, Rabbi Meir is referring to a non-Jew who studies his seven mitzvos. Rabbi Yochanan is referring to a non-Jew who studies mitzvos and Torah that have no application to him.*

---

[1] Deut. 33:4.

[2] The Braisa, as discussed in earlier lessons, is a statement of the oral Torah parallel and of equal authority to the Mishnah.

[3] Lev. 18:19.

## ANALYSIS OF SANHEDRIN 59A

[Proposition:] *Rabbi Yochanan said: A non-Jew who delves into Torah is liable to death, as it says: "The Torah was commanded through Moses as **the inheritance** of the Children of Jacob."[4] It is an inheritance for the Jews, not for the Non-Jews.*

As will all Talmudic discourse, this section opens with a proposition supported by a proof. Propositions are either supported by logic or a scriptural verse. In this case, Rabbi Yochanan invokes Deuteronomy 33:4 as his source for the proposition that, apparently, all non-Jewish Torah study is prohibited.

- [Question:] *Why is this [prohibition] not included explicitly in their seven laws?*

The Talmud is surprised that a prohibition serious enough for "liable to death" is not recorded explicitly as part of the Noahide laws. The Talmud explains that, though not specifically listed, it is part of the Noahide laws via derivation:

  o [Answer #1:] *One explanation is that "**the inheritance**" prohibits Non-Jews from delving into Torah because it would constitute stealing.*

By describing the Torah as an "inheritance" the Torah is telling us that it is the right of Israel alone, not of other nations. Therefore, one who misappropriates that right is, therefore, guilty of theft.

  o [Answer #2:] *Another explanation is that the word for "**the inheritance**" should be read as "betrothed." Therefore, a non-Jew who studies Torah is considered as having committed adultery with a betrothed woman.*

Both here and in Pesachim 49b, the Talmud points out that the word *Morasha*, inheritance, may also be read *Morasa*, betrothed. Both Answer #1 and #2 are explaining that the prohibition of non-Jewish Torah study is not recorded as a stand-alone prohibition because either answer places it conceptually under an existing category of prohibition: either theft or sexual immorality. Both of these answers, however, are difficult for reasons that we shall soon see.

Despite the proposition, Rabbi Yochanan's claim of a blanket prohibition of Torah study for non-Jews is contradicted:

[Challenge to the Proposition:] *They [the other Rabbis] challenged this teaching from a Braisa:[5]*

---

[4] Deut. 33:4.

[5] A *braisa*, as discussed in earlier lessons, is a statement of the oral Torah parallel and of equal authority to the Mishnah.

> *Rabbi Meir would say: From where do we know that even a non-Jew who delves into Torah study is like a Kohen Gadol [high priest]? For it is written: "…that **Adam**, a man, shall keep them and live through them."[6] The verse does not say that a Kohen, Levi, or Yisrael, shall do and live through them, but rather "a man."*

The word *Adam* can refer to mankind, a man, humanity, or the first man, depending on context and usage. Typically, in the *Tanach Adam* implies the nation of Israel.[7] Rabbi Meir argues that, in this verse, *Adam* should be understood in the universal sense of Jew and non-Jew alike.[8] The proof verse here teaches that all mankind can benefit from the Torah. The comparison of a non-Jew who delves into Torah with a high priest is derived from Shem, the Son of Noah. Shem was the leading scholar of the Noahide laws in his time and was praised as a "priest of God on High."[9]

The Talmud's challenge is essentially asking: how do we square Rabbi Yochanan's derivation of the prohibition of non-Jewish Torah study with Rabbi Meir's apparent endorsement of it?

- [Answer and resolution:] *There, in the Braisa, Rabbi Meir is referring to a non-Jew who studies his seven mitzvos. Rabbi Yochanan is referring to a non-Jew who studies mitzvos and Torah that have no application to him.*

**CONCLUSION**

The conclusion of the Talmud is, as is often the case, is that Rabbis Yochanan and Meir are not arguing. Rather, they agree and are teaching two sides of the same issue:

- Rabbi Yochanan: Non-Jews who study areas of the Torah that do not apply to them are liable to death.

- Rabbi Meir: Non-Jews who study the parts of the Torah which do apply to them are comparable to Shem, a priest of God.

Non-Jews may only study those portions of the Torah that are essential to their practice and faith as Noahides. Areas of the Torah that pertain only to Jewish mitzvos are prohibited.

---

[6] Lev. 18:19.

[7] See Ezekiel 34:31 and *Yevamos* 61a.

[8] See Rashi and Tosafos here.

[9] See Genesis 14:18. Rashi explains that Malchitzedek was Noah's son Shem.

## Liable to Death?

Assigning the death penalty for non-Jewish Torah study is deeply problematic.

Let's examine the issue again: The Talmud was bothered by the fact that Rabbi Yochanan claimed death as the apparent penalty for non-Jewish Torah study.
If this is such a serious prohibition, then why is it not prohibited explicitly as part of the 7 laws?

The Talmud's answer is puzzling: it teaches that the prohibition is learned by derivation from theft or from sexual immorality. That answer is fine for explaining how the prohibition fits into the Noahide laws. Yet, we are still left with the original question: If it is a death penalty issue, then why it is not mentioned explicitly? The assumption of the question is that something as serious as a death penalty crime is not learned by derivation or implication (this is, in fact, a truism of Torah law).

Another problem is the description of non-Jewish Torah study as "theft." A specific requirement of actionable theft under Torah law is the loss of tangible property. Non-Jewish Torah study does not result in the loss of any property to Israel. Therefore, the case couldn't even be tried! Similarly, if non-Jewish Torah study is compared to adultery, it certainly cannot be tried as adultery because actual adultery never happened.

Clearly, we see that the death penalty can never be administered for a non-Jew learning Torah. So, what is Rabbi Yochanan's point in telling us this?

**MAIMONIDES**

The Maimonides's all-seeing eye apparently noted the same issue, writing:

- From *Hilchos Melachim* 8:10 – *Moshe gave over the Torah and the Mitzvos only to Israel "an inheritance to the Children of Israel." It is also permitted for anyone who wants to convert.*

- From *Hilchos Melachim* 9:10 - *A Non-Jew who learns Torah is obligated to the death penalty. He may learn only his seven mitzvos. If he learned Torah, kept Shabbos, or took on new mitzvos, we beat him, punish him, and inform him that he deserves death.* **However, we do not actually kill him.**

The Rambam tells us that, although a non-Jew is obligated to death, he is not actually put to death. The *Meiri*, *Yad David*, *Kesef Mishnah*, and all other commentaries explain that a non-Jew who studies Torah is in fact liable to the death penalty. However, their sentence is only carried out by the hands of heaven and not human courts. We will discuss this point more in a future lesson.

## Types of Study & Types of Torah

In the above-quoted section of the Talmud (from Sanhedrin) it is important to note that, *lilmod ha-Torah*, the **study** of Torah, is never referred to. Instead, the Talmud only discusses *she-osek ba-Torah*, **delving** into Torah.

What is the difference between "delving" into the Torah and merely "learning" Torah? Also, what is called "Torah" for the sake of this prohibition? Does it mean the written Torah, or the oral Torah? What about kabbalah or Midrash?

**THE MEIRI ON SANHEDRIN**

The Meiri[10] summarizes the views of the sages as follows:

> *[The prohibition is only] if he is involved in Torah not for the sake of keeping the mitzvos, but only because he desires to fathom the wisdom of the written and oral Torahs.*

The Meiri is telling us three things:

1) That "delving" means learning deeply to "fathom the wisdom" of the Torah.

2) That the prohibition of delving applies to both the written and oral Torahs.

3) That "delving" is permitted for the sake of learning the Noahide laws, but not for learning any other areas of Torah. This implies that basic (non-delving) learning, even of areas not relevant to Noahides, is permitted.

## Delving vs. Learning

**THE MACHANEH CHAIM**

The distinction between delving and learning for the purpose of Torah law is explained by Rabbi Chaim Sofer in his *Machaneh Chaim*.[11] Rabbi Sofer divides Torah study into two categories: *mishnah* and *gemora*. Now, there are actual texts called Mishnah and Gemora (we have discussed them previously). However, the categories of *mishnah* and *gemora* discussed here refer categories of Torah study (for simplicity, we will refer to the texts of the Mishnah and Gemora with capital letters and the categories with lower case letters).

---

[10] As noted in prior lessons, practical application of the Meiri's opinions is not easy. In this case, though, the Meiri is summarizing the conclusions reached by many other commentaries.

[11] I: 7.

The category of *mishnah* refers to anything composed for the sake of basic knowledge, whether it is of the oral or written law. In contrast, *gemora* refers to the derivation of laws and exploration of the deeper meanings and structures within the text,[12] either oral or written. All study of *Mishnah* is permitted for Noahides, while the only *gemora* permitted is that which pertains to Noahide observance.

Another very important point here is that method of study and material of study are fundamentally the same thing. For example, if one studies the Torah text using the methods of the Talmud, or simply studies the text of the Talmud, both constitute *gemora* – delving. This is because they both accomplish the same type of prohibited study.

## What May Be Studied?

**THE WRITTEN TORAH & TANAKH**

It is permitted for a Noahide to read the 24 books of the Tanakh. This is clear from many sources, most notably Maimonides who writes that a non-Jew may even read from a Torah scroll.[13] A non-Jew may even learn commentaries on the text provided that the purpose of the commentaries is to explain the plain meaning of the text (i.e. *Rashi* and *Nachmanides* – these fall under the category of *mishnah*).

However, studying commentaries which delve into the intent of the text using methods similar to the Talmud are prohibited (this would constitute *gemora*). Such classic commentaries as the *Sifri* and *Mechilta* are, therefore, prohibited for study. One is also forbidden from learning the *Kabbalistic* and *Midrashic* interpretation of the Torah unless they pertain to Noahism.

**ORAL TORAH & WORKS OF LAW**

Any sections of Torah literature composed for the sake of basic knowledge, whether it be of the oral or the written law, is permitted for study (because it is *mishnah*). Therefore, the Mishnah, the Mishnah Torah (by Maimonides), and the Shulchan Aruch (Code of Jewish Law) are all permissible because they teach the laws and conclusions without delving into the reasons and methods of its derivation.

However, the commentaries on these works (including those printed in the margins) are prohibited for study.

---

[12] See also *Hagahos Yaavetz* on Sanhedrin 59a.

[13] *Hilchos Sefer Torah 10:8.*

## Do Noahides Make a Blessing on Torah Study?

There is no commandment of Torah study for Noahides. Intrinsically, a non-Jew never need study the Noahide laws. His only obligation is to obey them. Of course, this is not possible unless he studies them. By fiat of logic and necessity, Torah study is therefore part of Noahism.[14]

However, mere study of the Torah is not something that a Noahide receives particular praise for. It is a purely utilitarian activity.

Yet, for going beyond the mere utilitarian need for study and "delving" into his obligations, a Noahide is praised like a High Priest. This delving is a voluntary activity, while basic study is a necessary activity. Neither, however is a *Chov*, an obligatory commandment, upon which the blessing "...who has commanded us..." is said. Therefore, Noahides should not make a blessing on Torah study.

Nevertheless, a Noahide receives tremendous reward for his "delving" into the Torah, which is of great value in the eyes of heaven.

## Summary of This Lesson

- Any basic material (*mishnah*) may be studied whether it does or does not apply to Noahism.

- Any material which deals with deeper aspects, derivations, or analysis of the Torah (*gemora*) may only be studied if it is directly relevant to Noahide laws or practice.

- One who studies that which he is injucted against is liable to death at the hands of heaven.

**Examples of Texts Permitted for Basic Study – Complete Texts That May be Studied**

- Text of the Torah
- Text of the Prophets
- Text of the Writings
- The commentaries of Rashi, Ramban, Kli Yakar, Ibn Ezra, or Abarbanel on the above.
- Text of the Mishnah

---

[14] See Meiri, Sanhedrin 59a. See also *Maharsha* to Avodah Zara 3a.

- Text of any compilations of Torah law such as Mishnah Torah of the Rambam, Shulchan Aruch, or Kitzur Shulchan Aruch.

**Examples of Text Prohibited for Study Unless Pertaining to Noahide Practice**

- Talmud
- Zohar & Kabbalah[15]
- Midrash
- Topics on theology or philosophy which do not deal directly with Noahide practice.
- Commentaries on the Mishnah
- Works of law which explain the derivations of the laws such as the Mishnah Berurah, Aruch HaShulchan, Shulchan Aruch HaRav.
- Commentaries on Mishnah Torah of the Rambam, Shulchan Aruch, or Kitzur Shulchan Aruch.
- Any books on Jewish law which go beyond a practical presentation of the rules.

---

[15] See also Tos. Chagigah 13a.

THE YESHIVA PIRCHEI SHOSHANIM SHULCHAN ARUCH LEARNING PROJECT

# The Noahide Laws – Lesson Twenty One

**© Yeshiva Pirchei Shoshanim 2017**
This shiur may not be reproduced in any
form without permission of the copyright holder.

164 Village Path, Lakewood NJ 08701 732.370.3344
164 Rabbi Akiva, Bnei Brak, 03.616.6340

## Outline of This Lesson:

1. Introduction

2. *Chagigah* 13b: Teaching Torah to Non-Jew

3. *Bava Kamma* 38a: A Contradiction

4. A Curious Omission

5. What May and May Not Be Taught

6. Teaching Noahides

7. Summary

# Torah Study II

## Introduction

In the previous lesson we learned the Talmud in tractate Sanhedrin 59a that teaches that a non-Jew who delves into his laws deserves honor and respect like a *Kohen Gadol*, a high priest. However, a non-Jew who delves into Torah that he may not learn deserves death. This latter law applies only to in-depth or analytical Torah study. Superficial explorations of any part of Torah are permitted to anyone. In this lesson we are going to look at non-Jewish Torah study from "the other side:" the Jewish prohibition of teaching parts of Torah to non-Jews. While this prohibition devolves on Jews, it has implications for Noahides and is therefore important to know.

## *Chagigah* 13b: Teaching Torah to Non-Jews

In *Chagigah* 13b the Talmud states the following:

> Said Rav Ami: Do not give over the words of the Torah to a non-Jew for it is written: 'He did not do so to any other nation and of His laws they were not informed [Psalm 147:19-20].'

*Tosafos*[1] to *Bava Kamma* 13a understands this verse as commanding a positive *mitzvah* to Jews to safeguard their unique relationship with their Torah.

*Tosafos* to *Chagigah* 13b asks a very good question: If the Talmud has already stated an injunction against non-Jewish Torah study (Sanhedrin 59a), then Jews should be prohibited from teaching non-Jews Torah because of *lifnei iver* – placing a

---

[1] D.h. *Karu*.

stumbling block before the blind (see Lev. 19:14). After all, was a Jew to teach a non-Jew Torah, the Jew would be causing the non-Jew to transgress! Why then does *Chagigah* 13b instead learn the prohibition from Psalm 147?

*Tosafos* proposes the only answer that makes sense given the circumstances: the Talmud must be talking about a case where there is another Jew available who is willing to teach the non-Jew Torah. *Lifnei iver* – placing a stumbling block – only applies when a Jew directly enables another's transgression.

If the transgressor could accomplish their deed without the Jew's involvement, then there is no prohibition of *lifnei iver*. *Tosafos* understands our case as one in which there are Jews around who are willing to teach prohibited Torah to non-Jews. In such a case, there is no issue of *lifnei iver*. Nevertheless, the Talmud teaches that there is another prohibition in effect. That prohibition is this one learned from the words of Psalm 147.

From this selection and from *Tosafos*[2] we learn two things:

1) A Jew cannot teach Torah to non-Jews because of *lifnei iver*. However, if there are Jews available and willing to teach non-Jews Torah, then *lifnei iver* does not apply. In such a case,

2) All Jews are nonetheless prohibited by Psalm 147 from teaching Torah to non-Jews.

## Bava Kamma 38a: A Contradiction

The Talmud Bava Kamma 38a records the following:

> *The Roman government sent two officers to the sages of Israel. They said "Teach us your Torah!" They read it once, reviewed it, and then read it a third time*[3]...

In light of what we have just learned, this Talmud presents an obvious problem! What is the resolution? *Tosafos* again comes to the rescue, proposing two answers:

1) The decree against teaching Torah does not require one to give his life or suffer hardship rather than transgress. Since the teaching of these two officers was a decree of the Roman government, the sages acceded. Or,

---

[2] Tos. Rid to *Bava Kama* 38 proposes the same understanding as our *Tosafos* here.

[3] The Rashba explains that they either studied it with the Sages three times, or that the sages taught them three things: Tanakh, Mishnah, then *Gemora*.

2) Perhaps the two officials converted, in which case teaching them was certainly permitted.[4]

The *Yam Shel Shlomo* notes that *Tosafos* only provides two answers to a problem when one of the answers is somehow insufficient. The problem with *Tosafos's* first answer, he explains, is that it is far from certain that it represents actual *halakhah*, practice. Perhaps the teaching of Torah to non-Jews is prohibited even upon pain of death? Hence we need another explanation: perhaps the two romans converted.

From this *gemora* (section of the Talmud) and its commentaries, we learn a number of possible exceptions to the prohibition of teaching Torah to non-Jews.

## A Curious Omission

Though all of the Talmudic commentaries agree that there is a prohibition of teaching Torah to non-Jews, it is not recorded in any of the major *halakhic* (legal) codes. Many people who make their careers from teaching Torah to non-Jews have claimed to rely upon this omission to justify their actions. However, they are in grave error. Many, many *Acharonim* (later scholars) explain that this law is, in fact, <u>not</u> omitted in the later codes. Maimonides[5] and Shulchan Aruch[6] both codify a general prohibition against teaching Torah to those who should not receive it.

Later *poskim* understand that the prohibition against teaching Torah to non-Jews is subsumed within this general prohibition.[7] Furthermore, the Shulchan Aruch[8] records that it is forbidden to teach Torah to an *eved Kenaani* (a Canaanite

---

[4] Despite the text making no reference to conversion, it is entirely possible that they did convert. We can infer this by contrasting our passage with *Megillah 9a*. *Megillah* 9a teaches that the sages were forced to translate the Torah into Greek. However, to disguise the true meaning of certain passages, the sages made a number of subtle textual changes. Yet, *Bava Kamma* goes on to tell us that the sages taught the two officers the exact Torah. Why didn't the sages alter certain passages? It must be that the officers had converted. This answer has its own vulnerabilities, however.

[5] *Hilchos Talmud Torah 4:1*.

[6] YD 246:7.

[7] See also *Igros Moshe* YD III:89; *Minchas Chinuch* 232:3; See also *Beer Sheva Beer Mayim Chayim* 14. Though the *Beer Sheva* is doubtful as to the final *Halacha*, he acknowledges a prohibition of teaching to those who are unworthy. He notes that Moshe smashed the tablets because the Jews who participated in the sin were unfit to learn Torah. He goes on to draw a comparison between the Jews who participated in the golden calf and non-Jews to conclude that non-Jews are in the category of "not fit to study."

[8] YD 267:71.

indentured servant). This prohibition would naturally include teaching Torah to a non-Jew.

Just as the prohibition enjoining a non-Jew from learning Torah is not something to be taken lightly (it is punishable at the hands of heaven!), so too Jews should not take lightly the prohibition against teaching Torah to non-Jews.
To reinforce the seriousness of the issue, Rabbi Shlomo Luria, author of the aforementioned *Yam Shel Shlomo*, writes[9]:

> *Woe to those who teach Torah to non-Jews! Their sin is greater than they could ever possibly bear and they will not see the redemption of Zion.*[10]

## What May and May Not Be Taught

All of the scholars agree that the Oral Torah may not be taught to non-Jews. The status of the written Torah is not so clear.

Famously, Rabbi Tzvi Hirsch Chayes wrote in his commentary on the Talmud[11] that the *poskim* (decisors of Torah law) have decided that it is forbidden to teach the Oral Torah yet permitted to teach the Written Torah. Yet, for over 150 years scholars have been mystified as to what Rabbi Chayes is talking about. There are no prior *poskim* who make such a distinction![12]

Support, however, might be implied in an earlier source. The aforementioned *Yam Shel Shlomo*[13] seems to understand the Talmud's prohibition as directed only at teaching the Oral Torah.[14] We may infer that the *Yam Shel Shlomo* would permit teaching the written Torah.

There are plenty, though, who oppose teaching even the written Torah to non-Jews. Most important is the *Sheiltei Gibborim*[15] who holds that one may not teach the Chumash but may teach the Prophets and Writings.

---

[9] To *Bava Kamma* 4:9.

[10] In all fairness, his statement may only be in opposition to those who teach Oral Torah to non-Jews.

[11] To *Sotah* 35a.

[12] See *Sdei Chemed*, *Yabia Omer*, and many others.

[13] Ibid.

[14] This is how the *Tzitz Eliezer* XVI: 55 understands the *Yam Shel Shlomo*.

[15] To *Avodah Zarah* 6a, in the Rif.

The *poskim* have not reached a clear consensus on the issue. These are some of the opinions:

- Rabbi Naftali Tzvi Yehudah Berlin (the *Netziv*) holds[16] that it is permitted to teach the written Torah to non-Jews because God commanded Joshua to write the Torah in 70 languages. Therefore, it must be permissible to teach if God himself has ordered it made accessible to the non-Jews.

- The *Yehudah Yaaleh* permits teaching the Written Torah because the Talmud only prohibits non-Jews from "delving," which implies studying the Oral Torah.

- Rabbi Ovadia Yosef in his **Yabia Omer**[17] – Prohibits teaching Oral or Written Torah to non-Jews.

- Rabbis Moshe Feinstein[18] and Eliezer Yehudah Waldenburg[19] declined to decide completely between the *Yam Shel Shlomo* and the *Shiltei Gibborim*. Their conclusions are hedged: Ideally one should not teach the Written Torah to Non-Jews. If one does, he should not be rebuked because he has support upon which to rely. One may definitely teach the Prophets and Writings to non-Jews. Their view is the most widely relied upon.

- Rabbi Yosef Shalom Eliyashiv[20] - Based upon the Zohar, Rabbi Elyashiv states that one may teach no part of Torah whatsoever to non-Jews other than what is relevant to the Noahide laws.[21]

---

[16] *Meromei Sadeh, Chagigah.*

[17] VII YD 7.

[18] *Igros Moshe* YD III 90.

[19] *Tzitz Eliezer* XVI 55.

[20] *Kovetz Teshuvos* III YD 142.

[21] This is a very strange conclusion. The Rav decides solely according to the Zohar (unusual in and of itself), yet without taking into account or discussing the *Shiltei Gibborim* or other classic sources. In general, many of Rav Elyashiv's printed works are treated with suspicion; it is well known that he had no editorial control over their preparation or publication. This issue is discussed in Artscroll's biography of Rav Elyashiv.

## Teaching Noahides

The sages conclude[22] that Jews are permitted and even encouraged to teach non-Jews the parts of the Torah relating to their Noahide obligations. However, the extent of what may be taught is subject to some disagreement. The *Maharsha*[23] is strict that only the basic tenets of what is permitted and forbidden may be taught to Noahides, but not anything else. They should be left on their own to delve deeper. Others, such as Maimonides, are much more lenient.

The degree of instruction that Jews may provide in the Noahide laws is a matter of varying opinions.

## Attending Torah Classes

Non-Jews may only attend classes on material that is permitted for them to learn. Therefore, Noahides may attend classes on the weekly *parsha* or very basic classes in Mishnah or Torah law. However, classes on Talmud, Midrash, or Kabbalah are prohibited. If a non-Jew does sit in on such a class, must the Jewish teacher stop teaching until the non-Jew leaves?

Rabbi Moshe Feinstein was asked a very similar question[24]. He answered that the prohibition of teaching Torah applies only when the instruction is actually directed to or intended for non-Jews. If the instruction is intended for and directed to Jews, yet a non-Jew happens to sit-in, there is no transgression committed from the side of the Jew. However, the non-Jew is transgressing his own prohibition by studying that which is prohibited to him.

---

[22] See *Yabia Omer*, *Dvar Moshe*, *Tosafos Chagigah* 13a, and many others. Note, however, that there are some who opine that even teaching non-Jews the Noahide laws is forbidden. The *Yad Eliezer* and *Divrei Yissaschar* acknowledge that, even though a non-Jew who delves into his obligations is like a *Kohen Gadol*, it is still forbidden for Jews to teach him the Noahide laws. *Eyn Yaakov* on *Chagigah* quotes a *Tosafos* which states that teaching non-Jews about the Noahide laws was only a *mitzvah* before the giving of the Torah. After Sinai it became prohibited for Jews to teach them any Torah. This *Eyn Yaakov* must be discounted, however, because the *Tosafos* he quotes has never been located. See *Igros Moshe* YD III 89.

[23] To *Chagigah* ibid.

[24] *Igros Moshe* YD II 132.

## Summary of Lesson 21

1. Jews are prohibited from teaching Torah to non-Jews.

2. The sages agree that Jews should instruct non-Jews in the Noahide Laws

3. There is significant disagreement as to the extent and depth of this instruction. While non-Jews may delve as deeply as they wish into their obligations, many authorities do not permit Jewish assistance in this. There is a variety of contemporary rabbinic opinions and practices.

4. Jews may not teach the Oral Torah to non-Jews.

5. Whether or not Jews may teach the written Torah to non-Jews is a matter of some dispute. Nevertheless, it is accepted today that they may teach them the written Torah (including the prophets and writings).

6. Non-Jews should not attend any Torah classes that teach material prohibited to them.

7. If a non-Jew does attend such a class, the teacher does not need to stop teaching. However, his continued teaching should not be seen as condoning the non-Jew's participation.

THE YESHIVA PIRCHEI SHOSHANIM SHULCHAN ARUCH LEARNING PROJECT

# The Noahide Laws – Lesson Twenty Two

© **Yeshiva Pirchei Shoshanim 2017**
This shiur may not be reproduced in any
form without permission of the copyright holder.

## Outline of This Lesson:

1. Introduction
2. Classic *Semikhah*
3. Modern *Semikhah*
4. Problems With Modern *Semikhah*
5. Choosing a Rabbi
6. Kabbalah – Specialized Licenses
7. Honor Due to Torah Scholars
8. Honor Due to Torah Books

# Selecting a Rabbi

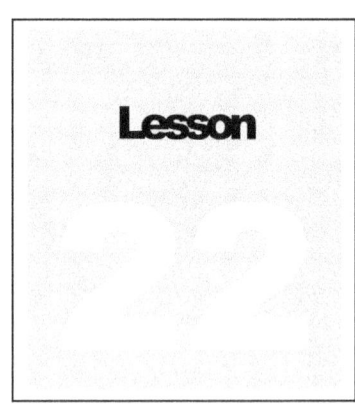

## Introduction

In previous lessons we examined the laws governing what Torah may be learned by non-Jews and what Torah may be taught to non-Jews by Jews. In this final lesson on Torah study, we are going to look at Rabbis, different types of Rabbis, and the requirement to show proper honor to Torah scholars and Torah books.

## Rabbinic Ordination: Classical *Semikhah*

*And Moses spoke to the Lord, saying: 'Let the Lord, the God of all flesh, set a man over the congregation, who may go out before them, and who may come in before them, and who may lead them out, and who may bring them in; that the congregation of the Lord be not as sheep which have no shepherd.' And the Lord said unto Moses: 'Take Joshua the son of Nun, a man in whom is spirit, and lay your hand upon him; and set him before Eleazer the priest, and before all the congregation; and give him a charge in their sight. And you shall put of your honor upon him that all the congregation of the children of Israel may hear. And he shall stand before Eleazer the priest, who shall inquire for him by the judgment of the Urim before the Lord; at his word shall they go out, and at his word they shall come in, both he, and all the children of Israel with him, even all the congregation.' And Moses did as the Lord commanded him; and he took Joshua, and set him before Eleazer the priest, and before the entire congregation. And he laid his hands upon him, and gave him a charge, as the Lord spoke by the hand of Moses.*[1]

*And Joshua the son of Nun was full of the spirit of wisdom; for Moses had laid his hands upon*

---

[1] Numbers 27:15-23.

*him; and the children of Israel hearkened unto him, and did as the Lord commanded Moses.*[2]

*And the God said to Moses: 'Gather unto Me seventy men of the elders of Israel, whom you know to be the elders of the people and officers over them; and bring them to the tent of meeting, that they may stand there with you. And I will come down and speak with you there; and I will take of the spirit which is upon you, and will put it upon them; and they shall bear the burden of the people with you, so that you should not have to bear it alone.*[3]

The "laying on of hands" and "placing the spirit" described in the above verses are the first examples Rabbinic ordination and the beginning of classical *Semikhah* (*Semikhah* is Hebrew for ordination). Joshua went on to ordain others, who in-turn taught and ordained their students down through the generations. This ordination was not a license to teach Torah or to lead a congregation – it was the transferring of divinely sanctioned authority from one scholar to another. This ordination imbued the holder with a spirit of wisdom, imparting holiness to his words and thoughts. *Semikhah* was required for certain roles; it was especially needed in order to serve in the Sanhedrin and other institutions of Torah law. Upon entry of the Jewish people into Israel, certain rules took effect governing how this ordination was given[4]:

- *Semikhah* could only be conveyed by a quorum of three judges, one of whom must himself have *Semikhah*.[5] *Semikhah* could be conferred verbally or in writing. The "laying on of hands" was only practiced in the earlier generations. It was not practiced beyond the generation of Moses and Joshua.

- Both the grantor and recipient must be in Israel at the time *Semikhah* is given.

- In order to receive *Semikhah*, one must be an expert in all areas of Torah law. He must also be of proper character and zealously observant of the mitzvos and words of the sages.

An important detail of rabbinic ordination is that it was tiered: ordination was given in specific areas of Torah knowledge. To receive any one of these ordinations, however, a scholar must be capable and fluent in all areas of Torah knowledge. The ordinations were, in ascending degrees:[6]

---

[2] Deuteronomy 34:9.

[3] Numbers 11:16-17.

[4] Most of this material is taken from Maimonides, *Hil. Sanhedrin* 4.

[5] *Sanhedrin* 13b-14a. *Hilchos Sanhedrin* 4:5.

[6] *Sanhedrin* 5a.

- *Yoreh Yoreh* (He shall instruct, he shall instruct) – This ordination was for matters of religious and ritual law.

- *Yadin Yadin* (He shall judge, he shall judge) – This ordination qualified the scholar to matters of civil, criminal, and monetary law.

- *Yatir Yatir* or *Yatir Bechoros Yatir* (He shall permit, he shall permit) – This ordination qualified its holder to rule on matters of animal sacrifices and ritual purity.

This chain of ordination passed unbroken for centuries until shortly after the Bar Kokhba rebellion (132 – 135 CE). In the wake of Bar Kokhba's failed attempt to re-establish Jewish autonomy, the Romans viewed *Semikhah* as a dangerous expression of the Jewish desire for self-rule. They also realized that, by ending *Semikhah*, they would destroy the Sanhedrin. What ensued was a brutal program of persecution and suppression. By imperial decree, giving *Semikhah* was made a capital offense with terrible consequences. Not only were the parties to the *Semikhah* executed, but absolute destruction was decreed for the city in which *Semikhah* was granted. To emphasize his point, the emperor also ordered the complete destruction of all villages and settlements located within 2000 *Amos* of that city's boundaries.[7]

By the fourth and fifth centuries the Romans had driven most of the rabbinic community across the border into what is now Iraq. With few sages remaining in Israel, the chain of *Semikhah* eventually broke.[8] For the next several centuries, the title "rabbi" would not be used.[9] Instead, a scholar would either be referred to as "*khokham*" (wise one) or, if he held a position of authority, as a *Gaon* (eminence).

### Rabbinic Ordination: Modern *Semikhah*

In modern times, *Semikhah* refers to a degree or diploma certifying one as having completed a course of study in halakhah, Jewish law. The impetus for this new *Semikhah* was the rise of the medieval university, which began to issue diplomas and degrees. Jewish communities, in constant flux, saw the value of credentialing its religious scholars. They called this academic degree *Semikhah* in

---

[7] *Sanhedrin* 14a.

[8] There are some Gaonic traditions indicating that ordination may have continued beyond the fourth century. See the *Kovetz Shaarei Tzedek*, p. 29-30 and *Sefer HaShtarot*, p. 132. However, even these concur that there is no modern *Semikhah*.

[9] The term "Rabbi" is not all that common in the Talmud either. There are many honorifics used in the Talmud for Torah scholars. However, most of them are referred to simply by their names or sobriquets.

commemoration of the classical *Semikhah*. While this *Semikhah* caught on in the European Jewish world, Sephardic communities did not adopt it until very late.

Today, *Semikhah* is given at three levels:

- **Rav U-Manhig** – The equivalent of a Bachelor's degree, this *Semikhah* originated in the 20th century at Ner Israel Rabbinical College in Baltimore, MD. It certifies the holder as a teacher and as knowing the basic laws of the synagogue ritual service and observance of the holidays. Not all yeshivas issue this *semikhah* or accept it as valid. Where accepted, the holder may use the title Rabbi.

- **Yoreh Yoreh** – Equivalent of a Master's degree. Based on the *classical Yoreh Yoreh*, this is usually awarded following a course of study in kashrus (dietary laws), Shabbat, *Niddah* (laws pertaining to married women), and *Aveilus* (mourning). Traditionally, the final exam is given in *Issur ve-heter* (a very detailed sub-section of the dietary laws). This is the most common *Semikhah* today. A Rabbi with this *Semikhah*, who holds a position of communal authority, may be called Rav.

- **Yadin Yadin** – Also based on the classical *Semikhah*, this ordination is the equivalent of a Ph.D. It requires extensive study of the laws of monetary and civil damages, as well as the laws of marriage and divorce. One who holds this ordination may be called a Rav or Dayan. In the US, however, they are usually called Rabbi or Rav.

There is a fourth level that is very uncommon in our times called *heter horaah* (although this term is confusingly applied to other ordinations as well) or *Semikhahs Moreh Horaah*. This is an all-encompassing *Semikhah* awarded to rare scholars who have mastered the entire body of Torah literature. Very few people receive this today.

## The Problems with Modern *Semikhah*

Students of Judaism and Noahism should be aware that there are many details (and problems) with modern *Semikhah*:

- *Semikhah* is first and foremost a certification in Torah Law. Biblical interpretation, philosophy, and theology, are rarely, if ever, part of the curriculum. *Semikhah* is only relevant to the study of Torah law – it is not awarded for knowledge of other areas.

- *Semikhah* is an academic degree attained after a course of study and examination. It is not awarded based on righteousness or character. There are people with *Semikhah* who are not particularly pleasant.

- One who has *Semikhah* at one level may not teach or answer questions about law from a higher level. Someone with *Yoreh Yoreh* should not answer questions about *Yadin Yadin* material.

- In the past 15 or 20 years, many yeshivas have begun awarding *semikhahs* in very specific areas of study. For example, someone may take a course in the laws of *Shabbos* and receive *semikhah* in *Shabbos* (this may even be done online). However, he may not know any other area of Torah law.

- Such a person must be very cautious about holding himself out as a Rabbi because he is not qualified to discuss anything other than the laws of Shabbat. There are many "area specific" Rabbis in the world today. Unfortunately, many hold themselves out as "Torah authorities" when, in actuality, they are woefully unqualified outside their narrow area of study. Of Rabbis who teach or rule on matters in which they are not thoroughly versed, Maimonides describes them as "evil, arrogant people."[10]

- Because it is possible to get *Semikhah* in only one narrow area, it means that one does have to be a Torah scholar anymore to be a Rabbi. Likewise, one doesn't need to be a rabbi to be a Torah scholar.

- One does not have to study at a yeshiva to attain *Semikhah*. Either a person can study at a yeshiva and receive *Semikhah* from the Yeshiva, or one can study privately and be examined by a renowned Torah scholar.

Ultimately, the world of Torah scholarship is a meritocracy – the greater scholars receive the greatest recognition and are accorded authority on the merits of their achievements. For this reason, many of the greatest Torah scholars and authorities of the past 150 years never bothered with *Semikhah*.

## Choosing a Rabbi

The only qualified Rabbis are those who are observant and received their training from orthodox institutions. If someone was ordained as a reform Rabbi, and subsequently became orthodox, their ordination remains invalid.

Know from where a Rabbi received *Semikhah*. Did he get it online, from a recognized Torah scholar, or from a Yeshiva? All three could be valid, depending

---

[10] *Hilchos Talmud Torah* 5:30.

on the source.

Also, what did the Rabbi have to study to receive his *Semikhah*? Was it one area (i.e. *Issur v'Heter*) or did he have to complete a long course of study? Most importantly – is the rabbi affiliated with a particular institution, or is he a "lone wolf?" "Lone wolf" rabbis who "do their own thing" should generally be avoided because they have no accountability to anyone other than themselves.

You must endeavor to find a Rabbi in whose scholarship you have confidence and who you believe will take your interests seriously. If you always agree with everything your Rabbi tells you, then your relationship with the rabbi is not healthy for you. You want to find a Rabbi who challenges you. Most important of all, you must find a Rabbi who is consistent in his teachings. A rabbi who changes his opinions to suit the audience at hand, or when he is challenged, should be avoided.

## Kabbalah – License

Besides ordination, there is another rabbinic credentialing called *kabbalah* – although this is similar to the Hebrew word for mysticism, it has an entirely different meaning here. A *kabblah* is a license to practice as a *mohel* (perform circumcision), *Sofer* (scribe) or *Shochet* (kosher slaughterer).

- **Mohel** – An unlicensed *mohel* should not be used. Additionally, unlicensed *mohalim* are exposed to tremendous liability. Besides the religious requirement for licensure, many countries have laws that enforce certification.

- **Sofer** – There is a tremendous number of unlicensed *soferim* (scribes) today. Many of these are producing non-kosher *mezuzos* and *Tefillin*. Without licensure, their work would still remain unacceptable because the work of an unlicensed *Sofer* (scribe) considered non-kosher even if the unlicensed Sofer is a Torah scholar and if their work is executed properly. Purchase of *safrus* from an unlicensed person is likewise prohibited.

- **Shochet** (a ritual slaughterer of animals) – The requirement of licensure for *shochtim* is very stringent. The meat of an unlicensed *Shochet* is treated as non-kosher even if he slaughtered the animal correctly. As a result the meat is either discarded or sold to non-Kosher meat companies.

## Honor Due to Torah Scholars

*Rise before an elderly person and stand before a wise man.[11]*

This teaches that we are obligated to show honor to a Torah scholar by standing in his presence. We must stand when a scholar enters or leaves a room if he is within six feet of us. For an exceptional scholar, we stand when he enters the room even from more than 6 feet away.

## The Honor Due to Torah Books

There are a number of rules that ensure the respectful treatment of holy books. The *Kitzur Shulchan Aruch* (Concise Code of Jewish Law), 28:4 to 10, summarizes these:

> *28:4 One should treat sacred books, even those other than a Torah scroll, with great respect. If placed on a bench, it is forbidden to sit on this bench unless the texts are placed on some object whose height is at least a handbreadth. It is surely forbidden to place such texts on the ground. A person should not put a sacred text on his lap and rest his arms upon it. When necessary, one may sit on a chest that contains other sacred books. However, this is forbidden if it contains a Torah scroll. Chumashim {The writing of the five books of Moses} may be placed on books of the Prophets and Sacred Writings. Books of the Sacred Writings may be placed on books of the Prophets and books of the Prophets may be placed on books of the Sacred Writings. However, we may not place books of the Prophets or of the Sacred Writings on Chumashim.*

> *28:5 A Torah scroll that has become worn should be placed in genizah. The same applies to other sacred texts, writings, and ritual articles. It is forbidden to burn them.*

> *28:6 One should not toss sacred texts or even works of Law or Aggadah. Similarly, it is forbidden to turn them upside down. If one finds one upside down, he should turn it the right way up.*

> *28:7 One should not urinate in the presence of holy texts. In an emergency, one should at the very least, see that they are placed ten handbreadths up.*

> *28:8 One should not make covers or mantles for a sacred article, from an article that was used for ordinary purposes. However, ex post facto, it is permitted. However, if it was made from an article that was used for idol worship, even after the fact, it is forbidden.*

---

[11] Leviticus 19:32.

*28:9      It is forbidden to use a holy text for one's own benefit - e.g., to stand it up for shade in the sun, or as a screen so that his colleague does not see what he is doing. However, if the sun is shining too brightly on the text that one is studying, one may use another text for shade, because one is not using it for one's own benefit. Similarly, to place a sacred text under another text from which one is studying to raise it, to make studying easier, is allowed. However, one should not place one text inside another, so that one will not need to search afterwards for the place one was learning. One should not rule a notebook on top of a sacred text since a notebook is not sacred until one has written in it. Similarly, one should not place paper and the like within a sacred text to be preserved.*

*28:10     One who destroys sacred texts transgresses a negative commandment, "Do not do so to the Lord, your God." We need to rebuke the binders of books, who (often) glue, in the covers of books, pages from sacred texts. Also great care should be taken when giving old holy texts to a gentile binder to rebind. One should remove the old covers and hide them, so the binder does not use them for secular books.*

THE YESHIVA PIRCHEI SHOSHANIM SHULCHAN ARUCH LEARNING PROJECT

# The Noahide Laws – Lesson Twenty Three

© **Yeshiva Pirchei Shoshanim 2017**
This shiur may not be reproduced in any
form without permission of the copyright holder.

## Outline of This Lesson:

1. Sanhedrin 58b – The Prohibition
2. Sanhedrin 58b – Commentary
3. Yevamos 48b – Shabbat & the Ger Toshav
4. Talmud Krisus 9a – A Similar Conversation & Conclusion
5. The Midrash Rabbah Explains...

# Shabbat I

## Introduction

The question of Noahide observance of Shabbat comes up a lot. Unfortunately, there is much confusion surrounding the issue. Some have encouraged Noahides to keep a form of Shabbat observance, mistakenly equating Noahides with *ger toshav* (as well as erroneously understanding the *ger toshav's* relationship to Shabbat). This confusion is understandable considering that the question involves advanced mechanics of Torah law and a beguiling array of often contradictory sources.

## Sanhedrin 58b – The Prohibition

*Said Reish Lakish: A non-Jew who refrains from labor for an entire day is liable for death, as it is written:*

> *"Day and night they shall not cease."(Genesis 8:22)*

*The master said: Their warning is sufficient to warrant their death.*

*Said Ravina: This is so even if a non-Jew refrained from work on Monday.*

*[Challenge:] If this is so, then let this prohibition be counted among the Noahide laws!*

*[Answer:] The Noahide laws are enumerated as prohibitions. They are not listed according to their positive aspects.*

## Sanhedrin 58b – Commentary

*Said Reish Lakish: A non-Jew who refrains from labor for an entire day is liable for death, as it is written:*

> *"Day and night they shall not cease."(Genesis 8:22)*

Explanation: This verse, at first glance, seems to refer to the progress of the seasons. However, Reish Lakish explains the word "they" as referring to man. Therefore, this verse is prohibiting Noah and his descendants from disengaging in the labor of the world for an entire day. This is a positive commandment that precludes observance of Shabbat. There is ambiguity though, as to whether this is a general prohibition on cessation of work or a specific prohibition on doing so for religious reasons.

*The master said: Their warning is sufficient to warrant their death.*

Explanation: This is the general rule for the transgression of a Noahide commandment for which a warning is evidenced in the Torah.[1] Certain prohibitions, however, are derived obliquely and are not subject to punishment by death.[2] The Rambam understands the punishment for keeping Shabbat as heavenly and not imposed by human courts.

*Said Ravina: This is so even if a non-Jew refrained from work on Monday.*

Explanation: The intent of Ravina's statement is unclear.

Rashi[3], Ridbaz[4], Rav Moshe[5] - They understand Ravina as telling us that gentiles are prohibited from establishing a particular 24-hour period to abstain from work for any reason. To take a day off occasionally for rest only, with no religious motivation, would be acceptable, however.

---

[1] See *Hilchos Melakhim* 9:14.

[2] See *Hilchos Melakhim* 10:6.

[3] Ad loc.

[4] Commentary to Rambam, *Hilkhos Melachim 10:9.*

[5] *Igros Moshe YD* II: 9.

> <u>Yad Ramah</u>[6] - This prohibition applies only if the rest is religiously motivated. It does not matter, according to them, whether this motivation is monotheistic or pagan. According to then, to establish a 24-hour period to rest from work for health reasons would be permitted.

*[Challenge:] If this is so, then let this prohibition be counted among the Noahide laws!*

*[Answer:] The Noahide laws are enumerated as prohibitions. They are not listed according to their positive aspects.*

> Explanation: Rashi and other Talmudic commentaries explain that the Noahide laws, meaning the general categories themselves, are listed according to their negative *(thou shalt not)* aspects only. Even though the laws may include positive commandments, these are sub-classes of the general prohibitions. As mentioned in a previous lesson, *dinim* (the requirement to establish courts) appear to be positive. Nevertheless, it is primarily negative in that it establishes courts to enforce the other negative prohibitions.

## <u>Yevamos 48b</u> – Shabbat and the Ger Toshav

Sanhedrin 58b is apparently contradicted by a <u>braisa</u> in Yevamos 48b. The Talmud there is discussing the laws of an *eved*, indentured servant, purchased before Shabbat and the prohibition of his performing work on behalf of his master. The same *braisa* concludes with a surprising statement:

> *[Six days you shall work, but on the seventh day you shall rest. Your ox and donkey shall have rest, the son of your maidservant,* **and the ger***, so that they may be refreshed. (Exodus 23:12)]*

"…and the ger" – *this refers to a* ger toshav *[resident alien]*.

> Explanation: Talmud tells us that the word *ger*, used in this verse, refers to a *ger toshav*. So, is this verse telling us that a *ger toshav* must observe Shabbat? How can that be? A *ger toshav* is not Jewish and, as the Talmud stated in Sanhedrin, non-Jews cannot observe Shabbat! Since the verse uses the generic term *ger*, it might be that the Torah means a *ger tzedek*, a convert to Judaism.

*You might question: How do we know this refers to a* ger toshav*? Perhaps it refers to a* ger tzedek*, [a regular convert to Judaism]? This cannot be so, because another verse states:*

---

[6] To Sanhedrin 58b.

*And the Seventh day is a Sabbath... you shall do no labor... both you and the* ger *within your gates.*
*(Deuteronomy 5:14)*

> Explanation: The Talmud understands the verse "*ger* within your gates" as referring to a *ger tzedek* – a full convert to Judaism. Since another verse has already taught us that a *ger tzedek* must observe Shabbos as a Jew, then our passage must be referring to a *ger tzedek*, the only other type of *ger*.

What are we to make of this? There are a number of explanations:

- **Rashi** – Rashi understands the Talmud simply: A *ger toshav* must keep Shabbat. Apparently, Rashi derives his position this from the Talmud in [Eruvin 69b.](#) There it states that one who desecrates Shabbat is like one who worships idolatry. Rashi applies this idea to a *ger toshav*. Since the *ger toshav* has disavowed idolatry, he must therefore keep Shabbat. Rashi must interpret the Talmud's prohibition (from Sanhedrin 58a) as only precluding idolaters from observing Shabbat.

- [Tosafos](#) **D. H. Zeh** – A *ger toshav* has no obligation to observe Shabbat and may not do so because of the aforementioned passage from Sanhedrin. The Talmud here is only discussing whether or not a non-Jew may do work for a Jew on Shabbat. This certainly seems the intent of the verse:

> *Six days you shall work, but on the seventh day you shall rest. Your ox and donkey shall have rest, the son of your maidservant,* **and the ger**, *so that they may be refreshed*

    The first part of this verse discusses animals or servants working on behalf of a Jew (they clearly have no intrinsic obligation to observe Shabbat). Correspondingly, the first part of the *braisa* discusses a Jew's servant working on his behalf. The second part of the *braisa* is explaining that a *ger toshav* is likewise prohibited from working on behalf of a Jew.

The basis of Rashi and *Tosafos's* disagreement appears to be that the other entities mentioned in the verse (ox, donkey, servant, etc.) are subject to the will of a master, while the *ger toshav* is not. A *ger toshav* is completely autonomous. *Tosafos* seems to interpret the verse's inclusion of *ger toshav* to mean: "You may think that a *ger toshav*, being a non-Jew who is not in your household, may labor on your behalf, but the verse is teaching that this is not so."

*Tosafos's* explanation is certainly consistent with the Talmud's discussion. Rashi's opinion, though, is very difficult to understand. First of all, Eruvin 69b is only describing Jewish desecration of Shabbat, not that of a *ger toshav*. To apply it to a *ger toshav*, we have to have some other pre-existing reason to equate Jewish desecration of Shabbat to that of a *ger toshav*. Moreover, the comparison is made for the unique purposes of explaining when a Sabbath desecrating Jew may be trusted or combined with other Jews for certain matters of *halakha*. In other words, it is only asking when a Jew is treated as an idolater in certain areas of Torah law. This entire issue is compounded by the lack of clarity as to how Rashi defines *ger toshav*.

Because of the difficulties in explaining Rashi, the Maimonides,[7] *Shulchan Aruch*,[8] and all other codifiers[9] decide the halakha like *Tosafos*. Therefore, even a *ger toshav* is included in the prohibition of gentile observance of Shabbat.

## Talmud *Krisus 9a*

There is similar discussion in the Talmud to Tractate *Krisus* 9a:

> Our Rabbis taught [in a braisa]: A ger toshav *does work for himself on Shabbat to the same degree as a Jew on the intermediate days of the festivals.*[10]
>
> Rabbi Akiva *said: As a Jew does on the festivals.*[11]
>
> Rabbi Yossi *said: A* ger toshav *does labor on Shabbat for himself just a Jew does on a weekday.*
>
> Rabbi Shimon said: Both a ger toshav, *an idolater, a resident slave, or maidservant do labor for themselves on Shabbat just as a Jew does on a weekday.*

The Talmud tells us that the *halakha* is like Rabbi Shimon.[12]

---

[7] Rambam, Hilkhos Shabbos 20:14.

[8] *Orach Chaim* 304.

[9] Ibid. See the Bais Yosef there for a lengthy discussion of the issues.

[10] On the intermediate days of the Passover and Sukkot festival Jews may only do labor that is needed for enjoyment of the festivals or to prevent a loss.

[11] On the festivals themselves Jews may cook as well as carry in the public domain.

[12] See emendations of the Shitta Mekubetzes here, note 12. See also Maimonides, Hilkhos Shabbos 20:14.

Thus far, we see have seen that there is nothing preventing a *ger toshav* from performing labor on Shabbat. Since a *ger toshav* is a de facto Noahide, we may infer that that there is nothing prohibiting a Noahide from doing labor on Shabbat.

At the same time, there is a positive commandment requiring the inhabitants of the world to constantly engage in the world. This requirement precludes observance of Shabbat.

## Midrash Rabbah

The Midrash[13] explains the idea behind this prohibition:

> *Rabbi Yossi, son of Chanina, said: A gentile who observes the Shabbat before being circumcised is liable to the death penalty. Why? Because he was not so commanded. But, what is your reason for saying that a gentile who observes the Sabbath is liable to the death penalty? Said Rabbi Chiya, the son of Abba, in the name of Rabbi Yochanan: If a king and queen are sitting in conversation and someone comes and barges between them, isn't he liable to death? So too is the Shabbat between Israel and the Holy One, blessed is He, as it is written:*

> *"[You shall speak unto the Children of Israel, saying: you must keep my Shabbat, for it is a sign] between me and the Children of Israel" (Exodus 31:13).*

> *Therefore, a non-Jew who comes and places himself between them before being circumcised is liable to the death penalty.*

Prior to the giving of the Torah, the rest of Shabbat was the privilege of God alone and man was not allowed to partake it. The commandment of observing Shabbat, the divine day of rest, was given to the Jews alone as part of their unique covenant with God.

In the next lessons we will look at further possible relationships between Noahides and Shabbat.

## Summary of Lesson

1. The Torah prohibits Noahides from observing Shabbat, requiring them to be involved constantly in the making of the world.

2. This prohibition only applies to religiously motivated resting.

---

[13] *Midrash Rabbah* to Deuteronomy 1:18.

3. A Ger Toshav has no obligation to observe Shabbat. They are likewise enjoined against observing Shabbat.

4. The Talmud in *Krisus* reiterates the Halakhah with regard to a ger toshav.

5. The Midrash Rabbah explains that the reason for the prohibition is because Shabbat is a matter between God and Israel alone.

THE YESHIVA PIRCHEI SHOSHANIM SHULCHAN ARUCH LEARNING PROJECT

# The Noahide Laws – Lesson Twenty Four

© **Yeshiva Pirchei Shoshanim 2017**
This shiur may not be reproduced in any
form without permission of the copyright holder.

164 Village Path, Lakewood NJ 08701 732.370.3344
164 Rabbi Akiva, Bnei Brak, 03.616.6340

## Outline of This Lesson:

1. Introduction

2. Talmud *Yoma 28b*

3. 1) The Labor of Noahides

4. 2) The Definition of a Day

5. 3) The Circumstances of Pre-Sinaitic Noahides

6. 4) The Patriarchs & Monotheism

    a. In Summary

    b. *Yoma 28a*

    c. The *Binyan Tzion* Remains

7. Summary

# Shabbat II: The Patriarchs & Shabbat

## Introduction

In the last lesson we saw there is a positive *mitzvah* upon all non-Jews to remain constantly engaged with the world (*Sanhedrin* 58b). This *mitzvah*, by default, prohibits non-Jews from observing any 24 hour rest period for religious reasons (Maimonides). This law applies equally to all non-Jews, including *ger toshav* and Noahides (*Tosafos* to *Yevamos* 48b and *Kerisus* 9a).

We saw from the Midrash that the Jews were commanded to partake in the divine rest of Shabbat. Their observance of Shabbat was established as a sign of their unique covenant with God. Anyone else is an interloper and even deserving of death!
Yet, we are also taught that the patriarchs kept all of the *mitzvos*. This would, of course, include observing Shabbat. Considering that the patriarchs were Noahides, how do we reconcile their behavior with *halakhah*?

## Talmud *Yoma* 28b

The source teaching us that the patriarchs kept the Torah is *Yoma* 28b:

> *Rav* Said: Our forefather Avraham kept the entire Torah, as it is written:
>
> "Because Abraham obeyed My voice [and observed my safeguards, My commandments, My statutes, and my laws.]"
>
> Rav Shimi bar Chiya said to Rav: Why not say that verse speaks only of the seven Noahide laws?

> *[Response]: It also referrers to circumcision, [therefore the verse must speak of more than just 7 laws.]*
>
> *[Rav Simi bar Chiya responded]: Then say it refers only to the seven Noahide laws and to circumcision!*
>
> *Rav said to him: If that were the case, then why does the verse state "My commandments… My laws?" This implies that Avraham kept the entire Torah.*
>
> *Rav Ashi said: Our forefather Avraham fulfilled even* eruvei tavshilin *[a rabbinic mitzvah] for it is stated "My Laws" [lit. "My Torahs"], implying both the written and oral Torahs[1].*

Many later commentaries hold like Rav Shimi bar Chiya, that the patriarchs only observed the Noahide laws plus the other *mitzvos* specifically commanded to them.[2] According to this understanding of the Talmud, the Patriarchs did not observe Shabbat.

There are a significant number of commentaries, however, who agree with Rav or Rav Ashi. According to them, the patriarchs observed the entire written Torah, oral Torah, and possible even later rabbinic decrees.[3]

Their view requires a lot of explanation. The most obvious question is: how did the patriarchs know the Torah before it was given? There are many good answers to this question, the most famous being that they knew it through *Ruach ha-kodesh*, a form of divine inspiration[4] just below prophecy.[5] This question, though, is nowhere nearly as difficult as the one posed by Leviticus 18:18:

> *Do not marry a woman and her sister…*

Yet, Yaakov (Jacob) married two sisters (Rachel and Leah) despite this explicit Torah prohibition. How was this possible according to those who say that he

---

[1] Occasionally the term Oral Torah includes rabbinic decrees as well. See Maharsha and Rashash.

[2] See Rashbam, Chizkuni, Ibn Ezra and many others to Genesis 26:5. See the Meiri and Rabbi Avraham ben HaRambam in their introductions to *Pirkei Avos*. Maimonides in *Hilchos Melachim 9:1* holds similarly.

[3] See Responsa of Rashba I: 94 and Radbaz II: 696. This is also the opinion of Rashi. However their opinions are still somewhat circumscribed.

[4] Prophecy and inspiration will be discussed in a future lesson.

[5] Ramban to Genesis 26:5.

observed the entire Torah! There are many examples of patriarchal behavior appearing to contradict the Torah.[6]

According to the literalist interpretation of Rav and Rav Ashi, the Torah observance of the patriarchs must be somehow qualified to explain these contradictions. Many of the greatest Torah scholars in history have tackled this question and arrived at a number of solutions. For example:

- Ramban to Genesis 26:5 – The patriarchs only observed the Torah in the boundaries of Israel. This may be tied into their knowledge of the Torah via *Ruach haKodesh*.[7]

- The Maharal of Prague[8] writes that the Patriarchs only kept the positive commandments, not the negative commandments.

- The Rama[9] writes that there are indeed problems explaining how Yitzchak and Yaakov kept the Torah. His solution is to simply disagree with the early commentaries, writing that only Avraham kept the Torah. Indeed, the Talmud only states that Avraham kept the Torah before it was given. Almost all other commentaries disagree, holding that Yitzhak and Yaakov kept the mitzvos as well.

- Ohr HaChaim to Genesis 49:3 – Though they kept the Torah, it had not yet been revealed and was not, therefore, truly binding. Their observance of the Torah could be modified by prophecy. When they deviated from the Torah, it was due to prophetic instruction.

- Daas Zekeinim to Genesis 37:35 and Nefesh HaChaim 21 – since the Torah had not been given, the patriarchs had no actual obligation to observe it. The patriarchs were empowered to make judgment calls for the sake of building a people and community.

---

[6] For example, Amram, father of Moshe, married his aunt. Kayin married his sister. Problems are also caused by simple chronology. For example, how could the patriarchs have observed the laws of *Teruma* and *Ma'aser* if there were no Kohanim yet? How did the patriarchs observe laws dependent on future events, such as remembering the exodus from Egypt or the persecution of Amalek?

[7] As mentioned in a previous lesson, there is a special relationship between the land of Israel and the powers of prophecy and inspiration.

[8] *Gur Aryeh* to 46:10 and 32:4; *Chiddushei Aggados* Chullin 91a.

[9] Responsa 10.

This sampling reveals a trend: Most explanations of how the Patriarchs kept the Torah render their observance of Shabbat irrelevant to modern Noahides (see above, *Maharal, Ohr HaChaim, Daas Zekeinim,* and *Nefesh HaChaim*). A further problem is that many commentaries explain that the Patriarchs were not 100% Noahides.

Once they accepted the covenant of circumcision, the patriarchs were considered Jewish to a degree permitting them to partake in Shabbat.[10] This also precludes their observance from having any relevance to contemporary Noahides.

Therefore, to learn anything useful from the patriarchs, we must serious narrow our question. The exact question should be:

> How do we explain Shabbat observance of the Patriarchs according to those who hold that the Patriarchs were 100% Noahides and those who hold that they kept the Torah exactly as we understand "keeping the Torah?"

Although many have written about how the Patriarchs kept the Torah, the cross-section of those commentaries discussing our specific question is very small.

## 1) The Labor of Noahides

Let's look again at the verse prohibiting Noahide Shabbat observance:

> *Day and night they shall not cease...*

When the Torah prohibits gentiles from observing Shabbat, it is telling them that they may not refrain from labor for an entire day. What type of labor are we talking about, though? The *Binyan Tzion*[11] makes a brilliant observation. The 39 prohibited labors, the Torah's conception of labor for the purposes of Shabbat, were not articulated until Sinai. Since the details of these labors were not previously known to the world, they could not be definition of labor used in regard to Noahides and their prohibition of observing Shabbat.

For example, according to the 39 labors defined at Sinai, carrying a needle in the public domain is considered a prohibited labor for a Jew on Shabbat. However, if a Jew carries a sofa up and down the stairs of his home on Shabbat, it is not considered labor and is permitted.

---

[10] *Beit HaOtzar* Maarekhet I: 1; *Parshat Derakhim* 1. Rabbi Asher Weiss in *Minchas Asher* 9 records that this is the opinion of *HaRav HaGaon* Chaim Kanievsky.

[11] No. 126.

Before Sinai, however, the definition of labor was entirely colloquial. Therefore, the prohibition of observing Shabbat for gentiles was only on refraining from the colloquial definition of labor, not on the Jewish definition of labor. When the patriarchs rested, they observed the Torah (Jewish) definition of labor, which was not prohibited for them as Noahides. However, they did not refrain from colloquially defined forms of labor.

According to this understanding, gentiles are only enjoined against setting aside a day to refrain from their jobs, yard work, home repairs, etc. because of religious reasons. However, observing the Jewish definitions of labor for Shabbat is not a problem; it is not the type of labor from which they are prohibited from resting.

## 2) The Definition of Day

The *Panim Yafos*[12] also makes a remarkable observation. The verse states:

> *Day and night they shall not cease…*

This verse indicates that the Shabbat that may not be observed by non-Jews is one lasting from daybreak to daybreak. After all, the verse states *day and night*, not *night and day*. However, the Jewish Shabbat, the one commanded at Sinai, lasts from nightfall to nightfall. The patriarchs kept the Jewish Shabbat (nightfall to nightfall), which was never prohibited for gentiles.

This opinion would apparently permit Noahides to observe Shabbat in the same way as Jews. However, the *Panim Yafos's* definition of "day" as daybreak-to-daybreak is disproven and rejected by numerous later authorities who find it at great variance with other established areas of *halakhah*.[13]

## 3) The Circumstances of Pre-Sinaitic Noahides

The Meiri[14] explains that the circumstances of the Patriarchs were fundamentally different from that of later Jews. He holds that the reason gentiles are prohibited from observing Shabbat is because a gentile is not permitted to imitate the Jewish faith. However, before the giving of the Torah, there were no Jews. Therefore, there is no point to prohibiting Shabbat observance.

---

[12] Commentary to Genesis 8:22.

[13] *Binyan Tzion* 126; Responsa Rabbi Akiva Eiger 121 (Hosifos); Cheker Halakhah 15; Yad Shaul YD 293:4; Pardes Yosef, Noah 22; Teshuvos Toras Chesed 25.

[14] To *Sanhedrin* 58b.

But, wait a minute, wasn't the key verse written in Genesis? This is long before the Jews were commanded to keep Shabbat. If there was no point at that time to prohibit non-Jewish Shabbat observance, then why is the verse written in Genesis?

The Meiri understands that it was written here for future generations. The Meiri would, therefore, prohibit any modern Noahide observance of Shabbat.

## 4) The Patriarchs & Monotheism

Rabbi Meir Dan Plotzki in his *Kuntres Ner Mitzvah*[15] offers an interesting and unexpected view. The Talmud states:[16]

> *Israel is not governed by* mazal.

*Mazal* is a broad term referring to the created agents and mediators (both angelic and physical) of God's providence in the world. It includes the motion of the stars and constellations and the physical and transcendent forces of the universe. These entities form a vast mechanism channeling God's providence into the world.

Before Sinai, all nations of the world were subjected to this mitigated divine providence. At Sinai, however, the Jews were taken out from this system and became subject to God's direct and unmitigated oversight. God signaled this new status by commanding the observance of Shabbat, by asking Israel to share in the divine rest of the seventh day. This is the intent of the verse:

> *Speak unto the children of Israel, saying: You must keep my Shabbat, for it is a sign between Me and you throughout your generations, that you may know that I am the Lord who sanctifies you. (Exodus 31:13)*

Given the Jews a portion in Shabbat was the sign that they were no longer subject to the cycles of time, seasons, and stars – the lesser providence.

The non-Jewish nations are subject to *mazal*, hence they must observe the cycle of time and days. When a non-Jew observes a religious Shabbat, it is an attempt to lay claim to the unique providence of Israel, to cast off the mitigating forces of creation. This is why the Midrash describes non-Jewish observance of Shabbat as an interposition between a king and queen – it is the usurping of a private, unique relationship.

---

[15] An important overview of the Noahide laws.

[16] *Shabbat* 156a and *Nedarim* 32a.

However, God commanded Avraham: *Exit from your stargazing! Israel is not governed by* mazal!<sup>17</sup>

God was telling Avraham that, from that point onward, he would merit God's direct providence and no longer be subject to the influences of *mazal*. Therefore, Avraham was permitted to observe Shabbat fully.

The *Chemdas Yisrael* further explains that Abraham merited this providence by disavowing idolatry.

This explanation fits well with Rashi's opinion that a *ger toshav* must keep Shabbat (assuming Rashi defines a ger toshav as one who only does not worship idols).

However, it appears from the Talmud[18] that, assuming a change in providence is the underlying factor, this change only applied to Abraham and his descendants, but to none other.

Furthermore, this interpretation does not work according to *Tosafos* (which is the *halakha*), who holds that even a *ger toshav* may not keep Shabbat.

**IN SUMMARY:**

***Binyan Tzion*** – Non-Jews are only prohibited from refraining from colloquially defined types of labor. They may choose to refrains from the 39 *Melachos*.

***Panim Yafos*** – The prohibition is only on observing a Shabbat of daybreak-to-daybreak. However, the definition of "day" as daybreak-to-daybreak is difficult. His interpretation is rebutted by many later authorities.

***Meiri*** – The Patriarchs were Noahides and did keep Shabbat. However, the prohibition against Shabbat observance did not apply at that time.

***Chemdas Yisrael*** – Because they were not idolaters, the patriarchs merited God's direct providence. Shabbat is the sign of such providence. This interpretation is precluded by *Tosafos*, though, and from *Yoma* 28a.

**YOMA 28A**

*Rav Safra Said: The time of the afternoon prayer of Avraham [minchah] is when the walls began to grow dark.*

*Rabbi Yosef said: We learn* halakha *from Avrham! [Surprised objection]*

---

[17] *Shabbat* 156a and *Nedarim* 32a, based upon Genesis 15.

[18] Note 15, above.

Rabbeinu Tam, the *Aruch*, *Ritva*, *Maharitz Chayes*,[19] and many others explain that *halakha*, practice, cannot be learned based on the conduct of the patriarchs before the Torah was given.[20] God's expectations for the world and the way in which we relate to God fundamentally changed at Sinai.

Therefore, the *Chemdas Yisrael's* conclusion is not practical.

**THE *BINYAN TZION* REMAINS**

From the above opinions, only the *Binyan Tzion*'s (regarding the nature of labor for Noahides) remains: the patriarchs kept the Jewish Shabbat yet engaged in the colloquial definition of labor.

This conclusion remains because it is a valid halakhic interpretation all to itself, and is not dependent on the behavior, status, or actions of the patriarchs.

However, it is virtually impossible to carry out this idea in practice. How does one keep the Shabbat according to the Jewish definition of labor while engaging in what is colloquially termed "work?" The two definitions overlap substantially. Additionally, observing the Jewish sabbatical restrictions may present a problem of *chiddushei dat*, which will be examined in the next lesson.

## Summary of This Lesson

1. The Talmud tells us that the patriarchs kept the Torah before it was given at Sinai.

2. This cannot be taken 100% literally, because there are examples of the Patriarchs not following Torah laws.

3. To learn from the Patriarchs observance of Shabbat to modern Noahides, we have to look at commentaries that both view the Patriarchs as 100% Noahides and that hold their Torah observance was identical to ours. There are very, very few views satisfying these conditions.

4. Of those meeting our conditions, most of them do not apply to modern Noahides.

5. There is a general rule that we cannot learn our practice from the behavior of the Patriarchs.

---

[19] All commenting to this page of the Talmud.

[20] This is only a general rule that is not without its exceptions.

6. The *Binyan Tzion's* interpretation, however, may have relevance to modern Noahides. However, it is impossible to apply it in practice.

THE YESHIVA PIRCHEI SHOSHANIM SHULCHAN ARUCH LEARNING PROJECT

# The Noahide Laws – Lesson Twenty Five

© **Yeshiva Pirchei Shoshanim 2017**
This shiur may not be reproduced in any
form without permission of the copyright holder.

## Outline of This Lesson:

1. Introduction & Review
2. Maimonides *Hilkhos Melakhim* 10:9
3. Rabbi Moshe Feinstein, *ztz"l*
4. In Conclusion
5. Letter of the Law vs. Spirit of the Law
6. Observance vs. Acknowledgement
7. Shabbat Suggestions
8. Summary

# Shabbat III: Practical Conclusions

## Introduction & Review Thus Far

This is a summary of what the sources have taught us so far:

- **Sanhedrin 58b** – Cites Genesis 8:22 which prohibits all mankind from keeping Shabbat. The verse prohibits cessation from work for a 24 hour period. Prior to Sinai, the respite of Shabbat was for God alone At Sinai, the Jews were commanded to partake in the experience of Shabbat as a sign of their unique status.

- **Rashi**, **Radbaz**, **Rav Moshe Feinstein** commenting on the **Rambam** – For the sake of this prohibition, it does not make difference as to why one rests for an entire day. Even if one sets aside an entire day only to recuperate from work, he still transgresses. The Radbaz clarifies, though, that this is only if one establishes a regular, fixed day. To take an occasional day off is permitted.

- **Midrash Rabba** – Explains that the prohibition of non-Jewish observance of Shabbat takes on special poignancy after the giving of the Torah. The Jews were commanded at Sinai to partake of the divine rest of Shabbat as a sign of their covenant. Anyone else who tries to do so is interposing between God and Israel.

- **The Patriarchs** – The patriarchs, we are taught, kept the Torah. However, both the nature of their observance and their identity as Noahides are not clear enough for us to draw any practical conclusions. Additionally, there is a principle that we do not learn *halakha*, practice, from the actions of the patriarchs.

## Maimonides *Hilkhos Melakhim* 10 : 9

§9 *A non-Jew[1] who delves into the Torah is obligated to die. They should only be involved in the study of their seven commandments.*

*Similarly, a non-Jew who rests, even on a weekday, observing that day similarly to a Shabbat, is obligated to die. Needless to say, this is also the case if he creates a festival for himself.*

> In the Torah, the Hebrew word "Shabbat" may refer to the Shabbat, the seventh day, or any day upon which labor is prohibited by the Torah. This would include festivals. The Radbaz quotes Rashi who writes[2] that any kind of rest for any reason should be prohibited. However, the Radbaz adds "This is if he establishes a day for rest; however, occasional cessation from labor is not prohibited."

*The general rule governing these matters is this: they may not originate a new religion or create/perform* mitzvot *for themselves based on their own reasoning. Either convert and accept all the* mitzvot *or uphold their commandments without adding or detracting from them.*

> Maimonides explains that the reason for the prohibition of Shabbat observance by non-Jews is *chiddushei dat*, originating a new religion (discussed at length in a prior lesson). *Chiddushei dat* would preclude Noahides from observing Shabbat even by refraining from the Jewish definition of labor; the 39 *melachot*.

*If a gentile delves into the Torah or Shabbat, or innovates a religious practice, he is beaten, punished, and informed him that he is obligated to die for his actions. However, he is not actually executed.*

## HaRav HaGaon Moshe Feinstein, ztz'l

Rabbi Moshe Feinstein[3] explains that *chiddushei dat* is a general prohibition against Noahides adopting Jewish practices as religious observances. However, the prohibition of observing Shabbat and the strictures on Torah study are singled out by Maimonides due to their severity.

---

[1] Many printed editions of the *Mishnah Torah,* being heavily censored, read *akum*, meaning *idolater*. However, almost all early manuscripts and critical editions read *goy*, a generic term for anyone who is not Jewish.

[2] Sanhedrin 58b.

[3] In a number of letters he discusses Noahide issues. See *Igros Moshe* OC II:25, V:18, YD I:3, I:6, II:7, II:8, III:90, IV:51:1, CM II:69.

## In Conclusion

According to Maimonides, Noahides may also not observe Shabbat by refraining from the Jewish definition of work (the 39 *Melachos*). This would be *chiddushei dat*.

*Chiddushei dat* would also prohibit Noahides from marking Shabbat in anyway by using Jewish rituals such as lighting candles, making Kiddush, making the blessing for bread over two loaves, etc.

The conclusion of the *poskim* is, therefore, that Noahides may not observe Shabbat in anyway by refraining from work for a 24 hour period or by adopting Jewish rituals. Noahides may neither establish a regular 24-hour period of rest even for non-religious reasons.[4]

## Letter of the Law vs. Spirit of the Law

A Noahide has two options as to how to deal with the question of labor on Shabbat. He may either take the liberal approach, which follows only the strict letter of the law, or he may take a pious, conservative approach acknowledging both the spirit and letter of the law.

**The Letter of the Law**

**The letter of the law** is that a Noahide may not commemorate Shabbat by regularly refraining from work for an entire day. It does not matter if one rests from daybreak-to-daybreak or from nightfall-to-nightfall. This approach implies that refraining from only some labors, or even from all labor but only part of the day, is not a problem. According to this approach, a Noahide should turn on a light, make a fire, write, or do at least one prohibited act so that his observance of Shabbat is not a complete observance. Otherwise he would transgress the prohibition of observing Shabbat.

We should keep in mind, though, that this observance of Shabbat is meaningless. "Observance" of Shabbat means resting from the 39 labors defined at Sinai. The purpose in a Noahide doing one prohibited labor is so that he does not run afoul of the prohibition of observing Shabbat. That means that his one-prohibited-labor invalidates the entire observance. Therefore, despite resting for a whole day, on account of the one labor he is required to do, he never kept Shabbat anyway!

Furthermore, as we mentioned earlier, God only asked Israel to share in Shabbat. A Noahide who does so is imposing his will upon God. As we saw in earlier lessons, this is a severe issue.

---

[4] See *The Divine Code*, 2nd ed. Pp. 64 – 74.

Although this mode of behavior is in step with the letter of the law, it fails to acknowledge the spirit of the law. It is a liberal approach to Torah law and Noahism.

**The Spirit and Letter of the Law: The Shabbat of a Pious Noahide**

One, who seeks to go beyond the letter of the law as a matter of piety, will refrain from any observance of Shabbat. A pious, God fearing, religious Noahide will not attempt to observe Shabbat in any way by resting. A Noahide who imitates Jewish observance of Shabbat by "resting" is a less observant Noahide than one who does not observe Shabbat at all!

## Observance vs. Acknowledgement

Until now, we have only discussed the *observance* of Shabbat. By *observance*, however, we mean refraining from labor or imitating other Jewish Shabbat obligations. However, this prohibition does not preclude Noahides having a positive, meaningful connection with Shabbat in another way.

At the beginning of creation, Shabbat was established as a day of rest for Hashem (only), but also as a commemoration of the work of creation, a testament that G-d created the world in seven days. According to many, this latter aspect of Shabbat should be acknowledged by all non-Jews.[5] The Midrash says:[6]

> *[The wicked Turnus Rufus][7] asked Rabbi Akiva: "From where can you prove to me that God wished to honor the Seventh Day?" ... Rabbi Akiva responded: "Verify it with [via necromancy,] because a spirit will ascend on any day of the week except for Shabbat – verify it with the spirit of your father!"... Turnus Rufus checked the veracity of Rabbi Akiva's claim with the spirit of his own father. His father's spirit ascended on every day of the week except Shabbat. On the following Sunday, Turnus Rufus again raised his father and asked him, "father, is it possible that you became a Jew after you died, that you now observe Shabbat? Why did you ascend every day of the week, but did not ascend on Shabbat?" He [Turnus Rufus's father] answered him, saying: "Anyone who does not willingly observe the Sabbath among the living is forced to do so among the dead!"*

---

[5] This also appears to be the opinion of the *Mishneh LaMelech, Melachim* 10:7 and *Kli Yakar* to Exodus 20:8. However, the *Maharanach* in his Torah commentary appears to hold that even verbal acknowledgment of Shabbat by non-Jews is prohibited. See *Toldos Noach, Matza Chein* 9:4 for a discussion and comparison of the sources.

[6] *Bereshis Rabbah* 11:5.

[7] The brutal Roman governor of Israel in the times of the Mishnah.

The *Maharzu*⁸ explains that the spirit of Turnus Rufus's father could not mean that non-Jews must observe Shabbat. Rather, it means that any non-Jew who denies the significance of Shabbat will be "forced to do so among the dead." What does it mean "forced to do so among the dead?" The Midrash goes on to explain that the wicked are punished with the fires of Gehinnom (purgatory) every day of the week, but are given respite on Shabbat. One who denies the existence and significance of Shabbat, even a Non-Jew, will apparently be held accountable.

Furthermore, Noahide acknowledgement of Shabbat goes back to the beginning of creation. There is a fascinating *Midrash*⁹ about Adam, Kayin, and the composition of Psalm 92:

> *Adam met Kayin and asked of him: "What happened? What was your judgment?"*
>
> *Kayin replied: "I repented and it was mitigated"*
>
> *Adam began slapping his own face and cried out: "Such is the power of repentance – and I didn't know it!" Adam immediately arose and declared:* Mizmor shir le-yom ha-Shabbat, a Psalm, a song for the Shabbos…

Psalm 92, recited by Adam for Shabbat, only mentions Shabbat in its opening. It then goes on to praise God's deeds and creations, curiously contrasting the permanence of His deeds with the temporary follies of the wicked, and then concludes with the praises of the righteous man.

What is the connection between the ideas of *teshuvah*, repentance, the temporary prospering of the wicked, and the Shabbos?

Speaking with Kayin, Adam realized the power of repentance and marveled at its greatness. *Teshuvah* is the great creation for which Adam praises God. God is also praised for His incredible kindness: He does not execute judgment immediately. Rather, He waits, allowing transgressors time to either do *teshuvah* or lose themselves further. Alternatively, Adam also realized that this world is the place of finite recompense. Here a person is rewarded for the minority of his deeds. Therefore, the wicked are often rewarded for their few mitzvos, while the righteous are often punished for their few *aveiros*, sins.

---

⁸ Rav Zeev Wolf Einhorn d.1862 – major expounder on the Midrash.

⁹ *Bereshis Rabbah* 22.

But what does this all have to do with Shabbos? When God rested on Shabbos, he beheld the goodness of His creation – he saw that it was well suited for its purpose. So too, Adam, in his revelation, suddenly understood the "big picture" – the greatness of God's world and the incredible potential that it offered.

In that revelation, he saw the "big plan" – he understood the nature of reward and punishment, the fate of the wicked, and the ultimate reward of the righteous. He understood his purpose and how the world was designed for it.

Rashi understands this Psalm as, primarily, an acknowledgement of the World to Come, the ultimate Shabbos.

We see that Adam's relationship to Shabbat was not one of rest. It was a relationship to Shabbos as the capstone of creation, the zecher le-maaseh bereshis, the commemoration of G-d's having created the world in seven days. If there is any aspect of Shabbos that is proper to be acknowledged by Noahides, then this is it.

It is therefore appropriate to base the Noahide acknowledgement of Shabbat on Psalm 92 and Adam's epiphany. In this way, Noahides are following in the way of Adam, to whom the Noahide laws were commanded.

THE YESHIVA PIRCHEI SHOSHANIM SHULCHAN ARUCH LEARNING PROJECT

# The Noahide Laws – Lesson Twenty Six

© **Yeshiva Pirchei Shoshanim 2017**
This shiur may not be reproduced in any
form without permission of the copyright holder.

## Outline of This Lesson:

1. Introduction: Torah Time
2. The Starting Point: Mishnah Rosh HaShanah 1:2
3. Connecting to the Festivals
4. One Day vs. Two Days
5. Rosh HaShanah: Introduction
6. The New Year?
7. Rosh HaShanah – A Day of Many Meanings
8. Elul – The Month of Preparation
9. Summary

# Festivals I: Introduction & Rosh HaShanah

## Introduction: Torah Time

The Torah establishes a spiritual calendar for the world. However, this calendar does not represent a single conception of time. Instead, the spiritual calendar is a complex affair of concentric, interlocking cycles.[1] For example, the Mishnah (*Rosh HaShanah 1:1*) tells us that there are several *Rosh Hashanah's* (New Years), each demarcating a unique cycle of time. These cycles run concurrently, overlaying each other, creating an ever-shifting mosaic of seasons:

> *There are four Rosh Hashanah's [New Years]: the 1st of Nissan is the New Year for kings and festivals, the 15th of Elul is the New Year for the tithing of animals (according to Rabbis Elazar and Shimon, this is on the 1st of Tishrei), the 1st of Tishrei for counting years, the Jubilee and Shemitta cycles, and the tithing of trees and produce. The 1st of Shvat is the New Year for trees according to the yeshiva [school] of Shammai. According to the yeshiva [school] of Hillel, it is on the 15th of Shvat.*

This flow of spiritual time is demarcated by a number of holy days that give it shape and meaning. For most of these holidays, their significance exists on two levels. One level is universal and important to all peoples. The other level is specific and narrowly applicable to Israel alone.

---

[1] The Hebrew calendar acknowledges and integrates a number of astronomical cycles. Contrary to popular belief, the Hebrew calendar is not a lunar calendar. Rather, it is a *lunisolar calendar*, a calendar based upon both the solar and lunar astronomical cycles. This resolution is necessary to keep the Torah's holidays within their designated seasons, as it is written: "These are festivals of the Lord that you shall proclaim in their appointed seasons." (Lev. 23:4). A purely lunar calendar results in an 11 day per-year drift in the holidays. This drift is the reason why the Islamic holidays, relying upon a purely lunar calendar, occur 11 days earlier each year. Furthermore, there is a larger solar cycle commemorated by *Birkas HaChamma* (a blessing on the renewal of the sun) every 28 years.

For example, let's look at the holiday of Sukkot. For Israel, it commemorates God's providence and guardianship of Israel via the *ananei ha-Kavod*, clouds of glory, which surrounded Israel as they traveled in the desert.[2]

The festival huts built on this holiday are in commemoration of these clouds.[3] We see that the *mitzvah* of building *sukkot*, huts, is of unique significance to Israel. This is true of many of the Torah's commandments pertaining to Sukkot.

However, Sukkot is also the holiday on which the world is judged for water.[4] This point is of universal significance; water is the life-blood of the world. It is fundamental to the survival of every living thing and to planetary ecology. The amount of rain and its geographic distribution is determined on this holiday. Some may be judged for drought, others for flood. However we pray that each nation and person will receive just the right amount.

Additionally, offerings were given on sukkot to atone for the nations of the world. While the Jews have *Yom Kippur*, the other nations of the world have sukkot.

For Noahides, these aspects of Sukkot are the most relevant. They transcend the specific observances of Israel, addressing common concerns for all of humanity and the world.

As we embark on our study of the Torah's holidays, our goal is to identify which holidays have universal significance, the nature of that significance, and how that significance may be positively expressed by Noahides.

## The Starting Point: *Mishnah*, **Rosh HaShanah 1:2**

*At four junctures, the world is judged: on Passover for grain, on Shavuot for fruits, on Rosh Hashanah all pass before him like sheep of the flock, as it is written, "He form their hearts as one, he understands all of their deeds." (Psalms 33). On Sukkot, the world is judged for water.*

---

[2] Specifically, Sukkot commemorates the return of the Clouds of Glory. See *Kol Eliyahu* 84. The clouds departed after the sin of the golden calf. It was only after their national atonement and the building of the Tabernacle that the clouds returned. This was on the 15th of Nissan. The specific observances of sukkot are mostly linked to this episode in the history if Israel.

[3] Bottom of *Sukkot* 11b.

[4] *Mishnah, Rosh HaShanah 1:2.*

This Mishnah teaches us which of the Torah's holidays hold universal significance and are important for the entire world. It also tells us the main themes of these holidays.

**A BRIEF OVERVIEW OF THE MISHNAH**

***On Passover for grain...*** – On Passover God decides upon the volume and distribution of the world's grain production. While the liberation from Egypt, observance of the Passover sacrifices, the *Seder*, etc. are all uniquely Jewish concerns; the concern for worldwide food resources is universal. For Noahides, this is the central concern of the Passover holiday.

***On Shavuot for fruits...*** – On Shavuot the world is judged as to whether the fruit trees will yield enough produce to sustain the world's population. Shavuot is also the commemoration of the giving of the Torah at Sinai. For Noahides, the giving of the Torah holds special significance because it was then that the Noahide laws were reaffirmed by Moses. On Shavuot, the original Noahide covenant was placed under the umbrella of Sinaitic obligation. For Noahides, these are the two central themes of Shavuot: the reaffirmation of the Noahide laws and the judgment on the produce of trees.

***On Rosh HaShanah all pass before him like sheep of the flock...*** – All the peoples of the world are judged according to their deeds on Rosh HaShanah. This includes Noahides as well as Jews. While the blowing of the shofar is unique to the Jews, the general idea of repentance and judgment is important to all. As we shall see, many of the customs of Rosh HaShanah (meaning non-*mitzvah* practices) are reasonable and relevant for Noahides as well.

***On Sukkot, the world is judged for water...*** – The abundance and availability of fresh water (for drinking, rains, rivers, etc.) is determined on the holiday of Sukkot. Additionally, this was the holiday upon which offerings and prayers were given on behalf of the 70 gentile nations. Sukkot therefore has two meanings for Noahides: It is the day upon which Noahides pray for and acknowledge the importance of water, one of the creations of the First Day.[5] It is also the time of atonement for the nations of the world.

---

[5] The creation narrative implies that water existed at the beginning of creation. However, the Midrash explains that it was impossible for anything to have existed prior to creation. The Midrash derives that ten things must have been created on the first day: the heavens and the earth, the *tohu* and *vohu* (void and primeval chaos), light and dark, wind and water, and the time of day and time of night (since the heavenly bodies were not yet created, day and night must have been defined as times instead of the products of planetary motion).

## Connecting to the Festivals

Noahides have no obligation to observe any of the Torah's festivals, even those that have universal relevance. Nevertheless, the importance of these festivals for the entire world compels their acknowledgement.

As we have mentioned many times in this course, Noahism has not existed as a living faith in over 1700 years. As a result, any customs, practices, or prayers unique to it have long since vanished. The goal of this project is not to attempt to recreate something that is long since lost, but to define the *halachic* (Torah practice) boundaries of Noahism and establish its parameters so that it can grow and flourish.

Much of what will be brought here are outlines of suggested customs and prayers for these holidays. The Noahide community will, undoubtedly and over time, develop their own liturgy and customs. Until then, these suggestions may serve as a springboard.

## One Day Vs. Two Days

Jews outside of Israel observe the Torah festivals for two days instead of one day (the exception, however, is Rosh HaShanah, which is always observed for two days whether in Israel or the Diaspora). An extra day was added to the holidays by the ancient sages due to a unique diaspora problem. At that time the new month was declared based upon the sighting and reporting of the new moon in Israel. Communicating the decree of the new month to the diaspora was fraught with problems. The issues involved often delayed the news of the new month from reaching diaspora settlements. At most, these delays could create a variance of one day in the diaspora calendar. Therefore, the ancient sages decreed that diaspora Jews should add an additional day to alleviate the calendrical doubt.

Nowadays, with our fixed calendar, there is no practical need for a second day. Nevertheless, the Jewish community still keeps this additional day because the original decree that established it was never abolished.

It is not known if the ancient Noahide communities observed or acknowledged the Torah festivals in any way. This fact, combined with the lack of continuity and voluntary nature of Noahide observance, makes it clear that the rabbinic decree of a second day is not relevant to Noahides.

Furthermore, by keeping only the Biblically ordained date of the holiday (as do the Jews in Israel), Noahides are making a positive distinction as to their unique relationship to the holidays.

# Rosh HaShanah: Introduction

> *...on Rosh Hashanah all pass before him like sheep of the flock, as it is written, "He forms their hearts as one, he understands all of their deeds."*

*...on Rosh Hashanah all pass before him like sheep of the flock,*

> Rashi comments on this Mishnah in Rosh HaShanah 18a. He explains that when a shepherd counts his sheep for tithes, he lets them pass one-by-one through a small opening into a corral. The opening, being too small for two sheep to pass at once, ensures that they can are counted properly as they pass through. It also gives the shepherd a chance to examine each sheep individually. According to this explanation, each person is responsible for his own judgment; it is between him and his "shepherd." Furthermore, Rosh Hashanah is a passage through a "narrow place." It is a day upon which all things hang in the balance. However,

*"He forms their hearts as one, he understands all of their deeds."*

> This verse is surprising, because it appears to contradict what we just learned! If Rosh HaShanah is a time of individual judgment, then why does this verse imply that it is a time of communal judgment? The Talmud explains that this verse means that on Rosh HaShanah God also sees the hearts of all mankind in a single glance.

The correct way to read this Mishnah, then, is that it is teaching us two things. One is that Rosh Hashanah is the time when one must face his creator as an individual, taking sole responsibility for his actions and being. The other, is that on Rosh Hashanah mankind and all its deeds is viewed as a whole. On Rosh Hashanah, God judges human society in all of its complexity and the vast network of interpersonal relationships therein.

# The New Year?

As we mentioned above, spiritual time is a complicated motion of wheels-within-wheels. The Mishnah tells us that there are a number of years running concurrently, each with their own Rosh HaShanah:

> *There are four Rosh Hashanah's [New Years]: the 1$^{st}$ of Nissan is the New Year for kings and festivals, the 15$^{th}$ of Elul is the New Year for the tithing of animals (according to Rabbis Elazar and Shimon, this is on the 1$^{st}$ of Tishrei), the 1$^{st}$ of Tishrei for counting years, the Jubilee and Shemitta cycles, and the tithing of trees and produce.*

*The 1ˢᵗ of Shvat is the New Year for trees according to the yeshiva [school] of Shammai. According to the yeshiva [school] of Hillel, it is on the 15ᵗʰ of Shvat.*

The Rosh HaShanah of the 1ˢᵗ of Tishrei is the BIG Rosh HaShanah. This is the Rosh HaShanah that determines how we actually count our years. However, the month of Tishrei is not the first month. The first month is actually Nissan.

It seems counter-intuitive to count years starting in the middle of the cycle of months. However, it makes sense when you think of the "year" as a number of years occurring at the same time. The first day of the first month, the month of Nissan, is the Rosh HaShanah for kings and festivals. This year deals with counting the reign of kings, dating of legal documents, and the cycle of festival offerings in the temple.

The BIG Rosh HaShanah, however, is concerned with the spiritual relationship between man and his creator. While months are counted according to the civil calendar, the BIG picture – years – is determined according to the spiritual cycle.

This point is reinforced by a fascinating dispute in the Talmud Rosh HaShanah 10b – 11a:

- Rabbi Eliezer offers evidence to prove that creation occurred in Tishrei (the seventh month).

- Rabbi Yehoshua offers evidence that creation happened in Nissan (the first month).

Rabbeinu Tam[6] points out that they are not actually arguing. There were actually two creations. The first, in Tishrei, was the creation of the world in thought. This was the purer, spiritual, creation of the world in abstract. The creation of Nissan, however, was the physical creation of the world. The *Mases Binyamin* notes[7] that this explains many differences between the year that beings in Nissan and the year that begins in Tishrei.

We count years according to the very beginning of God's thought: Tishrei. In doing so, we assign greater importance to the abstract, prime spiritual creation rather than the physical creation of Nissan.

---

[6] Tosafos Rosh HaShanah 27a.

[7] In Shu"t 101. He points out that we calculate years based on the assumption that the world was created in Tishrei. However, many other astronomical calculations are based on the assumption that the world was created in Nissan.

## Rosh Hashanah: a Day of Many Meanings

When Rabbi Eliezer tells us that the creation occurred in Tishrei, he means that the creation was completed in Tishrei on the first day of the month. The creation actually began on the 25th day of Elul, culminating with the creation of Adam on the final sixth day of creation.

Rosh Hashanah is, more properly, the birthday of Adam and the anniversary of the creation of man. However, the joy of this event is dampened by the fact that it is also the anniversary of Adam and Eve's fall.

Because Rosh HaShanah commemorates two events of opposing natures, it is a holiday full of paradoxical meanings. It is a day of celebration, yet also of judgment and trepidation. It is a day of joy, yet solemnity. It is also a time of great mercy, as well as great severity.

The preparation, prayers, and customs of Rosh Hashanah all acknowledge this subtle weave of meanings.

Rosh Hashanah is ultimately a time of renewal. It is the day when each person must search his deeds, evaluating his relationships both with God and his fellow men, righting wrongs and starting anew.

## Elul – A Month of Preparation

Preparations for Rosh Hashanah actually begin a month before the holiday, starting on the first of Elul. Since ancient times, the month of Elul has been a time of introspection and review. It was on the first of this month that Moses ascended Sinai to beseech forgiveness for the Jewish people. It is also during this month that creation began.

Starting on the first of Elul, every person should devote time daily to consider his relationship with God, his neighbors, and his family. A person should assess who he is now, who he wants to be, and how to attain these goals.

Our goal in the month of Elul is change; we set out to change who we are, to show God that we can be different, better people. In English, this process is called repentance. In Hebrew the term is *teshuvah*.

## Teshuvah: Technical vs. Colloquial Use

Colloquially, the term *teshuvah* is employed to mean any type of repentance. However, *Teshuva* also has very specific, technical meanings. In the course of your studies you may come across the statement: "There is no *teshuvah* for Non-Jews,[8]" or "There is no *teshuvah* for Noahides." When you see this statement, remember that it is dealing with the technical definition of *teshuvah*, which is far more complicated than the way the word is commonly used. The technical definition of *teshuvah* is only relevant to Jews. However, there are other types of repentance. For example, many explain that the type of repentance relevant to Noahides is called *charata*. The details of these technical distinctions, however, are entirely theoretical and have little-to-no practical impact on Noahide practice. There is certainly repentance for Noahides regardless of whether the technical term for that repentance is *teshuvah*, *charata*, or anything else. After all, the story of Jonah is all about non-Jewish repentance.[9]

**ACTION: PSALM 27**

The custom of Jews, starting on the first day of Elul, is to recite Psalm 27 daily, both in the morning and evening (around sunset or at night). The Midrash explains that this psalm contains a number of subtle references to the period of repentance and the holidays. It is certainly appropriate for Noahides to recite this psalm as part of their preparations for Rosh Hashanah. This twice-daily recitation of Psalm 27 continues from the 1st of Elul through the 21st of Tishrei.[10]

## Psalm 27

*To be recited in the morning and at sunset (or at night), daily, from the 1st of Elul to the 21st of Tishrei. Commentary is found in the footnotes.*

Of David: the Lord is my light[11] and my salvation.[12] Of whom shall I be afraid? The Lord is the strength of my life. Of whom shall I dread? When evil-doers – my

---

[8] See *Midrash Tanchuma*, Haazinu 4.

[9] Resolving *Midrash Tanchumah* against *Sefer Yonah* has elicited much discussion among the Acharonim. See *Sefer Ratz KeTzvi: Yerach HaEisanim* 13 for an extensive discussion of the issues.

[10] This, as we shall see, is the period of the holidays for Noahides and Jews.

[11] The Midrash understands this as a reference to Rosh Hashanah.

[12] The salvation mentioned here is the atonement of the holiday season. For Jews it refers to the atonement of Yom Kippur, for Noahides the atonement of Sukkot.

tormentors and opponents[13] – draw near to devour my flesh, it is they who stumble and fall. Though an army may besiege me, my heart will not fear. Should warfare arise against me, in this alone I shall trust.[14]

I have asked one thing of the Lord, only this have I sought: that I may dwell in the house of the Lord all the days of my life, to behold the pleasantness of the Lord, and to meditate within His sanctuary.[15]

On the day of evil He will hide me within His shelter. He will conceal me in the innermost shelter of his tent. He will lift me up upon a rock. And now he will raise my head above my foes who surround me. I will slaughter in his tent joyous offerings. I will sing and make music to the Lord. Lord, hear my voice when I call! Favor me and answer me! For your sake has my heart spoke to me: "Seek his presence!" O God, I seek your presence! Do not conceal your countenance from me! Do not repel your servant in anger! You have been my help. Do not forsake me, do not abandon me, O God of my salvation!

Though my father and mother have abandoned me,[16] the Lord shall gather me in. Teach me your way, O Lord, and on account of my watchful foes[17] set me upon a straight path. Do not give me over to their wishes for they have set against me false witnesses who breathe violence.

---

[13] The evil-doers and opponents mentioned in this psalm are primarily internal. They are the devices of the *yetzer ha-ra*, the evil inclination. They are also the memories and emotions associated with one's past misdeeds. These memories often torment a person and hamper their ability to return to God. This will be discussed more in a future lesson.

[14] Rashi and Radak explain that this refers to the opening line "The Lord is my light and my salvation," which is the process of Rosh HaShanah and subsequent atonement. One must trust in this process. Once a person has returned to God and reestablished a positive relationship with God, then God will protect and shelter him. Alternatively, Ibn Ezra explains that this phrase refers to the next sentence: *I have asked one thing of the Lord, only this have I sought: that I may dwell in the house of the Lord all the days of my life…* One should trust in God because he (the penitent) ultimately desires spiritual success and not the vain achievements of this world.

[15] Writes the *Malbim*, that despite the many desires and needs a person may have, the desire to know his creator is the ultimate, all inclusive desire of the soul.

[16] Sforno explains that once a person becomes an adult he must find his own way in the world. He can no longer rely upon his parents to make choices for him. He must choose his values and make his own decisions. Although his parents are no longer his guiding voice, the Lord is always there. God is eternally our father and guide.

[17] The Hebrew here is a little difficult to translate. The word for "Watchful foes" is related to the word for "staring" or "gazing." In the context of our verse, it refers to those who stare maliciously. The psalm is asking God to frustrate the wishes of those who maliciously watch and mock one who wishes to come back to God. See Radak.

Had I not believed[18] that I would see the goodness of the Lord in the land of life![19] Hope to the Lord! Be strong and He will give you courage[20] – and hope to the Lord!

## Studying For Elul: Works on Repentance

**ACTION: STUDY FOR ELUL**

In Elul, many prepare by studying works of *mussar* (personal development) or writings on *Teshuva* (repentance). There are, thank God, many, many books addressing these topics. The following are a few suggested titles:

- *Returnity*, by R' Tal Zwecker
- *The Power of Teshuvah*, by R' Heshy Kleinman
- *A Touch of Purity*, by R' Yechiel Spero
- *Teshuvah, Restoring Life*, by R' Reuven Leuchter
- *Teshuvah*, by S. Felbrand
- *Thirty Days to Teshuva*, by R' Zvi Miller
- *Crown Him With Joy*, by R' Hadar Margolin
- *Gates of Repentance*, by Rabbeinu Yonah

During Elul, many are accustomed to study and use the advice given by Rabbeinu Yonah in his *Gates of Repentance*, in a section called *The Foundation of Repentance* (the full text of *Gates of Repentance* is available in translation from Feldheim Publishers.) We have provided a translation of this section here:

---

[18] Rashi explains: Were it not for my faith in God, my enemies would have destroyed me and I would have never merited to achieve closeness to God.

[19] Meaning the World to Come. See *Brachos* 4a.

[20] Strength in faith is the ultimate source of all courage.

# Gate of Repentance: The Foundation of Repentance
## by Rabbeinu Yonah of Gerona c. 1250 CE

The Holy One, blessed is He, taught us through his servants, the prophets, and [specifically] through Yechezkel the prophet [Yechezkel 18:30-31]:

> *Repent, and cause others to repent, from all your transgressions so that they shall not be a stumbling block of iniquity for you. Cast away from yourselves all your transgressions and make for yourselves a new heart and a new spirit. Why should you die?*

You, who have transgressed and sinned, and now comes to seek refuge under the wings of the Divine Presence, to enter into the ways of repentance, I shall instruct you and enlighten you in the path to travel.

On that day,[21] you shall cast away all the sins that you have committed and consider yourself as if you were born today; as if you have neither merit nor fault. This day is the beginning of your deeds. Starting today, you shall weigh all your actions in order that your steps not veer from the good path. This path will bring you to repentance, a complete return, because it is as if you have cast from your shoulders the heaviness of all the transgressions you have committed. Thus your thoughts will neither haunt nor confuse you nor prevent you from repenting because of embarrassment from your sins. This is because [otherwise] your thoughts will say to you: "How could I be so brazen to repent after I have sinned and transgressed, doing such-and-such over and over? How could I raise my face before Him? [I am] like a thief who has been caught - I am too embarrassed to stand before Him! And how can I show myself in his courtyard, how could I keep his laws?"

Do not think like this! The evil inclination sits like a fly in the chambers of the heart, renewing himself every day, watching and waiting to make you stumble. He puts these destructive thoughts in your heart. Instead, you should remember that this is the nature of the Creator, may He be blessed: that His hand is outstretched to receive the penitent. Therefore, it is good for you to cast off your sins and make for yourself a new heart.

And so shall you do on the day that you decide to return: When your spirit moves you to become a servant of your Creator, you shall offer up your prayer before Him and say:

> "Please God, I have sinned and transgressed, (and such and such I did...) from the day I came upon the Earth until this very day. And now, my heart has moved me and my spirit has pressed me to return to You in

---

[21] Meaning the day one decides to return to God.

truth and with a good and complete heart – with all my heart, soul, and all that is dear to me – and to admit and cast aside my ways; to cast away from myself all my sins and to make for myself a new heart and a new spirit, and to be meticulous and careful in my fear of You. And You, Lord, my God, who opens His hand with repentance, helping those who come to purify themselves, open Your hand and receive me with complete repentance before You. Help me to strengthen myself in fear of You. Help me against the evil inclination, who wages war against me with cunning strategies, seeking to entrap my soul and destroy men, that it should not rule over me. Distance it from my 248 limbs and cast it into the depths of the sea. Thwart it so that it shall not stand at my right side to accuse me.[22] Help me so that I shall go in Your laws. Remove from me this heart of stone and grant me a heart of flesh.

Please O Lord, my God, listen to the prayer of Your servant and to his supplications and receive my return unto You. Do not let any sin prevent my prayer and return. May there come before Your holy throne upright defenders to defend me and bring my prayer before You. And if, on account of my many and great sins, there is no one to defend me, then make an opening from under Your throne of glory and receive my repentance so that I should not return empty from before You; for only you listen to prayer."

You should habituate yourself to always say this prayer.

And such is the path that you should walk and the actions to which you should accustom yourself so that you will be on guard from all sin. In the morning, when you wake from your sleep, you should think in your mind that you will repent and examine your ways. You should strive, in accordance with your ability, not to stray.

At meal-times, before you eat, you should confess your sins. If you strayed in anything, you should confess it. This confession will distance you from all sin and transgression. Because, if a sin comes your way, you will be cautious of it and say in your heart: "How could I do this great, evil thing and then confess on it later? Why, I would be of those of which it is said, [*Tehillim* 78:36] 'Nevertheless they did flatter him with their mouth, and they lied unto him with their tongues. For their heart was not right with him, neither were they steadfast in his covenant.' I would be like one who immerses [in a *mikveh*] while holding an impure creature! I would be foolish and with little intellect before my Creator for not having being able to stand up to my lusts even for a short time like this!"

---

[22] One's own evil inclination stands against Him as prosecutor.

And when you put this to your heart and spirit, you will then be guarded from sin.

You should be swift as a deer and strong as a lion to do the will of your father in heaven. This applies even to minor things because all your ways will be measured. And so King David said [*Tehillim* 49:6]:

> *Why should I fear in the days of evil, when the iniquity of my heels shall compass me about.*

This verse speaks of the sins and *mitzvot* that men trample with their heels (meaning sins that most people are not careful about) and consider them to be nothing.

When the time to eat comes, and you search yourself and find nothing, then you should thank and praise the Creator who has helped you against your enemies, and that you merited to have one hour of *teshuva* in this world. Like this you should then eat your meal. Afterwards, when the evening meal comes, you should confess beforehand everything, as I have said. And so you should do from the time of eating your evening meal until the time to sleep [meaning, a third confession before sleep].

We have, therefore, three daily opportunities for this confession. Thus should you do every day from the first day of your *teshuva* and afterwards, for one month or one year, until you are strengthened in the fear of the Creator and have succeeded in abandoning your bad habits.

And when you can guard yourself from the sins to which you were habituated, finding that you had many opportunities to transgress yet did not do so, you should no longer fear. From heaven you were helped... And regarding the previous sins that you had cast off from yourself, you should be always regretful and seek from God to erase them from the heavenly record. You should also chastise your soul over them. If you are of delicate constitution, and cannot tolerate difficult chastisement and fasts, you should at least restrict your desires, in particular those for food and drink.

So said said the pious Rabbi Avraham bar Dovid, "the best safeguard, the greatest and best, is to refrain from over-indulging in food." He explained his words, saying that this is not to mean that one should refrain altogether from eating meat and drinking wine. After all, what has already been forbidden is enough. Rather, he means that while you are eating and still desire to eat more, you should stop in honor of your Creator, and not eat according to your whole desire. This practice will save you from sin and remind you of the love of the Creator more than fasting once a week. That is because this practice is every day, always, when you eat or drinks – then you should refrain from your desire for the honor of your Creator.

You should put your heart to the Torah. If you were accustomed to learning one page each day, then you should learn two. This is because Torah study leads to action. And you should subjugate yourself, forcing your innate desires to be for Torah and the fulfillment of *mitzvos*…

You should not be haphazard in your service of the Creator. Rather you should serve Him with a complete heart. You should never neglect any matter because of laziness or embarrassment…

Even if the world mocks you, nevertheless you should be like a simpleton in their eyes rather than transgress even a small *mitzva* of the Creator's *mitzvos*. Regarding this it is written "in its love you shall be ravished always" (Mishlei 5:19), which means - for the love of a *mitzva*, you should be ravished and simple to leave all things and to work on it. We have found an example of this by Rebbi Elazar ben Pedas, who would sit in the lower market of Tzipori and toil in Torah while his cloak lay in the upper market of the town. He appeared like a simpleton in the eyes of the world because of his love of *mitzvos* and of the Creator [Talmud *Eruvin* 54b]. And if one does this and dies at half of his days, he is given reward as if he had lived all 70 years. This is what King Shlomo said in his wisdom [*Koheles* 5:11]:

> *The sleep of the working man is pleasant, whether he eats little or much.*

This means that whether one's days are many or few, the reward for the few is like the reward for the many.

Moshe toiled for the Jewish people 40 years, and Shmuel HaNavi only ten years, nevertheless the verse equates both of them as one, as it is written [*Tehillim* 99:6]:

> *Moshe and Aaron among his priests, and Shmuel among them that call upon his name.*

The penitent should not muse to himself and say: "Why should I toil in vain? I will waste my strength for nothing! How can my repentance stand against my sins? All that I am capable of doing will not help against all the sins that I have done!"

Don't say this. The Holy One, blessed is He, promised through the prophet Yechezkel that one's sins will not be recalled again, as it is written [*Yechezkel* 18:21-22]:

> *But if the wicked will turn from all his sins that he has committed, and keep all my statutes, and do that which is lawful and right, he shall surely live, he shall not die. All his transgressions that he has committed, they shall not be mentioned to him; in his righteousness that he has done he shall live.*

And there are many more verses for those haunted by their sins, to strengthen them to repent as is written [*Yechezkel* 33:10-11]:

> *Say to them, By My life, says the L-rd, I desire not the death of the wicked, but that the wicked turn from his way, and live. Repent, repent from your evil ways; why should you die, O children of Israel?*

And through all his servants, the prophets, He warned us many times on the matter of *teshuva*. And also our teachers, the Sages of the generations, warned us very much on *teshuva* saying "repent one day before your death" [*Pirkei Avot*].

And they said, "the level of the one who has repented is greater than that of the completely righteous." This is what they meant when they said "in the place where the penitent stands, the perfectly righteous does not stand" [Repentance] is one of the things created before the creation of the world. Likewise they said in the *Midrash Bereishis* [4:13] "*And Kayin said to God, 'is my sin too great to bear?'* - he repented."
Therefore this verse has 7 words, (hinting) that repentance rises up until the holy throne, the 7 firmaments, 7 realms…

Therefore, every God fearing person should put in his heart the fear of the Creator and repent from all his sins. He should prepare for himself a new, clean, pure heart with which to serve his Creator. He should accustom himself to all that has been written. He should use his intelligence to think of ways in which he could fear the Lord, the Great and Awesome One, and engage such matters between him privately, away from the eyes of men.

Fortunate is one who merits and causes others to merit. The entire world was created for such a person, as it is written [*Koheles* 12:13]:

*The end of the matter, all having been heard, is fear God and keep his* mitzvos, *for this is the sum of man."*

Our sages have expounded this verse to mean [Talmud *Berachos* 6] "The entire world was created as a companion for such a person."

THE YESHIVA PIRCHEI SHOSHANIM SHULCHAN ARUCH LEARNING PROJECT

# The Noahide Laws – Lesson Twenty Seven

© **Yeshiva Pirchei Shoshanim 2017**
This shiur may not be reproduced in any
form without permission of the copyright holder.

**164 Village Path, Lakewood NJ 08701 732.370.3344**
**164 Rabbi Akiva, Bnei Brak, 03.616.6340**

## Outline of This Lesson:

1. Introduction
2. When To Start Saying *Selichos*
3. The Custom Noahides Should Follow
4. In Practice
5. Action Point
6. Structure of *Selichos*
7. Suggested *Selichos* Service

# Festivals II: Selichos

## Introduction

The second phase Rosh HaShanah preparation is the recitation of *Selichos* – penitential prayers. These prayers are meant to prepare the soul for Rosh HaShanah. Since Rosh HaShanah is the day upon which the heart of every person (Jew and Noahide alike) is examined, it makes sense that every person should prepare. The recitation of *Selichos* is thus appropriate for both Jews and Noahides.

## When to Start Saying *Selichos*?

*Selichos* are usually said in the early, pre-dawn, hours and followed by one's regular devotions. As with all Noahide prayers, there is no quorum required for their recitation. They may be said by an individual or by a group of people. There are two different customs as to when to begin saying *Selichos*.

**The Sephardi Custom**  According to the Sephardi custom (the custom of the Jews of Spain, North Africa, and the Middle East), *Selichos* are said for the entire month of Elul. The reason for this is that Moses ascended Sinai on the first of Elul and remained there all month. He spent the time petitioning for his people and, eventually, received the second set of tablets. Selichos are recited for the entire month in commemoration and imitation of Moses's petitioning upon Sinai.

**The Ashkenazi Custom**  Ashkenazi custom (the custom of the Jews of Europe and most of America) is a little more complicated. The Ashkenazi custom has two requirements. First, is that there must be a minimum of four days of *Selichos* before Rosh HaShanah. Second, is that *Selichos* must start after the preceding Shabbat. Therefore, if Rosh

HaShanah starts on a Wednesday night, then *Selichos* start after the preceding Shabbat. However, if Rosh HaShanah starts on a Monday night, then *Selichos* starts after the Shabbat preceding the Shabbat before Rosh Hashanah. In such a case, *Selichos* are said for almost 10 days.

This custom has a fascinating source. In the Torah's list of the festival offerings[1] it states over and over: "You shall bring…" However, the offering of Rosh HaShanah says: "You shall make…" The sages have noted this subtle difference. On Rosh HaShanah, they explain, a person must make himself like an offering, a sacrifice, to God. He must prepare his soul in the same way in which a sacrifice is prepared for the Temple. Just as a sacrifice must be examined and watched for four days to ensure it is free of a disqualifying blemish, so too must a person search and examine his soul for at least four days prior to Rosh HaShanah.

What is the reason for always beginning after Shabbat? Beginning after Shabbat was originally a practical matter of synagogue logistics. Over time it became standard convention.

## Which Custom Should Noahides Follow if They Wish to Say Selichos?

It seems more appropriate for Noahides to follow the Ashkenaz custom with some slight modifications. There are many, many reasons why the Ashkenaz custom is preferable for Noahides. Namely:

1) Moses's ascending Sinai in Elul, the basis for the Sephardic custom, was about seeking atonement for the Jewish sin of the golden calf. This is less relevant to Noahides than the reason behind the Ashkenaz custom. Noahides, after all, have a share in the laws of offerings. In fact, a Noahide may, even today, offer certain sacrifices (something even a Jew cannot do!)

2) Almost all of the texts of the *Selichos* are inapplicable to Noahides. There are barely enough texts for the Ashkenaz custom and certainly not enough to fill out an entire month of *Selichos* according to the Sephardic custom.

---

[1] Numbers, Chapters 28 & 29.

**IN PRACTICE**

Since the Ashkenaz custom of starting *Selichos* after Shabbat began as a matter of synagogue logistics, it is not relevant to Noahides. For this reason, we suggest that Noahides say *Selichos* only in the four days before Rosh HaShanah. While Jews do not say *Selichos* on Shabbat, the reasons for this omission do not apply to Noahides. Therefore, Noahides who wish to say *Selichos* should began four days before Rosh HaShanah and say them for each of the four days. In 2015 Noahides will say Selichos as follows:

- Thursday, September 10, 2015 – First day of *Selichos* for Noahides. Jews will begin saying *Selichos* on the night of September 5.
- Friday, September 11, 2015 – Second day of *Selichos* for Noahides.
- Saturday, September 12, 2015 – Third day of *Selichos* for Noahides.
- Sunday, September 13, 2015 – Fourth and final day of *Selichos*. Rosh HaShanah begins at night.
- Monday, September 14 – Rosh HaShanah day.

**ACTION POINT**

There are very, very few existing *Selichos* texts that work for Noahides. The composition of uniquely Noahide *Selichos* is worthwhile and certainly needed for those who wish to say *Selichos*. An excellent source for the format and style of the *Selichos* is The Complete Artscroll Selichos. In the suggested Noahide service below, we have used Psalms associated with the themes of repentance as *Selichos* texts. However, these may certainly be changed out in favor of uniquely Noahide texts.

## The Structure of *Selichos*

The *Selichos* service consists of fixed prayers interspersed with the *Selichos* texts. The *Selichos* texts change daily, while the fixed portions remain the same. The outline is as follows:

- Opening Prayers - The *Selichos* service consists of fixed opening prayers.

- *Selichos* - Each *Selicha* (the singular of *Selichos*) is separated by a repeated prayer refrain.

- The Litany – Following *Selichos* we recite a confession.

- Supplication – The concluding prayer.

The following is a suggested *Selichos* service for Noahides. It is adapted from the traditional Ashkenaz *Selichos* service.

## *Selichos*

## The First Day

*Selichos may be said alone or with a congregation. This service is drafted for a congregation. An individual praying alone should say "I" instead of "we" and "my" instead of "our." An individual also omits congregational responses.*

### Opening Prayers

**Sanctification** — **Leader:** May His great name be ever exalted and sanctified (**Cong.:** Amen!) in the world that He created according to His will. May His kingship reign in our lifetimes and in our days, swiftly and soon, and we say: Amen!

**Cong.:** Amen! May His great Name be blessed forever and ever!

**Leader:** May His great name be blessed forever and ever. Blessed, praised, glorified, exalted, extolled, mighty, upraised, and lauded is the name of the Holy One, Blessed is He (**Cong.:** Blessed is He!) exceedingly beyond any blessing and song or praise and consolation that may be uttered in the world, and we say: Amen (**Cong.:** Amen!)

**All continue individually:**

**To you, Lord, is the righteousness...** — To you, Lord, is the righteousness and to us the shamefacedness. What can we plead? What can we say? What can be uttered? How can we justify ourselves? We will search our ways, inspect them, and then we shall return to you, for Your right hand is outstretched to accept those who return. Neither with kindnesses nor worthy deeds do we come before You. Rather, like the poor and needy do we knock upon Your doors. We knock upon your doors, O Merciful and Compassionate One! Please, do not turn us away from You unanswered! Our King, do not turn us away from You unanswered, for You alone hear prayer!

**All flesh shall come to You...** — All flesh shall come to You, the One who hears prayer. All flesh shall come to bow before You, O Lord. They will come and bow before you, my Lord, and will render honor unto Your name. Come! Let us prostrate ourselves and bow! Let us kneel before God, our maker. Let us come to His dwelling places, let us prostrate at His footstool. Enter His gates with thanksgiving and His courts with praise. Give thanks to Him and praise His name! Exalt the Lord, our God, and bow at His footstool for He is Holy. Exalt the Lord, our God, and bow at His holy mountain for holy is the Lord, our God. Prostrate yourselves before the Lord in His most holy place. Tremble before Him, all who are upon earth.

As for us, through Your abundant kindness we shall enter Your house. We shall prostrate ourselves toward Your holy sanctuary in awe of You. We will bow towards Your holy sanctuary and give thanks to Your name, for Your kindness and truth, because You have exalted Your promise beyond Your name. Come! Let us sing to the *Lord*, let us call out unto the Rock of our salvation! Let us greet Him with thanksgiving, let us call out to Him with praiseful songs. Let us share together in sweet counsel, let us walk in throngs within the house of God.

God is dreaded in the hidden-most counsel of the holy ones, inspiring awe upon all those who surround him. Lift your hands in the sanctuary and bless the Lord. Behold! Bless the Lord, all you servants of the Lord, who stand in the house of the Lord in the nights. For what force is there in heaven or earth comparable to Your deeds and power? For His is the sea and He perfected the dry land; His hands fashioned it. For in His power are the hidden mysteries of the earth; the mountain summits belong to Him. For the soul of every living thing is His – so too is the spirit of all human flesh. Heaven will gratefully praise Your wonders, O Lord. Your faithfulness [will be praised] in the assembly of holy ones. Your arm is great with power. You strengthen Your hand; You exalt Your right hand! The heavens are Yours and the earth too, the earth and its fullness, is yours for you founded them. You shattered the sea with your might; you smashed the heads of sea serpents upon the waters. You established order upon the earth; summer and winter – you fashioned them. You crushed the heads of the leviathan and You served it as food to the nation of legions. You split open fountain and stream, You dried the mighty rivers. The day is Yours and the night, as well, is Yours. You established luminaries and the sun – You, who performs great deeds that are beyond comprehension and wonders without number. For the Lord is a great God, a great king who is above all heavenly powers. For You are great and work wonders – You alone, O God. For Your kindness is exalted above the very heavens and Your truth is until the upper heavens. The Lord is great and exceedingly lauded. He is awesome above all heavenly powers. Yours, Lord, is the greatness, strength, splendor, triumph, and glory – even everything in heaven and earth! Yours, Lord, is the dominion and sovereignty over every leader. Who could not revere You, O King of the Nations, for in all their kingdom there is none like You. There is none like You, O Lord, for You are great and Your name is great with power. O Lord, God of legions, who is like you, O Strong One, O God? Your faithfulness surrounds you! O Lord, Master of Legions, enthroned above the Cherubim, You alone are God.

Who can express the mighty acts of the Lord, who can announce all His praises? For what in the sky is comparable to the Lord, that can be likened to Him among the angels? What can we say before You who dwells on high? What can we say to You who abides in the highest heaven? What can we say before You, Lord, our God? What can we declare? What justification can we offer? We have no mouth with which to respond. Neither are we so brazen as to raise our heads, for our iniquities are too numerous to count and our sins too vast to be numbered. For

Your Name's sake, O Lord, revive us and, with your righteousness, remove our souls from distress. It is Your way, our God, to delay Your anger against people, both evil and good, and for this You are praised. Act for Your sake, our God, and not for ours. Behold our condition – destitute and empty-handed. The soul is Yours and the body is Your handiwork; take pity on Your labor. (**All continue to the end, but The Leader concludes by reading the following sentences aloud:**) The soul is Yours and the body is Yours. O Lord, act for Your name's sake! We have come, relying upon Your name, O Lord. Act for Your name's sake and because of Your name's glory – for "gracious and merciful God" is Your name! For your name's sake, Lord, may You forgive our iniquity, abundant as it may be.

**Cong. first aloud, then repeated aloud by Leader:** Forgive us, our father, for in our abundant folly we have erred. Pardon us our King, for our iniquities are many.

## *Selicha* – Psalm 32

*The* Selicha *texts are poetic creations of the* paytanim *– ancient poets who were masters of the Hebrew language and Jewish liturgy. Their creations deal extensively with the experience of Israel in exile and the restoration of the unique relationship between Israel and God. Due to their specificity, the* Selichos *texts are mostly inapplicable to Noahides. As of today, there are no uniquely Noahide* Selichos. *For this service, we have used Psalms associated with repentance as* Selicha *texts. In the future, Noahides may compose their own unique poems to use in their place.*

*All recite Psalm 32 to themselves. The Leader, however, reads the last verse out loud.*

**Standing, all recite:**

**Oh God, King, Who sites upon the throne of mercy...**

Oh God, King, Who sites upon the throne of mercy, who acts with kindness, forgives iniquities, removes sin, and grants abundant pardon to careless transgressors and forgiveness to rebels – He Who deals righteously with every living being. You do not repay them according to their evil.

**Leader:** Please do not regard as sinful that which we have done foolishly and transgressed.

**Cong.:** We have erred, our Rock! Forgive us, O One who has formed us!

*The following four verses are recited responsively. Each verse is recited first by the Leader followed by the Congregation:*

**Hear our voice...**

Hear our voice, O Lord, our God, show us pity and compassion, and accept our prayer with compassion and favor.

Bring us back to You Lord, and we will return to you.

Do not cast us away from You, and do not remove Your holy spirit from us.

Do not cast us away in old age; do not forsake us when our strength is exhausted.

**All continue individually:**

Do not forsake us O Lord, our God, be not distant from us. Display for us a sign for good, so that our enemies may see it and be ashamed, for You, O Lord, will have helped and consoled us. To our sayings give ear, O Lord, perceive our thoughts. May the expressions of our mouth and the thoughts of our heart find favor before You, Lord, our Rock and our Redeemer. Because for You, O Lord, we have waited; You will answer, my Lord, our God.

# Confession

**All continue individually:**
Our God, may our prayer come before You. Do not ignore our supplication, for we are not so brazen and obstinate as to say before You, Lord, our God, that we are righteous and have not sinned, for in truth we have sinned.

*The confession is recited with head and body slightly bowed. Strike the left side of the chest with the right first at each bolded word.*

WE have **become guilty**, we have **betrayed**, we have **robbed**, we have **spoken slander**, we have **caused perversion**, we have **caused wickedness**, we have **sinned willfully**, we have **extorted**, we have **accused falsely**, we have **given evil counsel**, we have **been deceitful**, we have **scorned**, we have **rebelled**, we have **provoked**, we have **turned away**, we have **been perverse**, we have **acted wantonly**, we have **persecuted**, we have **been obstinate**, we have **been wicked**, we have **corrupted**, we have **been abominable**, we have **strayed**, and You have let us go astray.

We have turned away from Your commandments and from Your good laws but to no avail. Yet, You are righteous in all that has come upon us, for You have acted truthfully while we have caused wickedness.

We have acted wickedly and sinned willfully. Inspire our hearts to abandon the path of evil, as it is written by Your prophet: May the wicked one abandon his way and the vicious man his thoughts; may he return to the Lord and He will show him mercy - to our God, for He is abundantly forgiving.

Your righteous anointed one [David] said before You: "Who can discern mistakes? From unperceived faults cleanse me." Cleanse us Lord, our God, of all our willful sins and purify us, of all our contaminations. Sprinkle upon us pure water and purify us, as it is written by Your prophet: I shall sprinkle pure water upon you and purify you; I will purify you of all your contaminations and of all your abominations.

Micah, your servant, said before You: "Who O God is like You, who pardons iniquity and overlooks transgression for the remnant of his heritage? He who has not retained His wrath eternally, for he desires kindness! He will again be merciful to us; He will suppress our iniquities and cast all sins into the depths of the sea."

Daniel, the greatly beloved man, cried out before You: "Incline Your ear, my God, and listen; open Your eyes and see our desolation and that of the city upon which Your Name is proclaimed. Not because of our righteousness do we cast our supplications before you, but rather because of your abundant compassion. O my Lord, heed! O my Lord, forgive! O my Lord, be attentive and act! Do not delay, for your sake my God, for your Name is proclaimed upon Your city and Your people."

Ezra the scribe said before You: My God, I am embarrassed and ashamed to lift my face to You, for our iniquities have multiplied and our sins have extended unto heaven. You are the God of forgiveness, compassionate and merciful, slow to anger, and abundant in kindness. You have not forsaken us.

Do not forsake us, our Father, do not cast us off, our Creator, do not abandon us, our Molder, and do not bring about our destruction.

**Act for the sake...**

Act for the sake of Your truth, act for the sake of Your covenant, act for the sake of Your greatness and splendor, act for the sake of Your law, act for the sake of Your glory, act for the sake of Your meeting house, act for the sake of Your remembrance, act for the sake of Your kindness, act for the sake of Your goodness, act for the sake of Your oneness, act for the sake of Your honor, act for the sake of Your teaching, act for the sake of Your kingship, act for the sake of Your eternality, act for the sake of Your counsel, act for the sake of Your power, act for the sake of Your beauty, act for the sake of Your righteousness, act for the sake of Your sanctity, act for the sake of Your abundant mercy, act for the sake of Your presence, act for the sake of Your praise, act for the sake of Your beloved ones who rest in the dust, act for the sake of the desolation of your temple, act for the sake of the ruins of your altar, act for the sake of the martyrs for your holy name; act for the sake of those slaughtered for your oneness, act for the sake of those who entered fire and water for the sanctification of your name, act for the nursing infants who did not err act for the sake of the weaned babes who did not sin, act for the sake of the children at the schoolroom. Act for your sake, if not for ours. Act for your sake and save us!

**Answer us...**    Answer us, Lord, answer us.
Answer us, Our God, answer us.
Answer us, Our Father, answer us.
Answer us, Our Creator, answer us.
Answer us, Our Redeemer, answer us.
Answer us, He Who Searches Us Out, answer us.
Answer us, Faithful God, answer us.
Answer us, Steadfast and Kind One, answer us.
Answer us, Pure and Upright One, answer us.
Answer us, Living and Enduring One, answer us.
Answer us, Good and Beneficent One, answer us.
Answer us, You Who Knows Inclination, answer us.
Answer us, You Who Suppresses Wrath, answer us.
Answer us, You Who Dons Righteousness, answer us.
Answer us, King Who Reigns Over Kings, answer us.
Answer us, Awesome and Powerful One, answer us.
Answer us, You Who Forgives and Pardons, answer us.
Answer us, You Who Answers in Times of Distress, answer us.
Answer us, Redeemer and Rescuer, answer us.
Answer us, Righteous and Upright One, answer us.
Answer us, He Who is Close to Those Who Call Upon Him, answer us.
Answer us, Merciful and Gracious One, answer us.
Answer us, You Who Hears the Destitute, answer us.
Answer us, You Who Supports the Wholesome, answer us.
Answer us, You Who are Hard to Anger, answer us.
Answer us, You Who are Easy to Pacify, answer us.
Answer us, You Who Answers In a Time of Favor, answer us.
Answer us, Father of Orphans, answer us.
Answer us, Judge of Widows, answer us.

The Merciful One Who Answers the poor, may He answer us.
The Merciful One Who Answers the brokenhearted, may He answer us.
The Merciful One Who Answers the humble of spirit, may He answer us.

O Merciful One, answer us!
O Merciful One, have pity!
O Merciful One, have mercy upon us – now, swiftly, and soon!

## Concluding Supplication

*The following is recited seated.*

And David said to Gad: "I am exceedingly distressed. Let us fall into The Lord's hand for His mercies are abundant, but let me not fall into human hands.

O compassionate and Gracious One, I have sinned before you, O Lord, Who is full of mercy, have mercy on me and accept my supplications.

Lord, do not rebuke me in Your anger nor chastise me in Your rage. Favor me, O Lord, for I am feeble. Heal me, O Lord, for my bones shudder. My soul is utterly confounded. And You, Lord, how long? Desist, Lord, release my soul – save me as befits your kindness, for there is no mention of you in death. In the lower world, who will thank you? I am wearied with my sigh, each night my tears drench my bed and soak my couch. My eye is dimmed by anger, aged by my tormentors. Depart from me all evildoers, for the Lord has heard the sound of my weeping! The Lord has heard my plea. The Lord will accept my prayer. Let all my foes be shamed and utterly confounded; they will regret and be ashamed.

*The following is recited while standing:*

We know not what we do, but our eyes are upon you. Remember your mercies, Lord, and your kindnesses, for they extend from the beginning of the world. May your kindness be upon us, O Lord, as we have awaited You. May your mercies meet us quickly. Be gracious to us O Lord! Amid rage, remember to be merciful! For He knows our nature; He remembers that we are dust. **All continue to the end; the Leader reads this last verse aloud:** Help us, O God of our salvation, for the sake of Your glory. Rescue us and judge us favorably!

**Sanctification**

**Leader:** May His great name be ever exalted and sanctified (**Cong.:** Amen!) **Leader:** in the world that He created according to His will. May His kingship reign in our lifetimes and in our days, swiftly and soon, and we say: Amen!

**Cong.:** Amen! May His great Name be blessed forever and ever!

**Leader:** May His great name be blessed forever and ever. Blessed, praised, glorified, exalted, extolled, mighty, upraised, and lauded is the name of the Holy One, Blessed is He (**Cong.:** Blessed is He!) exceedingly beyond any blessing and song or praise and consolation that may be uttered in the world, and we say: Amen (**Cong.:**. Amen!)

# *Selichos*

## The Second, Third, and Fourth Days

*The service for these days differs slightly from that of the first day.*

## Opening Prayers

**Sanctification**

**Leader:** May His great name be ever exalted and sanctified (**Cong.:** Amen!) in the world that He created according to His will. May His kingship reign in our lifetimes and in our days, swiftly and soon, and we say: Amen!

**Cong.:** Amen! May His great Name be blessed forever and ever!

**Leader:** May His great name be blessed forever and ever. Blessed, praised, glorified, exalted, extolled, mighty, upraised, and lauded is the name of the Holy One, Blessed is He (**Cong.:** Blessed is He!) exceedingly beyond any blessing and song or praise and consolation that may be uttered in the world, and we say: Amen (**Cong.:.** Amen!)

*All continue individually:*

**To you, Lord, is the righteousness...**

To you, Lord, is the righteousness and to us the shamefacedness. What can we plead? What can we say? What can be uttered? How can we justify ourselves? We will search our ways, inspect them, and then we shall return to you, for Your right hand is outstretched to accept those who return. Neither with kindnesses nor worthy deeds do we come before You. Rather, like the poor and needy do we knock upon Your doors. We knock upon your doors, O Merciful and Compassionate One! Please, do not turn us away from You unanswered! Our King, do not turn us away from You unanswered, for You alone hear prayer!

**All flesh shall come to You...**

All flesh shall come to You, the One who hears prayer. All flesh shall come to bow before You, Lord. They will come and bow before you, my Lord, and will render honor unto Your name. Come! Let us prostrate ourselves and bow! Let us kneel before God, our maker. Let us come to His dwelling places, let us prostrate at His footstool. Enter His gates with thanksgiving and His courts with praise. Give thanks to Him and praise His name! Exalt the Lord, our God, and bow at His footstool for He is Holy. Exalt the Lord, our God, and bow at His holy mountain for holy is the Lord, our God. Prostrate yourselves before the Lord in His most holy place. Tremble before Him, all who are upon earth.

As for us, through Your abundant kindness we shall enter Your house. We shall prostrate ourselves toward Your holy sanctuary in awe of You.
We will bow towards Your holy sanctuary and give thanks to Your name, for Your kindness and truth, because You have exalted Your promise beyond Your name. Come! Let us sing to the Lord, let us call out unto the Rock of our salvation! Let

us greet Him with thanksgiving, let us call out to Him with praiseful songs. Let us share together in sweet counsel, let us walk in throngs within the house of God.

God is dreaded in the hidden-most counsel of the holy ones, inspiring awe upon all those who surround him. Lift your hands in the sanctuary and bless the Lord. Behold! Bless the Lord, all you servants of the Lord, who stand in the house of the Lord in the nights. For what force is there in heaven or earth comparable to Your deeds and power? For His is the sea and He perfected the dry land; His hands fashioned it. For in His power are the hidden mysteries of the earth; the mountain summits belong to Him. For the soul of every living thing is His – so too is the spirit of all human flesh. Heaven will gratefully praise Your wonders, O Lord. Your faithfulness [will be praised] in the assembly of holy ones. Your arm is great with power. You strengthen Your hand; You exalt Your right hand! The heavens are Yours and the earth too, the earth and its fullness, is yours for you founded them. You shattered the sea with your might; you smashed the heads of sea serpents upon the waters. You established order upon the earth; summer and winter – you fashioned them. You crushed the heads of the leviathan and You served it as food to the nation of legions. You split open fountain and stream, You dried the mighty rivers. The day is Yours and the night, as well, is Yours. You established luminaries and the sun – You, who performs great deeds that are beyond comprehension and wonders without number. For the Lord is a great God, a great king who is above all heavenly powers. For You are great and work wonders – You alone, O God. For Your kindness is exalted above the very heavens and Your truth is until the upper heavens. The Lord is great and exceedingly lauded. He is awesome above all heavenly powers. Yours, O Lord, is the greatness, strength, splendor, triumph, and glory – even everything in heaven and earth! Yours, O Lord is the dominion and sovereignty over every leader. Who could not revere You, O King of the Nations, for in all their kingdom there is none like You. There is none like You, O Lord, for You are great and Your name is great with power. The Lord, God of legions, who is like you, O Strong One, O God? Your faithfulness surrounds you! The Lord, Master of Legions, enthroned above the Cherubim, You alone are God.

Who can express the mighty acts of the Lord, who can announce all His praises? For what in the sky is comparable to the Lord, that can be likened to Him among the angels? What can we say before You who dwells on high? What can we say to You who abides in the highest heaven? What can we say before You, Lord, our God? What can we declare? What justification can we offer? We have no mouth with which to respond. Neither are we so brazen as to raise our heads, for our iniquities are too numerous to count and our sins too vast to be numbered. For Your Name's sake, O Lord, revive us and, with your righteousness, remove our souls from distress.

It is Your way, our God, to delay Your anger against people, both evil and good, and for this You are praised. Act for Your sake, our God, and not for ours.

Behold our condition – destitute and empty-handed. The soul is Yours and the body is Your handiwork; take pity on Your labor. **(All continue to the end, but The Leader concludes by reading the following sentences aloud:)** The soul is Yours and the body is Yours. O Lord, act for Your name's sake! We have come, relying upon Your name, Lord. Act for Your name's sake and because of Your name's glory – for "gracious and merciful God" is Your name! For your name's sake, O Lord, may You forgive our iniquity, abundant as it may be.

**Cong. first aloud, then repeated aloud by Leader:** Forgive us, our father, for in our abundant folly we have erred. Pardon us our king, for our iniquities are many.

**All continue individually:**

**O God - You are slow to anger...**

O God - You are slow to anger. You are called the Master of Mercy and You have taught the way of repentance. May You recall this day and every day the greatness of Your mercy and kindness. Turn to us in mercy for You are the Master of mercy. With supplication and prayer we approach Your presence. Turn back from Your anger. May we find shelter in the shadow of Your wings. Overlook sin and erase guilt. Give ear to our cry and be attentive to what we have said!

**As a father...**

As a father is merciful to his children, so too, Lord, may you have mercy upon us. The Lord, master of legions, praiseworthy is the person who trusts in You. Save, O Lord! May the King answer us on the day we call!

**Leader:** Forgive, please, our iniquity according to the greatness of your kindness! Forgive us as you granted forgiveness in your Holy Torah, as it is written:

**Cong.:** And said the Lord, "I have forgiven according to your word!"

## *Selicha* – Psalms
*On the second day, recite Psalm 62. On the third day, Psalm 75. On the fourth day, Psalm 51.*

**Oh God, King, Who sites upon the throne of mercy...**

Standing, all recite:
Oh God, King, Who sits upon the throne of mercy, who acts with kindness, forgives iniquities, removes sin, and grants abundant pardon to careless transgressors and forgiveness to rebels – He Who deals righteously with every living being. You do not repay them according to their evil.

**Leader:** Please do not regard as sinful that which we have done foolishly and transgressed.

**Cong.:** We have erred, our Rock! Forgive us, O One who has formed us!
*The following four verses are recited responsively. Each verse is recited first by the Leader followed by the Congregation:*

**Hear our voice...**   Hear our voice, O Lord, our God, show us pity and compassion, and accept our prayer with compassion and favor.

Bring us back to You O Lord, and we will return to you.

Do not cast us away from You, and do not remove Your holy spirit from us.

Do not cast us away in old age; do not forsake us when our strength is exhausted.

**All continue individually:**

Do not forsake us, Lord, our God, be not distant from us. Display for us a sign for good, so that our enemies may see it and be ashamed, for You, O Lord, will have helped and consoled us. To our sayings give ear, O Lord, perceive our thoughts. May the expressions of our mouth and the thoughts of our heart find favor before You, Lord, our Rock and our Redeemer. Because for You, Lord, we have waited; You will answer, my Lord, our God.

## Confession

**All continue individually:**

Our God, may our prayer come before You. Do not ignore our supplication, for we are not so brazen and obstinate as to say before You, O Lord, our God, that we are righteous and have not sinned, for in truth we have sinned.

*The confession is recited with head and body slightly bowed. Strike the left side of the chest with the right first at each bolded word.*

WE have **become guilty**, we have **betrayed**, we have **robbed**, we have **spoken slander**, we have **caused perversion**, we have **caused wickedness**, we have **sinned willfully**, we have **extorted**, we have **accused falsely**, we have **given evil counsel**, we have **been deceitful**, we have **scorned**, we have **rebelled**, we have **provoked**, we have **turned away**, we have **been perverse**, we have **acted wantonly**, we have **persecuted**, we have **been obstinate**, we have **been wicked**, we have **corrupted**, we have **been abominable**, we have **strayed**, and You have let us go astray.

We have turned away from Your commandments and from Your good laws but to no avail. Yet, You are righteous in all that has come upon us, for You have acted truthfully while we have caused wickedness.

We have acted wickedly and sinned willfully. Inspire our hearts to abandon the path of evil, as it is written by Your prophet: May the wicked one abandon his way and the vicious man his thoughts; may he return to the Lord and He will show him mercy - to our God, for He is abundantly forgiving.

Your righteous anointed one [David] said before You: "Who can discern mistakes? From unperceived faults cleanse me." Cleanse us Lord, our God, of all our willful sins and purify us, of all our contaminations. Sprinkle upon us pure water and purify us, as it is written by Your prophet: I shall sprinkle pure water upon you and purify you; I will purify you of all your contaminations and of all your abominations.

Micah, your servant, said before You: "Who O God is like You, who pardons iniquity and overlooks transgression for the remnant of his heritage? He who has not retained His wrath eternally, for he desires kindness! He will again be merciful to us; He will suppress our iniquities and cast all sins into the depths of the sea."

Daniel, the greatly beloved man, cried out before You: "Incline Your ear, my God, and listen; open Your eyes and see our desolation and that of the city upon which Your Name is proclaimed. Not because of our righteousness do we cast our supplications before you, but rather because of your abundant compassion. O my Lord, heed! O my Lord, forgive! O my Lord, be attentive and act! Do not delay, for your sake my God, for your Name is proclaimed upon Your city and Your people."

Ezra the scribe said before You: My God, I am embarrassed and ashamed to lift my face to You, for our iniquities have multiplied and our sins have extended unto heaven. You are the God of forgiveness, compassionate and merciful, slow to anger, and abundant in kindness. You have not forsaken us.

Do not forsake us, our Father, do not cast us off, our Creator, do not abandon us, our Molder, and do not bring about our destruction.

**Act for the sake...**  Act for the sake of Your truth, act for the sake of Your covenant, act for the sake of Your greatness and splendor, act for the sake of Your law, act for the sake of Your glory, act for the sake of Your meeting house, act for the sake of Your remembrance, act for the sake of Your kindness, act for the sake of Your goodness, act for the sake of Your oneness, act for the sake of Your honor, act for the sake of Your teaching, act for the sake of Your kingship, act for the sake of Your eternality, act for the sake of Your counsel, act for the sake of Your power, act for the sake of Your beauty, act for the sake of Your righteousness, act for the sake of Your sanctity, act for the sake of Your abundant mercy, act for the sake of Your presence, act for the sake of Your praise, act for the sake of Your beloved ones who rest in the dust, act for the sake of the desolation of your temple, act for the sake of the ruins of your altar, act for the sake of the martyrs for your holy name; act for the sake of those slaughtered for your oneness, act for the sake of those who entered fire and water for the sanctification of your name, act for the nursing infants who did not err act for the sake of the weaned babes who did not sin, act for the sake of the children at the schoolroom. Act for your sake, if not for ours. Act for your sake and save us!

**Answer us...**  Answer us, O Lord, answer us.
Answer us, Our God, answer us.
Answer us, Our Father, answer us.
Answer us, Our Creator, answer us.
Answer us, Our Redeemer, answer us.
Answer us, He Who Searches Us Out, answer us.
Answer us, Faithful God, answer us.
Answer us, Steadfast and Kind One, answer us.
Answer us, Pure and Upright One, answer us.
Answer us, Living and Enduring One, answer us.
Answer us, Good and Beneficent One, answer us.
Answer us, You Who Knows Inclination, answer us.
Answer us, You Who Suppresses Wrath, answer us.
Answer us, You Who Dons Righteousness, answer us.
Answer us, King Who Reigns Over Kings, answer us.
Answer us, Awesome and Powerful One, answer us.
Answer us, You Who Forgives and Pardons, answer us.
Answer us, You Who Answers in Times of Distress, answer us.
Answer us, Redeemer and Rescuer, answer us.
Answer us, Righteous and Upright One, answer us.
Answer us, He Who is Close to Those Who Call Upon Him, answer us.
Answer us, Merciful and Gracious One, answer us.
Answer us, You Who Hears the Destitute, answer us.
Answer us, You Who Supports the Wholesome, answer us.
Answer us, You Who are Hard to Anger, answer us.
Answer us, You Who are Easy to Pacify, answer us.
Answer us, You Who Answers In a Time of Favor, answer us.
Answer us, Father of Orphans, answer us.
Answer us, Judge of Widows, answer us.

The Merciful One Who Answers the poor, may He answer us.
The Merciful One Who Answers the brokenhearted, may He answer us.
The Merciful One Who Answers the humble of spirit, may He answer us.

O Merciful One, answer us!
O Merciful One, have pity!
O Merciful One, have mercy upon us – now, swiftly, and soon!

## Concluding Supplication

*The following is recited seated.*

And David said to Gad: "I am exceedingly distressed. Let us fall into the Lord's hand for His mercies are abundant, but let me not fall into human hands.

O compassionate and Gracious One, I have sinned before you, Lord Who is full of mercy, have mercy on me and accept my supplications.

Lord, do not rebuke me in Your anger nor chastise me in Your rage. Favor me, O Lord, for I am feeble. Heal me, Lord, for my bones shudder. My soul is utterly confounded. And You, O Lord, how long? Desist Lord, release my soul – save me as befits Your kindness, for there is no mention of You in death. In the lower world, who will thank You? I am wearied with my sigh, each night my tears drench my bed and soak my couch. My eye is dimmed by anger, aged by my tormentors. Depart from me all evildoers, for the Lord has heard the sound of my weeping! The Lord has heard my plea. The Lord will accept my prayer. Let all my foes be shamed and utterly confounded; they will regret and be ashamed.

*The following is recited while standing:*

We know not what we do, but our eyes are upon you. Remember your mercies, O Lord, and your kindnesses, for they extend from the beginning of the world. May your kindness be upon us, O Lord, as we have awaited You. May your mercies meet us quickly. Be gracious to us, Lord! Amid rage, remember to be merciful! For He knows our nature; He remembers that we are dust. **All continue to the end; the Leader reads this last verse aloud:** Help us, O God of our salvation, for the sake of Your glory. Rescue us and judge us favorably!

**Sanctification**

**Leader:** May His great name be ever exalted and sanctified (**Cong.:** Amen!) **Leader:** in the world that He created according to His will. May His kingship reign in our lifetimes and in our days, swiftly and soon, and we say: Amen!

**Cong.:** Amen! May His great Name be blessed forever and ever!

**Leader:** May His great name be blessed forever and ever. Blessed, praised, glorified, exalted, extolled, mighty, upraised, and lauded is the name of the Holy One, Blessed is He (**Cong.:** Blessed is He!) exceedingly beyond any blessing and song or praise and consolation that may be uttered in the world, and we say: Amen (**Cong.:**. Amen!)

Pirchei Publishing
164 Village Path / P.O. Box 708
Lakewood, New Jersey 08701
(732) 370-3344
www.shulchanaruch.com

Product Produced & Compiled by YPS:
Rabbi Shaul Danyiel & Rabbi Ari Montanari
www.lionsden.info/YPS

THE YESHIVA PIRCHEI SHOSHANIM SHULCHAN ARUCH LEARNING PROJECT

# The Noahide Laws – Lesson Twenty Eight

**© Yeshiva Pirchei Shoshanim 2017**

This shiur may not be reproduced in any
form without permission of the copyright holder.

## Outline of This Lesson:

1. Introduction

2. Judgment & Celebration

3. *Mitzvos* vs. *Minhagim*

4. Eve of Rosh HaShanah

5. Suggested Evening Prayers

6. Rosh HaShanah Night Meal

# Festivals III: Rosh HaShanah

## Introduction

Rosh HaShanah, the Day of Judgment, Birthday of the World – it is a time of tremendous celebration and tremendous solemnity. It is a day of ultimate connection with the Creator.

## Judgment & Celebration.

As we mentioned earlier, Rosh HaShanah is both a day of solemnity and rejoicing. We celebrate the completion of creation and the birthday of all mankind. However, it is also a day of judgment and solemnity for it is the day upon which Adam and Eve failed in their mission.

The observances of Rosh HaShanah strive to acknowledge the day's dual nature.

## Shofar on Rosh HaShanah?

The general rule with all Noahide practice is to avoid imitating those commandments ordered only to the Jewish people. Besides the fact that such imitation-of-practice limits the universal aspect of Noahism, it also creates serious problems in Torah law. Therefore, Noahides should not blow the shofar on Rosh HaShanah.

## Mitzvos vs. Minhagim

*Mitzvos* are those matters that God commanded to mankind, whether Noahide or Jew. However, *mihangim* (usually translated as "customs") are practices developed by man to enhance the spiritual experience of the holidays. While the law is that Noahides may not take on Jewish mitzvos (unless they provide some practical, real-world benefit; i.e. *Tzedaka* or honoring one's parents), Noahides may certainly take on established Jewish *minhagim*.

These *minhagim* are often rich with meaning and speak deeply to the human experience of the Torah. We will mention many such *minhagim* in the course of these lessons.

## Eve of Rosh HaShanah

Rosh HaShanah, as all of the Torah's festivals, beings at sunset on the previous evening. For example, Rosh HaShana 2015 is on Monday, September 14. However, it actually beings at sunset on Sunday, September 13.

By Rosh HaShanah eve, the house should be cleaned in honor of the holiday. One should also endeavor to get a haircut, cut his nails, and dress in clean, nice clothing to welcome the Great Day.

One should not rush into Rosh HaShanah. Instead, all of the preparations should be completed well before sunset so that one may enter the day in a spirit of peace, tranquility, and focus.

## Evening Prayers

*As with all of the liturgies brought in this course, they are based on the traditional Jewish prayers, yet adapted as needed for Noahide use. These prayer services are by no means the final or definitive forms of these prayers. Instead, these services are intended as a starting point for growth and development.*

## Introductory Psalm

*Psalm 96*
*The Leader reads the bold text aloud.*

**Sing to The Lord a new song! Sing to The Lord, all the Earth! Praise The Lord and bless His name! Announce His salvation from day to day!** Declare His honor among the nations and His wonders among all peoples. For the Lord is great and exceedingly praised; He is feared above all gods. For all the gods of the nations are worthless – but The Lord made the heavens! Majesty and glory are before him, strength and beauty are in His sanctuary. Render to The Lord, you families of the nations, render to The Lord glory and honor! Give The Lord the honor due to his Name. Bring offerings into His courtyards. Bow down before the Lord in abundant holiness and tremble before Him, everyone on Earth! Say among the nations, "The Lord reigns!" The world is firmly set, it shall not falter. He will judge the nations in righteousness.
Heaven will rejoice and the Earth will be glad! The oceans and their fullness will roar! The fields and all that is in them will exult! **The trees of the forest will sing with joy before the Lord – For He will have arrived, He will have come to judge the Earth. He judges the world in righteousness and the peoples in His truth!**

## Introductory Nighttime Psalm & Verses of Praise[1]

A Song of Ascents: Behold, bless The Lord, all you servants of the Lord who stand in the House of the Lord in the nights. Lift your hands in the Sanctuary and bless the Lord. May the Lord bless you from Zion, the Maker of heaven and earth.[2]

In perfect peace I will lie down and sleep; for You, O Lord, will set me apart and secure my dwelling.[3] At dawn, the Lord will command His kindness; at night His resting place is with me – a prayer to the God of my life![4] The salvation of the righteous is from the Lord; their might in a time

---

[1] Inclusion of these Psalm verses is adapted from *Nusach Sfard*, the Chassidic rite version of the *siddur*.

[2] Psalm 134.

[3] Ibid. 4:9.

[4] Ibid. 42:9.

of distress. The Lord helps them and enables their escape; He enables their escape from the wicked and will save them, for they have taken refuge in Him.[5]

## Sanctification

**Leader:** May His great name be ever exalted and sanctified (**Cong.:** Amen!) in the world that He created according to His will. May His kingship reign in our lifetimes and in our days, swiftly and soon, and we say: Amen!

**Cong.:** Amen! May His great Name be blessed forever and ever!

**Leader:** May His great name be blessed forever and ever. Blessed, praised, glorified, exalted, extolled, mighty, upraised, and lauded is the name of the Holy One, Blessed is He (**Cong.:** Blessed is He!) exceedingly beyond any blessing and song or praise and consolation that may be uttered in the world, and we say: Amen (**Cong.:.** Amen!)

## Call to Prayer (omitted by one praying alone)

**Leader:** Blessed is The Lord, the Blessed One!
**Cong.:** Blessed is The Lord, the Blessed One, for all eternity!
**Leader:** Blessed is The Lord, the Blessed One, for all eternity!

## Acceptance of Kingship

**All aloud:** Almighty God, we accept upon ourselves Your sovereign kingship and mastery:

**All continue individually:**

> You alone are our God,
> You alone are our King,
> You alone are omnipotent, and
> You alone are eternal.
>
> You alone are our creator,
> You alone are our savior.
> You alone do we worship, and to

---

[5] Ibid. 37:39 – 40.

You alone do we give thanks.

As it is written in Your holy Torah: "You shall know this day and take unto your heart that God alone is God; in the heavens above and upon the earth below – there is none other!"[6] And, "You shall love your God with all your heart, all your soul, and all your means,"[7] and to (**Leader recites aloud:**) **"Fear God, your God, and serve Him, and to vow in His name only."**[8]

**Leader:** The Lord shall reign for all eternity![9]
**Cong:** The Lord shall reign for all eternity!

## Silent Prayer

*During the silent Prayer, all should stand erect with the feet together. One should pray only loud enough to hear himself.*

### On God's Might

Your might is eternal, my Lord, the one who resuscitates the dead, who is abundant in salvations, who sustains the living with kindness, who revives the dead with abundant mercy, who supports the fallen, heals the sick, and releases the bound, Who upholds his faith to those who sleep in the dust. Who is like you, O Master of mighty deeds?

Who is comparable to You, O King, who causes death and restores life, who makes salvation bloom?

And You are faithful to revive the dead! Blessed are you, O Lord, who revives the dead!

### On God's Holiness

You are holy and Your Name is Holy, and the holy ones praise you every day, eternally. Therefore, bestow your awe upon all Your works and your dread upon all you have created. Let all your works revere you and all creations prostrate themselves before you. Let them all whole-heartedly

---

[6] Deut. 4:39.

[7] Deut. 6:5.

[8] Deut. 6:13.

[9] Exodus 15:18.

do your will. For, as we know HaShem our God, the dominion is yours. Might is in your hand and strength within your right hand; your name invokes awe upon all that you have created.

You are Holy and your name is awesome, and there is no god other than You, as it is written: The Lord, Master of Legions, will be exalted in judgment, and the Holy God will be sanctified in righteousness. Blessed are you, O Lord, the Holy king.

*On the Day of Judgment*

Our God, may there arise, come, reach, be noted, be favored, be heard, be considered, and be remembered a remembrance of ourselves before you for deliverance, for goodness, for grace, for kindness and compassion, for life, and for peace upon this Day of Judgment. Remember us on it, O Lord, for blessing and for life.
Be gracious and compassionate with us, favor us for salvation, compassion, and pity, for our eyes are turned to you, for you are God, the gracious and compassionate King!

Our God, reign over the entire universe in Your glory. Be exalted over the entire world in Your splendor. Reveal Yourself, in the majestic grandeur of Your strength, upon all that dwell within Your world. Let everything that has been made know that You are its maker and let everything that has been shaped understand that you are its sculptor. Let everything with the breath of life in its nostrils proclaim: "The Lord is King! His Kingship rules above all!" O God, purify our hearts to serve You sincerely, for You are the true God and Your word is true and eternal! Look down upon Your creation and judge it favorably! Grant us the opportunity to return to you! Grant us life, grant us salvation, and grant us favor! Blessed are you, O Lord, King over all, who sanctifies the Day of Judgment!

*Giving Thanks*

We thank you, for it is you who are The Lord, our God, and the Rock of our Lives. We shall thank You and relate Your praise for our lives, which are committed to Your power, and for our souls that are entrusted to You, for Your miracles that are with us every day, and for Your wonders and favors in every time – Morning, noon, and night. The Benevolent One, for Your benevolences were never exhausted, and The Compassionate One, for Your compassions are never ending – we place our hope in You.

Please, inscribe us all for a good life!

And all life will thank You and praise Your name, O God of salvation and help. Blessed are you, O Lord, Your Name is "The Benevolent one" and to You alone is it fitting to offer thanks!

*For Peace*
Establish peace upon the world and upon all peoples, for you are king, the master of peace!

May we be remembered and inscribed before You in the book of life, blessing, peace, and livelihood.

Blessed are you, O Lord, who creates peace.

*Concluding Supplication*
My God, guard my tongue from evil and my lips from speaking deceit. To those who would curse me, let my soul be silent; let my soul be like dust to all. Open my heart to your will so that my soul will pursue it. As for all those plan evil against me, quickly nullify their counsel, frustrate their designs. Act for Your Name's sake, act for Your right-hand's sake, act for Your sanctity's sake. Let Your right hand save and respond to me.

May the expressions of my mouth and the thoughts of my heart find favor before you, Lord, my Rock and my Redeemer.

*One takes three steps back at this point, as if taking leave of a king.*

*Bow to the left and say:* He who makes peace in His heights,
*Bow to the right and say:* May He Make peace upon us,
*Bow forward and say:* And upon the entire world.
*One straightens and concludes:* And we say: Amen.

*Remain in place for a moment, and then take three steps forward. The silent prayer is concluded.*


# Psalm 24

*When the majority of those present have concluded their silent prayer, the leader begins the following responsive recitation. The Psalm is recited responsively, verse by verse, Leader followed by Congregation*

Of David: a Psalm. The Lord's is the earth and its fullness, the inhabited land, and all those who dwell upon it.

For He founded it upon the seas, established it upon the rivers.

Who may ascend the Lord's mountain, and who may stand in the place of His Holiness?

One of clean hands and of pure heart, who has neither sworn in vain by My soul, nor deceitfully.

He will receive a blessing from The Lord and righteousness from the God of his salvation.

This is the generation of those who seek Him, those who strive for Your Presence.

Raise up your heads, O Gates! Be uplifted, O eternal entrances, so that the King of glory may enter!

Who is this king of glory? The Lord – the powerful and mighty! The Lord – Who is great in battle!

Raise up your heads, O Gates! Be uplifted, O eternal entrances, so that the King of glory may enter!

Who is this king of Glory? The Lord, the Master of Legions, He is the king of glory! Selah!

## We Bend Our Knees…

*One should bend the knees and bow down at the words in bold text, straitening up at …King of kings…*

We **bend our knee, bow down**, and give thanks, before the King of kings, the Holy One blessed is He, Who stretches forth the heavens and founded the earth, Whose honored abode is in the heavens above, and Whose powerful presence is in the most exalted heights. He is our God; there is none else. True is our king, and there is nothing besides Him, as it is written in His Torah: "Know this day and take to your heart that the Lord is God; in the heaven above and on the earth below - there is none other."

Therefore, we place our hope in You, Lord our God, that we may soon behold your mighty splendor; to banish idolatry from the earth. False gods will be utterly cut off; to perfect the world through the Almighty's sovereignty. All humanity shall call in Your Name, returning the wicked of the world unto you. Then all the inhabitants of the world will recognize and know that to you every knee should bend and to Your Name every tongue should pledge. Before You, Lord our God, they will bow and prostrate themselves, and render honor unto the glory of Your Name; they will all accept upon themselves the yoke of Your kingship so that You may reign over them, soon, forever and ever. For the kingdom is Yours and You will reign in all eternity, as it is written in Your Torah: "The Lord will reign forever and ever." And it is said: **"The Lord will be King over all the world – on that day the Lord will be One and His Name will be One."**

## Psalm 27

*Each congregant recites psalm 27 to his or herself. The leader recites the opening and concluding verses (in bold text) aloud.*

**Of David: The Lord is my light[10] and my salvation.[11] Of whom shall I be afraid?** The Lord is the strength of my life. Of whom shall I dread? When evil-doers – my tormentors and opponents[12] – draw near to devour my flesh, it is they who stumble and fall. Though an army may besiege me, my heart will not fear. Should warfare arise against me, in this alone I shall trust.[13]

I have asked one thing of The Lord, only this have I sought: that I may dwell in the house of The Lord all the days of my life, to behold the pleasantness of The Lord, and to meditate within His sanctuary.[14]

On the day of evil He will hide me within His shelter. He will conceal me in the innermost shelter of his tent. He will lift me up upon a rock. And now he will raise

---

[10] The Midrash understands this as a reference to Rosh HaShanah.

[11] The salvation mentioned here is the atonement of the holiday season. For Jews it refers to the atonement of Yom Kippur, for Noahides the atonement of Sukkot.

[12] The evil-doers and opponents mentioned in this psalm are primarily internal. They are the devices of the *yetzer ha-ra*, the evil inclination. They are also the memories and emotions associated with one's past misdeeds. These memories often torment a person and hamper their ability to return to G-d. This will be discussed more in a future lesson.

[13] Rashi and Radak explain that this refers to the opening line "HaShem is my light and my salvation," which is the process of Rosh HaShanah and subsequent atonement. One must trust in this process. Once a person has returned to HaShem and reestablished a positive relationship with G-d, G-d will protect and shelter him. Alternatively, Ibn Ezra explains that this phrase refers to the next sentence: *I have asked one thing of HaShem, only this have I sought: that I may dwell in the house of HaShem all the days of my life…* One should trust in G-d because he (the penitent) ultimately desires spiritual success and not the vain achievements of this world.

[14] Writes the Malbim, that despite the many desires and needs a person may have, the desire to know his creator is the ultimate, all inclusive desire of the soul.

my head above my foes that surround me. I will slaughter in His tent joyous offerings. I will sing and make music to The Lord. O Lord, hear my voice when I call! Favor me and answer me! For your sake has my heart spoke to me: "Seek his presence!" O God, I seek your presence! Do not conceal your countenance from me! Do not repel your servant in anger! You have been my help. Do not forsake me, do not abandon me, O God of my salvation!

Though my father and mother have abandoned me,[15] The Lord shall gather me in. Teach me your way, O Lord, and on account of my watchful foes[16] set me upon a straight path. Do not give me over to their wishes for they have set against me false witnesses who breathe violence.

**Had I not believed[17] that I would see the goodness of the Lord in the land of life![18] Hope to the Lord! Be strong and He will give you courage[19] – and hope to the Lord!**

## Greetings

*The traditional greeting for Rosh HaShanah is:*

May you be inscribed and sealed, immediately, for a good life and for peace.

*And,*

A good and sweet year!

---

[15] Sforno explains that once a person becomes an adult he must find his own way in the world. He can no longer rely upon his parents to make choices for him. He must choose his values and make his own decisions. Although his parents are no longer his guiding voice, HaShem is always there. HaShem is eternally our father and guide.

[16] The Hebrew here is a little difficult to translate. The word for "Watchful foes" is related to the word for "staring" or "gazing." In the context of our verse, it refers to those who stare maliciously. The psalm is asking G-d to frustrate the wishes of those who maliciously watch and mock one who wishes to come back to G-d. See Radak.

[17] Rashi explains: Were it not for my faith in G-d, my enemies would have destroyed me and I would have never merited to achieve closeness to G-d.

[18] Meaning the World to Come. See *Brachos* 4a.

[19] Strength in faith is the ultimate source of all courage.

## Night Meal

*The Blessing on bread is made by the leader on 1 loaf on behalf of all present. The custom is to use a round loaf during the holiday season.*

**Leader**: Blessed are You, O Lord, our God, King of the Universe, who brings forth bread from the Earth **(Guests: Amen!)**

*While still holding the loaf, the leader recites:*

**Leader**: Blessed are you, HaShem, our God, who has kept us alive, sustained us, and brought us to this season! **(Guests: Amen!)**

*The loaf is then cut and distributed. Each person should eat his or her slice with honey. One should refrain from speaking from after answering "Amen" until having partaken of the bread.*

## *Simanim* - Signs

*The custom of* Simanim *involves eating foods whose names or qualities invoke positive thoughts and ideas of blessing. On Rosh HaShanah, God looks into the heart of all peoples and renders judgment. Therefore, one's mind and heart should only look for the positive on Rosh HaShanah. To set the tone for the Rosh HaShanah meal, the custom of* Simanim *is placed at its beginning.*

*The source of the custom is found in the Talmud:*

> *Abaye taught: Since you have said that a* Siman *(the name or quality of an item) holds significance, a person should habituate himself at the start of each year to eat gourds, fenugreek, leeks, beets, and dates.*[20]

*The foods listed here are important because their names or other qualities invoke concepts of blessings.*

*Therefore, Jews have the custom to eat foods for* Simanim *whose names invoke positive qualities, or that taste sweet, or that have traits that are considered blessed.*

*There is no fixed order or list of* Simanim *foods; indeed, many families even invent their own!*

*Below is an example of a traditional* Simanim *order. Only the first* Siman, *apples, is universal.*

---

[20] *Horayos* 12a; *Kerisus* 6a.

## Apples

*Every guest takes a piece of apple, dips it in honey, and then each guest makes the following blessing for his or herself:*

Blessed are You, The Lord, our God, King of the universe, who creates the fruit of the tree.

*A small bit of the apple is eaten following this blessing. Then the leader then recites:*

**Leader:** May it be your will, Lord our God, that you renew us for a good and sweet year! **(Guests: Amen)**

## Carrot or Fenugreek[21]

*Each participant then takes a small piece of carrot or fenugreek. The leader recites:*

**Leader:** May it be your will, Lord, our God, that our merits increase! **(Guests: Amen)**

## Beets[22]

*Each participant takes a piece of beet and the leader recites:*

**Leader:** May it be your will, HaShem our God, that our adversaries be removed from upon us. **(Guests: Amen)**

## Pomegranate

**Leader:** May it be your will, HaShem our God, that our merits increase like the seeds of a pomegranate. **(Guests: Amen)**

## Fish

**Leader:** May it be your will, HaShem our God, that we be fruitful and multiply like the fish of the sea. **(Guests: Amen)**

*There are many, many, more* Simanim *that are, like these, based on Aramaic, Hebrew, or Yiddish wordplay. It is appropriate for Noahides to add more based on their own languages. Some people, in fact, eat raisins, praying for a "raise in...," followed by celery, for "salary!"*

*The only general rules for* Simanim *are: no bitter or sharp tasting foods, and that the prayer formula: May it be your will, Lord, our God... is recited before each Siman is eaten.*

---

[21] The reason for this *Simon* is that the Yiddish word for carrots is *mehren*, which also means *to increase*. Fenugreek is *rubya* in Aramaic, which also implies abundance and increase.

[22] Beets, in Aramaic, is *silka*. This is similar to the world *salek*, which means *to remove from upon*.

## Words of Torah

*During the course of the meal, those present should be careful not to speak ill of anyone or anything, focusing only on good things and good thoughts. The discussion should include much Torah, goals for the New Year, and prayers and blessings for spiritual and material successes.*

## Blessing After the Meal

*Psalm 67*[23]

For the Conductor upon the *Neginos*, a Psalm, a song: May God favor us and bless us, may He illuminate His countenance with us, *Selah*. To make known Your way upon the earth, among all the nations Your salvation. Then peoples will acknowledge You, O God, the peoples will acknowledge You – all of them. Nations will be glad and sing for Joy, because you will judge the peoples fairly and guide with fairness the nations on the earth, Selah! Then peoples will acknowledge you, O God, the peoples will acknowledge You – all of them! The earth will then have yielded its produce, may God, our God, bless us, May God bless us, and may all the ends of the earth fear him!

*At the conclusion of the meal, the following blessing is recited either by all together, each person to him or herself, or by the leader on behalf of all present, who respond "Amen."*

**Blessed is the God of the universe of Whose bounty we have eaten.**

---

[23] The Jewish practice is to recite Psalm 126 before concluding the meal. This psalm expresses the hope for redemption of the Jewish people. Psalm 67, however, is more appropriate for Noahides because it refers to the entire world and its peoples coming to know God. It also refers to God as the source of all blessing, food, and produce.

# The Noahide Laws – Lesson Twenty Nine

© **Yeshiva Pirchei Shoshanim 2017**
This shiur may not be reproduced in any
form without permission of the copyright holder.

## Outline of This Lesson:

1. Introduction
2. Yom Kippur & History
3. The Offerings of Sukkot
4. Sources of Judgment
5. *Nisukh HaMayim* – The Water Libation
6. Summary So Far
7. Sukkot & Yom Kippur
8. Tying it All Together

# Festivals III: Sukkot

## Introduction

The Festivals of the Torah and their meanings transcend any particular time or place. Nevertheless, each of the holidays is anchored to some event in history. Yom Kippur is the most important Jewish holiday after Rosh HaShanah. However, its historical anchor and meaning are both unique to Israel alone. The purpose and theme of Yom Kippur, though, has a universal parallel in the holiday of Sukkot. Furthermore, the historical anchor of Sukkot is directly related to Noahism.

## Yom Kippur & History

On the 7th day of Sivan, Moses ascended Sinai and remained there for 40 days and 40 nights (See Rashi to Ex. 32:1). At the end of this period, Moses received the first set of tablets (Ex. 31:18).

On the 16th of Tammuz, the Jewish people construct the Golden Calf (Ex. 32:1 – 5; See Rashi). They began worshiping it on the following morning (Ex. 32:6). God commands Moses to descend on that day, the 17th of Tammuz. Upon seeing the people's transgression, Moses cast down the tablets, breaking them against the mountain. He grinds the calf into dust; mixing it with water and makes the people drink it. The Levites are commanded to kill all of the transgressors (Ex. 32:7 – 9).

On the 19th of Tammuz, Moses ascends the mountain again (Ex. 32:30 – 34). During this ascent, Moses secured a tentative pardon for the people.

He descended at the end of 40 days, on the 29th of Av, to inform the people of this.

On the 1st of Elul, Moses ascended the mountain for a third time Ex. (34:4-17). During this third 40-day ascent, Moses finally achieved pardon for the Jewish people (Ex. 33:17, 8-10). At the end of this period, Moses descended with the second set of tablets (Ex. 34:1-2, 27 – 29). The date of this descent was the 10<sup>th</sup> of Tishrei – Yom Kippur.

This day would be designated as a day of atonement for the Jewish people for all times:

> *This shall remain for you an eternal decree: In the seventh month, on the tenth day of the month, you shall afflict yourselves and you shall not do any work, neither the native nor the convert among you, for on this day He shall provide atonement for you to cleanse you from your sins – before the Lord you shall be cleansed.*[1]

Yom Kippur's general theme, atonement, is anchored in the history of the Jewish people and the sin of the golden calf.

Being anchored in the historical experience of Israel and, being commanded only to Israel, Yom Kippur only provides atonement for Israel. As such, it is not a Noahide holiday and, therefore, does not have any relevance to Noahides. Does this mean, then, that Noahides have no means of atonement? No – it does not. God designated another time for Noahide atonement.

## The Offerings of Sukkot

As we have mentioned several times in previous lessons, many of the Torah's festivals have both universal meanings and specific meanings. The specific meanings of the festivals pertain only to the Jewish people. The universal meanings, however, are for the entire world. It is these latter, universal meanings which are the festival's meaning for Noahides.

The Mishnah tells us:

> *At four junctures, the world is judged: on Passover for grain, on Shavuot for fruits, on Rosh Hashanah all pass before him like sheep of the flock, as it is written, "He form their hearts as one, he understands all of their deeds." (Psalms 33).* **On Sukkot, the world is judged for water.**[2]

This Mishnah is teaching us the universally relevant themes of these holidays. For Sukkot, as we see, the theme is judgment for water. Superficially, this may seem

---

[1] Leviticus 16:29-30.

[2] *Mishnah, Rosh HaShanah* 1:2.

like an awfully narrow concept. However, there is much more going on than meets the eye. Let's start with the offerings given on the days of Sukkot:

> [Day 1:] And on the fifteenth day of the seventh month, there shall be a holy convocation for you; you shall not perform any mundane work, and you shall celebrate a festival to the Lord for seven days. You shall offer up a burnt offering, a fire offering for a spirit of satisfaction to the Lord: **thirteen young bulls**, two rams, fourteen lambs in the first year; they shall [all] be unblemished. And their meal offering [shall be] fine flour mixed with oil; three tenths for each bull for the thirteen bulls, two tenths for each ram for the two rams. And one tenth for each lamb, for the fourteen lambs. And one young male goat for a sin offering, besides the continual burnt offering, its meal offering, and its libation.
>
> [Day 2:] And on the second day, **twelve young bulls**, two rams, and fourteen lambs in the first year, [all] unblemished. And their meal offerings and their libations, for the bulls, for the rams, and for the lambs, according to their number, as prescribed. And one young male goat for a sin offering, besides the continual burnt offering, its meal offering, and their libations.
>
> [Day 3:] And on the third day, **eleven bulls**, two rams, and fourteen lambs in the first year, [all] unblemished. And their meal offerings and their libations, for the bulls, for the rams, and for the lambs, according to their number, as prescribed. And one young male goat for a sin offering, besides the continual burnt offering, its meal offering and its libation.
>
> [Day 4:] And on the fourth day, **ten bulls**, two rams, and fourteen lambs in the first year, [all] unblemished. Their meal offerings and their libations, for the bulls, for the rams, and for the lambs, according to their number, as prescribed. And one young male goat for a sin offering, besides the continual burnt offering, its meal offering and its libation.
>
> [Day 5:] And on the fifth day **nine bulls**, two rams, and fourteen lambs in the first year, [all] unblemished. And their meal offerings and their libations, for the bulls, for the rams, and for the lambs, according to their number, as prescribed. And one young male goat for a sin offering, besides the continual burnt offering, its meal offering, and its libation.
>
> [Day 6:] And on the sixth day, **eight bulls**, two rams, and fourteen lambs in the first year, [all] unblemished. And their meal offerings and their libations, for the bulls, for the rams, and for the lambs, according to their number, as prescribed. And one young male goat for a sin offering, besides the continual burnt offering, its meal offering, and its libations.

> *[Day 7:] And on the seventh day, **seven bulls**, two rams and fourteen lambs in the first year, [all] unblemished. And their meal offerings and their libations, for the bulls, for the rams, and for the lambs, according to their number, as prescribed for them. One young male goat for a sin offering, besides the continual burnt offering, its meal offering, and its libation.*[3]

As you may have noticed, the number of offerings remains essentially the same each day with the exception of the bull offering. Each day of Sukkot, the bull offering is reduced by one. The total number of the offerings is 70: 13 + 12 + 11 + 10 + 9 + 8 + 7 = 70. Why 70?

**Sukkot 55b**

> *Rabbi Eliezer said: "To what do these 70 bulls correspond? They correspond to the 70 nations of the world." …*
>
> *Rabbi Yochanan said: "Woe to the non-Jews who don't even realize what they lost! As long as the temple stood, the altar atoned for them…*

Rabbi Eliezer is telling us that the 70 bulls were offered by Israel as atonement for the 70 nations of the world. Rabbi Yochanan laments that the non-Jews who destroyed the temple didn't realize what they were losing: it was the temple that gained them divine forgiveness and atonement each year through the bull offerings!

## Sources of Judgment

**Braisa**, Talmud Rosh HaShana 16a

> *Rabbi Yehuda said in the name of Rabbi Akiva: Why did the Torah tell us to bring the Omer offering on Passover [see Lev. 23:9-14]? Because Passover is the time for judgment on grain. The Holy One, Blessed is He, said "Bring before me the Omer on Passover so that the produce in the fields will be blessed for you." Why did the Torah tell us to bring the two loaves on Shavuot [Lev. 23:17]?*[4] *Because Shavuot is the time*

---

[3] Num. 29:12-34

[4] The offering brought on Shavuot was from wheat, which is not actually a fruit. However, the two wheat loaves were brought as a prerequisite to the bikkurim, the offering of first fruits. Alternatively, it could be that this Braisa is according to Rabbi Yehuda's own opinion that the tree from which Adam and Eve ate was a "wheat tree." According to many, bread grew directly from trees before the sin of Adam. It was only afterwards that wheat was diminished, requiring harvesting, winnowing, grinding, and baking. See Machshavos Charutz 60; Sanhedrin 70b and Eyn Yaakov there. Therefore, wheat is offered as atonement for man's original sin of eating from the tree. It is by this mechanic that the wheat offering of Shavuot provides good judgment upon the fruit trees.

*for judgment on the fruits of the trees. The Holy One blessed is He, said: "Bring before me the two loaves on Shavuot so that the fruits of the tree will be blessed for you."*

*Why did the Torah tell us to pour water libations on Sukkot? Because the Holy One, Blessed is He, said: pour water before me on Sukkot so that the rains may be blessed for you…*

This *braisa* is telling us that the offering commanded on each holiday hints to the judgment of that holiday. Now, for each of the festivals mentioned here, as well as for Rosh HaShanah, there are verses in the Torah that allude to the festival offering. The one exception is Sukkot. Our *braisa* tells us about a water libation on sukkot. What is this and why is it not mentioned in the Torah?

## Nisukh HaMayim – The Water Libation

In the times of the temple, every peace offerings and burnt offering was accompanied by a flour offering and a wine libation. On Sukkot, however, there was an additional libation of water. This water libation, the *Nisukh ha-Mayim*, was poured upon the altar at the giving of the morning sacrifice. This offering consisted of two stages: the *Semichas beis ha-shoeivah* (water drawing ceremony), and the actual *Nisukh ha-Mayim* (pouring of the water).

Each morning, the Levites and Kohanim drew three *lugin* of fresh water with a golden vessel from the Shiloach, a stream that ran to the south of the Temple mount.

The ceremony of drawing water for the libation was an occasion for tremendous joy. The Talmud states:

*One who has not witnessed the celebration of water-drawing has never seen real joy.*[5]

The joy was so great that even brought some to the spirit of prophecy:

*Why is the celebration called* beis ha-sho'evah *[the celebration of the place of water drawing]? Because from there [from the ceremony itself] one draws the spirit of holiness. .. Yonah ben Amitai was one of the pilgrims who ascended to Jerusalem on the Festival. He went to the* Semichas bet ha-sho'evah *and [from the intense joy] the spirit of holiness rested upon him and he attained prophecy. This teaches us that the spirit of holiness rests upon a person only when his heart is filled with joy.*[6]

---

[5] *Sukkah* 51a.

[6] *Yerushalmi Sukkah* 5:1.

Following the water drawing was the libation ceremony itself, which was also celebrated with great fanfare.

However, the ceremony of the water libation is not mentioned anywhere in the Torah. The sages tell us that this *mitzvah* is a *Halacha le-Moshe mi-Sinai*, a direct commandment given to Moses at Sinai. It is part of the *Torah SheBaal Peh* – the Oral Torah.

## Summary So Far

Let's look at what we know so far:

- On Sukkot a water offering was given – the *Nisukh ha-Mayim*.

- Following the lead of the *braisa* mentioned above, this would indicate that the world is judged for water on Sukkot.

- Unlike the offerings associated with all other festivals, this offering was given as part of the *Torah SheBaal Peh* – the Oral Torah. This makes this Sukkot, its offering, and its judgments uniquely different from those of the other festivals

- On sukkot, 70 bull offerings were given in atonement for the 70 nations.

- Rashi writes that their atonement by way of these offerings is connected to the judgment for rainfall.

- Sukkot is the only holiday upon which the Jews gave offerings on behalf of the nations of the world.

We see from all of these points that there is something very special and very unique about Sukkot.

## Yom Kippur & Sukkot

**Midrash 32:5**  *And I will blot out all of the Yekum that I have made…*[7]

*R' Berachya said: It means "all that exists." Rav Avun Says: It means "The inhabited world." Rabbi Levi said in the name of Reish Lakish: It refers to Kayin, who had been hanging, suspended, until the flood came and swept him away.*

Bereshis Rabbah 22:13 tells us that Kayin repented before God and received a mitigated judgment. We have already seen what happened next:

*Adam met Kayin and asked of him: "What happened? What was your judgment?" Kayin replied: "I repented and it was mitigated"*

*Adam began slapping his own face and cried out: "Such is the power of repentance – and I didn't know it!" Adam immediately arose and declared:* Mizmor shir le-yom ha-Shabbat, *a Psalm, a song for the Shabbos…*

Let's look at this Midrash very carefully. It appears from this Midrash that Adam was aware of *teshuva*, repentance, but unaware of how great its power really was. When Adam saw Kayin's success in repenting, he realized something that he did not know. What was this realization? The commentaries explain:[8]

It seems that Adam was originally under the impression that *teshuvah* only helps when the sin is truly a thing of the past. If the sin is something that continues to cause harm and affect the world, then *teshuva* is ineffective. Since Adam's sin introduced death into the world, he could not repent from it. As long as people continue to die, Adam's sin continues to exert influence on the world. Therefore, from Adam's point of view, *teshuva* wasn't possible.

Applying Adam's understanding of *teshuva* to Kayin, it would seem that *teshuvah* was of no help to him either. After all, by killing Avel, Kayin prevented countless future generations from being born.

Yet, we see that Kayin was able to do *teshuva*. Why?

---

[7] Gen. 7:4.

[8] See *Beis Yitzchok* to Bereshis 7:4-5. See also the following commentaries to *Bereshis Rabbah* 32:5: Maharzu; *Eitz Yosef*; *Yefeh Toar* to *Bereshis Rabbah* 22:12. See Also *Matnos Kehunah*,

The answer is fascinating: God knew that there was an end in sight, a time when the effects of Kayin's sin would cease: the flood. In the flood all life, except that of one man and his family, would be destroyed. Even if Avel had descendants, they would not have survived. Since there was a time when Kayin's sin would cease to affect the world, God agreed to accept Kayin's repentance. However, it was only a partial acceptance. God would not grant atonement until the full effects of the sin were removed from the world at the time of the flood (we will discuss this point more in the live class).

Adam suddenly realized that, for him too, there was a time when his sin would cease to affect the world – the time of the World to Come. That is why Adam composed Psalm 92 – a psalm in praise of the eternal Shabbat of the world to come.

We see that the flood provided atonement for the sin of Kayin - it was, effectively, the first Day of Atonement in history. This atonement was carried out through water.

The sin of Kayin, his repentance, and the atonement of the flood is the historical anchor for Sukkot in the same way that the sin of the golden calf, the repentance of the Jews, and the atonement at Sinai is the historical anchor for Yom Kippur.

## Tying it All Together

We now understand the connections between the offerings, rain, and the atonement for the nations. On Sukkot, offerings are given in the temple in atonement for the nations. Since the first atonement was brought about through water, that day also became the time for judgment of the world's water supply. The pouring of water upon the altar was part of the ceremony for securing a favorable judgment for rain. Atonement for the nations came about through the offerings of the bulls. The reason for offerings of bulls may be because the Talmud[9] tells us that the angel of rain, called Ridayah or Af Bri, appears as a bull.

---

[9] *Taanis* 25b. See also Rashi there as well as *Tosafos* to *Niddah* 16b, d.h. *Malach*. We should note that, according to *Taanis* 2a, only God decides when and where rains are to fall. The task of this angel is only to execute God's decision. See *Tosafos HaRosh* to *Nidda* ad loc.

THE YESHIVA PIRCHEI SHOSHANIM SHULCHAN ARUCH LEARNING PROJECT

# The Noahide Laws – Lesson Thirty

© **Yeshiva Pirchei Shoshanim 2017**
This shiur may not be reproduced in any
form without permission of the copyright holder.

## Outline of This Lesson:

1. Introduction

2. Observance of Sukkot

3. The Sukkot of Future Times

4. Sukkot Today

5. Prayers So Far...

6. Shemini Atzeres / Simchas Torah

# Festivals V: Sukkot II

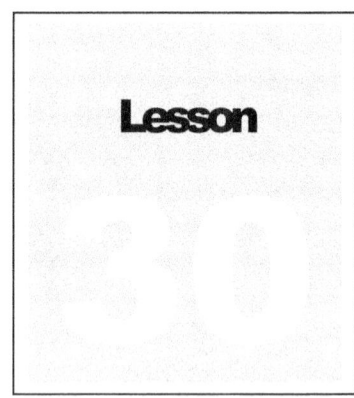

## Introduction

As we saw in the previous lesson, Sukkot is a holiday of major importance for both Jews and Noahides. This lesson is concerned with the greater question of acknowledging this importance. How can Noahides connect with the holiday of sukkot in our times?

## Observances of Sukkot

The Torah commands a number of observances to Israel on sukkot, most of which are impossible to fulfill in our times. Without the temple, we cannot perform the water libations, offerings, or many other mitzvos. Today, there are only two that remain:

> *Also in the 15th day of the seventh month, when you have gathered in the fruit of the land, you shall keep a feast to the Lord seven days; on the first day shall be a Sabbath, and on the eighth day shall be a Sabbath.* **And you shall take on the first day the boughs of goodly trees, branches of palm trees, and the boughs of thick trees, and willows of the brook; and you shall rejoice before the Lord your God seven days.** *And you shall keep it a feast to the Lord seven days in the year. It shall be a statute forever in your generations; you shall celebrate it in the seventh month.* **You shall dwell in booths seven days;** *all who are Israelites born shall dwell in booths. That your generations may know that I made the people of Israel to dwell in booths, when I brought them out of the land of Egypt; I am the Lord your God.*[1]

However, these two *mitzvos*, of taking the four species and dwelling in sukkot, were commanded only to Israel. This fact creates a problem of *chiddushei dat* for Noahides. Additionally, there are no *minhagim* (customs) for Sukkot that translate

---

[1] Lev. 23:39-43.

from Jewish to Noahide practice. In what way, then, can Noahides form a meaningful connection with the holiday of Sukkot?

## The Sukkot of Future Times

Though it is clear that Noahides do not observe the Jewish mitzvos of Sukkot, this is apparently only in our times. The prophet Zechariah tells us:

> *And it shall come to pass, that every one that is left of all the nations that came against Jerusalem shall go up from year to year to worship the King, the Lord of hosts, and to keep the feast of tabernacles. And it shall be that whoever of the families of the earth that does not go up to Jerusalem to worship the King, the Lord of hosts, upon them there shall be no rain.*[2]

We see, therefore, that the nations of the world who survive the war of Gog and Magog will keep sukkot in the future, and that it will continue to be the time for judgment of water.

On a tangential note – there is a fascinating *aggadic* (non-legal or ethical) understanding of the non-Jew's future observance of sukkot brought in Avodah Zarah 3b. We will discuss it in the live class.

## Sukkot Today

In much the same way that the Jews would offer sacrifices on behalf of the non-Jews of the world, taking a proactive role on their behalf, it appears that the Jewish community should take a more proactive role even now in making sukkot relatable to non-Jews.

If there is any holiday in which Noahides and Jews should come together, it is on Sukkot.

Ideally, sukkot is the time that Jews should share communal meals with Noahides in the Sukkah and that both should rejoice in their common goal: a Torah-based redemption of mankind.

However, this ideal is not as easy as it sounds. The tragic 2000-year history of Jews and Non-Jews has created a situation in which the Torah-observant community is insular and uninterested in engaging with non-Jews. It is difficult for

---

[2] Zech. 14:16-17.

30 years of Noahide interest in Torah to sway a mindset established by 2000 years of unimaginable oppression, brutality, and bloodshed. The idea of non-Jews having any positive interest in Torah is still something novel and strange to most of the Jewish world. Does the Torah-observant Jewish world trust Noahides? As a whole, the answer is "no."

This "No" must be understood in the context of history. See, for example, *Codex Judaica* by Rabbi Matis Kantor. This is an excellent year-by-year overview of Jewish history from the creation of the world until the modern era. Starting in the early middle ages, you will see that hardly a year passes without mass executions, state persecution, burnings, exile – it is a non-stop record of sorrows. Each year, tens of thousands of Jews were brutally exterminated and no one – absolutely no one – batted an eye. The world was indifferent to the Jewish oppression and suffering. As a result, the Jews had to develop a mentality that placed their own survival above all else. This mentality is still needed and still governs the Jewish attitude toward outreach. Remember, the holocaust, the last major attempted destruction of Jewry, was only 69 years ago. For the past several decades, the Jewish world has been struggling to rebuild a basis upon which their future survival can be guaranteed. All efforts are being devoted to stopping assimilation, establishing Jewish schools, encouraging mitzvos observance, and much more. In short: the Torah world today is still concerned and fighting for its own survival. The recent advent of Noahism needs more time before it can gain the necessary attention, trust, and resources trust of the mainstream Jewish world.[3]

## Prayers

As with all of the holidays, the prayers are the most important part – and on Sukkot there is a LOT for which to pray.

Before getting into the prayers of Sukkot, let's do a quick review of the liturgical calendar so far:

- **1st of Elul** – We began introspection and intense self-examination in preparation for the Day of Judgment, Rosh HaShanah.

- **26th of Elul** – Noahides began saying Selichos, penitential prayers.

---

[3] Unfortunately, there are many who have lost support or become persona-non-grata in the Jewish world. To maintain support and keep an audience, they have turned to teaching Torah to Noahides, Christians, and other non-Jewish groups. Unfortunately, the fact that a Rabbi is teaching non-Jews is viewed in the Jewish world as a sign that Rabbi has lost legitimacy in his own community. This fact means that Noahides must be extremely cautious when deciding who to learn from and whose advice to accept.

- **1st of Tishrei, Rosh HaShanah** – Prayer and joyful evening meal with Simanim. Day prayers followed by a meal. Prayers of this day are a mixture of Joy and prayers for forgiveness.

- **From the 2nd of Tishrei through the seventh day of Sukkos**, it is appropriate to continue reciting Selichos. However, these Selichos are in preparation for the atonement period of Sukkot. We have provided Selichos for the four days prior to Rosh HaShanah, yet it is appropriate for Selichos to continue through the final day of Sukkot.

- **15th of Tishrei** – First day of Sukkot. Prayers for this period include festive meals with friends. It is appropriate for Jews to have Noahides as guests and to share meals in the Sukkah. The day time prayers of each of the Seven days include mention of the offerings of that day.

- **21st of Tishrei** – The final day of Sukkot. On this day, the prayer for rain is said in the congregation in the morning. The day service includes prayers for atonement. The day should be one of celebration and confidence that God will hear everyone's prayer and hearken to it.

## Shemini Atzeret / Simchas Torah

The holiday of Shemini Atzeret, which falls out on the eight day after the start of Sukkot, is not part of the Sukkot holiday. Instead, it is an independent holiday.[4] The Torah discusses Shemini Atzeret in two places:

> *Seven days you shall bring an offering made by fire unto the Lord; the eighth day shall be a holy convocation to you; and you shall bring an offering made by fire unto the Lord; it is a day of solemn assembly; you shall do no manner of servile work.*[5]

And,

> *On the eighth day ye shall have a solemn assembly: ye shall do no manner of servile work.*[6]

---

[4] See Sukkot 48a.

[5] Lev. 23:36.

[6] Num. 29:35.

Curiously, though, the Torah gives no reason for this holiday.

Even the name of the holiday, *Shemini Atzeres*, yields little insight. *Shemini* means "the eighth," while the word "Atzeres," connotes "ingathering," and "assembly," as well as "holding back," and "tarrying."

The sages explain the meaning of *Shemini Atzeres* using a parable: A king throws a banquet for several days, inviting guests from all over his country. This includes his sons, who travel to be with him. At the end of the celebration, all the guests leave. However, the king asks his sons to linger, to spend one more day with him.

Similarly, the holiday of Sukkot is a seven day banquet for all the nations of the world. However, once it concludes, God asks Israel to tarry for one more day. This holiday's only purpose is to make a distinction between Israel and the non-Jewish nations. As such, it is inappropriate for Noahides to observe it.

What about *Simchas Torah*, the holiday that coincides with *Shemini Atzeres*? *Simchas Torah* is the celebration marking the renewal of the weekly cycle of Torah readings. However, there is no source for this holiday. It is not mentioned in the Torah, Talmud, or any of the foundational literature. Where does it come from?

It appears that Simchas Torah began in the $10^{th}$ century. However, it was not until several hundred years later that it became universally observed in the Jewish world. Most of the customs of the holiday developed in Europe during the $14^{th}$ and $15^{th}$ centuries.

Is it relevant to Noahides? Possibly.

The celebration of Simchas Torah is a custom which has developed around another custom. The annual Torah cycle is also a custom developed primarily in the diaspora. In fact, it was only recently that an annual cycle has become almost universal.

THE YESHIVA PIRCHEI SHOSHANIM SHULCHAN ARUCH LEARNING PROJECT

# The Noahide Laws – Lesson Thirty One

**© Yeshiva Pirchei Shoshanim 2017**
This shiur may not be reproduced in any
form without permission of the copyright holder.

**164 Village Path, Lakewood NJ 08701 732.370.3344
164 Rabbi Akiva, Bnei Brak, 03.616.6340**

## Outline of This Lesson:

1. Introduction
2. Cheshvan / MarCheshvan
3. Kislev
4. The Timeline of the Flood
5. Curious Things…
6. The Meaning of a Rainbow
7. The Noahide Covenant vs. The Noahide Laws
8. The First of Kislev

# Festivals VI: Cheshvan & Kislev

## Introduction

Following Sukkot and the conclusion of the month of Tishrei, we enter the months of Cheshvan and Kislev. Cheshvan contains no holidays, yet its relationship to Kislev is important for reasons that we shall see.

## Cheshvan / MarCheshvan

The 2nd month of the new year (and 8th month over all) is Cheshvan. Cheshvan is commonly referred to as *Marcheshvan*, which literally means "bitter Cheshvan." Why is this month called bitter? One reason is because it is the only month with no holidays. Another is that a number of tragic events happened to Israel in this month. For example, on the 5th of Cheshvan the Chaldeans murdered the sons of king Tzidkiyahu, blinded him, and took him into captivity. On the 15th of Cheshvan Yarovam ben Nevat aroused God's wrath against Israel.

However, *mar* may also refer to the flood of Noah. According to most chronologies of the flood, the rains began on the 28th or 27th of Cheshvan. Curiously, Cheshvan is called *Bul* in Melachim I 6:8. Many commentaries explain that this term *Bul* is derived from the word *mabul*, which means flood. *Mar* can also mean "a drop of water," as we see from Isaiah 40:15. Of course, Cheshvan is also the start of the rainy season in Israel, and *mar*, meaning "drop," may be an indication of this quality.

## Kislev

The month of Kislev follow Cheshvan. Kislev is famously known for the holiday of Chanukah. Beginning on the 25th of Kislev, Chanukah commemorates the Jewish victory over the Seleucid Greeks and the miracles wrought for Israel in their fight for religious freedom.

Given that Chanukah is an entirely rabbinic holiday commemorating a Jewish victory, it has no relevance to Noahides and should not be observed. However there is a major historical event that occurred in Kislev which is of extreme importance to Noahides.

## The Timeline of the Flood

It is very difficult to pin down the exact chronology of the events of the flood. Nevertheless, most commentaries agree that it began at the end of Cheshvan (on the 27th or 28th of that month) and ended one year later, with Noah emerging from the Ark on the 28th of Cheshvan.

Upon Noah's exit from the Ark, he had much to do:

> *And Noach built an altar to God. He took from all of the pure animals and all of the pure fowl and he sacrificed burnt-offerings upon the altar.*[1]

It was only after these offerings that God was appeased:

> *And the Lord smelled the sweet savor, and the Lord said in His heart: "I will not again curse the ground any more on account of man; for the thoughts of man's heart is evil from his youth;*[2] *neither will I again smite any more everything living, as I have done.*[3]

Upon making this decision, God blessed Noah and his family, and stuck a new covenant with mankind:

> *And God blessed Noah and his sons, and said unto them: 'Be fruitful and multiply, and replenish the earth. And the fear of you and the dread of you shall be upon every beast of the earth, and upon every fowl of the air, and upon all that teems on the ground, and upon all the fish of the sea: into your hand are they delivered. Every moving thing that lives shall be for food for you; as the green herb have I given you all.*[4]

---

[1] Gen. 8:20.

[2] This curious statement will be discussed below.

[3] Gen. 8:21.

[4] Gen. 9:1-3.

At this point, God completed the commanding of the Noahide laws with the seventh and final commandment:[5]

> *Only flesh with the life thereof, which is the blood thereof, shall ye not eat.*[6]

God then gave mankind a sign of this covenant:

> *And God spoke unto Noah, and to his sons with him, saying: 'As for Me, behold, I establish My covenant with you, and with your seed after you; and with every living creature that is with you, the fowl, the cattle, and every beast of the earth with you; of all that go out of the ark, even every beast of the earth. And I will establish My covenant with you; neither shall all flesh be cut off any more by the waters of the flood; neither shall there again be a flood to destroy the earth.' And God said: 'This is the token of the covenant which I make between Me and you and every living creature that is with you, for perpetual generations: I have set My bow in the cloud, and it shall be for a token of a covenant between Me and the earth. And it shall come to pass, when I bring clouds over the earth, and the bow is seen in the cloud, that I will remember My covenant, which is between Me and you and every living creature of all flesh; and the waters shall no more become a flood to destroy all flesh. And the bow shall be in the cloud; and I will look upon it, that I may remember the everlasting covenant between God and every living creature of all flesh that is upon the earth.' And God said unto Noah: 'This is the token of the covenant which I have established between Me and all flesh that is upon the earth.'*[7]

When did all of this occur? According to most commentaries, it couldn't have been on the 28th of Cheshvan, the day that Noah emerged from the ark. The building of the altar and preparations for the sacrifices would have taken at least a few days. Therefore, the covenant of the rainbow was most likely given on or shortly after the first day of Kislev.[8]

---

[5] This is according to Maimonides in *Hilchos Melachim* 9:1. Tosafos, as mentioned in a prior lesson, however, holds that all seven were commanded to Adam. In the times of Noah the details of the seven *mitzvos* were only modified and reaffirmed. Either way, this covenant marks an important point in the commanding of the Noahide laws.

[6] Gen. 9:4.

[7] Gen. 9:8-17.

[8] See *Sefer Todaah*, *hakdama* to Kislev.

## Curious Things…

The events surrounding Noah's exit from the ark are riddled with mysteries. Particularly striking is this passage:

> *And the Lord smelled the sweet savor, and the Lord said in His heart: "I will not again curse the ground any more on account of man;* **for the thoughts of man's heart are evil from his youth**;[9] *neither will I again smite any more everything living, as I have done.*[10]

This passage seems to state that, because man is inherently evil, he not culpable for his actions. At a minimum, culpability for his actions is not at such a level so as to warrant destruction of the earth. Yet, this cannot be the correct understanding of this passage. Consider what is written before the flood:

> *And the Lord saw that the wickedness of man was great upon the earth,* **and that every impulse of the thoughts of his heart was evil, always**.[11]

The "evil in man's heart" cannot be both the reason for bringing the flood (as stated before the flood) and the justification for never again bringing a flood (as stated after the flood)!

The relationship of these two verses is one of the most difficult concepts to understand in the Torah, and many commentaries have wrestled with it. To be clear, there are two issues at play:

1) What does it mean that "… every impulse of the thoughts of his heart was evil, always?" Is man inherently evil? It is a difficult proposition to entertain in light of everything else that we have learned. And,

2) How do we resolve the first use of this phrase (pre-flood) against the second (post-flood)?

A particularly attractive interpretation of these two questions is offered by the *Bina Le-Ittim*.[12]

---

[9] This curious statement will be discussed below.

[10] Gen. 8:21.

[11] Genesis 6:5.

[12] Cited in R' Yehudah Nachshoni's *Hagos B'Parshios HaTorah* on *Parshas Noah*.

**BINAH LEITTIM**

The Torah writes:

> *And God saw everything that He had made, and, behold, it was very good.*[13]

The Midrash explains:

> *R' Nachamn bar Shmuel bar Nachman said in the name of Rav Shmuel bar Nachman: … "And, behold, it was very good." This refers to the evil inclination. But, is the evil inclination "very good?" If not for the evil inclination, man would never build a house, take a wife, reproduce, or conduct any business. So too said Solomon: "[And I saw that all labor and all skillful enterprise] spring from man's rivalry with his neighbor."*[14]

When the Torah states that *…for the thoughts of man's heart are evil from his youth*, and *… that every impulse of the thoughts of his heart was evil, always*, it is referring to man's evil inclination, the *yetzer ha-ra*.

Before the flood, the world only used the *yetzer ha-ra* for evil. Its desires were only to be indulged and enjoyed. After the flood though, when Noah offered his offerings to God, God saw that the *yetzer ha-ra* was once again being used as a tool for good. This is why, before the flood, God criticizes man for his *yetzer ha-ra*. After the flood, however, the reference to the desires of man's heart is actually in praise of man.

What, though, does it mean that Noah, in offering the sacrifices, was using his *yetzer ha-ra* for good? We will discuss this further in our live class.

## The Meaning of a Rainbow

God's choice of a rainbow as the sign of his renewed covenant with man has been the subject of many interpretations, some of which are more fanciful and creative than others. Here is an anthology of the approaches of the classical scholars of the Torah:

- **Talmud** Chagigah 16a - *Anyone who does not care about his Creator's honor, it would be merciful for him had he not been created. In other words, better off that this person was never created. Who is such a person? Rabbi Abba says this is one who stares at a rainbow. As it says, 'Like the appearance of the rainbow that will be in the clouds on a rainy day, so was the appearance of the brilliance all around.' (Ezek. 1:28) That was the appearance of the similitude of God's honor'.* According to this *gemara*, God's presence is manifested somehow in the appearance of a rainbow. Just as one may not

---

[13] Gen. 1:31.

[14] Ecc. 4:4.

stare at any manifestation of the *shechina*, the divine presence, so too one may not stare at a rainbow. To do so is to slight God's honor. This passage also tells us that staring at a rainbow damages one's sight.

- ***Bereshis Rabbah* 35:2 & Kesubos 77b** – When Eliyahu HaNavi was studying Torah with Rabbi Yehoshua ben Levi, they encountered a difficulty in a statement of Rabbi Shimon bar Yochai, the author of the Zohar. Since Rabbi Shimon bar Yochai was no longer living, the two of them ascended to *Gan Eden* to ask Rabbi Shimon for clarification of his words. Eliyahu approached Rabbi Shimon first. Rabbi Shimon asked him: "Who is this with you?" Eliyahu HaNavi answered: "Rabbi Yehoshua ben Levi, one of the great ones of his generation." Rabbi Shimon turned to Rabbi Yehoshua and asked: "Has a rainbow ever been seen in your generation?" Rabbi Yehoshua answered: "yes," to which Rabbi Shimon replied: "If a rainbow has been seen in your generation, then you are not fit to learn from me!" The commentaries explain that the fact that a rainbow had appeared in Rabbi Yehoshua's generation indicated that his generation was worthy of destruction. Therefore, Rabbi Yehoshua was not of sufficient righteousness or purity to speak to the holy Rabbi Shimon. The *gemora* in Kesubos 77b, however, tells us that a rainbow never appeared in the generation of Rabbi Yehoshua. Why then did Rabbi Yehoshua tell Rabbi Shimon that a rainbow had appeared? The *gemora* explains that Rabbi Yehoshua did not want to be seen as haughty.

- Rashi **to Gen. 9:14** – Based on the Midrash, Rashi explains that when God desires to bring punishment upon the world, he places the rainbow as a sign of the covenant, as a reminder that He will not destroy the world. Therefore, the appearance of a rainbow is not a good sign. Rather, it is a sign that things are not right between God and the world and, were it not for the covenant, God would again destroy the world! In fact, the *Mishnah Berurah*,[15] the most widely accepted interpretation of the Shulchan Aruch today, states that if one sees a rainbow, even though it is something upon which we bless, one should not inform others because it is not a good sign.

- Nachmanides **(the Ramban)** – The Rainbow appears like a bow without a string. Instead of aimed from heaven downwards, it is upturned, away from the earth. This symbolizes that God does not "hold destruction over the earth." Furthermore, the unstrung bow is a sign of peace. The Ramban further writes that we see that rainbows are a natural phenomenon caused by water refracted through moisture. Therefore, they must have existed since the

---

[15] 229:1.

beginning of creation. It was only after the flood that a particular meaning was assigned to the rainbow. This is implied by the verse's wording: "I have **set** my rainbow…," implying that the rainbow already existed. This is also the opinion of Rav Saadya Gaon.

- Ibn Ezra & Radak – The rainbow did not exist prior to the flood.

- Chizkuni – The appearance of opposite colors together symbolized a resolution of opposite ends. Blue against red, for example symbolized the resolution of fire and water, of mercy and harsh judgment.

- Rav Shimshon Rafael Hirsch – Rav Hirsch, an exceedingly deep thinker of 19th century Judaism, offered the following interpretation of the rainbow:[16]

*Perhaps, the appearance of the rainbow's colors is closest in meaning [to the actual meaning of the rainbow] than all these aforementioned interpretations. By it, our attention is repeatedly drawn to the fact that, despite all the variances in the degrees of the development of mankind, God would never again decree the downfall of the entire human race. Rather, the differences and varieties found among humanity would serve as the basis for mankind's gradual education towards its godly purpose. For the rainbow is nothing other than a single, pure ray of light broken into seven degrees of seven colors. [It ranges] from the red rays nearest to the light to violet – the most distant from the light and the nearest to darkness. Yet, from one to the other, are they not all but rays of light, and do they not all combine to form a single, pure, white ray? Could this not, perhaps, be intended to say that the whole array of living creatures, from Adam, the most alive and whose name means "red one," the nearest to God, all the way down to the lowest, humblest worm in whom there is a living soul of flesh, and even moreso all of the variety and shades of humanity among the races of mankind – from the brilliant intellectuals to those in whom there is hardly a glimmer of the spiritual - that God unites them all in a common bond of peace. All are fragments of one life; all are refracted rays of the one spirit of God. [Is not] the lowest, darkest, most distant one not still a son of the light? Thus we see later on that our sages describe the different spiritual and moral degrees of the righteous using the metaphor of degrees of light; from the bright illuminating rays of the sun to the gleam of the menorah in the temple. All is light, yet it only appears different according to the difference of the material, [as it is written:] "There are seven groups among the righteous… and their faces shine like the sun,[17] like the moon,[18] like the firmament,[19] like lightening,[20] like the stars,[21] like the blossoms,[22] and like the menorah[23] in the holy temple."[24]*

---

[16] Commentary of Rav Hirsch to Gen. 9:16. Editor's translation from the original German.

[17] See Song of Songs 6:10.

It is important to note that all of the above interpretations embody that quality that we have seen so many times in this course: paradox. The rainbow, a sign of peace, potential, and resolution, is also a sign of warning and displeasure. These apparent opposites both exist simultaneously, underscoring the complex relationship between God and his creation. God is both merciful father and true judge, the immanent and the transcendent, the destroyer and creator, the giver of life and one who decrees death, the God of light, dark, and all of the colors in-between. Perhaps, the expression of this complicated paradox is part of the full meaning of the rainbow.

For Jews, Kislev is deeply connected with Chanukah, a commemoration of the triumph of Torah over the onslaught of Greek thought and subjugation. For Noahides, Kislev is associated with the original Noahic covenant. Should this association be commemorated? May a Noahide celebrate the 1st of Kislev as a commemoration of the original covenant?

## The Noahide Covenant vs. The Noahide Laws

We must make a careful distinction as to what the first of Kislev commemorates. It was on or about the first of Kislev that God gave man permission to eat meat, blessed Noah and his sons, and guaranteed that He would no longer destroy the world on account of man.

However, it is not a commemoration of the giving of the Noahide laws. Even though the Noahide laws were completed (or modified to their final form, according to some)[25] at this time, their binding authority today is from Sinai, not from the covenant with Noah. It is not appropriate to commemorate the first of Kislev as a time of the giving of the Noahide laws – that honor belongs to

---

[18] Ibid.

[19] Dan. 12:3.

[20] Nahum 2:5.

[21] Dan. 12:3.

[22] A poetic reference to the prophets. See Psalm 69:1.

[23] Zech. 4:2.

[24] This statement shows up in many places. See *Midrash Tehillim* 16:12; *Pseikta d'Rav Kehana*, 27:2.

[25] See note 5, above.

Shavuot, the commemoration of the revelation at Sinai. Recall that Sinai is the basis for modern observance of the Noahide laws, not the Noahic covenant.

## The First of Kislev

If one wishes, he may commemorate the 1<sup>st</sup> of Kislev as an historical milestone. However, one should keep in mind that the day is of limited religious significance; its primary religious significance was supplanted by the events at Sinai. Nevertheless, it is appropriate to recall the rainbow as a sign of God's promise and to pray that all man will return to God.

THE YESHIVA PIRCHEI SHOSHANIM SHULCHAN ARUCH LEARNING PROJECT

# The Noahide Laws – Lesson Thirty Two

### © Yeshiva Pirchei Shoshanim 2017

This shiur may not be reproduced in any
form without permission of the copyright holder.

THE YESHIVA PIRCHEI SHOSHANIM SHULCHAN ARUCH PROJECT
THE NOAHIDE LAWS | FESTIVALS VII | LESSON 32

## Outline of This Lesson:

1. Introduction
2. *Tu B'Shvat*: The New Year For Trees
3. *Tu B'Shvat, Terumos & Maasros*
4. *Tu B'Shvat, Orlah, Neta Reavi*
5. Are *Terumos & Maasros* Relevant to Noahides?
6. Maimonides
7. An Ongoing Dispute?
8. Jewish Commemoration of *Tu B'Shvat*
9. The Evolution of a Custom

# Festivals VII: Tu B'Shvat

## Introduction

Shvat is the month that follows Kislev. The only holiday occurring in this month is *Tu B'Shvat*. However, there is some uncertainty as to whether or not this day is relevant to Noahides. Exploring this question will be the main topic of our lesson.

## Tu B'Shvat: The New Year for Trees

The Mishnah[1] teaches us:

> *There are four* Rosh Hashanahs *[New Years]: the 1st of Nissan is the New Year for kings and festivals, the 15th of Elul is the New Year for the tithing of animals (according to Rabbis Elazar and Shimon, this is on the 1st of Tishrei), the 1st of Tishrei for counting years, the Jubilee and Shemitta cycles, and the tithing of trees and produce. The 1st of Shvat is the New Year for trees according to the yeshiva [school] of Shammai.* **According to the yeshiva [school] of Hillel, it is on the 15th of Shvat.**

Since the *halakhah*, practice, always follows Hillel,[2] then we see that *Tu B'Shvat* is established on the 15th of Shvat. In fact, the name "Tu B'Shvat" literally means "the 15th of Shvat."

---

[1] *Rosh HaShanah* 1:1.

[2] There are, however, six exceptions to this rule in the Talmudic canon.

## Tu B'Shvat, Terumos & Maasros

A number of standard agricultural tithes were given each year in ancient Israel. There were also variable tithes dependent on the seven year *shemitta* cycle. The cycle was as follows:

- **Year 1** – *Terumah Gedolah, Maaser Rishon* (and *Terumas HaMaaser*) & *Maaser Sheni*

- **Year 2** – *Terumah Gedolah, Maaser Rishon* (and *Terumas HaMaaser*) & *Maaser Sheni*

- **Year 3** – *Terumah Gedolah, Maaser Rishon* (and *Terumas HaMaaser*) & *Maaser Ani*

- **Year 4** – *Terumah Gedolah, Maaser Rishon* (and *Terumas HaMaaser*) & *Maaser Sheni*

- **Year 5** – *Terumah Gedolah, Maaser Rishon* (and *Terumas HaMaaser*) & *Maaser Sheni*

- **Year 6** – *Terumah Gedolah, Maaser Rishon* (and *Terumas HaMaaser*) & *Maaser Ani*

- **Year 7** – *Shemitta Year*. Land may not be worked; Remission of debts.

**Terumah Gedolah** – This was the first separation and was given to the *Kohanim*, [**Priests**] of the temple. The minimum amount of this tithe varied depending on whether the owner of the produce was poor or wealthy.

**Maaser Rishon** – A tithe of $1/10^{th}$ removed after *Terumah Gedolah*. This was gifted to the Levites.

**Terumas HaMasser** – From the *Maaser Rishon* they received, the Levites were obligated to give $1/10^{th}$ to the *Kohanim*. This amounts to $1/100^{th}$ of the total produce.

***Maaser Sheni*** – This tithe (another 1/10th of the remaining produce) was separated only in the 1st, 2nd, 4th, and 5th years of the *shemitta* cycle.

***Maaser Ani*** – This tithe, given to the poor, was given only in the 3rd and 6th years of the *shemitta* cycle.

An important part of these laws was the rule that one may not satisfy the tithing obligation of one year with the fruit produced in another year. For fruit trees, *Tu B'Shvat* marks the demarcation line between one year and the next for the purposes of these tithes.

## Tu B'shvat, Orlah & Neta Revai

*Tu B'Shvat* is also important for two further *mitzvos*: *Orlah* and *Neta Revai*.

- **Orlah** – One may not eat fruit yielded by a tree in its first three years. While the start of this three-year period is based on the 1st of Tishrei, the end of this period is after the *Tu B'Shvat* of the third year of the tree's life. For example, if one planted trees before Rosh HaShanah, the fruit of those trees would be prohibited until after the third *Tu B'Shvat* after the Tree was planted.

- **Neta Revai** – Fruit produced by a tree in its fourth year is similar to *Maaser Sheni*; it may only be consumed in Jerusalem. Alternatively, one may redeem this produce and use the money to buy food to consume in Jerusalem. *Tu B'Shvat* is also used to calculate the fourth year for *Neta Revai*.

## Are Terumos and Maasros Relevant to Noahides?

It is clear that Noahides are not obligated in *Terumos* and *Maasros*. This is the universal conclusion of the *halachic* authorities.[3] After all, these *mitzvos* were commanded only to Jews. Therefore, Noahide performance of these *mitzvos* can only be voluntary at best.

The Mishnah[4] certainly implies this, stating that such a voluntary tithing is valid:

---

[3] See Rambam 4:15; Ridvaz ad loc; Sefer Mitzvos HaShem (Shteif), Mitzvos Bnei Noach. This is also the implication of the Mishnah, as we shall see.

[4] Terumos 3:9.

> *The Terumah of a non-Jew or Cuthean is Terumah, their tithes are valid tithes, and their sanctified gifts are sanctified gifts.*

However, there is significant doubt as to whether or not the validity of these separations is biblical or rabbinic in nature. If it is biblical, then *Tu B'Shvat* is a significant date for Noahides. However, if it is rabbinic, then *Tu B'Shvat* might not be relevant to Noahides.

Most authorities appear to hold that the validity of a Noahides voluntary separations is only rabbinic. However, things are not so clear.

## Maimonides

In his Mishnah Torah,[5] Maimonides explains the reason for the rabbinic decree:

> *When a gentile separates Terumah from his own produce, according to Biblical Law, the separation is ineffective because he has no obligation to do so. [Our Rabbis] decreed that his separation should be effective, though, because of the wealthy, lest the money belong to a Jew and he say that it belong to a gentile to make it exempt. We cross-examine the gentile who separates Terumah. If he says: "I separated it so that it should be like a Jew's," we give it to a priest. If not, it should be entombed, for perhaps his intent was [to dedicate it] to heaven. When does the above apply? In Eretz Yisrael. Our Sages did not, however, issue a decree if a gentile separates Terumah in the Diaspora. We tell him that he is not obligated to do this and the produce is not Terumah at all.*

According to what is written here, the tithes of a non-Jew are only acceptable in the Temple because of a rabbinic decree made to address a problem in the Jewish world. Apparently, wealthy people would occasionally falsify ownership of their crops and produce, claiming they belonged to a non-Jew, in order to escape paying the regular, obligated tithes. If a non-Jew came to voluntarily offer tithes, there was suspicion that it may be a ruse.

While this passage implies that Maimonides holds of only rabbinic validity to these tithes, this is not definite.

Maimonides, commenting on our aforementioned Mishnah from Terumos 3:9, writes:

> *Non-Jews, even though they are not obligated in these separations or tithes, they receive a little benefit by giving them... therefore they are valid.*[6]

---

[5] Terumos 4:15.

[6] Peirush al Hamishnayos.

This remark certainly implies that, though not obligated in *Terumos* and *Maasros*, non-Jews may separate these tithes and they are accorded a *mitzvah* for doing so. It appears that Maimonides acknowledges the biblical validity of these tithes.

## An Ongoing Dispute?

*Tosafos* to Kiddushin 41b implies that this question may be an ongoing Talmudic dispute. There are a number of possibilities as to how we can understand the relationship of the texts involved.[7]

1) The Mishnah is saying the same thing as Maimonides, that the tithes and separations of non-Jews are only valid per force of Rabbinic decree. The disagreement in the Talmud, however, is only relevant to determining whether or not the validity of a non-Jew's *Terumah* is comparable to a Jew's for the purpose of acting as a Jew's agent in separating these tithes. It is not directly relevant to whether or not non-Jews can validly separate *Terumah* and *Maaser*.

2) The Mishnah states that, on a biblical level, the separation of *Terumah* and *Maaser* by a non-Jew is valid. Maimonides agrees to this (as we see in his commentary on the Mishnah). However, in the Mishnah Torah Maimonides is only addressing the issue from the "Jewish side" of things; in a situation of doubt caused by possibile dishonesty. We cannot determine anything about the validity of a true Noahide separation of *Maaser* or *Terumah* from what Maimonides writes there. The Talmud in Kiddushin may not be relevant for the same reason mentioned earlier – it is only discussing validity for the purposes of agency.

So, what is the conclusion? Are the voluntary *Terumos* and *Maasros* of a non-Jew valid because of the rabbinic decree mentioned by the Rambam, or is because they are intrinsically valid? There isn't a clear answer. Yet, this isn't the end of things…

---

[7] See Toldos Noach 13:10.

## Jewish Commemoration of *Tu B'Shvat*

How do Jews commemorate *Tu B'Shvat*? Many have the custom to plant trees on this day. However, this custom is very recent. It only began in 1890 in Zichron Yaakov, an agricultural commune in pre-state Israel. The practice was adopted in the early 1900's by a number of early religious Zionist movements has since become prevalent in the Reform and Conservative movements.

Traditionally, Tu B'Shvat was not celebrated as a holiday. Other than omitting certain supplications from the regular liturgy, there are no assigned commemorations for this holiday.

However, in the middle ages some began to acknowledge the day with a quasi-ceremonial eating-of-fruit. The origin of this custom seems to come from Rashi's commentary to *Rosh HaShanah* 14a. Rashi comes to answer an obvious question: Why is the 15th of Shvat the New Year for trees and not some other day? Though the Talmud loosely connects *Tu B'Shvat* to the lifecycle of fruit trees, Rashi makes things much clearer for us. According to Rashi, *Tu B'Shvat* is the day on which an internal process begins within the tress of the world. On this day, they begin to draw their sap up from the roots to nourish the tree through the winter season. Botanically, this marks the renewal of the lifecycle of the tree - a cycle eventually culminating in fruit. Today, when the *Trumah* and *Maaser* cycle is mostly inapplicable,[8] it would seem that that this quasi-ceremonial fruit eating is an acknowledgement of the physical process taking place in the world on Tu B'Shvat.

## The Evolution of a Custom

Over the next few hundred years, the custom of eating fruit on this day became more commonplace and widespread. The ceremony also became more elaborate, eventually culminating in a standardized Seder. The form of this ceremony was fixed by the Ari Za"l and his students, in whose hands the custom took on deep mystical significance.

I numerous places, man is compared to a tree. For example, Deut. 20:19 states:

> *When you besiege a city for many days to wage war against it to capture it, you shall not destroy its trees by wielding an ax against them, for you may eat from them, but you shall not cut them down. Is the tree of the field a man, to go into the siege before you?*

---

[8] In the land of Israel, there are some remaining, residual requirements of tithing. However, they are not given to Kohanim in our days.

The language of this verse is such that it can be read as saying "A man is but a tree of the field…" From here the Talmud draws a number of comparisons between a man and a tree.[9] Jeremiah 17:8 also compares a righteous person to a tree planted by water. Such comparisons are also common in the Psalms, Midrashim, and other sources.

The Ari Za"l and his school explained that these comparisons are far more than parables or literary devices. On a very deep level, they allude to the connection between the soul of Adam, both as the first man and as all of mankind, and the original tree – the Tree of Knowledge.

Their *Seder* for this meal invokes themes of restoring and repairing the spiritual damages caused by man's very early transgressions.

From a perspective of Torah law, the Noahide relationship to *Tu B'Shvat* is only to the degree that voluntary *Terumah* and *Maaser* may be brought according to the agricultural calendar. However, from a perspective of natural phenomena (see Rashi's opinion above) and kabbalah, there is certainly enough connection to warrant commemoration of the holiday using the Ari's *Seder*.

Yeshiva Pirchei Shoshanim has prepared a translated and annotated edition of the Ari Zt"l's *Seder* for *Tu B'Shvat*. We have included it with this lesson.

---

[9] See Taanis 7a.

THE YESHIVA PIRCHEI SHOSHANIM SHULCHAN ARUCH PROJECT

# The Noahide Laws – Lesson Thirty Three

© **Yeshiva Pirchei Shoshanim 2017**
This shiur may not be reproduced in any
form without permission of the copyright holder.

## Table of Contents:

1. Introduction
2. 7th of Adar
3. Month of Nissan
4. Nissan as the Rosh HaShanah for Kings and Festivals
5. New Year for Kings
6. Judgment for Grain
7. *Birkas Hallanos* – Blessing on the Trees
8. *Birkas HaChama* – The Blessing on the Cycle of the Sun
9. Summary

# Adar & Nissan

## Introduction

The next month in the calendar is Adar. The only major holiday in Adar is Purim, a Rabbinic celebration commemorating the victory of the Jews over their Persian oppressors. Like Chanukah, this day is of little significance to Noahides. However, there are other days, though not as well-known as Purim, that are nevertheless significant. In this lesson, we will also look at the month of Nissan and the holiday of Passover.

## The 7th of Adar

The 7th of Adar is the anniversary of both Moses's birth and death. Though are no special commemorations for this day, there are a number of customs that have grown up around it. However, most of these customs are not universally observed. In the past, there were some who had the custom to fast on the 7th of Adar and to recite a special prayer. However, this is uncommon in our days. There are some who light a *yahrzeit* (memorial) candle in memory of Moses. In many communities, Jewish burial societies hold their annual meetings on the 7th of Adar.

For Noahides, Moses is a significant figure in the transmission of the Noahide laws and it is certainly important to acknowledge his role. The 7th of Adar is the appropriate day to do so.

- As a general rule, fasting is discouraged unless one has a particularly compelling reason to do so. Nevertheless, one may still recite the prayer for the 7th of Adar (this will be provided to the group in the near future).

- Lighting a 24-hour memorial candle in memory of Moses is an appropriate custom.

This year the 7th of Adar is Thursday, February 26. 2015.

In a Hebrew leap year, when there is an extra month of Adar, the 7th of Adar is commemorated in Adar II.

## The Month of Nissan

The Month of Nissan is second only to Tishrei in religious significance. As with all of the major festivals of the Torah, it has levels of specific meaning relevant only to Israel and broader meaning relevant to the world. Let's take a look again at our source Mishnah's:

> *There are four* Rosh Hashanah's *[New Years]:* **the 1st of Nissan is the New Year for kings and festivals**, *the 15th of Elul is the New Year for the tithing of animals (according to Rabbis Elazar and Shimon, this is on the 1st of Tishrei), the 1st of Tishrei for counting years, the Jubilee and Shemitta cycles, and the tithing of trees and produce. The 1st of Shvat is the New Year for trees according to the yeshiva [school] of Shammai. According to the yeshiva [school] of Hillel, it is on the 15th of Shvat.*[1]

> *At four junctures, the world is judged:* **on Passover for grain**, *on Shavuot for fruits, on Rosh Hashanah all pass before him like sheep of the flock, as it is written, "He form their hearts as one, he understands all of their deeds." (Psalms 33). On Sukkot, the world is judged for water.*[2]

For Jews, the Month of Nissan is all about Passover, the liberation of Israel from the slavery of Egypt. However, the universal meaning is two-fold:

1) The 1st of Nissan is a Rosh HaShanah for Kings and festivals.

2) On the 15th of Nissan, Passover, the world is judged upon the abundance of grain.

---

[1] Mishnah Rosh HaShanah 1:1.

[2] Mishnah Rosh HaShanah 1:2.

## Nissan as the Rosh HaShanah for Kings and Festivals

Before Israel exited Egypt, the months of the Hebrew calendar were all counted from varying starting points. Either the months were counted from creation, from the cessation of the flood, or the birth of Abraham. After the exodus, however, God commanded Israel to count all of the months beginning from Nissan:

> *And the Lord spoke unto Moses and Aaron in the land of Egypt, saying: "This month shall be unto you the beginning of months; it shall be the first month of the year to you."*
> *(Exodus 12:1-2)*

Having established Nissan as the first month, Pesach (Passover) is thus reckoned as the first of the festivals. This is important for calculating the window one has to fulfill a vows pertaining to offering (this detail will be discussed in the live class). This aspect of Nissan may be relevant to Noahides and will be discussed in greater detail in a future lesson.

This year, the first of Nissan falls on Saturday, March 21, 2015.

## The New Year for Kings

The Talmud clarifies that Nissan is only considered the New Year for the reign of Jewish kings. This is because of the unique status of Nissan for Jews as the month of Redemption. For gentile kings, their reign is counted from the time of creation, the month of Tishrei.

We see that the status of Tishrei as a Rosh HaShanah for kings is only relevant to Jews. Yet, as a Rosh HaShanah for festivals, it may be relevant to Noahides.

## Judgment for Grain

The 15$^{th}$ of Nissan is Passover for the Jews – a holiday primarily concerned with commemorating the exodus from Egypt. For the rest of the world, its primary relevance is as a day of judgment for grain.

It is on this day that God determines which nations will prosper and which will have famine. As such, it is important to pray for the sustenance of the world at this time.

On Passover, we also recite the prayer for dew. The reason for this prayer is that the rains that fall after the 15$^{th}$ of Nissan are damaging for the grain harvest. An excess of moisture at this time can cause the drying grain to rot. Therefore, on the 15$^{th}$ of Nissan we pray for dew, asking God for a sufficient amount of moisture to sustain the crops and the world without harming the drying grain. This prayer is recited on the first day of Passover during morning prayers.

Communal are certainly appropriate at this time. It is also appropriate to eat bread and food from grains at this meal.

For Noahides, the 15th of Nissan is a one-day holiday. This year it falls on Saturday, April 4, 2015.

## Birkas Hallanos – Blessing on the Trees

Nissan is strongly associated with spring, renewal, and the emergence of the world from its winter slumber. During this month, upon seeing fruit trees in bloom, we make a special blessing upon them. This blessing may be made only once each year. Some have the custom to gather in groups, making the occasion one for celebration. This blessing is subject to the following rules:

- The blessing is said only upon fruit bearing trees. It a dispute as to whether or not this blessing may be said in any month other than Nissan.

- The blessing is only recited when one sees at least two fruit bearing trees together. These trees should be over 3 years old.

- According to some, this blessing should not be made on the seventh day or on a holiday.

- If one has already seen blossoming trees, then the blessing is not recited.

- The blessing is not recited upon a tree that is actually laden with fruit, only upon a tree that is blossoming.

This is the blessing on blossoming fruit trees:

**Blessed are You, Lord, our God, King of the Universe, in Whose universe nothing is lacking, and in which He created good creatures and good trees, in which mankind takes joy.**

## *Birkas HaChama* – The Blessing on the Cycle of the Sun

The Blessing on the Sun is a blessing recited once every 28 years. Due to its infrequency, this blessing has become a special occasion for rejoicing. The Talmud writes:

> *One who sees the sun at the beginning of its cycle ... recites: Blessed in the One who makes the creation. And when is this? Abaye said: Every 28 years.*[3]

Conventional wisdom, that the sun rises in the east and sets in the west, is only mostly true. The exact positions of its rising and setting vary from season-to-season. Near the summer solstice, the sun rises and sets at its northernmost point. However, near the winter solstice, the sun's rising and setting is at its southernmost place. The midpoint of the sun's southern journey is the autumnal equinox, while the midpoint of its northern journey is the spring equinox. The interval between the reoccurrence of these phases is the solar year, which is approximately 365 ¼ days, or 52 weeks and 1 ¼ day.

Due to the additional 1 ¼ day, these solar benchmarks shift forward slightly each year. For example, if the spring equinox is at 12:00 PM on a Sunday, then it will fall on Monday at 6:00 PM in the following year. The next year, it will fall at midnight on Tuesday, and so on.

After 28 years will the sun have returned back to its original position at the same time we began our count.

The sun was placed in the heavens during the first hour on the evening of the fourth day of the week (a Tuesday night).[4] According to the sages, this was the Spring Equinox. Therefore, the first sunrise occurred twelve hours later on the morning of the fourth day. It is at that time, every 28 years that we make the blessing on the sun.

2009 was the last time that the blessing was made. The next occasion for this blessing is April 8, 2037.

---

[3] Brachos 59b.

[4] The details here are all summarized from Brachos 2a & 59b, Eruvin 56a, Rosh HaShanah 10b.

This blessing is recited according to the following laws:

- The blessing is cited as soon as the entire disk of the sun has risen above the horizon.

- The blessing may only be said until the third hour of daylight. According to some, if one misses that time, then he may recite it until noon.

- It is preferable that this blessing be recited by as many people together as possible.

- Women do not recite this blessing. This is because, in the times of the Prophet Jeremiah, worship of the sun became widespread among women of the time.
- It is customary for the congregation to assemble before sunrise for their prayers, timing them so that they have ample time afterwards to make the blessing.

- Following the blessing, the custom is to celebrate with song, music, and food.

The blessing is:
**Blessed are You, Lord our God, who makes the work of Creation.**

## Summary of the Lesson

1. Nissan, as a Rosh HaShanah may be relevant to Noahides because it established the window of time during which one must fulfill a vow to bring a voluntary offering.

2. Nissan, as a Rosh HaShanah for kings, is not relevant to Noahides

3. The 15th of Nissan is important as a day of judgment for grain and produce.

4. On the 15th of Nissan we recite the prayer for dew.

5. During Nissan, we recite the blessing on blooming fruit trees.

6. Every 28 years, we make a blessing upon God's renewal of the cycle of the sun.

# The Noahide Laws - Lesson Thirty Four

THE YESHIVA PIRCHEI SHOSHANIM SHULCHAN ARUCH PROJECT

© **Yeshiva Pirchei Shoshanim 2017**
This shiur may not be reproduced in any
form without permission of the copyright holder.

164 Village Path, Lakewood NJ 08701 732.370.3344
164 Rabbi Akiva, Bnei Brak, 03.616.6340

## Table of Contents:

1. Introduction
2. The Noahide Covenant & Man
3. Judgment on the Fruit of the Trees
4. Observances for *Shavuos*
5. *Tisha B'Av* – the 8th of Av
6. Jewish Observances of *Tisha B'Av*
7. *Tisha B'Av* & Noahides – Mourning the Temples
8. Summary

# Sivan & Av

## Introduction

The next important holiday is *Shavuos*, which is on the 6th of Sivan. For Jews, *Shavuos* is primarily the *zman matan Torosaynu* – the time of the giving of the Torah. However, for Noahides it carries a different yet equally important connotation. In this lesson we will look at *Shavuos* and the remaining holidays of the year from a Noahide perspective.

## The Noahide Covenant & Man

To understand the Noahic significance of Sinai, we must place it within the context of God's historical relationship with man. When God created man, He did so with a number of hopes and expectations. However, God also gave man free will. By giving man free will, God also gave man the ability to disappoint Him as well as to please Him. As a result the God/man relationship is never a static one; is it constantly in flux as man provokes and God responds, or God provokes and man responds. The history of humankind, since the beginning of creation, is a chronicle of this dynamic and evolving relationship.

- **Year 1 / - C3760** – God creates Man. The Noahide laws, either all or in part, are communicated to Adam and Eve. This constitutes the first covenant with man.

- **Year 1536/-2225** – By this time man had completely forgotten, or willfully ignored, the original covenant. The world is completely corrupted and man follows his desires with no thought as to God's will. In this year, Noah began construction of the Ark.[1]

- **1657/-2104** – Noah and his family had remained in the Ark for a full solar year (the equivalent of one lunar year and 11 days).[2] Noah, his family, and all that was with him exited the Ark on the 27th or 28th of Cheshvan. Sometime during the waning days of Cheshvan and the first days of Kislev, Noah and his sons named the constellations in the sky.[3] Noah also gave offerings from the clean animals. At this time, God was appeased and resolved to never again destroy the world on account of man. God designated the rainbow as a sign of this covenant. God also commanded (or, according to some, only modified) the last of the Seven Universal Laws – the commandment against eating meat from the limb of a living animal.[4] Noah and his descendants were also granted all living things as food.

- **1996/-1765** – Within only a few hundred years the world had fallen back into idolatry and, with the exception of a very few individuals, the Noahide laws had been forgotten. In this year the peoples of the world were dispersed and their languages mixed as a result of the Tower of Babel.[5] According to many, it was at this time that Abraham recognized God's complete unity.[6] God also recognized the uniqueness of Abraham.

---

[1] See *Zohar, Bereshis 58b*; Rashi to Gen. 5:29.

[2] *Midrash Rabbah, Bereshis* 33:7.

[3] *Mishnah Torah, Yesodei HaTorah* 3:7.

[4] According to Maimonides, *Hilchos Melachim 9*:1, the first six Noahide laws were given to Adam and the remaining one given to Noah after the flood. *Tosafos*, however, holds that all seven were given to Adam and only modified in the times of Noah.

[5] See *Midrash, Yalkut Divrei HaYamim* I 1073.

[6] *Midrash Rabbah Bereshis* 64:4 and *Seder HaDoros*. Although Abraham rejected idolatry earlier in his life, it appears that it was not until age 40 or 48 that he came to a fully developed, monotheistic recognition of God. See Maimonides, *Hil. Avodah Zarah* 1:3 with *Hagahos Maimonios* and *Kesef Mishnah*.

- **2018/-1743** – God's relationship with Abraham ascended as the world fell deeper and deeper into idolatry and immorality. Therefore, God chose to make a new covenant with Abraham alone. In this year, the *Bris Bein HaBsarim* (Covenant of the Parts) is made with Abraham.[7]

- **2048/-1714** – The covenant of circumcision is made with Abraham.

- **2084/-1677** – Abraham and Isaac, his 36 or 37 year old son[8], were tried by the *Akeida* – the binding of Isaac. Their special relationship is further established with God.

- **2185/-1576** – Jacob dreams of the ladder. At this time, God continues his covenant with Jacob.

- **2238/-1523** – Jacob and his family descend into Egypt. Egypt is a furnace of idolatry, magic, necromancy, and everything antithetical to the faith of Abraham, Isaac, and Jacob. Nevertheless, in this, the capital city of spiritual impurity, despite 210 years of slavery and oppression,[9] the descendants of Jacob (known now as the Children of Israel) maintained their monotheism and allegiance to God.

- **2448/-1313** – God redeems the children of Israel from Egypt. He leads them to Sinai, where He establishes an eternal covenant with the entire people and reveals the Torah. Although Israel was God's primary concern at Sinai, it was not God's only concern. By the time of Sinai, the rest of the world had entirely abandoned the Noahide laws. With Israel's triumph of faith, God took new hope in the future of his creation. As He commanded Israel in the Torah, He also seized the opportunity to reaffirm the Noahide laws and command them anew to the world.

---

[7] See *Mechilta Shemos* 12:40; *Tosafos Berachos* 7b & *Shabbos* 10b; *Maharsha* to *Megilla* 9a; *Seder HaDoros*.

[8] This is based on the accepted chronology found in the *Midrash* and *Seder HaDoros*.

[9] Abraham is told that his ancestors will go into exile for 400 years; however this count began with Isaac and not with the actual descent into Egypt. The actual time of Israel in Egypt was only 210 years. See *Mechilta, Shemos* 12:40-41; *Seder HaDoros*.

From Sinai onwards, God's expectation for humanity was to observe the Noahide laws not because of their having been commanded to Adam or Noah, but because of their having been affirmed by Moses at Sinai. From this time onwards, the Noahide laws would be bound up with and subject to the interpretation and study of the Torah as revealed and entrusted to the Jewish people at Sinai.

Although the Seven Noahide Laws were commanded to the world in the times of Noah and Adam (as part of God's evolving relationship with man), their final form was established at Sinai. For Noahides today, Sinai is the origin, purpose, and motivation for keeping the Noahide laws.

This is the reason for Maimonides's words in the Mishnah Torah:[10]

> *All who accept the Seven Mitzvos and are careful to observe them are called* MiChasidei Umos HaOlam *(of the Pious Peoples of the World) and they have a share in the World to Come. This is provided that one accepts and observes them because they were commanded to him by the Holy One, in his Torah, and reaffirmed by Moses. However, one who observes them based on intellectual reason alone is neither called a Ger Toshav nor MiChasidei Umos HaOlam (of the Pious Peoples of the World). He is, rather, "of the wise ones" of the gentiles.*[11]

*Shavuos*, the anniversary of the giving of the Torah is the time to connect with the obligation of observing the Noahide laws, accept them anew, and celebrate the fact that God affirmed them anew at Sinai.

## Judgment for the Fruits of the Trees

Our Mishnah, which we have seen many times, states:

> *At four junctures, the world is judged: on Passover for grain,* **on Shavuos for fruits**, *on Rosh Hashanah all pass before him like sheep of the flock, as it is written, "He*

---

[10] **Hilchos Melachim** 10:11.

[11] The text of this last phrase differs in the *editio princeps* (Rome, 1480) and almost all subsequent printed editions. These versions read : ... *one who observes them based on intellectual reason alone is neither called a* Ger Toshav *nor* MiChasidei Umos HaOlam *(of the Pious Peoples of the World),* **and is not** *"of the wise ones" of the gentiles.* This is almost certainly the error of a careless copyist (the mistake being in the transcription of a single letter). Many of the earliest manuscript versions read ... *He is, rather, "of the wise ones" of the gentiles.* Later scholars also cite this version of the text as correct. See Teshuvos Maharam Alashkar 117, Rav Yosef ben Shem Tov's *Kevod Elokim* 29a, and, more recently, Iggros Reiyah I:89. Recent critical editions of Maimonides have corrected this text to read ... *He is rather "of the wise ones" of the gentiles.* See Rabbi Shabtai Fraenkel's edition of the *Mishneh Torah*. See also the editions prepared by Rabbi Yosef Qafih and Yeshivat Or Vishua.

*form their hearts as one, he understands all of their deeds." (Psalms 33).  On Sukkot, the world is judged for water.*

On *Shavuos*, the world is judged upon fruits.  As such, it is an appropriate time to pray for the produce of trees.

## Observances for *Shavuos*

Shavuot will next fall on May 24, 2015.  Like all the holidays, it actually begins at nightfall on the preceding evening.

**Decorating the Synagogue**

There is a custom to decorate the Synagogue with greenery and flowers in commemoration of the revelation at Sinai, a mountain "full of greenery." The *Bnei Yissaschar* further connects this custom to the Midrash, which states the following:

> *To what can this [the revelation at Sinai] be compared? A king had a garden that had become overgrown with thorns. The king brought in gardeners to cut down the entire garden. Just then, the king saw a single rose blooming. He said: "For the sake of this rose, let the entire garden be saved!" Likewise, God declares: "In the Merit of the Torah, the entire world shall be saved!"*

In giving the Torah to Sinai, God took renewed hope in the world.  This is confirmed by the fact that the Noahide laws were re-commanded to the World at Sinai. It is, therefore, appropriate for Noahides to decorate their places of worship or homes for the holiday in accordance with this Midrash and the other reasons that we have stated.

**Renewed Acceptance of the Noahide Laws**

Since this is the anniversary of God's affirmation of the Noahide laws to the world, this is an appropriate time to both individually and communally accept and affirm the Noahide laws. This acceptance does not require a Beis Din or witnesses, but may be done individually or personally.  There is no set text for this acceptance; indeed Maimonides says that this is a matter entirely dependent upon the heart.  However, should one wish to make a public declaration of his faith, we suggest the following text:

> *I accept upon myself the Seven Commandments of the Children of Noah, including the general and specific prohibitions of idolatry, murder, theft, sexual immorality, blasphemy, eating of flesh torn from a living animal, and the general and specific commandments to establish a system of justice, as commanded to Noah, Adam, and their descendants, by the mouth of The Holy One, creator of the universe, as reaffirmed and transmitted by His servant Moses at the giving of the Torah at Sinai.*

**Prayers**

Prayers should express the desire that the entire world acknowledge the revelation at Sinai and come to accept the Noahide laws.

Prayers should also include petitions for favorable judgment upon the produce of trees.

**A Vigil of Torah Study**

There is a Jewish custom to remain awake for the entire night of Shavuos, studying Torah in anticipation of the arrival of daybreak. There are a number of reasons for this custom, many of which connect it directly to events relevant to Israel. The *Magen Avraham*, for example, explains:

> *The Zohar says that the early pious ones would stay awake all night on Shavuos and learn Torah. Nowadays, our custom is for most learned people to do so. Perhaps the reason is based on the fact that the Israelites slept all night long and God had to wake them when He wanted to give them the Torah, as it says in the Midrash, and therefore we must repair this.*[12]

The Midrash records that Israel overslept on the Morning of receiving the Torah. For this reason, proposes the Mogen Avrohom, the Jews remain awake all night on *Shavuos*.

However, the Zohar records other reasons for this custom:

> *R. Shimon used to sit and learn Torah at night when the bride joined with her spouse. It is taught: The members of the bride's entourage are obligated to stay with her throughout the night before her wedding with her spouse to rejoice with her in those perfections (tikkunim) by which she is made perfect. [They should] learn Torah, Prophets and Writings, homilies on the verses and the secrets of wisdom, for these are her perfections and adornments. She enters with her bridesmaids and stands above those who study, for she is readied by them and rejoices in them all the night. On the morrow, she enters the canopy with them and they are her entourage. When she enters the canopy, the Holy One, blessed be He, asks about them, blesses them, crowns them with the bride's adornments. Blessed is their destiny.*[13]

This passage describes the giving of the Torah as a "wedding" of The Holy One to His Presence, the *shekhina*. Kabbalistically, this refers to the rectification and restoration of God's kingship in the world. This spiritual wedding is accompanied by the bridesmaids, the Jewish people, who learn Torah all night as an adornment of the bride. The Zohar offers further descriptions of this custom:

---

[12] *Mogen Avraham OC 494*.

[13] *Zohar* I:8a

> *Therefore, the pious in ancient times did not sleep that night but were studying the Torah, saying, "Let us come and receive this holy inheritance for us and our children in both worlds." That night, the Congregation of Yisrael is an adornment over them, and she comes to unite with the King.*
> *Both decorate the heads of those who merit this. R. Shimon said the following when the friends gathered with him that night: Let us come and prepare the jewels of the bride... so that tomorrow she will be bejeweled... and properly ready for the King.[14]*

It appears that the custom of staying awake all night is unique to the closeness of Israel and God. Nevertheless, it is appropriate to increase Torah study on this day and to prepare spiritually for the morning of Shavuos. It is, therefore, appropriate to gather and study the Noahide laws and Midrashim pertaining to the Noahide laws and the giving of the Torah until late at night. The morning prayers should be held early as well.

## Tisha B'Av – the 9th of Av

*Tishav B'Av*, the 9th day of the month of Av, is the darkest day on the Hebrew calendar. On this date, innumerable tragedies befell the Jewish people throughout their history. Most importantly, both of the holy temples were destroyed on this day, albeit 500 years apart.

However, this day was fixed as a time of mourning long before, while Israel still wandered in the wilderness:

> *The Lord spoke to Moses saying, "Send out for yourself men who will scout the Land of Canaan, which I am giving to the children of Israel. You shall send one man each for his father's tribe; each one shall be a chieftain in their midst." So Moses sent them from the desert of Paran by the word of the Lord. All of them were men of distinction; they were the heads of the children of Israel...*

> *They returned from scouting the Land at the end of forty days... They brought them back a report, as well as to the entire congregation, and they showed them the fruit of the land... They spread an [evil] report about the land which they had scouted, telling the children of Israel, "The land we passed through to explore is a land that consumes its inhabitants, and all the people we saw in it are men of stature...* **The entire community raised their voices and shouted, and the people wept on that night.**[15]

---

[14] *Parashat Emor* 88a.

[15] Numbers, chapters 13 & 14.

The Midrash explains that God, upon hearing the people weep, said: "Since you have cried on this night for no reason, I will give you a reason!"

Because of the *lashon hora*, evil speech, which was perpetrated on this day against the land of Israel, the 9th of Av became designated as a day of sadness for all future generations.

## Jewish Observance of *Tisha B'Av*

*Tisha B'Av*, the 9th day of Av, is a day of mourning for the Jewish people - not only for the Temple, but for all the tragedies of their history. Although a Holocaust memorial day has been recently established, it is not acknowledged by most observant Jews. Rather, they remember the Holocaust along with all other tragedies on *Tisha B'Av*. This is because *Tisha B'Av* is the root, the source, of all of these tragedies.

On this day, Jews fast from sundown until after sundown. Additionally, they gather in the synagogue and recite laments while seated upon the floor. There are a number of other observances expressing mourning that are kept as well. For example, Jews do not greet each other on this day. Additionally, they do not wear leather shoes or bathe. For Noahides, who do not share in the tragic history of the Jewish people, they cannot relate to much of the meaning of this day. However, Noahides do have a share in the most fundamental concern of the day – mourning the destruction of the Holy Temple.

## *Tisha B'Av* & Noahides – Mourning the Temples

Though the service and responsibility of the Temple was given to the Jewish people, the Temple was of benefit to the entire world (as we have discussed much in our previous lessons). In fact, the sages tell us:

> *If the nations of the world had only known how much they needed the Temple, they would have surrounded it with armed fortresses to protect it!*[16]

On *Tisha B'Av*, Noahides, should they wish to fast in mourning for the temple, may certainly do so. However, it is suggested that this only be a half-fast, from sunset until noon of the following day. Additionally, it is appropriate to compose and recite

---

[16] *Bamidbar Rabbah 1:3.*

laments upon the destruction of the temples. These should be appropriate to the Noahide relation to the temples.

**Point of Action: Noahide *Kinnos***

The Jewish laments for *Tisha B'Av*, called Kinnos, are mostly relevant only to Jewish history and Jewish experience. It is appropriate for Noahides to compose their own *kinnos*, laments, for the day. These should be recited both at night and morning prayers.

*Tisha B'Av* is an opportunity to recognize the importance of the Temple, and to express to God the desire to right the wrongs of the world.

A service for the Noahide commemoration of *Tisha B'Av* is being drafted as part of this course.

Tisha B'Av will next fall on Sunday, July 26, 2015. As will all holidays, it actually begins on the preceding evening at nightfall.

## Summary of the Lesson

1. While Jews celebrate Shavuos as the giving of the Torah, Noahides celebrate it as the day upon which the Noahide laws were renewed and a day of judgment for the fruit of trees.

2. The place of worship or the home should be decorated with greenery.

3. It is a time for reaffirmation and acceptance of the Noahide laws.

4. Torah study should be increased on this day.

5. On Tisha B'Av it is appropriate for Noahides to mourn the loss of the Temple and to meditate upon its meaning for the Nations of the world.

6. If Noahides wish to fast on Tisha B'Av, it should only be until midday on the day of Tisha B'Av.

7. It is appropriate for Noahides to recite laments for the destruction of the two Temples. This is a point of action for Noahides – to compose laments appropriate to their relationship with the temple.

THE YESHIVA PIRCHEI SHOSHANIM SHULCHAN ARUCH PROJECT

# The Noahide Laws - Lesson Thirty Five

© **Yeshiva Pirchei Shoshanim 2017**
This shiur may not be reproduced in any
form without permission of the copyright holder.

## Table of Contents:

1. Introduction
2. When Was the Mitzvah Given?
3. *Tzaar Baalei Chaim* – Animal Cruelty
4. The Commandment to Noah
5. *Ever Min HaChai vs.* the Verses
6. To Which Animals Does it Apply?
7. What is Called *Basar* – Flesh?
8. Summary

# Lesson 35

## Introduction to Ever Min HaChai

### Introduction

We now begin our study of the dietary laws applicable to Noahides. The most important prohibition in this arena is *ever min ha-chai*, that of a limb taken from a living animal. Though it may, at first, seem like a narrow prohibition, it actually involves a number of details.

### When Was *Ever Min HaChai* Given?

As we should recall from a very early lesson, the Talmud derives all Seven laws from Genesis 2:16:

> *And the L-rd, God, commanded the man, saying: "Of every tree of the garden you may surely eat."*

*Ever Min HaChai*, besides being derived from this verse, was also commanded directly to Noah after the flood. There are two opinions as to the reason for this repetition. Both of these interpretations are tied to another Talmudic debate as to whether or not Adam was permitted to eat meat:[1]

---

[1] See Sanhedrin 57a, 59b.

- Rashi[2] & Tosafos[3] – Both hold that, as the Talmud states, all seven laws were given to Adam at the time of creation. This would include *ever min ha-chai*. Of course, *ever min ha-chai* would only be relevant if Adam was permitted to eat meat at this time. According to Rashi and Tosafos, Adam was permitted to eat meat; however, he was not allowed to kill animals for food. Adam was only allowed to eat animals that had died on their own. It was not until after the flood that Man received permission to kill animals for food.

- Maimonides[4] – Maimonides understands the Talmud's derivation of the Noahide laws from Genesis an *Asmachta*, a supporting allusion to the existence of the laws prior to the time of Noah. It is not a hard-and-fast source for their derivation. Based upon a much simpler reading of the Torah text, Maimonides proposes that man was not given permission to eat meat at all until after the flood. Therefore, Adam could not have been commanded regarding *ever min ha-chai*. It was only after the flood, when man was permitted from eating meat, that God gave the commandment against *ever min ha-chai*.

Both **Tosafos, Rashi** and **Maimonides**, however, agree to the following points:

- At creation, Adam was given the right to use animals for any useful tasks as the Torah teaches:[5]

    *And God blessed them; and God said unto them: 'Be fruitful, and multiply, and replenish the earth, and subdue it; and have dominion over the fish of the sea, and over the fowl of the air, and over every living thing that creeps upon the earth.'*

- This permission, however, did not extend to killing animals for food.[6]

---

[2] To Sanhedrin 57a.

[3] To Sanhedrin 56b.

[4] *Mishneh Torah, Hilchos Melachim* 9:1.

[5] Gen. 1:28.

[6] Sanhedrin 59a.

Considering these two points, of the utility of animals for human need vs. the prohibition of killing them for food, the question naturally arises: Was Adam allowed to cause pain or suffering to animals?

## Tzaar Baalei Chaim – Animal Cruelty

The prohibition against animal cruelty, *tzaar baalei chaim*, applies to Noahides.[7] The exact details of this prohibition will be examined in greater detail in a future lesson. For the purposes of this lesson, though, we at least need to know that it applies and will be relevant to our study of the laws of *ever min ha-chai*.

## The Commandment to Noah

In the times of Noah, all agree that man was given permission to now to kill animals for the sake of food:

> *The fear of you and the dread of you shall be upon every beast of the earth and every bird of the sky, upon everything that moves on the earth and upon all fish of the sea; into your hand they are given. Every moving thing that has life shall be yours for food; I have given them unto you like the green herbage.*

The commandment of *ever min ha-chai* was either given here for the first time, or reaffirmed in light of this permission to kill animals for food:

> *But flesh with its soul, its blood, you shall not eat.*[8]

The Talmud in Tractate Sanhedrin 59a explains that this verse is the prohibition of *ever min ha-chai*.

## Ever Min HaChai vs. the Verses

The term *ever min ha-chai* is a Talmudic paraphrase of the source verse for the prohibition. It is a much more convenient and, indeed, specific way of referring to the law. However, it contains a subtle weakness.

---

[7] See *Sefer Toldos Noach* I: 26:11; *Sefer Sheva Mitzvos HaShem* IV: 1 Haarah 3. See also *Sefer Chassidim* 666.

[8] Gen. 9:4.

*Ever min ha-chai* is often translated as "a limb torn from a living animal." This is a terrible translation! The verse in the Torah states simply:

> *But Flesh with its soul, its blood, you shall not eat.*[9]

The Talmud rephrases this prohibition as *ever min ha-chai*, which literally means "a limb/part from the living." Let's break it down:

- ***Ever***, "a limb/part" – The verse states "flesh," a broad term we will have to winnow down. Although the Hebrew word for "flesh" is sometimes used specifically for "meat," in this context it means almost any edible part taken from an animal. The Talmud rephrases it with the term *ever* to capture the broader meaning of the word for "flesh." The intent of the prohibition is to prohibit any edible, solid parts separated from an animal while it lives.

- ***Min***, "from" – The verse does not say anything about material being "taken" or "torn" from a living animal. Therefore, the method by which the material is separated from the animal is irrelevant. A limb remains prohibited even if it falls from an animal on its own. We should note that, according to this point and the previous one, one might incorrectly assume that even milk and eggs should be prohibited. We will therefore discuss milk and eggs in the next lesson.

- ***HaChai***, "the living" – This last term is very broad. In fact, it is too broad, because the actual verse contains a qualification that limits the types of "the living" creatures to which this this applies:

> *But **flesh with its soul, its blood**, you shall not eat.*[10]

Note that this verse draws a distinction between the flesh and the blood of the animal. This distinction actually has an important place in Torah law.

For example, for Jews consuming horse blood violates their injunction against consuming blood (the punishment for which is *Kares*, spiritual excision). Eating the meat of a horse, however, is prohibited to Jews for a

---

[9] Gen. 9:4.

[10] Gen. 9:4.

separate reason: the prohibition against eating the meat of non-kosher species (the punishment for which is lashes).

Our verse states the qualification *...flesh with its soul, its blood...* to teach us that the prohibition of *ever min ha-chai* only applies to animals for which the Torah makes legal distinctions between their **flesh** and their **blood**.[11]

There are many animals for which the Torah makes no distinction between their flesh and their blood. For these animals, the entire animal and all of its parts and pieces are included under one prohibition against eating. Since the Torah makes no distinctions for these animals, then *ever min ha-chai* does not apply to these animals.

## To Which Animals Does it Apply?

*Ever min ha-chai* does not apply to *sheratzim*, a class of eight animals mentioned by the Torah in Lev. 11:29-30. This is because there is no distinction between their blood and flesh in Torah law. All of the commentaries agree that the common mouse and, most likely, the monitor lizard are among these eight creatures; however, there is disagreement as to the identity of the remaining 6. In practice, one should not eat any *ever min ha-chai* from any animal in which the application of *ever min ha-chai* is doubtful or a matter of dispute.

The following are the *sheratzim* with various opinions as to their identity:

- **Choled** – The Talmud describes this as a predatory, burrowing animal that tunnels underneath houses.[12]
    - Weasel/ermine/martin, mole, or mole-rat - According to the *Arukh*
    - Rat – *Targum Onkelos*, *Tosafos Yomtov*
    - Field Mouse – *Targum Yonasan*

- **Akhbar** – Most agree that this is the common mouse. Some include the rat under this term.

- **Tzav** – The Talmud[13] implies that it is similar to a salamander or snake.

---

[11] Sanhedrin 59a – b.

[12] See Shabbos 107a.

- Toad – This is the opinion of Rashi to Lev. 11:29 and Niddah 56a. The Mishnah,[14] and indeed many of the *Rishonim*, seem to compare it to a frog.
- Tortise – *Meam Loez, Tiferes Israel*.[15]

- *Anakah*
  - Hedgehog or beaver – Radak.
  - Gecko – Rabbeinu Saadia Gaon

- *Ko'ach*
  - Lizard – According to *Radak*. From the descriptions of the various commentaries, it is most likely the monitor lizard.[16]

- *Leta'ah*
  - Another species of lizard or great gecko.

- *Chomet*
  - Snail – Rashi.
  - Many other commentaries identify this as a skink.

- *Tinshemes*
  - Mole – Rashi to Chullin 63a.
  - A Burrowing lizard of some sort.

Further exempted from the prohibition of *ever min ha-chai* are all creatures that live entirely in the sea, insects, arachnids, and snakes, frogs, and lizards. It is therefore permitted consume limbs from dolphins, crabs, lobster, etc. before the animal has actually expired. However, it is preferable done in a manner that minimizes the suffering of the animal (because of the prohibition of *tzaar baalei chaim* – cruelty to animals). There are some further important clarifications to make:

---

[13] Chullin 127a.

[14] Tohoros 5:1. See Mishnah and Rishonim there.

[15] To Tohoros ibid.

[16] See Rav Saadia Gaon, in particular.

- **Rodents** – because of the uncertainty in identifying all of the *sheratzim*, and the doubt is on a biblically prohibited matter, one must treat all rodents as if *ever min ha-chai* applies to them. The exception, however, is the common mouse. It is certain that the mouse is a *sheretz* and that *ever min ha-chai* does not apply to it.

- **Seals, otters, walruses, etc.** – these mammals all live in the water as well as on land. Are they to be treated as sea creatures, and exempted from *ever min ha-chai*, or as land mammals and included in *ever min ha-chai*?

    - **Maimonides**[17] - Classifies sea lions as sea creatures, which implies that they are exempted from *ever min ha-chai*.

    - **Chullin 127a** – If a mammal can travel on land of its own power, then it is considered a land animal in *halakhah*.

    - **Mishnah, Keilim 17:13** – The carcass of a sea lion is subjected to certain types of ritual impurity that do not apply to sea animals. Therefore, the sea lion must be a land animal.

    - *Tzafnas Paneach* on Maimonides – Based on many of the cited rebuttals, *Tzafnas Paneach* rejects Maimonides as the law.

    - **In practice,** seals, otters, walruses, and similar creatures are considered land animals and subject to *ever min ha-chai*.

## What Is Called *Basar* - Flesh?

The source verse prohibits *Basar* – flesh – from a living animal. This means that one is only liable for punishment for having eaten *Basar* from a living animal. However, this is a broad term which applies in various ways. Additionally, any prohibition against eating something only applies if that item is considered fit for consumption. The criteria for this determination are complex and require the expertise of a *posek*.

The following is a basic guide to what is and is not permitted. Again, note that we are dealing with what is called *basar* for the sake of liability. Eating any solid body parts

---

[17] *Hilchos Maachalos Assuros 2:12.*

from a species of living animal to which this prohibition applies is prohibited even if one does not incur punishment for doing so:

- **Bones** – Because bones are not considered fit for human consumption, they are not called *Basar*.[18] One should not eat them, however.[19] However, bone marrow is considered *Basar* – flesh.[20]

- **Tendons & Sinews** – Although not considered *Basar*, their consumption is prohibited. However, one is not liable to punishment for eating them.[21]

- **Hooves, horns, feathers** – These parts, even their soft inner parts, are not called *Basar*, and therefore *ever min ha-chai* does not apply.[22] Again, however, they should not be consumed.[23]

- **Flesh of Birds** – Although the prohibition applies to birds just as it does to land mammals, one is not liable to punishment for consuming bird flesh.[24]

- **Hides & Skins** – Some types of hides and skins are called *basar* and some are not. Any questions of *ever min ha-chai* that may arise regarding hides or skins should be presented to a *posek* who is an expert in the Noahide laws.[25]

- **Placenta** – A placenta expelled naturally by an animal may be eaten and is not included at all in the prohibition of *ever min ha-chai*. However, if it is removed from the animal before it gives birth, then it is prohibited as *ever min ha-chai*.[26]

---

[18] *Hilchos Maachalos Assuros 4:18.* This is true even if the bones are ground or powdered. Even soft chewable bones are exempted. See *Hilchos Avos HaTumah* 3 and *Hilchos Korban Pesach* 10.

[19] Rama, YD 62.

[20] *Tosefta, Pesachim* 6:8.

[21] See *Hilchos Korban Pesach* 10:8 and the commentary of the *Raavad* there.

[22] *Hilchos Maachalos HaAssuros* 4:18 & 9:7. See also *Avos HaTumah* 1, 3:9.

[23] See n. 19, above.

[24] *Hilchos Melachim* 9:10 and *Kesef Mishnah* there.

[25] Maimonides, *Hilchos Maachalos Assuros* 4:18, states that hides and skins are not considered fit for consumption and that ever min ha-chai does not apply to them. This is even in a case when they are fully cooked and made appetizing (see Rashi to Chullin 77b). However, this is only the law for certain hides. "Soft" hides are considered Basar and are subject to ever min ha-chai. See Rashi to Chullin 122a and *Maachalos Assuros* 4:20-21.

- **Blood** – Blood is not included in the prohibition of *ever min ha-chai*. As we mentioned above, the Hebrew word *basar* – flesh – is broad and includes almost all solid parts of the animal. However, the source verse makes a clear distinction between blood and flesh:

> But **flesh with its soul, its blood**, *you shall not eat.*

Maimonides[27] and [Kesef Mishnah],[28] based on Sanhedrin 59a, explain that this prohibits *Basar* taken from an animal while it is living, but not blood taken from an animal while it is living. Blood may be consumed by Noahides even if it is taken from an animal while it is living.

## Summary of the Lesson

1. *Ever min ha-chai* was either given to Adam or to Noah. This depends on whether or not Adam was permitted to eat meat from animals that died on their own.

2. Noahides are enjoined against cruelty to animals. The details of this will be discussed in a future lesson.

3. The prohibition applies to any *basar* – flesh – that came from an animal while it was living. It does not matter how this flesh was removed from the animal.

4. The prohibition applies to animals for which the Torah makes a legal distinction between their blood and their flesh. This means that aquatic animals, bugs, and reptiles and amphibians are not included in this prohibition.

---

[26] This distinction may be derived from [Maachalos Assuros 5:13] and the comments of the [Raavad] there.

[27] [Maimonides Hilchos Melachim 9:10].

[28] Ibid.

5. Only that which is defined as edible and is called *basar* is prohibited as *ever min ha-chai*. Nevertheless, one should refrain from eating anything solid that is separated from a living species of animal to which this prohibition applies. Though one may mistakenly think that this prohibition includes eggs and milk, we shall explain their details in a future lesson.

THE YESHIVA PIRCHEI SHOSHANIM SHULCHAN ARUCH PROJECT

# The Noahide Laws - Lesson Thirty Six

**Written by Rabbi Avraham Chaim Bloomenstiel**
© **Yeshiva Pirchei Shoshanim 2014**
This shiur may not be reproduced in any
form without permission of the copyright holder.

164 Village Path, Lakewood NJ 08701 732.370.3344
164 Rabbi Akiva, Bnei Brak, 03.616.6340

## Table of Contents:

1. Introduction
2. Amount for Liability
3. The Life of the Animal
4. Strict Liability
5. Removing the Prohibition
6. Kosher vs. Non-Kosher Slaughter
7. Possible Leniencies
8. Practical Advice
9. Eating Out
10. Eggs and Milk
11. Summary

# *Ever Min HaChai II*

## Introduction

Last week we saw the basis of *ever min ha-chai* and the scope of its application. This week we are going to look at more of the fundamentals of this prohibition and some challenges presented by the contemporary food industry.

## Amount to Trigger the Prohibition

There is no minimum amount that a Noahide must consume to incur liability for *ever min ha-chai*.[1] Even the smallest amount of *ever min ha-chai* is enough to incur punishment. However, swallowing an entire living creature is not prohibited. After all, the prohibition only applies to meat which is "from" a living creature.[2]

## The Life of the Animal

*But flesh with its soul, its blood, you shall not eat.*[3]

---

[1] Maimonides, Hilchos Melachim 9:10.

[2] This issue is debated in Chullin 102b. *Tosafos* rules like Rabbi Yehudah, that eating an entire living creature is not forbidden. Although Rashi disagrees, Maimonides upholds *Tosafos*. See *Hilchos Maachalos Assuros* 4:3.

[3] Gen. 9:4.

Rashi and *Targum Yonasan* make an important observation on this verse: that it applies to eating flesh while the animal's soul is "in/with its blood." As the sages understand this, the prohibition of *ever min ha-chai*, to trigger punitive liability, only applies while the animal from which the flesh was taken is still living. Once the animal dies, eating the flesh that was taken from it does not incur liability. However, the sages state that meat removed from an animal while it was living remains prohibited for everyone for all time - even after the animal has died:

> *Flesh that becomes detached from it [while it is dying] is considered like flesh detached from a living creature and is prohibited to a Noahide even after the animal has expired.*[4]

This point is very important and we will revisit it shortly.

## Strict Liability

One only incurs strict liability, meaning capital punishment, if one transgresses *ever min ha-chai* by eating:

- Meat,

- From a land mammal,

- Removed from the animal while it is living,

- Eaten while the animal is still living, and

- Eaten in the normal manner.

All other possible "eatings" do not incur the death penalty, but are nonetheless forbidden. Therefore, though one is not punished for eating the flesh taken from a bird while it is still living, it is still forbidden to do so.[5]

---

[4] *Chullin 121b*. Although this is the law, the Talmud's exact reasoning behind the statement is a little unclear. According to many, it is a Rabbinic decree. Of course, this interpretation raises the debate as to if, how, and to-what-degree rabbinic decrees apply to Noahides. Others, however, take a much stricter approach. Nevertheless, all agree that the meat remains prohibited for all time even after the animal has died.

[5] See *Hilchos Melachim 9:10* with the *Kesef HaMishnah*.

## Removing the Prohibition

There is a big difference between Jewish law and Noahide law as to when the prohibition of *ever min ha-chai* ceases to apply to an animal. For Jews, the process of *shechita*, Jewish ritual slaughter, removes the prohibition of *ever min ha-chai*. Once the majority of the trachea and esophagus of an animal has been severed according to Torah law, the prohibition of *ever min ha-chai* ceases to apply. At that point, a Jew may remove a limb or meat from the animal even if the animal is still in its death throes. That flesh would be permitted for a Jew to eat.[6] However, for a Noahide, the prohibition of *ever min ha-chai* does not depart from the animal until its heart has ceased beating.[7] This fact creates a contradiction between Jewish and Noahide law:

- If an animal is slaughtered properly, in accordance with the laws of Jewish ritual slaughter, it is considered "dead" for all intents and purposes even it is still moving about. A Jew may then sever and consume meat from that animal even before its heart and breath have ceased.

- However, the meat severed from that animal remains forbidden for Noahide consumption as *ever min ha-chai*. This is because Noahides do not rely upon ritual slaughter to remove the prohibition of ever min ha-chai, rather, they rely upon the death of the animal.

If you have been paying close attention, you will note a subtle problem: this situation appears to contradict our general rule from the Talmud that Noahide law cannot be more prohibitive in scope that Torah law.

The Talmud[8] and many *poskim* (most notably the *Shakh*[9]) explain that when a Jew slaughters meat for Jewish consumption, this slaughter completely removes the prohibition of ever *min ha-chai* in its totality - even for a non-Jew! This unique rule is subject to the following conditions, though:

---

[6] This is only in respect to *ever min ha-chai*. Practically, the animal remains prohibited for eating until it actually dies. See *Yoreh Deah 27*.

[7] See *Shulchan Aruch HaRav OC 329:3*. At that point we assume that all motion and breath have stopped. If the animal has ceased moving and breathing, and has bled copiously, then we may assume that the heart has stopped.

[8] Chullin 121b.

[9] To *Yoreh Deah 27*.

- It must be the slaughter of a kosher species,

- It must be slaughtered by a qualified *shochet* (slaughterer) according to all of the details of kosher *shechita*,

- It must be slaughtered for Jewish consumption,

- Once the animal has been slaughtered properly, meat may be removed from it even before it has stopped moving. However, one should wait until the animal has died before actually eating the meat.

Once these conditions are met, the meat of the animal is permitted for all, Jews and Non-Jews alike. Needless to say, kosher slaughter today is carried out according to all of these requirements. Therefore, non-Jews may consume kosher meat without any concern for *ever min ha-chai*.

But what about non-kosher meat production? Does non-kosher industrial slaughter present any problems for Noahides today?

## Kosher vs. Non-Kosher Slaughter

The standard procedure in most non-kosher slaughter houses is to stun the animals (usually by electric shock) immediately prior to actually killing them. Although stunning may stop the animal's breath temporarily, it does not render the animal "dead enough" for the purposes of our removing the prohibition of a limb torn from a living animal.[10]

As for the actual methods of slaughter employed by most slaughterhouses, most of them do not bring about the immediate death of the animal (meaning complete cessation of cardiac and neuromuscular activity). Should the animal be conveyed to processing prior to the cessation of cardiac activity, a problem would arise as to the *kashrus* of the meat for Noahides.[11] This is because the animal would, effectively, be carved up before it has actually died and the meat rendered *ever min ha-chai*.

---

[10] See *Chasam Sofer YD* 339; *Shu"t Igros Moshe YD* II:146.

[11] These methods do, however, mortally wound the animal. In such cases, the meat is forbidden, yet one does not incur capital liability for having eaten it. See Radvaz to *Hilchos Melachim* 9:13 and *Sefer Sheva Mitzvos HaShem* IV:3:2, *haarah 71*.

According to Dr. Temple Grandin, one of the world's leading experts on industrial slaughter, the interval between slaughter and processing is so long that it is very rare for an animal's heart to continue beating until the time of processing. However, this generalization is not true of smaller slaughterhouses and specialty slaughterhouses (i.e. those that produce exotic meats). Although the stunning and slaughter of animals is strictly regulated by USDA policy, regulations pertaining to the time between slaughter and processing are uncommon at both state and federal levels and do not apply equally to all sectors of the meat industry.

Although the chances of getting *ever min ha-chai* at the grocery store are low, the only way to ensure beyond any doubt that your average grocery store meat is acceptable for Noahides is to know with certainty how the animal was slaughtered, and the policies of the slaughterhouse as to determining the death of the animal.

Considering that any amount of *ever min ha-chai* is prohibited for consumption, it is not unreasonable to be wary of commercially produced meat. By eating meat which has been slaughtered according to the laws of *shechita* (Jewish ritual slaughter) and relying upon the ruling mentioned above, any suspicion is removed.

## Possible Leniencies

However, there are many possible leniencies for Noahides with regard to buying regular, grocery store meat. Unfortunately, these leniencies depend on whether or not certain mechanics of Torah law carry over into Noahide law. For example:

- **Safek** – Cases of doubt. The resolution of doubts as to whether or not an item is prohibited is governed by many principles and canons. Although these rules could create leniencies for Noahides with regard to non-kosher slaughtered meat, it is uncertain as to whether or not these rules apply in the Noahide legal system.[12]

---

[12] This question of *safek issur* by Noahides is discussed at great length by the *poskim*. Unfortunately, there is no consensus on the issue. The problem depends on a number of unresolved questions. First – are Noahides obligated in Rabbinic laws? Second – is the concept of *safek d'oraisa lechumra* ("biblical doubts are resolved stringently") itself sourced in the Torah (like Rasbha, *Chiddushim* to *Kiddushin* 73a) or in rabbinic legislation (like Maimonides in *Avos HaTumah 9:12*). If it is a matter of Torah law, then Noahides must avoid even doubtful transgressions of the Noahide laws. However, if it is rabbinic, then everything depends on whether or not Noahides are bound by rabbinic laws. This is an extremely complicated question. See *Toldos Noach* I:18:45 for an extensive survey of the literature. Incidentally, it is possible to prove from the *mitzvah* of *dinim* (establishing courts) that Noahides are obligated in Rabbinic law. For the purpose of this course, we take the

- ***Rov*** – Nullification by majority. If a prohibited item is mixed with a majority of permitted items to the point that we cannot distinguish between the two, then the prohibited item is considered "nullified" in the majority. It unclear if this principle applies to the Noahide laws.[13] If it does, then all mass produced meat may be considered "in a mixture" and, thus, the minority of meat coming from living animals is nullified in the majority of acceptable meat.

Though the application of these leniencies is doubtful, so too is the very presence of *ever min ha-chai* on the regular, commercial grocery market. Although each factor (*rov* or *safek*) by itself is not enough to permit the consumption of over-the-counter grocery store meat, taken together, most contemporary authorities agree that they may be relied upon to permit the consumption of regular grocery store meat.

## Practical Conclusions

Despite the uncertainties as to the aforementioned leniencies, there are strong reasons to permit the Noahide consumption of regular, grocery store meat. As we said, though, there are reasons to dispute on this permissive approach.

Therefore, there is a stringent option for those who wish to adopt it. As we mentioned above, the act of Jewish ritual slaughter removes any doubt of "a limb taken from a living animal." Although regular non-kosher meat is permitted, should a Noahide wish, he may elect to consume only meat that was slaughtered according to Jewish ritual law. By doing so, all questions of *ever min ha-chai*, a limb from a living animal, are removed. According to many, this approach is proper and strongly supported by the aforementioned authorities on Torah law. However, one who does not wish to adopt this stringent approach has what to rely upon.

So, there are two approaches to dealing practically with the question of flesh from a living animal:

1) Regular, grocery store meat is 100% acceptable for Noahides. Even though there are uncertainties as to whether or not the concepts of

---

approach that Noahides are only obligated in the Rabbinic laws that apply to those *mitzvos* in which Jews and Noahides have equal obligation and that have logical application to both.

[13] As with cases of doubt, the rule of majority also depends on how we understand many of the underlying mechanics.

"nullification by majority" and "doubt" apply to Noahides, there are also uncertainties as to whether or not meat from living creatures is even present in the marketplace. Noahides may rely upon these two uncertain factors in combination to permit regular grocery store meat.

2) Because there are some who would question this leniency, a Noahide may voluntarily, and <u>as a stringency only</u>, elect to only eat meat that was slaughtered according to Jewish ritual practice.

**This second approach *does not* advocate or imply that Noahides are in any way obligated or expected to keep Kosher – the Jewish dietary laws.** The *only* reason for electing to consume kosher-slaughtered meat is that, by doing so, one can be guarded from any suspicion of *ever min ha-chai*, flesh taken from a living animal, according to most authorities. Observing this elective stringency does not constitute *chiddushei dat*, creating a new religion. The reason it is not *chiddushei dat* is that one observes this stringency only in order to avoid eating *ever min ha-chai*, flesh from a living animal. **One does not observe this stringency to "keep kosher" or in any way imitate Jewish practice**; after all, a Noahide has no share or obligation in such laws.

Keep in mind that, while this stringency is strongly supported and proper according to many, it is not necessary and purely voluntary. Practicing it has nothing to do with "keeping kosher" because the only reason for a non-Jew to eat meat slaughtered according to Jewish ritual law is because this is one of many possible ways of avoiding the prohibition of *ever min ha-chai*.

## Eating Out

If a Noahide chooses to only eat kosher slaughtered meat, he will encounter problems when it comes to eating out. Non-kosher restaurants will have used their utensils and equipment for non-Kosher grocery store meat. Is it permitted for Noahides who have taken this voluntary stringency upon themselves to eat in such restaurants? Does a Noahide who has taken this voluntary stringency upon himself have to be concerned for the flavor of possibly *ever min ha-chai* meat that has been absorbed into the vessels?

The issue of absorptions in utensils is a major part of the Jewish dietary laws. The *poskim* disagree as to how or if it affects the Noahide laws.

- <u>*Chasam Sofer*</u>[14] - Pots and utensils that have been certainly used for *ever min ha-chai* may never be used by non-Jews.[15]

- **Darchei Teshuvah**[16] - The *Darchei Teshuvah* and many other *poskim* hold that there is no prohibition on Noahides using utensils that were previously and even certainly used with *ever min ha-chai*.

A Noahide who is careful to eat only meat slaughtered according to Jewish ritual practice may rely upon the *Darchei Teshuvah* and other *poskim* who permit utensils that had been used with *ever min ha-chai*. This is due to a solid *heter* (permissive ruling) from the *Darchei Teshuvah* combined with a number of other potential leniencies.

Of course, this only means that although Noahides who have accepted such a stringency may eat out at restaurants that serve regular, non-kosher meat, they may not eat any food containing actual meat at the restaurant. Again – this is only applicable to those who have elected such a stringency. However, this stringent approach is not at all required or expected.

## Eggs & Milk

Technically, eggs and milk should be included in the prohibition of *ever min ha-chai*.[17] After all, they are material separated from the animal while it was living. This possibility does not create a problem for Jews, because the Torah explicitly permitted eggs and milk to them:

- "…A land flowing with milk and honey…"[18] The Talmud says that by praising Israel with milk, this verse is permitting milk, exempting it from the prohibition of *ever min ha-chai*.[19]

---

[14] *Shu"t YD 19*, at the very end.

[15] According to the *Chasam Sofer*, the *heter* of *linas laila* and *taam pagum* does not apply to Noahides.

[16] 62:5.

[17] Talmud *Bechoros* 6b to 7a and *Tosafos Chullin* 64a, d.h. *Sheim rikmah*.

[18] This phrase appears in many verses in the Torah.

[19] See Talmud ibid.; Rosh 1:5.

- The Torah states: "If you chance upon a birds nest on your way, in a tree or on the ground, with young ones or eggs, and the mother is sitting upon the young, or the eggs, you shall not take the mother with the young[20]" This is understood as releasing eggs from the prohibition of *ever min ha-chai*.[21]

These verses, however, were only given to Israel – they do nothing for Noahides. Are Noahides are still prohibited from eating eggs and milk?[22]

Although the *Chasam Sofer*[23] suspects that certain eggs are, in fact, prohibited to Noahides, almost all other *poskim* disagree. Virtually all *poskim* permit milk for Noahides.[24]

The reasons that milk and eggs are permitted for Noahides will be discussed in the live class.

## Summary of the Lesson

1. Although the requirements to trigger punishment for transgressing *ever min ha-chai* are very narrow, the scope of the prohibition is very broad.

2. Technically, one is not liable for punishment for *ever min ha-chai* unless the animal from which the meat is taken is still living at the time the meat is consumed.

3. There a number of potential issues with commercially produced non-Kosher meat. These issues do not exist with meat slaughtered according to Torah law. For many reasons it is advisable, according to many, for

---

[20] Deut. 22:6.

[21] See *Bechoros* ibid.; *Chullin 140a; Tos. Chullin 64a*.

[22] Practically speaking, nearly all *poskim* agree that milk and eggs are permitted for Noahide consumption. However, their reasons for permitting them are greatly varied and not at all simple.

[23] YD 19.

[24] Rabbi Shlomo Kluger in his *HaElef Lecha Shlomo YD* 322 brings a proof from Avraham, who served dairy to his guests.

Noahides to eat meat that is slaughtered by a Jew according to the laws of Jewish ritual slaughter law. Nevertheless, regular grocery store meat is permitted for Noahide consumption.

4. Noahides who observe the stringency of eating only meat slaughtered according to kosher practice may eat out at any restaurants as long as they do not eat the meat served there.

5. Milk and eggs are permitted for Noahide consumption even though there are theoretical reasons to consider them *ever min ha-chai*.

THE YESHIVA PIRCHEI SHOSHANIM SHULCHAN ARUCH PROJECT

# The Noahide Laws - Lesson Thirty-Seven

© **Yeshiva Pirchei Shoshanim 2017**
This shiur may not be reproduced in any
form without permission of the copyright holder.

164 Village Path, Lakewood NJ 08701 732.370.3344
164 Rabbi Akiva, Bnei Brak, 03.616.6340

## Table of Contents:

1. Introduction
2. Two Reasons
3. Modern Applications
4. *Stam Yayin* - Wine
5. *Chalav Akum & Gevinas Akum* – Milk & Cheese
6. *Pas Akum* – Baked Goods
7. *Bishul Akum* – Non-Jewish Cooking
8. *Sheichar Akum* – Social Drinking
9. Transporting Kosher Foods
10. Summary

# Kashrus III

## Introduction

In this last lesson on dietary laws we are not going to discuss Noahide prohibitions, rather, we are going to discuss a number of prohibitions that apply only to Jews. The reason we are discussing these laws here is because they affect the relationship between Jews and non-Jews. Food is a major factor in building social bonds and relationships. All too often, the Jewish dietary laws present challenges for Jews and non-Jews. The issue, however, is not merely one of ingredients. As we shall see, Torah law places limits on Jewish and non-Jewish social interactions, using food to define the boundaries of these relationships. It is important to understand the basis and reasons for these restrictions so that either group does not offend one another or come to misunderstanding.

## Two Reasons

These prohibitions are motivated by two concerns. Some are due to the possibility that non-kosher material may be present. Others were established for the express purpose of limiting social contact between Jews and non-Jews. This group of prohibitions was established out of concern for intermarriage between Jews and non-Jews; an extremely severe prohibition with equally severe consequences.

## Modern Applications

Even though many of the reasons behind these prohibitions are not relevant anymore in our times, they nevertheless continue to apply. This is because of a principal in Torah law called *davar she-biminyan*.[1] This principle teaches that decrees established by ancient courts cannot be overturned by later courts unless they are equal in number and eminence to the original court.

## Stam Yayin - Wine

Wine that is owned or made by a non-Jew is prohibited for Jewish consumption. This is so even if all of the ingredients and utensils used in the process of manufacture are kosher. Included as well is any wine or grape product has been touched, moved, or poured by a non-Jew. The rabbis made this decree out of concern for the intent of the non-Jew at the time of handling the wine. If the non-Jew had any thoughts or intent for idolatry at that time, the wine would become biblically prohibited to Jews like an idolatrous offering. Today, this law applies in a slightly different way than it did in ancient times. This is because the idolatry of today differs from ancient idolatry. Nevertheless, many elements of this law are still an application to all grape-juice, wine, and grape derivatives. Because of *davar she-biminyan* (discussed above), this law applies even to wine touched by Noahides and even those in the process of conversion to Judaism.

Though this prohibition applies to all grape juice, wine, and grape byproducts, it does not apply to wine or grape juice that has been boiled or cooked. This is because the ancient forms of idolatry that motivated the original prohibition did not consider cooked wine fit for religious use.

Therefore if you are at a gathering of Jews at which wine is served, make sure that the wine is *Mevushal*, cooked, before handling it. If it is not cooked, then it should not be handled or moved. Similarly, if bringing wine to a dinner, one should only give wine that is *Mevushal*. This is usually indicated on the label, near the *hekhsher* (symbol of kosher approval):

---

[1] *Beitza 5a.*

Lastly, kosher wine that remains corked and sealed cannot be rendered prohibited until it is opened.

## *Chalav Akum & Gevinas Akum* - Milk & Cheese

Milk and cheese produced by non-Jews, even if all of their ingredients are kosher, is nevertheless prohibited for Jews. This is because non-kosher material may have been mixed into the milk or the cheese. In order for non-Jewish milk or cheese to be kosher, a Jew must have been present while the cheese was made or the milk was milked.

These laws have very little impact on regular Jewish and non-Jewish interactions. Nevertheless it is good to be aware of them.

## *Pas Akum* - Baked Goods

Bread and other baked goods baked by a non-Jew for personal use are prohibited for Jewish consumption. This is even in a case when all of the ingredients and the oven involved were kosher. This decree was made purely to limit the social interaction between Jews and non-Jews. Resultantly, bread that was baked for commercial purposes, meaning for sale and not for consumption, may be eaten by a Jew and is not subject to this prohibition. Therefore, a Jew cannot eat cookies baked for him by a non-Jewish friend, but a Jew can purchase the exact same item at the grocery store.

## *Bishul Akum* - Non-Jewish Cooking

Many other items cooked by a non-Jews are prohibited for Jewish consumption. This is, again, even if all of the ingredients and utensils used are kosher. However, this law only applies to foods which have a certain degree of "significance." The details of what is considered "significant" for the purposes of this law are complicated and not always a matter of consensus. Generally speaking, very basic staple foods, such as coffee and tea, and certain basic snacks (like potato chips, according to some) prepared by a non-Jew may be eaten by a Jew.

However, almost all other items are considered prohibited for Jewish consumption. As well, the utensils used by the non-Jew in preparation of these foods are also prohibited for use by a Jew. If food is later cooked by a Jew in these utensils, that food would also prohibited for Jewish consumption.

Practically speaking, this prohibition makes it impossible for a Jew to ever permissibly eat food of any kind that has been prepared in the home of a non-Jew. This was, after all, the fundamental intent of this law.

The only exception to this law is if a Jew has minimal participation in the cooking. Ashkenazim and Sephardim have different understandings as to what is called "minimal participation."

## Sheichar Akum - Social Drinking

This prohibition is one that, unfortunately, is not even known by many Jews.

Jews are not permitted to drink socially with non-Jews. Specifically, this refers to gatherings in which the purpose is to socialize and drink. It does not apply to situations in which the gathering has a primary purpose and alcohol just happens to be served. For example, if a Jew attends a conference with his coworkers, and beers happened to be served, or there is an open bar, a Jew may be allowed to have a drink. However, this is only if the occasion is infrequent. If the event or circumstances occur regularly, the Jew would not be allowed to drink. For example if a company gets together once a week to discuss business matters, and alcohol is always served at these meetings, a Jew would be prohibited from partaking in the beverages.

Similarly Jew cannot accept an invitation from a non-Jew to "come over and have a beer." However, if the Jew is in your home for some other reason (business, helping you move, etc.) then he may accept the offer of a drink. This law also forbids Jews from attending bars - an environment designed for social drinking. According to some authorities, this law does not only apply to alcohol, but to all "social beverages." Therefore, getting a cup of coffee at Starbucks would also be

---

[2] YD 114. The application of this law depends greatly on existing social conventions and other details that change with time. As a result, the *Shulchan Aruch* is not the final word on this prohibition. Deciding questions pertaining to this law require familiarity with the decisions of later *poskim*. This section is based mostly on *Sefer Bein Yisrael LeNochrim* 11:8:23; *Chelkas Binyamin* 114:12; *Shut Halachos Ketanos* 9; *Bais Yehudah* 21; *Sheeilas Yaavetz* II:142; *Chochmat Adam* 66:14; *Shut Rivevot Ephraim* 6:79; *Shut Chai HaLevi* 4:53:6-7.

prohibited. Most authorities, though, point out that coffee houses are not places of socializing like bars. After all, people who congregate in coffeehouses usually do so in small groups or individually and rarely speak to strangers. Therefore, a Jew may get coffee in a coffee house, but is prohibited from getting alcohol in a bar. Nevertheless a Jew may not regularly go out regularly with non-Jews or a non-Jewish group and get coffee for the purpose of socializing.

## Transporting Kosher Foods

Food transported or entrusted to a non-Jew, even if being sent from one Jew to another, is subject to a number of rules.

- All food requires at least one seal. The type of seal will be discussed in the live class.

- Wine, meat, chicken and fish require two seals.

In certain situations, the absence of such seals will render the food non-kosher when it arrives at its final destination. This *Halacha* contains a number of nuanced details. A *posek* should be asked in any situation in which a question arises.

# Summary of the Lesson

1. Certain prohibitions were decreed on non-Jewish foods either out of concern for kashrus or to limit social interactions.

2. These prohibitions apply today regardless of whether or not the underlying reasons for the prohibitions still exist.

3. Wines owned, made, touched, poured, or handled by non-Jews become prohibited for Jewish consumption. The exceptions are wines that remain fully sealed and corked or that are *Mevushal*.

4. There are similar laws pertaining to milk and cheese, however these don't have much practical effect on Jewish/Non-Jewish interactions today.

5. Anything baked by a non-Jew for consumption is prohibited to Jews. This is true even if all the ingredients are kosher. However, if baked goods are made for commercial sale, then they are permitted.

6. Any food cooked by a non-Jew is prohibited for Jewish consumption. This is even if the food is cooked in a Jew's home using the Jew's utensils. The pots and pans used for this cooking are even rendered non-kosher. The only way to permit a Jew to eat non-Jewish cooking is if a Jew participates, even minimally, in the cooking. There are differing opinions between Ashkenazi and Sephardi authorities as to what is called "minimal participation."

7. Social drinking between Jews and non-Jews is prohibited. A Jew cannot get a drink at a non-Jewish bar. Although this prohibition would technically include coffee houses as well, most authorities do not extend the prohibition that far.

8. A non-Jew cannot transport or hold onto food on behalf of a Jew unless the food is wrapped and sealed. Different foods require different types of seals.

THE YESHIVA PIRCHEI SHOSHANIM SHULCHAN ARUCH PROJECT

# The Noahide Laws - Lesson Thirty-Eight

© **Yeshiva Pirchei Shoshanim 2017**
This shiur may not be reproduced in any
form without permission of the copyright holder.

**164 Village Path, Lakewood NJ 08701 732.370.3344**
**164 Rabbi Akiva, Bnei Brak, 03.616.6340**

## Table of Contents:

1. Introduction
2. Sexual Morality & Derivations of the Laws
3. Example: The Canaanites
4. Categories of Prohibited Relations
5. Source of the Basic Subdivisions
6. Prohibited by Early Decree
7. Permitted, yet not Practiced
8. Male & Female Liability
9. Precautionary Laws
10. Summary

# Lifecycle I: Male & Female

## Introduction

The next several lessons will cover the Noahide lifecycle from birth to death. In this lesson we will start just before birth: with the details of dating and marriage. This lesson will cover acceptable marriage partners, details of interactions between the genders, and issues of modesty in these areas.

## Sexual Morality & Derivations of the Laws

The Noahide laws prohibit acts of sexual immorality. As discussed in a very early lesson, the Talmud learns these laws, by way of implication, from Genesis 2:16. Like all the Noahide laws, though phrased in the negative, it also implies positive aspects. Laws that prohibit sexual immorality also imply the converse: the embracing of acts of sexual purity and endorsing sexual morality.

As we have further seen, the seven Noahide laws are "families" of laws instead of discrete prohibitions unto themselves. Indeed, "sexual immorality" is too broad a term to mean anything without subdivision and definition. These laws, however, are unique because the Torah itself appears to provide many examples of what is and is not acceptable behavior.

For example:

- The behavior of Pre-Flood Society:

    *The land was corrupt before G-d... For all flesh had corrupted its way.*

> The Talmud states: *A braisa of the academy R' Yishmael has taught: anywhere that the term "corruption" is used, it is only in reference to sexual matters or idolatry.*[1]

- Sodom & Gemorah

- The abominations of Egypt: *You shall not commit the deeds of the Land of Egypt wherein you dwelt.*[2]

    Although this was commanded to Jews, the Torah and Midrashim describe Egypt's deeds as "abominations." Many commentaries discuss whether this implies that the deeds of Egypt are prohibited to Noahides as well.

- Behavior of the Canaanites:

    > *Likewise, the deeds of the land of Canaan, the where I shall bring you, you not do; neither shall you walk in their statutes*[3]; and,

    > *There shall not be found among you one who asses his son or daughter through the fire, one who uses divinations, and illusionist, an auger, or a sorcerer… because of these abominations, Hashem your G-d is banishing them from before you.*[4]

    The Talmud states: *God would not punish these nations unless he had warned them against such acts.*[5]

The implication of these examples is not always clear. Let's take a close look at the Canaanites.

---

[1] Sanhedrin 57a.

[2] Lev. 18:3

[3] Lev. Ibid.

[4] Deu. 18:10-12.

[5] Sanhedrin 56b.

## Example: The Canaanites

The Torah, in Lev. 18:3, introduces the list of Jewish prohibited relationships with the following:

*You shall not commit the deeds of the Land of Egypt wherein you dwelt. Likewise, the deeds of the land of Canaan, the where I shall bring you, you not do; neither shall you walk in their statutes.*

The Torah then goes on to list all of the relationships prohibited to Jews in verses 6 to 24. The Torah concludes by stating that the Canaanites lost their land to Israel as punishment for transgressing the laws of sexual morality:

*And the land was defiled, therefore I visited their iniquity upon it, and the land vomited out its inhabitants. Therefore, you shall keep My statutes and My ordinances, and shall not do any of these abominations; neither the native-born, nor the convert, for all these abominations have been committed by the men of the land who came before you, and the land is defiled...*[6]

Does this Lev. 18:3, referring to the "deeds of Canaan," imply that the succeeding list of prohibited relationships (verses 6 to 24) equal the abominations committed by Canaan? If we say "yes," then all of the relationships mentioned in 6 to 24 are also prohibited to Noahides. However, if we say "no," then we cannot assume that all relationships in the list are prohibited to Noahides.

A proof may be adduced from the Talmud, Sanhedrin 56b. Deut. 18:10-12 lists a number of prohibited forms of sorcery and divination, stating that these were also reasons Canaan was driven from its land. The Talmud states: *God would not punish these nations unless He had warned them against such acts.*

However, things are not so simple. The Talmud[7] notes that there are relationships mentioned in the list that are, elsewhere, defined as permitted to Noahides. Therefore, the list in verses 6 to 24 cannot be defining the prohibited Canaanite practices. Furthermore, not all of the Tannaim agree to the idea that *God would not punish these nations unless He had warned them against such acts.* If so, then why then does the Torah appear to list these relations as the prohibited "abominations" of Canaan?

As we see from this example, the Torah's many references to what is or is not acceptable for Noahides, based on ancient practices, cannot be taken at face value.

---

[6] Lev 18:28.

[7] Sanhedrin 56b.

## Categories of Prohibited Relations

There are a number of categories in this prohibition:

- **Relationships that are biblically forbidden** – We will see shortly how these are derived.

- **Relationships that are prohibited by decrees of ancient Noahides (i.e. Shem)** – the sages record a few relations that, although permitted by the Torah, were prohibited by ancient Noahides and their courts. Their ability to make such prohibitions, as we shall see, derives from the *mitzvah* of *dinim*, establishing rule of law. A few of these decrees continue to apply today, yet there are others that either do not apply today or whose application is uncertain.

- **Permitted, Yet Not Practiced** – As mentioned in the above discussion, the Torah refers to a number of relationships as "abominations" even though they are fundamentally permitted to Noahides. Is this term meant to imply that they are only abominations from the viewpoint of the Jewish *mitzvos*? Or, is it saying that they are abominations even when committed by non-Jews? The problem is the word "abomination," a term meaning socially, morally, or emotionally repulsive behavior. It is out-of-place in a discussion of law. Yet, if the permission/prohibition of an act is based on a social judgment or emotional reaction to an act, then the act must have been considered repulsive even before it was prohibited by law. Yet, we see that many of the acts called "abominations" in Lev 18:6-24 are not prohibited to Noahides. The conclusion, as we shall see, is that these acts are permitted, yet should not be practiced.

## Source of the Basic Subdivisions

*Therefore, a man shall leave his father and mother and cling to his wife and they shall become one flesh.*[8]

From this verse the Talmud derives five prohibitions for the descendants of Adam:

---

[8] Gen. 2:24.

- ***Therefore, a man shall leave his father...*** The Talmud explains that "leaving his father" means that one cannot have relations with that which is or was his father's, meaning his father's current or former wife. This applies for all time, even if one's father has died or has divorced the woman.[9] What makes the woman prohibited to the son (or the son to her) is that she and the father had formed a bond of marriage. This bond created the prohibition. The definition of this bond will be discussed below.

- ***...and mother...*** Using a similar reasoning as in the previous case, this prohibits incest between a man and his mother. The prohibition of relations between a man and his biological mother is prohibited even if the woman was never actually married to the man's father.[10]

- ***...and cling to his wife... His*** wife and not the wife of another man. This forbids adultery between a man and a woman who is another man's wife. This prohibition is based on the marital bond, which will be explained below. We should note that polygamy is permitted to Noahides as it is for Jews. However, Jewish courts universally banned the practice over 1000 years ago. For reasons that will be discussed in the class, this should not be practiced by Noahides either.

- ***...to his wife...*** This forbids male homosexual relationships. *Wife*, being of female gender, precludes a relationship between a male and a male. Lesbianism, although it cannot be derived from this verse, is nevertheless prohibited. The source for its prohibition is not agreed upon by all. Some view it as a subcategory or derivation from male homosexuality. Others prohibit it because it is one of the "abominations" practiced in Egypt, in combination with a number of other concerns. It may also be the subject of an earlier decree.

    The Talmud indicates that granting civil recognition to homosexual unions (equating them with marriage) is prohibited for Noahides.[11]

---

[9] *Hilchos Melachim 9:6.*

[10] *Hilchos Melachim ibid.*

[11] In Chullin 92b, Ulla laments that the Non-Jews of his time were sunk in the grossest forms of idolatry and immorality. However, he praised them for retaining three practices: 1) they did not write a marriage contract for homosexual unions, 2) they did not sell flesh in the marketplace (it is unclear to what this refers – see Rashi), and 3) despite all of their idolatry and immorality they still showed respect for the Torah.

- **...and they shall become <u>one flesh</u>.** This indicates the ability of a man and a woman to create *one flesh*, a child, through their union. This precludes relations between species that cannot produce offspring. Hence, all forms of bestiality are prohibited, whether one is male or female, or the active or passive partner.

There is a sixth biblical prohibition of incest between siblings. However, this prohibition does not have as clear a derivation as the others:

*And Avimelech said to Abraham: 'What motivated you to do such a thing [to say "she is my sister"]?' And Abraham said: 'Because I thought: Surely the fear of God is not in this place, and they will slay me on account of my wife. And moreover she is indeed my sister, the daughter of my father, but not the daughter of my mother; and so she became my wife.*

From here, the authorities derive that a maternal half-sister, and all the more-so a full sister, is prohibited. The bond of marriage between any of the parents of these siblings is irrelevant here. Biological relation is enough to establish the prohibition.[12] Curiously, this only prohibits a sister with whom one is maternally related. Paternal half-sisters are permitted for marriage.[13] It appears that having the same mother is the benchmark for the biblical definition of siblings for the purpose of this prohibition. The exact reasons for this are a matter of interpretation.[14]

## Prohibited by Early Decree

We know of a few prohibitions prohibited by early decree. However, it is clear that this category included many other relations not mentioned here. The "abominations" that are fundamentally permitted to Noahides may be relations that were voluntarily prohibited by the early Noahides. Therefore, although they are permitted, they are unacceptable. The following decrees, however, we know with certainty to be binding even today:

---

[12] *Issurei Biah 2:2-4.*

[13] Maimonides *Hilchos Melachim 9:5* and *Hilchos Issurei Biah 14:10.*

[14] The Jerusalem Talmud, *Yevamos 11*, however, derives the prohibition of sibling incest from Gen. 2:24, along with all of the other biblical prohibitions. However, even the Jerusalem Talmud debates as to whether or not it applies to all type of siblings.

- **Father and Daughter** – Another omission from this list is relations between a daughter and her father. Fundamentally, such relationships are not prohibited.[15] However, Nachmanides[16] and Rashi[17] write, that this practice was banned in the very early days of mankind as a repulsive practice.

- **Noahide & Idolater** - In the story of Judah and Tamar, we have to ask: by what authority was Judah able to decree death for Tamar? The Talmud in Avodah Zarah 36b records that, in ancient times, Shem and his court prohibited Noahide cohabitation and marriage with idolaters. The reason is that a family's religious commitment cannot be built on two faiths. Inevitably, one will be forced to assimilate or be subjugated to the other. Therefore, Noahides may not marry practicing idolaters. The commentaries explain that his decree stands until today.

    **This is only discussing when a committed Noahide knowingly marries an idolater. Any other situation (i.e. one becomes a Noahide after having already married) is not included in this decree. Any practical questions as to how this applies must be presented to a competent *posek*. We will discuss this in much greater detail in the live class.**

## Permitted, yet Not Practiced

There are a number of other unions that, although fundamentally permitted, the Torah appears to condemn them as "abominations."[18] This is an extremely murky area. For reasons that will be discussed in the live class, caution is appropriate in all of the acts defined as "abominations" of Egypt and Canaan. Such acts include:

- One should not marry his mother's full or maternal half-sister. However, a paternal half-sister of his mother is completely permitted.[19]

---

[15] Sanhedrin 58b; Shulchan Aruch YD 29:3.

[16] Gen. 19:32.

[17] Gen. 20:1

[18] See *Sifrei* and *Peirush HaMishnayos,* Sanhedrin 7. These are derived from many of the above mentioned verses pertaining to the Canaanites and Egyptians. Although these acts are fundamentally permitted, and one does not incur punishment for doing them, the Torah itself may dissuade them, calling them "abominations." See Maimonides Hilchos Issurei Biah 14:10.

[19] Nachmanides to Yevamos 98; Shulchan Aruch Yoreh Deah 269:3.

- Some hold that some paternal aunts are also called "abominations."[20] However, this conclusion is doubtful.[21] [Editor's Note: I do not see sufficient reason for stringency in this particular situation; it would be a *chumra yeseira* – an unsubstantiated stringency. The reasoning of the *Shach*, who bring this rule, is far more than just "doubtful." See footnote 21]

- Marrying a both woman and her daughter (his stepdaughter). Although it is fundamentally permitted,[22] it is also called an abomination.[23]

- Uncle, brother, or son's ex-wife.[24]

This is only a partial list and many other relationships may be included. There is ample proof[25] that the generations immediately after the flood took on additional, voluntary prohibitions in sexual matters. Although it is unclear as what all of these prohibitions are, they may have included these things labeled "abominations" in Egypt and Canaan that are, technically, permitted to Noahides. If this is the case, then all of these "abominations" would be called "prohibited by early decree."

## Male & Female Liability

All of the above categories of prohibited relations apply equally from both the female and male sides. The Talmud learns this from the phrase "...***they*** shall become one flesh." Therefore, a woman's maternal half-brother is prohibited to her just as a man's maternal half-sister is prohibited to him. A woman is prohibited to her son just as a man's mother is prohibited to him.

---

[20] *Shach to Yoreh Deah* 269:4.

[21] [Rabbi Bloomenstiel: This *Shach* contradicts the generally held view of the Rishonim. As we saw in very early lessons, an *Acharon* (i.e. the *Shach*) cannot contradict a consensus of *Rishonim*. This particular issue depends on a dispute between Rabbi Eliezer and Rabbi Akiva in Sanhedrin 58b. Though the Shach follows Rabbi Eliezer, this is against the majority of the Rishonim (Maimonides, Nachmanides, Smag, etc.) who conclude that the law is like Rabbi Akiva.]

[22] Nachmanides, *Rashba, Nemukei Yosef* and other Rishonim to Yevamos 98.

[23] *Mitzvos HaShem* p. 398. *This is among the relations termed "abominations" by the Sifra to Lev. 18:3.*

[24] Ibid. and Shulchan Aruch Yoreh Deah 269.

[25] *Bereshis Rabbah* 70:12 & 80:6.

## Defining Marriage

The details of Noahide marriage will be dealt with at great length in a future lesson. We must at least define marriage here because many of the prohibitions we have discussed depend upon it. Marriage is a means by which a woman becomes prohibited to all other men except for her husband. The man, by way of marriage, accepts certain obligations of support and protection for his wife.[26] By pursuing the ideal of Marriage, both parties are fulfilling the divine expectation of *yishuv haaretz*, settling and civilizing the world (which we will also discuss in a future lesson). For Noahides marriage involves, minimally, two components:

1) **A mutual agreement to accept the status of husband and wife and the prohibitions and expectations that come with that status.** Once this agreement has been made, the man and woman are considered betrothed. At this point, all the prohibited relations discussed above take effect. However, one is not yet liable for punishment for transgressing them.

2) **Consensual intercourse.** Once this has taken place, the man and women are liable for both transgression and punishment for all of these prohibitions.

Once a couple has fulfilled these two requirements, they are considered husband and wife in Torah law.

A man and woman who live together for an extended period of time may acquire the status of "betrothed," even if they have never agreed to do so. In certain situations, they may even be considered married.[27] As such, both would acquire the prohibitions and statuses implied therein. For this reason, it is not advisable for a man and woman to live together prior to marriage.

## Precautionary Laws

In Jewish law there are a number of restrictions on interactions between the genders. For example, a man and woman who are prohibited to each other may not hug, hold hands, kiss, or engage in any other expression of physical intimacy (this does not apply to parents and their children or siblings – a parent may kiss or

---

[26] These obligations, however, are not explicit Torah obligations. According to many, they may fall out under the family of *dinim*, establishing rule of law, because society determines the moral and legal expectations of a man for his wife. For Jews however, these obligations are very strictly defined by the Torah.

[27] This issue impacts both Noahides and Jews. See *Hilchos Kiddushin 1*.

hug his child). Similarly, such a couple may not be isolated together in an inaccessible or locked room.

Do these prohibitions apply to Noahides as well?

- *Minchas Chinuch*[28] – Yes. These prohibitions on contact and situations are not safeguards. Rather, they are intrinsically part of the biblical prohibitions. One does not transgress the biblical prohibition only by sexual congress, but by any pleasurable physical contact. This view is heavily disputed by other authorities and may only apply to Jews.

- **Bereshis Rabbah 70:12 & 80:6** – Yes. The generation after the flood accepted extra precautions on issues of sexual morality. However, we cannot use the Midrash as a proof because it is not clear if these precautions were general precautions on physical contact and intimate situations. We only know for certain that these measures included precautions on specific relations between specific partners.

- *Chavas Yair*[29] and *Chida* as cited in the *Sdei Chemed*[30] - No. A proof can be made by comparison of the laws pertaining to relations between Jews and non-Jews and the laws of relations between Noahides and Noahides. However, it is not clear that the situations mentioned are analogous. In the laws pertaining to relations between Jews and non-Jews, all of the restrictions involved fall on the Jew's side, not on the Non-Jew's. The fact that these prohibitions (from the Jew's side) are the dispositive ones is not proof that Noahides have no such prohibitions (we will clarify this in the live class).

- *Mitzvos HaShem*[31] – Yes. Noahides are forbidden to have contact or create situations that could lead to transgression. However, this purely is a logically compelled practice, and not an actual Torah obligation.

The *Mitzvos HaShem*'s point is the most compelling. It makes sense because there is a general principle that we can never trust ourselves when it comes to the sexual desire.[32]

---

[28] Mitzvah 188.

[29] 108.

[30] III: 38.

[31] P. 479.

[32] This is repeated many times in the Talmud and other Torah literature.

Since these precautions have a practical motivation, a Noahide may practice them even according to the Jewish laws. Many recent writers and teachers on Noahism have advocated that Noahides do so.

With tremendous deference and respect to these writers, it appears that their endorsement of this practice for Noahides may not be fully thought-out (this will be discussed more in the live class). For many reasons, Noahides must determine their own boundaries in these matters within a very broad set of guidelines.

For example, Noahides should use only Jewish law to determine what is permitted to them in these areas, and not what is forbidden in these areas. For example:

- A doctor seeing a female patient in an examination room – since this is permitted for Jews it is certainly permitted for Noahides.

- Socially acceptable forms of greeting (handshakes), since fundamentally permitted to Jews, are always permitted for Noahides.

As far as prohibitions are concerned, their determination is based on sensibility. Rabbi Bloomenstiel has suggested that any situation in which a wife would just have to "trust her husband," or a husband would have to "trust his wife" would be a situation that calls for precautions. The nature of these precautions is up to Noahides to determine. Such situations would include:

- **A man taking a business trip with a married female co-worker.**

- **A girl living in a college dorm.** Technically, premarital intimacy is permitted for Noahides. However, there are reasons to be strict that will be discussed in the live lesson.

- **A woman allowing another man into her home for a social visit if her husband is out of town. This is in a case when they would be alone.**

- **A man sleeping in or sharing a room with a man who is suspected of homosexual desires or activity.**

Socially acceptable forms of greeting (handshakes, etc.) are always permitted for Noahides.

Contact that implies intimacy should not be had between those who are prohibited to each other. The exceptions are normal expressions of love between immediate family members. This will be discussed in the live lesson.

# Summary of the Lesson

1. Even though the Torah includes many apparent examples of sexual immorality pre-Sinai, these examples are not always clear prohibitions.

2. The fundamental prohibitions are learned from Gen 2:24 and from Abraham's words to Avimelech.

3. Many relations were prohibited by Noahides in ancient times. Only a few are known for certain to be in effect today. However, this may have included those things permitted for Noahides, yet called "abominations."

4. There are a number of relations that are fundamentally permitted, yet should not be practiced.

5. Liability for transgressing these prohibitions falls upon both the male and female transgression of these laws.

6. Marriage is the result of 1) agreeing to become man and wife, and 2) consensual sexual relations.

7. Logical precautions should be observed to avoid coming to transgress these laws.

THE YESHIVA PIRCHEI SHOSHANIM SHULCHAN ARUCH PROJECT

# The Noahide Laws - Lesson Thirty-Nine

© **Yeshiva Pirchei Shoshanim 2017**
This shiur may not be reproduced in any
form without permission of the copyright holder

164 Village Path, Lakewood NJ 08701 732.370.3344
164 Rabbi Akiva, Bnei Brak, 03.616.6340

## Table of Contents:

1. Introduction
2. Source for Marriage
3. Implications of the Marital Concept
4. The Obligation of *Yishuv HaAretz*
5. Marriage
6. Beyond the Minimum
7. Sources & Suggested Elements for a Marriage Service
8. Common Law Marriage
9. Summary

# Lifecycle II: Marriage & Pre-Marriage

## Introduction

In the last lesson we saw the various prohibited relations and the need for reasonable precautions when it comes to interactions between the genders. In this lesson, we are going to discuss pre-marriage and marriage.

## Source for Marriage

*Therefore a man shall leave his father and his mother and cling to his wife, and they shall become one flesh.*[1]

We have learned that this verse is the source of five of the six punishable prohibited relations. However, this verse also states that a man should "cling to a wife." This implies that marriage is the ideal relationship between men and women.

Yet, we must ask: Does marriage even apply to Noahides? This question hinges on a principle that we learned in an earlier lesson: **Anything stated before Sinai only applies to Noahides if it was repeated at Sinai.**[2] Therefore, if marriage was mentioned at Sinai, this repetition would be sufficient proof that the concept of marriage applies to all man. Sure enough, Deut. 22:13 states:

---

[1] Genesis 2:24.

[2] This is a fundamental principle of deriving the Noahide laws from Sanhedrin 59a.

*When a man takes a wife…*

In fact, the Talmud devotes an entire tractate, *Kiddushin*, to identifying and analyzing the numerous post-Sinaitic references to marriage. We see then that marriage applies to Noahides as well as to Jews.

## Implications of the Marital Concept

*Therefore a man shall leave his father and his mother and cling to his wife, and they shall become one flesh.*

Having established that the concept of marriage applies to Noahides, we have to then consider both its positive and negative implications.

**The positive implication of marriage** is that a committed, legally defined, consensual relationship is the ideal for Noahide men and women.

**The negative implication of marriage** is that noncommittal, undefined, or nonconsensual relationships are the opposite of that ideal. Nachmanides to Gen. 2:24 writes that the verse warns against promiscuity and licentiousness. However, the *poskim* do not derive or specify any prohibited acts of licentiousness (premarital sex, prostitution, etc.) The negative implications of our verse are too broad to imply specific prohibitions. Keeping this point in mind, let's examine another factor.

## The Obligation of *Yishuv HaAretz*

*The Lord, Creator of the Heavens, He is the God, the one Who formed the earth… He did not create it for emptiness,* **he fashioned it to be inhabited**…[3]

The phrase …*he fashioned it to be inhabited*… carries *halachic*, practical, weight.

---

[3] Isaiah 45:18.

**Talmud Gittin 41a-b**

The Talmud in Gittin 41a-b discusses the case of a Canaanite indentured servant who is granted partial release by his employers.[4] In this situation, his status is in serious doubt. Is he a Jew or a Non-Jew? The Talmud, Tosafos,[5] Rashi, and other commentaries explain that this "half-free" status is untenable. In such a state the person cannot marry a Jew or a non-Jew and, as the commentaries explain, cannot fulfill his obligation of *yishuv ha-aretz*, making the world settled and civilized. We see that *yishuv ha-aretz* is an obligation for Noahides.

*Yishuv HaAretz*, settling and civilizing the world, appears to be part of the commandment of *dinim*, establishing civil law. Along with the ideal of marriage and its negative implications against promiscuity, these concepts create a general obligation to avoid licentiousness and socially corrosive sexual behaviors.

However, the specifics of these obligations are not mentioned in any of the *halachic* codes. It may be that these general, conceptual prohibitions were the basis upon which the court of Shem and other early leaders decreed specific prohibitions for Noahide society.[6] This view may also explain the wording of I Kings 14:24, which states:

> ...*and also prostitution was in the land, and they did all the abominations of the nations*...

The verse separates prostitution and the other "abominations" (prohibited relations), implying that they are problematic for different reasons. According to our understanding, prostitution had reached the point that it ran afoul of *yishuv haaretz* and the implications of the marital ideal. However, the "abominations," as we mentioned in the last lesson, may have been things that were decreed as prohibited by Shem and early Noahide courts. Therefore, they are "abominations," socially and morally reprehensible behaviors. However, prostitution is not called an "abomination," because it was connected to an actual prohibition.

---

[4] Once a Canaanite becomes a servant to a Jew, he is no longer a Jew or a Non-Jew. Instead, he attains a halfway-conversion of sorts: partially non-Jew and partially Jew. Upon gaining complete release from his servitude, the Canaanite is now a Jew in all respects. The situation under discussion is the status of a Non-Jew who is granted incomplete release. What then is his status?

[5] *Tosafos* to *Gittin* and also to *Bava Basra* 13a.

[6] As discussed in the previous lesson.

Prostitution and premarital relations, though not intrinsically prohibited, become problems when they impinge on the aforementioned obligations. Therefore, they are not punishable offenses. Noahides have an obligation, though, to regulate or discourage such behaviors as needed to preserve society.[7]

## Marriage

Maimonides, based on the Talmud's discussion of pre-Sinaitic marriage,[8] writes in Hilchos Ishus 1:1 that prior to Sinai Noahides became married via a two-stage process.[9] This process is not meant to represent the ideal method of marriage, but only the absolute minimum requirements to affect marriage within the Noahide laws. Let's look closer at what these two factors entail:

1) **Agreement to become married:**

    a. The man and woman must be biblically permitted to each other. No bond of marriage exists between parties who may not marry each other on a biblical level.[10]

    b. No one can marry another against his or her will.[11]

    c. Additionally, one must be mature enough to understand the seriousness of the commitment and the prohibitions and the obligations that it entails. Therefore, there is a minimum age for marriage. This age is certainly no less than the age-of-obligation[12] within the Noahide laws, and may even be higher. If a man and women are not capable enough for marriage, then allowing them

---

[7] See *Even HaEzer* 177 and Rashi to Num. 22:5.

[8] Sanhedrin 57b – 58b.

[9] See Maimonides and Sanhedrin ibid; *Kiryas Sefer* and Maggid Mishneh on Maimonides ibid.; Minchas Chinuch 35:13 & 19; Shut Rivash 398. See also Tosafos HaRid to Bava Basra 16b, Rashi to Sotah 10a. There are far more sources and authorities than can be listed here.

[10] *Parshas Derakhim* and many others. See also Shevus Yaakov I:20 who clarifies that no status of marriage can exist between Jew and non-Jew either.

[11] Nachmanides *Milchamot* to Sanhedrin 8; *Nemukei Yosef* Sanhedrin 8; Ran to *Pesachim* 2; See also Rashi to Gen. 24:57.

[12] There is a dispute as to whether this is a fixed age or is dependent upon the individual's intelligence and understanding. This age will be the topic of a future lesson.

to marry is actually a detriment to society. Noahides should make these determinations for themselves.[13]

d. Both parties must understand and consent to the prohibitions and obligations that marriage creates. For example, the woman becomes prohibited to all other men. Similarly, the man must knowingly accept any obligations he may have to his wife.[14]

e. Once the couple has made this agreement, the woman is considered *meorasah*, "betrothed." At this point she is prohibited to all other men. However, she would not be liable for punishment if she should transgress.[15]

2) **Consensual marital relations:**

a. Having become betrothed, the marriage is consummated through consensual, normal[16] relations with the specific intent of creating the marital bond.[17]

b. Once the marital act is completed, the woman is considered a *be'ulas ba'as*, a fully married woman.[18]

## Beyond the Minimum

There is no requirement for witnesses or ceremony for a Noahide marriage. However, we must keep in mind that that *halacha* – Torah law – provides a skeleton, an outline, in which to cultivate meaning, relevance, and importance. It is essential to make Noahide ceremonies meaningful, personal, and relevant to the spouses and their families.

---

[13] The Acharonim discuss the issues in this paragraph at great length. See *Shut Chasam Sofer YD* 317; *Minchas Chinuch 190*; Rashi to Nazir 29b; *Sdei Chemed Peas HaSadeh III*; *Hilchos Melachim* 10:2.

[14] A Noahide man has no biblical obligations to his wife. However, there are certain expectations that are compelled by the concept of marriage and *yishuv haaretz*. We will see these soon.

[15] See note 8 for sources.

[16] "Normal relations" refers to vaginal intercourse in the normal manner. See *Talmud Yerushalmi Kiddushin 1:1*.

[17] See Maimonides *Hilchos Ishus 1:1*; *Shut Rivash* 398; *Minchas Chinuch* 35:13 & 19.

[18] See note 8 for sources.

Additionally, since the process of marriage changes the status of the partners involved, it is appropriate to hold a service in which their new statuses are witnessed and announced to the world.

## Sources and Suggested Elements for a Marriage Service

- **Wedding Canopy** – Getting married beneath a canopy is a requirement of Jewish law. Some *Rishonim*, however, imply that it is not a Jewish innovation. Indeed, they state that it was part of the marriage ceremony even in ancient pre-Sinaitic times. This is certainly not enough evidence to imply that one *should* use a marriage canopy. However, it is enough to prove that it is acceptable for Noahides and doing so is not considered *chiddushei dat*. After all, the symbolism of the canopy applies equally to both Noahides and Jews (this will be discussed in the live class).

- **Wedding Rings** – the Talmud in Sanhedrin 58a writes that when a Noahide's marriage ends, the woman "uncovers her hair in the marketplace." In other words, she goes about bareheaded in public. Some have cited this passage as proof that married Noahide women should cover their hair.[19] However, it appears that the issue is not covering hair, but that the woman should have a public sign that she is married. Since this is the underlying reason, then covering the hair would not accomplish this purpose. After all, most people would not interpret it as a sign of marriage. However, a wedding ring certainly accomplishes this in America. Therefore, it is appropriate to give rings as part of the ceremony of marriage. Once the couple is married, they should be careful to wear their rings whenever in public.

- **Marriage Document** – Because accepting the obligations and prohibitions associated with marriage requires full knowledge and consent of the parties, these obligations and expectations must be specified and known to both the man and woman. The best way of guaranteeing this is for the parties to write vows and acknowledge them to each other. These vows should mention the prohibitions created by marriage and the obligations of marriage. Alternatively, and perhaps more effectively, would be to draft a list of the mutual agreements

---

[19] *Sefer Sheva Mitzvos HaShem VI:6:9.*

of the husband and wife. The following is a suggested outline for such an agreement:

*On the _____ day of the week, the _____ day of the month of _____ in the year _____, here in the city of _____, ___(groom)___ said to his bride, _____: "Please become my wife according to the laws of Noah as commanded to the world in ancient times and reaffirmed through the hand of Moses at Sinai. I pledge to _____, and I accept all of the expectations and obligations of a husband unto his wife, as well as any prohibitions created unto me by becoming your husband. Together we will build a home and, together, fulfill the divine vision of yishuv ha-aretz, settling and civilizing the world according to God's will."*

*On this day, _____ said unto her groom: "I will become your wife, according to the laws of Noah as commanded to the world in ancient times and reaffirmed through the hand of Moses at Sinai. I pledge to_____, and I accept all of the expectations and obligations of a wife unto her husband, as well as any prohibitions created unto me by becoming your wife. Together we will build a home and, together, fulfill the divine vision of yishuv ha-aretz, settling and civilizing the world according to God's will."*

*Before all of the undersigned, the bride and groom have together entered into the bond of betrothal with the intention of creating a complete bond of marriage.*

_____          _____
        *Groom*                               *Bride*

_____
        *Witnesses*

## De Facto (Common Law) Marriage

We should note that an unrelated man and woman who live together without being married may acquire the de facto status of marriage or betrothal.[20] For this reason, it is not advisable that Noahide men and women share living spaces together prior to marriage.

---

[20] See *Hilchos Ishus 1:1* and commentaries. This is written about extensively in the *poskim* and commentaries.

# Summary of the Lesson

1. Gen. 2:24 introduces the concept of marriage. The fact that it is iterated at Sinai indicates that it applies to Noahides as well.

2. Marriage implies not only what is appropriate, but what is inappropriate. However, it does not do so with enough specificity to imply particular prohibitions.

3. The Talmud states that *yishuv haaretz*, settling and civilizing the world, is an obligation of all mankind. For Noahides it implies certain prohibitions and responsibilities.

4. Minimally, marriage requires full agreement to accept the status of marriage and consummation via relations.

5. Although this is the minimum, it is important that the deeper, human and spiritual aspects of marriage be acknowledged and celebrated.

6. Noahides may use a wedding canopy.

7. One should possess a sign that she is married.

8. Since complete knowledge is required to accept the status of marriage, it is advisable that the bride and groom have some sort of a marriage document or vows that acknowledge their obligations and expectation.

THE YESHIVA PIRCHEI SHOSHANIM SHULCHAN ARUCH PROJECT

# The Noahide Laws - Lesson Forty

© **Yeshiva Pirchei Shoshanim 2017**
This shiur may not be reproduced in any
form without permission of the copyright holder.

164 Village Path, Lakewood NJ 08701 732.370.3344
164 Rabbi Akiva, Bnei Brak, 03.616.6340

## Table of Contents:

1. Introduction
2. Reproduction & *Yishuv HaAretz*
3. Conception & Contraception
4. *Coitus Interruptus*
5. The Marital Bond & Sexual Intimacy
6. Condoms
7. Surgical Sterilization
8. Pharmaceutical Contraceptives
9. Summary

**THE YESHIVA PIRCHEI SHOSHANIM SHULCHAN ARUCH PROJECT**
**THE NOAHIDE LAWS | NOAHIDE LIFECYCLE III | CONCEPTION & CONTRACEPTION | LESSON 40**

# Lifecycle III: Conception & Contraception

## Introduction

In the last lesson we explored marriage, the beginning of the Noahide lifecycle. In this lesson we move onto the next stage: starting a family. This lesson will address questions of conception and contraception, touching on a number of other issues along the way.

## Reproduction & *Yishuv HaAretz*

Adam and Noah were both commanded in "be fruitful and multiply." However, this commandment was not repeated at Sinai. As we learned in prior lessons: any *mitzvah* given before Sinai, yet not repeated at Sinai, applies only to Jews.[1] Therefore, *peru u'revu*, be fruitful and multiply, is not a Noahide *mitzvah*.

In the last lesson, we learned about the obligation of *yishuv haaretz*, settling and civilizing the world. This commandment includes the expectation of reproduction and building a family. What is the difference, though, between the commandment of *yishuv haaretz* and *peru u'revu*, "be fruitful and multiply? If they are the same, then why do we need them both?

---

[1] Sanhedrin 59a.

There are big differences between the two *mitzvos*:

- **Yishuv HaAretz** is a general obligation to reproduce, raise children, and through doing so build and perfect human society. This applies to both men and women.

- **Peru U'Revu,** "be fruitful and multiply" is a very specific commandment applying only to Jewish men. One fulfills this commandment by fathering at least 1 boy and 1 girl. Furthermore, it creates a number of de facto negative commandments. For example, contraception is technically prohibited until this *mitzvah* is fulfilled.[2]

## Conception & Contraception

May contraception be used by Noahides? What if a man and woman want to wait to have children? What if pregnancy would pose medical risks to the woman? There is no Torah-based reason to prohibit contraception for Noahides. However, certain methods of contraception may pose problems. Let's examine them one-by-one:

## Coitus Interruptus

At first glance, it appears *coitus interruptus* is absolutely prohibited. After all, the Talmud tells us this practice is one of the acts that brought the flood.[3] Furthermore, Er and Onein, the sons of Judah, were specifically punished for doing this.[4]

However, things are not as clear as they look. Before Sinai, Noahides were obligated in "be fruitful and multiply." After Sinai, they were not.[5] Therefore, we have to ask the question:

---

[2] There are a number of allowances for contraception depending on the circumstances of the couple. Jewish couples must consult a *posek* to determine when contraception may be used.

[3] Rashi to Niddah 13a; Sanhedrin 108b. Genesis 6:12 states: "All flesh has corrupted its way upon the earth," is understood by the Talmud as a reference to onanism.

[4] Gen. 38:9. See Yevamos 34b for the Talmud's discussion of their deaths.

[5] Sanhedrin 59a.

Were Er, Onain, and the generation of the flood punished for an independent transgression of spilling seed? Or, was it because they had spurned their obligation of "be fruitful and multiply?"

If they were punished for spilling seed, then it may apply even to Noahides today. However, if it was due to "be fruitful and multiply," then it is not relevant to Noahides today.

Another issue depending on this question is the permissibility of male masturbation. If the prohibition is only because of spurning "be fruitful and multiply," then male masturbation may be permitted to Noahides. However, if it is an independent prohibition of spilling seed, then male masturbation is specifically prohibited.

Tosafos to Sanhedrin 59b takes the latter approach: Er, Onan, and the generation of the flood were punished for spurning "be fruitful and multiply." Since this obligation does not apply to Noahides today, there is no reason why the acts of Er, Onan, etc. should be prohibited.

However, Nachmanides[6] holds that spilling seed is a prohibition independent of "be fruitful and multiply."[7] All of the other major Rishonim (Rashba, Ran, Ritva and others) concur with him. This would mean two things:

1) *Coitus interruptus* is a prohibited form of contraception, and
2) Male masturbation is prohibited.

Accordingly, any form of contraception that wastes seed should be prohibited. This would preclude the use of condoms. The same reasoning would also prohibit sexual relations with a woman who is infertile. However, there is another factor to consider.

---

[6] In his novellae on the Talmud.

[7] There is some disagreement as to Nachmanides's underlying reasoning. See *Mateh Aharon* cited in *Sdei Chemed* VII and *Mishneh LaMelech* to *Melakhim* 10:7. They read Nachmanides as saying that this is a biblical prohibition. However, *Toras Chesed* to *Even HaEzer* 43 argues that Nachmanides's understands this is a rabbinic prohibition. However, *Pnei Yehoshua* II EH 44 brings strong proofs that this prohibition is biblical. According to the *Pnei Yehoshua*, anytime the Torah says something is "wicked in God's eyes," it is communicating an absolute biblical prohibition upon all peoples.

## The Marital Bond & Sexual Intimacy

Part of the marital bond, and even a prerequisite of it, is the sexual intimacy between a man and a woman.[8] Sexual intimacy is as much a special part of the marriage as emotional, spiritual, and intellectual intimacy. The sex act does exist merely for procreation, but is essential to establishing a bond between a man and a woman. Sex is not viewed in Torah religious thought as sinful, taboo, or purely utilitarian. In the right context it is meant to be indulged and enjoyed.

The *poskim*[9] have written extensively on this topic and their conclusions are universal: expelling seed during intercourse is part of the act of sexual intimacy between a man and woman. Therefore, even though a woman may be infertile, there is no issue for her husband from the side of "spilling seed." However, as we see from the example of Er and Onan, the semen must not be expelled outside of the woman's body.

## Condoms

The problem with condoms is that the man's semen is collected within and then discarded. Obviously, this should violate the prohibition of "spilling seed." However, it is not so clear. Since expelling seed is permitted as part of marital intimacy, perhaps the use of a condom is permitted. After all, the seed is not expelled outside of the woman's body when a condom is used.

The *poskim* discuss and compare condoms to IUDs, which are permitted.[10] Both devices block semen from reaching the uterus, and all agree semen that later exits the woman's body poses no issue for the man. He is only liable for semen actually expelled outside the woman's body. The question comes down to whether or not the complete imposition of a condom between the man and woman makes it as if the semen is expelled outside the woman's body and therefore is not truly part of the marital act.

---

[8] Most *poskim* learn this from the implication of the phrase in Gen 2:24: "…shall cling to his wife…" the word for "clinging" in Hebrew connotes sexual as well as other forms of intimacy.

[9] The conclusion brought here is accepted as a fact in Torah law by all *poskim*. For specific details of the derivations and proofs, see Rabbeinu Asher cited in Bais Yosef to *Even HaEzer* 23. See also Rama, Bach, and *Bais Shmuel* cited there.

[10] See *Shut Achiezer* III:24; *Shut Maharshag* II:243; *Pri HaSadeh* III:53; Igros Moshe EH I:63.

Although the *Sefer Sheva Mitzvos HaShem* (*The Divine Code*) permits the use of condoms, the issue does not appear to be conclusively decided.[11]

## Surgical Sterilization

The Tannaim[12] dispute whether or not sterilization is an independent biblical prohibition for Noahides. Rabbi Chidka and the School of Manasseh hold that it is a biblical prohibition from the verse:

> …*swarm on the earth, and multiply upon it…*[13]

However, the other Tannaim view this verse as a statement of blessing, not a commandment.

The Rishonim and Acharonim are divided as to which Tannaic opinion is the *Halacha*, actual practice:

- There is an independent prohibition of sterilization – The Talmud rules that a Jew may not have a Noahide to castrate his (the Jew's) animal.[14] The reason, apparently, is that a Noahide is enjoined against castration.[15] The Jew, by asking the Noahide to carry out such an act, is "placing a stumbling block before the blind."

- There is no prohibition against sterilization – Most later *poskim* reject this line of reasoning, pointing out that a Jew is also prohibited from asking a Noahide to do anything that he himself, as a Jew, cannot do. Since Jews are biblically prohibited from sterilization, they may not ask a Noahide to

---

[11] Pirchei Shoshanim consulted a number of *poskim* on this question. Of the two American *poskim* consulted, one tentatively permitted condom use and the other held it was prohibited. Rav Bloomenstiel consulted *HaRav HaGaon* Chaim Kanievsky, *shlit"a*, one of the leading *poskim* in the world, who said: "Possibly, it is permitted. There is no liability [punishment] for doing so." The Rav was clear that this was not a *psak*, a conclusive statement. Similarly, *HaRav HaGaon* Shmuel HaLevi Wosner, *ztz"l* said that he has not yet seen any strong proofs to decisively permit or prohibit condom use for Noahides and that the issue still requires study.

[12] Sanhedrin 56a.

[13] Gen. 9:7.

[14] Bava Metzia 90b and numerous commentaries.

[15] See *Kiryas Sefer* on Issuerei Bia 16:13. See also the discussion in the *Beis Yosef* on *Even HaEzer* 5.

do so. However, there is no implication that Noahides are also prohibited from castrating animals.[16]

Although the issue continues to be debated, it appears as if this discussion has passed into the realm of academic speculation. The large majority of *poskim* permits sterilization to Noahides and bring strong reasons for their rulings.[17]

While the *Halacha* is that there is no independent prohibition of sterilization for Noahides, *sterilization* poses another issue.

As we will learn in future lessons, a person is forbidden from causing any destruction or permanent damage to his body.[18] This includes many surgeries not deemed medically necessary.[19] Without a compelling medical reason, surgical sterilization should not be used as a method of contraception.

Tubal ligation however, does not appear to pose a problem.[20] Today, it is a relatively minor, reversible procedure causing no permanent damage to the body.

## Pharmaceutical Contraceptives

Pharmaceutical contraceptives (such as "the pill") which do not result in any permanent physical damage are certainly permitted.[21] Similarly, a woman may use contraceptive film or foam.

---

[16] See Maimonides, *Issurei Biah* 16:13 with the *Maggid Mishnah*. See also the *Maggid Mishneh's* commentary to *Hilchos Sechirus* 13:3; Rosh, Rashi, and others to Bava Metzia 90a.

[17] It is difficult to find any contemporary *poskim* who rule there is a prohibition of sterilization for Noahides. The following is just a sampling of the more authoritative and extensive treatments of the subject: *Arukh HaShulchan, Even HaEzer* 5; *Shut Nishmas Chaim* 133; *Shut Zivchei Tzedek CM* 2; *Chelkas Yaakov Even HaEzer* 28; *Shut Ateres Paz* I, YD 14 & EH 7.

[18] The *Minchas Chinuch*, though he appears to hold that sterilization is an independent prohibition, adds that causing harm is another reason to prohibit.

[19] Cosmetic surgery, in many situations, is an exception to this rule. We will discuss it in a future lesson.

[20] *Igros Moshe, Even HaEzer* III:15.

[21] *Shulchan Aruch, Even HaEzer* 5:12.

## Summary of the Lesson

1. Noahides are not obligated in *peru u'revu*, be fruitful and multiply. However, they are obligated in *yishuv haaretz*.

2. Contraception is permitted for Noahides. However, certain methods pose issues.

3. *Coitus interruptus* is prohibited to both Noahides and to Jews.

4. Sex is not purely utilitarian in Torah thought. It is part of forming the bond between husband and wife and is meant to be enjoyed.

5. Condoms are a permitted form of contraception for Noahides.

6. Surgical sterilization is prohibited if it renders one permanently sterile.

7. Pharmaceutical contraception is permitted.

THE YESHIVA PIRCHEI SHOSHANIM SHULCHAN ARUCH PROJECT

# The Noahide Laws - Lesson Forty-One

© **Yeshiva Pirchei Shoshanim 2017**
This shiur may not be reproduced in any
form without permission of the copyright holder.

164 Village Path, Lakewood NJ 08701 732.370.3344
164 Rabbi Akiva, Bnei Brak, 03.616.6340

## Table of Contents:

1. Introduction
2. WARNING
3. Abortion in the Noahide Laws
4. At What Point is Abortion Prohibited
5. When the Mother is Endangered
6. Die or Transgress
7. *Rodef*: The Pursuer
8. Summary

# Lifecycle IV: Abortion

**Lesson 41**

## Introduction

Abortion is an issue that evokes strong responses from everyone. Unfortunately, the possibility for nuanced and sensitive discussion of the important questions involved is marred by the existence of two dogmatic camps: "pro-life" and "pro-choice."

The Torah view of abortion does not fall clearly in either camp; both are contrary to the Torah view. From an ethical standpoint, the Torah views abortion negatively. The Zohar states:

> *Three drive the divine presence from this word and make it impossible for the Holy One, blessed is He, to fix His abode in the universe... And the [third] is one who destroys a fetus in the womb, for he destroys the craft of the Holy One, blessed be He, and his workmanship... on account of these abominations the Holy Spirit weeps...*[1]

Practically speaking, though, the approach to abortion is not so black-and-white. The eminent Rabbi Dr. Tzvi Hersh Weinreb, former CEO and Executive Vice President Emeritus of the Orthodox Union, accurately described the Torah approach as follows:

> *... in actual practice the Torah view of abortion is very different from the conservative views of the Catholic Church and from the liberal views of [many] Jewish groups. It is nuanced, complex, and depends upon such a variety of factors that categorizing Torah Judaism as either pro-life or pro-choice is almost a caricature of our position.*[2]

---

[1] *Zohar Shemos 3b.*

[2] "Orthodoxy in the Public Square" in *Tradition* 38:1 (Spring 2004), p. 34

Abortion is one of the few topics in the Noahide Laws for which there is extensive literature. The downside of so much being written is that even a cursory survey of the literature is far beyond the scope of this course.

## A WARNING

Any practical questions of abortion <u>must</u> be asked to a competent *posek*. Issues of life and death cannot be determined by most Rabbis, <u>especially those who are experts in the Noahide laws.</u> The question must be asked to an impartial noted authority in Jewish Law [*posek*]. Any *posek* capable of ruling on such issues will have expertise in the application of these laws to Noahides far beyond that of any expert or specialist in the Noahide laws.

## Abortion in the Noahide Laws

Abortion falls under the category of murder within the Noahide laws. In Jewish law, abortion is also prohibited. However the details and sources of the prohibitions are different. They are so different that by studying the Jewish laws of abortion it is possible to come to the conclusion that killing a fetus is not murder for Noahides. The Talmud, however, teaches us that this is not so.

Rebbi Yishmael[3] makes an observation on the following verse:[4]

> *One who spills the blood of man; by man shall his blood be spilt.*

In Hebrew, this is an odd construction:

> *Shofeikh dam ha-adam ba-adam damo yishafeikh*

It is ambiguous, able to take a comma in two possible places. The first possibility is:

> *Shofeikh dam ha-adam, ba-adam damo yishafeikh*

Punctuated like this way, the verse yields the translation we have given above.

---

[3] Sanhedrin 57b.

[4] Gen. 9:6.

However, an alternate punctuation results in an altogether different meaning:

*Shofeikh dam ha-adam ba-adam, damo yishafeikh*

One who spills the blood of a **person who is within a person**, his blood shall be spilt.

Regarding this reading, the Talmud states:

> They [the sages] said in the name of Rebbi Yishmael: "Noahides are liable for killing a fetus. What is the reason for Rebbi Yishmael? For it states in the verse: 'One who spills the blood of a person who is within a person, his blood shall be spilt.' Which is a 'person who is within a person?' You would answer that this is a fetus."

The *halacha*, Torah law, follows the opinion of Rebbi Yishmael and the sages. Maimonides rules as such, writing:

> A gentile who slays any soul, even a fetus in its mother's womb, is executed as penalty for its death.[5]

## At What Point Is Abortion Prohibited?

The contemporary political and religious debates on abortion have hinged upon the definition of embryonic/fetal life. This factor is the most important, yet by no means exclusive, consideration shaping the Torah's approach to the issue.

**Abortion during the first 40 days following conception**

The Talmud indicates in many places[6] that the embryo does not have the status of a "fetus" or a living being during the first 40 days following its conception. Rather, the embryo is termed *mayim bealma*, "only fluid." This is the *halacha*[7] and reflects a general principle that Torah law is not concerned with that which is microscopic or barely visible. At this stage in its development, the embryo has no *halachic*, practical, existence. Therefore, should a Jewish woman miscarry at this stage she is not subject to the impurity described in Leviticus 12:2-5.[8] As well, the spiritual impurities (*tumah*) associated with corpses are not assigned to a miscarried

---

[5] *Hilchos Melachim* 9:4.

[6] *Yevamos* 69b; *Niddah* 30a; *Bechoros* 47b.

[7] See *Shulchan Aruch* YD 305:23.

[8] See *Niddah* ibid.

embryo at this stage.⁹ This fact allows for the possibility of abortion during the first 40 days.

However, life is not so simple – after all, it among the Holy One's greatest creations. The *Beer Halachos Gadolos*, one of the earliest and most important codes of Torah law, rules that a Jew may transgress Shabbat for the sake of saving an unborn life even during its first 40 days.¹⁰

The *Beer Halachos Gadolos* obviously considers the embryo "alive enough" to permit a Jew to transgress Shabbat on its behalf. It appears that there are different definitions of life for different purposes of Torah law.

During the first 40 days after conception an embryo:

- Is not considered life for the laws of miscarriages,¹¹
- Is not considered life for the laws of impurities caused by the dead,
- It is considered life enough to warrant violation of Shabbat in order to save it.

We must ask: Where is the threshold of life for the sake of the prohibition of abortion? This is a topic of **extensive** discussion.

Some *poskim* have taken a very simple approach: if we are permitted to violate Shabbat to save the embryo, it must be prohibited at that point to abort the embryo. The *Chavas Yair*¹² writes that it doesn't make sense for Jews to be allowed to violate Shabbat to save a life that they could voluntarily terminate.

However, the reasons for permitting Shabbat violation for the life of the embryo may be more nuanced.

---

⁹ *Mishneh LaMelekh* to *Hilchos Tumas Meit* 2:1.

¹⁰ Cited in Nachmanides's *Toras HaAdam, Shaar HaSakanah* II:29. *Rosh* and *Ran* also cite this as *halacha* in their commentaries to *Yoma 82a*.

¹¹ As mentioned above.

¹² 31.

**Human trafficking & abortion – what do they have in common?**

Rashi[13] writes that the prohibition against selling someone into involuntary servitude applies even to an unborn child. Yet, the unborn child lacks full human status. Why then should it be included in this law?

Since the child will, as a matter of natural events, inevitably become fully human, it is treated as if fully human even at this point in its development.[14] Rav Issar Yehudah Unterman proposed[15] that this logic also underlies the *Beer Halachos Gadolos*'s permit to save an embryo during its first 40 days. In other words - the saving of *potential* life (an embryo during its first 40) is enough to warrant Jewish transgression of Shabbat.

According to this understanding, the fetus is not *actual*, yet only *potential* life during its first 40 days. Rav Unterman's thesis has significant support in earlier literature as well as from later *poskim*.

The implication of this approach for Noahides is important. From the Talmud's discussion of the Noahide prohibition of abortion, it is clear that Noahides are only liable for the taking of *actual* embryonic life, not *potential* embryonic life. This is indicated by the term "a *person* within a *person*" - one is only liable when the life of the fetus is comparable to that of the mother. Therefore, there may be no prohibition on Noahide abortion during the first 40 days after conception.

However, Rav Unterman's explanation is not accepted by all *poskim*.[16] Alone, it is not enough to permit abortion during the first 40 days. However, it is a significant factor when combined with other mitigating concerns.

## Abortion When the Mother is Endangered

When a woman's life or health is put at serious risk by pregnancy, may the pregnancy be terminated? There are a number of factors to take into account, four of which are especially important:

1) Must a Noahide give her life rather than transgress?

---

[13] To Sanhedrin 85b.

[14] The idea that an object that will inevitably reach a state of obligation is considered in such a state even now is a principle occurring many times in Torah law.

[15] *Shevet MiYehudah* I:9.

[16] See notes to the summary below.

2) What is the status of the life of the embryo/fetus?

3) Does the law of *rodef*, a pursuer, apply to Noahides?

4) Is the embryo/fetus considered a *rodef*?

We will examine these four questions in no particular order.

## Die or Transgress?

II Kings 5:14-19 records that Naaman (a Noahide) asked Elisha if he had committed a transgression when visiting his master, the King of Aram. The king had placed his hand upon Naaman, forcing him to bow down before an idol. Elisha replied: "Go in peace."

The Talmud, Sanhedrin 74b explains that Naaman's question was if he should have given his life rather than transgress. After all, the king had to force Naaman down with his own hands. Had Naaman resisted completely, he would have been risking his life! Elisha's reply, "go in peace," indicates that Naaman did nothing wrong. From this incident (involving idolatry no less!) the Talmud learns *a fortiori* that a Noahides has no obligation to give her life in lieu of transgressing any of her laws.[17] Therefore, a Noahide should be able to commit murder to save her life. By this reasoning, abortion is permitted to save the life of the mother (however, only the mother would be able to carry out the abortion, not another).

**Does this apply to murder?** The problem with this line of thought is that murder may be the exception to this rule. The Talmud, Sanhedrin 74a states as a logical fact that "no man's blood is redder than that of another." In other words: we do not make relative comparisons as to the values of individual lives.

Maimonides elaborates on this idea as it pertains to Jews in *Hilchos Yesodei HaTorah, Chapter 5*. The *Parshas Derakhim*[18] notes that Maimonides views this concept as a universal principle, applicable to Jews and non-Jews. This interpretation of Maimonides is corroborated by the Jerusalem Talmud, Shabbos 14 and Avodah Zarah 2:5.

---

[17] The Yad Ramah and Rashi had a slightly different version of the Talmud's text. According to their reading it comes out that a Noahide may be required to give up his life rather than transgress in public. Naaman, however, was permitted to bow because he was in private. However, Tosafos had a different reading in which Noahides are never required to give up their lives for their mitzvos. This latter reading is corroborated by most other Rishonim, including Rabbeinu Tam, Chiddushei HaRan, and Maimonides. It appears to be the one held as correct by most poskim.

[18] *Darsuh II, d.h. VeDah.*

They clearly view this idea as a logical principle applying to all mankind. Assuming this is so, a woman would not be permitted to abort (murder) the fetus to save her own life.

Yet, Maimonides, in discussing the Noahide laws, writes the following:

> *A gentile who is forced by another person to violate one of his commandments is permitted to transgress. Even if he is forced to worship false gods, he may worship them,* **for gentiles are not commanded to sanctify God's name.**[19]

Without making any distinctions, Maimonides permits a Noahide to transgress any of the Noahide laws when her life is in danger. Many authorities reject the *Parshas Derakhim*'s opinion based upon this passage, holding that Noahides may commit murder rather than suffer death (therefore permitting abortion to save the mother's life).[20]

The *Sefer Mitzvos HaShem* and other contemporary *poskim* have suggested a compromise of sorts. In the section quoted above Maimonides is only writing as about whether or not Noahides have a biblical obligation to give their life rather than transgress. This is why he writes "...**gentiles are not commanded to sanctify God's name."** However, Maimonides in *Hilchos Yesodei HaTorah* teaches that there is a logical, yet non-biblical reason for Noahides to give their lives rather than transgress murder.

Many *poskim* agree with the *Parshas Drakhim*. Whether or not a Noahide must die rather than commit murder is too uncertain a matter to help us in the case at hand.

## *Rodef*: The Pursuer

> *If a burglar is found tunneling into a home,*
> *and is discovered and killed, there is no liability.*
> Exodus 22:1

The Talmud, Sanhedrin 72a explains this verse. The assumption is the thief is armed and poses immediate danger to the residents of the house. Sanhedrin 73a cites further verses allowing, and even encouraging, the killing of one who poses immediate danger to another. This is known as the law of the *rodef*, the pursuer:

---

[19] Hilchos Melachim 10:2.

[20] The *Parshas Derakhim* states this as a possibility and cites those who hold accordingly. See *Maharash Yafeh* on *Bereshis Rabbah* 44:5. See also *Maskil LeDovid* on *Parshas Vayishlach*.

If a person is actively endangering the life of another, the one causing the danger must be neutralized by whatever means necessary.

We must ask two questions on this law:

1) Does the law of *rodef* apply to Noahides, and
2) In the case of a pregnancy, when the woman's life is endangered by the fetus, does the fetus have the *din*, law, of a *rodef*, a pursuer?

**Does *rodef* apply to Noahides?**

On the first question, the Talmud, Sanhedrin 57a appears to assume that the law of *rodef* applies to Noahides.[21] Most *poskim* concur, however they are uncertain as to who may kill the pursuer.[22] Is it permitted only for one being pursued, or is any onlooker permitted to kill the pursuer?

**Is the fetus a *rodef*?**

The Mishnah in *Ohalos* 7:6 states:

*If a woman's labor endangers her life, the fetus must be cut up within her womb and removed piecemeal, for her life takes precedence over its life. If its greater part has already come forth, it must not be touched, for its life cannot supersede her life.*

The Mishnah does not tell us the reason for this ruling. However, the Talmud, discussing the law of the pursuer,[23] asks if a pursuer requires warning before he is killed. Along the way, they ask about our Mishnah, because a fetus cannot be warned:

*Rav Chisda asked from the Mishnah: If a fetus is endangering the mother, we kill it. Once the head leaves the womb, we do not kill it. We do not kill one person to save another.*

*[Answer:] That case is different. There, baby has no choice.
Heaven is threatening the life of the mother.*

By asking if the fetus requires warning, the Talmud obviously assumes this is a case of a *rodef*, pursuer.

However, the Talmud's answer implies this is <u>not</u> a case of a pursuer because the baby has no intent nor is actively threatening the mother. Rather, the natural circumstances of birth are endangering the mother: "Heaven is threatening the life

---

[21] See *Minchas Chinuch* 296:5. While most *poskim* agree in principle, the details are hotly debated.

[22] See *Toldos Noach*, *Matza Chein* IV: 32 for an exhaustive overview of the sources.

[23] Sanhedrin 72b.

of the mother." The fetus is, apparently, only a tool to accomplish heaven's "pursuit."

Rashi, understands that *rodef*, the law of a pursuer, is not the operative permit for aborting the fetus (indeed, the Mishnah doesn't even mention it). Rashi writes that although the fetus is "alive enough" to render abortion prohibited, "as long as it has not emerged into the light of the world, it is not a [fully] human life." According to Rashi the value of the fetus's life does not trump that of the mother's; the mother's blood is redder than that of the fetus. This implies that the Talmud's dictum of not comparing life-to-life only applies to life that has fully emerged into this world. Once the head of the baby has emerged, it is considered fully human, equal to mother, and cannot be killed.

Maimonides learns that the fetus is a pursuer:

> *Our Sages ruled that when complications arise and a pregnant woman cannot give birth, it is permitted to abort the fetus in her womb, whether with a knife or with drugs,* **for the fetus is considered a rodef of its mother.** *If the head of the fetus emerges, it should not be touched, because one life should not be sacrificed for another. Although the mother may die, this is the nature of the world.*[24]

Why then does the emergence of the infant's head change the law according to Maimonides?

Many have explained that Maimonides views the life of the mother and infant as equal even before the head of the baby emerges. Therefore, unlike Rashi, there can be no permit to kill the fetus unless it is a pursuer.

The emergence of the head thus removes the law of "pursuer" from the baby. It appears that once the head has emerged, the infant is considered fully independent of the mother and cannot be considered a pursuer at that point.

The *Nodah BiYehudah*[25] and many others[26] have explained that the fetus is not actively "pursing" the woman, but is only a passive tool of heaven's pursuit. Once the head has emerged, the fetus is considered independent of the woman's body

---

[24] *Hilchos Rotzeach 1:9.*

[25] *Tinyana* CM 59.

[26] *Chavas Yoir* 31; *Chiddushei R' Chaim HaLevi, Rotzeach* 1:9. *Even HaAzel Rotzeach* 1:9 has a slightly altered understanding, however.

and it is only the circumstances of delivery, not the baby, that are endangering her life.

The Shulchan Aruch[27] establishes the Halacha like Maimonides. We should note, however, that there are numerous means of understanding Maimonides's reading of the Talmud. Some of these opinions have bizarre ramifications in Torah law and affect the laws for Noahides.[28]

See the summary with footnotes, below, for a practical overview of what emerges from this lesson.

## Summary of the Lesson

1. During the first 40 days after conception, all agree that the "life" of the embryo is markedly different than after 40 days.

2. Therefore, in a case of even non-lethal medical risk to the mother, the pregnancy may be terminated at this stage.[29] Other situations (rape, incest, medical risks to the fetus, etc.) may also permit abortion at this stage.[30] However, they must be dealt with on a case-by-case basis bay a competent *posek*.

3. After 40 days, abortion of the fetus is considered murder in Noahide law.

---

[27] CM 452:2.

[28] There are some who prohibit abortions for Noahides under all conditions. However, these opinions are contrary to the majority of poskim. There are others who distinguish between cases of disease that endanger the pregnancy and danger resulting directly from the pregnancy. The following discuss the possible ramifications of Maimonides's reasoning on the halacha: Achiezer II:72; Sridei Eish III 342; Chemdas Yisrael, Maftechos ve-Hosafos p.32; Shu"t Koach Shor 20; Pachad Yitzchok (Lampronti), Erekh Nefalim 79b;

[29] R. Ovadiah Yosef, Yabi'a Omer, IV Even Ha-Ezer 1: 8-10 even permits abortions in such cases through the first trimester. See also Igros Moshe CM II:69 & 71. Seridei Eish I:162. See also Sheelas Yaavetz 43. This is an extremely controversial responsum, yet may be permitted for Noahides. See also Toras Chesed Even HaEzer 42:32. There are many who rule very severely on this issue, but the hanhaga of poskim today appears more lenient. See Levushei Mordekhai CM 36; Koach Shor 21.

[30] *Seridei Eish* ibid.

4. If the mother's life is endangered by the fetus during this period, abortion may be permitted. This is because the fetus is considered a *rodef*, a pursuer.

5. In cases of medical complications for the fetus or other factors (such as rape, incest, etc.) a *posek* must be consulted. Typically, the further along the pregnancy, the higher the risk standards must be to permit termination. If it is medically determined that the fetus will not live for 30 days after birth, abortion may also be permitted.[31]

6. For Noahides, there is uncertainty as to who may kill a *rodef*. If at all possible, the mother should herself use chemical or pharmaceutical methods (under the strict guidance and assistance of a physician) to terminate the pregnancy when permitted.

7. If the doctor must actively terminate the pregnancy (i.e. embryotomy), it is better that the mother use a Jewish rather than non-Jewish doctor. This is will be discussed more in the live lesson.

8. Once the head has emerged from the womb, the baby may not be harmed in any way.

---

[31] See *Hilchos Rotzeach* 2:6; *Maharam Shick* OH 142; *Minchas Chinuch* 34.

THE YESHIVA PIRCHEI SHOSHANIM SHULCHAN ARUCH LEARNING PROJECT

# The Noahide Laws – Lesson Forty Two

© **Yeshiva Pirchei Shoshanim 2017**
This shiur may not be reproduced in any
form without permission of the copyright holder.

164 Village Path, Lakewood NJ 08701 732.370.3344
164 Rabbi Akiva, Bnei Brak, 03.616.6340

## Outline of This Lesson:

1. Introduction
2. Talmud *Yoma 28b*
3. Sanhedrin 59b
4. The Descendants of Keturah/Hagar
5. Voluntary Circumcision
6. Possibly Prohibited
7. Conclusions
8. Summary

# Lifecycle V: Circumcision

## Introduction

Circumcision is one of most well-known of Jewish obligations. Although Abraham and his household were commanded in circumcision, this has very little relevance to today's non-Jews. Nevertheless, may a Noahide elect to voluntarily circumcise himself? This is the topic of our lesson.

## Talmud Sanhedrin 59b

Sanhedrin 59b discusses in detail the relevance of circumcision to Abraham, his household, and his descendants. The following summary is based upon Sanhedrin 59b and its commentaries.

Genesis 17:10 – 13 states:

> *This is My covenant that you shall keep between Me,* **you,** *and* **your offspring after you:** *every male* **among you** *shall be circumcised. You shall be circumcised in the flesh of your foreskin and it shall be a token of the covenant between Me and you. He* **among you** *that is eight days old shall be circumcised, every male throughout* **your** *generations that is* **born in your house** *... He that is born in your house... must be circumcised; and My covenant shall be in your flesh for an everlasting covenant.*

The Torah is very specific in commanding circumcision only to Abraham, his household, and his offspring. In the first generation of this commandment, it applied only to Abraham, Isaac, and Ishmael. However, Genesis 21:12 later states:

> *Whatever Sarah tells you, heed her voice, since through Isaac will your offspring considered yours.*

We see that only Isaac and his offspring were, in distinction to Ishmael, considered heirs to Abraham's spiritual legacy. Therefore, circumcision was only obligatory for the descendants of Isaac. Similarly, Isaac said to Jacob:

*And God will give to you and your descendants the blessings of Abraham.*[1]

We see from here that God designated Jacob, not Esau, as the heir to the Abrahamic legacy of which circumcision was the sign. Those descendants of Jacob/Israel are the Jewish people of today.

## The Descendants of Keturah/Hagar

The Torah states:

*Vayosef Abraham and took a wife whose name was **Keturah**.*[2]

The Midrash[3] and Torah commentaries[4] note two anomalies in this verse. The first is the word *Vayosef*, which is a strange construction for introducing marriage, implying "gathering in" or "adding."[5] Furthermore, Keturah is not a proper name, but a title meaning "restrained" or "controlled." Some commentaries also interpret the name as a reference to *ketores*, incense, meaning that she and her deeds were pleasing. The Midrash explains that Abraham remarried Hagar, taking her again as his wife. Hagar had remained faithful to Abraham, reconciling with him following the death of Sarah.

Abraham and Hagar produced six children from this union (see Gen. 25:2). The commentaries explain that these children and their descendants were obligated in circumcision. After all, they were born into Abraham's home and, unlike Ishmael and Esau, were never actually excluded from the command of circumcision.[6]

The descendants of these children eventually intermarried with the descendants of Ishmael to the point that they are indistinguishable from the Ishmaelites.

---

[1] Gen. 28:4.

[2] Gen. 25:1.

[3] *Tanchuma* 5; *Bereshis Rabbah* 61:4.

[4] *Rashi*; *Ramban*; many others to this verse.

[5] See *Targumim*.

[6] See the *Malbim* and *Zohar* who discuss the differences between Ishmael and these siblings.

Therefore, the modern Ishmaelites, those of paternal Arab ancestry, are obligated in circumcision.[7] Maimonides summarizes the Talmud's conclusions in *Hilchos Melachim* 10:7-8:

> *§7 Only Abraham and his descendants were commanded in circumcision, as Genesis 17:9-10 states: "Keep My covenant, you and your offspring... you shall circumcise every male." The descendants of Ishmael are excluded by Genesis 21:12: "It is through Isaac, that your offspring will be called." Esau's descendants are also excluded, for Isaac told Jacob in Genesis 28:4: "May God grant Abraham's blessing to you and your descendants," implying that only he is the true offspring of Abraham who maintained his faith and his righteous behavior. Thus, they alone are obligated in circumcision.*
>
> *§8 Our Sages related that the descendants of Keturah, who are the offspring of Abraham that came after Isaac and Ishmael, are also obligated in circumcision. At present, the descendants of Ishmael have become intermingled with the descendants of Keturah. Therefore, they are all obligated to be circumcised on the eighth day.*

## May A Noahide Voluntarily Undergo Circumcision?

The Talmud teaches:

*Rabbah Bar Bar Chanaha said in the name of Rabbi Yochanan: a ger toshav who allows 12 months to pass without circumcising himself is like any other idolater. [The Sages responded:] That is in a case when he vowed to circumcise himself and failed to do so.*[8]

Explanation: this case is of a non-Jew who, when accepting the seven Noahide laws to become a *ger toshav*, voluntarily vows to circumcise himself. If he hasn't done so after 12 months, we assume that his vow was insincere. If he was insincere at the time of his vow, we must also doubt his sincerity in accepting the Noahides laws.[9]

We learn a number of things from this passage. For one, it appears that a *ger toshav* may circumcision himself. We also see that circumcision is voluntary – a *ger toshav* is certainly not obligated to circumcise himself.

---

[7] The minimum of circumcision required to fulfill this commandment is different than for Jews. While Jews must remove the entire foreskin, the Bnei Keturah fulfill this mitzvah with the removal of the outer foreskin. See *Shaagas Aryeh*; *Minchas Chinuch* 2.

[8] Avodah Zarah 65a.

[9] See commentaries to *Avodah Zarah* ibid.

Maimonides writes in his discussion of *ger toshav*:

> **Anyone** *who agrees to circumcise himself and allows twelve months to pass without doing so is considered an idolater.* [10]

In contradistinction to the rest of the section, Maimonides applies the Talmud's statement to "**anyone**." Shall we understand this to mean that the Talmud's statement is not unique to *ger toshav*, but applies to any non-Jew who accepts the Noahide laws? If it applied to "anyone," even modern Noahides, then who exactly "considers him an idolater?"

Also, when is this "vow to circumcise himself" made? Is it connected to the acceptance of the obligation of the Noahide laws, or is it talking about any religiously motivated circumcision? Perhaps, we are reading too much into Maimonides. Perhaps "anyone" should be read in context, meaning any *ger toshav*. Even in this case, though, it may be that circumcision is permitted to any Noahide.

Each possibility leads to a variety of possible conclusions that we will summarize shortly.

## Possibly Prohibited?

Rabbenu Yerucham[11] *paskened*, decided, that it is prohibited to circumcise a non-Jew for any reason other than conversion to Judaism. The Rama agrees and cites this as the *halacha*, law, in the Shulchan Aruch.[12] Additionally, we note that a Jew may circumcise a non-Jew for medical purposes.[13] Taking these two *halachos* together, it appears that a Jew is precluded from circumcising a Noahide for religious purposes. Yet, if Noahides may practice circumcision (as the Talmud certainly implies), then why would it be prohibited for Jews to assist them?

The *poskim* who come after the Rama are very uncertain as to the reason for this law and details of its application. Indeed, it poses a number of contradictions to other statements in the Talmud and *poskim*.[14] It is possible that the source is from

---

[10] *Hilchos Melachim* 8:10.

[11] In his *Toldos Adam VeChavah*, cited in *Bais Yosef* at the end of YD 266.

[12] *Yoreh Deah* 263:5.

[13] See *Avodah Zarah* 26b with the comments of the *Chiddushei HaRitva*, *Rashi*, and *Tosafos*. See *Otzar HaBris* I p.59 in the *Ohalei Shem*. *Shulchan Aruch* paskens such in YD 268:9.

[14] Many of the *nosei kelim* on *Shulchan Aruch*, both on YD 263:5 and 268:9, debate the reasons. The Taz holds that by assisting a non-Jew the Jew is nullifying circumcision as a sign of the covenant. This would present a basis for prohibiting Noahide circumcision. However, it is not clear that the

the *Zohar*,[15] which writes that Joseph sinned by encouraging the Egyptians to adopt circumcision. This was despite Joseph's intent being for the sake of heaven. However, it appears that these were forced circumcisions, which would be prohibited in any case.

## Conclusions

There does not appear to be any reason in Torah literature to assume that Noahides are prohibited from circumcising themselves. To the contrary, it appears that circumcision was a sign of commitment to the creator even before Abraham was commanded in it. After all, the Midrash[16] states that Adam, Shes, and Noah all came into the world circumcised, attaching special significance to this.

Furthermore, if there was a prohibition on Noahides practicing circumcision, then the prohibition would upon them, and not as a prohibition upon Jews against circumcising them.

It seems that the Talmud permits any Noahide to voluntarily circumcise himself. Maimonides, citing the Talmud, does so only for the issue of trusting a *ger toshav's* acceptance of the Noahide laws. There is no reason to assume that there should be any difference here between Noahides and *ger toshav*. There are further reasons to permit voluntary circumcision to Noahides that will be discussed in the live class.

It is possible to object to Noahide circumcision based on the prohibition against wounding oneself. However, it does not appear that voluntary circumcision would fall under this prohibition.[17]

Although Noahides may voluntarily circumcise themselves, using a Jewish doctor or *mohel*, circumciser, may present problems for the Jew.

---

Taz himself would oppose Noahide circumcision (this will be discussed in the live lesson). It is possible that this logic would have prohibited Noahide circumcision before matan Torah, yet not afterwards. See also Levush; Meil Tzedaka 14:2; Otzar HaBris ibid. for further discussion of the underlying reasons.

[15] *Miketz*.

[16] *Tanhuma Noach* 6:5.

[17] For perspectives on this issue, see *Panim Yafos* to *Lech Lecha*; *HaMikneh*, end of *Kiddushin*; *Glyoni Shas* (Engil) to Avodah Zarah 10b; *Meshech Chochmah Vayishlach* 34:22.

This is because of the prohibition of a Jew circumcising a gentile.[18] In such a case, the *mohel* or doctor may decline.

We will discuss practical aspects and reasons for voluntary Noahide circumcision more in the live lesson.

## Summary of This Lesson

1. Noahides have no obligation in circumcision.

2. However, those of paternal Arab ancestry may be obligated in circumcision because of being *Bnei Keturah*.

3. Voluntary circumcision appears permitted to Noahides for reasons that will be discussed in the live class.

4. However, there is a prohibition prohibiting a Jew from circumcising a non-Jew. The reasons for this prohibition are very unclear. However, it seems unrelated to the question of whether or not a Noahide may voluntarily undergo circumcision.

---

[18] Although it is possible to find room for leniency (especially based upon the *Shach*, however his views are problematic, as proven by the *nekudas hakesef*), most *poskim* are conservative. See *Shu"t Har Tzvi* YD 215; *Minchas Yitzchok* I:36.

# The Noahide Laws - Lesson Forty-Three

THE YESHIVA PIRCHEI SHOSHANIM SHULCHAN ARUCH PROJECT

© **Yeshiva Pirchei Shoshanim 2017**
This shiur may not be reproduced in any
form without permission of the copyright holder.

## Table of Contents:

1. Introduction
2. Possibilities
3. Definitions
4. Possible Torah Hints
    a. Adam
    b. Shechem
    c. Shimon & Levi
5. The Rishonim
    a. Rashi
    b. The Rosh
6. The Acharonim
    a. Chasam Sofer
    b. The Gaon of Rogatchov
7. Maimonides?
8. Age of Obligation for Women
9. Conversion of a Minor
10. Bar Chiyuv
11. Summary

# Lifecycle VI: Growing Up

## Introduction

No system of law can hold liable a person who is incapable of understanding or learning what the law expects of him. Naturally, a child too young to comprehend God's expectations of him cannot be bound by those expectations However, there is a point in a child's development when he becomes aware of right, wrong, rules, and the nature of divine obligation. This would be the "age of obligation," the point at which he becomes bound by the Noahide laws. Determining this age is very important not only for understanding the application of the laws, but also for the education of the young.

As with abortion, this is a question that has generated a tremendous amount of literature, particularly among the Acharonim. The discussion is complicated and far reaching, having ramifications for both Jews and Non-Jews.

## Possibilities

Torah literature discusses at length how to determine the age of obligation for the *mitzvos*. Is the standard of maturity determined purely by intellectual development? Or, perhaps, maturity requires both intellectual and physical signs of maturity? We know that it cannot be based on physical development alone, because this would completely disregard the importance of comprehension. Or, could it be that physical development and mental development go hand in hand?

## Definitions

The Torah literature notes it is the way of the world for boys to have begun biological maturity by age 13 and girls by age 12. These ages create a dividing line between two statuses:

- **Katan** – a "minor." A *katan* is one who is under the age of 13 for a boy and 12 for a girl.

- **Gadol** – an "adult." A *Gadol* is one over 13 if male or 12 if female.

## Possible Torah Hints

**Adam**

*When Adam received the Noahide laws, he was not even one day old. This proves that even those younger than the biological ages of maturity are obligated in the laws.*

This possibility is proposed by the *Shoel UMaishiv*.[1] He attempts to prove that the age of obligation is based upon understanding and not any chronological age. However, this is not a convincing proof. We can certainly learn from this fact that chronological age is not the *only* determining factor for obligation in the Noahide laws. After all, Adam was created biologically mature and with full understanding. This only shows that one who is biologically and intellectually mature is obligated in the *mitzvos*. Perhaps we only consider a person to have reached this point once they are over 12 or 13? Perhaps understanding alone is not enough to obligate one in the *mitzvos*? This verse doesn't really tell us anything about age at all.

**Shechem**

*The residents of the city of Shechem were all put to the sword. Maimonides writes:*

> *The inhabitants of Shechem transgressed [by not establishing rule of law] and were executed.*[2]

*Maimonides is teaching us that all of the residents were executed, even the minors. We see that they were all held liable, and therefore, Noahides minors can be held liable for transgression of the Noahide laws.*

---

[1] *Tinyana* I:14.

[2] See *Melachim* 9:14.

This possibility is also cited by the *Shoel UMashiv*. However, Gen. 35:29 states that Shimon and Levi captured the *tapos* - the "young ones" – of Shechem. We see that it *cannot* be assumed that minors were executed Shechem.[3]

**Shimon & Levi**

*Shimon and Levi… each ish [man] took his sword…*[4]

This verse uses the term *ish*, meaning an "adult man," to refer to Shimon and Levi. According to the chronology of the Torah, Levi would have been 13 at the time. This would make him the youngest person to be called an "adult man" in the Torah. In his commentary on the Talmud, Rashi[5] writes that this this verse establishes 13 as the age of maturity and, therefore, obligation in the *mitzvos*. Rashi repeats this opinion in several of his other commentaries.[6] Rashi appears to understand 13 as a natural benchmark for both biological and intellectual maturity.

[Editor's Note: Rashi could have also cited Gen. 25:27, which states *vayigdlu haNaarim,* "and the youths became adults," referring to Yaakov and Esav. According to Torah chronology, Yaakov and Esav would have been 13 years old at that time. This verse is a stronger proof than Gen. 34:25. We know from Rashi's commentary to Gen. 25:27 that he was certainly aware of the verse's implications. I am uncertain why he preferred Gen. 34:25 in his commentary to the Talmud.]

## The Rishonim

There are two opinions in the Rishonim as to the age of obligation: Rashi (which we have already seen) and the Rosh. The differences between their positions have far reaching consequences both for Jews and for Noahides and are the subject of a lot of Acharonic writings.

**Rashi**

Rashi understands the Torah as stating a natural fact: 13 is a developmental benchmark age at which one enters the beginning of physical and mental maturity. Both are required for one to be fully obligated in the *mitzvos*.

However, Rashi's view is not without weaknesses:

---

[3] This and other rebuttals to the *Shoel UMaishiv* are brought in the *Sdei Chemed* II:85:1.

[4] Genesis 34:25.

[5] To *Nazir* 29b.

[6] See Rashi to *Avos* 5:21 and to Sanhedrin 69b.

- It does not establish the minimum age of adulthood for females, only for males (this will be discussed more at the end of the lesson).

- It only says that a male of 13 is an adult, it doesn't tell us that one under 13 is not an adult. it is possible that a 12 year old is an adult!

**Rabbeinu Asher ben Yechiel – The Rosh**

Perhaps because of these difficulties, the Rosh took a different approach. The Rosh[7] writes that the ages of obligation for girls and boys are *halachos lemoshe misinai*- they are part of the rules of interpretation of the Torah communicated at Sinai and are not necessarily mentioned in the text of the Torah.

The Rosh adds a further point that directly affects Noahides. All measures and amounts for liability and obligations in the *mitzvos* are part of a family of *halachos, laws,* called *shiurim,* literally "amounts." These laws define, for example, how much non-Kosher meat a Jew must eat to be liable for punishment. Noahides, we know for a fact, were never commanded in *shiurim*.[8] Since the Rosh holds that the ages of 12 and 13 for Jewish liability are *shiurim,* they do not apply to Noahides at all, only to Jews.

If 12 and 13 are not benchmarks for Noahides, then how would the Rosh determine the age of obligation for Noahides? In his Tosafos to Sanhedrin 69b, the Rosh writes that prior to Sinai an 8 year-old who manifested signs of puberty would be considered an *ish,* man. This implies that the Rosh bases pre-Sinaitic obligation upon physical signs of maturity alone.[9]

However, the *Chavatzeles HaSharon*[10] writes that the Rosh may mean to say that the early onset of puberty only defines one as an *ish,* "man," from a biological standpoint. The Rosh holds that actual obligation in the *mitzvos* requires further mental development.

This point from the *Chavatzeles HaSharon* illuminates what may be the central issue dividing the positions of Rashi and the Rosh: a fundamental disagreement as to how to understand the word *ish,* "man," in the Torah.

---

[7] *Teshuvos* 16:1.

[8] This is the consensus of the *poskim* based on Maimonides, *Hilchos Melachim* 9:9.

[9] The Rosh implies this also in *Tos. HaRosh* to *Yevamos* 12b.

[10] to Gen. 34:25. *Chavatzeles HaSharon*, by Rav Mordechai Carlebach, is an acclaimed commentary on the Torah that discusses many *halachic* issues via the weekly *parhsa*.

Does *ish* imply the beginning of overall maturity (meaning one is a *gadol*), or only physical maturity (meaning one is only an *ish*, not a *gadol*)? Rashi understands *ish* as the former, yet the Rosh appears to understand *ish* as the latter.

**The Ramifications for Noahides**

- **RASHI** - If the *halacha*, practical law, is like the Rashi then the age of 13 should be the age of obligation for Noahide as well as Jewish men (will discuss women soon).

- **ROSH** - If the *halacha* is like the Rosh, then the ages of 12 and 13 are not relevant to Noahides. Obligation is determined by comprehension alone and is not connected to physical or chronological benchmarks.

## The Acharonim

The most important *posek* to discuss the question was the <u>Chasam Sofer, Rav Moshe Schreiber (Sofer)</u>.

***Chasam Sofer, Shu"t YD 317***

Rav Moshe was asked to rule on the sale of a Jew's cow to a non-Jew. At the time, the Jew thought that the Non-Jew was at least a teenager. It turned out that the boy was a very big 9 year-old! Was the sale valid? The *Chasam Sofer* follows the Rosh, concluding that the boy was of mature enough mind and understanding that the sale was valid.[11]

The <u>Shoel UMeishiv</u>[12] and <u>Minchas Chinuch</u>[13] also uphold the Rosh in their writings.[14]

The *Chasam Sofer's* precedent aside, many other <u>Acharonim</u> identified fundamental difficulties with the Rosh:

- The Rosh's assumption that age of majority is included in *shiurim*, "measures" is questionable.[15] **[Editor's note: The reasons this is**

---

[11] *Shu"t Chasam Sofer YD 317.*

[12] Ibid.

[13] 190:8; 26:17; 34:8.

[14] The *Chasam Sofer's* reliance on the Rosh, however, is difficult to resolve against the *Talmud Nazir 62b*. See *Minchas Chinuch 26* and <u>Ohr Somayach</u> *Issurei Biah 3:2* and in his novellae to *Nazir* for possible resolutions.

questionable are complex and involve issues of advanced Torah learning. Consider this question: By all other *shiurim* we have a concept of *chatzi shiur assur min ha-Torah*, but by the *shiur gadlus* there is no *chiyuv* of *chatzi shiur*, only a *d'rabbaon* of *chinuch* on the parents! If *chatzi shiur* has no *chalos* by *shiur gadlus*, then *shiur gadlus* is obviously not comparable to other *shiurim she-nasan bi-Sinai*. This remarkable insight is from HaRav HaGaon Asher Weiss, Shlit"a.]

- That the ages of 12 and 13 are divinely ordained and completely independent of biological benchmarks is not correct. Biological and developmental factors do impact, to a degree, the determination of the age of obligations for Jews.[16]

- Why would the Jewish obligation be tied to the ages of 12 and 13 and not to developmental factors, while the opposite would apply to Noahides? Is this is a situation of Noahide law being more stringent than Jewish law?

- There is significant evidence that Maimonides understands the age of obligation like Rashi and not the Rosh.

**Tzafnas Paneach, the Gaon of Rogatchov**

The famed Gaon of Rogatchov, Rav Yosef Rosen, had serious questions on the Rosh's opinion. In his responsa,[17] the Rogatchover held against the Rosh in favor of Rashi. He held that 13 and 12 are the ages of obligation for Noahides as well as for Jews.

---

[15] *Toras Ben Noach* 9:49; *Minchas Asher Bamidber* 6 concedes that when Maimonides wrote that Noahides were not commanded in *shiurim*, he may only have intended food related prohibitions. (this is a very difficult conclusion to uphold, though). However, Rav Weiss adduces further proof that these aged are not *shiurim* in his *Kovetz Darkhei Horaah* 11. Similar conclusions can be reached from Chemdas Yisrael 38. See also *Shut Minchas Chaim* I:10; *Shu"t Bris Yaakov* OC 21.

[16] The relationship of developmental factors to the age of obligation is much easier to understand according to Rashi. Nevertheless, it is a much-discussed topic. See *Shitta Mekubetzes* to *Bava Metzia* 56b; *Kovetz Shiruim Pesachim* 2; *Tzafnas Paneach Ishus* 2:9; *Maharit* I:1. See also *Shut Minchas Chaim* I:10; *Shu"t Bris Yaakov OC 21* for discussion of this question according to the Rosh, specifically.

[17] *Shu"t Tzafnas Paneach* 101.

## Maimonides?

Is it possible to know what any other Rishonim held besides the Rosh and Rashi? What about Maimonides? Maimonides has been argued both ways - as supporting the Rosh or Rashi. However, the arguments that he supports the Rosh are, at best, only inferred (see examples from the *Shoel UMaishiv* quoted at the beginning of this lesson).

Many later Acharonim have made a strong argument that Maimonides holds like Rashi. Maimonides writes:

*A child, from the time of his birth until the age of 13 is called a **katan, a minor.**[18]*

At the end of the same section where he makes this statement, he concludes:

*We have defined herein twenty terms [pertaining to the stages and ages of obligation]... Keep these terms in mind at all times; do not forget their meaning, so that their intent will not have to be explained whenever they are mentioned elsewhere.[19]*

And then later, in reference to the liabilities for transgressing the Noahide laws, Maimonides writes:

*In any case, a **katan, a minor**, is never punished for their transgression.[20]*

This chain of statements indicates that Maimonides understood the age of obligation for Noahides to be 13, just as for Jews.[21]

The *Sdei Chemed*, *Rav Ovadia Yosef*,[22] and many other *poskim* have noted this.

## Age of Obligation for Women

If the *Halacha* follows Rashi, and we assume that the age of obligation of 13 for men is the result of developmental reality, then from where do we know the age of obligation for girls? Knowing that obligation is based on the age at which physical

---

[18] Ishus 2:10.

[19] Ibid. 2:27.

[20] Melachim 10:2.

[21] The Sdei Chemed ibid.

[22] Yabia Omer II YD 17.

and intellectual maturity are assumed to have begun, we can assume this age is slightly earlier for girls as is such way of the world.

The Talmud says explicitly that women reach maturity earlier than men, using this fact to establish the age of 12 as the age of obligation for women.[23]

## Conversion of a Minor

It is beyond the scope of this course, but the position of the Rosh runs counter to *halachic* practice for the conversion of minors to Judaism. The *Halacha* is that a minor is not considered mature enough to accept the mitzvos as required in the conversion process. Therefore, their conversion is only conditional, not taking full effect until the boy or girl turns 12 or 13. If a Noahide is considered a *halachic* adult even at an earlier age, then why should their acceptance not be considered valid? Doubt as to the validity of a minor's acceptance of the mitzvos could create serious problems should the child decide to reject their "conditional" conversion as an adult. On account of these issues, the Ritva, commenting on the laws of conversion,[24] adopts Rashi's approach. We will discuss this issue more in the live lesson.

## Noahide *Bar Chiyuv*

Whether we hold like the Rosh or Rashi, all would agree that age 12 or 13 is an important milestone because all agree that a boy or girl is fully obligated in the Noahide laws at this point in his or her life. As such, it makes sense to celebrate it as a milestone that involves formal acceptance of the Noahide laws.

## Summary of the Lesson

1. Rashi holds that the age of obligation is based upon the age at which we assume that one has begun his transition to adulthood both biologically and intellectually.

---

[23] See Niddah 45b and commentaries there. It is possible that this presents a further difficulty to the Rosh.

[24] *Chiddushim* to Kesubos 11.

2. This is not a legal, but a physical and developmental reality. For boys the age is 13, for girls, 12.

3. Since this is stated before the giving of the Torah, it should apply equally to Noahides. This is a statement of reality, not of law or *mitzvah*.

4. The Rosh holds that development is irrelevant for Jews; the ages are divinely ordained. According to the Rosh, before Sinai the age of obligation would be based on the intellectual development of the individual.

5. Although there are a few *poskim* who rule like the Rosh, the Rosh's opinion is rife with problems.

6. Nevertheless, by age 13 or 12 a boy or girl is certainly a *bar Chiyuv*, obligated, according to all. This transition is a life event that, by logic, deserves to be marked somehow.

THE YESHIVA PIRCHEI SHOSHANIM SHULCHAN ARUCH PROJECT

# The Noahide Laws - Lesson Forty-Four

© **Yeshiva Pirchei Shoshanim 2017**
This shiur may not be reproduced in any
form without permission of the copyright holder.

164 Village Path, Lakewood NJ 08701 732.370.3344
164 Rabbi Akiva, Bnei Brak, 03.616.6340

THE YESHIVA PIRCHEI SHOSHANIM SHULCHAN ARUCH PROJECT
THE NOAHIDE LAWS | NOAHIDE LIFECYCLE VII | PARENTS | LESSON 44

# Table of Contents:

1. Introduction
2. Are Noahides Obligated in Honoring Parents?
3. Obligated From Another Source?
4. *Mitzvos Muskalos* – Logically Compelled *Mitzvos*
5. Mitzvos Muskalos – Obligation or Liability?
6. Honoring Parents as a Logical *Mitzvah*
7. The Commandment is Only to Honor One's Parents
8. Anthology of the Laws of Honoring Parents
9. Summary

# Lifecycle VII: Growing Up

## Introduction

In the Torah we learn that G-d has expectations on certain relationships. There are mitzvos that set certain boundaries for the relationships between man and woman, king and subjects, and rabbis and students. One of the most important relationships is between a child and his parents. We know that the Torah commands Jews to honor their fathers and mothers. What does the Torah expect for Noahides? Are Noahides obligated in this mitzvah as well? This question is the topic of this lesson.

## Are Noahides Obligated in *Kibbud Av VeEim*, Honoring Parents?

It is clear that Noahides are not obligated in the *mitzvah* of *kibbud av ve-eim*, honoring one's father and mother, as stated Exodus 20:12 and Deuteronomy 5:16.

Four places in the Talmud discuss the Noahide relationship to this commandment:

- Sanhedrin 56b & Bechoros 8b

    *The Israelites accepted ten mitzvos at Marah[1] — the seven commanded to Noah, plus the additional, new mitzvos of Shabbos, civil laws, and honoring one's father and mother.*

    The Talmud separates the commandments of Shabbos, civil laws, and honoring one's parents from the universal, Noahide laws. This means that these commandments are specific to Jews alone.

- Kiddushin 31a

    *Asked Rabbi Eliezer: "What is the extent of kibud av ve-eim, honoring one's parents?" They replied, "Go and observe the behavior of a certain Non-Jew in Ashkelon named Dama ben Nesinah. The sages requested of him certain precious stones for the ephod[2] for 60,000. The key to the chest where the stones were kept rested under his father's pillow. He refused to disturb his father's sleep in order to retrieve the key. The following year, he was rewarded with a red heifer.[3]" Rav Chaninah said: "We see the reward of one who is **not commanded** and does, just imagine then the reward of one who is commanded and does!"*

    This passage states that Dama ben Nesinah's observance of this *mitzvah* was voluntary. Therefore, he could not have been obligated in the commandment.

- **Nazir 61a** - Rashi and Tosafos point out the Talmud's implicit assumption is that Noahides are not obligated in honoring their fathers and mothers.

## Obligated In Honoring Parents From Another Source?

Although the Torah verses explicitly mentioning honoring parents do not apply to Noahides, this does not mean that Noahides are not obligated in this *mitzvah*.

---

[1] See Exodus 15:26 which refers to commandments given at Marah. The Talmud *ad loc.* and in many other places derives which *mitzvos* the Torah is referring to.

[2] One of the priestly vestments.

[3] The value of a red heifer (see Numbers 19) was far more than the jewels.

As we mentioned in earlier lessons, Noahides may observe any *mitzvah* that is compelled by logic. According to most *poskim*, however, observance of these "logical commandments" is obligatory.

## Mitzvos Muskalos – Logically Compelled Mitzvos

Rav Nissim Gaon writes:[4]

*Regarding all those mitzvos that depend on reason and the nature of the heart, all are* **already obligating** *in them from the time God created man and for all generations that follow.*

Additionally, Rav Saadia Gaon explains that all men, Jews and Noahides, are compelled by force of reason to do good and to pray for their needs.[5]

Most *poskim* agree that Noahides are obligated in logically compelled *mitzvos*. However, we have to determine the nature of this obligation.

## Mitzvos Muskalos – an Obligation or a Liability?

It is not entirely accurate to say that Noahides are "obligated" in logically compelled *mitzvos*. It is more accurate to say that Noahides are "liable" for the logical *mitzvos*. What is the difference between "obligated" and "liable?"

We are taught that the city of Sodom was destroyed primarily for nullifying the practice of charity and encouraging rampant cruelty.[6] Rav Avraham Grodzinski in his **Toras Seichel HaEnoshi** notes that Sodom was not punished for insufficient charity, but only for actively rejecting the concept of charity.[7]

It appears from Sodom (and many other examples) that Noahides are only liable for punishment for actively and communally rejecting *mitzvos* compelled by logic, yet not for failing to be proactive in the performance of such *mitzvos*.[8] The active

---

[4] In his introduction to the Talmud found in Tractate Brachos.

[5] *Emunah VeDeos* III:1.

[6] Sanhedrin 104b.

[7] The *Toldos Noach, Matza Chein* I: 54:2 discusses this at length.

[8] Again, see the extensive discussion in the *Toldas Noach*, ibid.

performance of such *mitzvos* is entirely voluntary, though. One may even elect to perform such *mitzvos* according to the Jewish details of the *mitzvah*.[9]

## Honoring Parents as a Logical *Mitzvah*

The *Sefer Ha-Chinuch*[10] says in no uncertain terms that honoring one's parents is, first and foremost, a logically compelled *mitzvah*. He writes:

> *It is appropriate for a person to recognize and do kindness with those who have done so for him. One should not act as a degenerate, alienating [those who have helped him] and being ungrateful, for this is a bad and completely repulsive trait before both God and man. One should remember that his father and mother are the cause of him being in this world. Therefore, in truth, he should accord them all due respect and benefit, for they brought him into this world.*

The **Sefer Ha-Chinuch** further explains that honoring one's parents is a means by which one comes to recognize and appreciate the good that The Holy one does for him. Similarly, our sages have taught other parallels between honoring parents and honoring God:

> *It is said "**Honor** your father and your mother" (Ex. 20:12) and "**Honor** the Lord..." (Prov. 3; 9). Thus the Torah equates the honor due to parents to the honor due to God. It is also said "Every man must **revere** his mother and father and keep my Shabbat, I am the Lord Your God" (Lev. 19:3). It is also said "The Lord your God shall you **revere**" (Deut. 13:4). The Torah compares the reverence of parents to the reverence for God. It is said "He who curses his father or mother **shall surely be put to death**" (Ex. 21:17) and it is also said "Whoever curses his God **shall bear his sin**" (Lev. 24:15). Thus the Torah is equating cursing parents to cursing God... This equation makes sense because of the three are partners in creating an individual. Our Rabbis have taught: There are three partners in creating a person: God, a father, and a mother. When a person honors his father and his mother, God says. "I credit them as if I dwelled among them!" A Tanna said before Rab Nachman: "When a person curses his father and mother, God says 'I did right in not dwelling among them, for had I dwelt among them they would have cursed me too!'"*[11]

---

[9] As discussed in earlier lessons.

[10] 33

[11] Kiddushin 30b -31a.

## The Commandment is Only to Honor One's Parents

It is interesting to note that the *mitzvah* is to honor one's parents and not to love them or have any other emotional obligation to them. As the *Chinuch* has written, we are compelled to honor our parents because of a basic, human obligation to show gratitude. This point doesn't imply that one shouldn't love his parents, but only that it is not the same as honoring one's parents.

Unfortunately, many people do not have comfortable relationships with their parents. Nevertheless, their feelings do not change what God expects of them. It is important to remember that the Torah's ideal for both Jewish and Non-Jewish society is that it is obligation-based, not rights-based. A parent has no rights to a child's respect. Rather, the child has an obligation to show respect to his parent. This obligation does not come from the parent, but is a divine expectation from God himself.

For a person whose parental relationships are strained, it may be hard, taking even herculean effort to honor them properly. The more effort it takes, though, the more precious is the *mitzvah* on high.

However, the obligation to honor one's parent is mitigated if the relationship between parent and child is abusive or otherwise pernicious to one's self or one's family. In such a case, one should seek rabbinic as well as professional counseling.

## An Anthology of the Laws of Honoring Parents

**Training Children in the *Mitzvah***

- Parents should not be demanding of respect or honor. Any parent who insists, demanding his child's honor, will ultimately alienate his children and be despised by them. Rather, a parent should be forgiving, overlooking occasional slights. He should train his children gently, and not insist that the children honor him, but their mother. Likewise, a mother should teach the children to honor the father.[12]

---

[12] *Shulchan Aruch* Y.D. 240:19.

- Similarly, when speaking to a child a parent should never command him or order him about. Instead, a parent should speak pleasantly: "Do you mind getting me…." or "Would it be possible for you to…"[13]

- Parents may absolve their children of the duty to honor them.[14]

- A child who wants to honor a parent despite the parent having absolved him is praised and fulfills a *mitzvah*.[15]

- Although a parent can forego his honor, it appears that he may not allow a child to actively insult or abuse him.[16]

**Father vs. Mother**

- If one's father and mother ask for something at the same time, the father's needs take precedence.

- If one's parents are divorced and both request a task at the same time, the child may choose whose request he wishes to fulfill first.[17]

**Husband vs. Parent**

- It appears that a married woman's obligations to her husband take precedent over those to her parents.[18]

**In Laws**

- It is appropriate to show honor to one's in-laws as well.[19] One's actual parents, however, take precedence.

**Step Parents**

- Children are obligated to honor their father's wife, even if she isn't their mother, as long as the father is living. Doing so is a way of honoring their father.

- Likewise, they are obligated to honor their mother's husband, even if he isn't their father, as long as their mother is living.

---

[13] *Sefer Kibud Av V'Eim, ha'arah* 46.

[14] *Shulchan Aruch Y.D.* 240:19.

[15] *Shu"t RadVaz* 524.

[16] *She'iltos Parshas Mishpatim, She'Ilta 60 im He'emek Sh'eila*.

[17] *Shulchan Aruch Y.D.* 240:14. See *Nosei Keilim Sham*.

[18] *Shulchan Aruch Y.D.* 240:17 and *Shach*.

[19] *Shulchan Aruch Y.D.* 240:24

- Although there is no obligation to honor a step-parent after the passing of the parent, it is still a praiseworthy thing to do.[20]

**Grandparents**

- There are many diverse opinions as to how the obligation of honoring one's parents applies to grandparents. It is clear that honoring one's own parents takes precedence. However, in a case where parents and grandparents are all in one room, then the grandfather's needs take precedence over one's father's needs.[21]

**Sitting in a Parent's Place**

- If one's father or mother has a designated spot to stand for certain gatherings or for regular prayers, it is forbidden for a child to stand in that spot.[22]

- A child may not sit in a place in the home that is designated for a parent to sit. Standing in the place that a parent sits, however, is permitted.[23]

- If a parent has a specific chair (not a specific place, but a particular piece of furniture) it is prohibited to sit in it, even if it is moved out of its usual place. One stand on a parent's chair for a moment for a specific purpose (i.e. in order to change a light bulb).[24]

- It appears uncertain as to whether the practices regarding a parent's seat apply also to the parents sleeping place. Once should ask a parent before sleeping in their bed.[25]

- Should a child (or son-in-law) take his father into his home to live with his family, there is no obligation for the father to be seated at the head of the table. Rather the son (or son in law) may keep his seat at the head of the table as head of the household. Nevertheless, his father should be seated beside him.

---

[20] *Shulchan Aruch* Y.D. 240:21

[21] *Shu"t Teshuva M'Ahava* 178.

[22] *Aruch HaShulchan Yoreh Deah* 240:9

[23] *Shulchan Aruch* Y.D. 240:2

[24] *Pischei Teshuva*. Y.D. 240:16.

[25] *Taz* to Y.D. 240.

- Some people have the custom, when their father or father in law comes for a visit, of seating the father at the head of the table and allowing him to lead the meals. This is a custom that is greatly praised because it sets a precedent for the children and grandchildren who are present.

- However, when the food is served one's parents should be served first even though the son or-son-in-law is the head of the household.[26]

### Standing for One's Parents

- Children are obligated to stand for their parents when they enter a room. The custom is to do so once during the day and once during the night.

- If a parent is blind, there is still an obligation to rise when he enters the room. Honoring one's parents does not depend on the parent being aware of the honor.[27]

### A Sleeping Parent

- A child may not awaken a sleeping parent.

- However, if the reason is to prevent a monetary loss or some other direct benefit the parent will appreciate, the child should wake his parent.

- Similarly, one may awaken a parent for the sake of a *mitzvah*.[28]

### Referring to a Parent by Name

- One may not refer to or address a parent by first name; rather a parent must be referred to as "my father," "my mother," "Dad," "Mom," etc.[29] This rule even applies to a deceased parent.[30]

---

[26] *Aruch HaShulchan* YD 240:11

[27] Rav Akiva Eiger to *Shulchan Aruch* Y.D. 240:7.

[28] *Chayei Adam* 67:11

[29] *Shulchan Aruch* Y.D. 240:2.

[30] *Kesef Mishna Hilchos Mamrim* 6:3.

## Speaking to & Contradicting a Parent

- One should speak to his parents softly and with respect. Imagine how one would speak to a king.[31]

- It is prohibited to contradict a parent.[32]

- If a parent has a verbal disagreement with another person, and the child says to the other person "I concur with your view," it is considered contradicting the parent and is prohibited.[33]

- According to some *poskim* this prohibition is only in the presence of the parent. Other *poskim*, however, maintain that even not in the presence of the parent it is prohibited.[34]

- If the issue is a Torah discussion and the child has clear proofs against his parent, many *poskim* allow the son to contradict the father, even in his presence (albeit he must do so respectfully).[35]

- If the parent asks the child for his or her input, there is no prohibition in giving it.[36]

- If a parent does or says something that is against the Torah, the child should not say "You transgressed a Torah prohibition", as not to cause the parent embarrassment. Rather, the child should say something to the effect of: "Does it not say in the Torah one should not…." in a way that sounds like a question and not rebuke. Allow the parent to realize on his own that he has made an error.

## Caring for Ill or Elderly Parents

- A child must take responsibility for the care of an elderly or ill parent. He must ensure that they have food, drink, and appropriate clothing. One should also endeavor to arrange for the parents transportation as needed.

---

[31] *Sefer Chareidim Perek* 12 (4 in older editions).

[32] *Shulchan Aruch* Y.D. 240:2.

[33] *Shach. YD* 240:2.

[34] *Shach, Taz* ibid. *Biur HaGra* 240:3.

[35] *Chazon Ish. Even HaEzer* 47 d.h. *V'lo soser es devarav.*

[36] *Aruch HaShulchan* 242:23.

Ideally, one should tend to these matters personally.[37]

- One should tend to his parent's needs with a pleasant approach, without making it appear as a burden. Even if one provides his parent wit the finest food and luxury, yet does so in ill temper, he receives heavenly punishment.[38]

- Although a child is obligated to ensure the parent's needs are met, the cost of doing so does not need to be entirely borne by the child. The child may use the parent's money.

- If the parents cannot afford food, and the child can afford food, the child must to pay for this food. Courts are empowered, from the standpoint of Noahide law, to compel a child to do so.

- The obligation to provide for parents is divided amongst all the children proportionate to their respective means. If some of the siblings are poor, the obligation to provide needs for the parents falls only on those who can bear it.

- Irrespective of monetary or material support, a child is obligated to personally do things that are requested of him his parent, even it is will indirectly cause him monetary loss (it is unlikely that Noahides have to go to this extent).

- Tending to a parent's needs take precedence over another positive *mitzvah*. If there is time to tend to both, the parent should be taken care of first.[39]

- If one's parent is insane or is otherwise incapable of thinking intelligently, the child should try to treat the parent respectfully and attend to their needs as possible. Of course, one should hire professional care as needed.[40]

---

[37] *Shulchan Aruch Y.D.* 240:4.

[38] *Shulchan Aruch Y.D.* ibid.

[39] *Shulchan Aruch Y.D.* 240:12.

[40] *Shulchan Aruch Y.D.* 240:10.

- When caring for very ill or incapacitated parents, we must remember that out parents did the same for us when we were born. They cleaned us, bathing us, dressed us, etc. In the parent's illness or old age, it is now time for us to reciprocate. This is, indeed, the greatest expression of the logically compelling aspect of the *mitzvah*.

**Difficult Parents**

- The Talmud[41] and Shulchan Aruch[42] cite the following example:

    *If a son is dressed in finery and sitting at the head of a table presiding over a congregation and his mother or father approach him, tear his clothing, hit him on the head, and spit in his face, he should not retaliate or insult them. Instead, he should remain silent and fear the King of Kings who commanded him to do so.*

    The *poskim* debate the exact application of this idea. Most *poskim* rule that this only applies to a parent suffering from dementia, Alzheimer's or a similar condition, but does not apply to normal, healthy parents who should know and behave better.[43] Although one is not obligated to bear such insult if the parent is in full control of his faculties, it is praiseworthy nonetheless.

- According to those who hold that the above applies even to a well parent, one may take action to prevent his parent from creating such a public spectacle. However, they hold that once the attack starts, the child must bear it.[44]

- If a parent is a wicked or abusive to a child, most *poskim* indeed rule that the child need not suffer and take the abuse, and should defend themselves and rebuke the parent for their inexcusable actions. The child should do anything necessary to save himself from an abuse.

- If someone is in such a situation a Rabbi as well as a therapist should be consulted for the best course of action.

---

[41] Kidushin 31a.

[42] *Yoreh Deah Siman 240:3.*

[43] *Tosafos* to Kiddushin ibid. d.h. *U'bas imo.*

[44] *Yam Shel Shlomo Kidushin 31a. Siman 64.* at length.

## Summary of the Lesson

1. Noahides have no obligation in honoring parents from the versus of the Torah.

2. However, Noahides have an obligation from the side of *mitzvos muskalos* – logically compelled mitzvos.

3. "Obligated," is not the best term to use when describing these commandments. Rather, one is liable for avoiding such *mitzvos* on principle.

4. There is no obligation to love one's parents; only to honor them as an expression of gratitude. Therefore, even if one has a difficult relationship with his parents, he must strive to honor them anyway.

5. If a relationship is abusive, this obligation is mitigated.

THE YESHIVA PIRCHEI SHOSHANIM SHULCHAN ARUCH PROJECT

# The Noahide Laws - Lesson Forty-Five

© **Yeshiva Pirchei Shoshanim 2017**
This shiur may not be reproduced in any
form without permission of the copyright holder.

## Table of Contents:

1. Introduction
2. Spiritual vs. Physical Illness
    a. Sickness as an Impetus to Repentance & Self Betterment.
    b. Sickness is not only a message for the sick.
3. Visiting the Sick
4. Nature of the Mitzvah: Rabbinic or Biblical?
    a. Rabbinic?
    b. Biblical?
5. Spiritual Purpose of the Mitzvah
    a. Spiritual Purposes
    b. For the Patient
    c. For the Visitor
6. Practical Reasons for the Mitzvah
    a. Physical Needs
    b. Emotional Needs
7. Who is Called Sick?
8. Guidelines for Visiting the Sick
9. Summary

# Lifecycle VIII: Sickness

## Introduction

Sickness is as much a part of the human lifecycle as birth and death. In this lesson we will discuss the significance of illness and the special *mitzvah* of visiting those who are ill.

Visiting the sick is a positive *mitzvah* and an obligation for Jews. However, it is not part of the Noahide laws. Nevertheless, visiting the sick, for many reasons, is beneficial to society and logically compelling. Therefore, it is one of the *mitzvos hamuskalos* – the logically compelled *mitzvos* – that Noahides may adopt and practice even according to the details of the Jewish *mitzvos*.

Although the details of this *mitzvah* appear self-evident, they carry deep theological significance. In this lesson we will examine the origins of this *mitzvah* and the various details of its fulfillment.

## Spiritual vs. Physical Illness

The Talmud makes a fascinating statement regarding illness:

> *All illnesses are from heaven except for common colds.*[1]

The Talmud and commentaries explain that some illnesses are decreed from heaven while others are the result of simple negligence; failing to bundle up in the cold or over exerting oneself in the sun.

---

[1] This statement appears in many places. *Kesuvos 30a; Bava Metzia 107b*.

However, any illness that cannot be explained by negligence on the part of the aggrieved is the result of heavenly decree. For example:

> *No one so much as bruises a finger on Earth unless it was decreed against him in heaven.*[2]

**Illness as an Impetus for Repentance & Self Betterment**

While prayer is appropriate and helps for all sickness (even those a person may bring upon himself), it is of special importance for illnesses decreed by heaven. These maladies come upon a person as a "wake up call," an impetus for him to examine his deeds and relationship with God:

> *When a person sees that suffering has come upon him he should carefully examine his behavior.*[3]

and,

> *R' Alexandri said in the name of R. Chiya bar Abba that one who is sick cannot be healed unless he is first forgiven for all his sins.*[4]

and,

> *Rabbi Meir used to say: Two people take to their beds with the same illness. One recovers while the other does not. One prays and is answered; the other prays and is not. Why is one answered and the other not? Because this one prayed with true sincerity while the other did not.*[5]

One of the great Chassidic masters summed things up well: "A small hole in the body means a big hole in the soul."[6]

**Sickness is Not Only a Message for the Sick**

Not only should the ill individual examine his deeds and pray, but others should pray for him as well:

---

[2] *Chullin 7b.*

[3] *Brachos 5a.*

[4] *Nedarim 41a.*

[5] *Rosh HaShanah 18a.*

[6] Attributed to the Maggid of Mezritch.

> *If a person is sick for more than a day,*
> *he should let people know so that they will pray for him.*[7]

The prayers of the righteous are particularly important:

> *Someone who has a sick person in his house should go to*
> *a Sage and ask him to pray for him.*[8]

Prayer always helps, even when HaShem does not answer it with the outcome that we desire.

## Visiting the Sick

In many places in the Talmud and holy writings it is brought that we should endeavor to imitate the attributes of God.[9] One of the many attributes of God is that He visits his presence upon the sick. Genesis 18:1 records:

> *Now the Lord appeared to him [Avraham] in the plains of Mamre, as he was sitting at the*
> *entrance of the tent when the day was its hottest.*

The Talmud, *Bava Metzia 86a*, tells us that this this occurred on the third day after Avraham's circumcision, when his pain and discomfort was at its greatest.

God's appearance was a distinct and separate visitation from the appearance of the other three visitors. We know this because when the three visitors appear in verse 2, Abraham took leave of the Lord before tending to them:

> *And he said, "My lords, if only I have found favor in your eyes,*
> *please do not pass on from beside your servant.*[10]

Why did God appear to Abraham? This visitation seems superfluous in the context of the narrative. The Talmud and Midrash both explain that God visited Abraham to comfort him and inquire about his welfare.[11]

---

[7] *Brachos 55b.*

[8] *Bava Basra 116a.*

[9] *Sotah 14a, Bava Metzia 30a.*

[10] Gen. 18:3.

[11] Of course, God knows all; inquiring of Abraham's welfare was part of visiting him and providing comfort.

## Nature of the *Mitzvah*: Rabbinic or Biblical?

Is this a biblical or a rabbinic commandment for Jews? The answer to this question depends on the reason for the *mitzvah*.

**Rabbinic?** If the reason is that we are imitating the qualities of God, then all agree that the commandment is only Rabbinic in origin. The reason is the fact that God acts a certain way does not create a biblical obligation for us to act in the same way. Indeed, this is a dangerous approach to deriving *mitzvos*. After all, God can do whatever He wants while man is limited by His will. God can strike down, judge, and reward as He sees fit. Man, however, must obey God's laws even when we disagree with them or do not understand them. Even with positive *mitzvos*, God's behavior does not establish an obligatory biblical precedent for man. For example: Jews keep Shabbat because they were commanded to do so, not because the Torah tells us that God rested on the seventh day.

**Biblical?** Another possible reason for the *mitzvah* is that it may be included in a general *mitzvah* of *gemilus chasadim* – increasing or creating kindness in the world.[12] This view makes it a biblical commandment.[13]

The overwhelming opinion is that the specific *mitzvah* of visiting the sick and all its details are the result of rabbinic decree.[14] However, one does receive some biblical merit for kindnesses committed during the fulfillment of the *mitzvah*.

For Noahides, the *mitzvah* is compelled by the fact that it is a logical act of kindness that is beneficial to the individual and society. In any case, the *mitzvah* accomplishes many of the same purposes and goals as the Jewish rabbinic *mitzvah*.

## Spiritual Purpose of the *Mitzvah*

Visiting the sick is beneficial both practically and spiritually for the patient and the visitor.

---

[12] *Maharsha*, Nedarim 39b, d.h. biku.

[13] *Ran* to Brachos 3 holds this is a *d'oraisa*. See also *Rabbeinu Yonah*, Brachos 11b. Modern *poskim* who discuss the origins are the *Teshuvos VeHanhagos* 2:592; *Yabia Omer* YD III:22:23.

[14] *Kol Bo 112*; Maimonides, *Hilchos Avel 14:1*; *Tur* 33; *Levush* 1. *Maharatz Chayes* to Nedarim 39b curiously holds that it is a *halacha leMoshe miSinai*.

**Spiritual Purposes**

The Talmud in Tractate *Nedarim*[15] and elsewhere[16] learns that the *shechina*, divine presence, hovers above the head of one who is ill. In much the same manner that God visited Abraham, God continues to visit those who are ill.

**For the Patient**

Since illness is a form of atonement and an impetus for the patient's repentance, the *shechina* stands ready, as it were, to receive his prayers. However, as we saw above, others should pray for the patient as well. Therefore, one who visits the sick person should take the opportunity to pray and wish for the patient's recovery before the *shechina*.[17]

**For the Visitor**

It is important to realize that the sickness is not only for the patient. When a person takes ill, the message of his condition is intended for all those who know him. Therefore, for the visitor too, seeing one in the condition of suffering and atonement is meant to make an impression. The visitor should be moved to pray for his own health as well and to search his own deeds.[18]

## Practical Reasons for the *Mitzvah*

**Physical Needs**

A practical aspect of the *mitzvah* is making sure that the ill person has all of his physical needs taken care of: medical supplies, clothing, food, etc. For patients staying in a hospital, this is not the main focus of the *mitzvah* because the hospital staff is charged with taking care of these matters.[19]

**Emotional Needs**

Today, one of the most important aspects of visiting the sick is their emotional needs. Being sick is an emotionally as well as physically challenging situation. For

---

[15] 40a.

[16] *Levush* 3; *Kitzur Shulchan Aruch* 193:2; *Chochmas Adom* 151:2; *Aruch Hashulchan* 7; Refer to *Vayikra Rabbah* 34:1.

[17] According to many, this is the fundamental reason for the mitzvah. See, for example: *Toras HaAdam Shaar HaMichush* 1; *Kol Bo* 112; *Levush* 1 4; *Chochmas Adam* 151:3; *Kitzur Shulchan Aruch* 193:3; *Aruch HaShulchan*; *Igros Moshe* YD 4:1. According to many of these authorities, a Jew who visits a sick person but does not pray for him has not fulfilled his obligation. This is not speaking of one who fails to pray for the sick person in his presence; rather it is speaking of a person who does not pray at all for the patient. We must note that one may visit the person and pray for them later in another place.

[18] See *Toras HaMincha* 4 on *Vayeira* who holds that this is one of the fundamental reasons for the mitzvah of visiting the sick.

[19] *Tzitz Eliezer V* in the *Ramos Rachel* 3.

those in a hospital it can be a particularly lonely, depressing experience. Providing company is a tremendous aide to the wellbeing of the patient. Rav Moshe Feinstein[20] points out that when God visited Abraham, God did not say anything to him. Presence alone provides tremendous comfort.

## Who is Considered "Sick" for the Purposes of this *Mitzvah*?

Let's start with the extremes: It applies to anyone who is dangerously ill.[21] However, it does not apply to a person with a minor ailment (headache or cold). Between these two extremes, there are many guidelines in *Halacha* as to who is considered "sick."[22]

- Anyone whose body is hampered in its ability to move due to pain or illness is considered sick. The **Maharal of Prague**[23] learns this from Abraham. During the first two days following his *bris*, he was "injured" in a single limb. This "injury" did not affect his entire body until the third day when he was in great pain. Accordingly, one who has a broken arm is not considered sick once the pain has subsided to such a point that he is up and about. It is nevertheless proper (as an act of kindness) to see if the person requires assistance.

- For one who is not dangerously ill, there is no *mitzvah* to visit him unless his illness is of the type we have described and has persisted for two days. As we see, God did not visit Abraham until after two days had passed.[24] According to many, this exemption applies to others but not to the patient's family.[25]

- The *mitzvah* certainly applies to a woman who is on bed rest or to someone who is confined to their home.

---

[20] *Doresh Moshe* on *Vayeira*.

[21] *Nedarim 40a*.

[22] There are many different customs and interpretations as to how these are applied. We have presented a very general summary here of some common approaches.

[23] Commentary on Gen 18. See also *Piskei Teshuva 242*.

[24] See *Biur Halacha OC 219, Kegon*.

[25] *Psak* attributed to **Rav Chaim Kanievsky.**

- It is unclear how this *mitzvah* applies to the mentally ill.

## Guidelines for Visiting the Sick

*The most important guideline is this: do not make your visit into a burden or annoyance. All too often, when visiting the sick, the visitor will overdo their expressions of concern to the point of causing unnecessary stress. Be pleasant, ask the patient what they need, and don't insist on doing anything for the patient unless they clearly appreciate it.*

### Plan Ahead

- Check with the sick person first to find out if he wants visitors.

- Find out from the family and the sick person the best time to visit.

- No surprises – Knock before entering.[26]

### When to Visit

- Relatives and very close friends may visit immediately. However, others should wait until after two full days have passed. If you are doubtful, wait two days.[27]

- One should avoid visiting a sick person during the first three or last three hours of the day.[28] However, if there are no other times, one may visit provided that it is ok with the patient's attendants and the patient himself.[29]

---

[26] *Niddah 16b*. Even HaShem hates those who enter unannounced.

[27] *Levush 335:1; Rav Chaim Kanievsky; Tzitz Eliezer V, Ramos Rachel 7*.

[28] *Ahavas Chesed 3:3; Tzitz Eliezer ibid.* See also Maimonides, *Hilchos Avel 14:5*. There are many reasons for this that we will discuss during the live class.

[29] The *Aruch HaShulchan 335:8* holds that there are no restrictions on the time of day to visit. However, we only rely upon this opinion if there are no other convenient options.

## In Groups?

- As long as a group will not cause stress or inconvenience, it is not an issue.[30]

## Comportment

- Because of the presence of the *shechina*, one should make himself presentable before going to visit. He should wear respectable clothing.[31]

## Where to Sit

- One should not sit on a level higher than the patient. If the patient is lying upon the floor, for example, the visitor should sit on the floor.[32]

- According to the *Zohar*, one should not sit behind or right alongside the head of the patient because of the presence of the *shechina*. If a patient is dangerously ill, the visitor should not sit directly at the patient's feet. That is the position of the *malakh ha-maves*, the angel of death.[33]

## Praying for the Sick

- The visitor must pray for the welfare of the sick individual. It is praiseworthy that this be done in the sick person's presence. However, this prayer must not be done in a way that makes the patient self-conscious or uncomfortable.

- "May you merit a full recovery" or "May HaShem heal you soon" or some other simple expressed is sufficient.[34]

- It is not proper to mention the name of the ill person when praying for them in their presence.[35] We learn this from Moses who, when praying for his sister's

---

[30] See *Igros Moshe YD 4:51; Yalkut Yosef VII*, p. 125. The *Sheiltos* recommends visiting one at a time. However, this is not the prevalent custom. See *HaEmek HaSheilah 93:7*.

[31] *Bikkur Cholim B'Halakha U'BiAgadah* p. 77, *haarah 9; Tzitz Eliezer 5* in the *Ramos Rachel*.

[32] *Shulchan Aruch 335:3; Chochmas Adam 151:2; Aruch HaShulchan 335:7*.

[33] See *Aruch HaShulchan ibid.; Gesher HaChaim I:1:5*.

[34] Rav Shlomo Zalman Auerbach, ztz"l in *Halichos Shlomo 8, haarah 63; Shevet HaLevi V:184*.

[35] *Brachos 34a; Mogen Avraham OC 119:1*. See also *Rivevos Efraim VII:335*.

recovery, did not mention her by name.[36] Doing so can actually bring harsh judgments upon the sick.[37]

### If the Patient is asleep or Unconscious

- Since the fundamental reason for visiting the sick to pray for their recovery, it does not matter if the patient is aware of the presence of the visitor. Therefore, it is still a *mitzvah* to visit a sick person if they are in coma, unconscious, or asleep.[38] However, if visiting the patient would disturb his sleep, then he should not be visited until he is awake.

### Effect upon the sickness

The Midrash[39] and Talmud[40] both state that visiting a sick person removes 1/60th of his illness. The exact meaning of this statement is uncertain,[41] but anyway we interpret it the gist is that visiting the sick person is of great benefit to healing him.

## Summary of the Lesson

1. Sickness is sometimes the result of the patient's fault and sometimes the result of divine decree.

2. Sickness comes upon a person from heaven as an impetus for repentance and self-betterment.

3. The message of sickness is not just for the sick person, but for others as well.

---

[36] Numbers 12:13.

[37] *Chasam Sofer* to *Nedarim 40a*; *Ben Yehoyada*, *Brachos 34a*; See also *Yalkut Reuveni,s Vayeira 18:1*.

[38] *Avnei Yushfei 1:230; Mitzvos Bikkur Cholim* pp.184 to 185. See also *Rosh* to *Vayeira* 18:1.

[39] *Vayikra Rabbah 34:1*.

[40] *Nedarim 39b; Bava Metzia 30a*.

[41] This saying is cited and discussed extensively. See *Kol Bo 112; Tur 335; Shach 335:1; Chochmas Adam 151:1; Aruch HaShulchan 335:5; Rivevos Ephraim IV:355:8; Toras Chaim to Bava Metzia 30a; Keren Orah to Nedarim 40a*.

4. For Jews, this is a Rabbinic *mitzvah*.

5. The divine presence stands ready above the head of a sick person to accept prayers.

6. When visiting a sick person, one must not only pray for his well-being, but also check that the patient has all of his basic needs met.

7. Sick, for the purpose of this mitzvah, means ill to the degree that one is not "up and about" for two days or that one is dangerously ill.

THE YESHIVA PIRCHEI SHOSHANIM SHULCHAN ARUCH PROJECT

# The Noahide Laws - Lesson Forty-Six

© **Yeshiva Pirchei Shoshanim 2017**
This shiur may not be reproduced in any
form without permission of the copyright holder.

## Table of Contents:

1. Introduction
2. When This a Chance of Recovery
    a. Praying for the Very Ill
    b. Changing the Name
3. When the Doctors Have Given Up Hope: The Inevitable End
    a. Praying for the Terminally Ill
    b. Praying for the Death of One Who is Suffering
    c. Euthanasia
4. Near Death
    a. Respirator
5. Organ Donation
6. Summary

# Lifecycle IX: Life Threatening Illness & End of Life

## Introduction

Illness and injury, especially when life-threatening, are stressful for the patient as well as for his family, friends, and community. The outcome is usually uncertain and, as in all situations of uncertain outcome, it is all too easy to panic and lose one's bearings. It is important to remember that everything, especially life and death, is in the hand of the Holy One, blessed is He. In the fog and fear of uncertainly our faith in God is the all-important beacon that guides us through the storm.

Our approach to the spiritual challenges posed by dangerous illness depend on the patient's chances for recovery

## When There is a Chance of Recovery

**Praying for the Very Ill**

When someone is very sick and, God forbid, their life is threatened it is proper for anyone who is capable to pray for the patient's recovery. The Talmud states:

> *One who can pray for the ill and does not is called a sinner.*[1]

The prevalent custom is to say Psalms for the merit of the sick person. Most Jewish editions of the Psalms include lists of those appropriate (we have also enumerated these in an earlier lesson).

---

[1] *Brachos 12b.* However, some say that this only applies to *tzaddikim*.

Many Jewish communities have *Tehillim*/Psalm groups that gather weekly to recite *Tehillim*/Psalms for the sick. This practice is appropriate for the Noahide community as well. Not only does it provide the benefit of healing the sick, but it also builds cohesion among Noahides as well as a sense of unity.

**Changing the Name**

When a person is gravely ill and their life is seriously threatened, it is appropriate to change the name of the sick person. This is usually done when recovery is uncertain. There are a number of reasons for this custom and it appears, in general, to apply non-Jews as well as to Jews.

.By changing one's name the heavenly decree against him also changes.[2] According to some, it has a metaphysical effect on the soul and destiny of the sick person.[3] The name should be changed to that of a relative or righteous person who lived a very long life. It is also appropriate to change the name to Raphael – the name of the angel of healing.[4]

Changing the name may also be accomplished by adding a name to the patient's existing name. When doing so, the new name is added to the beginning of the patient's name preceding his original first name. [5]

This practice is rooted in mystical concepts whose exact relevance to Noahides needs more research and study. Therefore, many of the specific practical details are still a little unclear. For example, there is an established Jewish service for changing or adding a name. However, there is no corollary service for Noahides. It is uncertain if such a ceremony is even necessary.

## When the Doctors Have Given Up Hope: The Inevitable End

Once the doctors have given up hope for the patient's recovery and all that remains is waiting for the end, our approach to the sick person changes slightly.

---

[2] *Darchei Moshe 2, Rama 10;* <u>*Kitzur Shulchan Aruch 192:2;*</u> <u>*Aruch Hashulchan*</u> *335:12. See also Rosh Hashanah 16b with Maharsha; Minchas Elazar 2:27;* <u>*Sefer Chassidim*</u> *245.*

[3] *Ritva to Rosh Hashanah 16b, Sefer Ha-Chinuch Mitzvah 311; Levush 10.*

[4] *Keser Shem Tov p. 643.*

[5] *Sefer Keroei Shmo p. 305.*

**Praying for the Terminally Ill**

There is a principle in Torah thought called *ain somchin al ha-nes*, we do not rely upon miracles.[6] The theological import of this idea is vast and far beyond the scope of this lesson. In short, a person should never expect God to perform miracles for him. On a practical level, this principle extends to praying for miracles as well. When God has established something as natural or scientific order, we do ask God to change that order. We will discuss this concept in greater detail in the live lesson.

Once the doctors have given up hope on a patient, according to many we must be careful to temper our prayers so that we do not ask for miracles. Some suggest[7] that we pray instead that the suffering of the sick person and his family be removed, or that God's will be done in the way that minimizes their suffering. Alternatively, we should pray for the welfare of the patient's body and soul. Manny hold that, at this point, any prayers specifically requesting healing or recovery are, de facto, requests for the miraculous. Accordingly, some hold that once the doctors have given up hope on a patient there is no obligation to continue praying.[8]

However, there are authorities who understand the prohibition against praying for miracles to be inapplicable to cases of life and death.[9] Others hold that this prohibition only applies to praying for miracles which would be beyond natural explanations.[10] Therefore, one may pray for a very unlikely yet naturally explicable cure.

Once the doctors have given up hope it is advisable to the situation with a Torah Scholar to determine the best spiritual course of action.

---

[6] *Brachos 54a & 60a* and many other sources. This principle is universally accepted and a fundamental concept in Torah thought. However, its exact application is sometimes unclear. According to *Bekhor Shor* to *Shabbos 21b* and *Gevuras Ari, Ta'anit 19a* the prohibition does not apply to an exceptionally righteous person.

[7] *Halichos Shlomo Tefillah 8, haarah 56.* See also *Sefer Chassidim 794*; Rav Akiva Eiger on O.C. 230:1.

[8] See source in *Mitzvas Bikur Cholim* pp. 237.

[9] *Einayim Le-Mishpat, Berakhot 10a, 60a.*

[10] *Bechor Shor*, ibid.

**Praying for Death of One Who is suffering**

The Ran[11] permits prayer for the death of one who is suffering. The *Aruch HaShulchan 335:3* agrees with the Ran as do many *poskim*.[12] According to these *poskim*, even in such cases we should not pray explicitly for the person to die, but only that God take his soul and end his suffering.

This Ran is controversial and has created vigorous debate among many, many Torah scholars. Most modern *poskim* accept the Ran's view as theoretically correct, but practically unusable.[13] Others outright reject it.[14] According to this latter group, the Ran's was only commenting in explanation of the Talmud's discussion and not making any practical statement of law.

Any practical question about this issue must be asked to a competent rabbi.

**Euthanasia**

Killing someone who is in the process of dying or very near to death is still murder.[15] We do not have the right to choose when a person deserves to die. Nevertheless, a Noahide may passively allow another person to die to relieve their suffering.[16] Similarly, if a Noahide of sound mind[17] refuses medical attention it is permissible to grant his wish.

---

[11] *Chiddushim Nedarim 40a, d.h. Ein.*

[12] See also *Tiferes Yisrael* to *Yoma 8:7*. The *Minchas Shlomo 1:91:24* records this as the position of Rav Shlomo Zalman Auerbach. *Yalkut Yosef, Yoreh De'ah 335* and the latest edition of the *Yalkut Yosef* on *Hilkhot Bikur Holim* and *Aveilut* 63-66 both state that Rav Ovadia Yosef accepted the Ran as Halacha and actually relied upon it in practice.

[13] See the *Shevet HaLevi* X:292:3; *Chikrei Lev YD 150*; *Igros Moshe* CM II:74:1. See also *Teshuvos Ve-Hanhagos* II:82.

[14] *Tzitz Eliezer* V, *Ramos Rachel 5*. The *Shome'ah Tefillah II:24* cites other *poskim* who agree with the *Tzitz Eliezer*.

[15] Maimonides, *Hilchos Melakhim 9:4*; *Rotzchim 2:7*.

[16] This is because non-Jews are not commanded in Lev. 19:16. See also Tosafos to Sanhedrin 59a.

[17] If a person is not of sound mind, then we may not listen to him. *See Igros Moshe CM II: 73 to 75.*

## Near Death

When death is close at hand, and one could pass at any moment, it is prohibited to move or even touch the patient since any disturbance could extinguish the fragile flame of life.[18] This does not apply when one is trying to help save the person or alleviate his suffering.

**Respirator** If a patient is on a respirator, the machine may be turned off once the patient is considered clinically dead.[19]

## Organ Donation

Organ Donation is praiseworthy and a great fulfillment of the *mitzvah* of *chesed* – doing kindness for others. The harvesting of organs is often problematic. Many hospitals harvest organs when the patient is very close to death yet not actually dead. Many times, the life of the patient is extended artificially in order to allow for the harvesting.

This practice is not permitted under Noahide law.[20] Harvesting the organs at this point hastens the death of the patient and is akin to murder. The patient must be clinically dead before the organs may be removed for transplant.

This is prohibited even if the recipient of the donated organ is gravely ill.[21] As we learned in the prior lesson on abortion, it appears that Noahides may violate any of their commandments for the sake of preserving life. However, it is extremely doubtful if this includes the transgression of murder.

---

[18] *Shulchan Aruch YD 339; Igros Moshe CM II: 73* writes explicitly that this is the *halacha* for Noahides as well.

[19] *Tzitz Eliezer XIII: 89.*

[20] This can be derived from the Jewish law; see *Igros Moshe YD II:174.*

[21] *Igros Moshe ibid.*

## Summary of the Lesson

1. When there is a chance for recovery, we must pray for the sick person.

2. When the chances of recovery are uncertain, it is often proper to chance the name of the sick person. The details of this for Noahides are a little fuzzy, however.

3. We may not pray for a miracle. Therefore, when death is a medical inevitability we must be cautious with how we order our prayers. It is a good idea to discuss the issue with a Torah scholar when the sickness has reached such a point.

4. If the patient is suffering greatly, and death appears close, there are those who permit praying for the person's death. However, this is a very sticky subject. Since no two people pass in the same way, each case needs to be treated according to its unique details. A Torah scholar should be consulted.

5. Euthanasia, even for those who are suffering, is considered murder.

6. It is permitted, though, to passively allow a patient to die if they are suffering tremendously.

7. When death is close at hand it is prohibited to touch or move the patient.

8. A patient may not me removed from a respirator until they are clinically dead.

9. Similarly, organs may not be harvested from a donor unless the patient is actually deceased.

THE YESHIVA PIRCHEI SHOSHANIM SHULCHAN ARUCH PROJECT

# The Noahide Laws - Lesson Forty-Seven

© **Yeshiva Pirchei Shoshanim 2017**
This shiur may not be reproduced in any
form without permission of the copyright holder.

164 Village Path, Lakewood NJ 08701 732.370.3344
164 Rabbi Akiva, Bnei Brak, 03.616.6340

## Table of Contents:

1. Introduction
2. Body & Soul
3. Autopsy
4. Delaying Burial
5. Embalming
6. Cremation vs. Burial
    a. Caskets
    b. Cemetery
7. Funeral Service
8. Mourning
9. Summary

# Lifecycle X: Death, Burial & Other Issues

## Introduction

For Jews, the laws of death and burial are wrought in tremendous detail. Many of these laws are Rabbinic, yet predicated on values and beliefs expressed in the written Torah; beliefs as to the nature of body and soul, faith in the eventual resurrection, the afterlife, etc.

Unlike Jews, Noahides do not have any specific commandments on treatment of the dead. However, the value statements and beliefs found in the written Torah (upon which much of the Jewish laws are based) apply equally to Noahides. Therefore, while Noahides do not have specific religious duties to their dead, their actions are informed and guided by Torah beliefs and values.

Although there are many verses and episodes in Tanakh that imply burial practices for Noahides, these instances do not create any actual obligations. The Tanakh's many references to burial and treatment of the dead are discussed at length in the Torah literature. However, a full exploration and explanation of these references would require far more than one (or even several) written lessons. We will provide only a general overview of the issues here and save specific questions for the live class.

## Body & Soul

*Then the Lord God formed man of the dust of the ground, and breathed into his nostrils the breath of life; and man became a living soul.*[1]

---

[1] Gen. 2:7.

This verse is teaches us the most important dichotomy of the human condition: we are both physical and spiritual beings. The creator "breathed" a soul into man and, like breath, it is ethereal, invisible, and absolutely essential. The body, however, was molded from the earth. It is dense, physical, and entirely material.

When God decides that a person's time has come, the two elements that comprise man return to their primordial sources. The soul returns back to its completely spiritual existence while the body rejoins the earth:

> *By the sweat of your brow you shall eat bread until you return unto the ground; for out of it you were taken; for you are dust and unto dust you shall return.*[2]

This verse does not command us to bury our dead;[3] it merely describes the natural decay of the body as part of God's design.

## Created in the Image of God

*And God said, "Let us make man in our **image**, after our **likeness**, ... And God created man in His own **image**, in the **image** of God created He him...*[4]

As we know, God and the Angels have no physical form or shape. What is meant by the terms *image* and *likeness*? Rashi summarizes the interpretations for us:

> **...*after our likeness...;***
>
> *Meaning that man, unlike the other creations, is similar to his creator in that he has the ability to understand and discern.*
>
> ***And God created man in His image...***

---

[2] Gen. 3:19.

[3] The Jewish commandment for burial is learned from Deut. 21:23. See Sanhedrin 46b.

[4] Gen. 1:26 to 27.

*Meaning that God created man in the form that was made for him. Everything else was created with a commandment ["let there be"], whereas man was created by God's own "hands," as it is written (Psalms 139:5): "...and You placed Your hand upon me." Man was made with a stamp, like a coin, which is made by means of a die.*[5]

### ...in the image of God He created him...

*It explains to you that the image that was prepared for him was the image of the likeness of his Creator.*[6]

Rashi is teaching us that man is unique from all other creations in two primary aspects. First, unlike all other creations, man has the ability to understand, discern create, etc. This is describing the nature of the human soul and mind. Second, we were made in the "image" of God. The Hebrew here, *tzelem*, is a difficult word to translate. It can mean diagram, picture, or mold. Rashi is pointing out that God Himself directly designed, shaped, and formed man. This is in contrast to all other elements of creation that came about via the verbal command of God: *Let there be…* God simply ordered something to exist and it was so. However, He never ordered the existence of Man. Rather, as Rashi writes …*man was created by God's own "hands"…*

While the "likeness" of God refers to the spiritual, mental, and creative aspects of man, the "image" or "design" of God refers primarily to the physical aspect of man.
Therefore, once the soul is taken from the body, the "likeness" of God is also removed. However the body remains as a testimony to the unique care with which God fashioned man and His special love for him:

*[Rabbi Akiva] would say, 'Man is beloved because he was created in the image of God. It is an even greater love that this was made known to mankind, as it says, "and in the image of God was man created."*[7]

Therefore, the body, the testimony of God's love and handiwork, should be treated with great respect. This idea does not create liability or obligation, but is a value that should guide the decision making process of the family when making arrangements for the deceased.

---

[5] See *Midrash Tehillim* to 139:5; Sanhedrin 38a.

[6] See Bava Basra 58a.

[7] Avos 3:14 (3:13 in some editions).

## Autopsy

Autopsies are generally prohibited under Jewish practice for the reasons we have mentioned above.[8] Though not prohibited for Noahides, autopsies run contrary to Torah values. Autopsies should be discouraged unless there is a specific reason or need.[9]

## Delaying Burial

Jews are prohibited from delaying burial of the dead for any reason. However, delays necessary for the sake of the deceased and his honor are permitted. While these rules do not apply to Noahides, it is not respectful to the deceased to allow it to remain unburied for any unessential period of time.[10]

## Embalming

God, in his wisdom, designed the human body to return to its source once the soul has departed. Embalming is a corruption of this design and is not considered respectful to the deceased.

## Cremation vs. Burial

There is no prohibition of cremation for Noahides. However, cremation is the destruction of God's handiwork and should be discouraged.

**Casket** — Burial in the ground allows the body to decay according to God's design. This process is facilitated by using a casket that is also biodegradable. Many funeral homes offer plain wooden caskets (often marketed as "traditional Jewish caskets") that break down over time or are perforated to allow the body to decay and return to the earth.

---

[8] There are other reasons as well. See Bava Basra 115a.

[9] See Bava Basra ibid. Chullin 116; *Nodah BiYehuda YD* 210; and *Shu"t Chasam Sofer YD* 336. For Jews autopsies are only permitted in an extremely narrow range circumstances.

[10] There are some who may hold it is prohibited to even delay Noahide burial. See *Toldos Noah* 13:21 and *Matza Chein* 13:29.

**Cemetery**  Noahides may not be buried in Jewish cemeteries (this is a prohibition from the Jewish side; Jews are not allowed to bury non-Jews in Jewish cemeteries). Burial in any other place is permitted.

## Funeral Service

There is no set service for Noahide funerals. This is one of a number of areas in which Noahism requires development. Keeping in line with the ideology of the Torah, the following principles are suggested:

- The service should not in any way allow for denial of the condition or reality of death. This is unhealthy and has long-term consequences.

- The service should allow open mourning and crying for the deceased. Expressions of grief are exceptionally important for both spiritual and psychological reasons. Unexpressed or unresolved grief is a most poisonous emotion, producing unexpected results (and, sometimes, even entire religions…)

- Eulogizing of the deceased by those close to him is important because it opens the hearts of those who are present and honors the deceased.

- The funeral should offer the opportunity for closure, forgiveness, and for those present to "bury the hatchet" with the deceased.

- Open casket funerals should be discouraged for a number of reasons that will be discussed in the live class.

## Mourning

In the Jewish world, mourning is a highly developed process, crafted to ensure emotional as well as spiritual health. Its details are obligatory and involve many very formal elements. Noahides have no such obligations or mourning customs. This is another area in which development is needed. We should note, however, that Noahides in earlier times observed a set period of mourning:

*For in another seven days, I will make it rain upon the earth for forty days and forty nights, and I will blot out all beings that I have made, off the face of the earth.*[11]

The Talmud, Sanhedrin 108b explains that the flood was delayed for seven days to allow mourning for the righteous Methuselah. As Rashi writes:

### For in another seven days…

*These are the seven days of mourning for the righteous Methuselah, for whom the Holy One, blessed be He, showed honor by delaying punishment. If you calculate the chronology of Methuselah you will find that he passed in the six-hundredth year of Noah's life.*

Noahides certainly have a solid precedent from this verse for observing seven days of mourning for their dead.

In the next lesson we will finish the lifecycle series.

## Summary of the Lesson

1. Man is composed of body and soul; physical and spiritual entities.

2. Man's mind, wisdom, intelligence, and creativity are all part of the "likeness of God" and set man apart from animals and other elements of creation.

3. Man's physical aspect, however, was formed by God. What is more, this physical aspect was designed and formed directly by God. It was not merely commanded into being.

4. As such, the physical aspect of man is a testament of God's love of man and of His handiwork. Therefore, dishonoring it is dishonoring one of God's most prized creations. Though not implying any obligations or liabilities, it is a value which informs burial practice.

5. Autopsies and embalming are discouraged.

---

[11] Gen. 7:4.

6. Burial should not be delayed unless it is for the sake of the deceased.

7. Burial in the ground is ideal. In locales that require use of a casket, it is best that the body be buried in a casket that allows for full decay of the body"

8. There is no set Noahide funeral service. This is an area of development for Noahides.

# The Noahide Laws - Lesson Forty-Eight

THE YESHIVA PIRCHEI SHOSHANIM SHULCHAN ARUCH PROJECT

© **Yeshiva Pirchei Shoshanim 2017**
This shiur may not be reproduced in any
form without permission of the copyright holder.

164 Village Path, Lakewood NJ 08701 732.370.3344
164 Rabbi Akiva, Bnei Brak, 03.616.6340

## Table of Contents:

1. Introduction
2. Avraham & Eliezer
3. Talmud, Kiddushin 17b to 18a
4. Who Inherits?
5. Sons or Daughters
6. Equal Inheritances?
7. Basic Summary So Far
8. *Havaras Nachala*
9. Mitigating Factors
10. Practical Examples of Partial Inheritance
11. Summary

# Lifecycle XI: Inheritance

## Introduction

In our time on this Earth we tend to accumulate a lot of stuff (in fact, we usually end up with more than we could ever need!) In death, however, our ownership of all things material ceases. The only possessions accompanying us into the afterlife are our *mitzvos* – our fulfillments of God's will. Ultimately, all material possessions and wealth have very little meaning.

It is unfortunately very common that, when a loved one dies, their death results in a "battle for stuff," creating strife and disagreement over who inherits the deceased's estate. In the midst of these conflicts everyone seems to miss the greater point: no matter who gets the inheritance, it won't be theirs for long. Eventually, everyone dies and, as the Yiddish expression goes, shrouds have no pockets.

The Torah is very concerned with the details of inheritance. The Talmud and later scholars devote much labor to clarifying the details of inheritance. In this lesson we will look at the general principles of inheritance as they apply to Noahides.

## Avraham & Eliezer

Before getting into things in detail, we need to first note the following passages in the Torah and Talmud:

> *After these incidents, the word of the Lord came to Abram in a vision, saying, "Do not fear, Abram, for I am your Shield; your reward is exceedingly great." And Abram said, "O Lord God, what will You give me? I am going childless and the steward of my household is Eliezer of Damascus!" And behold, Abram said "Behold, You have given me no offspring and one of my*

*household will inherit me." And, behold, the word of the Lord came to him, saying: "This man shall not inherit you; only one that shall come forth from within you shall be your heir."*[1]

The commentaries explain that Abram was uncertain about God's promise of material reward. Knowing the vanity of such things, Abram saw little point considering that he had no heir to whom to pass anything. The best he could do, said Abram, was to leave everything to Eliezer, the head of his household. God replies and assures Abram that he will have offspring to inherit his estate.

However, Abram's complaint is strange. After all, he had other relatives. Why couldn't his nephew, Lot, inherit him? What about Abram's brothers? The *Kovetz Haaros*[2] and *Kovetz Shiurim*[3] both point out that Abram did not consider these other relatives as his natural heirs; he only considered his offspring as natural heirs.

## Talmud, Kiddushin 17b to 18a

An indentured servant's period of servitude ends in the *shemitta* (remission) year. However, a servant who does not desire his freedom and, instead, wishes to instead remain a servant must serve his master until the *Yovel* (Jubilee) year.

The Torah records the details in the following verses:

*If you purchase a Jewish servant, he shall serve for six years and go completely free in the seventh year… But if the servant says: "I love my master… I will not go out free," then his master shall bring him before God, to the door or door-post, and his master shall bore his ear through with an awl; he shall then serve him **forever**.*[4]

The Talmud and Torah commentaries explain that "forever" here means until the end of the Jubilee cycle.

In Kiddushin 17b to 18a the Talmud discusses the sale of such a bound servant to a Non-Jew. The Talmud notes that although the servant's commitment becomes the property of the Non-Jew, it cannot be inherited by the Non-Jew's children.

---

[1] Gen 15.

[2] 64:3.

[3] Bava Basra 358.

[4] Exodus 21:2-6.

The source, says the Talmud is:

*And he shall calculate with him who bought him from the year that he sold himself to him until the year of jubilee; and the price of his sale shall be according unto the number of years; according to the time of a hired servant shall he be with him.*[5]

The Talmud points out that the servant's servitude is only between his master and the indentured servant. If the master dies, then the agreement of servitude does not pass to the master's heirs. In the course of this discussion, however, Rava Raises an interesting point:

> *From the fact that the Torah needed to teach that a Non-Jew does not inherit his father's servant, we see that a Non-Jew inherits his father on a biblical level.*

In other words, when a Non-Jew dies his possessions are not entirely ownerless. Rather, they pass to the owner's children. Therefore, the Talmud had to teach the exception of an indentured servant. According to the Talmud, there are two sources for this law:

1. *…I will not give you of their land, no, not so much as for the sole of the foot to tread on; because **I have given mount Seir unto Esau for an inheritance**.*[6]

2. *And the Lord said unto me: 'Be not at enmity with Moab, neither contend with them in battle; for I will not give thee of his land for a possession; because **I have given Ar unto the children of Lot for an inheritance**.*[7]

These verses both demonstrate the concept of inheritance from parents to children. The Talmud's derivation is further bolstered by the aforementioned incident with Abram.

## Who Inherits?

Although the story of Abram clearly implies that only children have a right of inheritance, this learning is not reflected in later writings. For example, Maimonides writes:

---

[5] Lev. 25:50.

[6] Deut. 2:5.

[7] Deut. 2:9.

> *According to Scriptural Law, a gentile inherits his father's estate. With regard to other inheritances, we allow them to follow their own customs.*[8]

According to Maimonides, only children inherit their father's estate. In all other situations, Noahides should follow the customs of their lands and laws. For example, if a woman dies without any children, then her estate is divided according to the probate law of the land.

The Meiri,[9] however, has an entirely different understanding than Maimonides. He writes that a son and all other immediate family members inherit the deceased's property.

Rav Shlomo Zalman Auerbach z"l,[10] based on the *Chidushei HaRitva*, offers a very deep analysis of the entire question of inheritance that brings the opinions of Maimonides and the Meiri into greater focus. Let's start with a question: When a person dies, what is the status of his property? Absent any concept of inheritance, the property is *hefker*, ownerless. If it is *hefker*, than anyone can freely take it and their actions are not considered theft.

Yet, the Torah tells us that this is not so. When a person dies, the ownership of his property transfers automatically to another party. If another takes this property he commits theft.

According to the Meiri, ownership of the deceased's property passes to his immediate family. The exact division and of who-gets-what is entirely the result of law and social custom. However, the Meiri holds that these customs have the force of biblical law. Therefore, if someone steals from the deceased's possessions, he is liable for theft on a biblical level!

Maimonides holds that a son automatically inherits and that this right cannot be mitigated by custom. It is only in the absence of a son that the division of property among the remaining relatives is (as the Meiri holds) determined by custom.[11]

The *Halacha*, practice, is like Maimonides.[12]

---

[8] *Hilchos Nachalos* 6:9.

[9] To Kiddushin ibid. In previous lessons we mentioned that the validity of the Meiri as a practical halachic source is a complicated issue.

[10] *Minchas Shlomo* 86.

[11] The *Minchas Chinuch* 400, however, has a different understanding of Maimonides.

[12] See *Chochom Sofer* YD 127; *Minchas Shlomo* Ibid.; *Pri Yitzchok* II:60; many others.

## Sons or Daughters?

The *Minchas Chinuch* and others[13] write that a son inherits his father's estate. Should we understand their use of the Hebrew term "son" as limiting inheritance to the son only? Or, perhaps their use of "son" is non-specific and daughters also their father. Tosafos[14] appears to hold that, when there is a son, no one else inherits the father; not even a daughter.

The *Kovetz Haaros*[15] and *Kovetz Shiurim*[16] point out that, in the aforementioned conversation between God and Abram, Abram only complains that he has no offspring to inherit him. He makes no distinction between sons and daughters.[17] Therefore, the *Kovetz* holds that they both inherit. Later authorities appear to agree the *Halacha* is sons and daughters both inherit their fathers.

## Equal Inheritances?

While sons and daughters inherit their father, do they receive equal portions? Jewish law dictates that the son's inheritance takes precedence. This is learned from the following verse:

> *And you shall speak unto the children of Israel, saying: If a man dies and has no son, then you shall cause his inheritance to pass to his daughter.*[18]

Do these rules also apply to Noahides? The answer appears to be "no." After all, this verse was never commanded to Noahides!

---

[13] See *Pri Yitzchok* II:60.

[14] Bava Basra 115b *d.h. Melamed* as analyzed in the *Kovetz Shiurim*, Bava Basra 357.

[15] 64:3.

[16] Bava Basra 358

[17] The *Chavatzeles HaSharon* 468 discusses this issue at length and finds the *Kovetz* to be a compelling proof. Note that the passage in Genesis 15 goes out of its way to avoid any gender distinction.

[18] Numbers 27:8.

Rashi to Yevamos 62a[19] writes there is no distinction between a son and a daughter for the sake of Noahide inheritance. This approach is echoed in the later commentaries as well.[20] It must be noted that there are a number of possible differences between the inheritances of sons and daughters that remain unclear.

## Basic Summary So Far

We will discuss the practical ramifications of this lesson in the live class. However, the basic takeaway is as follows:

- When a person dies intestate, his estate automatically passes to his sons and daughters according to Torah law.

- His estate should be divided equally between his sons and daughters.

- If a person has no children, he may divide his estate as he wishes or allow it to be divided according to the probate laws of his country.

## Havaras Nachala

The Torah's requirements for inheritance constitute a *mitzvah*. Correspondingly, one who circumnavigates the Torah's obligations commits an *aveira*, a sin, of *havaras nachala* – disrupting the order of inheritance[21] (admittedly, further study is needed as to the exact severity of and scope of this prohibition for Noahides.)[22] Therefore, should not completely disinherit a Torah-designated heir.

---

[19] *D.h. Nakhriosan.*

[20] See *Toldos Noach* 13:20 and *Matza Chein* 13:27. Though most later Acharonim equate sons and daughters for inheritance, there many minor detail in which there is much uncertainty.

[21] *Mishnah* Bava Basra 133b; *Teshuvos HaRosh* 85:2; *Kenesses HaGedolah* CM 282:2.

[22] Its exact application for Jews is often unclear. Some limit this transgression to real estate bequests. See *Sdei Chemed Maareches Lamed* 3:11.

Most authorities note that one transgresses this *aveira,* sin, even by intentionally diminishing his estate in his lifetime in order to lessen the inheritance of rightful heirs. Therefore, *inter vivos* gifts ("lifetime bequests") are ideal.[23]

All Torah authorities agree that, even though *havaras nachala* is prohibited, a will or bequest that does so remains valid.[24]

## Mitigating Factors

In many families, there are complex dynamics and concerns that affect how one may wish to have his estate divided upon his death. When such factors exist, it is possible to make special arrangements for one's estate without shirking the Torah obligations of inheritance.

**Partial vs. Complete Disinheritance**

According to the majority of *poskim,* the issue of *havaras nachala* is, for Jews, only when one completely disinherits a Torah-designated heir. However, partial distributions between Torah-designated and "outside" heirs are permitted when there are mitigating concerns. This understanding has been relied upon for centuries in the Jewish world and is a foundation of Torah-observant estate planning. The same principle appears to apply to Noahides.

**The Amounts of Partial Distributions**

According to the *rishonim,* partial distributions are permitted as long as the testator leaves "four *zuz*" (a Talmudic currency) to his Torah-designated heirs.[25] As long as that amount has been ensured, the remainder of the estate may be divided as one chooses. What is "four *zuz*?" Translating ancient measurements into modern currency is very tricky. There are many ways of doing these calculations, all of which reach different answers. Rav Moshe Feinstein, *ztz"l* explains that the four *zuz* measurement is not exact – rather it only means to indicate a significant portion of one's estate.[26] According to Rav Moshe, either of the following is sufficient:

- **Portion of the Estate** – What constitutes "a significant portion" varies from place to place and estate to estate. 1/5 of one's estate, however,

---

[23] See *Pischei Choshen, Yerusha* 4:2.

[24] *Choshen Mishpat* 282.

[25] *Shu"t Tashbetz* III:147; *Maharshal* 49. See further *Avkas Rochel* 92; *Taz Even HaEzer* 113:1; *Ketzos HaChoshen* CM 282:2; *Birkey Yosef* YD 249:15.

[26] *Igros Moshe, Choshen Mishpat* II:50.

should be enough to satisfy this requirement.[27]

- **Actual Monetary Amount** – If we assume that the "four *zuz*" is a firm amount, then we must realize that there are many ways to calculate it. $1000 would cover most all possibilities.[28]

- **Real Estate** – Leaving one's house or residence to halachic heirs is also sufficient and considered enough.[29]

There is no requirement to choose the largest of these amounts; rather one should choose what is appropriate for the situation. Once one of these amounts has been left to the Torah-designated heirs, the remaining estate may be divided as needed.

## Practical Examples of Partial Inheritance

Common situations where one may want to use a partial distribution are:

- **A spouse** – If one has a spouse and children, then by Torah law his children inherit his entire estate. However, if one is concerned for the welfare of his spouse then he may leave the "four *zuz*" equivalent to his children and the rest of his estate to his wife.

- **Adopted vs. biological children** – The Torah obligation is to one's biological children. Under Torah law, adopted children have no automatic entitlement to inheritance. As long as one leaves at least "four *zuz*" to his biological children, the remainder of his estate may be left to his adopted children.

- **Children vs. Grandchildren** – One may leave his biological children one of the amounts mentioned above, and leave the rest to his grandchildren if needed.

---

[27] *Igros Moshe, Choshen Mishpat* II:49.

[28] *Igros Moshe, Choshen Mishpat* II:50.

[29] *Igros Moshe, Even HaEzer* I:110.

## Summary of the Lesson

1. The Torah provides extensive laws of inheritance for Jews.

2. The Talmud explains that the mechanism of inheritance, that property passes from the deceased to the living (although by logic it should become ownerless), applies to Noahides as well.

3. The commentaries discuss whether the ownership of the Non-Jew's property passes to all of his immediate family or only to his children. The *Halacha* appears to be like Maimonides that ownership passes to one's children.

4. Inheritance appears to pass to sons and daughters equally.

5. It advisable that Noahides draft a will that is both *Halachically* and legally valid.

THE YESHIVA PIRCHEI SHOSHANIM SHULCHAN ARUCH PROJECT

# The Noahide Laws - Lesson Forty-Nine

© **Yeshiva Pirchei Shoshanim 2017**
This shiur may not be reproduced in any
form without permission of the copyright holder.

164 Village Path, Lakewood NJ 08701 732.370.3344
164 Rabbi Akiva, Bnei Brak, 03.616.6340

## Table of Contents:

1. Introduction
2. The Sources
    a. *Halacha LeMoshe MiSinai*
    b. Deut. 25:4
    c. Exodus 23:5
    d. *Ever Min HaChai*
    e. Balaam, Adam & Noah
3. Elucidating the *Sefer Chassidim*
4. Are Noahides Obligated?
5. In Practice

# Animal Issues I: Tzaar Baalei Chaim - Cruelty to Animals

## Introduction

Animals, be they insects, mammals, birds, or slugs, are man's constant companions on this planet. They were created before man, yet are clearly subservient to him, as the Torah tells us:

*The fear and dread of you shall be upon every beast of the earth, every fowl of the air, and upon all that teems on the ground and all the fishes of the sea; into your hand are they delivered. Every moving thing that lives shall be for food for you; as the green herb have I given you all.*[1]

Despite the subservient position of animals, man's relationship to them is not without boundaries. Man cannot do to them whatever he pleases. In this and the following lesson we will explore the Torah's expectations for man's relationship with his fellow creations.

## The Source for *Tzaar Baalei Chayim* – The Prohibition of Causing Pain to Living Things

The Torah prohibits causing the suffering of any living creature without valid necessity ("valid necessity" will be defined later in this lesson). Though the Talmud[2] states that this prohibition is biblical, there are varying traditions as to its exact source. For Noahides, making such a determination is important for knowing whether or not the law applies to them.

---

[1] Genesis 9:2-3.

[2] Bava Metzia 32a to 32b.

The *Gedolim*, great Torah scholars, have proposed a number of possible sources.

**Halacha LeMoshe MiSinai**

Ritva[3] & Rabbeinu Peretz[4] explains the prohibition as a *Halacha le Moshe miSinai*, a precept communicated directly by God to Moses without explicit textual source in the Torah.

However, it only tells us that Jews were commanded via *Halacha le Moshe miSinai* and implies nothing about Noahides.

**Deuteronomy 25:4**

Shita Mekubetzes & Raavad offer Deuteronomy 25:4 as a source for the prohibition against cruelty to animals:

> *You shall not muzzle an ox while he is treading out the grain.*

Muzzling an ox during threshing, thus preventing it from feeding as necessary is cruel. This verse does not come to teach only this specific prohibition, but a broader prohibition against cruelty to animals.

However, this verse was only communicated to the Jews and not to Noahides.

**Exodus 23:5**

According to Rashi[5] the prohibition is from Exodus 23:5:

> *If you see your enemy's donkey lying under its burden would you refrain from helping him? You shall surely help along with him.*

Regardless of one's relationship to the donkey's owner, Rashi holds that one must relieve the donkey of its suffering. However, this verse, as Deuteronomy 25:4 above, was never commanded to Noahides. Therefore, it does not tell us anything about Noahide obligations.

---

[3] To Bava Metzia ibid. *D.H. Teida.*

[4] Bava Metzia ibid.

[5] To Shabbos 128b.

**Part of Ever Min HaChai**

Maimonides[6] & Nachmanides[7] write that an underlying purpose of the prohibition of *ever min ha-chai* (flesh taken from a living animal) is to prevent causing cruelty to animals. Such an interpretation means that the prohibition of causing suffering to animals is intrinsically part of the Noahide code. Maimonides further cites the incident of Balaam and his donkey as proof of the prohibition's inclusion in the Noahide laws:

> *The she-donkey saw the angel of the Lord, and it crouched down under Balaam. Balaam's anger flared, and he beat the she-donkey with a stick. The Lord opened the mouth of the she-donkey, and she said to Balaam,* **"What have I done to you that you have struck me these three times?"** *Balaam said to the she-donkey, "For you have humiliated me; if I had a sword in my hand, I would kill you right now." The she-donkey said to Balaam, "Am I not your she-donkey on which you have ridden since you first started until now? Have I been accustomed to do this to you?" He said, "No." The Lord opened Balaam's eyes, and he saw the angel of the Lord standing in the road, with a sword drawn in his hand. He bowed and prostrated himself on his face. The angel of the Lord said to him,* **"Why have you beaten your she-donkey these three times?"**[8]

**Balaam, Adam & Noah**

The *Sefer Chassidim*[9] also understands the story of Balaam as referring to the prohibition of *tzaar baalei chaim*. However, the *Sefer Chassidim* offers a fascinating insight into the *mitzvah*:

> *A person is punished for any actions that cause suffering to his fellow. This is even if one causes needless suffering to an animal; for example, if one places upon it a burden so heavy that it [the animal] cannot walk and he then hits it. In the future, such a person will have to give an accounting for this, for causing suffering to animals is a biblical prohibition. As it is written by Balaam: "Why did you strike your donkey?" As punishments often correspond to the crime, because Balaam said "If there was a sword in my hand I would kill you right now!" he was himself killed by the sword [see Joshua 13:22]. The warning is learned from the fact that Noahides were not commanded in "dominion." Adam, who was not allowed to eat meat, was given dominion over the animals. However, Noah, who was given permission to eat meat, was not given dominion.*

---

[6] *Moreh Nevuchim* III: 48.

[7] To Genesis 1:28.

[8] Numbers 22:27 to 32

[9] 666.

## Elucidating the *Sefer Chassidim*

The *Sefer Chassidim* connects the prohibition against cruelty to animals to the permission given to Noah to eat meat and to the blessings given to Noah and Adam. At first glance, the *Sefer Chassidim's* intent is a little unclear. Let us start by comparing the blessings given to Adam and to Noah:

**The Blessing Given to Adam**

*And God blessed them and God said to them: "Be fruitful and multiply, replenish the earth, and subdue it; and have **dominion** over the fish of the sea, and over the fowl of the air, and over every living thing that creeps upon the earth."*[10]

Compare the language of this blessing very carefully to that of the blessing given to Noah

**The Blessing Given to Noah**

*And God blessed Noah and his sons, and said to them: "Be fruitful and multiply, and replenish the earth. And the **fear of you and the dread of you shall be upon** every beast of the earth, and upon every fowl of the air, and upon all that teems upon the ground, and upon all the fishes of the sea: into your hand are they delivered."*[11]

The Midrash[12] notes a significant change in language in these two passages:

*Fear and dread returned [after the flood], but not dominion.*

In the blessing to Adam, God granted man dominion over all other life on earth. God's blessing to Noah is virtually identical, except that God did not grant Noah dominion. Rather, He only instilled the fear of man upon the other creatures of the world.

In God's original vision of creation man was given the world for domination as a king rules over his dominion. In this state, Adam's task was to preserve the order and well-being of the world created for him. His power over the lesser creatures was intrinsic: Adam was given dominion. It appears that as a king Adam was not permitted to eat meat – doing so would be to eat his own subjects!

However, this divine vision was corrupted beyond all measure:

*And God saw the earth and, behold, it was corrupted, for all flesh had corrupted its way upon the earth.*[13]

---

[10] Genesis 1:28

[11] Genesis 9:2.

[12] *Bereshis Rabbah* 34:12.

Man debased himself and lost his position as a ruler. In the blessing to Noah, we see that man's inherent "dominion" was replaced with "fear and dread."

As we see from the above-cited Midrash and its commentaries that before the flood man was feared because of his inherent dominion. After the flood God placed the fear-of-man upon the animals because man lost his dominion.

At this point man was, for lack of a better way of putting it, only "the top of the food chain" and not a ruler. Therefore, man could eat animals. However, unlike a ruler, man was not allowed to do with the animals as he saw fit.

Eating meat and the prohibition of causing suffering are both, therefore, signs of man's debasement and lowered position following the flood.[14]

## Are Noahides Prohibited from Causing Other Creatures Pain?

If the source of *tzaar baalei chaim* is *Halacha le-Moshe mi-Sinai* (a command given directly to Moses) or from Deuteronomy 25:4 or Exodus 23:5, then it is clear that the prohibition does not apply to Noahides. This is because the verses cited, as well as *halachos leMoshe miSinai*, were not commanded to Noahides. The *Aishel Avraham (Buczacz)*[15] and the *Pri Megadim*[16] hold *Bnei Noach* are not obligated in *tza'ar ba'alei chaim* based upon these sources.

According to Maimonides and the *Sefer Chassidim*, however, Noahides are biblically enjoined against causing unnecessary suffering to other living beings.

Upon closer examination it appears these sources are not mutually exclusive. Although the *Aishel Avraham* and *Pri Megadim* hold that Noahides are not obligated in *tzaar baalei chaim*, this appears to only be in regard to the Torah verses related to the commandment; after all, these verses explicitly reference the Jewish Sinaitic obligation.

---

[13] Genesis 6:12.

[14] This understanding of the *Sefer Chassidim* sits well. However, it is not 100% clear this is the intended understanding of the *Sefer Chassidim*. There are other possible explanations.

[15] *Magen Avraham* 13 on *Orach Chaim* 305.

[16] *Mishbitzos Zahav*, *Orach Chaim* 468:2.

Nevertheless, the *Aishel Avraham* and *Pri Megadim* would certainly agree that, independent of the Torah verses, Noahides have an obligation to not cause harm to other creatures.

Admittedly, there are a number of subtle issues inherent in Maimonides's and the *Sefer Chassidim's* derivations (we will discuss these issues in the live class). Regardless of these issues, there are many other reasons to assume Noahides are prohibited from causing suffering to animals, namely on account of it being of the *mitzvos ha-muskalos* – the logically compelled *mitzvos*.[17]

## In Practice

Because the prohibition may be biblical in nature (as opposed to being logically compelled) it is advisable that Noahides practice the obligations according to their full exposition in Torah law. The following is a compilation of the laws of *tzaar baalei chaim*:

### To Which Animals Does it Apply?

1) The prohibition applies to all animals and, apparently, insects as well.[18]

### When Does the Prohibition Not Apply?

2) Causing pain to animals is only restricted to unnecessary pain. Man was given the right to use animals for his needs (food, clothing, etc.)[19] Discomfort that is necessary as part of such uses is not prohibited.[20]

3) The "need" must be genuine and tangible. For example, to force feed an animal so that its meat should look more appealing is not acceptable.[21]

---

[17] For further perspectives see the *Sefer Chareidim* 14:1; *Chiddushei Chasam Sofer* to Bava Metzia 32; *Matza Chein* 54:11 to *Toldos Noach* 1:26.

[18] *Igros Moshe Choshen Mishpat* II: 47. There is some disagreement in the *poskim* as to fish; see *Siach Yitzchok* 387

[19] Sanhedrin 59b. See also *Taz, Yoreh Deah* 117:4.

[20] See also *Even HaEzer* 5:14; *Rama, Even HaEzer* 5:19; *Terumas HaDeshen* 105.

[21] *Igros Moshe Even HaEzer* IV: 92.

4) Even when one is permitted to harm an animal for a valid need, he may not cause more suffering than is necessary.[22]

5) Medical experimentation on animals for the benefit of human health is permitted.[23] In such cases, though it is praiseworthy to do so, there may not be any actual requirement to endeavor to lessen the suffering of the animals involved.[24]

6) Cosmetics testing on animals are permitted according to most *poskim*. Others have expressed reservations, however. This issue will be discussed more in the live class.

7) Castration or sterilization of an animal for the benefit of its owner is considered a valid need and is permitted.[25]

8) Similarly, declawing a cat is permitted under certain conditions.[26] This will be discussed in the live class.

9) Human financial need is also a valid waiver for the prohibition of *tzaar baalei chaim*.[27]

## Your Animal vs. That of Another

10) One may feed another animal to his dog or other pet. Since he owns the pet, he is responsible for its welfare. However, one should kill the food animal first as to minimize its suffering.[28]

---

[22] See the sources cited above.

[23] *Tzitz Eliezer*, 14:68; *Sridei Eish* YD 91.

[24] *Shevus Yaakov* III: 71 holds that because of the importance of medical testing for humans, the need to mitigate pain to the animal is not present.

[25] Shabbos 110b.

[26] This will be discussed more in the live lesson.

[27] Avodah Zarah 13b.

[28] *Shulchan Aruch, Yoreh Deah* 1:5 and commentaries there.

11) One may not kill an animal to feed it to another's dog or an ownerless animal.

12) One has an obligation to feed and care for his own animal. Denying the animal food or care is considered cruel. However, Noahides have no obligation to provide food for other animals. It is certainly praiseworthy to alleviate the hunger of a starving animal, though.

### Relieving the Suffering of an Animal and Mercy Killing

13) One is only prohibited from causing unnecessary suffering to an animal. One has no obligation to alleviate an animal's existing suffering.[29]

14) Euthanasia of suffering animals is a much discussed topic in Torah literature. It hinges on this question: is the act itself of killing an animal considered *tzaar baalei chaim*? Some hold that the act of killing is always *tzaar balei chaim*,[30] while others hold that it is not.[31] Furthermore, the act of ending the animal's life must be viewed in terms of benefit-to-the-owner vs. benefit-to-the-animal. This issue must be determined on a case by case basis.

### Dangerous Animals & Pests

15) Animals that pester, sting, or annoy humans may be killed even if they will suffer in the process. This includes insects, dangerous dogs,[32] or other pests and vermin.

---

[29] Although one may claim from Exodus 23:5 that there is such an obligation, this argument has already been rejected by most *poskim*. See *Shulchan Aruch HaRav, Ovrei Derakhim* 3.

[30] *Shoel UMashiv Tinyana* III: 5.

[31] *Nodah BiYehudah Tinyana* YD 10; *Yam Shel Shlomo* to Bava Kamma 10:38; *Taz, Yoreh Deah* 116:6.

[32] *Taz, Yoreh Deah* 116.

16) Nevertheless, it is better that they be killed in a passive manner (traps, etc.) so that a person does not become accustomed to killing and taking life.[33]

## Labor Animals

17) Labor animals may be struck or prodded as minimally necessary to direct their labor. This is considered necessary for human benefit.

## Hunting

18) Hunting, unless an actual necessity for food or hide is considered a cruel endeavor and should not be done. The only people described as hunters in the Torah are cruel people such as Nimrod and Eisav.[34]

19) Capturing animals for human benefit is certainly permitted. Zoos, therefore, pose no issue as long as the animals are properly cared for.

---

[33] *Igros Moshe, Choshen Mishpat* II: 47.

[34] *Nodah BiYeshuda* ibid.

THE YESHIVA PIRCHEI SHOSHANIM SHULCHAN ARUCH PROJECT

# The Noahide Laws - Lesson Fifty

© **Yeshiva Pirchei Shoshanim 2017**
This shiur may not be reproduced in any
form without permission of the copyright holder.

## Table of Contents:

1. Introduction
2. Braisa, Sanhedrin 56b
3. Sanhedrin 60a Elucidated
4. Where were Noahides Originally Commanded in These Mitzvos?
5. Maimonides
6. Explaining Maimonides
7. Summary of Laws
   a. Determining Different Species
   b. The Prohibition Against Cross-Breeding Animals
      i. To What Does it Apply?
      ii. How Does One Transgress?
      iii. Artificial Insemination & Genetic Engineering
      iv. Status of Hybrid Offspring
   c. The Prohibition Against Grafting Different Species
      i. What is Called "Tree," "Vine," and "Fruit"
      ii. To Which Combinations Does this Prohibition Apply?
      iii. Discovering Grafted Trees or Vines on One's Property
      iv. The Fruit & Branches of a Hybrid Tree

# Animal Issues II: Cross-Breeding Animals & Grafting Trees

## Introduction

In the last lesson we reviewed issues pertaining to causing pain to animals. In this lesson we are going to examine *mitzvos* applying to animal cross-breeding and grafting trees.

## Braisa, Sanhedrin 56b

A *braisa* in tractate Sanhedrin discusses the source of the Noahide *mitzvah* to not cross-breed animals or graft different species of trees:

> The Rabbis taught in a braisa that seven commandments were given to the children of Noah: justice, not cursing the divine name, not committing idolatry, against acts of sexual immorality, against murder, against theft, and against eating a limb from a living animal.
>
> Rabbi Chananya ben Gamla says: "Also against eating blood [taken from a live animal]."[1]
>
> Rabbi Chidka says: "Also against sterilization."[2]
>
> Rabbi Shimon says: "Also against sorcery." Rabbi Yossi says: "A Noahide is also warned against every act stated in the section on sorcery [Deut. 18:12]…"

---

[1] The Talmud later rejects this proposition.

[2] Most later authorities understand the Talmud as rejecting this proposition.

Rabbi Eliezer says: "Noahides are also warned against Kilayim [prohibited mixtures of species]. Noahides are, however, permitted to wear [clothing made from mixtures of wool and flax]³ and to plant Kilayim [meaning to plant different plant species of vegetation in the same plot]. However, Noahides are prohibited from mating different species of animals and from grafting one species of tree onto another.

**Talmud, Sanhedrin 60a**

The Talmud then embarks on a lengthy, detailed examination of the Torah sources and allusions to each of the propositions brought in this *braisa*. On page 60a the Talmud turns its attention to Rabbi Eliezer:

*From where is this derived [that Noahides may not cross-breed animals or graft different types of trees]?*

Shmuel [offering an explanation of Rabbi Eliezer] says: "Because the verse states:⁴

**'My decrees you shall observe[: You shall not mate your animal with another kind; you shall not plant your field with diverse species,** *and a garment of mixed species shall not come upon you].'*

**'You shall not mate your animal with another kind; you shall not plant your field with diverse species…'** Just as **"your animal,"** prohibits mating, **"your field"** prohibits grafting trees.

## Sanhedrin 60a Elucidated

Let's take a closer look at Sanhedrin 60a:

*From where is this derived [that Noahides may not cross-breed animals or graft different types of trees]?*

Shmuel [offering an explanation of Rabbi Eliezer] says: "Because the verse states:

**'My decrees you shall observe [: You shall not mate your animal with another kind; you shall not plant your field with diverse species,** *and a garment of mixed species shall not come upon you].'*

---

³ Compare to Leviticus 19:19 and Deut. 22:10-11 that record a Jewish prohibition against doing so.

⁴ Lev. 19:19.

Rashi explains **My decrees you shall observe...** is an unusual turn-of-phrase for the Torah. Normally, God issues his decrees without any introduction. So, whenever we see such a preface we must question its purpose. Here, it implies that these statutes were already known to man; God is only adjuring man to preserve them.[5] Shmuel explains that these statutes are ancient Noahide prohibitions against cross-breeding species and grafting trees.

> *'You shall not mate your animal with another kind; you shall not plant your field with diverse species...' Just as "your animal," prohibits mating, "your field" prohibits grafting trees.*

Shmuel is telling us that the Hebrew expression **You shall not plant your field with diverse species...** refers specifically to grafting trees in one's orchard and not to planting multiple species of plants in a single field. Rashi and Ritva[6] explain that just as two animal species may not be joined by mating them, so too, two plant species may not be joined by mating/grafting them together.

What about the last part of the Lev. 19:19 prohibiting wearing "mixtures?" The *Yad Ramah* explains that the preface **My Statutes...** only comes to introduce the first two prohibitions (cross breeding animals and cross-grafting trees) and not to the third prohibition of wearing *Kilayim* (garments made of wool and linen). Therefore, Noahides may wear garments made of wool and linen, but Jews may not.

## Where were Noahides Originally Commanded in These *Mitzvos*?

According to Shmuel's interpretation of Rabbi Eliezer, the whole world was previously commanded against cross-breeding animals and cross-grafting trees. We know from Lev. 19:19's preface **My decrees you shall observe...** that such a prior mitzvah existed. Is any evidence of such a *Mitzvah* found anywhere else in the Torah?

Yes, it is! See Genesis 1:11 to 12:

---

[5] *The Talmud, Sanhedrin ibid. points out other instances of non-Noahide commandments being prefaced with similar language; see Lev. 18:5, for example. However, these instances do not imply earlier Noahide obligations. These passages use different word order and terminology than the verse at hand.*

[6] *To Kiddushin 39a.*

*And God said, 'The earth shall sprout forth vegetation, herbage that produces seed; **Edible trees that produce fruit of their own species**' ... And the earth produced vegetation, herbage that produces seed of its own species and trees that bear seed-bearing fruit of their own species.*

We see here that even though all herbage produced "its own species," only the trees were actually commanded to produce fruit identical to their own species. From here, we have learned that Adam was charged with keeping animal species separate as well. Therefore, the original Noahide laws appear to have included these prohibitions.[7]

## Maimonides

**Hilchos Melachim 10:6**

Maimonides in *Hilchos Melachim 10:6* include these prohibitions as part of the Noahide Laws:

> §6 *According to the Oral Tradition* [*meaning* Halacha leMoshe miSinai], *Noahides are forbidden to cross-breed animals and graft different species of trees together. However, they are not executed for violating this prohibition.*

At first glance, things appear straight-forward. However, Maimonides's words include a subtle difficulty. He writes **According to the Oral Tradition...**, not "According to Rabbi Eliezer or Shmuel." This fact demonstrates that Maimonides does not hold of the Talmudic exposition of this commandment.

## Explaining Maimonides

This difficulty is troubling for a number of reasons. Why does Maimonides not hold of Rabbi Eliezer/Shmuel's explanation of the laws? From where does he know that there is such a *Halacha* if he does not hold of their derivation?

Many, many pages have been written exploring Maimonides's learning of these prohibitions. This is a fascinating and advanced topic beyond the scope of this lesson. In short, there are many explanations and reactions to Maimonides. Some have even argued on Maimonides, rejecting entirely the existence of any Noahide prohibitions on cross-breeding plants or animals.[8]

---

[7] *Yerushalmi,* Kilayim 1:7; See *Gra* to *Yoreh Deah* 295:2.

[8] *Ritva,* Kiddushin 39a *D.H. Amar Rabbi Yochanan; Shach,* Yoreh Deah 297:3.

An important aspect of this difficulty is that **Rabbi Eliezer** is a lone opinion. If **Rabbi Eliezer** is learning these prohibitions as direct, biblical prohibitions, then he is *de facto* arguing for an eighth Noahide law. This position would pit him against the majority of sages who only hold of seven. Therefore, the *Halacha* cannot be like **Rabbi Eliezer/Shmuel**.

On the other hand, **Rabbi Eliezer's** proposition, unlike many others in the same *braisa* (i.e. against eating blood and sterilization), is not rejected by the Talmud. It is then possible that Maimonides understands **Rabbi Eliezer/Shmuel** as offering an *asmachta*, an allusion to these prohibitions, and not an actual source for these prohibitions. Since they are not explicitly commanded in the Torah, they are not independent Noahide laws, but rather subsumed within one of the larger categories.

The question then becomes: which of the larger categories includes these prohibitions? **Rabbi Shmuel bar Chofni Gaon** appears to place these prohibitions under the header of *ever min ha-chai*. However, The **Rama** MiFanu places them under the injunction against sexual immorality.[9]

Despite the dissenting arguments, most *poskim* agree with Maimonides that Noahides may not cross-breed animals or graft trees. However, the uncertainties work to create leniencies in certain situations.[10]

## A Summary of the Laws of Cross-Breeding Animals & Grafting Different Species of Trees

### Determining Whether Two Species Are the Same or Different

1) Torah law differs from modern science in its methods for classifying and identifying species of plants and animals.

2) For example, many scientific taxonomists consider dogs, coyotes, and wolves to be of the same species. Halacha, however, does not.[11] Therefore, one may not breed these animals to each other.

---

[9] These classifications of the Noahide laws were discussed in an earlier lesson.

[10] See *Chazon Ish*, *Kilayim* 1:1.

[11] See Mishnah, Kilayim 1:6.

3) A very general rule is that *halachic* species determination follows the names of the items rather than their biological qualities. For example, even though a dog and a wolf may be biologically similar, one is called a dog and the other a wolf. They are, therefore, considered different species.

4) This rule of following the name is only a general guideline and certainly does not help us for determining leniencies. For example, some citrus fruits, even though they have different names, might be considered one species in *Halacha*.[12]

5) Anytime there is a doubt as to whether two animals or plants are considered the same species, a qualified rabbi should be consulted.

## The Prohibition Against Cross Breeding Animals

### To What Does it Apply?

6) Broadly, this prohibition applies to all animals that mate via genital/cloacal coupling.[13] This would include all mammals (both land and sea[14]), reptiles,[15] most amphibians, and birds.[16]

7) This prohibition also applies to mating hybrid species with a pure species. For example: one may not mate a mule with a horse. The reason is that a hybrid species is considered a new species unto itself.

8) One may, however, mate two of the same hybrids provided that their mothers and fathers were, respectively, of the same species. For example: a mule whose mother is a donkey and father is a horse may mate with another mule whose mother is a donkey and father is a horse. However, a mule whose mother is a donkey and father is a horse may not mate with a mule whose mother is a horse and father is a donkey.[17]

---

[12] See *Chazon Ish*, Kilayim 3:7.

[13] In many species of insects and aquatic animals the female will deposit her eggs and the male will fertilize them later. The entire process takes place without any contact between the animals. See *Tosafos, Bava Kama 55*a discussing fish.

[14] *Tur* 297 with commentary of the *Prisha*.

[15] Chullin 127a.

[16] *Shulchan Aruch, Yoreh Deah* 297.

[17] *Shulchan Aruch*, Ibid.

9) It appears that this prohibition applies to mating animals of differing species even when they cannot produce viable offspring.[18]

10) One may not crossbreed his own animals, those of another, or those that are ownerless.[19]

### How Does One Transgress Cross-Breeding Animals?

11) In order to transgress this *mitzvah*, one must directly cause the mating to occur by either placing the animals in the mating position or using means that will likely lead to mating.[20]

12) Merely placing animals in physical proximity, even though they may actually mate with each other, is not considered direct involvement and is permitted.[21]

13) However, one should avoid placing two animals of different species in physical proximity if it is almost certain that they will try to mate. For example, one should not place a male wolf in a pen with a female dog that is in heat. One should similarly avoid placing a horse in a pen with a mule if it is likely that they will mate.[22]

### Artificial Insemination & Genetic Engineering

14) According to many *poskim*, artificial insemination of one species with the semen of another transgresses this prohibition.[23] An animal produced by such procedures has the status of a new, hybridized species as mentioned above.

---

[18] *Chasam Sofer to Yoreh Deah 297.*

[19] *Maimonides, Hilchos Kilayim 9:1.*

[20] *Biur HaGra to Yoreh Deah 297.*

[21] *Shulchan Aruch, Yoreh Deah* ibid.

[22] *This is a dispute among the authorities. Although it seems fundamentally permitted too merely place them in the same enclosure, this should be avoided if possible.*

[23] *Minchas Shlomo* III: 98. *The Ramban to Lev. 19:19 understands that purpose of the* mitzvah *is to keep the various species distinct.*

15) It is questionable whether genetic engineering involving the manipulation and splicing of genes on a molecular level is included in this prohibition. This is an exceedingly complicated question that continues to evolve alongside the science that drives it.

**Hybrid Offspring**

16) The hybrid offspring may be kept and maintained by its owner.

17) The animal is permitted or consumption.

18) All the laws of *tzaar baalei chaim* apply to this animal.

## The Prohibition against Grafting Different Species of Trees

What is Called "Tree," "Vine," and "Fruit?"[24]

19) Any perennial plant with a trunk (or a structure resembling a trunk) is called a "tree" for the sake of this prohibition. Therefore, Grapes, Peaches, apples, blackberries, bananas, etc. are all called trees.

20) This prohibition also applies to combinations of trees and fruit bearing vines. A "vine" is a plant that produces leaves and fruit yet does not possess a trunk. It doesn't matter whether or not the vine is perennial. This would include many species we consider vegetables such as tomatoes, gourds, cucumbers, etc.

21) A "fruit" is anything the fruit or vine yields that may be used as sustenance for living creatures. Therefore, a tree or vine producing fruit that only animals eat (i.e. a Bois d'Arc tree) is included in this prohibition. However, trees that produce spices (cinnamon, for example) are not included.

To Which Combinations Does this Prohibition Apply?[25]

22) The prohibition of grafting different species only applies to the following combinations:

---

[24] *Except where otherwise noted, this section is based on Shulchan Aruch, Orach Chaim 202 & 203; Chasam Sofer to Shulchan Aruch Yoreh Deah 287; Talmud Yerushalmi, Kilayim; Maimonides, Hilchos Kilayim 5.*

[25] *Unless otherwise noted, this section is based on the Tur and Shulchan Aruch, Orach Chaim 295, and commentaries there.*

a. A fruit tree grafted to a different species of fruit tree.

   b. A fruit tree grafted to a species of fruit bearing vine.

   c. A fruit bearing vine grafted to a species of fruit bearing tree.

23) One may graft a fruit-bearing species of tree or vine to a non-fruit-bearing species of tree or vine. One may also graft two different species of fruit-bearing vines to one another.[26]

24) The prohibition of grafting only applies to the parts of the plants or vines that are above ground. It does not apply to roots.

## If One Grafts a Tree or Discovers a Grafted Tree on His Property

25) When one buys property, he should examine the fruit trees and vines therein to ensure that none of them are grafted. Many species of trees are commonly grafted even when still in the nursery. For example, peach trees are almost always grafted onto almond stalks. Nectarines are commonly grafted onto peach or plum stalks. We will talk about the practicalities of this in the live class.

26) If one finds a grafted tree or vine on his property, its law depends on whether or not the graft has yet fused. If the graft has fused, then one may keep the tree. However, the tree should not be watered, pruned, or maintained for its own benefit (we will discuss this more in the live lesson). Doing so is considered as contributing to the grafting process.

27) If the graft has not yet fused, then the graft must be taken apart even if this will cause the death of the plant.[27]

28) Before the graft has fused it is also prohibited to uproot and replant the tree elsewhere. Once the graft has fused, the tree may be replanted.

---

[26] *This is permitted for Noahides, but not for Jews.*

[27] *Shulchan Aruch, Yoreh Deah 295. The Sefer Sheva Mitzvos HaShem applies this ruling to Noahides. However, it is possible that Noahides may have leniencies not afforded to Jews in such a situation.*

## The Fruit & Branches of a Hybrid Tree

29) The fruit of a grafted tree or vine/tree combination may be eaten.[28]

30) The branches of a hybrid tree may be cut and replanted. They are not themselves considered grafted entities. Rather, they are only the hybrid produce of such a graft.

31) A branch from a grafted tree is, like a hybrid animal, considered a new species and may not be grafted to either of its parent species. It may, however, be grafted to another identical hybrid.

---

[28] Maimonides, Kilayim 1:7 and Shulchan Aruch, Yoreh Deah ibid.

# THE YESHIVA PIRCHEI SHOSHANIM SHULCHAN ARUCH PROJECT
# The Noahide Laws - Lesson Fifty-One

**© Yeshiva Pirchei Shoshanim 2017**
This shiur may not be reproduced in any
form without permission of the copyright holder.

164 Village Path, Lakewood NJ 08701 732.370.3344
164 Rabbi Akiva, Bnei Brak, 03.616.6340

## Table of Contents:

1. Introduction
2. Origin of Idolatry
3. Maimonides, *Hilchos Avodah Zarah* 1:1-2
4. What is Idolatry?
5. Maimonides
6. Modes of Idolatrous Worship
7. Belief Alone: Permitted or Prohibited?
8. *Shituf*
9. *Shituf*, Christianity, & Other Religions
10. Creating New Religions
11. Summary

# Idolatry I: Introduction

## Introduction

The term "idolatry" is used today, for the most part, in a metaphorical or homiletic sense. We use "idolatry" to refer to anything that receives undue or inappropriate human attention. This use of "idolatry" does not even come close to conveying the concept and actions the Torah prohibits or that *HaShem*, the One True God, finds so offensive.

True, absolute idolatry is virtually non-existent in our times. The influence of Abraham has touched almost all peoples and all corners of the world. Even faiths that we may think of as "idolatrous" are still not entirely comparable to the ancient forms and concepts of idolatry prohibited by the Torah. To understand the relevance of the prohibition of idolatry in our times requires a careful examination of the Torah's intent.

## The Origins of Idolatry

The Torah makes a curious statement in Genesis 4:26:

> *And for Seth, to him also a son was born and he named him Enosh. Then* **hukhal** *to call by the name of HaShem.*

The phrase *...to call by the name of HaShem...* refers to prayer or worship of God. We see that something happened to worship and prayer in this era. However, the term used, **hukhal**, is an ambiguous, carrying two possible meanings:

- **Hukhal** - "it became common." Used this way, the verse reads: *Then it became common to call by the Name of HaShem.* This would indicate that prayer and worship of God began in this generation.

- *Hukhal* – "it became profaned." Used this way, the verse reads: *Then calling in the name of HaShem became profaned*. This reading would indicate that something went horribly wrong in that generation's relationship with God.

Whenever the Torah uses a term that has two clear implications, it usually intends both meanings. Considering this fact, the intent of the verse should be:

> *Then the prayer and worship of God [calling by the name of HaShem] became widely/commonly [***hukhal***] profaned.*

Rashi and all other commentaries apply this reading of the verse. A number of ancient Midrashim and other texts record what transpired in that generation. Maimonides summarizes their accounts follows:

## Maimonides, *Hilchos Avodah Zarah* 1:1-2

**§1** *In the time of Enosh,[1] mankind made a great error. The wise men of that generation gave reckless counsel. Enosh himself was one of those who erred.[2] Their error was as follows: They said God created stars and spheres with which to control the world. He placed them on high and treated them with honor, making them as servants who minister before Him. Accordingly, it is fitting to praise and glorify them and treat them with honor. [They perceived] this to be the will of God,[3] blessed be He, that they should exalt and honor those who He exalted and honored just as a king desires that the servants who stand before him be honored. Doing so is, in fact, an expression of honor to the king.*

*After formulating this idea, they began to build temples to the stars and to offer sacrifices to them. They would praise and glorify them with words and prostrate themselves before them. This is because, by doing so, they would - according to their false ideas - be fulfilling the will of God. This was the essence of the worship of false gods and the rationale of those who served them. They would not say that there is no other god except for this star. This message was conveyed by Jeremiah, who declared (10:7-8): "Who will not fear You, King of the nations, for to You it is fitting. Among all the wise men of the nations and in all their kingdoms, there is none like You.*

---

[1] Adam's grandson, Enosh lived from 3525 BCE to 2620 BCE.

[2] Shabbat 118b implies that Enosh did not take part in the idolatry. However it is evident from the Sheiltos of Rav Achai Gaon and others that there is a slightly different version of this gemora which may be the source of the Rambam's statement.

[3] This is the "… it became common/profaned to call in the name of HaShem…"

*They have one foolish and senseless idea; a teaching as empty as wood;" i.e., all know that You alone are God. Their foolish error consists of conceiving of this "emptiness" as Your will.*

*§2 After many years, there arose false prophets who claimed that God had commanded them to speak and say: Serve this star (or all stars), sacrifice to it, offer libations to it, build a temple for it, and make an image of it so that all people - including women, children, and the common people - may bow to it. He would inform them of an image he had conceived, and tell them that this is the form of the particular star, claiming that this was revealed to him in a prophetic vision.*

*In this manner, the people began to make images in temples, under trees, and on the tops of mountains and hills. People would gather together and bow to them and they would say: "This image is the source of benefit or harm. It is appropriate to serve it and fear it." Their priests would tell them: "This service will enable you to multiply and be successful. Do this and this, or do not do this or this." Subsequently, other deceivers arose and declared that a specific star, sphere, or angel had spoken to them and commanded them: "Serve me in this manner." He would then relate a method of service: "Do this, do not do this." Thus, these practices spread throughout the world. People would serve images with strange practices – each one more distorted than the other - offer sacrifices to them, and bow down to them. As the years passed, His glorious and awesome name was forgotten by the people of the world, in both their speech and thought, so that they no longer knew Him. Thus, all the people, the women, and the children would know only the image of wood or stone and the temples of stone to which they were trained from their childhood to bow down and serve, and in whose name they would make oaths. The wise men among them thought there is no God other than the stars and spheres for whose sake, and in resemblance of which, they had made these images. The Eternal Rock was not recognized or known by anyone in the world, with the exception of some individuals, for example: Chanoch, Metushelach, Noach, Shem, and Ever. The world continued in this fashion until the pillar of the world - the Patriarch Abraham - was born.*

## What is Idolatry?

Idolatry is a severe prohibition and a concept whose rejection is a core tenet of the Torah. Torah scholars have devoted centuries of study and thought to defining idolatry. This is one of those areas to which we could devote an entire library of books. For the sake of this course, we are going to present an overview of the basic, practical issues you may encounter today

Broadly speaking, idolatry includes:

- The worship of any created thing as God or as embodying any part of God.

- Worshiping any created thing in the manner of Enosh and his generation; by believing in the One True God, yet honoring Him by worshipping one of His creations.

- Worshiping, praying to, or considering any created thing as an intermediary between man and God.

- Behaving in a worshipful manner toward any two or three dimensional representation of either *HaShem* or any other created thing.

- Ascribing to God the form of any of his creations.

- Ascribing to God multiplicity instead of oneness.

There are many variations of idolatry besides these. We will address them when they arise.

## Modes of Worship

When we say it is "prohibited to worship" idolatry, what do we mean? Simply put, one commits a sin by engaging in a specific act of idolatrous "worship." However, acts of idolatrous "worship" are often very different from what we may consider "worship."

The different types of idolatry described above each developed their own specific forms of worship. These methods express the unique, underlying beliefs specific to that form of idolatry. Therefore, one is only liable for transgressing idolatrous worship when he employs a mode appropriate to the particular idol he is worshipping.[4]

There are four actions, however, that are prohibited regardless of the type of idolatry:[5]

- **Bowing** before idolatry.

- **Slaughtering** to idolatry.

- **Burning an offering** before idolatry.

---

[4] For examples, see Maimonides, *Hilchos Avodas Kokhavim* 3.

[5] Maimonides, *Hilchos Avodas Kokhavim* ibid.

- **Offering a libation** to idolatry.

These four actions are reserved for the service of HaShem in the holy temple and may not be used in the service of any other entity.

We should note that an object once worshipped or designated for idolatrous worship becomes prohibited for ownership or benefit. We will discuss this in greater detail in the next lesson.

## Is Belief Alone Prohibited or Permitted?

Acts of idolatrous worship may be prohibited, but what about the mere belief in another god in addition to HaShem? For Jews, belief in any other power or deity is clearly prohibited as idolatry. For Non-Jews, however, the status of belief in a secondary deity is not as clear.

- **Maimonides & Nachmanides** - In many, many places Maimonides asserts that belief in idolatry is the essence of the prohibition.[6] Nachmanides echoes this opinion in several places his own commentary to the Torah.[7] It goes without saying that acting upon this belief, via worship, is also prohibited.

- **Rashi** - Rashi, however, holds that the essence of idolatry is only the act of worshiping idolatry.[8] Belief alone, according to Rashi, is not prohibited to Noahides.

What would be the practical difference between these two views? According to Rashi, one can believe in another god besides God, however any act of worship for that false deity would be prohibited.

This idea that idolatrous belief is possibly permitted to Noahides (though practice is not), lays at the heart of the concept of *shituf*.

---

[6] See *Hilchos Avodas Kokhavim* 2:1-2; *Hilchos Teshuva* 3:7.

[7] To Exodus 20:3; 22:19; 23:25.

[8] See Rashi to Exodus 20:3.

## Shituf

*Shituf* is the belief in another divine entity besides HaShem, God. For Jews, this is an absolute prohibition and equal to outright idolatry. Its acceptability for Noahides however, has long been a topic of study. Though Maimonides and many others consider *shituf* idolatry for Noahides as well, the majority of *poskim*, including the Shulchan Aruch (Rama[9]) permit *shituf*. However, it is subject to the following limitations:

- The Torah views non-Jewish belief in another god in addition to the true God to be mistaken. It is not a prohibition, but it is unrighteous and one who does so, though not viewed as a sinner, is not considered *MiChasidei Umos HaOlam* – of the Pious Nations of the World - and will not receive his full reward for observing the Noahide laws.[10]

- *Shituf* pertains only to **belief** in a secondary divine being, <u>not</u> to the **worship** of a secondary god. Any expression of worship for this secondary deity is prohibited as idolatrous practice.

- It is only the belief in another god in addition to the true God that is not punishable. Conflation of the true God with another entity or the assigning of corporeality to the true God may create issues of actual idolatry. The Torah definition of idolatry is not only limited to the worship of idols, but pertains to how we conceive and represent the nature of the one true God.

## Shituf, Christianity, and Other Religions

Many have tried to qualify Christianity as an acceptable belief for non-Jews using the concept of *shituf*. Though true that many authorities have suggested so, this opinion must be put in context.

---

[9] *Orach Chaim* 156.

[10] *Sefer Sheva Mitzvos HaShem* 1, *haarah* 7.

The exact status of Christianity in the eyes of the Torah is difficult to determine. There have been thousands of pages written on this topic, and even a basic survey of the literature is far beyond the scope of this course. In short: Christianity has many elements that are clearly idolatrous from a Torah perspective (i.e. its various rituals and modes of worship), but some that are difficult to pin down (i.e. is it truly monotheistic or polytheistic?). Its difficult status makes its exact classification doubtful.

Historically, Sephardic Rabbis, living in Muslim-ruled lands, were free to rule stringently. They criticized Christian belief as outright idolatry. However, rabbis living in Christian lands had to be very clever and cautious in what they said and wrote. Given the shadow of the church and the constant threat of exile and death, they were not free to even intimate that Christianity may be outright idolatry. Given their precarious situation, they had to take a tempered position. In these Rabbis' theological writings they often declare Christian belief *shituf* and therefore acceptable for non-Jews. However, in their writings on *halakha*, Torah law, they held that Christian ritual and worship was to be treated as idolatry.[11] They were often able to get these views past censors because *halachic* (legal) writings were not so thoroughly vetted as the church censors usually lacked sufficient understanding of the material.

Were it not for the threat of the church, these Ashkenazi rabbis very well may have taken the stringent view of their Sephardi co-religionists and condemned Christianity as idolatry.

Nevertheless, even if Christian belief is *shituf*, the practice of Christianity would remain idolatrous. The practical conclusion, for a number of reasons, is that Christianity is to be treated as absolute idolatry.[12] Namely, it is not merely the worship of another secondary deity, but is an idolatrous conception of God Himself.[13] Therefore, Christianity is treated as absolute idolatry for Noahides in

---

[11] See Rama YD 141:1 and 150 who rules that crosses to which a non-Jew has bowed are prohibited as idolatrous images. This is a subtle yet definitive statement since such a conclusion is only possible if, fundamentally, the Rama believes that the concept of the trinity is idolatry.

[12] See *Hilchos Avodas Kokhavim 9:4, Maachalos Assuros 11:7, Hilchos Melachim 11:4*. See also Rambam's *Perush HaMishnayos* to the beginning of tractate Avoda Zarah (note, however, that the modern editions are heavily censored). See also *Minchas Elazar* I: 53-3; *Yechaveh Da'as* IV: 45. An extensive list of opinions is brought in *Yayin Malchus*, pp. 234-237.

[13] See the *Vikuach* of Nachmanides. See also his commentary on the Torah to Deut. 16:22. The idea that God ever took on corporeal manifestation, had a mother, was born, or exists as a tripartite deity are all heretical concepts according to the Torah.

both belief and practice.[14] As we will discuss in the live lesson, however, it is not "absolute idolatry" in the same sense as the ancient idolatries described in Tanakh and the Talmud.

What about Islam? Islam is not idolatrous[15] and, rather, has a strong theological resonance with Torah thought and belief.[16] From the perspective of the prohibition of idolatry, it is 100% monotheistic and an acceptable belief system[17], [18] However, Islam presents a different problem altogether.

## Creating New Religions

Both Jews and non-Jews are enjoined against the creation of new religions.[19] One who creates a new religion is, by default, rejecting belief in the truth of the Torah,

---

[14] It should be pointed out that believing Christians do not themselves have the status of full idolaters. See *Shulchan Aruch*, Y.D. 148:12; *Shut Yehudah Yaaleh* YD 170.

[15] *Maachalos Assuros 11:7*; *Tur* YD 124; *Beis Yosef* YD 146; *Rama* YD 146:5; YD 124:6; *Taz* YD 124:4; *Shach* YD 124:12; See *Ben Ish Chai* on Parshas Balak for a discussion of the issues. There are a few who hold that Islam is prohibited as idolatry. It seems that this is due to certain customs of the Haj. See note 24.

[16] For example, a Jew may not enter a Church for any reason because it is a place of idolatry (see *Igros Moshe* YD 3:129-6 and many, many others), yet it is permissible to enter and even pray within a mosque *(Avnei Yashfei 1:153 quoting Rav Elyashiv, ztz"l; Yabia Omer VII YD 12:4;* and others). In fact, a Muslim contemporary of Maimonides, the historian Ibn al-Qifti, records that in Egypt the Maimonides would occasionally pray in a Mosque (see *al-Qifti's Tarikh al-Hukama)*. Of course, this is not an ideal situation and may have been done only in special circumstances. One recent authority, Rabbi Boruch Efrati, has advised traveling Jews to pray in airport mosques (a common amenity overseas) rather than pray among the hustle and bustle of the terminal. This ruling, though, pertains only to praying in the physical space of the mosque. One may not take part in actual Islamic prayer services. It should be noted that another recent authority, the *Shu"t Tzitz Eliezer* XIV:91, cites the Ran (see note 26 below) and prohibits Jews, or for that matter Noahides, from entering mosques. Although his opinion is not agreed to by other authorities, all agree that one should not enter a mosque without a compelling need or reason.

[17] While the belief system of Islam is acceptable theologically, many customs of the Haj are problematic. This may be the reasons for the *Ran Sanhedrin 61b* and other dismissals of Islam. See Meiri to Avodah Zarah 57a.

[18] However, an interesting difference emerges with regard to teaching Torah. Maimonides writes in a responsum (ed. Blau #149) that because Christians accept the Torah as part of God's revelation (as the "old testament"), there are unique permits and leniencies with regard to Jews teaching them Torah. Yet, because Islam rejects the Torah's authenticity (substituting the Quran), Jews may not teach Torah to Moslems.

[19] *Hilchos Melachim Perakim* 8 & 10.

Moses (the greatest prophet in history), and in God's authority. The Torah, containing both the Noahide and Jewish laws, were given to stand for all eternity. The Torah states this in no fewer than 24 places![20]

New religions denying the eternal authority of the Torah are not to be given legitimacy. This principle would apply equally to Christianity, Islam, Buddhism or any religion coming after the Torah, regardless of whether or not these religions observe all or part of the Noahide laws.[21]

## Summary

1. Idolatry began in the third generation after Adam. It was originally conceived as a means of honoring HaShem, but quickly devolved.

2. Idolatry is not only the worship of statues or stars. It is the worship of any created thing as divine.

3. Idolatry includes the worship of any created thing as a means of honoring HaShem or as an intermediary between man and God.

4. Ascribing to God the form of any of His creations is considered idolatrous.

5. Idolatry includes ascribing to God any multiplicity.

6. One only transgresses the prohibition of idolatry by either serving the object in a mode appropriate to it or by 1) Bowing to it, 2) Slaughtering to it, 3) Bringing a burnt offering before it, 3) Offering a libation before it.

7. An object worshiped as or designated for idolatry becomes prohibited.

8. Belief in a secondary deity to HaShem is permitted for Noahides. However, it is unrighteous and they are not considered *Chasidei Umos HaOlam* for doing so.

---

[20] Exodus 12:14, 12:17, 12:43, 27:21, 28:43, Leviticus 3:17, 7:36, 10:9, 16:29, 16:31, 16:34, 17:7, 23:14, 23:21, 23:31, 23:41, 24:3, Numbers 10:8, 15:15, 19:10, 19:21, 18:23, 35:29, Deuteronomy 29:28.

[21] See *Igros Moshe* YD II: 7.

9. Even though one may believe in *shituf*, one may not actually worship this other deity.

10. Christianity is treated as idolatry for all intents and purposes, but it is not 100% identical to ancient forms of idolatry.

11. All religions after the giving of the Torah are inherently false even if they are entirely monotheistic.

THE YESHIVA PIRCHEI SHOSHANIM SHULCHAN ARUCH PROJECT

# The Noahide Laws - Lesson Fifty-Two

**© Yeshiva Pirchei Shoshanim 2017**
This shiur may not be reproduced in any
form without permission of the copyright holder.

## Table of Contents:

1. Introduction
2. The Injunction Against Noahide Idolatry
3. Noahide vs. Jewish Prohibitions of Idolatry
    a. Capital Idolatry
    b. Lesser Forms of Idolatry
4. Idolatry in Thought or Intellect: The Prohibition of "Turning to Idolatry"
    a. Thoughts and Theologies
    b. Books of Idolatry
    c. Learning From Deviant Believers
    d. Deniers of the Torah & Scorners
    e. Debating Idolaters & Atheists
5. Verbal Idolatry
    a. Oaths
    b. Referring to Idols
    c. When it is Permitted
6. Summary

# Idolatry II: Fundamentals

## Introduction

In the last lesson we did a very general overview of the origins and nature of idolatry. This lesson begins our practical overview of the subject.

Idolatry exists in two realms:

1) **Idolatry of thought, belief, and words,** and
2) **Acts of idolatry.**

Although all forms of idolatry are prohibited, one is only culpable in earthly courts for committing **acts of idolatry**. This lesson will address **idolatry of thought, belief, and words.** We will examine acts of idolatry in the next lesson.

## The Injunction Against Noahide Idolatry

Genesis 2:16 states:

> *And the Lord,* **God,** *commanded unto Adam…*

This verse goes out of its way to specify that the Lord, *HaShem*, is God. The Talmud in Sanhedrin 56b notes the implication of this verse is that *HaShem*, and only *HaShem* is God. This idea carries positive and negative *mitzvah* connotations:

- **Negative: Not to "exchange" God** - This is the specific prohibition of idolatry. The Torah defines idolatry as the replacement or "exchange" of God. This concept is much larger than the singular idea of worshiping a graven image. It includes the worship of any natural object or abstract force. Included as well is the worship of any image representing God.

Since God has no form, there can be no item that depicts Him. Therefore, if one worships such an image, he is by default <u>not</u> worshipping *HaShem*. Similarly, to worship any physical item as an embodiment of God (or part of God) creates a similar problem because God has no corporeal or physical manifestation in this world.

- **Positive: One must fear/awe/respect God** – As the creator and master of all things, giver of life, and ultimate power, God demands and deserves our fear, awe, and respect. It is true that we must also strive to love and be grateful to God. However, full acceptance of God's authority and law requires respect and awe of Him.

## Noahide vs. Jewish Prohibitions of Idolatry

For Jews, there are many acts and types of idolatry that incur the death penalty. However, there are other types of idolatry for which a Jew would not receive death, but which are nevertheless prohibited. For example, a Jew is not liable to death for embracing or kissing an idol, even though doing so is prohibited.[1]

Are Noahides executed for all types of idolatry? Or, are they perhaps liable only for those for which Jews would be liable to death?

**Capital Idolatry: *Braisa* Sanhedrin 56b**

The Talmud cites the following *braisa* as authoritative:

> *Anything [idolatrous] for which a Jewish court would execute [Jews], Noahides are warned against. Anything [idolatrous] for which a Jewish court would not execute [Jews], Noahides are not warned against.*[2]

This *braisa* teaches that any Jewish act of idolatry that incurs capital punishment for Jews also incurs capital punishment for Noahides. Therefore, capital forms of idolatry are the same for both Jews and non-Jews.

**Lesser, Non-Capital Forms of Idolatry**

What about acts of idolatry that are prohibited for Jews, but for which they are not executed? What is the Noahide liability for these lesser forms of idolatry? Are they even prohibited to Noahides? For example: is a Noahide prohibited from embracing or kissing an idol?

---

[1] Sanhedrin 60b.

[2] Sanhedrin 56b.

Though the *braisa* certainly says they are not executed for doing so, is it prohibited nevertheless? The Talmud actually asks this exact question and concludes that Noahide liability is identical to Jewish liability. Therefore, Maimonides writes:

> *A gentile is sentenced to death for any type of idolatrous worship for which a Jewish court would impose capital punishment [upon a Jew]. However, a gentile is not executed for a type of idolatrous worship for which a Jewish court would not impose capital punishment. Even though a Noahide will not be executed for these forms of worship, he is nevertheless forbidden from engaging in any of them.*[3]

The definitions of prohibited forms of idolatry, whether they incur capital liability or not, are equally the same for both Jews and Noahides. As we shall see, idolatry's definition, never changes: idolatry is idolatry regardless of who commits it.[4]

## Idolatry of Thought or Intellect: The Prohibition of "Turning to Idolatry"

The Torah states:

> *Do not turn toward the idols…*[5]

and

> *Beware … lest you seek to find out how these nations serve their Gods.*[6]

**Idolatrous Thoughts & Theologies**

These verses prohibit contemplating, studying, or investigating the thoughts or theologies of idolatrous religions. Therefore, one may not entertain idolatrous thoughts, contemplations, or other such musings. One is also prohibited from planning or contemplating prayer or worship to an idol. Heaven punishes a person for this even if the plan is not actually carried out.[7]

---

[3] *Hilchos Melachim* 9:2.

[4] The only one exception may be the concept of *shituf* – belief in Hashem plus another entity. While it is considered idolatry for Jews, it is not for non-Jews according to *halakhah*.

[5] Lev. 19:4.

[6] Deut. 12:30.

[7] *Kiddushin* 39b with *Tosafos*.

**Books of Idolatry**

As well, books of idolatrous faiths are forbidden and may not be studied or even owned. Such books should be destroyed so that their falsehoods will not persist in the world.[8] The "new testament" is a book of idolatry and must likewise not be owned or read. Even though the central figure was a Jew, the theology and even the apparently wise sayings therein contain many deep, subtle and carefully crafted distortions and misrepresentations of Torah thought. From start to finish, it is a bastardization of Torah thought and belief. Due to its thorough corruption, it is no different from nor does it have any more relevance to Torah than any other pagan or idolatrous book. However, it is more dangerous than other pagan books because of its superficial similarities and seeming parallels to parts of Rabbinic literature as well as its historical connection to Judaism (or to "a Jew," to be precise).

One may only learn or own such texts if the purpose is to understand how to recognize and better avoid that which is prohibited or to save others from the trap of such material.

**Learning from Deviant Believers**

Also included in the prohibition of "turning to idolatry" is learning personally from a *min*, a person whose beliefs or conceptions of God are fundamentally wrong. There are five basic types of *minim* (the plural of *min*), deviant believers, brought in Torah literature:[9]

- One who does not believe in any god or guiding force to the universe,

- A polytheist – one who believes in more than one god,

- One who believes in one god, yet believes that he has now or has ever had a form, body, or other physical manifestation,

- One who denies creation's fixed beginning ex nihilo from God's command,

- One who believes in, serves, or worships any natural or man-made item as an intermediary between man and God.

These beliefs are idolatrous and prohibited.

---

[8] *Shulchan Aruch*, *Orach Chaim* 334:21.

[9] *Hilchos Yesodei Teshuvah* 3:7 and 8 with the commentaries of the *Kesef Mishnah* and the *Raavad*; *Hilchos Mamrim* 1:1-2 & 3:3.

**Deniers of Torah & Scorners**

The following are not called *minim*, deviant believers, but are called "scorners" or "deniers of the Torah," and one should not learn from them:

- One who does not believe in prophecy or that God communicates with man,

- One who denies God's omniscience,

- One who believes that the *mitzvos* are manmade or were in any way devised by man,

- One who believes that the Oral Law is manmade or in any way a human invention.

- One who believes that God replaced or altered any part of the Torah or any *mitzvah* after the revelation at Sinai.

This latter group of beliefs is erroneous, yet not idolatrous. Believing in any of them is tantamount to denial of the Torah in its entirety. Therefore, it is not possible for one to be called a believing Jew or Noahide if one believes in any of these things. One may not learn from any of these deviant or erring believers even if such learning is for a constructive purpose like recognizing or countering prohibitions.[10]

**Debating Idolaters and Atheists**

The prohibition of "turning to idolatry" also includes debating idolaters and atheists. However, discussion with them for the sake of exposure to Torah and the Noahide laws is permitted.[11]

## Verbal Idolatry

The Torah states:

> ...you shall not mention the names of other gods...[12]

---

[10] Shabbat 75a with Rash; *Shulchan Aruch, Yoreh Deah* 179 (end) and *Shach*. We should note that there has been serious debate for centuries over Maimonides's reliance upon Aristotle. There is not sufficient room to discuss the issue here, but only note that Maimonides's use of Aristotle is no proof that we may learn or study Aristotle's works.

[11] See *Hilchos Avodah Kokhavim* 2:5 along with its commentaries.

[12] Exodus 23:13.

The Talmud and Maimonides explain that this verse comes to prohibit praising or giving any credence to the name of idolatry.[13] Therefore, there are a number of restrictions on using the names of idols.

**Oaths**  One may not pledge or swear an oath in the name of an idol or adjure others to do so.[14] This is even prohibit if one swears but does not mean it sincerely or have any sincere belief in the idol.[15]

**Referring to Idols**  It is prohibited to refer to any idol in a respectful manner. For example, many of the catholic saints are actual idols. When referring to them, one should not use the honorific of "saint." Casual or neutral references to the names of idolatry are permitted. Nevertheless, it is praiseworthy not accustom oneself to using the name of an idol even in a casual sense.

**When it is Permitted**  One may mention the names of idols when teaching the prohibitions of idolatry.

**Verbal Acceptance of an Idol**  In all of these cases, one does not incur capital punishment. However, if one verbally accepts an idol upon himself as his god he has committed a capital crime.[16]

## Summary

1. Idolatry is prohibited in thought as well as deed. Idolatrous thoughts, however, are not punishable by a human court.

2. Idolatry is the "exchanging" God or the true conception of God for any other god or idea of God.

3. Whatever is considered idolatrous for Jews (whether idolatry of thought or deed) is also considered idolatry for Noahides. It doesn't matter whether it is a capital form of idolatry or a lesser form of idolatry.

---

[13] *Hilchos Avodas Kokhavim* 5:10.

[14] The laws of making such oaths are found in *Hilchos Avodas Kokhavim* 1:2, 5:10; *Hilchos Shevuos* Ch. 11.

[15] *Radvaz* V:256.

[16] *Hilchos Shegagos* 1:2 with commentaries. See further *Nekudos HaKesef* YD 148; *Hilchos Avodas Kokhavim* 9:5.

4. One may not contemplate idolatrous theologies or ideas.

5. One may not own or study the books of idolatrous religions. Such books should be destroyed.

6. One may not learn religion or even Torah from one whose beliefs are corrupted.

7. It is prohibited to debate those who hold such corrupted beliefs.

8. One may not swear in the name of an idol or refer to them in a praiseworthy manner.

THE YESHIVA PIRCHEI SHOSHANIM SHULCHAN ARUCH PROJECT

# The Noahide Laws - Lesson Fifty-Three

© **Yeshiva Pirchei Shoshanim 2017**
This shiur may not be reproduced in any
form without permission of the copyright holder.

## Table of Contents:

1. Introduction
2. Idolatry for Jews & Non-Jews
3. The Elements of Idolatry
4. Prohibitions of Benefit
5. Objects of Idolatry
    a. Representational Idols
    b. Natural Idols
    c. Decorative Figures
    d. Appurtenances to Idolatry
6. Modes of Worship
    a. Idol Specific
    b. Methods Reserved for HaShem
    c. Placing Items Before an Idol
7. Secondary Services & Practices
8. Nullification

# Idolatry III: Idolatry in Deed

## Introduction

In the last lesson we examined some of the fundamentals of idolatry and especially idolatry in thought and belief. One is not liable to earthly punishment for these types of idolatries. However, idolatry in deed is much more severe and may actually incur such liability. In this lesson we are going to examine the *halachos* of practical idolatry.

## The Elements of Idolatry

Idolatry usually involves the confluence of four factors:

1) The **object** of idolatry (the idol),
2) The **method** of worshipping the idol,
3) The **utensils** of worship, and
4) The **worshipper** himself.

When a person commits a culpable act of idolatry, there are ramifications for all four factors:

1) The **object of idolatry** usually (but not in all cases) becomes prohibited (we will discuss what this means shortly),

2) The **act of worshipping** that item incurs a transgression that may be deserving of death or punishment at the hands of heaven,

3) The **utensils of worship** become prohibited whether they are decorations or offerings to the idol,

4) The **worshipper** himself has committed a grievous transgression for which he is either subject to punishment at the hands of heaven or liable to punishment by earthly courts. It also gives him the halachic identity of an "idolater" that affects how Jews and Noahides may interact with him (this will be discussed in the next lesson).

## Prohibitions of Benefit

What do we mean by "The object of idolatry becomes prohibited?" It means that one may neither own nor derive any benefit whatsoever from such items.[1] These items must be destroyed or nullified ("nullification" will be described below). Once the item is nullified, it may be owned and even benefited from.[2]

**An important note to keep in mind: one person cannot render prohibited an item that does not belong to him unless he physically alters it in some way.**

## Objects of Idolatry: "Idols"

An object of idolatry is either **representational** or **natural**:

- **Representational idols** - A man-made statue or image that either represents a deity, is believed to be the deity, is believed to be an intermediary between man and a deity, or is believed to contain or embody some aspect of a deity. Not only may one not worship such idols, but one may not make or own any two dimensional or three dimensional representation of anything for the purpose of worship or to represent God or a god.[3] Owning such items is also prohibited.[4] There is a slight difference between representational idols made by Jews and those made by non-Jews:

    - **Made by a non-Jew for the sake of idolatry** - it is immediately prohibited as an item of idolatry.

---

[1] *Shulchan Aruch, Yoreh Deah* 146:14. See also Ramban's commentary to *Avodah Zarah* 59b.

[2] *Hilchos Avodas Kokhavim* 8:9.

[3] *Hilchos* Avodas Kokhavim 3

[4] See Rashi and *Mechilta* to Exodus 20:3.

- o **Made by a Jew for the sake of idolatry -** If a Jew makes such an item, it does not become prohibited until it is actually worshipped.[5]

- **Natural idols** – A natural idol is not man made, but is something created by God. This includes trees, rocks, animals, streams, rivers, mountains, etc. There are two type of natural idols:

  - o **Natural idols in their naturally occurring condition** – A naturally occurring item in its original condition, unaltered in any way for the sake of idolatry, does not become prohibited for benefit if it is worshipped.[6] Therefore, the rocks and stones of an idolatrous mountain are permitted for benefit. Waters from an idolatrous wells or rivers are also permitted as are animals. So too, the fruits of a tree worshipped as an idol are permitted. Anything offered to such an idol remains permitted for benefit. However, any adornments fashioned to honor or beautify the idol are prohibited for benefit.

  - o **Natural idols that are altered (with idolatrous intent) from their naturally occurring conditions** - Any naturally occurring item whose condition is altered for the sake of idolatry becomes prohibited like an item fashioned as an idol. The item itself is prohibited as is anything offered to the idol. For example, if a stone is rolled to a new location for the sake of idolatry, then it becomes prohibited and anything offered to it also becomes prohibited. However, if the stone was worshipped in its original, naturally occurring position, then neither it nor anything offered to it become prohibited. Another example: a tree in its natural condition does not become prohibited as idolatry if worshipped. However, if it was planted for the sake of idolatry, or if it is in any way altered for the sake of idolatry, then it is prohibited and so too is anything offered to it.

---

[5] *Hilchos Avodah Zara* 7:5

[6] These *halachos* and those in the following section are found in the *Shulchan Aruch, Yoreh Deah* 145 and Maimonides, *Hilchos Avodah Kokhavim* Chapter 8.

- **Decorative figures** – The Torah additionally prohibits the making of any three-dimensional representations of humanoid or angelic figures for the purpose of decoration.[7] This includes making sculptures of angels, demons, and mythical humanoid creatures (satyrs, mermaids, etc.) If such sculptures are not used for the purpose of decoration, then they may be made.[8] Therefore, mannequins, medical models, and CPR dummies may be constructed. Whether it is permitted for Noahides to own a prohibited item is unclear and a dispute between many Torah authorities.[9] If one wishes to keep such an item for decoration, it should be nullified; altered in such a way as to make it an imperfect form. For example, if the item is a sculpture of a hand, then a finger should be removed. If a face, then the nose should be cut off. This is nullification, and will be discussed in more depth below. One may make two dimensional representations of other humanoid or angelic forms.

- **Appurtenances to idolatry** – Besides the idol itself, there are many other objects involved in acts of idolatry:

    o **Items offered to idols** – These fall into three categories:

    - **Items offered to man-made idols** – are prohibited for benefit.

    - **Items offered to unaltered natural idols** – do not become prohibited.

    - **Items offered to natural idols that have been altered for the sake of idolatry** – are prohibited from benefit.

    o **Vessels of service**[10] – Goblets, bowls, or other containers made for use in serving the idol are also prohibited.

---

[7] *Shach, Yoreh Deah* 141:20 to 21.

[8] See for a more detailed examination of these laws, see *Chasam Sofer* 128.

[9] The *Tur, Rema,* and *Shach* to *Yoreh Deah* 141:4 concur that there is no Torah prohibition on owning such items. However, the *Maharam M'Rottenberg, Ramban, Rambam, Rif,* and *Maharit* disagree and hold it is a biblical prohibition. Nevertheless, Jews are prohibited from owning such items due to rabbinic injunction. Although Noahides have no such injunction, the great disparity of opinion among the Rishonim is enough to give pause to anyone who owns such items. Therefore, many *poskim* conclude that Noahides should not own or use such items.

[10] These laws are found in *Shulchan Aruch, Yoreh Deah* 139.

- **Decorations for the idol**[11] – Any items made for decoration or enhancement of the idol are prohibited for benefit. This is not limited to items that are attached or in contact with the idol, but includes candles, rugs, incense,[12] etc. Flowers and other items, though natural, are also prohibited. One may not smell or otherwise use them.

- **Buildings or structures erected for the idol** – Any house or building constructed for the purpose of idolatrous worship or later renovated for such a purpose is prohibited for benefit.[13] Such a structure must be destroyed or nullified. Churches have the status of houses of idolatry. Therefore, a Noahide should not enter or admire such places. When family events are held in churches, and one's absence would cause strife, it is possible to attend. However one should be very, very cautious to neither participate in any religious aspect of the service nor admire nor benefit from the things within the church. Nevertheless, one may enter a church for any practical purposes (i.e. work requirements). One may enter a mosque for any reason because it is not at all idolatrous.

- **Music of idolatry** – One may not benefit from music of idolatry if there is not a practical purpose for doing so.

## Modes of Worship

All forms of idolatry are forbidden.[14] However, one only incurs capital liability and prohibits the items involved by worshipping idols in one of the following ways:

- **In a method specific to the idol** – If one worships an idol in a way that is established as particular to that idol, he transgresses and the idol and items involved become prohibited.

---

[11] *Shulchan Aruch ibid.*

[12] Meaning incense burned to enhance the environment and not as an offering.

[13] *Shulchan Aruch, Yoreh Deah* 145.

[14] *Hilchos Melachim* 9:2.

- **Using any action reserved for *HaShem* in the temple** – Certain methods of worship are specific to the worship of the Holy One, Blessed is He. If one uses any of these methods in worship of an idol, even if this method is not particular to that idol, he transgresses and renders the idol and all items involved prohibited. There are four modes unique to the Temple:[15]

  - **Bowing** – One is capitally liable if he bows to an idol and brings his face to the ground.[16] This is even if bowing is not the normal method of worship for this idol. However, if bowing even less than this amount is customary for this type of idolatry, then even a lesser form of prostration incurs liability. If one bows as a sign of respect, but not intending to recognize the idol as a God, one still transgresses because the act of bowing is itself an act of submission and acceptance.[17] However, if the bowing is in no way intended to be a sign of respect, but instead one bows for some other reason (i.e. fear of persecution or death), he is not liable.[18] Similarly, one may bow down to avoid danger.

  - **Slaughtering an animal** – This is incising an animal's neck on either its front or the back,[19] or chopping the neck with a sword or axe.[20] The species of animal is irrelevant.[21]

---

[15] Both of types of liability are discussed in *Nodah BiYehudah* II: 148 and *Minchas Chinuch* 26. According to some (*Tzafnas Paneach Tinyana, Avodas Kokhavim* 3), singing before any idol is also prohibited because it was a form of worship in the Temple (see *Hilchos Kli HaMikdash* 3:3). It is not clear if this opinion is recognized the majority of *poskim*. It should be avoided, however, because it is a normative method of worship in most idolatrous faiths.

[16] *Hilchos Avodah Kochavim* 6:8. See also *Shu"t Tashbatz* III: 315.

[17] *Ritva*, Shabbos 72b.

[18] Sanhedrin 61b.

[19] *Hilchos Avodas Kokhavim* 3:3.

[20] *Shulchan Aruch, Yoreh Deah* 139:4.

[21] *Shulchan Aruch, Yoreh Deah* 139:4. The *Shulchan Aruch* does not rule like Maimonides, but instead follows the *Raavad* that the act of slaughter, not the object of slaughter, is what transgresses the prohibition. Therefore, even if one slaughtered a locust to an idol, even though a locust is not fit to be offered in the temple, the act is prohibited. See Avodah Zara 51a; *Hilchos Avodah Kokhavim* 3:4 with *Kesef Mishnah* and *Raavad*.

- o **A burnt offering** – Burning anything for the sake of the idol is prohibited.[22]

- o **Offering a libation** – This is the throwing or pouring for the sake of an idol of any substance that can splash or splatter. This includes oil, blood, water, etc.[23] It does not include solid material or hard substances like clay.[24]

**Placing an Item Before an Idol**

- **Placing items before an idol** - Merely placing any item before an idol is not automatically an act of idolatrous worship unless it is the normal mode of service for that idol. However, if such a "placing" involves items resembling those offered in the temple, then the action and the items are all prohibited in all cases.[25] Such "placings" include:

  - o The meat of any species of sacrificial animals, such as sheep, cows, or goats.

  - o Whole doves.[26]

  - o Wine, bread, oil, salt, water, blood, wheat, or grapes.[27]

## Nullification

Once an item has been made into an idol, what do we do with it? Since it is prohibited for benefit, it cannot be owned or used by anyone for any purposes. The *Halacha*[28] depends on who made the item into an idol:

---

[22] *Shulchan Aruch, Yoreh Deah* 179:19. This even includes anything that was not burned on the altar in the temple. The issue is the act of burning, not the item being burned or offered.

[23] This would even include materials such as honey and fruit juices that were not offered on the altar in the Temple. See *Shulchan Aruch Yoreh Deah* 139.

[24] See Shulchan Aruch 139:3. Note that the Shulchan Aruch and most *poskim* do not agree with Maimonides, Avodah Kochavim 3:4 on this point.

[25] See *Shulchan Aruch, Yoreh Deah* 139.

[26] *Taz, Yoreh Deah* 139:5.

[27] See *Tosafos* and *Rosh* to *Avodah Zarah* 50a.

[28] These laws are in *Shulchan Aruch, Yoreh Deah* 146.

- **The idol of a Jew** – An idol made prohibited by a Jew can never be nullified. It must be destroyed as completely as possible.

- **The idol of a non-Jew** – A non-Jewish idol can be *mevatel*, nullified. This allows it for benefit and ownership. One nullifies an idol by marring it in a conspicuous way with the intent of removing its status as an idol. For example, if the idol is a human face, then the nose should be cut off. If it is a hand, then a finger should be removed. Any non-Jew can nullify the idol of any other non-Jew. A Jew, however, cannot nullify anyone's idol.

## Secondary Services & Practices

The Talmud in Sanhedrin 56b states that Noahides are warned against numerous forms of divination, sorcery, and necromancy. Though many of the Torah's specific examples of divination are no longer practiced,[29] the types of divination mentioned remain prohibited.[30] These acts are not actual idolatry, but are secondary practices. While prohibited, they do not incur capital liability. The following are prohibited forms of divination:[31]

- Any forms of fortune telling, such as tarot, scrying, etc.

- Interpreting events and sights as omens for the future. This includes casting lots or dice and interpreting the results as signs for the future.

- One may not select a sign for himself, saying, "If such and such occurs, then I will do such and such." This is forbidden when there is no logical connection between the sign and the person's action.

---

[29] See Deut. 18:9-12.

[30] Maimonides does not mention these prohibitions in his summary of the Noahide laws. However, he mentions them in other places as either outright idolatry or, it appears, as part of the prohibition against turning to idolatry. See *Hilchos Avodah Kokhavim* Ch. 6, Ch. 11:6; *Peirush HaMishnayos Avodah Zarah* 4:7; *Sefer HaMitzvos* N9; and many, many other locations).

[31] These are based on <u>*Hilchos Avodah Kokhavim* Ch. 6</u> & <u>Ch. 11</u>; *Shulchan Aruch, Yoreh Deah* 179.

- It is permitted to look back and appreciate the connections between past events and the results of those events, saying "That was good for me, everything got better after that."

- One may not practice incantations, meaningless words believed to have magical effects.

- One should not try to command supernal, supernatural, or spiritual forces for his own needs.

- One may not attempt to contact the dead.

- Astrology is permitted for Noahides. It may be foolish or inappropriate but it is not prohibited.[32]

## Summary

1. The definition of idolatry is the same for both Jews and non-Jews.

2. Idolatry is the worship of both man-made idols and natural items. When one worships a man-made idol or a natural idol that has been altered for idolatrous reasons, the item, its offerings, and the utensils of worship all become prohibited. Neither a natural item in its natural condition nor the items offered to it ever become prohibited for benefit. However, the decorations that are upon the item do become prohibited.

3. One may not make a three-dimensional representation of any humanoid or angelic figure.

4. All idolatrous decorations, texts, and offerings (except as mentioned above) are prohibited from benefit.

5. A non-Jew's idol can be "nullified" by defacing it. The resulting item may be used and owned.

6. Divination, scrying, and necromancy are all prohibited.

---

[32] Jews, however, are explicitly prohibited from such things. Noahides are not – see Shabbos 156a.

7. Astrology is permitted, although it may be foolish or inappropriate.

THE YESHIVA PIRCHEI SHOSHANIM SHULCHAN ARUCH PROJECT

# The Noahide Laws - Lesson Fifty-Four

© **Yeshiva Pirchei Shoshanim 2017**
This shiur may not be reproduced in any
form without permission of the copyright holder.

## Table of Contents:

1. Introduction
2. Man as God
3. A Man With an Idol or Image Upon Him
4. In Business
    a. As a Seller
    b. As a Buyer
    c. An Accidental Purchase
    d. Idolatrous Festivals
5. Inheriting Idolatry
6. Attending Idolatrous Festivals
7. Entering Places of Idolatry
8. Summary

## *Idolatry IV: Idolaters*

### Introduction

So far, we have looked at the fundamentals of idolatry and its prohibitions in thought, speech, and deed. In this lesson we will look at the interpersonal aspects of idolatry and the *halachos* pertaining to idolaters. Recall that we have already learned that it is prohibited to learn from or debate idolaters or those who hold corrupt beliefs.

### Man as God

Bowing or honoring any man who has made himself into a god is prohibited. However, bowing before such a person is permitted in the case of fear or out of honor for one's position (examples will be discussed in the live class).

### A Man with an Idol or Image upon Him

It is forbidden to honor or show respect before a person who has an idol embroidered upon his clothing or is wearing an image of the idol.[1] "Showing respect" includes methods of honor such as:

- Bowing,

- Removing one's hat,

---

[1] *Orach Chaim* 113:8; *Yoreh Deah* 150.

- Kissing another's hand,

- Standing when the other enters the room,

- Curtsying.

This prohibition is limited only to showing honor because of the idol itself or the idolatry associated with the person's position. If the idol carried upon the person is unrelated to any reason for the individual's honor, then it is permitted to bow or kiss the person's hand.

For example, may one stand or remove his hat for someone who is wearing a crucifix? It depends:

- If the person is a priest or minister, then honoring him is prohibited,

- If the person is a powerful official of a secular government (whose position deserves honor) then it is permitted even though the individual is wearing a crucifix.

**Idolatrous Vestments** The clothing and vestments of idolatrous priests are not themselves idolatrous unless they include an image of the idol. They wear these garments for their own honor and position, not for the sake of the idol.

## In Business

**As a Seller** A Noahide may not sell items known to be idolatrous. Also, he may not sell any item, even a non-idolatrous one, to a Noahide if he knows for certain that it is going to be used for idolatrous purposes.[2] Therefore, selling Xmas lights to idolaters is permitted because their purpose is not intrinsically prohibited. However, one may not sell idolaters candles or other utensils of actual worship. If the items are readily available at the same or better price elsewhere, and the Noahide's livelihood is affected, then he may sell it to the idolater because he is not contributing directly to the idolater's act.[3]

---

[2] *Shulchan Aruch, Yoreh Deah* 151:2.

[3] *Shulchan Aruch, Yoreh Deah, Rama* 151 and 151:6.

**As a Buyer**  One may not buy goods or donate money or other materials when such resources would go directly to perpetuate idolatrous institutions or activities (i.e. a church bake sale).[4] However, one may donate or purchase goods when the funds are going to be used for other things as well (i.e. a church bake sale to raise money for a homeless shelter).

**An Accidental Purchase**  If one buys many items from an idolater and unwittingly purchases or receives idolatrous items, he does not need to nullify or destroy the items. Rather he may return them to the idolater (the reasons will be discussed in the live class).[5]

**Idolatrous Festivals**  The Talmud and *Halacha* prohibits conducting any business with idolaters both on their festivals and in the days immediately preceding them.[6] This includes repaying loans,[7] buying, and selling.[8] The concern is that the business will prompt the idolater to thank his god on the festival.

This prohibition has very limited application in the western world today. The reasons will be discussed in the live class.

## Inheriting Idolatry

If ones parents or other relatives leave him an inheritance that includes idolatrous items, he may not give the items to his siblings or other idolaters. Rather, he must take possession of the items and then destroy or nullify them.[9] Remember, however, that idolatrous items inherited from a Jew cannot be nullified; they must be destroyed.

## Attending Idolatrous Festivals

It is prohibited to attend idolatrous festivals at which idols are served by any acts of idolatry or prayer. As long as there is no prayer or actual idolatrous service, one may

---

[4] *Shulchan Aruch, Yoreh Deah* 143.

[5] *Shulchan Aruch, Yoreh Deah* 146:3.

[6] *Talmud Avodah Zara* 2a; *Shulchan Aruch, Yoreh Deah* 148:1.

[7] *Hilchos Avodah Zarah* 9:1.

[8] See the *Rosh* 1:1 to *Avodah Zara* at length for a discussion of the details.

[9] *Shulchan Aruch, Yoreh Deah* 146:4 with the *nosei Keilim*.

attend the gathering even if it has religious or seasonal connotations. Therefore, one may attend an office Xmas party since the main purpose is not relevant to idolatry or religion.

## Entering Places of Idolatry[10]

Buildings dedicated to or constructed for idolatry are prohibited. One may not use these buildings or benefit from them in any way. While there is no actual prohibition against Noahides entering these structures,[11] one should avoid doing so.[12] Entering a church or other place of idolatry is fraught with potential problems and pitfalls.

Today, almost all Noahides have relatives who are involved with idolatrous religions. This fact makes lifecycle events, often held in churches, awkward for believing Noahides. There is a much literature pertaining to Jews entering such places or attending such events. However, there is very little material addressing the Noahide situation. The following is a summary of the *halachos* according to the available responsa literature.

**The Type of Event**
Lifecycle events that are idolatrous in their very purpose or nature may not be attended under any circumstances. This would include church confirmations, christenings, ordinations, etc. Similarly, if one has a relative who is singing or performing in an idolatrous service, one may not attend to hear her perform since the essence of the gathering is idolatrous. Weddings, however, are not intrinsically idolatrous since the concept of marriage is almost universal.

**Held in a Sanctuary**
If the event is held in a church, yet the event is not intrinsically idolatrous, he should still not attend unless his absence would create conflict or strife. In that case, one may attend, but should be very cautious to not participate in any way in the service; one may only passively observe the event. One should also avoid any action that may be perceived as idolatrous (examples will be discussed in the live class). It is best to stand or sit at the back of the congregation so that his non-participation will not be conspicuous or cause ill will.

---

[10] This summary of the *halachos* is based on *Shulchan Aruch, Yoreh Deah* Ch. 142, 148, and 150.

[11] Jews, however, are abjured against entering such places.

[12] There some authorities who have argued that Noahides are actually prohibited from entering churches. However, it appears to this author that this is not on account of any actual injunction against doing so, but only as a practical issue.

**In Another Part of the Church**   One may attend an event that is not intrinsically idolatrous and not held in a church sanctuary (meaning, that it is held in a social hall or other room). This is even if one's absence would not create strife. However, one may not participate in the service if it includes any religious overtones.

**Entirely Secular Events**   One may attend an entirely secular event held in a church (concert, town meeting, etc.) provided that he avoids any action that appears to give deference to the idols therein.

**Summary of the Halacha**

|  | Sanctuary | Other Room or Building in the Facility | Entirely Secular Facility (i.e. Non-Denominational Wedding Hall) |
|---|---|---|---|
| Idolatrous | May not attend. | May not attend. | May not attend. |
| Not-Intrinsically Idolatrous | May attend if one's absence would cause strife. Must not participate or appear to honor the idols therein. | May attend even if absence would not create strife. Should still not participate in the service. | May attend even if absence would not create strife. Should still not participate in the service. |
| Entirely Secular | May attend, but should not appear to honor the idols therein. | May certainly attend. | May certainly attend. |

**For Practical Purposes**   A Noahide may enter a church or other such place for certain business purposes or other practical reasons.

## Summary

1. One may not bow or honor any man who is believed to be a God.

2. One may not honor any person with an idol upon his person. However, if there are reasons for honoring the person independent of the idol, then one may show him honor.

3. It is prohibited to sell any idolatrous item. It is also prohibited to sell any regular item if it is known with certainty that it will be used for idolatry.

4. One may return accidentally purchased idolatrous items.

5. If one inherits items from his family, they must be nullified or destroyed.

6. Attending the festivals of idolaters is permitted providing that the festivals are not actually idolatrous.

7. Entering idolatrous places for idolatrous services is always prohibited. There are cases when one may attend a church for family or lifecycle events.

# The Noahide Laws - Lesson Fifty-Five

THE YESHIVA PIRCHEI SHOSHANIM SHULCHAN ARUCH PROJECT

© **Yeshiva Pirchei Shoshanim 2017**
This shiur may not be reproduced in any
form without permission of the copyright holder.

164 Village Path, Lakewood NJ 08701 732.370.3344
164 Rabbi Akiva, Bnei Brak, 03.616.6340

## Table of Contents:

1. Introduction
2. Monetary Mitzvos for Jews vs. For Noahides
3. Maimonides & Others
4. The Minimum Amount Considered Theft
5. Restitution?
    a. Eruvin 62a
    b. Rashi
    c. Other Rishonim

# Monetary Law I: Introduction & Concepts

## Introduction

Presenting the monetary laws of the Torah includes several unique challenges. For one, this is a large body of material that continues to grow ever larger as we invent and adapt new mechanisms of trade, payment, commerce, and investing. Because of the size and ever-changing application of these laws, it is virtually impossible to present them point-by-point. Instead, we will have to introduce only general concepts of monetary law. To successfully fulfill the God's expectations requires regular study and reflections on the specific business and monetary situations we encounter in our daily lives.

Another difficulty in teaching this subject is the Torah's monetary laws, for both Jews and Noahides, are often much stricter than what secular law permits. This means many business practices we consider acceptable, possibly even essential, are actually prohibited by the Torah! Sadly, because of the tremendous *yetzer hora* (destructive desire) for money, it is common for Jews and Noahides to ignore, sidestep, or outright reject the Torah's strictures. A believing Jew or Noahide must be willing to lose money, pass on deals, and even lose everything he has to uphold the Torah's monetary laws. Indeed, one of the *Gedolim* (leading Torah sages) once said "Anyone who has never walked away from a valuable deal or who has never lost a tremendous amount of money because of his religious convictions has not yet upheld the Torah's monetary laws."

By the same token, some of the Torah's monetary laws are more lenient than secular monetary law. In these cases, one cannot transgress secular law using the Torah as his justification. Believe it or not, this happens a lot.

## Monetary *Mitzvos* for Jews vs. Noahides

Looking at the Torah closely, we see that God commanded Jews in many specific monetary *mitzvos*, yet only commanded non-Jews against theft. Nevertheless, the Talmud is thick with exhaustive analyses and examinations of monetary laws and business ethics as they apply to both Jews and non-Jews, apparently extending non-Jewish monetary concerns well beyond the basic issue of theft. How do we explain this apparent disparity?

Answering this question requires a comprehensive grasp of the Talmudic literature involved. Thankfully, many Sages with just such a grasp have provided answers.

## Maimonides & Others

Maimonides in *Hilchos Melachim UMilchamos* 9:9 summarizes the Talmud's various discussions of non-Jews and theft as follows:

> *A non-Jew is liable for transgressing the prohibition of theft if he stole from another gentile or from a Jew. This applies to one who forcefully robs an individual or steals money, a kidnapper, an employer who withholds his worker's wages and the like, even a worker who eats from his employer's produce when he is not working. In all such cases, he is liable and is considered as a robber.* **With regard to Jews, the law is different.**

The concluding line of this passage is mysterious: **With regard to Jews, the law is different.** In what way is the "law different for Jews?" Indeed, the Torah specifically forbids a Jew in all of these prohibitions!

The [Kesef HaMishnah]() and many other commentaries explain the difference as being in the source of their obligations. Jews are obligated in all of these acts from a number of specific, separate commandments given at Sinai. Noahides, however, are equally obligated in all of these acts, yet from the simple injunction against theft.

All of the various, specific Jewish monetary laws which are conceptually linked to theft are included within the general Noahide prohibition of theft.

Note the structure of the passage:

> **A gentile is liable for violating the prohibition against theft whether** he *stole from another gentile or from a Jew. This applies to one who forcefully robs an individual or steals money, a kidnapper, an employer who withholds his worker's wages*

*and the like, even a worker who eats from his employer's produce when he is not working.* **In all such cases, he is liable and is considered as a robber.** *With regard to Jews, the law is different.*

It is clear that Maimonides is defining theft very broadly and only naming a few examples of what is included therein. What actions fall under the umbrella of "theft" for Noahides? The Talmud, Sanhedrin 57a appears to equate the definitions of theft for Noahides to those for Jews. This understanding, that acts of theft are the same for both Jews and Noahides, is the *Halacha*.[1]

## The Minimum Amount Considered Theft

Maimonides, in *Hilchos Melachim UMilchamos* 9:9 concludes with the following:

> *Similarly, a gentile is liable for stealing an object worth less than a perutah.*

Jews are only liable or theft for stealing an amount more than a *perutah*, which is defined as the smallest usable amount of money. As discussed in an earlier lesson, Noahides were not commanded in *shiurim*, limits and amounts for liability. Therefore, a Noahide is liable for taking any amount to which he was not entitled. We should make clear, however, that this means liability for committing a sin, not necessarily liability for capital punishment. Most of the situations of theft we will discuss here do not incur capital punishment even though they are forbidden.

However, taking an item or amount that is too small to quantify monetarily is permitted. This permit applies to amounts truly insignificant such that the owner would neither notice, miss, nor prevent one from taking it. The classic example is taking a tiny sliver of wood from another's wood pile to use as a toothpick. Such a small item has no quantifiable monetary value and its absence makes no difference to the owner.

In some situations, however, even this is prohibited. For example: if it is common practice for many people to wantonly take slivers of wood then eventually all those little slivers will amount to a big loss to the owner! In such a case even taking a small sliver is considered theft. A pious person will refrain even from taking such a small amount in permitted circumstances.[2]

---

[1] See Maimonides ibid.; *Minchas Chinuch* 516; *Shulchan Aruch HaRav Hilchos Gezeilah* 23.

[2] See *Ben Ish Chai* on *Ki Seitztzi*.

## One Who Has Stolen – Restitution?

As with all of the Noahide laws, the punishment for transgression is death. However, most acts of theft will not actually warrant capital punishment. What is to be done in these situations? Even though the Torah commands Jews to return stolen objects and to make restitution, no such commandment was given to non-Jews. Or, was it?

The Torah specifically commands Jews in making restitution:

> *When he becomes guilty of such a sin, he must return the stolen article…*[3]

Is this positive commandment considered part of the body of legislation common to both Jews and Noahides? Or, perhaps, positive commandments regarding theft are not included in the general Noahide negative prohibition against theft.

**Talmud, Eruvin 62a**

The Talmud states:

> *A Noahide is punishable by execution for theft of an amount less than one perutah; he cannot return it.*

This statement may be read a number of ways. Perhaps it is only discussing a case involving less that a *Peruta*. Or, maybe it means that a Noahide can never return a stolen item. Since it is discussing a case of capital liability, maybe it only exempts a Noahide from restitution in cases of capital punishment; however, in a case when capital punishment is not administered the perpetrator should return the item.

The Rishonim have discussed this passage in detail and generally reached two conclusions:

- **Rashi** – There is no need for a non-Jew to make restitution because the verse commanding restitution[4] was only commanded to the Jews. A court cannot either force him to do so because it would be imposing a penalty of which they have no right to administer.

---

[3] Leviticus 5:23.

[4] Leviticus 5:23.

- **Tosafos** and **Other Rishonim**[5] – The point is that restitution does not exempt a Noahide from capital liability. He must make restitution in any case and the court has the right to force him to do so.

It would appear, according to **Tosafos** and the **Other Rishonim** that a thief must make restitution for what he stole even in a case where capital punishment is not given. The disagreement between **Rashi** and **Other Rishonim** may be viewed as a disagreement over one or all of three issues:

- **Positive Commandment of Restitution** – Is the positive commandment of restitution included in the Noahide prohibitions against theft? Rashi clearly says no. However, the Other Rishonim hold it is. As we have seen, Noahides are commanded in all of the Jewish *mitzvos* related to theft, which may include the positive commandment to make restitution.

- **Restitution is a Positive Implication of the Negative Commandment** - Or, perhaps, Tosafos agrees with Rashi that Noahides are not explicitly required to make restitution; the Jewish positive commandment from Lev. 5:23 is not included under the general umbrella of the Negative Noahide prohibition of theft. However, Tosafos may hold that restitution is a positive implication of the negative injunction against theft.

- **As Repentance** – Transgressions of civil law are also spiritual transgressions: one who steals commits a crime as well as a sin. The court may impose a penalty for the criminal aspect, yet the thief must return the item as part of his repentance for the spiritual aspect of the transgression.[6] This idea has some support from the Talmud in Taanis 16a. In describing the repentance of Nineveh[7] the Talmud tells us that the citizens demolished their houses in order to remove and return the wooden beams and joists they had stolen from others. The implication is that full repentance was not possible as long as the stolen items remain in their possession.[8]

---

[5] *Rabbeinu Chananel, Ritva, Ran, and Rashba to Eruvin* ibid. See also *Ritva* to Avodah Zarah 71b. These commentaries are in general agreement on this principle.

[6] *Shu"t Yad Eliyahu* 40.

[7] The city of sin to which the prophet Jonah was sent.

[8] The Talmud understands this as the meaning of Yonah 3:8 that each man "… repented from the *chamas* that is in their hands."

The *Halacha*, as we may have deduced by now, follows the majority who hold a Noahide must make restitution. This is the case when a Noahide steals any amount from either a Jew[9] or another Noahide.

## Summary

1. Jews are commanded in a number of specific mitzvos pertaining to theft and monetary propriety. Noahides are also obligated in all of these specific commandments; however their *mitzvos* are all included in the general injunction against theft.

2. Noahides are liable for stealing even an amount less than a *perutah* – the minimum usable amount of money.

3. Nevertheless, there is no prohibition on an amount so small as to be impossible to quantify monetarily and that the owner would certainly forgive.

4. If the taking of such a small amount will over time result in a definite loss, and people commonly take such small amounts, then it is prohibited to do so.

5. A pious person will refrain even when it is permitted to take such small amounts.

6. One must return the item that he stole. This is the opinion of the majority of Rishonim. The details of how restitution is to be made will be the subject of a future lesson.

---

[9] According to some understandings of the aforementioned Rishonim, a Noahide is not required to make restitution to a Jew for less than a *perutah*. According to them, this is because the Jewish threshold for liability is a *perutah* and Jews are not particular to demand restitution for less than that amount (such a view is not, therefore, imposing the *perutah* as a measure for liability for Noahides). This might be a valid leniency in certain pressing situations. .

THE YESHIVA PIRCHEI SHOSHANIM SHULCHAN ARUCH PROJECT

# The Noahide Laws - Lesson Fifty-Six

© **Yeshiva Pirchei Shoshanim 2017**
This shiur may not be reproduced in any
form without permission of the copyright holder.

## Table of Contents:

1. Introduction
2. The Prohibition Against Theft
3. Robbery vs. Theft
4. Transactional Law
   a. Overcharging, Undercharging & Price Gouging
   b. Formulating Covetous Thoughts & Schemes
   c. Against False Weights & Measures
   d. Against Owning False Weights & Measures
   e. Requirement to Maintain Honest Weights & Measures
5. Debts
   a. Against Withholding Payment When One Has Means to Pay
   b. Falsely Denying a Debt

# Monetary Law II: Overview of the Laws of Theft

## Introduction

A complete exposition of every way in which monetary laws apply is impossible (to attempt it would require at least a 10 year course!). The landscape of modern business and finance is constantly shifting as new methods of commerce, trade, and payment are created and adapted. The only way to successfully navigate these *halachos* is to be aware enough of the guiding issues to know when to do more research or to seek assistance.

The following is a list of the specific types of theft alluded to in the Torah and that are common to both Jews and Noahides. This list is based upon Maimonides's *Hilchos Gezeilah*, *Hilchos Geneiva*, and *Sefer HaMitzvos*.

## The Prohibition Against Theft

The Torah says many times:

> *You shall not steal.*

Its first occurrence, in Exodus 20:15, does not refer to the theft of money or goods, but rather to the theft of another person: kidnapping (this will be discussed in the near future).

Lev 19:11 is the first time *Do not steal* appears with full force as a prohibition against the theft of another's property. [1]

---

[1] See *Mechilta* to this verse.

We must note that this prohibition is specifically against "theft," called *Geneiva* in Hebrew. *Geneiva* specifically refers to the taking of another's property by stealth and without the victim's awareness.[2]

*Geneiva*, theft, as will all other associated prohibitions, is transgressed whether one takes the item with intent to return it or pay for it later[3] or as a practical joke.[4] This would include taking an item that is normally rented with the intent of returning it later and paying for the time.[5] Even taking an item from a store and leaving money behind without the shopkeepers' approval is not permitted.[6]

One may not steal from another even for a constructive purpose. For example, one cannot steal from someone to teach him to better guard his belongings.[7]

Furthermore, one may not steal from one who has cheated him in the past.[8] One may also not steal an item from another thief.[9]

In short: a person may never take the possessions of another person unless the other person has granted permission. The intent of the one taking the items makes no difference.

An exception to the rule, however, is in the case of a person who cannot sufficiently guard his property due to disability or infirmity. In such a case it is

---

[2] See Maimonides, *Hilchos Geneva* 1:3.

[3] Maimonides, *Hilchos Geneiva* 1:2. *Shulchan Aruch, Choshen Mishpat* 348.

[4] See *Sefer HaMitzvos, Lo Saaseh* 244; *Sefer HaChinuch* 224. *Minchas Chinuch* 224, however, appears to disagree as to the liability of Noahide in these cases. However, his reasoning is difficult to understand considering it is well established that Noahides are as equally obligated as Jews in these prohibitions.

[5] *Sefer Sheva Mitzvos HaShem, Geneiva* 1:6 citing *Sheiltot* 4 and *HaEmek HaShaila*.

[6] There are a number of reasons to refrain from this that will be discussed in the live lesson.

[7] *Sefer Sheva Mitzvos HaShem, Geneiva* 1:8.

[8] *Shulchan Aruch HaRav, Hilchos Gezeila* 1. The rights of an owner to seize back that which is his will be discussed in a future lesson.

[9] *Hilchos Melachim* 9:9. Stealing a stolen item in order to compensate the owner will be discussed in a future lesson.

permitted (and sometimes perhaps meritorious) for another to take and guard his possessions if necessary.[10]

## Robbery vs. Theft

Leviticus 19:13 states:

> *You shall not commit robbery.*

The Talmud in Bava Kamma 79b explains that robbery, *Gezeila*, is different from *Geneiva*, theft. While *Geneiva*, theft, is stealing carried out in secret, *Gezeila*, robbery, is stealing executed by force and with full knowledge of the victim.[11] As proof the Talmud cites II Samuel 23:21 which refers to a spear being forcibly taken from a person.

This would include armed robbery, using threats and intimidation, and blackmail.

## Transactional Law

**Overcharging, Undercharging & Price Gouging**

Leviticus 25:14 states:

> *When you sell an item to your neighbor or purchase something from him, do not **victimize** each other.*

The name for this prohibition is ***Ona'ah*** – meaning victimization or deception. The Talmud explains at length the implications of this verse:[12]

- One transgresses this prohibition by charging another by more than 1/6 (16.67%) of the fair market price for an item.

- The seller must return the overage to the buyer. The overage is considered stolen even though the buyer paid it willingly.

- Alternatively, the buyer may demand that the entire transaction be voided.

---

[10] *Sefer Chassidim* 585.

[11] Maimonides, *Hilchos Gezeilah* 1:3.

[12] The primary discussion in found in Bava Metzia 49b to 50b, 61a. However, the topic is discussed further in many places in the Talmud. The practical *Halacha* is brought in Maimonides, *Hilchos Mechira* 12; *Shulchan Aruch, Choshen Mishpat* 227.

- Similarly, this prohibition applies on the buyers end as well – if a buyer underpays by more than 1/6 (16.67%) then the seller may demand the difference be paid to him or that the sale be voided completely.

- There is a statute of limitations on such transactions. Usually, it is the amount of time needed to complete due diligence and determine whether or not the item was priced correctly. Depending on the item, this time varies from a 6 to 24 hours.

- This law does not apply to all goods. The following goods are exempted from the laws of *Ona'ah*:

  - **Real Estate** – While buyers and sellers do not have any recourse to demand compensation or void a real estate transaction, some hold that *Ona'ah* remains prohibited. According to many scholars, there is not even a prohibition.

  - **Collectables** – Collectables, antiques, and other items having no real utilitarian value are not subject to *Ona'ah*. This is because the value of these items is entirely based on desire.

  - **Items whose value is determined by appraisal** – this category is not always so clear, however.

  - **Auction & Barter** – Items that are sold via auction or commonly bartered in exchange for other goods.

**Pressing Another into a Sale**

This commandment is one of the most commonly misunderstood (and transgressed) by Jews, Noahides, and everyone. Exodus 20:14 states:

> *Do not covet* [lo sachmod] *your neighbor's house...*

This verse cannot prohibit the feeling of envy. As we shall see, there is another commandment specifically addressing the desire for another's property. What is more, the language of *lo sachmod* is unusual and unclear.[13] The sages point to Exodus 7:25 as proof of its full connotation:

---

[13] Ibn Ezra.

*You shall burn in fire the graven image of their gods. You shall not covet [lo sachmod] the gold and silver that is upon them and take it for yourself…*

We see that *lo sachmod* involves the actual taking possession of another's property. This prohibition cannot come to forbid seizure by force – that would already be prohibited as robbery. So, what type of "taking" is implied by this prohibition? The Talmud discusses this question in many places and its conclusions are summarized for us by Maimonides:

> *Anyone who covets a servant, maidservant, house, or utensils belonging to a colleague, or [who covets] any other article that can be purchased from him, and then he pressures him with friends and requests until he [the owner] agrees to sell it, violates a negative commandment. This is even though he pays much money for it. It is stated: 'Do not covet...' One does not violate this commandment until one actually takes possession of the item he covets, as alluded to in the verse, 'Do not covet the gold and silver upon them and take it for yourself.' Implied here is that the word* sachmod *refers to coveting accompanied by an action.*[14]

At what point, however, does a solicitation to buy become harassment to sell? The *Betzeil Ha-Chochmah*[15] brings a strong proof that a solicitation to buy becomes harassment only after three attempts have already been made. However, this is only in a case when the two parties are of equal standing and influence to each other. If one party has particular influence over the other, then the situation may change greatly. For example, if the buyer is the landlord to the unwilling seller, then even fewer than two attempts may be called harassment. If the buyer knowingly uses his position to influence the sale, then even one attempt is problematic.

We should also note that this involves making repeated attempts under the same price and terms. If, with each attempt, the buyer offers terms or prices more advantageous to the seller, then it is called a "first attempt."

A very important question is if the prohibition works in the reverse: Does a salesman who desires the money of a customer transgress this prohibition by pushing the customer to buy?

---

[14] *Hilchos Gezeilah 1:9.*

[15] III: 43. Rav Betzalel Stern (1910 – 1988) was a Hungarian rabbi who settled in Melbourne, Australia after the holocaust. Along with his brother, Rabbi Moshe Stern (author of the *Beer Moshe*), he played a crucial role in rebuilding Judaism post-Holocaust.

This question has been discussed by many, many *poskim*. While some hold *lo sachmod* is a problem even in these situations, most are lenient.[16]

As well, this prohibition applies to gifts.

**Formulating Covetous Thoughts & Plans**

In addition to actually pressing another party into a sale, the Torah also forbids entertaining plans and thoughts by which to deprive another of his property. Deuteronomy 5:18 states:

> *Do not desire* [lo sisaveh] *your neighbor's house.*

The phrase *lo sisaveh* is commonly mistranslated as *you shall not covet*. A correct translation, however, *you shall not desire*. The sages explain that entertaining the desire for another's property is the first step toward near-inevitable transgression. This is also implied by Michah 2:2:

> *They desired fields and so robbed them.*

Once a person begins to plan and scheme to gain the property of another, the *yetzer hora*, destructive desire, takes strong hold of the person's judgment. It is only a slight step from there to *Aveira* – sin. If the one who desires the object then presses or forces the owner to sell it to him, then the buyer has transgressed two prohibitions: 1) Against desiring and, 2) Against pressing another to part with his property.

Many commentaries cite I Kings 21 as a cautionary tale on such desire. There are many interesting questions raised by this prohibition that we will be discussed in the live class.

**Against False Weights & Measures**

The prohibition against using false weights and measures is brought in Leviticus 19:35:

> *Do not be dishonest in* **law**, *measures, weights, or volumes.*

The Talmud's discussion of this prohibition includes many examples of deceptive practices such as:

- Soaking weights in salt water.

---

[16] See *Minchas Asher* to Parshas Yisro. This is a complicated subject. In short, most *poskim* understand that one must desire a specific item in order to transgress this prohibition. Money is not considered enough of a specific item to incur the prohibition. The salesperson wants to bring in money, but he doesn't necessarily want a particular $20 bill or one person's money over another's.

- Using the same measuring rope in the summer and the winter, in spite of the variations in length caused by changes in the weather.

Even though the variations are slight, they incur full transgression of the *mitzvah*.

The *Sifra* explains the term *law* used in the source verse refers to the representations one makes as to his weights and measures.[17] By extension, this prohibition includes false advertising and other misrepresentations ones may make as to his merchandise.

The laws are codified in the *Shulchan Aruch, Choshen Mishpat* 231.

**Against Owning False Weights & Measures**

Not only is it not permitted for one to misrepresent the weights, measures, and other details of his merchandise, but a person may not own or possess items used for transactional fraud or deceit. This is learned from Deuteronomy 25:13-14:

> *Do not have two stones in your bag, one large and one small. Do not have in your house two ephos [measuring units] one large and one small].*

One is not even allowed to keep such an item if he intends to use it for an honest purpose (i.e. keeping a false weight to use as a paperweight). The details of this prohibition are discussed in the Talmud, Tractates Bava Metzia 61a and Bava Basra 89b

**Honesty (Positive Requirements) in Weights and Measures**

In addition to prohibiting misrepresenting the weights, measures and other properties of one's merchandise (and against owning the instruments of such fraud), we are required to maintain and ensure that our weight, measures, and other representations are correct. This is learned from Leviticus 19:36:

> *Just balances, just weights, a just* ephah *[measure],*
> *and a just* hin *[another measure], you shall have…*

This commandment establishes a positive mitzvah of quality control to ensure that customers are not charged improperly.

---

[17] *Sifra* explains that the clause *Do not be dishonest in law…* cannot refer to passing legal judgment, for this was already commanded in Lev. 19:15.

## Debts

**Not Withholding Payment When One Has Means to Pay**

Leviticus 19:3 states:

*Do not withhold that which is due…*

This verse prohibits withholding payment owed when the debtor has full ability to repay the creditor. This applies to any case in which one owes another a debt. Therefore, employers must pay employees and debtors must pay creditors.

This prohibition is not only transgressed by flat denial, but also by pushing off payment with excuses and delays.

**Falsely Denying a Debt**

Similarly, it is prohibited for one to falsely deny a debt, as Leviticus 19:11 states:

*Do not deny it…*

A person is also prohibited from falsely denying that another entrusted him with an item or money. A person may also not falsely deny he borrowed an item.

By denying a debt or that one has another's property in his possession, even though the other party may have entrusted items to him willingly, one commits a form of passive theft. True, the perpetrator never took the items. However, his brazen denial of having the items or money in his possession is considered a type of unlawful seizure.

## Summary

1. Theft is the taking of another's property without the victims' immediate knowledge.

2. Robbery is taking an item with force and with the victims' immediate knowledge.

3. One may not overcharge by more than 16% of the fair-market value. Similarly, underpaying by more than 16% also creates problems. There are many items and situations to which this prohibition does not apply.

4. It is prohibited to pressure another into selling an item that he does not want to sell. This does not apparently apply to pressuring another into buying an item.

5. One may not make covetous plans or entertain such thoughts.

6. False weights and measures are prohibited. This includes false advertising or other business deceptive practices.

7. One may not even own such items.

8. One has a duty to maintain such weights and measures.

9. If one has the capacity to repay a debt, he must do so. It is prohibited to hold the funds in such a case.

10. One is forbidden from denying a debt or committing other forms of passive theft.

THE YESHIVA PIRCHEI SHOSHANIM SHULCHAN ARUCH PROJECT

# The Noahide Laws - Lesson Fifty-Seven

© **Yeshiva Pirchei Shoshanim 2017**
This shiur may not be reproduced in any
form without permission of the copyright holder.

164 Village Path, Lakewood NJ 08701 732.370.3344
164 Rabbi Akiva, Bnei Brak, 03.616.6340

## Table of Contents:

1. Introduction
2. Workplace Theft
3. Summary of Laws of Workplace Theft
   a. Hourly Wage Employees
   b. Hourly Employees & Side Businesses
   c. Office Supplies & Resources
   d. Leftover Material
   e. Partaking of Produce
   f. Partaking of Office Property?
4. Land
5. Kidnapping
6. Making Restitution
7. Summary

# Monetary Law III: Laws of Theft Cont.

## Introduction

In this lesson we will complete our very general overview of the monetary laws. Remember, the main purpose of this overview is to get a sense of the underlying concepts in order to spot potential issues and know when to seek further guidance.

## Workplace Theft

Deuteronomy 23:25-26 serves as the source for two *halachos* pertaining to laborers:

*When you come into your neighbor's vineyard, you may eat grapes at will until you are satisfied; but you shall not put any in your vessel. When you come into your neighbor's standing wheat, you may pick stalks with your hand, but you shall not take a sickle unto your neighbor's standing wheat.*

The Talmud, Bava Metzia Ch. 7, dissects and examines these two verses in great detail. At first glance, the intent of these two verses is obscure. Why is a person allowed to take grapes from another's vineyard? Why is this not theft? The Talmud explains the terminology of "coming into a field" (as opposed to "walking through a field" or any other phrasing) as meaning coming into a field to harvest.[1] These verses give workers limited rights to partake of the produce of the field while directly engaged in the harvest. However, the two phrases: *…you shall not put any in your vessel…* and *… you shall not take a sickle unto your neighbor's standing wheat…* come to teach restrictions on this right.

---

[1] This is also the translation of the verse according to <ins>Onkelos</ins>.

One is only allowed to eat while the harvest is under way. Once the harvest is completed, there is no permit to take from the produce. Additionally, one is only allowed to take of the produce while working if this does not cause a net loss to or harm to the employer (we will discuss specific examples in the live class). This is the implication of ...*you shall not put any in your vessel*... and ... *you shall not take a sickle unto your neighbor's standing wheat*... both of these actions would abuse the right and cause a net loss to the employer. Such actions would constitute theft.

Many *halachos* applicable to the modern workplace are implied by and derived from these verses. A complete description of these *halachos* would require many, many lessons. Therefore, we will present here only a summary. For further study, see the seventh chapter of tractate Bava Metzia (starting at 87a), Maimonides's *Hilchos Sechirus*, Chapter 12 (included as an appendix to this lesson), and in the *Shulchan Aruch, Choshen Mishpat*.[2]

## Summary of Laws for Employees

**Hourly Wage Employees**

One who is paid by the hour must be very careful not to waste time while "on the clock." Otherwise the employee is *de facto* committing theft of his employer's money. If one is hired to complete a specific task and is paid by the hour for his labor, then he must let his employer know when he has completed the work.[3]

**Hourly Employees & Side Businesses**

An employee paid by the hour may not engage in other work or enterprises while on-the-clock. For example, one who is employed in an office may not work on his own internet business while at work.[4]

**Office Supplies & Resources**

An employee cannot use office materials for his own business while off-the-clock if such usage would cost the employer money or depreciate the value or utility of the items.

**Leftover Material**

It often happens that a craftsman is given material by a client to complete a task. If the craftsman has material leftover, who owns the material? If the amount of the material is enough to be of use or value to the client, then the craftsman must inform the client and return the material to him. This question is practically relevant to tailors, jewelers, and other such craftsman.

---

[2] We will cite the references from *Choshen Mishpat* as appropriate below.

[3] *Shulchan Aruch, Choshen Mishpat* 331.

[4] *Shulchan Aruch, Choshen Mishpat* 337.

## Partaking of Produce

The source verses mention both a restriction and a right to the employer's produce. Clearly, Noahides are included in the restrictions as they fall under the rubric of theft. What about the right to partake of produce during the harvest? The Talmud includes Noahides in this positive *mitzvah*. In discussing prohibitions of theft common to both Noahides and Jews, the Talmud[5] states:

> *If [a vineyard worker] ate of the produce while engaged in the actual harvest, then he is permitted to do so. Yet, if he ate of it while doing other work such as pruning, then it constituted theft...*

Nevertheless, some authorities[6] are uncertain whether Noahides are merely permitted to do so (meaning it is not called theft) or have an actual right to eat of the produce during harvest. The practical difference is whether or not the employer has the right to prohibit the employee from partaking of the produce during harvest. Even according to those who hold this is only a permit and not a right, it is appropriate for the employer to allow the worker to partake of the produce.

## Partaking of Office Property?

Outside of an agricultural/harvest situation, this permit/right has little application. Therefore, an employee should not take or use any of his employer's equipment or supplies for his own benefit. He must receive permission from the employer to do so.

## Land

Deuteronomy 19:14 states:

> *Do not move your neighbor's boundary marker.*

This verse prohibits the theft of real estate by moving a boundary marker.

## Kidnapping

Exodus 20:15 states simply:

> *Do not steal.*

---

[5] Sanhedrin 57a.

[6] *Sefer Sheva Mitzvos HaShem* II:13

As explained in an earlier lesson, the Torah uses this phrase in two places to teach two separate prohibitions. One is the general prohibition against theft while Exodus 20:15 teaches the specific prohibition against kidnapping.

## Making Restitution

Leviticus 5:23 states:

> *If he has transgressed and is found guilty, then* **he shall restore that which he took** *by robbery or the thing which he gained by extortion, or the deposit which was deposited with him [and he denied it]…*

As discussed in the first lesson on monetary law, a Noahide must make restitution for whatever he took. This applies to all of the aforementioned subspecies of theft.

The Talmud[7] points out the phrase … **he shall restore that which he took…** requires the return of the actual object that was stolen in its original condition:

> *If it is as it was when it was stolen, then he shall return it intact. If it is not [in its original condition] then he must pay the victim [the value of the object].*

The following is a summary of the details pertaining to restitution:

- When the victim has hope of getting back his property or money, then the thief must return the actual item that was taken. One is considered to have reasonable hope of getting back his property when the perpetrator was seen or there is a good chance that he can be otherwise identified.[8]

    - In this case, the thief must return the stolen item. The rightful owner, however, has the right to demand payment in lieu of getting the item back. In such a case, the stolen item becomes the purchased property of the thief once the thief has tendered payment.[9]

---

[7] Bava Kamma 66a.

[8] *Shulchan Aruch, Choshen Mishpat* 361.

[9] *Aruch HaShulchan, Choshen Mishpat* 360:1.

- o If the stolen item no longer exists, then the thief must return the monetary value of the items.[10]

- o If the thief has altered the stolen item in a permanent manner, he cannot return the item. He is considered the owner of the item, but must pay its pre-alteration value to the victim.[11]

- If the victim has despaired of getting back his property, then the thief is only obligated to return the monetary value of the item itself. The victim is assumed to have despaired in a case when the perpetrator is not known or it is unlikely that the perpetrator will be found.[12]

- When a stolen item appreciates or depreciates of its own accord while in the hand of the thief or as a result of market forces the issue of restitution can become very complicated. One should consult with an expert in the monetary laws.

- All of these laws of restitution apply absent an established legal system. As we shall see in a future lesson, each society must establish courts and laws as needed to impose order and meet the needs of the community. Therefore, the Torah's laws of restitution may be modified or supplanted by the needs of the courts.

---

[10] Bava Kamma 66a.

[11] See *Hilchos Gezeilah 2:1*; Shulchan Aruch, *Choshen Mishpat* 353.

[12] *Rema*, *Choshen Mishpat* 368. However, it is possible that this is not the law for Noahides. Rather, it may be that Noahides are not considered to have despaired until they have witnesses who can attest to their state of mind. See *Shach, Choshen Mishpat* 368:1.

## Summary

1. Employees may eat of the produce of their employee during the harvest. However, there are many restrictions on this right to prevent workplace theft.

2. Hourly wage employees must be very careful to make the most of their time.

3. One should not use any office or workplace resources without the employer's permission if the use would depreciate the items or cause a loss to the employer.

4. If a person entrusts material to a craftsman for a specific purpose, the craftsman must return the excess if it is a significant amount or of value to the owner.

5. The right of partaking of produce during the harvest has little corollary outside of agricultural harvest.

## Appendix: Maimonides, *Hilchos Sechirus* 12

### Derivations from Deuteronomy 23:25-26

### Translation Reprinted From Chabad.org

§1 When workers are performing activities with produce that grows from the earth,' but the work required for it has not been completed, and their actions bring the work to its completion, the employer is commanded to allow them to eat from the produce with which they are working. This applies whether they are working with produce that has been harvested or produce that is still attached to the ground.

This is derived from Deuteronomy 23:25, which states: "When you enter the vineyard of your colleague, you may eat grapes as you desire," and *ibid: 26,* which states: "When you enter the standing grain belonging to your colleague, you may break off stalks by hand." According to the Oral Tradition, we learned that these verses are speaking solely about a paid worker. For if the owner of the produce did not hire him, what right does the person have to enter his colleague's vineyard or standing grain without his permission? Instead, the interpretation of the verse is that when you enter the domain of your employer for work, you may eat.

§2 What are the differences in the application of this mitzvah between a person who performs work with produce that has been reaped and one who works with produce that is still attached to the ground? A person who performs work with produce that has been reaped may partake of the produce as long as the work necessary for it has not been completed. Once the work necessary for it has been completed, he may not eat. By contrast, a person who performs work with produce that is still attached to the ground - e.g., a harvester of grapes or a reaper of grain - may not partake of the produce until he has completed his work.

For example, a person harvests grapes and puts them into a large basket. When the basket is filled, it is taken away and emptied in another place. According to Scriptural Law, the worker may eat only when the basket has been filled. Nevertheless, in order to prevent the owner from suffering a loss, the Sages ruled that the workers may eat while they are walking from one row to another and while they are returning from the vat, so that they will not neglect their work to sit down and eat. Instead, they were granted permission to eat while they are performing their work, so that they will not neglect it.

**§3** When a person neglects his work and eats or eats when he has not completed his work, he transgresses a negative commandment, as Deuteronomy 23:26 states:

"You shall not lift a sickle against your colleague's standing grain."

According to the Oral Tradition, it is explained that as long as the worker is involved in reaping, he should not lift a sickle in order to partake of the produce himself. Similar laws apply in all analogous situations.

Similarly, a worker who carries home produce with which he had worked or who takes more than he can eat himself and gives to others transgresses a negative commandment, as *ibid.:28* states: "You may not place in your containers." The violation of these two prohibitions is not punishable by lashes, because a person who ate when one should not have or took produce home is liable to make financial restitution.

**§4** A person who milks an animal, one who makes butter, and one who makes cheese may not partake of that food, for it is not a product of the earth.

When a person hoes around onion heads and garlic heads, even though he removes small ones from the larger ones, or the like, he may not partake of them, because this activity does not constitute the completion of the task.

Needless to say, watchmen over gardens, orchards and fields where any crops are grown - e.g., cucumber gardens and gourd gardens - may not partake of the produce growing there at all.

**§5** A person who separates dates and figs that have already been harvested and are stuck together] may not partake of them, for the work that obligates the performance of the mitzvah of tithing has been completed.

A person who works with wheat and the like after they have been tithed - e.g., a person was hired to remove pebbles from grain, to sift the kernels or to grind them - may partake of them, for the work that obligates the performance of the mitzvah of *challah* has not been completed. When, however, a person kneads dough, bastes loaves or bakes, he may not partake of the food, because the work that obligates the performance of the mitzvah of *challah* has become completed. And a worker may not partake of produce except when the work that obligates the performance of the mitzvah of tithing or *challah* has not been completed.

**§6** If the cakes of figs belonging to a person become broken up, his barrels of wine become open, or his gourds become cut, and he hires workers to tend to the produce, they may not partake of it, for the work necessary for them has been completed and they have become obligated to be tithed. Indeed, they are *Tevel*.

If, however, the owner did not notify the workers, he must tithe the produce and allow them to partake of it.

Workers may not partake of the crops in a field that was consecrated to the Temple treasury. This is derived from [Deuteronomy 23:25](), which speaks of "your colleague's vineyard."

**§7** When a person hires workers to work with produce that is *Neta Reva'i*, they may not partake of it. If he did not inform them that it was *Neta Reva'i*, he must redeem it, and allow them to partake of it.

**§8** Workers who reap, thresh, winnow, separate unwanted matter from food, harvest olives or grapes, tread grapes, or perform any other tasks of this nature are granted the right to partake of the produce with which they working by Scriptural Law.

**§9** Watchmen for vats, grain heaps and any produce that has been separated from the ground, for which the work that obligates tithing has not been completed may partake of the produce because of local convention. They are not granted this privilege according to Scriptural Law, because a watchman is not considered to be one who performs an action.

If, however, a person works with his limbs whether with his hands, his feet or even with his shoulders, he is entitled to partake of produce according to the Torah.

**§10** A worker who is working with figs may not partake of grapes. One who is working with grapes may not partake of figs. These laws are derived from [Deuteronomy 23:25](), which states: "When you enter the vineyard of your colleague, you may eat grapes."

When a person is working with one vine, he may not eat from another vine. Nor may he partake of grapes together with other food; he should not partake of them together with bread or salt. If, however, the worker set a limit concerning the quantity that he may eat, he may eat the produce with salt, with bread or with any other food that he desires.

It is forbidden for a worker to suck the juice from grapes, for the verse states: "And you shall eat grapes." Neither the worker's sons nor his wife may roast the kernels of grain in a fire for him. This is implied by the above verse, which states: "You may eat grapes as you desire." The implication is that you must desire the grapes as they are. Similar laws apply in all analogous situations.

**§11** It is forbidden for a worker to eat an inordinate amount of the produce with which he is working. This is implied by the above verse, which states: "You may eat... as you desire, to your satisfaction." It is permitted, however, for him to delay eating until he reaches the place of higher quality grapes and eat there.

A worker may eat even a *dinar's* worth of cucumbers or dates even though he was hired to work only for a silver *me'ah*. Nevertheless, we teach a person not to be a glutton, so that he will not close the doors in his own face. If a person is guarding four or five grain heaps, he should not eat his fill from only one of them. Instead, he should eat an equal amount from each one.

**§12** Workers who have not walked both lengthwise and laterally in a vat may eat grapes but may not drink wine, for at that time they are still working solely with grapes. When they have treaded in the vat and walked both lengthwise and laterally, they may eat grapes and drink the grape juice, for they are working with both the grapes and the wine.

**§13** When a worker says: "Give my wife and my children what I would eat," or "I will give a small amount of what I have taken to eat to my wife and my children," he is not given this prerogative. For the Torah has granted this right only to a worker himself. Even when a *Nazarite* who is working with grapes says, "Give some to my wife and children," his words are of no consequence.

**§14** When a worker - and his wife, his children and his slaves - were all employed to work with produce, and the worker stipulated that they - neither he nor the members of his household - should not partake of the produce, they may not partake of it.

When does the above apply? When they are past majority, because they are intellectually mature, responsible for their decisions, and willingly gave up the right the Torah granted them. If, however, the children are minors, their father cannot pledge that they will not eat, for they are not eating from his property or from what the employer grants them, but rather from what they were granted by God.

# The Noahide Laws - Lesson Fifty-Eight

THE YESHIVA PIRCHEI SHOSHANIM SHULCHAN ARUCH PROJECT

© **Yeshiva Pirchei Shoshanim 2017**
This shiur may not be reproduced in any
form without permission of the copyright holder.

164 Village Path, Lakewood NJ 08701 732.370.3344
164 Rabbi Akiva, Bnei Brak, 03.616.6340

## Table of Contents:

1. Introduction
2. The Basics of *Dinim*
   a. Maimonides, *Melachim* 9:14
3. Sanhedrin 56b: R' Yochanan & R' Yitzchok
4. Katzenellenbogen & Bragadini v. Guistiniani, Venice 1550
   a. Rav Moshe Isserles, *Shu"t HaRama*, No. 10
5. Reception of the Rama's Ruling
   a. *Aruch LaNer*
   b. *Asmachta* vs. *Horaah*
   c. The *Netziv*
   d. The Talmud itself...
   e. Pre-Sinai vs. Post-Sinai
   f. Precedents
6. Summary

# Dinim I: Introduction

**Lesson 58**

## Introduction

The *mitzvah* of *dinim*, civil law, is one of the trickiest of the Noahide laws to both define and understand in terms of its real world applications. Much of this difficulty is historical in origin. Since the Jewish world has always maintained and used its own religious courts to judge monetary disputes, there was never a practical occasion or need to address the Noahide laws of *dinim*. This was the case until 1550 when a legal dispute prompted a massive evaluation by scholars of Noahide *dinim*.

## The Basics of *Dinim*

Although the Talmud reads the earliest reference to *dinim* from Genesis 2:16, the Torah is abound with references to the concept and need for justice. For example, Genesis 9:5-6:

*I will certainly demand the blood of your lives; at the hand of every beast I shall require it, and at the hand of man, even at the hand of every man's brother, I shall require the life of man. Whoever spills a man's blood, by man shall his blood be spilled...*

This verse clearly states a judgment and punishment for a murderer, requiring the punishment to be carried out at the hands of man. The Midrash expounds upon many other examples of pre-Sinaitic expectations for justice. Maimonides distills these allusions into the following description from *Hilchos Melachim* 9:14:

**Maimonides, Hilchos Melachim 9:14**

*How do the gentiles fulfill the commandment to establish laws and courts? They are obligated to set up judges and magistrates in every major city to render judgment concerning these six mitzvot and to admonish the people regarding their observance.*

*A gentile who transgresses these seven commands shall be executed by decapitation. For this reason, all the inhabitants of Shechem were obligated to die. Shechem kidnapped. They observed and were aware of his deeds, but did not judge him.*

Maimonides's makes three very important points:

1) **They are obligated to appoint judges and magistrates in every major city...** *Dinim* obligates Noahides in the establishment of courts.[1] The purpose of these courts, and indeed the essence of *dinim,* is to establish order between man and his fellow. This is because God places more emphasis on harmony between men than between Himself and man. Rashi[2] points out that this is the reason the generation of the flood and Sodom and Gomorrah were destroyed, while the generation of the Tower of Bavel was only dispersed. In the times of the flood and of Sodom and Gomorrah, the main sins were between man and his fellow. Therefore, they were destroyed. However, in the times of the tower, their sins were primarily between man and God, therefore God was lenient with them.

2) **...to render judgment concerning the other six mitzvos...** What is the content of the laws of *dinim*? Maimonides states that these laws are fundamentally procedural: they apply to the courts and consist of rules and methods for administering judgment for the other Noahide laws. It does not appear, according to Maimonides, that *dinim* includes matters of substantive law – actual prohibitions or demands on societal or individual behavior.

3) **... and to admonish the people in their observance.** It is a requirement of the courts to engage in public education of the Noahide laws.[3]

According to Maimonides, it appears that Noahide courts fulfilling these three fundamental purposes meet the standards for *dinim*. However, this proposition is

---

[1] See Sanhedrin 56b.

[2] Gen. 11:9.

[3] See *Chemdas Yisrael* 9:29; *Machaneh Chaim* II:22.

not so simple. The question of content, point #2 above gets us into complicated waters.

## Sanhedrin 56b: R' Yochanan & R' Yitzchok

To grasp the issues involved, we first have to look at a passage from **Sanhedrin 56b**:

> *From where is this [the Seven Noahide Laws] learned? Rabbi Yochanan says it is from the verse:*
>
>> *"HaShem, God, **commanded** unto the man, saying: Of evert tree of the garden you may surely eat.[4]"*
>
> *...**commanded**... This alludes to dinim, for it [the Torah] says similarly:*
>
>> *"For I know him - that he will **command** his children and his household after him that they may keep the way of HaShem to do justice...[5]"*

*When Rabbi Yitzchok arrived, he taught the opposite:*

> *...**commanded**... This alludes to idolatry.*
> *...**God**... This alludes to dinim.*

*It is understandable that ...**God**... alludes to civil law, for it is written:*

> *"The master of the house shall approach the elohim, judge.[6]"*

*However, from where do we see that ...**commanded**... is an allusion to idolatry?* **Rav Chisda** *and* **Rav Yitzchok bar Avdimi** *each found a source. One said it was:*

> *"They have turned aside quickly from the way that I **commanded** them.[7]"* [Referring to turning away from God and to idolatry]

*The other said it from:*

---

[4] Genesis 2:16.

[5] Genesis 18:19.

[6] Exodus 22:7.

[7] Exodus 32:8.

> "*Suppressed is Ephraim, crushed by judgment, because he willingly walked after the* **commandment** *[of the idolaters]*[8]

*What are the practical differences between these two verses?*

The Talmud then embarks on a comparison of the implications and ramifications of the two verses pertaining to idolatry. However, the Talmud does not likewise examine any implications of the two verses referring to *dinim*. 1200 years later, this subtle omission would play an important role in a copyright dispute between two Venetian printers.

## Katzenellenbogen & Bragadini v. Guistiniani, Venice 1550

In 1550 Alvise Bragadini, a Venetian non-Jewish printer/publisher, partnered with Rav Meir Katzenellenbogen to publish a landmark edition of Maimonides's *Mishneh Torah* with Rav Meir's critical emendations. It was a massive undertaking that required tremendous money and labor. At the same time, Marco Antonio Guistiniani, Bragadini's chief competitor and rival (also not Jewish), was preparing a virtually identical edition that also incorporated Rav Meir's work, albeit uncredited.

The copyright law of the Venetian Republic would provide little protection for Rav Meir and Bragadini's project. Realizing the secular courts were of no help, Bragadini and Rav Meir appealed to the court of Rav Moshe Isserles (the Rama), the famed Rosh Yeshiva and *halakhic* authority of Krakow, to judge whose copyright was valid. They knew Rav Isserles's ruling would carry tremendous weight in the Jewish community and, if in their favor, would ensure their success.

For the first time in over 1000 years, a Jewish court was asked to judge a case between two non-Jews: did Guistiniani infringe on Bragadini's copyright? This case brought up a fundamental question: should the printers be judged according to Torah law, or Noahide law? If Noahide law, then what procedures and standards are dictated by their *mitzvah* of *dinim*?

---

[8] Hoshea 5:11.

**Rav Moshe Isserles: *Sheelos U'teshuvos HaRama*, No. 10**

The Rama begins his analysis by noting the omission we observed in Sanhedrin 56b: Why did the Talmud not bother comparing the implications of the verses cited by Rabbis Yochanan and Yitzchok on *dinim*? The Rama writes that there was no reason for the Talmud to explain the differences between R' Yochanan and R' Yitzchok's verses because the differences are extremely obvious, "as clear as the noonday sun." The Rama explains:

> Rabbi Yochanan says **dinim** are learned from …**commanded**… and we know that …**commanded**… implies **dinim** this because of its use in Genesis 18:19. Note that this verse was stated prior to the giving of the Torah's judicial laws. Therefore, according to this verse the expectation was for Noahides to base their laws and customs of justice on their own needs and customs.

> Rabbi Yitzchok says **dinim** are learned from …**God**…, citing Exodus 22:7. This verse was stated after the giving of the Torah and specifically refers, in context, to the Torah's civil laws. Rabbi Yitzchok holds, therefore, that Noahides are expected to judge according to the statutes of Torah civil law.

The Rama concludes that the *halacha* is like **Rabbi Yitzchok**: in all matters of monetary and civil law, Noahide law is administered and applied identically to Jewish law (except when clear exceptions are demonstrated in the Talmud). In his examination of copyrights, it is clear that the Rama extends this principle even to rabbinic laws! Therefore, according to the Rama, *dinim* obligates Noahides to set up courts and administer justice (procedural), but it requires the court, for all intents and purposes, to judge two Noahides as a *beis din* would judge Jews. Therefore, *dinim* mandates that the substance of the monetary laws is, from the court's perspective, no different than the Jewish laws.

## Reception of the Rama's Ruling

This opinion is difficult in the extreme and few later authorities accept it entirely. Though many later authorities accepted the Rama's basic assertion that Noahide and Jewish monetary law is the same,[9] many have disagreed, raising major issues with the Rama's ruling:

1) **Aruch LaNer** – Takes issue with the Rama's opening premise: that the reason for the Talmud not comparing the implications of Rabbis Yochanan and Yitzchok's verses is that their implications are "as clear as the noon-day sun." According to the *Aruch LaNer*, the opposite is actually the case: The Talmud doesn't compare them because they do not imply

---

[9] I.e. *Tumim* 110:3; *Responsa Nachalas Yaakov* 3.

any practical differences. When distinctions between verses are implied, the Talmud discusses and examines them. For example, the verses dealing with idolatry warranted further comparison because one verse is from the Torah while the other is from the Prophets. Since they are from two different levels of scriptural authority, they <u>must</u> apply in different ways. The **Aruch LaNer** therefore rejects the entire premise of the Rama that these verses imply anything about the nature of *dinim*.

2) **Asmachta vs. Horaah** - Most commentators understand Sanhedrin's citation and discussion of Genesis 2:16 as *asmachta* – evidence of or reference to the Noahide laws – and not as the actual derivation of the Noahide laws (*horaah*). If so, then the Rama's analysis is misplaced.[10]

3) <u>Rabbi Naftali Tzvi Yehudah Berlin (the Netziv)</u> **in his** *HaEmek HaShaila*[11] - In Chagigah 13a the Talmud supports the prohibition against Jews teaching Torah to non-Jews from the verse:

*He relates his word to Jacob, His statues and laws to Israel. Yet, He did not do so for any other nation; Mishpatim [civil and monetary laws] they shall not know.*[12]

This verse specifically teaches that the Jewish civil and monetary laws were <u>not</u> commanded to non-Jews. Furthermore, by making Noahides subject to all the Torah requirements for civil and monetary laws, the prohibition against non-Jewish Torah study is rendered pointless! In order to carryout *dinim* according to the Rama, Noahides would have to study almost the entire Torah to the same level and degree as Jews!

4) **The Talmud itself** - The Talmud's main presentation of the Noahide laws is according to Rav Yochanan. Furthermore, the Midrash also explains *dinim* according to Rav Yochanan.[13]

5) **Before Sinai vs. After Sinai** - If Noahides civil and monetary law is the same as Jewish law, then what was *dinim* before Jewish law existed

---

[10] See *Kesef Mishnah* to *Hilchos Melachim* 9.

[11] 2.

[12] Psalms 147:19-20.

[13] See *Midrash Tanchuma, Parshas Shoftim; Shemos Rabbah* 30:9.

(meaning before Sinai)? The Rama notes this question and, in answering it, offers a proof to his position based on Sanhedrin 56b:

> *Dinim* – are Noahides actually commanded in this? Was it not taught in a *braisa*: "Ten commandments were given to Israel at Marah:[14] the seven the Noahides had previously accepted upon themselves, to which were added dinim, the Shabbos, and honoring ones parents." *[This Braisa implies that dinim, the obligations of civil and monetary law, were only given to Israel. If the Noahides were already commanded in dinim, then why was Israel again commanded in it?]*

The Talmud proposes a number of answers to this question, all of which are rejected. The Rama points out that there is an obvious and excellent answer that the Talmud neglects to consider: prior to Marah, the Israelites were commanded in *dinim* according to the Noahide laws. However, at Marah, the specific Jewish details of the laws were added to preexisting Noahide *dinim*.

The Rama writes that the fact that this answer was <u>not</u> proposed by the Talmud indicates the Talmud assumed the Jewish details of *dinim* were already part of the Noahide *mitzvah* of *dinim*.

The problem with this proof is that the Talmud, at the end of its discussion of this b*raisa*, concludes that the *beraisa's* implications are irrelevant because this *braisa* does <u>not</u> represent the *halacha* – in fact, according to this *braisa* Noahides were <u>never</u> commanded in the laws of *dinim*! The Rama's point, that the Talmud could have answered that the specific Jewish details of *dinim* were added at Marah, is a good point. However, since the whole discussion is only theoretical (because the *braisa* is rejected as *Halacha*) it cannot prove anything as to what the Talmud teaches as halachic fact.

6) **Precedents?** A final problem is that the Rema appears to, uncharacteristically, not have considered the *rishonic* evidence contradicting his ruling. Instead, the Rama goes directly to the Talmud, skipping over the <u>Rishonic</u> literature.[15] Two Rishonim, in particular, need to be noted.

---

[14] During the encampment at Marah, the Torah says that Israel was given a number of *mitzvos* (Exodus 15:25). However, it does not specify what these commandments were.

[15] There are many *rishonim* who clearly contradict the Rema. See *Maimonides, Hilchos Melachim* 10:10; *Shu"t Ritva* 14 in *Bais Yosef, CM* 66:18; *Tosafos, Eruvin 62a*; *Sefer ha-Ikkarim* 1:25. However, we were unable to find a clear precedent for the Rema's opinion anywhere in the *rishonim*.

**Maimonides**  The Rama tries to muster proof from Maimonides, citing the fact that Maimonides holds that many details of the Noahide prohibitions (i.e. theft, idolatry, etc.) are identical to Jewish prohibitions. However, these attempts do not succeed. Consider that Maimonides also wrote the following:

> *When two non-Jews come before you to have their dispute judged according to Jewish law, then if they both desire to be judged according to Torah law, they should be judged so. If one desires to be judged according to Torah law and the other does not, they are forced to be judged according to their own laws.*[16]

According to this ruling, Noahides have no obligation to be judged according to Torah law. Later scholars have noted that further examinations of Maimonides's writings reveal it is impossible to read Maimonides as supporting the Rama; rather, Maimonides explicitly contradicts him![17]

Furthermore, there is not a single *rishonim* that explicitly supports the Rema. In fact, the *rishonim* disagree with the Rema; some explicitly and others by implication.[18]

For us to accept such a controversial idea as *halacha*, it is essential that we establish the Rema's opinion within *mesorah*. We do so by finding explicit evidence of an earlier tradition supporting him. Are there any precedents that support the Rama? We will save this question for the next lesson.

### Summary

1. The two basics requirements of *dinim* are: the establishing of courts, and public education.

2. There is the additional question of the substance of *dinim*. Maimonides holds it is merely procedural law as to how to judge and administer the remaining Noahide laws.

---

[16] *Hilchos Melachim* 10:12.

[17] See *Minchas Shlomo I: 86; Shu"t Yechaveh Daas IV: 65; Tzitz Eliezer XVI: 55.*

[18] *Maimonides, Hilchos Melachim* 10:10; *Shu"t Ritva* 14 in *Bais Yosef, CM* 66:18; *Tosafos, Eruvin* 62a; *Sefer ha-Ikkarim* 1:25.

3. The Rambam holds that *dinim* is procedural. The Rama also holds that it is procedural but has a substantive aspect as well: it obligates Noahides in all the details of Jewish civil and monetary law. This apparently includes rabbinic as well as biblical edicts.

4. Virtually no later authority accepts the entirety of the Rama's ruling. Many, however, accept his conclusion that Noahide monetary and civil law are fundamentally the same as Jewish monetary and civil law.

5. Despite its acceptance by some, the Rama's ruling was not well received by most of the rabbinic community. It presents a number of fundamental challenges in both substance and method that are atypical of the Rama.

THE YESHIVA PIRCHEI SHOSHANIM SHULCHAN ARUCH PROJECT

# The Noahide Laws - Lesson Fifty-Nine

© **Yeshiva Pirchei Shoshanim 2017**
This shiur may not be reproduced in any
form without permission of the copyright holder.

164 Village Path, Lakewood NJ 08701 732.370.3344
164 Rabbi Akiva, Bnei Brak, 03.616.6340

# Table of Contents:

1. Introduction
2. Shechem
   a. Maimonides
   b. Nachmanides
3. "Comparable?"
4. Conclusions
5. The Rema Revisited
6. Summary

# Dinim II: Nachmanides

## Introduction

In the last lesson we learned that the first in-depth examination of *dinim* came from the pen of Rabbi Moshe Isserles, the Rema, in the 16th century. His conclusions and methods for reaching them, however, are puzzling. A big problem is that the Rema's ruling contradicts precedents found in the *rishonim*. Are there any *rishonim* that support the Rema? If not, then it becomes much harder to understand and accept the Rema's ruling. There is, possibly, one *rishon* who would support the Rema. To get to this *rishon* we first have to turn to the Torah.

## Shechem

Genesis 34 records that Shechem, the prince of his eponymous city, abducted Dina, the daughter of Jacob. In doing so he violated Noahide injunction against theft. The citizenry, however, took no initiative to bring Shechem to justice. Shortly thereafter, Shimon and Levi put the entire city to the sword.

**Maimonides**  Maimonides refers to this incident in his presentation of the law of *dinim*:

> How must the gentiles fulfill the commandment to establish laws and courts? They are obligated to set up judges and magistrates in every major city to render judgment concerning these six mitzvot and to admonish the people regarding their observance.
>
> A gentile who transgresses these seven commands shall be executed by decapitation. For this reason, all the inhabitants of Shechem were obligated to die. Shechem kidnapped. They observed and were aware of his deeds, but did not judge him.[1]

---

[1] *Hilchos Melachim* 9:14

According to Maimonides, the people of Shechem violated the *mitzvah* of *dinim* by not bringing their prince to justice.

**Nachmanides**

Nachmanides, however, disagrees with Maimonides on many points, namely:

- If Shimon and Levi were justified in executing the people of Shechem, then why did Jacob chastise them for it? If the people of Shechem were truly liable for death, then Jacob himself should have put them to the sword!

- *Dinim* is a positive commandment, yet Noahides are only liable to the death penalty for the transgression of negative *mitzvos*. Therefore, any punishment they deserved could not have been for transgressing the *mitzvah* of *dinim*.

Based upon these two difficulties (and others), Nachmanides takes issue with Maimonides's description of *dinim*. Most important for our discussion, Nachmanides writes:

> *As I understand it, the mitzvah of* dinim *enumerated among the seven noahide laws does not mean [as Maimonides writes] only the requirement to establish judges in every place, rather,* **God also commanded them in the laws of theft**, *price gouging, withholding wages, bailees…the laws of creditors and debtors, buying and selling…* **comparable to the to the civil laws commanded to Israel.**

Nachmanides is making two crucial points:

1) **Point #1: *God also commanded them in the laws of theft…*** *Dinim* is not, as the Rambam holds, merely procedural. *Dinim* also includes substantive monetary and civil laws, and

2) **Point #2: *…comparable to the civil laws commanded to Israel…*** These monetary and civil laws are "comparable" to those commanded to Israel.

## "Comparable?"

In what way is the substantive portion of *dinim* "comparable" to Jewish law? There are, generally speaking, two approaches to this question:

1) **Nachmanides supports the Rema** – *Dinim* equally obligate Noahides and Jews in the Torah's civil and monetary laws. However, there are some

differences in how these laws apply to Noahides. Because of these differences, Jewish and Noahide monetary/civil laws are called "comparable," but not "identical." Read this way, Nachmanides and the Rema are saying the same thing. Therefore, Maimonides and Nachmanides's dispute is a continuation of the supposed dispute between R' Yohanan and R' Yitzchok in the Talmud. The Rema follows the line of Rabbi Yitzchok and Nachmanides while Maimonides follows R' Yochanan. This is how things are understood by *Minchas Chinuch* 1:8; *Nachal Yitzchak* CM 91; *Maharsham* IV:86; *Avnei Neizer* CM 55. Shu"t Maharam Shick, OC 142.

2) **Nachmanides is irrelevant to the Rema** – Nachmanides is <u>not</u> saying the same thing as the Rema; the Maimonides/Nachmanides disagreement is entirely unrelated to the Rema. In fact, it even contradicts the Rema!

## Another Reading of Nachmanides

There is another was of reading Nachmanides that brings his words in-line with the understanding of many other *rishonim*. Let's return to Nachmanides's:

> *God also commanded them in the laws of theft, price gouging, withholding wages, bailees…the laws of creditors and debtors, buying and selling… comparable to the to the civil laws commanded to Israel.*

There is an obvious problem here: how is it that *dinim* includes the laws of theft? Are not the laws of theft <u>already</u> included under… the Noahide prohibition of theft! Indeed, many of the specific areas of law mentioned by Nachmanides as part of *dinim* (i.e. price gouging, withholding wages) have already been enumerated under theft!

Therefore, according to many, Nachmanides is <u>not</u> saying that *dinim* obligates the courts to judge Noahides according to Jewish law. Rather, he understands *dinim* as a two-fold obligation that includes <u>both</u> procedural and substantive laws. However, he defines the substantive aspect very differently from the Rema:

1) **Procedural** – Like Maimonides, *dinim* requires the establishment of courts and administration of justice.

2) **Substantive** – Unlike Maimonides, Nachmanides holds that there is a substantive aspect to *dininm*. Unlike the Rama, Nachmanides holds that this substantive aspect does not impose Jewish monetary and civil laws. Rather, the substantive aspect of *dinim* requires courts to make <u>additional</u> laws and decrees as needed to preserve order and maintain society. These

additional regulations fall out under *dinim* and not under any other category of Noahide law.[2] Therefore, if a Noahide court decides to impose a range of punishments for cruelty to animals, such penalties would fall under *dinim*, and not *ever min ha-chai* (assuming this is the parent prohibition of animal cruelty). These additional laws do not need to resemble Jewish law in any way. Put another way: *dinim* includes 1) the procedural laws of running courts, hearing cases, and administering justice, and 2) a legislative power for the courts to make additional laws as needed to keep society running smoothly.

According to this reading, Nachmanides is actually disagreeing with the Rema!

This reading is given weight by Nachmanides himself. In a responsum,[3] it seems Nachmanides does not hold that Noahide *dinim* is equivalent to Jewish law. See also Nachmanides's commentary on the Torah, beginning of *Parshas Mishpatim*, and to Exodus 26:1.

**Other Rishonim**  This reading of Nachmanides is consonant with many other *rishonim*. For example, Rabbi Yaakov of Anatol writes in his *Malmud*:[4]

> *When the Noahides were commanded in* dinim, *they were obligated to create a legal order… The judges must draw up rules of equity* **that shall be appropriate for their country and for the customs in which such things are handled.** *It is also incumbent upon merchants and tradesmen* **to establish their own rules and regulations…** *Whatever is established as law in this way is the law and carries biblical authority. Anyone who breaks this [established] law violates the Torah.*

This also appears to be Rashi's understanding based on his comments to the Talmud, Gittin 9b.

Furthermore, many *poskim* point out that even Maimonides may agree to this interpretation of *dinim*.

---

[2] See *Chasam Sofer, Likkutim* 6:14 for another way of understanding this issue of classification. Although the *Chasam Sofer* holds that the Maimonides/Nachmanides dispute is unrelated to the Rema, he nevertheless upholds the Rema's ruling in *Shu"t CM* 91.

[3] *Shu"t HaRamban* #225. It is unlikely that these responsa were widely available in earlier generations. It should be noted that many responsa published in Nachmanides's name were actually written by his students. They were later misattributed to Nachmanides. Many of these have been identified as authored by the Rashba, Nachmanides's main student. Therefore, it is not with 100% certainty that the *teshuva* cited here is actually by Nachmanides.

[4] Cited in *Margolios HaYam*, 56b:9.

## Summary

So, either Nachmanides is **supporting the Rema**, or his words have **nothing to do with the Rema**. If he is **supporting the Rema**, then the Rema has a precedent upon which to rely (albeit, a lone one). If Nachmanides has **nothing to do with the Rema**, then the Rema is left without precedent among the *rishonim*. In that case, his opinion is substantially weakened by the fact that many *rishonim* openly contradict him.[5]

## Conclusions

This debate about the nature of *dinim* has gone on since 1550. A full survey of Torah literature since then reveals that an overwhelming majority of later *poskim* disagree with the Rema, accepting instead the approach of Maimonides, Nachmanides, and Rabbi Yaakov of Anatol:

- **Rema, Tumim,**[6] **Nachalas Yaakov,**[7] **Chasam Sofer**[8] – Noahide *dinim* are identical to the laws of the Torah except in specific cases mentioned in the Talmud and codes.

- **Nachal Yitzchak,**[9] Chazon Ish,[10] Even Ha-Azel,[11] Aruch Ha-Shulchan He-Asid,[12] Ha-Emek She'elah,[13] Rav Avraham Yitzchok Kook,[14] Har Tzvi,[15] Yechaveh Daas[16] **4:65,** Minchas Yitzchok,[17] Rav

---

[5] For example, see *Maimonides, Hilchos Melachim* 10:10; *Shu"t Ritva* 14 in *Bais Yosef, CM* 66:18; *Tosafos, Eruvin 62a*; *Sefer ha-Ikkarim* 1:25.

[6] 110:3.

[7] 3.

[8] CM 91.

[9] *Choshen Mishpat* 91

[10] *Hilchos Melachim* 10:10 and Bava Kama 10:3.

[11] *Chovel uMazik* 8:5.

[12] *Melachim* 79:15.

[13] 2:3.

[14] *Eitz Hadar* 38, 184.

_Meir Simcha of Dvinsk,_[18] _Ksav Sofer_[19] - They hold there is no requirement for Noahide civil/monetary laws to be based upon Torah law. Rather, their legal systems should be based upon the needs and customs of their countries and cultures (like the latter interpretation of Nachmanides).

In the next lesson we will see how these *poskim* incorporate all of the considerations discussed thus far into actual practice.

## The Rema Revisited

The Rema's ruling in Bragadini v. Guistiniani is puzzling in the extreme and most *poskim* do not accept it. It is hard to imagine that the Rema would, *ab initio*, take such a difficult approach. However, there is a subtle detail to the Rema's case that we must note: he not issuing a *psak* (ruling) for Noahide courts. His actual task was to establish whether or not a Jewish court (his court) should judge non-Jews according to Jewish law or their own laws. What is more, Bragadini v. Guistiniani was not purely a case of Noahide law. The entire dispute between Bragadini and Guistiniani was brought to the Rema by Bragadini's partner, Rav Meir Katzenellenbogen, a party to the litigation. Therefore, it was really a dispute between Jews and non-Jews. The curious wording of the Rema's conclusion seems to acknowledge this fact: "We have clarified and proven that non-Jews are judged according to the laws of Israel, **and therefore a dispute between a non-Jew and a Jew just like a dispute between two circumcised people.**"

A close reading of the later *poskim* who agree with the Rema reveals that their rulings, like the Rema's, obliquely address the content of Noahide *dinim*. Their primary relevance is for the conduct of Jewish courts judging cases between Jews and non-Jews.

The language of the Rema, however, definitely discusses *dinim* in a general way and not in a manner unique to his situation. Does this fact imply that the Rama would even hold by his ruling for Noahide courts judging solely between non-Jews? It certainly seems so. However, certain historical factors may have influenced the

---

[15] *Orach Chaim II, Kuntres Mili d'Brachos* 2:1.

[16] IV:65.

[17] IV:52:3

[18] *Meshech Chokhma, Vayeira; Ohr Somayach, Melachim 3.*

[19] *Parshas Mishpatim.*

Rema's approach and presentation of his ruling. We will discuss these in the live class.

## Summary

1. According to Maimonides, *dinim* is primarily procedural. It dictates the requirement to establish courts and judge cases. He learns many details of *dinim* from the incident of Shechem.

2. Nachmanides takes issue with Maimonides's interpretation of the events surrounding the massacre of Shechem. He makes two curious points: 1) *Dinim* includes more than just procedural laws, and 2) That the Noahide *dinim* laws are comparable to the Jewish monetary/civil laws.

3. Nachmanides's intent is unclear. Although some view him as supporting the Rema, most see the Nachmanides/Maimonides dispute as irrelevant to the Rema.

4. Most *poskim* do not accept the Rema as *halacha*.

5. The Rema's ruling is puzzling for many reasons. It is possible that it was influenced by unusual external factors.

THE YESHIVA PIRCHEI SHOSHANIM SHULCHAN ARUCH PROJECT

# The Noahide Laws - Lesson 60

**© Yeshiva Pirchei Shoshanim 2017**
This shiur may not be reproduced in any
form without permission of the copyright holder.

# Table of Contents:

1. Introduction
2. Dinim = Procedural Laws & Substantive Decrees
3. Substantive Decrees
4. The Torah Requirements of Dinim
5. Courts That Only Observe or Enforce Part of the Noahide Code
6. Capital Punishment
7. Modern Courts: Conclusions
8. Modern Courts According to the Rema
9. Can Noahides Elect to Be Judged in *Bais Din*?
10. Summary

# Dinim III: Practical Summary

## Introduction

In the last lesson we delved deeply into the Rishonim in search of support for the Rema's opinion that Noahide *dinim* requires application of the Jewish civil and monetary laws. At the end, we saw that most *poskim* do not agree with the Rema's conclusion. Of particular significance was the opinion of Nachmanides. We saw that some *poskim* have read Nachmanides as a precedent for the Rema. However, most *poskim* hold that Nachmanides's views on *dinim* are either unrelated to or even contradict the Rema

In this lesson we will see will explore the practical issues of *dinim* in our times.

## Dinim = Procedural Laws & Substantive Decrees

In the last lesson we cited many, many *poskim* who hold that Noahide *dinim* is neither based upon nor identical to *choshen mishpat* – Jewish monetary and civil law.

The majority of the *poskim* hold that *dinim* has two aspects:

1) **Procedural** – *Dinim* requires the establishment of courts and administration of justice to judge the other Noahide laws.

2) **Substantive/Legislative** – The courts are empowered and expected to make additional laws and decrees as needed to preserve order and maintain

society.[1] These additional regulations fall out under *dinim* and not under any other category of Noahide law.

## Procedural Requirements of *Dinim*

The procedural requirements of *dinim* include:

- Noahide courts must enforce the other Noahide laws.[2]

- Noahide courts must judge the Noahide laws according to their Torah details as commanded to Noahides. They apparently have no right to judge otherwise when it comes to the other six laws.[3] (However, Noahides may judge other decrees established by their courts as needed).

- Noahide courts must also judge according to the minimum procedural requirements of *dinim*.[4]

- Noahide courts must also administer the death penalty for infractions of Noahide law.[5]

## Substantive/Legislative Requirements

*Dinim* grants Noahides the right to make laws and judge according to the needs of their own societies and cultures. These laws, in so much that they preserve society, have biblical authority.[6] Therefore, if the courts declare certain financial transactions illegal, even though the Torah permits them, those transactions become biblically prohibited under *dinim*. Their transgression is not only a civil

---

[1] See the list of *teshuvos* mentioned in the previous lesson as well as *Shu"t Ezras Kohein* 22.

[2] As we saw from Maimonides in the first lesson on *dinim*.

[3] See *Shu"t Mishneh Halachos* VII:254.

[4] This is also clear from Maimonides. We have decided not to get into the procedural details of *dinim* since these are mostly theoretical today (as we shall see).

[5] *Mishneh Halachos* ibid.

[6] According to Nachmanides and Rabbi Yaakov of Anatol. There are differing views on how Maimonides would characterize such laws.

crime, but also a religious sin. A court may also impose any punishments reasonably required to penalize the guilty and deter other would-be criminals.

Note that the courts are <u>only</u> empowered to make such laws that benefit society and preserve order.[7] The courts <u>may not</u> pass wicked or decadent laws (i.e. like Sodom and other corrupt peoples).[8]

The courts may not only make additional laws, but may judge these laws as they deem necessary.

## Modern Courts & *Dinim*

**Modern courts – do they fulfill *dinim*?**

Obviously, modern courts do not fulfill the procedural requirements of the Noahide laws. They do not enforce all of the Noahide laws, nor do they punish properly those that are enforced. Does this lack of proper enforcement mean that these courts are not fulfilling the *mitzvah* of *dinim*? If they are not fulfilling *dinim*, then are they valid courts of law in the eyes of the Torah? Does this fact invalidate the substantive decrees these courts make? This is a grave question with serious consequences:

- **If valid** – It is a *mitzvah* to use those courts, to participate in the justice system, and to respect its rulings.

- **If invalid** – Then it is forbidden to use these courts, participate in them, or even participate in the government that maintains them. The monetary rulings of such courts constitute theft, and should they impose the death penalty they would be guilty of murder!

## Courts That Only Observe or Enforce Part of the Noahide Code

Today's courts do not enforce all of the Noahide laws. Furthermore, the judges, lawyers, witnesses, and other officials of the court do not themselves conscientiously observe all of the Noahide laws. Even if they do, it is usually only on account of reason and not religious motivation.

---

[7] This is the fundamental purpose of *dinim*, as mentioned in the first lesson.

[8] See Rashi to Sanhedrin 56b.

However, observance of the Noahide laws for such a reason is nevertheless valid; they are Noahides, but only *chakhmei umos haolam* (of the wise) and not *chasidei umos haolam* (of the pious).

**Chazon Ish: Rabbi Avraham Yeshaya Karelitz**

The *Chazon Ish*,[9] in an important discussion of the *mitzvah* of *dinim*, proves that this level of observance is certainly enough to grant secular courts legitimacy under *dinim*. He makes a distinction regarding the validity of courts for procedural and substantive aspects of the law:

- **Procedural** – For a Noahide court to judge others according to Noahide law and the requirements of the Torah, the judges and officials must themselves be believing, religiously motivated Noahides. It makes no sense to empower an idolater to judge Noahides according to Noahide law.

- **Substantive** – For the laws passed to preserve society, we may appoint judges and courts as needed. These officials do not need to be committed Noahides, because they are not judging or administering the purely Noahide aspects of *dinim*.

Collectively speaking, modern courts derive their authority from the **substantive aspect** of *dinim*. Therefore, they are fulfilling the *mitzvah* of *dinim*, which, at its root, is about preserving order between man and his fellow (see the first lesson on *dinim* for more on this). Therefore, they are valid courts of judgment.

Yet, the individuals running our courts, are, generally, not committed Noahides. Therefore, they are not valid to administer the **procedural aspects** of *dinim*.

However, this fact produces an interesting result.

## Capital Punishment

Since most judges, officials, and witnesses are valid only according to the customs and needs of society, they may only administer matters governed by the substantive laws and decrees they have made. However, they cannot judge or administer the procedural aspects. The *Chazon Ish* draws a very important conclusion from this: modern courts are not empowered to give the death penalty for transgressions of Noahide law. Courts can only impose the death penalty when most of society and the courts keep the Noahide laws and do so for the right reasons.

---

[9] Bava Kamma 10:16.

Therefore, courts today <u>do not</u> have any right to impose the death penalty, even for murder! Most *Torah* authorities oppose the death penalty for this very reason. However, for the sake of preserving order, it may be imposed if society absolutely requires it as a criminal deterrent.[10] In that case, the death penalty would fall out under the substantive aspect of *denim* and not the procedural aspect.

## Modern Courts According to the Rema

Most *poskim* maintain that even those who hold of the Rema, that *dinim* imposes the Jewish legal system upon non-Jews, would agree to the validity of modern secular courts. The *Minchas Yitzchok*,[11] discussing this issue, concludes that the Rema holds Noahides may not initially establish their own legal system in lieu of the Jewish legal code. However, once established such a legal system is binding and valid.[12]

## Can Noahides Elect to Be Judged in *Bais Din*?

Technically, yes. But why? Some Noahides have asked to have their cases judged by *bais din* because they want to be judged according to "God's law." However, *dinim* is also God's law! It is true that modern courts are not fulfilling *dinim* in the ideal way, but todays *batei din* are not operating ideally either (as discussed in an earlier lesson). We see that Jews and Noahide are both far from their ideals. God has nevertheless provided us both with our own, unique pathways to Him. As different as the paths may look, they both start and end in the same place: the wellspring of the holy Torah.

---

[10] *Igros Moshe* CM II:68.

[11] IV:52.

[12] This is also the ruling of *Shu"t Keter Dovid* 18; *Kenesses HaGedolah*; *Chelkas Yoav* and many others cited by the *Minchas Yitzchok*.

## Summary

1. Many *poskim* read Nachmanides as disagreeing with Rema and supporting Maimonides and the other Rishonim.

2. *Dinim* operates on two levels: fixed requirements of procedural law, and decrees of substantive law that are made as per the needs of society.

3. Substantive decrees are valid only if just and beneficial to society.

4. Even though today's courts do not enforce all of the Noahide laws, they are nevertheless valid courts and fulfill *dinim* on the most basic level.

5. However, their fulfillment is not enough to empower them to impose the death penalty.

6. In general, Jews and Noahides are not in favor of the death penalty. However, in rare situations, they acknowledge that it may be justified if it would deter similar crimes in the future.

THE YESHIVA PIRCHEI SHOSHANIM SHULCHAN ARUCH LEARNING PROJECT

# The Noahide Laws
# Epilogue

© **Yeshiva Pirchei Shoshanim 2017**
This shiur may not be reproduced in any
form without permission of the copyright holder.

164 Village Path, Lakewood NJ 08701 732.370.3344
164 Rabbi Akiva, Bnei Brak, 03.616.6340

# Epilogue

We cannot express to you, collectively and individually, what a pleasure and honor it has been to research, write, and teach this course. We have made many wonderful friends and learned a lot along the way.

The purpose of this course was not to cover the entirely of the Noahide Laws. To do so would take years. Our intention was to explore the foundations and fundamentals of Noahism, discovering where it distinct from Judaism, and where it has similarities. By doing so, we hoped to help those taking this course to find their "place" within the Torah.

All mankind has a "place" within the Torah and God wants every person to find his or her "place." However, finding this "place" is a lifelong process of study and exploration. This is because both Judaism and Noahism are, at their cores, about building a relationship with Hashem. Any relationship requires work – hard work. This is an inviolable rule of being human: if we want productive relationships with our spouses, children, neighbors, and friends, then we must work to build those relationships.

Know this – Jews do not automatically feel closer to God or find it easier to build this relationship than Noahides. A Jew must struggle, study, endure, and work for a long time to bind himself to his Creator. It is no different for Noahides – we are all the same in our struggle to come close to God.

However, we are different in that the Jewish struggle is given its structure and shape by 613 mitzvos, while the Noahide struggle is shaped and directed by 7 categories of *mitzvos*. Many Noahides, though, often look at the Noahide laws, compare them to the Jewish laws, and conclude that the Noahide laws are somehow insufficient for their spiritual needs. As a result, they make the mistake of simply trying to imitate Judaism and find connection-to-God within the Jewish *mitzvos*.

This is a grievous error and one that is based on misperception and misinformation. It stems mostly from the fact that the Jewish path is clearly defined, while the Noahide path has suffered from centuries of neglect. Many areas of it are unclear. This lack of clarity is often mistaken for a sort of "incompleteness." In short, the Noahide path requires rediscovery. This process can only happen by a commitment to study, work, and growth. You and your fellow students have made a major commit to this rediscovery, study, and growth of the Noahide path. May God bless you with continued success, inspiration, and a long fruitful bond with the Creator of all life and all souls!

## What to Do Now?

There are basically three things to do going forward:

1) **Practice** – Live as a Noahide and identify as a Noahide. Embrace this identity and make it the motivation for your good works in this world. Pray regularly and look for opportunities to make the world better and to honor your Creator.

2) **Study** – this will be discussed below.

3) **Build the Noahide community** – This is incredibly important. The Noahide world has not existed as an identifiable community in over 1000 years. Today, it is a collection of individuals and a few organizations striving to discover their place within the Torah. Unity and cooperation are vitally important to bring that goal to fruition. See below for more info.

## Torah Study

There are three areas of study that are important whether Noahide or Jew:

1) **Text** – Study of the original texts, whether Torah, Talmud, Midrash, or Mishneh Torah, that apply to Noahides,

2) **Practice** – Study of books on the actual living and fulfillment of *halacha*, practice,

3) **Faith & Inspiration** – It is vitally important to stay focused on the good in this world and the love, mercy, and kindness of Hashem. The study of works dealing with faith and inspiration remind us of these truths.

When studying Torah, the following advice will prove helpful:

- Create a learning schedule. Set aside fixed times to read and study. The amount is not as important as is the consistency and regularity. A lot of study inconsistently is not as beneficial as a little done regularly.

- Select a material from at least two of the areas mentioned above and try to keep two tracts of study going at all times.

- Any time you come across a *mitzvah* (commandment), *minhag* (custom), or a concept, always ask yourself: is this relevant to Noahides or to Jews? Until uniquely Noahide versions of all of these texts become available, Noahides have to adapt information from Jewish sources. In general, anything from Exodus 20 onwards is not relevant to Noahides.

- Is the topic a *mitzvas muskalos* – a logically compelled *mitzvah*? If so, it may be studied and practiced according to even its Jewish precepts. However, be on guard and question constantly whether any particular practice is uniquely a product of Jewish history (as a custom or institution of later sages), or if it stems directly from the concept behind the *mitzvah*. This is necessary because there are not yet specifically Noahide guidebooks on many of these topics. Therefore, you must become skilled at evaluating and adapting material from books written for Jews. Specifically Jewish details of the *mitzvos* are not relevant to Noahides. If you need assistance, email Noahide Nations.

- Logically compelled *mitzvos* include, but are not limited to:

    - Honoring parents,
    - Cruelty to animals,
    - Interpersonal relationships,
    - Many monetary laws today,
    - Charity,
    - Caring for the sick,
    - Prayer & blessings,
    - Educating children in the Noahide Laws

## Suggested Material for Study:

| | |
|---|---|
| **Chumash (Torah) & Nakh (Prophets & Writings)** | **Chumash** (Artscroll Ed. Item# STOH) – Bilingual edition of the Torah with an anthology of the classic commentaries.

**Tanakh** (Artscroll Ed. Item# STGS) – Bilingual edition of the entire Hebrew scriptures with minimal commentary and reference.

**Midrash Rabbah: Bereshis & Noach** (Artscroll Kleinman Ed. Item# MRBR1) – Moral, ethical, and homiletic insights into the subtle nuances of the Torah's narrative. Lots of material relevant to Noahides.

**Rashi's Commentary on the Torah** (Artscroll Sapirstein Ed. Item# SRAHS) – Rabbi Shlomo Yitzhaki's commentary lays draws upon the entire corpus of |

Midrash, Talmud, etc. to explain the events of the Torah. Although Rashi writes many times "I only come to explain the plain meaning of the text," his commentary does much more than deal with "plain meanings." Rashi is viewed as the "starting point" for any question on the Chumash.

**Ramban's Commentary on the Torah** (Artscroll Ed. Item# SRBNS) – in the 13th century Ramban (Rabbi Moshe Bar Nachman, also called Nachmanides) wrote a commentary analyzing Rashi's remarks and considering alternative explanations. Reading Rashi alongside the Ramban really conveys the "whole picture."

**The Torah Anthology: Beginnings [Beraishis & Noah]** (Moznaim Item# 930153-2) – an 18th century commentary by Rabbi Yaakov Culi. Originally entitled *Me'am Loez*, it weaves together commentary, law, ethics, and mysticism to flesh out a practical understanding of the Torah. It is also very enjoyable to read.

**Artscroll Tanach Series: Bereshis/Genesis, In 2 Volumes** (Artscroll Item #BERH) - In depth commentary on the book of Bereshis/Genesis. Excellent for study.

**Talmud**

**Tractate Sanhedrin** (Artscroll Schottenstein Ed. Vol. 48 Item# DTSA2) – These pages contain most of the Talmud's discussion of the Noahide laws. Remember that not all of the opinions brought in the Talmud are actual law. Knowing and deriving the Talmud's conclusions is a skill that must be learned. It is important to learn this with a study partner or someone who has established skills in learning Talmud.

**Mishneh Torah**

Maimonides compiled the first complete statement of all Torah law from the Talmud, Midrashim, and other texts. It a monumental work, yet not without its flaws. Notably, Maimonides rarely quoted his sources or explained his rationales. Torah scholars have spent centuries reconstructing his reasoning and methods for understanding the Torah. Of course, this may be exactly what Maimonides wanted. Although the *halacha*, actual law, does not always follow Maimonides, his writings are essential for both Jews and Noahides desiring to know God's expectations of them:

- **Vol. 1: Yesodei HaTorah – Foundatons of the Torah** (Moznaim Item# 963669-1) – The foundations of Torah belief.

- **Vol. 2: Hilchos Deos - Attributes** (Moznaim Item# 963669-2) – Human traits and qualities.

- **Vol. 3: Avodas Kokhavim – Idolatry & Idolaters** (Moznaim Item# 963669-3) – Laws of idolatry & idolaters.

- **Vol. 4: Laws of Teshuvah** (Moznaim Item# 963669-4) – Principles of repentance.

- **Vol. 26: Sefer Nezikin – Monetary Laws** (Moznaim Item# 963669-26) – Monetary and civil law.

- **Vol. 29: Sefer Shoftim – Kings & Judges** (Moznaim Item# 963669-29) – includes Maimnonides's writings on the Noahide Laws.

**On Noahide Halacha**

The Seven Laws of Noah by Rabbi Aharon Lichtenstein

The Divine Code Vol. I by Rabbi Moshe Weiner

The Divine Code Vol. II by Rabbi Moshe Weiner (in preparation)

**Prayer**

Suggested Prayers for Noahide Community Services & Personal Worship by Rabbis Moshe Weiner and J. Immanuel Schochet

Prayers, Blessings, Principles of Faith, and Divine Service for Noahides by Rabbis Moshe Weiner and J. Immanuel Schochet

The Order: Noahide Prayers Book for Individuals, Communities, Holidays, and Lifecycle Events (in preparation)

**Psalms** (Artscroll Bilingual Full Size Ed. Item# TEHH; Pocket Sized Ed. Item# TEPH)

**Faith, Belief, and Thought**

**The Handbook of Jewish Thought, Vol. 1 & 2** (Moznaim Item# 505075-1 & 505075-2) – Excellent compendia of the basics of Torah belief. Though geared toward Jews, it contains much material relevant to Noahides as well.

**The Universal Garden of Emunah by Rabbi Shalom Arush**

**Restore My Soul** (Moznaim Item# 58620) – Rav Nachaman of Breslov's writings on repentance translated by Rabbi Aryeh Kaplan.

**Outpouring of the Soul** (Moznaim Item# 61578) – Rav Nachaman of Breslov's writings on prayer translated by Rabbi Aryeh Kaplan.

**Our Amazing World** (Artscroll Item# WOWH) – Seeing God's wonders in the world around us.

**Our Wondrous World** (Artscroll Item# AMAH) – Sequel to **Our Amazing World.**

**Other Laws and Practices**

Interpersonal
- **The Laws of Interpersonal Relationships** (Artscroll Item #JTVH)

Proper Speech
- **Chofetz Chaim Lesson a Day** (Artscroll Item# LADH)
- **Chofetz Chaim: The Family Lesson a Day** (Artscroll Item# FLADH)
- **Positive Word Power** (Artscroll Item# PWPH)

Business
- **Money in Halacha** (Feldheim Item# 6980)
- **Halachos of Other People's Money** (Feldheim Item# 3721)
- **Cases in Monetary Law** (Artscroll Item# CAM1H)

Blessings
- **The Laws of Brachos** (Artscroll Item# LOBH)

Family
- **The Fifth Commandment: Honoring Parents** (Artscroll Item# FIFH)
- **My Father, My Mother & Me** (Artscroll Item# MFMMH)

Sickness
- **Visiting the Sick** (Artscroll Item# VTSH)

Charity
- **The Laws of Tzedakah & Maaser** (Artscroll Item# LOTH)
- **The Tzedakah Treasury** (Artscroll Item# TZTH)

Teshuvah/Repentance

- Returnity, by R' Tal Zwecker (Menucha Publishers)
- The Power of Teshuvah, by R' Heshy Kleinman (Artscroll Item# POTP)
- A Touch of Purity, by R' Yechiel Spero (Artscroll Item# TPUEI)

**Polemics**

- **26 Reasons Jews Don't Believe in Jesus** (Feldheim Item# 4412)
- **Permission to Believe by Lawrence Kelemen** (Menucha Publishers)
- **Permission to Receive by Lawrence Kelemen** (Menucha Publishers)
- **The Real Messiah by Rabbi Aryeh Kaplan** (Artscroll Item# U-REMP)

**Learning Hebrew**

- HaYesod (Feldheim Item# 1734)

## Building Community

Every faith community really needs three things to have an identity:

- **Ethic** – a sense of what constitutes correct behavior and expectations for man. The Noahide laws clearly have this.

- **Ethos** – a worldview and philosophy. This is also part of the Noahide laws and is, generally, the same as the Jewish worldview. However, this is a topic that is not as easy to grasp as the "thou shalls" and "thou shalt nots" of practice. Study and practice together form and shape this aspect.

- **Ethnos** – a sense of community, commonality, and fellowship. This is what is lacking the most in the Noahide world today and what must be developed. The following are actions points that, to me, seem to be where more work is needed.

## Action Points

**Worship**

There is no official Noahide liturgy. Noahide Nations and Ask Noah International and have each developed liturgies for Noahide communities and individuals. However, these are only starting points. As the Noahide community grows and develops, their prayers must change to suit the needs of the community. Certain prayers still need to be written. For example:

- Selichos, penitential prayers, for the repentance season.
- Prayers for the festivals expressing the Noahide relationship to these festivals.

**Services** It is important to develop regular communal prayer services based upon the liturgies mentioned above. Special holiday services should also be part of this.

**Music** Music for Noahide worship is vital. It allows everyone to participate in worship and creates a sense of elevation. It also makes worship fun!

**Food** Feeding people is the most powerful way to build communities and peaceful relationships. Communal meals are ABSOLUTELY essential to building fellowship and community.

**Community Torah study** In addition to individual Torah study, it is important to come together and study Torah as a community. This includes regular study sessions as well as scheduling special events & speakers.

***Chesed*** The most important activities that Noahides can engage in, even more important than communal prayer or regular community Torah story, are acts of kindness that improve the world. Noahides should build charitable organizations and use these as their vehicles for outreach and performing their *mitzvos*. Noahide communities should arrange *chesed*, "kindness projects" for members of the community needing assistance. For example:

- When family has a birth, organize meals for the family for a week or two. Similarly, when a family experiences a tragedy, or a parent goes into the hospital, meals and basic needs should be arranged by the community.
- Regular prayer gatherings for the sick.
- Volunteerism for good causes (soup kitchens, habitat for humanity, etc.)
- Fundraisers for those in need.
- Food drives
- Arrange a lending organization for baby supplies, medical needs, etc.

Noahides should organize their communities around such acts of kindness. Ideally, Noahide congregations should start as 501(c)(3) charitable organizations devoted to acts of *chesed*.

THE YESHIVA PIRCHEI SHOSHANIM SHULCHAN ARUCH PROJECT

# The Noahide Laws - God

© Yeshiva Pirchei Shoshanim 2017
This shiur may not be reproduced in any form without permission of the copyright holder.

Rechov Rabbi Akiva 164, Bnei Brak, Israel 03.616.6340
360 Valley Ave #23, Hammonton, N.J. 08037. 732.370.3344 fax 1.877.Pirchei

THE YESHIVA PIRCHEI SHOSHANIM SHULCHAN ARUCH PROJECT
THE NOAHIDE LAWS | BELIEF | GOD

# Table of Contents:

1. Introduction
2. God the Transcendent and Immanent
3. The Transcendent Aspect of God
4. The Immanent Aspect of God
5. The Experience of God vs. The Reality of God
6. God's Incorporeality
7. Other Issues
8. Overview
9. Summary

# God

## Introduction

This week's lesson will begin our parallel series of lessons on Noahide belief and thought. We will begin with where all things began: God.

## God: The Transcendent and Immanent

God is easy and simple – utterly uncomplicated in any way.[1] However, our ability to comprehend Him is another matter. Anything we can say about God is more about how we perceive Him than about God himself. This is because God, as we shall see, is entirely transcendental. His essence is utterly beyond all comprehension. In fact, God is indescribable and ultimately unknowable.[2] However, God is also immanent and involved with His creation. From this feature of God we can learn a lot about Him, deriving His desires and values. This is perhaps the most famous example of God's essence versus our perception of God: although God is ultimately simple, we perceive Him as both transcendent and immanent. This idea is at the heart of much Torah theology and a good starting point for our discussion.

## The Transcendent Aspect of God

The prayer Shema states: "Hear O Israel, The Lord our God, The Lord is one!" This declaration of God's unity is not merely about the mathematics of faith. It is more correctly understood as a qualitative rather than quantitative idea. God is

---

[1] See *Derech HaShem* I: 1. Although God is entirely simple and in no way possesses any plurality, we describe his influence upon creation using a variety of attributes (mercy, justice, love, etc.). These relate to our understanding, however, not to God's actual essence. See also *Ohr HaShem* I: 3:4; *Shnei Luchos HaBris* (in the Bris Dovid) I: 42; *Mishnah Torah Yesodei HaTorah* 2:10.

[2] *Shomer Emunim* 2:11. See also *Mishnah Torah Hil. Teshuva* 5:5 and *Emunos Ve-Deos* II.

not simply "one." Instead he is "oneness," the ultimate unity.[3] The problem with ultimate one-ness is that its nature precludes two-ness. For that matter, it precludes three-ness, four-ness, or anything-else-ness at all! If that is the case, then how do we exist? The answer is an important concept called *tzimtzum*: constriction. Before God could create anything at all, He had to create a space in which creation could take place. In order to do so, He "constricted" his presence, creating a space in which the essence of one-ness was diluted enough to allow creation to endure. This empty space is known as the *Chalal ha-Penui* (or *Chalal*, for short), the vacated space. Between God's eternal, unified essence and the *Chalal* a barrier called the *Pargod*, the veil, or partition.[4]

The *Chalal* is the canvas upon which all creation took place. Anything that is not-God exists as a created entity within the *Chalal*. As God Himself said: "I am God; I make all things."[5]

This distinct separation between God and His creation yields a number of conclusions about God:

- As creator of all things, God must therefore be, in essence, entirely separate from all things.[6] There is nothing in the created world that can represent or approximate Him. As it states in Isaiah: "To whom will you then liken God?"[7] Similarly: "There is none like you among the heavenly powers…"[8] Since God must be distinct from the creation, Judaism and Noahism must reject any concept of pantheism.

- Since God created all things, his existence can in no way be predicated upon anything in creation. We cannot therefore define God as love,

---

[3] See Rambam *13 Principles of Faith* and *Peirusha al HaMishnayos* Sanhedrin 10:1.

[4] This entire paragraph is a summary of the initial creation as explained by the Zohar and early mystics.

[5] Isaiah 44:24.

[6] *Shomer Emunim* 2:11.

[7] 40:18.

[8] Psalms 86:8.

morality, or any kind ethical force.⁹ God may have those attributes, but they are not God and vice versa.¹⁰

- Since He created all matter, God must not be made of matter.¹¹ Similarly, since God created space and time, He cannot exist within space and time.¹²

What emerges from the above is a picture of a God who is entirely transcendent and beyond is creation. The danger of such a conception, however, is the erroneous conclusion that God is absent from His creation. To the contrary - God is intimately involved with His creation.

## The Immanent Aspect of God

*Tzimtzum* does not mean that God totally removed Himself from the *Chalal*. It only means that he restricted his essence to a degree necessary for creation to endure. Yet, God's presence still permeates and fills the *Chalal*.

How do we know this?

In Nechemiah 9:6 we are told:

> *You have made the heavens… the earth and all that is on it… you give life to them all.*

The last clause is in the present tense: God gives life and is continuously giving life. There are many other references to God as the perpetual creator throughout the Tanakh.¹³

---

⁹ *Pardes Rimonim* III: 1; *Yesodei HaTorah* 1:4; *Zohar* I: 22a.

¹⁰ *Kuzari* II: 2; *Ikkarim* II: 22.

¹¹ See *Kuzari* 4:3. Because of His complete detachment from any element of the physical world he is called "pure" and "holy" in many places in Tanakh.

¹² *Emunos VeDeyos* II: 11 & 12 and Shvil *Emunah* ad loc.; *Ikkarim* II: 18; *Asara Maamaros Choker Din* I: 16. This is the Torah's answer to the famous paradox of free will vs. fore-knowledge. If God knows all things before they occur, then how do we have free will? The paradox arises from the assumption is that our choice is a result of God's fore –knowing. However, this cause and effect relationship only exists from our perspective. From God's perspective, in which time is irrelevant, cause does not precede nor follow effect. Our choice and God's knowledge have no temporal relationship to one-another and, therefore, there is no paradox.

Since creation's continued existence depends constantly upon God's will, then His will must extend into the *Chalal*. However, since God is an absolute unity, then his will and his essence must be one in the same. Therefore, God's essence must extend into the *Chalal*.

In this sense, God is immanent: He is continuously and intimately involved with His creation. He directs and sustains it, He hears and answers the prayers of His people; He gives it life and deals with it in kindness and justice. We see this on every page of the Tanakh.

## The Experience of God vs. the Reality of God

We must be reminded, however, that this is a dual perception of God, and not relevant to God himself. It is a product of the finite mind's striking against an infinite reality. It is not a perception limited only to humans, however. This dual experience of God is alluded to in the song of the angels in Isaiah 6:3. The angels sing:

> *Holy, Holy, Holy us the God of hosts, the whole world is filled with his glory.*

This verse refers to the immanent experience of God. However, the angels also sing

> *Blessed is God's glory from His place.*[14]

Here the angels refer to God in the transcendental sense, as occupying a place that is His, only His, and that of none other.

Similarly, we say in the *Shema*: "Hear O Israel, the Lord our God, the Lord is one." Before declaring that God is an unknowable and transcendent unity ("the Lord is One"), we first declare that he is "the Lord our God," both imminent and ruling.

Furthermore, in every blessing we open with the words: *Blessed are you, our God, king of the universe.* We declare God as both *our God*, imminent and close, and as a king who is transcendent and lofty.

---

[13] Perpetual creation is fundamental and intrinsic to all Torah theology. See *Kuzari* 4:26; *Ibn Ezra Shemos* 3:2; *Ramban Bereshis* 1:4; *Yesodei HaTorah* 2:9; Zohar III:31a; *Pardes Rimonim* 6:8; *Reishis Chochmah Shaar HaYirah* I; there are too many sources to list here – this is only a sampling.

[14] Ezekiel 3:12.

The moving prayer *Ovinu Malkeinu*, recited several times during the year, repeats the refrain *Ovinu Malkeinu – Our father, our King!*, referring to God as both our imminent father and our transcendent king.

**For Discussion**

*In the live class we will discuss the following questions: if we know that God is the ultimately one, then why do we seem to focus this dual perception in our prayers and other sacred writings? For that matter, why do we speak of God as "angry" or "loving" if these are all only facets of our perception? Isn't there a better way to approach God?*

## God's Incorporeality

As mentioned above, since God is the creator of all matter and all space, he cannot be made of matter or subject to space. This fact precludes God having any material manifestation. God himself warns us to never think of him corporeally, saying:

> *Take heed of yourselves for you saw no matter of form on that day that God spoke to you at Horeb…*[15]

**Nevertheless**, the Torah often speaks of God using anthropomorphism – describing Him as if he had physical qualities. For example, in many places we find reference to the hand of God[16] or the eyes of God.[17] In all such situations the Torah is not telling us that God has a body. Rather, the Torah is borrowing from the language of man in order to express something about His relationship to His creation.[18]

**Similarly**, when the Torah describes God's voice, it is referring to a prophetic voice within the mind, but not to an actual divine voice in the sense that we understand voice.[19]

You wonder then why man is described as being created in God's image if God has no actual "image?"

---

[15] Deuteronomy 4:15.

[16] Exodus 9:15.

[17] Psalms 15:3.

[18] See *Ramban* to Genesis 46:1;

[19] *Kuzari* I: 89; *Emunos VeDeyos* 2:12.

This is not a description of the physical attributes of man – rather it means that man can affect and interact with the world using many of the same attributes perceived in God.[20] For example, Man and God both share free will and creative ability.

## Other Issues

Any descriptor for God must be qualified and considered carefully. For example, God is often referred to as "He," in the masculine. However, this is merely an effect of the Hebrew language which has no neuter grammatical gender.

In the same vein, even terms that seem accurate must be kept in perspective. For example, God is often described as "eternal." As apropos as this may appear, it is still a limited description. Not being bound by time, the human concept of "eternity" doesn't even fit properly. "Eternal" is only the closest term we can use to describe God-in-time.

## Overview

Although God is utterly beyond any description, comprehension, or corollary in the created universe, he is nevertheless intimately involved in it.

We see His impact upon reality at every turn, which informs us as to his will and attributes.

Nevertheless, these attributes are only products of our perception of God's action and not intrinsic to God Himself. We can only understand God's essence by knowing what it is not. In this sense, Torah theology is called "negative theology."

---

[20] *Nefesh HaChaim* I: 1; *Avodas HaKodesh, HaYichud* 18; *Mechilta Shemos* 14:29; *Hilchos Teshuva* 5:1.

## Summary of the Lesson

1. God is beyond any words, description, form, or comprehension.

2. Since God created time, space, and matter, He is not subject to any of them.

3. Although God is entirely transcendent, he is also completely immanent and involved with the world.

4. This dual perception of God is only a perception and is not the reality of God. We are limited in our ability to perceive the infinite.

5. God is incorporeal and without form. Anthropomorphism is used by the Torah, however, to convey by way of allegory God's attributes in this world.

6. Any positive description of God is only a description of God's actions and influence, not of God himself. The essence of God can only be truly communicated by contemplating what God is not.

THE YESHIVA PIRCHEI SHOSHANIM SHULCHAN ARUCH PROJECT

# The Noahide Laws - Man

© Yeshiva Pirchei Shoshanim 2017
This shiur may not be reproduced in any form without permission of the copyright holder.

## Table of Contents:

1. Introduction

2. The Purpose of Creation

3. Partaking of True Good

4. Free Will

    a. Internal Aspects: Yetzer Tov vs. Yetzer Hara

    b. External Aspects: Man vs. the World

5. Reward & Punishment

    a. Reward in This World

    b. *Middah Keneged Middah* – Measure for Measure

# Man, Reward, and Punishment

## Introduction

In our last lesson on theology and belief we discussed the Torah conception of God. In this lesson we will explore man.

## The Purpose of Creation

"Why did God create the world?" is perhaps the hardest question ever asked. To answer it, we have to presuppose an understanding of God's exact will and innermost thoughts before creation. If you studied the prior lesson on God carefully, then you will realize that this is impossible[1].

To further complicate things, consider that God is an absolute perfection, without lack or needs. He didn't need to create us. Therefore, his ultimate reasons for doing so are unfathomable.

Any discussion of God's purpose is only possible from our perspective as the beneficiary of creation.

## The Greatest Act of Love

Taking into consideration all that we cannot know, it informs us as to what we do know. If G-d is perfect and had no need to create us, then the act of creation must

---

[1] See *Moreh Nevukhim* 3:13; Yoma 38a; *Avos d'Rabbi Nasan* 41.

stand as the ultimate act of altruism.² The Psalms speak of creation as such, describing it as an act of love:

> *The world is built of love.³*

It is also an act of the ultimate goodness:

> *God saw all that He made and – behold! It was very good!⁴*

Since God is perpetually creating all reality,⁵ it means that His goodness and love is constantly sustaining all creation:

> *God is good to all; His love is upon all his works.⁶*

At every instant God's pure desire for us flows throughout every atom of creation.

## Partaking of True Good

> *You let me know the path of life; in your presence is the fullness of joy. In your right hand is eternal bliss.⁷*

> *I am The Lord your God who instructs you for your own reward…⁸*

---

[2] *Emunos VeDeos* I:4; *Reshis Chochma Shaar HaTeshuva* I; *Derech HaShem* I:2:1; *Sheni Luchos HaBris, Beis Yisroel* I:21b; *Likutei Moharan* 64.

[3] 89:3.

[4] Genesis 1:35.

[5] This is the doctrine of perpetual creation discussed in an earlier lesson.

[6] Psalms 145:9.

[7] Psalms 16:11.

[8] Isaiah 48:17.

This first verse tells us that God is the ultimate goodness[9]. The second verse tells us both that Man is capable of partaking of that ultimate goodness and that God instructs us as to how we should do so.[10]

However, in order to be aware of divine goodness, we must know its absence. This is another reason for *tzimtzum*, the restriction of God's presence in the physical creation.[11] By reducing the everyday immanent experience of God, true experiences of His goodness can be fully recognized.

## Free Will

> *I call heaven and earth to witness against you this day: I have put before you life and death, blessing and curse. Choose life…*[12]

This verse alludes to man's free will – his ability to choose whether to partake of God's goodness or to turn away from it.

If man had no free will, then enjoyment of God's goodness would not be true enjoyment. It would be a compulsory, rote experience devoid of greater meaning. Once he has the ability to desire and choose God's goodness, only then does the experience becomes valuable.[13]

Therefore, God created man with free will. Besides God, man is the only being who can act upon his free choice. In this sense, man resembles God. This is the fundamental understanding of man having been created "in the image of God."[14]

Free will, however, requires both an internal and external mechanism in order to function.

---

[9] *Ibn Ezra ad* loc; *Emunos VeDeyos* III. See also *Derech HaShem* I:2:1.

[10] *Emunos VeDeos* I:4.

[11] See the lesson on God.

[12] Deuteronomy 30:19.

[13] There is a massive amount of literature on the necessity of free will. For a basic overview, see *Hilchos Teshuva* 5; *Emunos VeDeyos* IV:4*; Reishis Chochmah Shaar Teshuva* I; *Zohar* I:23a.

[14] See *Derech HaShem* I:2.

**Internal Aspects: Yetzer Tov vs. Yetzer Hara**

Internally, man is imbued with two opposing forces:

- The *yetzer tov* – the desire for good, altruism, self-betterment, and mitzvos.
- The *yetzer hara* – the desire for evil, selfishness, self-destruction, and transgression.

This dual nature of man explains the apparent contradiction between these two verses:

> *And God created man in his image; in the image of G-d he created him.*[15]
> and
> *The desire of man's heart is evil from his youth.*[16]

The first verse refers to man's divine potential – the *yetzer tov*, the desire for good. The second refers to man's base desires – his *yetzer hara*, the desire for evil.

In the Talmud,[17] Rabbi Nachman bar Rav Chisda sees an allusion to both aspects in the verse

> *And God formed [וייצר] man…*

Rabbi Nachman points out that the word וייצר is spelled with and extra yud. He sees the two yuds in the word as an allusion to God's having formed man with two desires (also, the word *yotzer*, formed, is a cognate of the word *yetzer*, desire).

In Torah thought all of man's actions and choices are the result of a struggle between these two inclinations. One seeks the holy, the other the profane - one desires knowledge, the other wants only physical pleasure.

One might think that the goal of man is to entirely ignore his evil desire. This is not so. The ideal for man is to subdue his bad desire to his good desire, thus making it a tool of divine service.

---

[15] Genesis 1:27.

[16] Genesis 8:21.

[17] *Berachos* 61a.

**External Aspects: Man vs. the World**

In order for Man to have free will, he must be placed in an environment that allows him to exercise his power of choice. Therefore, God created a world filled with opportunities for both good and evil in which all things speak to his ultimate purpose:

> *God has made everything for his own purpose, even the wicked...*[18]

> *I form light and create darkness. I make peace and create evil. I am God – I do all these things.*[19]

In this environment, any and every decision a person makes is the direct result of a nuanced struggle between these opposite inclinations.

How man decides to use or pervert the opportunities God offers is man's choice alone and one for which he bears 100% of the responsibility:

> *If a person sins... he bears full responsibility for his action.*[20]

Since the potential for evil resides within man and is evenly matched with his capacity for good, the Torah rejects any concept of an all-evil being or devil who temps people into sin. To iterate: people are 100% responsible for their own sins.

## Reward & Punishment

We tend to think that we are rewarded *for* our good deeds and punished *for* our transgressions. This view is true only of laws created and administered by man. Spiritual reward and punishment operate according to a different mechanic. Just as God created the natural world with its own principles of cause and effect, He did the

---

[18] Proverbs 16:4.

[19] Isaiah 45:7.

[20] Leviticus 5:17.

same with the spiritual world.[21] Within this system reward and punishment are *direct results* of one's actions rather than things meted out *for* one's actions.[22]

This idea runs throughout *Tanakh*:[23]

*A wicked man's sins shall entrap him; he will be bound in the binds of his own transgression.*[24]

*God is known by the judgment he carries out when the wicked man is ensnared in the work of his own hands.*[25]

*He who digs a pit shall fall into it.*[26]

These two verses make clear that God's justice is programmed into the spiritual law of the universe and operates as a direct result of one's own actions. The same applies to reward.[27] However, there is a difference: while punishment is precisely meted out, reward is given liberally.[28] Furthermore, the ultimate reward for good lasts for eternity while the punishment for evil is only temporary. Because the nature of reward and punishment differ, good deeds cannot cancel out evil and vice versa. This is learned from a verse in the Torah:

---

[21] Just as with His natural law, it is only altered in very rare circumstances. See *Shemos Rabbah* 30:6; *Vayikra Rabbah* 35:3; *Yerushalmi Rosh HaShanah* 1:3.

[22] Numerous Midrashim discuss this idea. *See Koheles Rabbah* 3:11; *Vayikra Rabbah* 19:6; *Yalkut Shimoni* 2:938.

[23] For more examples see Proverbs 13:6; Obadiah 1:15; Psalms 18:25-26.

[24] Proverbs 5:22

[25] Psalms 9:17.

[26] Proverbs 6:27.

[27] *Sotah* 1:8; *Tosefta Sotah* 4:1; *Bava Metzia* 86a; *Sotah* 17a; *Chullin* 89a; *Sefer Chassidim* 53. There are many, many, sources and examples.

[28] See *Sotah* 9b; *Sefer Chasidim* 698; *Tos. Yom Tov* on Sotah 9:8; *Tos. Sotah* 11a s.v. Miriam. Again, there are many, many, sources and examples.

*God does not give special consideration or take bribes.*[29]

What does it mean that God does not take bribes? Our sages explain that God does not take the exchange of good deeds for evil ones.[30]

An individual is punished for all the evil he does and rewarded for all of the good.

However, the punishment that one deserves for his transgressions can be changed into the merit of a mitzvah by sincere, loving repentance.[31]

**Reward in This World?** As we will see in a future lesson, the primary place for reward and punishment is *Olam Haba*, the World to Come. Nevertheless, under certain circumstances, a person can receive reward and punishment for part of his deeds in this world. We will discuss this more in future lessons.

***Middah Keneged Middah*** Many times, but not always, there is an obvious correspondence between the deed and its reward and the crime and its punishment. This relationship is called *middah keneged middah – measure-matching-measure*. When this happens it is in order to demonstrate God's law and further reveal his kingship in the world.[32]

---

[29] Deuteronomy 10:17.

[30] See Ramban ad loc.; *Avos* 4:22 and numerous commentaries ad. loc.;

[31] *Yoma* 86a; *Yerushalmi Peah* 1:1; *Ikkarim* 4:25; *Shemos Rabbah* 31:1; *Bamidbar Rabbah* 10:1; *Shir HaShirim Rabbah* 6:1 and much more.

[32] See *Ikkarim* IV: 9; *Mekhilta Shemos* 14:26 and 18:11; *Shabbos* 105b; *Sanhedrin* 90a; *Nedarim* 32a and many, many more examples.

## Summary of the Lesson

1. God's innermost reasons for wanting to create the world are mysterious and cannot be understood. We can only understand His reasons from our perspective as the beneficiaries of creation.

2. Creation was the greatest, truest, and purest act of love and altruism. Since God is constantly creating, His love and goodness are constantly being sustaining the world.

3. It is possible for man to partake of and experience the underlying goodness that sustains creation. He does so by keeping the mitzvos and serving and clinging to God.

4. In order to know this good, we much know its absence. This is another reason for the idea of *tzimtzum*.

5. Man must voluntarily earn this good; otherwise his benefit would not be true benefit. Only by choosing it voluntarily does man truly enjoy it. Therefore God gave man free will.

6. In this aspect of free will man, in a very small way, resembles his Creator. This is the idea of man having been made in God's image.

7. To enable free will, man was given two conflicting internal drives: a desire to do good and a desire to do bad. Man was also placed in an environment which provides him with choices and contexts in which to exercise his will.

8. Reward and punishments are best conceived as the effects of our choices rather than judgments that are meted out. Reward and punishment are the effects of a "spiritual law" established by God and similar to natural law.

9. One's mitzvos cannot cancel out his transgressions. A person is rewarded for all of his mitzvos and punished for all of his sins. However, sincere repentance can convert ones sins into merits.

10. The primary place for reward and punishment is not in this world. Nevertheless, some reward and punishment is possible in this world depending on the circumstances.

11. Occasionally the relationship between the mitzvah/reward and the sin/punishment is obvious. Sometimes it is not.

'THE YESHIVA PIRCHEI SHOSHANIM SHULCHAN ARUCH PROJECT

# The Noahide Laws – The Soul

© Yeshiva Pirchei Shoshanim 2014
This shiur may not be reproduced in any form without permission of the copyright holder.

**164 Village Path, Lakewood NJ 08701 732.370.3344**
**164 Rabbi Akiva, Bnei Brak, 03.616.6340**

## Table of Contents:

1. The Material Body & the Immaterial Soul
2. The Glassblower
3. The Three Expressions of the Soul
4. The Five Expressions of the Soul
5. The Expressions of the Soul in This World
6. The Lower Soul
7. The Immortality of the Soul
8. *Gilgul HaNeshomos* – Reincarnation

# The Soul

## The Material Body & the Immaterial Soul

*God formed man out of the dust of the ground and breathed into his nostrils a breath of life. Man then became a living being.*[1]

This famous verse describes man as a being created of two natures: the physical (the dust of the ground) and the spiritual (the soul – the breath of life). A subtle nuance of this verse is that man was animated with God's breath – an exhalation from the innermost being of God. This is in contrast to the rest of creation, which was created by G-d's speech – with sound waves created by God – which is a lower level of divine intimacy, one that is distanced from God's essence.[2]

**Of course,**

> God does not actually have breath. This is a merely a descriptive metaphor enabling us to discuss the concepts involved. It is an extremely apt one, however, and is elaborated upon greatly by our Sages.

## The Glassblower[3]

The parable used by many sages to describe the nature of the soul is that of a glassblower creating a vessel. The glassblower dips one end of his tube into molten glass and places the other end against his lips. The breath originates at the lips, flows down the tube, and comes to rest in the molten glass below, forming it and shaping it into its final form as the glass blower rotates and turns the whole apparatus. Now, where is the soul in this analogy? Is it upon the lips of the glass blower, in the tube, or in the burgeoning glass bulb at the end? The answer is all three.

---

[1] Genesis 2:7

[2] See *Likutey Amazim, Sefer Shel Beinonim II; Nefesh HaChaim* 11:15.

[3] See the *Derech HaShem* of Rabbi Moshe Chaim Luzzatto (1707 – 1746).

## The Three Expressions of the Soul[4]

The soul is constantly being "blown" into the being by God. As such, the soul exists in a constant dynamic relationship with its creator. This ongoing emanation of the soul means that the soul constantly exists in three expressions. Many writers have described these three expressions as levels, or components of the soul. However, such descriptions are misleading. I prefer to call it three "expressions" of the soul:

1) **Neshamah**, meaning "soul," and derived from the word *Neshima*, meaning "breath." In our parable, this is the exit of the breath from the lips of the divine glassblower. This is the essence of the soul and its highest and most intimate connection to God.

2) **Ruach**, meaning "spirit," and derived from the word for wind. This is the moving, blowing of the soul into the world, representing the raging conduit and connection between man's soul and God.

3) **Nefesh**, often translated as "soul," yet better translated as "life-force," is from the word *Nafash*, meaning "to rest." It alludes to the divine breath coming to rest in the vessel of the body of man.

These three expressions exist simultaneously and in constant interaction with each other. While the *Neshama* is the closest to God and the place at which the soul's truest essence resides, it is bound to the *Nefesh*, the component that enlivens the body and interacts with the rest of creation, via *Ruach*, the conduit of divine breath.

These soul-elements form a chain binding man's soul to G-d:

*The* Nefesh *is bound to the* Ruach, *the* Ruach *is bound to the* Neshama, *and the* Neshama *to the Holy One, Blessed is He.*[5]

## The Five Expressions of the Soul

The Midrash,[6] however, adds two more levels to the soul:

---

[4] Based upon the *Nefesh HaChaim* of Rabbi Chaim Vital.

[5] Zohar 3:25a.

1) *Chayah*, "living essence," and,

2) *Yechidah*, "unique essence."

Our scholars understand these as two higher, almost completely imperceptible levels of the soul. They are, like God Himself, both immanent and transcendent in relationship to the lower levels of the soul.

If the *Neshama* is the breath of God, the glassblower, then *Chayah* is the body of the glassblower, the vehicle which gives motion to and exhales the divine breath. Note, though, that the breath exhaled by the glassblower is not intrinsic to His being.

Therefore,

> The lower levels of the soul originate from His "body," so to speak, yet are not "of" his body; they are a separate, created entity independent of, yet intimately originating from, the creator.

*Yechidah*, however, is something totally transcendent. It represents the true, inexpressible aspect of the creator. It is the innermost part of the creator which desires to create and knows its own purposes. In our parable, *Yechidah* is the soul of the glassblower, the innermost essence of God.

Man can only access the three lower levels of the soul: *Neshama*, *Ruach*, and *Nefesh*. The upper two levels belong to God Himself.

## The Expressions of the Soul in This World

Each expression of the soul exerts its own influence over particular areas of human activity.

*Nefesh*, the lowest level, governs man's physical interaction with the world. It transfers will into the animation of the body. It also binds the rest of the soul to the physical matter of the body.

*Ruach*, the motion of the divine spirit, is the source of the power of speech. It is responsible for the articulation and organization of inspiration into thought. This power, combined with *Ruach's* duty as the conduit between the lower and higher

---

[6] See Midrash Koheles Rabbah to Koheles 3:21 and Bereshis Rabbah 14:9.

expressions of the soul, also makes it the conduit for divine inspiration. Divine inspiration, in Hebrew, is called *Ruach ha-kodesh*, or holy *Ruach*. Ruach is also the realm of the emotions.

*Neshama* influences the higher realm of human faculties such as thought, intellect, and the spiritual sensibilities.

## The Lower Soul

We tend to think of the soul as a purely spiritual entity, which it is. However, what about animals? Do they have souls? The answer is "yes." However, their souls are not spiritual. Instead, they are the most ethereal of physical entities.[7]

What is more, all living beings possess this *nefes ha-behamis* – this "animal soul." This includes man as well.[8] This animal soul is the most basic force needed to maintain life. It is the animating force that governs the "natural laws" of physiology and most basic needs for survival.

This soul is what the Torah refers to when it states:

*The soul of the flesh that is in the blood.*[9]

This animal soul is essential for guaranteeing the survival of the organism. Without it, the spiritual soul would never eat, engage in reproduction, or do anything other than pray and pursue connection to God. This physical soul is what is also known as the *yetzer hora*, the evil desire discussed in earlier lessons.[10]

---

[7] See *Derech HaShem* on the soul.

[8] Eitz Chaim 49:3; Derech HaShem III: 1:1; Zohar II: 94b; Ramban to Genesis 1:20, Leviticus 17:14, and many, many more sources.

[9] Leviticus 17:11; Targum ad loc.

[10] Brachos 5a, 54a, 60b, 61b; Sanhedrin 91b; Derech HaShem I: 3:1 and II: 2:2.

## The Immortality of the Soul

All souls that will ever exist were created at the beginning of time. Since then they have been kept in a celestial repository until God deems them to be born.[11] Upon death, the soul ascends to a new place, the *olam ha-neshamos*, where it resides until the coming of the messiah. However, it doesn't always work out this way.

## Gilgul HaNeshomos – Reincarnation[12]

Reincarnation, though subject to some debate in the past[13], is an accepted part of Torah belief.[14] However, reincarnation is a loaded term with lots of non-Torah connotations. We must, therefore, be cautious not to assume anything about the Torah's doctrine lest we color our understanding with the convoluted perversions of pop-culture.

In the Torah's view, reincarnation is neither an automatic nor a common event. It is also neither a punishment nor a reward. Instead, reincarnation is an act of divine compassion. God gives many *neshamos*, souls, a "second chance" to fulfill mitzvos that they may have missed in a previous life. This is sometimes needed to allow particular souls to accomplish unique *tikkunim*, repairs to the world, for which those souls are uniquely suited.

---

[11] Niddah 13b; Chagigah 12b; Eitz Chaim 26:2. There is some disagreement between the Kabbalists and rational philosophers over this detail. See Emunos VeDeos 6:3.

[12] This entire section is a summary of *Shaar Gilgul HaNeshamos* from the *Kisvei HaAri*.

[13] Even though the concept predated them, reincarnation was rejected strongly by Rav Saadia Gaon, R' Yosef Albo, and Raavad I (not to be confused with Raavad II, the Rambam's famous disputant). However, Rav Hai Gaon argued with Rav Saadia in defense of reincarnation. In the medieval era, it was upheld by the Ramban and Rabbeinu Bachya ben Asher. Throughout the renaissance it gained further scholarly attention and support.

[14] The Ari and Ramak's systematization of kabbalah provided a full theological defense and context for reincarnation. Their study let to its acceptance by both the Baal Shem Tov and the Vilna Gaon.

However, *neshamos*, souls, are not always reincarnated in whole or in the same form held in their previous life. Sometimes only some of the components of the soul (*Nefesh*, *Ruach*, or *Neshamah*) are reincarnated, carved away from their fellows. The reincarnated souls, or parts of souls, may also not come back in human form.

Reincarnation is not common, and full reincarnation in human form is exceptionally rare. However, it does happen. Noahides are subject to the doctrine of *Gilgul ha-neshamos*, reincarnation as are Jews.

## Summary of This Lesson

1. Man was created with a physical being and a spiritual soul. The imbuing of the spiritual soul was a more intimate act of creation than the creation of the physical body. The body was created by speech, the soul by breath.

2. The soul is a single entity which emanates into the world, radiating as three distinct expressions. These expressions are a chain which binds the soul in this world to its origin.

3. Each expression influences particular human qualities.

4. There are higher expressions of the soul, but these are rooted in the being of God Himself and essentially unknowable to us.

5. Man, as all living creatures also has a natural, animal soul, which animates the basic, rote physiological processes and desires needed for survival. This soul is the root of the *yetzer hora*, the evil desire.

6. The soul is immortal. All souls were created at the beginning of creation and set aside by God until their time to be born. When a person dies, their soul is transferred to another repository to await the World to Come.

7. Some souls or portions of souls are reincarnated as an act of divine compassion. They are not always reincarnated in human form, however.

THE YESHIVA PIRCHEI SHOSHANIM SHULCHAN ARUCH PROJECT
# The Noahide Laws - Afterlife

© Yeshiva Pirchei Shoshanim 2017
This shiur may not be reproduced in any form without permission of the copyright holder.

**164 Village Path, Lakewood NJ 08701 732.370.3344**
**164 Rabbi Akiva, Bnei Brak, 03.616.6340**

**THE YESHIVA PIRCHEI SHOSHANIM SHULCHAN ARUCH PROJECT**
**THE NOAHIDE LAWS | BELIEF | THE AFTERLIFE | LESSON D**

## Table of Contents:

1. Introduction
2. Keeping Perspective
3. "Heaven" and "Hell"
4. *Gan Eden*
    a. The Lower Garden
    b. The Upper Garden
5. *Shoel / Chibbut HaKever*
6. *Gehinnom*
7. *Olam HaBa*

# The Afterlife, Messiah, and Redemption

## Introduction

As we learned a few lessons ago, both Judaism and Noahism believe in the immortality of the soul. Naturally, this entails belief in an afterlife. Yet, there is a very sharp distinction between the western, Christianized view of the afterlife and the Torah's view.

## Keeping Perspective

Compared to other belief systems, Judaism and Noahism focus very little on the afterlife. The afterlife is a particular pre-occupation of Christianity and Islam and an obsession that establishes the afterlife as the ultimate goal of all worldly activity. However, Torah references to the afterlife are almost non-existent. In fact, discussion of the afterlife is almost taboo and distasteful in many circles.

Many authors note this ongoing de-emphasis of the afterlife in Torah thought, connecting it to the exodus from Egypt. Egypt was a society obsessed with the afterworld to the point of corruption. Their afterlife was more real, immediate, and relevant than anything of this world.

Part of God's plan in taking the Jews out of Egypt was to cleanse them of this undue focus and set their priorities straight. God wants us to fulfill His will in <u>this</u> world – that is the purpose of creation. Therefore, the Torah is conspicuously devoid of any mention of the afterlife. The little we know about the afterlife and the World-to-Come is from scant references in the prophets, writings, and Oral Torah.

What is more, the rabbinic world has followed this trend, placing all of its emphasis on defining the fulfillment of God's will in this world. The study of the afterlife has remained a "fuzzy" topic for scholars.

While we know the general principles and order of things, the specific details are unclear. We must recall that no one has ever seen the afterlife. What we know about it we believe to be true with absolute faith. However, we must also have the humility to admit that which we do not know.

Taking this fact into account, scholars have realized that attempting to pin down a precise vision of the afterlife is not only impossible, but ultimately not a good a use of their time.

## "Heaven" and "Hell?"

Judaism and Noahism do not believe in heaven and hell. The idea of eternal damnation and suffering without relief just doesn't work. Consider that we believe God punishes commensurate with deeds. Eternal punishment isn't commensurate with anyone's deeds because no one, now, never, or ever, is infinitely evil or has committed an infinite number of evil deeds.

Another problem with hell is that God's purpose for creating the world was the bestowal of good. Let's imagine that a theoretically infinitely-evil person exists and does get sent to hell for all eternity. Now, if God's purpose is good, yet this person will receive none if it ever again, then why does this evil person continue to exist at all? Is it that God is sadistic and wants to make our evil person suffer forever? It is possible to argue that eternal suffering exists as a deterrent from transgression. However, this is not a compelling argument; there are better ways to discourage sin.

The concept of Heaven is equally perplexing. A place where everyone gets the same reward regardless of their deeds?

Also, where do heaven and hell leave the early realm? In this paradigm of the afterlife, this world is has little purpose; the emphasis is entirely on the future life.

Christianity, well aware of these problems, has wrestled with them for centuries. Rather than coming to compelling consensus, their doctrine has become highly fragmented. This fracturing of belief is the source of many doctrinal disputes and widely differing eschatologies.

Judaism and Noahism, on the other hand don't suffer from this doctrinal schizophrenia because we have a very different vision of the afterlife.

## Gan Eden

*The following description of the afterlife and future worlds are summarized from* Gesher HaChayim, The Bridge of Life, *by Rabbi Yechiel Michel Tukachinsky,* Derech HaShem, The Way of God, *by Rabbi Moshe Chaim Luzzatto, and* An Essay on Fundamentals, *also by Rabbi*

*Luzzatto. This presentation is a general overview of the beliefs, yet is nothing here is an iron-clad fundamental-of-the-faith.*

God prepared a number of places for the soul. In this physical world at this time, the place of the soul is the body. However, when the body is no longer available, God prepared another repository: *Gan Eden*, the Garden of Eden. The Garden has an upper garden and a lower garden.

**The Lower Garden**  While both gardens are entirely spiritual, the lower one is a "shadow," a spiritual simulacrum of the physical world. In this lower realm the souls maintain an image of their physical form. Similarly, the delights of this lower realm are limited, experienced much as greatest pleasures of the physical world.

**The Upper Garden**  The upper garden, however, is a place where souls exist in their abstract, truest essence; they do not maintain the "shadow" of their physical form. Likewise, the delights of this upper garden are abstract and uniquely spiritual, devoid of corollary in the physical world.

The Gardens are not static. They experiences "seasons" and a spiritual "time" all of its own. Its delights, the fruits of the garden, change regularly with the seasons.

## Shoel / Chibbut HaKever

However, the ability to enter these spiritual gardens necessitates the soul's detachment from the physical realm. The committing of transgressions has the effect of binding and entangling the soul with the physical world. In order for the soul to ascend, it must be carefully dis-entangled from *olam ha-zeh*, material existence.

Recall from our previous lesson on reward and punishment that punishment is not a "punishment for" as much as a "natural consequence of" sin.

We can now understand what this means. The "punishment" of sin is the disentanglement of the soul from the body. By nature, this is an unpleasant process, like disentangling a cotton ball from a thorn bush. The greater the transgressions, the more entangled the soul the longer and more unpleasant the experience.

**Burial and Decomposition**  This process begins with burial and the process of decomposition. Upon placement of the body in the grave (*shoel*), the "physical trap" of the soul returns to its source, losing its form and illusory autonomy. For approximately 12 months the soul hovers above the grave "grieving" and "mourning" for the loss of the body. This is the implication of the verses:

> *His soul mourns for him,*[1]
>
> and,
>
> *His flesh grieves for him.*[2]

This process, called *chibbut ha-kever*, the atonement/purification of the grave, is of tremendous anguish to the soul.

## Gehinnom

Once the soul has completed this *chibbut kever*, purification of the grave, it is then judged. At this point, the soul stands before the ultimate truth and must confront all of its deeds. This part of the afterlife is known as *Gehinnom*.

Since this is a purely spiritual process, it cannot be adequately described in words. Nevertheless, the Talmud, Midrash, and other sources attempt to convey the experience of the soul using graphic, often terrifying parables. For example, the description of *Gehenom* as a place of fire refers to the shame the soul experience as it stands before the ultimate truth.

The process of *Gehenom* is by not a permanent one; it lasts, at most, for only 12 months. After this point, the soul may ascend to the gardens.

## Olam HaBa

*Gan Eden*, the Garden, *Gehinnom* – all of these places are temporary. The permanent place of man's reward is the World to Come, *Olam HaBa*. This future era, ushered in by the coming of the Messiah and resurrection of the dead (topics of future lessons), is one of the most mysterious and least-understood of God's creations.

Although the World to Come is a creation of G-d, no two souls experience it the same way. Rabbi Chaim of Volozhin, in his *Nefesh HaChayim* describes the unique experience of the world to come as follows:

---

[1] Job 14:22. See Shabbos 152a.

[2] Ibid.

*A person's own deeds constitute his reward in the World to Come. Once the soul has departed the body, it arises to take pleasure and satisfaction in the power and light of the holy worlds that have been created and multiplied by his good deeds. This is what the Sages meant when they said: "All of Israel have a portion <u>to</u> the World to Come," and not <u>in</u> the World-to-Come. <u>In</u> implies that the World to Come is prepared and awaiting a person from the time of Creation, as if it was something existing on its own and of which man may receive as a reward. In truth, the World to Come is built of the expansion and multiplication of ones deeds into a place for himself... so too with the punishment of Gehenom, the sin itself is his punishment.*

The structure and space of the world to come is directly related to the mitzvos of an individual. Within that space, the eternal reward of his *mitzvos* is received. The amount of reward, however, is directly tied to the merit one accumulated in this world.

There is a lack of clarity and agreement as to whether the World to Come is physical or entirely spiritual. There is also confusion as to the various roles within that world, the nature of *mitzvos*, and the purpose of worship, holidays, and the third temple.

In truth, though, these details are not entirely for us to know, but to find out eventually.

For those wanting to read more, see the *Bridge of Life* by Rabbi Yechiel Michel Tukachinsky (published by Moznaim) and the *Way of God* by Rabbi Moshe Chaim Luzzatto (published by Feldheim).

## Summary of the Lesson

1. Upon death and burial, the process of decay begins. This atonement for the physical flesh via the grave is called *shoel*, literally, the grave.

2. As the soul decomposes, the soul undergoes a process of disentanglement from the body. This is known as *chibbut ha-kever*, the atonement/purification of the grave.

3. Following *chibbut ha-kever*, the soul then undergoes the first of a series of judgments. This is called *Gehenom*.

4. *Gehinnom* is the laying bare of one's sins in the light of complete truth. The many metaphors for *Gehinnom* found in the sources speak primarily to the emotional experience of *Gehinnom*.

5. The entire process of *Shoel*, *chibbut ha-kever*, and *Gehinnom*, takes 12 months at most.

6. Once the soul has been judged and is freed from its attachments to the physical, it ascends to *Gan Eden*, the Garden of Eden.

7. The Garden contains upper and lower gardens for different souls of different natures.

8. The Gardens experience seasons, fruits, and all the other varieties to be expected in a physical garden. Of course, these are all allegories for a non-physical place.

9. The soul awaits in the Gardens until the coming of the messiah. At this time the souls are reborn, experiencing resurrection.

10. The resurrection and rebirth is into a new world called *Olam Haba* – the world to Come.

11. The World to Come is a not well understood; it is also experienced differently by each soul commensurate with the *mitzvos* of that soul during its first lifetime.

THE YESHIVA PIRCHEI SHOSHANIM SHULCHAN ARUCH PROJECT

# The Noahide Laws – The Supernatural

© Yeshiva Pirchei Shoshanim 2017
This shiur may not be reproduced in any form without permission of the copyright holder.

## Table of Contents:

1. Introduction
2. Supernatural vs. Natural
3. Ghosts
4. Apparitions
5. Angels
6. *Dybbuk & Gilgul*
7. Exorcism
8. The *Shedim*
9. Summary

# The Supernatural

## Introduction

HaShem's creation is amazing and diverse, including far more than our physical senses allow us to perceive. The parts of creation lying beyond the senses are usually, and often erroneously, called "supernatural." However, these "supernatural" elements are actually far more natural than they may seem. They are part of the world and, in a sense, almost commonplace. Once we accept the paranormal as normal, the question of natural vs. unnatural becomes one of what constitutes natural vs. unnatural relationships to these entities. Most of the material cited here is summarized from the *Sefer HaBris*, *Derech HaShem*, and the writings of the Ari Zt"l. Know that this is a big topic – we will only give the scantest overview here.

## Supernatural vs. Natural

It is a common mistake to assume that the sages made no distinction between natural and supernatural causation. For example, while many ancient peoples attributed disease to demons and spirits, the sages had a far more advanced understanding. There Talmud provides us with many examples:

- Kesubos 110b – The Talmud acknowledges that moving and other stressful life-changes might cause digestive problems.

- Taanis 21b – Rabbi Yehudah decreed a fast due to an epidemic among pigs. The Talmud asked: "Does Rabbi Yehudah hold that an epidemic of one species will spread to another?" The answer is surprising: "No, but the biology of pigs and humans is similar enough that they are likely to suffer from the same diseases."

- Bava Metzia 107b – Chills and colds are the result of wind; one did not bundle up sufficiently against the cold.

- And many, many, more…[1]

The Talmudic understanding is that there are unseen, yet natural causes for disease and other phenomena while, concurrently, there are also metaphysical and spiritual causes. It is very important to realize that, unlike many ancient peoples, the Sages did not simply attribute supernatural agency to events for which they lacked scientific or natural explanations.[2]

## Ghosts

The soul's existence is entirely independent of the physical. However, the soul's ability to affect and benefit from this world is dependent on its remaining bound to the body. When the body ceases its biological function, the soul's existence continues, unhindered, upon its own plane. At that point, it has four options: it can either ascend to the gardens (as discussed previously), become reincarnated, seek refuge in another body (possession), or continue disembodied. The disembodied existence of an unclothed soul is only possible for a brief period of time. During this period the disembodied soul is not visible, yet can be sensed by the higher faculties of another soul.[3] Animals in particular are sensitive to such things and often sense them with greater ease than people.[4]

## Apparitions

Apparitions are the auditory and/or visible manifestation of a soul that is no longer carried by a body. The most famous example of an apparition is from I

---

[1] Kesuvos 20a, 77a; Brachos 25a; Bava Kamma 60b; Sanhedrin 9a. There are many more sources.

[2] This isn't to imply that the sages always understood the scientific causation of things. After all, there are many examples of apparent scientific error in the Talmud. The most famous are Shabbos 107b, Pesachim 94b, and Chullin 127a. The Rambam famously wrote (*Moreh Nevuchim* 3:14) that the Sages relied upon the best science of their time, which was not always correct. There is significant dispute and debate as to how to understand these apparent errors and to what degree they impact religious practice. The important point is that the sages understood that there were phenomena whose exact causes, though invisible, were not by default supernatural. By the same token, they also understood there to be events of apparently natural mechanism whose roots were entirely supernatural. The result is a complicated world-view of subtle interplay between the physical causes of the spiritual and vice-versa.

[3] Megillah 3a – "Though he does not see, his *mazal* sees…"

[4] See Bava Kamma 60b and Maharal *Beer HaGolah* V, p. 98.

Samuel 28, in which King Saul used a necromancer to summon the soul of the prophet Samuel. A close reading of this event reveals that, while the necromancer was able to see the prophet, only Saul was able to converse with it. Similarly, Saul was able to communicate with Samuel, but could not see him. Ralbag[5] explains that only the necromancer was able to see Samuel because her imagination was focused on the visual appearance of Samuel. Saul, however, needed information from Samuel and, therefore, focused his mind on the conversation alone. This implies that the apparitions of the voice and appearance of the prophet did not exist physically. Instead, they were only projected into the minds of those attuned to perceiving them.

This is true of all apparitions, be they of spirits or angels. Daniel 10 buttresses this understanding:

*I lifted up my eyes and looked and beheld a man clothed in linen… And I Daniel alone saw the vision, for the men that were with me saw it not; nevertheless, a great trembling took hold of them, and they fled…*

Daniel alone perceived a form for the entity, while the others only sensed its presence. In truth, the entity had no form for it was an entirely spiritual presence.

Maimonides, in his *Hilchos Yesodei HaTorah*, writes:

*One can never see matter without form or form without matter… The forms that are devoid of matter cannot be perceived with the physical eye, but only with the mind's eye.*[6]

In every recorded instance of an apparition it required the presence of an observer.

It should be noted, that the conjuring of an apparition from the souls of the dead is a sever prohibition.

## Angels

God cannot breach the veil between his essence and *Chalal* – the void in which all creation came to be. Were God's essence to intrude into this arena, all creation would immediately cease to be. The reason is that in the presence of God's

---

[5] Rabbi Levi ben Gershom (1288 – 1344). One of the great medieval bible commentators, a noted physician, and astronomer.

[6] 4:7.

absolute oneness, no other existence is possible. Therefore, to act directly upon this world, God needs an agent, a tool. These are the *Melakhim*, angels. They are mechanistic beings which exist to execute specific aspects of God's will upon the created world. The name of an angel alludes to its purpose:

- *Raphael* – From the words *rofe*, healer of, *Eyl*, God. This angel is the Healer of God, the one who brings healing to those who need it.

- *Gavriel* – From *gibor*, the mighty one, *ayl*, of God. This angel, the Mighty One of God, carries out acts of power and destruction.

- *Uriel* – From *Ohr*, light of, *Eyl*, God. The Light of God is the angel who illuminated, interprets, and explains.

- *Someil* – This angel, <u>whose name we never say</u>, is the Poison of God. His duty is to prosecute the wicked and execute God's punishment. He is sometimes called the *Soton* – the adversary.

Angels have no will independent of God's will. As purely spiritual beings, they have no physical appearance or shape. Instead, they exist as abstract forms. What then, are we to make of the many descriptions of angels found in the Tanakh?

Writes Maimonides:

> …*For the angels have no physical bodies, only abstract forms. What then is meant when the prophets report having seen a being of fire or with wings? These descriptions are part of the prophetic vision and should be understood allegorically.*[7]

We see that the vision and appearance of the angel, as experienced in the mind of the prophet, is part of the prophetic experience and part of the prophetic message.

## Dybbuk & Gilgul

When a disembodied soul can no longer endure the limbo of being out-of-body, it may seek refuge in a living body currently inhabited by a soul. This is called a *Dybbuk*, a clinging spirit. There are many types of *Dybbuk im*, the most common of which is a *Dybbuk ibur*. This spirit clings to another body silently and has no influence or effect on the host. It merely rides along until the host achieves a certain condition spiritually that is of benefit to the *dybbuk*. Keep in mind,

---

[7] *Hilchos Yesodei HaTorah* 2:3-4.

however, that the soul has a number of parts. Either the entire soul may become a *dybbuk*, or only certain parts of the soul.

Similarly, a soul may be either entirely or partially reincarnated, in which case it is a *Gilgul*. The main difference between a *Gilgul* and a *dybbuk* is that a *Gilgul* has returned to the higher realms and been sent back, while a *dybbuk* has never ascended. Additionally, a *Gilgul* is usually one soul in one body, while a *dybbuk* is multiple souls or parts of souls in one body.

## Exorcism

In incredibly rare cases, a *dybbuk* might assert influence upon its host. In these rare instances, the *dybbuk* has been given permission from on high in order that it may be exorcised. It must be understood that a *dybbuk* is neither evil nor demonic. Rather, the process of possession and exorcism is a rare opportunity for the atonement of both the *dybbuk* and the person within whom it resides. The process of exorcism is one of assisting the soul in making *tikkunim*, repairs, and helping it to repent in whatever way possible absent a body. Once this process is completed, the soul is then capable of ascending.

However, this process is only possible with the assistance of another soul, an exalted soul that can invoke the will of *Shamayim*. This would be the soul of a *tsaddik* or scholar who is capable of assisting the *dybbuk*. Without the proximity of such an individual, an exorcism is not possible. Since an exorcism is not possible, there is no point to the possession. Therefore, it won't happen.

There are very specific criteria for determining legitimate cases of possession. These are incredibly exact requirements and preclude any known physiological, psychiatric, or medical cause for the condition.

Since there are no people capable of exorcising a soul nowadays, legitimate cases of possession do not occur. The last verified case was in Lithuania in the 1930's and involved the Chofetz Chaim, Rabbi Yisrael Meir Poupko (Kagan).

## Shedim

Any time that you come across the word "demon" in translations of the Talmud or Midrash, it is almost always a translation of the Hebrew term *Sheid*. Like many translations of Hebrew words, though, it is polluted by Christological connotations.

*Shedim* are odd creatures, having both qualities of men and angels. Although they must eat and drink, they are only loosely bound by the constraints of time and space. Unlike angels, they can manifest physical form, yet only subject to certain conditions.

Additionally, they are bound by their own concept of Torah law, for which they may be held liable and judged in *Bais Din*, Rabbinic Courts. They also live subject to their own strict social order and are subjects of their own king.

In the past, man had frequent interactions with the *Shedim*. Their relationship to man was complicated and involved a lot of confusion and headache. A major problem is that non-Jewish nations constantly took to worshiping the *Shedim* as deities. The Talmud records that the sages made a number of laws limiting their relationship with man. This legislation culminated with the banishment of *Shedim* from all inhabited areas. Nevertheless, certain *halachos*, religious laws, exist that pertain to them. For example:

- One should not enter a house or other property that has been abandoned for 7 years.

- When remodeling a house, one should not completely seal up any of the doors or windows.

- When building an extension onto a home, one has to verify if it involves extending the property over land onto which a drainpipe or gutter opens. If so, then about a foot of dirt on either side, in front of, and beneath the drainpipe opening must be dug and transported to an uninhabited area.

There are a number of other *halachos* related to *Shedim*. However, most of them are not observed anymore due to the rarity of *Shedim*. A noted Kabbalist once told this author that their interaction with people is so rare that it is as if they do not even exist anymore.

*Shedim* are not singled out as evil or unusual in anyway. They are as much an ordinary part of creation as cows, the sun, spiders, or cats. Like any other animal or person, however, one should not seek to provoke them. The Talmud tells us that if you don't care about them, then they won't care about you.

## Summary of This Lesson

1. The sages were not superstitious. They did not assign supernatural causes to phenomena simply because they did not understand its physical causes.

2. A ghost, for lack of a better term, is a disembodied soul. It can be sensed, but has no physical form.

3. Souls and angels have no physical form or existence at all.

4. An apparition is the perception of a disembodied soul by the mind's eye. To intentionally conjure such an apparition is a severe prohibition.

5. Angels are messengers of God that exist to carry out very specific missions. Their names indicate their mission and purpose.

6. Angels have no will independent of God's will. In this sense, they are solely a tool or mechanism used by God.

7. All or part of a soul that has become disembodied and attached to another living person is a *dybbuk*.

8. All or part of soul that has ascended and returned again is a *Gilgul*.

9. Rarely, a *dybbuk* may be allowed to assert itself for the purpose of being exorcised. This is for the benefit of the *dybbuk* and the possessed individual.

10. This only occurs when there is one in proximity who is capable of exorcising the *dybbuk*. The last confirmed case of a full *dybbuk* was over 80 years ago. Since that time there has not been anyone capable of exorcising one.

THE YESHIVA PIRCHEI SHOSHANIM SHULCHAN ARUCH PROJECT

# The Noahide Laws – Moshiach Part I

© Yeshiva Pirchei Shoshanim 2017
This shiur may not be reproduced in any form without permission of the copyright holder.

**164 Village Path, Lakewood NJ 08701 732.370.3344**
**164 Rabbi Akiva, Bnei Brak, 03.616.6340**

## Table of Contents:

1. Introduction

2. The Pre-Messianic Era

    a. Changes in Religion and Belief

    b. Rise of Atheism

    c. Social & National Upheaval & Decline

    d. Increase in Secular Knowledge

3. Ingathering of Exiles

    a. Restoration of Prophecy

    b. Cultivation of the Land

4. The War of Gog and Magog

5. The Two Messiahs

6. Eliyahu HaNavi – Elijah the Prophet

7. Summary

# The Messiah I

## Introduction

The pre-Messianic era, Messianic era, and identity of the Messiah himself are complicated and often misunderstood topics that involve a number of people and a process of unfolding events. While the grand details are known with certainty, specific elements must remain speculation until the actual time comes. In this lesson we will review the facts and questions regarding the coming of the Messiah.

## The Pre-Messianic Era

Numerous scriptural prophecies, Midrashim, and other sources tell us that, as the time of the Messiah draws near, the world will experience changes and upheavals. Many of these will be positive, while others will be devastating.

**Changes in Religion and Belief**

> *Truth will* ne'ederes *[fail]*...
> Isaiah 59:15

The Talmud[1] explains that the word *ne'ederes* is also related to the word for "flocks." The implication of the verse is that truth will fail because the Torah world will be divided into various groups, or flocks, each of which will claim the truth for its own. True Torah and faith will become indistinguishable from that which is false.

**Rise of Atheism**

Atheism will engulf the world and religious studies will become despised in the era preceding the Messiah.[2] The Jewish world will not be spared from this calamity – many Jews will abandon the Torah and their faith as well. However, the wise will recognize that this torrent of disbelief is a test and that they must remain firm in their faith. This is the interpretation[3] of the verse:

---

[1] Sanhedrin 97a.

[2] *Sichos HaRan* 35.

[3] See Rambam *Iggres Teiman* and *Sichos HaRan* 35, 220.

> *Many shall purify themselves – make themselves white and be refined; but the wicked shall do wickedly; and none of the wicked shall understand; but they that are wise shall understand.*
> Daniel 12:15

There are many who are far from Torah and truth, however, who will see what is happening and realize its import. They will return to God, yet they will suffer ridicule for abandoning the norms of secular culture. This is the meaning of the verse:

> *He who departs from evil will be considered a fool.*
> Isaiah 59:15.

**Social & National Upheaval & Decline**

This decline in religious unity will be, partially, the result of a general global decline in values, morals, and important social institutions.[4] Because change will advance so rapidly, parents and children will experience the world on radically different terms.[5] As a result, there will be no respect of the elderly or for one's parents. Governments will become godless and economies will fail.[6]

This will all be accompanied by a sudden increase in world population.[7]

This will be a time of tremendous strain. The Midrash states:

> *One-third of the world's suffering will come in the generation before the Messiah.*[8]

**Increase in Secular Knowledge**

According to some recent authorities,[9] there will be an explosion of secular and scientific knowledge before the coming of the Messiah. This is understood from a passage in the Zohar:

> *In the 600th year of the 6th millennium, the supernal gates of wisdom and the lower wellsprings of wisdom will open. This will prepare the world to enter the 7th millennium just as man prepares for Sabbath before sunset.*[10]

---

[4] Sotah 49b; Sanhedrin ibid. See also *Shir HaShirim Rabbah* 2:13. Also Zohar 3:67b.

[5] See Kaplan, *Handbook of Jewish Thought* II 24:12.

[6] Sanhedrin 97a – "The son of David will not come until the last penny has gone out from the purse."

[7] *Tosafos* to Niddah 13b s.v. ad *she-yikhlu*.

[8] *Midrash Tehillim* 22:9.

[9] Most notably Rabbi Aryeh Kaplan in a number of his books and essays.

This prophecy establishes the Hebrew year 5600 (1839/1840) as the start of a new era in Human knowledge. Though we cannot tie this Zohar to any specific even in that year, it does correspond to the onset of the scientific revolution and modern technological era.

## Ingathering of Exiles

*He will gather the dispersed of Israel*
Psalms 147:2

*God will then bring back your remnants and have mercy on you. God your Lord will once again gather you from among all the nations where He scattered you.*
Deuteronomy 30:3

Either after or concurrent with the pre-messianic upheavals there will be a return of the Jewish people to their ancestral land. The unfolding of this process, whether gradual or sudden, miraculous or natural, is uncertain.[11] However it occurs, it will only be completed by the Messiah himself:

*On that day, God will stretch forth his hand a second time to recover His people... He will send up a banner for the nations, assemble the dispersed of Israel, and gather together the scattered of Judah from the four corners of the earth.*
Isaiah 11:11-12

**Restoration of Prophecy**  Besides the prophetic indications of a national return, it is also a necessary component of the redemptive process. It appears that the coming of the Messiah is concomitant with a return of prophecy.[12]

---

[10] Zohar I:117a

[11] It is not 100% clear if the current resettlement of Israel constitutes this pre-Messianic ingathering. On one hand, Kesubos 111a discourages the en-masse return to Israel prior to the coming of the Messiah (according to many). However, there are opinions that the return will began with some sort of political independence (see Rabbi Chama in Sanhedrin 98a) and possibly involve the consent and assistance of other nations (Ramban on Song of Songs 8:13, Radak to Psalms 146:3, Abarbanel to Psalms 147:2, and many, many more). Nevertheless, we should pray that the current Jewish resettlement of Israel is this much anticipated messianic prequel.

[12] See Joel 3:1 to 5 and Rambam *Igros Teiman*. Additionally, the Messiah will be king. Kings can only be anointed by a prophet. As well, the Messiah himself will be a prophet (see *Hilchos Teshuva* 9:2)

However, this can only happen when a number of other conditions are fulfilled, one of which is that the majority of the Jewish population must reside in the land of Israel. Therefore, there must be a resettlement prior to the advent of the Messiah.

**Cultivation of the Land**

*O mountains of Israel, let your branches sprout forth and yield your fruit to My people Israel, for they are at hand to come.*
Ezekiel 36:8

*I will open rivers on the high hills and fountains in the midst of the valleys. I will make the wilderness a pool of water and the dry land springs of water. I will plant in the wilderness cedar, the acacia, myrtle, and the oil-tree. I will set in the desert cypress, the plane-tree, and the larch together so that they may see, and know, and consider, and understand together, that the hand of HaShem has done this, and the Holy One of Israel has created it.*
Isaiah 41: 18 - 20[13]

These passages are only a sampling of those prophesying a renewed cultivation of the land of Israel prior to the redemption.[14]

## The War of Gog and Magog

One of the final steps in the messianic advent is the War of Gog and Magog. The Book of Ezekiel, chapters 38 and 39, prophecies a war in the era immediately preceding the Messiah. This war, according to the Zohar[15], will take place in the vicinity of Jerusalem. It will be the final showdown for the Land of Israel, a battle royale for the soul of the land. Upon its conclusion, the Jews will live free of harassment in their land.[16] According to Rabbi Akiva[17], the war will last one year.

---

[13] See interpretation of Rabbi Abba, Sanhedrin 98a.

[14] See also Isaiah 49:18 – 22, Jeremiah 33:10-11.

[15] 2:32a.

[16] *Sifrei* Bamidbar 76, Deuteronomy 43. See also Sanhedrin 97b.

[17] Eduyos 2:10.

Though the names of Gog and Magog appear early in Tanakh[18], the exact identities of these nations in modern terms is uncertain. According to the Talmud[19], the second Psalm is a reference to this eventual conflict

## The Two Messiahs

It is little known that there actually are two Messiahs: Moshiach ben David (Messiah, son of David) and Moshiach ben Yosef (Messiah, son of Joseph – sometimes called Moshiach ben Ephraim). This is alluded to in numerous places:

*And you, son of man, take one stick, and write upon it: For Judah, and for the children of Israel his companions; then take another stick, and write upon it: For Joseph, the stick of Ephraim, and of all the house of Israel his companions; and join them one to another into one stick, that they may become one in your hand.*
Ezekiel 37:16-17

*Ephraim's envy will depart and Judah's enemies will be cut off. Ephraim will not envy Judah and Judah will not envy nor harass Ephraim.*
Isaiah 11:13

Of particular importance is the latter verse teaching that each of the Messiahs will have their own missions uniquely suited to their strengths. They will not envy one another nor interfere with their respective jobs. Each Messiah will have his own era, as well, with the Era of Moshiach ben Yosef coming first.[20]

**Moshiach Ben Yosef**

All messianic tasks up to and including the War of Gog and Magog will be the duties of Moshiach ben Yosef. It is he who will wage the war and conquer:

*The house of Jacob shall be a fire, and the house of Joseph a flame, and the house of Esau stubble. They will set them ablaze and consume them; there will be no survivor of the house of Esau, for God has spoken.*
Obadiah 1:18

---

[18] I.e. Genesis 10:2.

[19] Avodah Zara 3b.

[20] There is some disagreement about the exact order of these two eras. *Tosafos* Eruvin 43b presents an argument that ben Yosef must precede ben David. However, Rashi *ad loc.* disagrees. Most scholars agree with Tosafos. There is a tremendous amount written on this subject..

It appears that this Messiah will die in battle, though, and be mourned by Israel:

*They shall look to Me because they have pushed him through, and they shall mourn for him as one mourns for a first born son.*
Zechariah 12:10

According to some scholars, however, the decree of death for Moshiach ben Yosef was rescinded. [21]

## Eliyahu HaNavi

Following the War of Gog and Magog[22], the prophet Elijah will herald the impending messianic age:

*Behold! I will send Elijah the Prophet before the coming of the great and awesome day of God! He will turn the hearts of the fathers to their children and of the children to their fathers…*
Malachi 3:23

As we see in the verse, he will turn people back to truth and rectify much of the world's pre-messianic decline. Immediately following his arrival, the final Messiah, ben David, will be revealed. [23]

In the second part of this lesson, we will examine the qualifications and duties of Moshiach ben David.

---

[21] See *Kol HaTor* 1:6 and 8. The Ari Z"l also says that the death of ben Yosef is not an absolute certainty.

[22] *Emunos VeDeyos* 8:2.. Some, however, maintain that Eliyahu will come before the war.

[23] Eruvin 43b and *Tos. Ad loc.* See also Rash on Eduyos 8:7, *Hilchos Nazirus* 4:11.

## Summary of This Lesson

1. There are a number of stages to the coming of the Messiah.

2. The first is a period of social, spiritual, and political decline.

3. According to contemporary understandings of the Zohar, there will be an explosion of secular wisdom concurrent with these travails.

4. There will be tremendous difficulty discerning truth from falsehood in these times. The wise will see and recognize the greater significance of these events.

5. Concurrent with or following this era will be a return of the Jews to their ancestral land. This return is an intrinsic part of the eventual return of prophecy.

6. The land will be cultivated and bloom again.

7. As the population increases and the former glory is Israel approaches its return, there will be a Great War: the War of Gog and Magog.

8. This war will be waged on behalf of God by Moshiach ben Yosef, one of the two Messiahs.

9. Either immediately before or after this war (after, according to most) Elijah the prophet will appear to announce and make final preparations for the final Messiah, Moshiach ben David.

THE YESHIVA PIRCHEI SHOSHANIM SHULCHAN ARUCH PROJECT

# The Noahide Laws – Moshiach Part II

© Yeshiva Pirchei Shoshanim 2017
This shiur may not be reproduced in any form without permission of the copyright holder.

**164 Village Path, Lakewood NJ 08701 732.370.3344**
**164 Rabbi Akiva, Bnei Brak, 03.616.6340**

## Table of Contents:

1. Introduction
2. Criteria for the Davidic Messiah
    a. When Will the Messiah Arrive?
3. A Descendant of David
    a. Jewish Ancestry
    b. From the Tribe of Judah
4. A King of Israel
5. Return of the Jewish People to Israel
6. Rebuilding of the Temple
    a. Reestablishment of the Sanhedrin
    b. The Temple Service
7. Establishing Peace and the End of All Wars
8. He Will Bring Awareness of God
    a. Free Will
    b. Conversion
9. The Messiah's End
10. Summary

# The Messiah II

## Introduction

In our previous lesson we examined the events of the pre-messianic era and the coming of *Moshiach ben Yosef* (Messiah son of Joseph). *Moshiach ben Yosef*, however, is only one of two messiahs. The second, final messiah is *Moshiach ben David*, the Davidic messiah. When most people speak of the messiah, they are referring to this final messianic figure. In this lesson we will examine the criteria for identifying the messiah, his duties, and the messianic age.

## Criteria for the Davidic Messiah

The Torah belief[1] is that the final Messiah, *Moshiach ben Dovid*, will be identified by six criteria:

1) He will be a direct descendant of King David,
2) He will be anointed as king of Israel,
3) He will complete the return of the Jewish people to Israel,
4) He will rebuild the temple in Jerusalem,
5) He will bring peace to the world, ending all war,
6) He will bring knowledge of God to the world.

These six criteria are not metaphorical – they are literal, observable, verifiable facts. They are the minimum that one must accomplish before he is accepted as the Messiah.

---

[1] Hilchos Melachim 11:1.

Writes the Rambam[2]:

> *If there arises a ruler from the family of David, immersed in the Torah and its mitzvos as was his ancestor David, who observes both the Oral and Written Torahs, who leads Israel back to the Torah, strengthening its observance and waging God's battles, then we may presume that he is the Messiah. If he then succeeds in rebuilding the temple upon its original site and gathering in the exiles of Israel, his identity as Messiah will then be confirmed.*

Once a candidate meets criteria 1, 2, 5 and 6, we may presume he is the messiah. Once he completes stages 3 and 4, he is confirmed as the messiah. Our sages teach us to nevertheless remain skeptical of messianic claims:

> *Said Rabbi Yochanan ben Zakkai: If you are holding a sapling in your hand and someone tells you, 'Come quickly, the messiah is here!', first finish planting the tree and then go to greet the messiah.*[3]

### When Will the Messiah Arrive?

The messiah can come at any time and will arrive (reveal himself) on any day except a Shabbat or a Holiday.[4]

However, we should never try to calculate or predict the time of the arrival of the messiah. The sages curse[5] those who attempt to predict the dates and times of his arrival because doing so ultimately damages the faith of others:

> *Rabbi Shmuel ben Nachmani said in the name of Rabbi Yonatan, "The bones of those who calculate the end should rot! For they would say that since the predetermined time has arrived and yet he has not come, he will never come. Rather wait for him, as it is written, 'Even though he might delay, wait for him'*[6]

Furthermore, studying, fixating, or obsessing on the messiah as a goal of one's religious thought and practice is discouraged:

---

[2] *Hilchos Melachim* 11:4.

[3] Avos 31b.

[4] Eruvin 43a.

[5] Sanhedrin 97a.

[6] Isaiah 30:18

*A person should not involve himself with the Aggadot [Talmudic sections regarding Mashiach] nor with the words of the Midrash that speak about this topic. Do not make them the prime focus, because they do not bring a person to love or fear of God. Also do not calculate the end [time of Mashiach's arrival] ... Rather wait for him and believe in the general principle, as we have explained.[7]*

The goal of our study and service of God should be to fulfill His will in this world at every moment. Focusing on the future redemption only diminishes one's *Avodah* (divine service) in the here-and-now.

## 1. A Descendant of David

*A shoot will come forth from the family of Jesse and a branch will grow from his roots*
Isaiah 11:1

This is one of many verses indicating that the messiah will arise from the family of David.[8] As mentioned, this is not a metaphor – he will actually be able to trace his lineage definitively to King David. There are many, many Jewish families today who can trace their ancestry to King David. Many of them are descendants of the Maharal, Rabbi Yehudah Loewy (1512 to 1609). Rabbi Loewy was a descendant of King David via his *Geonic* ancestry.

**Jewish Ancestry**

*I see him, but not now; I behold him, but not nigh; there shall step forth a star <u>out of Jacob</u>, and a scepter shall rise **out of Israel,** and shall smite through the corners of Moab, and break down all the sons of Seth.*
Numbers 24:17

*When you come into the land which the Lord your God gave you, and shall possess it, and dwell within it, and say: 'I will set a king over me like all the nations that are around about me,' then you will set over you as king a wise man whom the Lord your G-d shall choose. You shall set one from among your brethren as king over you. You may not place a stranger over you who is not your brother.*
**Deuteronomy 17:14-15**

---

[7] *Hilchos Melachim* 12:2.

[8] See the commentaries of Ibn Ezra and Radak to Isaiah. See also Sanhedrin 98a and *Eikhah Rabbah* 1:51.

These two versus inform us that the messiah must be Jewish. Since the messiah will also be anointed as a King of Israel, he must be Jewish. Jewish is defined as born of a Jewish mother.[9]

**From the Tribe of Judah**

*The scepter shall not depart **from Judah** nor the ruler's staff from between his feet as long as men come to Shiloh; and unto him shall the obedience of the peoples be.* Genesis 49:10.

The messiah must come from the tribe of Judah. Tribal affiliation is only passed through the father's lineage.[10]

## 2. A King of Israel

The term *Moshiach*, messiah, literally means "anointed with oil." Throughout the Tanakh there are many individuals who are called *Moshiach* on account of being anointed. Anointing with oil at the hands of a prophet was one of the many requirements for Jewish kingship. For example, the prophet Samuel anointed both Kings Saul and David with oil.[11]

Since the messiah will be crowned king, he must be anointed by a prophet. This is one of the reasons for the prophet Malachi's prophesy that Elijah would return prior to the messiah.[12]

## 3. Return of the Jewish People to Israel

*He will arise a banner for the nations and assemble the castaways of Israel; and He will gather in the dispersed ones of Judah from the four corners of the earth.*
Isaiah 11:12

*It shall be on that day that Hashem will thresh, from the surging [Euphrates] River to the Brook of Egypt, and you [Israel] will be gathered up one by one, O Children of Israel. It shall be on that day that a great shofar will be blown, and those who are lost in the land of Assyria and those cast away in the land of Egypt will come [together], and they will prostrate themselves to Hashem on the holy mountain in Jerusalem.*

---

[9] See Lev. 24:10 and Ezra 10:2-3. Kiddush 68.

[10] See Numbers 34:14, Numbers 1:18-44, Leviticus 24:10.

[11] See I Samuel 15:1, 16:1 to 13.

[12] Malachi 3:23-24.

Isaiah 27:12-13

*I will return the captivity of Judah and captivity of Israel, and will rebuild them as at first.*
Jeremiah 33:7

The return of the Jewish people to the land is not only part of the restoration of the glory of Israel, but is necessary for the return of prophecy. As we saw in the previous lesson, the Messiah will be the greatest prophet ever, second only to Moses.[13] As it is written:

*He will be filled with the spirit of God; he will not judge by what his eyes see or decide by what his ears hear.*
Isaiah 11:13.

Among the many requirements for prophecy is that the majority of the Jewish people live in the land of Israel. [14]

**Restoration of Tribal Identities**

Using his power of prophecy, the messiah will clarify the tribal identities of the Jewish people. In particular, he will determine the legitimacy of the *Kohanim* and *Leviim*.[15] He will then divide the land according to the ancestral heritage of each.

## 4. Rebuilding of the Temple

*I will seal a covenant of peace with them; it will be an eternal covenant with them; and I will emplace them and increase them, and I will place My Sanctuary among them forever. My dwelling place will be among them; I will be a God to them and they will be a people to Me. Then the nations will know that I am Hashem who sanctifies Israel, when My Sanctuary will be among them forever.*
Ezekiel 37:26-28

---

[13] *Hilchos Teshuva* 9:2.

[14] See Yoma 9b, Sanhedrin 11a, Brachos 57a, Sukkah 28a, Bava Basra 134a and many, many others.

[15] See Malachi 3:3.

> *It will be in the end of days that the Mountain of the Temple of Hashem will be firmly established as the most prominent of the mountains, and it will be exalted up above the hills, and peoples will stream to it.*
> Micah 4:1

> *It will happen in the end of days; The Mountain of the Temple of Hashem will be firmly established as the head of the mountains, and it will be exalted above the hills, and all the nations will stream to it. Many peoples will go and say, 'Come, let us go up to the Mountain of Hashem, to the Temple of the God of Jacob, and He will teach us of His ways and we will walk in His paths.*
> Isaiah 2: 2, 3

The Messiah will accomplish the rebuilding of the Third temple according to the details prophesied by Ezekiel.[16] According to many,[17] this is the act which definitively proves the identity of the messiah.

Many details of the rebuilding, such as the precise location of the altar, must be determined using prophecy.[18] For this reason, we know that the messiah must have prophecy. This also means that rebuilding the temple prior to the advent of the messiah is impossible.

**Reestablishment of the Sanhedrin**

The Messiah will also reestablish the Sanhedrin, which is a precursor to the re-establishment of the Temple:

> *I will restore your judges as at first, your counselors as in the beginning. Afterwards you will be called the city of righteousness, the faithful city. Zion shall be redeemed with justice…*
> Isaiah 1:26-27.

At some point between the coming of Elijah and the reestablishment of the Sanhedrin, formal *Semicha* (rabbinic ordination) will be restored. This is necessary for one to serve on the Sanhedrin. The chain of ordination from Moses was broken by Roman oppression in 358 CE. The possibility of renewing this ordination and reconstituting the Sanhedrin prior to the Messiah has been raised in the past, in particularly by Rabbi Yaakov Beirav in Tsfas in the 16th century.

---

[16] Chapters 40 to 48.

[17] *Hilchos Melachim* 11:4.

[18] *Zevachim* 62a. When Ezra rebuilt the temple only a few decades after its destruction, prophecy was required to locate the place of the altar. So too it will be needed to rebuild the final temple.

However, the attempt failed upon the ruling of the Radbaz, Rabbi Dovid ben Zimra, that the establishment of Semicha was not possible in our times.

**The Temple Service**

The messiah will also restore the sacrificial system to whatever degree it will apply in the Messianic era. He will also reestablish the Sabbatical and Jubilee year observances.

## 5. Establishing Peace and the End of All Wars

*I will seal a covenant of peace with them; it will be an eternal covenant with them; and I will emplace them and increase them, and I will place My Sanctuary among them forever.*
Ezekiel 37:26

*He will judge between many peoples, and will settle the arguments of mighty nations from far away. They will beat their swords into plowshares and their spears into pruning knives; nation will not lift sword against nations, nor will they learn war anymore.*
Micah 4:3

*He will judge among the nations, and will settle the arguments of many peoples. They shall beat their swords into plowshares and their spears into pruning hooks; nation will not lift sword against nation and they will no longer study warfare.*
Isaiah 2:4

The Messiah will be a great political leader who will make peace among the nations. All war will come to an end and the nations will work for the mutual benefit of the world.

## 6. He Will Bring Awareness of God

*They will neither injure nor destroy in all of My sacred mountain; for the earth will be as filled with knowledge of Hashem as water covering the sea bed.*
Isaiah 11:9

*The glory of Hashem will be revealed, and all flesh together will see that the mouth of Hashem has spoken.*
Isaiah 40:5

*For then I will change the nations [to speak] a pure language, so that they all will proclaim the Name of Hashem, to worship Him with a united resolve.*
Zephaniah 3:9

*They will no longer teach - each man his fellow, each man his brother-saying, "Know Hashem! For all of them will know Me, from their smallest to their greatest - the word of Hashem - when I will forgive their iniquity and will no longer recall their sin.*
Jeremiah 31:33

The most important mission of the Messiah will be to bring awareness of God to the world. Under his leadership all mankind will effortlessly achieve the highest levels of divine inspiration.

**Free Will** Man will still have free will at this time and the potential to do evil will still exist. However, the awareness of God will be so intense and immediately apparent that there will be no incentive to do evil.[19] Instead man will endeavor only to understand God and his Torah.

**Conversion** As the messiah approaches, many non-Jews will rush to convert to Judaism.[20] Once the Messiah ben David is revealed, however, converts will not be accepted anymore.[21]

## The Messiah's End

The Messiah will be a human being like any other.[22] He will have human parents and, like all men, will die a human death.[23] However, his reign will last for a very, very long time because lifespans in *Olam HaBa* (the messianic world) will be greatly extended.

---

[19] Sotah 52a; Zohar I:109a; See also Ramchal *Maamar Ikkarim*.

[20] See Zephania 3:9; Avodah Zarah 24a; Berachos 57b.

[21] Avodah Zarah 3b and *Maharal Chiddushei Aggados* ad loc.

[22] *Hilchos Melachim* 11:3.

[23] See Rambam to Sanhedrin 10:1.

## Summary

- There are six criteria that one must fulfill in order to be the messiah:

    1. He will be a direct descendant of King David,
    2. He will be anointed as king of Israel,
    3. He will complete the return of the Jewish people to Israel,
    4. He will rebuild the temple in Jerusalem,
    5. He will bring peace to the world, ending all war,
    6. He will bring knowledge of God to the world.

- The Messiah will be human, born of human parents, and will die a human death.

- Calculating the time at which he will arrive is forbidden and those who do so are cursed.

- While the messiah is a tenet of Torah faith, it should not be overly emphasized. Our duty is to fulfill Gods will in the here and now.

THE YESHIVA PIRCHEI SHOSHANIM SHULCHAN ARUCH PROJECT

# The Noahide Laws – Prophecy and Inspiration

© Yeshiva Pirchei Shoshanim 2017
This shiur may not be reproduced in any form without permission of the copyright holder.

## Table of Contents:

1. Introduction
2. *Siyata D'Shmaya* – Divine Assistance
3. *Ruach HaKodesh* – Divine Inspiration
4. *Nevuah* – Prophecy
    a. Conditions for Prophecy
        i. Land of Israel and Her People
        ii. The Ark of the Covenant
        iii. Worthiness of the Individual
        iv. Master & Guide
    b. The Experience of Prophecy
    c. Public Prophecy
    d. The Prophecy of Moses
    e. Prophecy's End

# Prophecy & Inspiration

## Introduction

The Tanach is replete with examples of divine inspiration, whether mere assistance or outright prophecy. What is prophecy? Does it exist today? How does God speak to us? In this lesson we are going to provide an overview of divine assistance, inspiration, and prophecy.

## Siyata D'Shmaya - Divine Assistance

The lowest level of inspiration is what we can best call "divine assistance.[1]" Though not uncommon, it is so that those who have it are usually unaware of it.[2] This level of inspiration is given to all of those who teach Torah in public with the proper motivations and fear of God.[3] This level of inspirations is alluded to in many places. For example in Psalms 25:14:

> *The counsel of HaShem is with them that fear Him; and His covenant, to make them know it.*

This was the minimal level of inspiration possessed by all leaders in the Tanach and Talmud. Any Torah leader whose works have been accepted by all or a substantial portion of Israel is assumed to have possessed this level of inspiration. This level can be attained by any person in any time or place.

## Ruach HaKodesh – Divine Inspiration

Ruach HaKodesh is the next highest level of inspiration. At this level a person is aware that God is guiding his actions.[4] However, it is still not prophecy.

---

[1] Moreh Nevuchim II:45.

[2] Kuzari II:14, III:32, and III:65

[3] Shir HaShirim Rabbah 1:8 – 9.

[4] See Ramban to Shemos 28:30 and Derech HaShem III:3:1 – 3.

Prophecy, as we shall see, is a communication between God and man. *Ruach HaKodesh* is not communication. Rather, it is inspiration and guidance. Through it a person develops unique intuition as to future events[5] and even the thoughts and actions of others.[6] There are ten qualities a person must perfect before he is even minimally worthy of this inspiration:[7]

- **Torah** – he must be unceasingly involved in the study and teaching of Torah.

- *Zehirus*, caution - He must be extremely careful to never violate a negative commandment.

- *Zerizus*, zeal – he must zealously perform every positive commandment.

- *Nekius,* cleanliness – he must be clean of sin in thought and desire.

- *Perishus,* abstention – he must sanctify himself even in that which is permitted and abstain from it if it may possibly lead to untoward desires or actions.

- *Tahara,* purity – he must have repented and cleanse himself of all sin, having righted all his past wrongs.

- *Chasidus*, piety – complete dedication to God beyond the letter of the law, but in the spirit of the law as well.

- *Anavah,* humility – complete nullification of ego and self.

- *Yiras Chet* – Dread and fear of sin.

- *Kedusha,* holiness – separation from worldly needs and desires.

Once these qualities have been mastered, then the initiate may engage in meditations, certain rituals, or methods of intense Torah study in order to merit *Ruach ha-kodesh*.

---

[5] R' Bachya to Lev. 8:8 and Derech HaShem ibid.

[6] Eliahu Rabbah to OC 101:8. See also Maharitz Chayes to Shabbos 12b.

[7] See Avodah Zarah 20b. Mishnayos Sotah 9:14.

Within this level there are many gradations that may be attained in greater or lesser measure.

The *Ketuvim*, Writings, were written in a state of *Ruach haKodesh*, divine inspiration, while the Prophets were written in a state of *Nevuah*, prophecy. That is why the Prophets are on a higher level than the writings. [8]

## Nevuah - Prophecy

At first, prophecy was attainable by all human beings. Moses, however, prayed that it be granted to Israel alone – a request to which God agreed:

*And he [Moses] said unto Him: 'If Your presence go not with me, carry us not up. For wherein now shall it be known that I have found grace in Your sight - I and Thy people? Is it not in that you go with us, so that we are distinguished, I and Thy people, from all the people that are upon the face of the earth?' And HaShem said unto Moses: 'I will do this thing that you have spoken, for you have found grace in My sight, and I know you by name.'* [9]

This restriction went into effect upon completion of the tabernacle.[10] From that moment on, prophecy was not granted to non-Jews unless it was for the sake of Israel.[11] Even in these instances, however, the prophetic vision was the bare minimum needed to convey the message. It would come secretly, at night, and in a vague form. This is the statement of the prophet:

*Now a word was brought to me secretly.*[12]

---

[8] Moreh Nevukhim II:45. There are numerous, vast discussions about the relative holiness of these books.

[9] Exodus 33:16-17; see Brachos 7b and Bava Basra 15b for explanation and interpretation.

[10] Vayikra Rabbah I:12 and Shir HaShirim Rabbah II:12.

[11] See the previous footnote for sources.

[12] Job 4:12.

## CONDITIONS FOR PROPHECY

Even with the restriction of prophecy to Israel alone, a number of conditions must exist for prophecy to take place:

### Land of Israel and Her People

Prophecy is only possible in the land of Israel when the majority of the Jewish people are living there:

> HaShem, your G-d, with raise up a prophet for your, **from your midst, from your brethren**, like me. To him shall you listen.[13]

The bold section indicates that prophecy is only possible in Israel when it is inhabited by the Jewish people. This is because prophecy requires a particular degree of *Kedushah*, holiness, which is only possible in Israel and in the midst of the people of Israel.[14]

Once a prophet has mastered prophecy in Israel, he can then attain prophecy even outside of Israel.[15] However this prophecy will be harder to achieve and only granted in specific circumstances.[16]

### The Ark of the Covenant

Full prophecy is only possible when the Ark of the Covenant rests in the temple. At that time, the influence of the Ark, the root of prophecy in this world extended to the boundaries of the land of Israel.[17]

### Worthiness of the individual

There are a number of qualities a person must possess as a prerequisite to prophecy:

- Must be of pure Israelite lineage[18] and a direct descendant of Abraham.[19] Moses alluded to this when he said:

---

[13] Deuteronomy 18:15.

[14] Sifrei; Yalkut Shimoni I:919.

[15] See commentaries to Ezekiel 1:3.

[16] Kuzari II:14; Maharitz Chayes to Moed Katan 25a; Mekhilta to exodus 12:1.

[17] Sefer Ikkarim III:11.

*God, your Lord, will elevate a prophet from you... **from your brethren, just like me**[20]* - meaning of Israelite ancestry like Moses himself[21]

- o This is a general rule, however. Exceptions have been made for those of special merit, such as Obadiah.[22]

- A potential prophet must possess a number of personal qualities as pre-requisites:[23]

    - o Must be mentally healthy and stable[24]
    - o Must have a mature intellect which has maximized its potential[25]
    - o Must be an expert in all areas of the Torah.[26]
    - o Must have what he needs and be materially completely satisfied with no desires materially for more or less.[27]

- The generation must be capable of meriting prophecy. Prophecy is only granted for the sake of God's people.[28] Even if an individual is worthy and

---

[18] See Kiddushin 70b & Tos. Ad loc. See also Yevamos 47b and Niddah 13b. See also Kuzari I:114.

[19] See Bamidbar Rabbah 12:4; Rashi to Sanhedrin 39b.

[20] Deuteronomy 18:15

[21] Sifrei, Yalkut Shimoni I:919. See also Rashi there and Rambam in the Iggeros Teiman.

[22] See Sanhedrin 39b.

[23] Shabbat 92a and Nedarim 38a.

[24] Moreh Nevukhim II:36.

[25] Moreh Nevukhim Ibid; Nedarim 38a; Hil. Yesodei HaTorah 7:1.

[26] See Shu"t HaRashba 548.

[27] Moreh Nevukhim ibid.; Avos 4:1; Shemonah Perkim 7.

[28] Mekhilta Shemos 12:1. See also Rashi to Devarim 2:16 and Shelah to Taanis II:137a.

capable of receiving prophecy, it will not be bestowed if the Generation is not worthy or capable of recognizing true prophecy.[29]

Once these minimum benchmarks are met, the candidate may begin to prepare for prophecy. This involves techniques of meditation and focus to attain the state required for prophecy.[30]

**Master & Guide** Every potential prophet must have a master to guide him and constantly give him "reality checks."[31] Without a master to teach him and keep him on the right track, the result of his efforts will be psychosis and hallucinations.[32]

**The Experience of Prophecy** Prophecy, being a skill and a craft, is something the prophet works to perfect over a long period of time.[33] His first early prophecies will be flawed, unfocused and possibly unrecognizable as prophecy.[34]

As his prophecy is perfected, it may be experienced as either a waking vision or a nocturnal dream:[35]

> *And He said: 'Hear now My words: if there be a prophet among you, I HaShem will make Myself known unto him in a vision, I will speak with him in a dream.*[36]

The type of prophetic experience indicates greater and lesser degrees of prophetic ability. In ascending order of ability:

- A Waking vision is always higher than a dream vision.

---

[29] Sanhedrin 11a; Brachos 57a; Succos 28a; Bava Basra 134a.

[30] See Hil. Yesodei HaTorah 7:4. These techniques are discussed in a number of sources.

[31] See Derech HaShem III:4:4.

[32] See Maharsha to Shabbat 149b and Sanhedrin 89a. See also Derech HaShem III:4:6.

[33] Derech HaShem Ibid.

[34] Derech HaShem Ibid.

[35] Pirkei R' Eliezer 28. Yesodei HaTorah 7:2. Derech HaShem III:5:2.

[36] Numbers 12:6.

- Hearing words is higher than seeing visions.
- Seeing the speaker of the words is higher than only hearing them.
- Seeing an angelic speaker is higher than seeing a human speaker.

The prophetic experience cannot be had if the prophet is depressed or angry.[37] He must be in a pleasant, content, happy mood in order to enter the prophetic state.[38] For this reason, we often see music connected to the prophetic experience.[39]

According to many, the voice one hears in a prophecy is the Prophet's own.[40] The face he may see is his own as well.[41]

**PUBLIC PROPHECY**

Most of a prophet's visions are private and meant only for the prophet himself.[42] However, a prophet is sometimes sent with a message for others. In such a case, the prophet is forced to reveal it even against his will:

*And if I say: 'I will not make mention of Him, nor speak any more in His name', then there is in my heart as it were a burning fire shut up in my bones, and I weary myself to hold it in, but cannot.*[43]

Not all public prophecies were recorded and canonized. Only those prophecies that apply to all of Israel at all times were recorded as part of Tanakh.[44]

---

[37] Shabbat 30a; Pesachim 66b and 117a.

[38] Yerushalmi Sukkah 5:1; Bereshis Rabbah 70:8. See also Tos. Sukkos 50b.

[39] I Samuel 10:5; II Kings 3:15; I Chronicles 25:1. Yesodei HaTorah 7:4.

[40] Shoshon Sodoth. See Brachos 45a that God spoke to Moses with the Voice of Moses.

[41] Shoshan Sodoth.

[42] Derech HaShem III:4:6.

[43] Jeremiah 20:9.

[44] Megillah 14a.

## THE PROPHECY OF MOSES

None of the aforementioned applies to Moses. Moses's prophecy was of an entirely different type than all other prophets.[45] Moses spoke to God as one speaks to his fellow, face to face.[46] His prophecy was not in the form of symbols, visions, or dreams, but as a waking, absolutely normal experience. Moreover, Moses was able to engage in direct conversation with God at any time.[47]

## PROPHECY'S END

Prophecy was very common during the first temple era. Many times there were over 1,000,000 people who had prophecy.[48]

The period of Prophecy lasted from about 1313 BCE until about 40 years after the building of the second temple (about 313 BCE). Prophecy had begun to wane when the majority of the Jewish people refused to return to Israel with Ezra.[49] Additionally, the Ark was displaced after the destruction of the first temple, which weakened the potential of prophecy. Sadly, there is no prophecy in our times.

---

[45] Bereshis Rabbah 76:1; Zohar I:171a; Hil. Yesodei HaTorah 7:6.

[46] Exodus 33:11.

[47] See Numbers 12:6-8.

[48] Megillah 14a. See also Shir HaShirim Rabbah 4:22 and Ruth Rabbah 1:2.

[49] Yoma 9b.

## Summary

- There are three types of heavenly inspiration that exist. Each has its own numerous gradations and subdivision.

- The lowest level is Divine Assistance, and this granted to all those who teach Torah in public for the right reasons. All may attain this.

- The second level is Divine Inspiration. It is rarer than the first type. There are a number of personal qualities that the initiate must possess. This is a form of divine guidance granting the holder unique insight and intuition.

- The highest level is *Nevuah – prophecy*. This is an experience of communication with God via a vision or dream. Prophecy does not exist anymore in our days.

www.ingramcontent.com/pod-product-compliance
Lightning Source LLC
Chambersburg PA
CBHW080718230426
43665CB00020B/2557